MOTHERLAND

MOTHERLAND

A FEMINIST HISTORY OF MODERN RUSSIA,

FROM REVOLUTION TO AUTOCRACY

JULIA IOFFE

ecco
An Imprint of HarperCollins*Publishers*

Without limiting the exclusive rights of any author, contributor or the publisher of this publication, any unauthorized use of this publication to train generative artificial intelligence (AI) technologies is expressly prohibited. HarperCollins also exercise their rights under Article 4(3) of the Digital Single Market Directive 2019/790 and expressly reserve this publication from the text and data mining exception.

MOTHERLAND. Copyright © 2025 by Julia Ioffe. All rights reserved. Printed in the United States of America. No part of this book may be used or reproduced in any manner whatsoever without written permission except in the case of brief quotations embodied in critical articles and reviews. For information, address HarperCollins Publishers, 195 Broadway, New York, NY 10007. In Europe, HarperCollins Publishers, Macken House, 39/40 Mayor Street Upper, Dublin 1, D01 C9W8, Ireland.

HarperCollins books may be purchased for educational, business, or sales promotional use. For information, please email the Special Markets Department at SPsales@harpercollins.com.

hc.com

Ecco® and HarperCollins® are trademarks of HarperCollins Publishers.

FIRST EDITION

Designed by Alison Bloomer

Library of Congress Cataloging-in-Publication Data

Names: Ioffe, Julia, author
Title: Motherland : a feminist history of modern Russia, from revolution to autocracy / Julia Ioffe.
Description: First edition. | New York : Ecco, 2025. | Includes bibliographical references and index.
Identifiers: LCCN 2025010562 (print) | LCCN 2025010563 (ebook) | ISBN 9780062879127 hardcover | ISBN 9780062879110 trade paperback | ISBN 9780062879134 ebook
Subjects: LCSH: Women—Soviet Union—History | Women—Russia (Federation)—History | Sex role—Soviet Union | Sex role—Russia (Federation) | Feminism—Soviet Union | Feminism—Russia (Federation) | Soviet Union—Social conditions | Russia (Federation)—Social conditions—1991
Classification: LCC HQ1662 .I64 2025 (print) | LCC HQ1662 (ebook)
LC record available at https://lccn.loc.gov/2025010562
LC ebook record available at https://lccn.loc.gov/2025010563

For Emma

Introduction xi
A Note on Transliteration xv

PART I

VALKYRIE OF THE REVOLUTION 3
INESSA 13
A FAIRY-TALE COUNTRY 23
RIVA 33
THE FIRST FIRST LADY 40
BUZYA 52
NADYA 63
TRAITORS TO THE MOTHERLAND 69
REQUIEM 84
WAR 92
THE HOME FRONT 108
VICTORY 127

PART II

SVETLANA 139
BERIA'S HOUSE 146
HERO MOTHERS 159
KHINYA AND EMMA 175
LONELY MOTHERS 187

NOMENKLATURA 199
OLGA 212
PERESTROIKA 219
RAISA 225
RECKONING 238
END OF THE FAIRY TALE 249
MOTHERLAND 264

PART III

JULIA 279
THE HUNT 289
LYUDMILA 305
THE WEAKER SEX 318
A MANLY MAN 329
PUSSY RIOT 336
WOMEN'S ZONE 356
GASOLINE 369
FIRST LADY 390
BRING THE BOYS HOME 406
LAND OF MOTHERS 420

Acknowledgments 437
Notes 441
Bibliography 461
Index 473

MY MATERNAL LINE

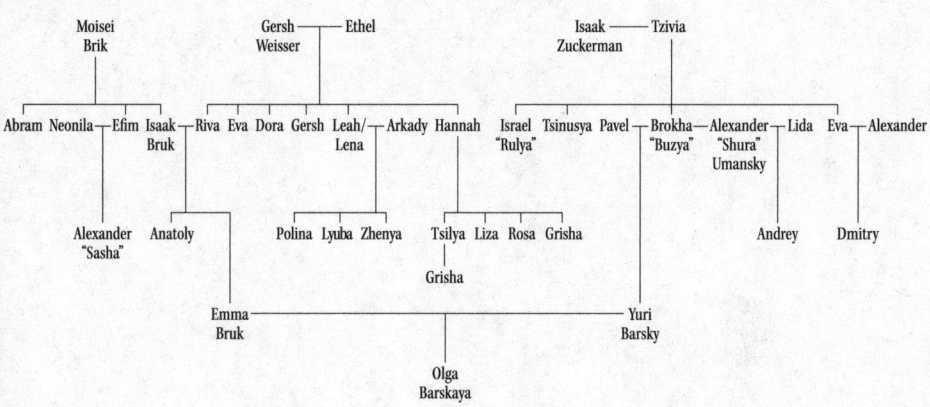

MY PATERNAL LINE

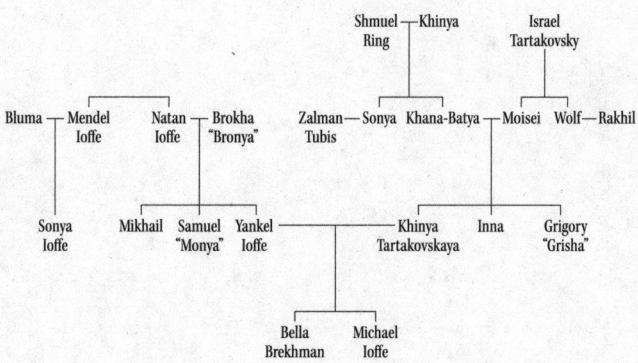

INTRODUCTION

HOW DO YOU TELL THE STORY OF ORDINARY PEOPLE LIVING IN extraordinary times?

My little sister, an oncologist, is the fourth generation of women in our family to practice medicine. She follows our mother (a pathologist), our mother's mother (a cardiologist), and our mother's mother's mother (a pediatrician). In fact, two of our great-grandmothers were doctors. Another was a PhD in chemistry who, in the 1930s, ran her own lab and published scientific papers at a time when her peers in the West still needed their husbands' permission to do much of anything. (Our other grandmother, for what it's worth, was a chemical engineer who oversaw the lab at a water filtration plant that supplied the Kremlin's drinking water.) Any American who hears this lineage assumes one thing: that the women in my family were extraordinary. That is because they measure them against American history and their own American families: even in educated families, most of my peers' grandmothers didn't attend college.

But, measured against the history of their own country, the Soviet Union, the women from whom I descend were perfectly average people. They were ordinary women who happened to be the subjects—and products—of one of the most radical social experiments in history: the attempt to emancipate women and build a new Soviet person. This book is, in part, an effort to explain the extraordinary circumstances that transformed the lives of my rather ordinary foremothers.

When the Bolsheviks seized power in October 1917, they embarked on a campaign to erase gender and dismantle the bourgeois family, which, in their view, imprisoned women in marriages based on economics rather than love and mutual respect. In just a couple of years, Soviet women were granted freedoms and rights that their Western counterparts would have to fight for, in most cases, for another several decades. By 1917, Soviet women had the (increasingly irrelevant) right to vote, years before their Western peers. They had the right to no-fault divorce and child support, paid maternity leave, and free higher education, including in the sciences, by 1918. By 1920, they had the right to abortion, provided by the state for free.

These changes were introduced in part by Alexandra Kollontai, a revolutionary who would become the world's first female cabinet minister and first credentialed female ambassador for a country that would put the first woman in space, two decades before Sally Ride. The experiment in erasing the legal, educational, and social differences between men and women was so successful that the first post-Revolutionary generation of Soviet women took up arms to fight the Nazis en masse. When Hitler's army invaded the USSR in the summer of 1941, tens of thousands of young women, most of them teenage girls, swarmed recruitment posts all over the country. Eventually, nearly a million of them would serve in the Red Army, as machine gunners and medics, as sappers and artillery officers, as snipers and fighter pilots in all-female squadrons. This was without parallel among any of the countries fighting in World War II. As one of the female Soviet veterans told historian Anna Krylova, "We are a generation not from this universe."[1] By the time my mother entered medical school in 1977, 70 percent of doctors in the Soviet Union were women.

A century after that experiment began, I found myself living in Russia for the first time since we emigrated when I was a child. This country was the successor state to the Soviet Union, but its women seemed different from my mother and grandmothers. Women there were obsessed with men—as husbands, as sugar daddies, as inseminators. The Russian women around me—educated, intelligent, cosmopolitan women—oriented their entire lives around attracting men and tricking them into staying put. The pinnacle of their fantasies was to become a stay-at-home wife. And when Vladimir Putin returned to power in 2012 for his third term as president, things only got worse. He revamped his entire governing ideology from the fiction of "managed democracy" to one of cultural and religious revanche. He weaponized traditional values as a means of political control and incorporated the Russian Orthodox Church into the Kremlin's political hierarchy. What,

I began to wonder, had happened? How had the country of Kollontai and women fighter pilots become a country of women who wanted nothing more than to become housewives?

In trying to answer these questions, I also conducted an experiment of my own: How do you tell the story of a country through its women? I drew on my personal fatigue with the West's fixation on Putin, on historians' fixations on Lenin, Stalin, Khrushchev, and the rest. The focus is merited: they are the dictators who set the course for a country of tens of millions. But the women in that history had been overlooked and underappreciated by historians who were, of course, mostly male. This book takes a different approach. It interweaves the unfurling of big history (as embodied here by the wives of leaders such as Lenin, Stalin, and Gorbachev, all of them influential in their own right) with what it felt like to live through that history (as told through my foremothers and other regular women).

In the end, though, it is a story of my family, of the women I descend from, and the country that shaped them and failed them, lured them in and cast them out. It is an extraordinary country, in the good sense and the bad, this land of my mothers, my Motherland.

A NOTE ON TRANSLITERATION

Place-names are spelled the way they would have been spelled at the time that is being described, so the capital of Ukraine is rendered as Kiev when the story takes place in Soviet times, and as Kyiv when we go to independent Ukraine.

PART I

Who knows four?
I know four!
Four are the mothers
—PASSOVER HAGGADAH

VALKYRIE OF THE REVOLUTION

IT WAS THE WOMEN WHO STARTED THE RUSSIAN REVOLUTION.[1]

The events that toppled the three-hundred-year-old Romanov dynasty began on International Women's Day—February 23, 1917, or March 8 in the Western calendar. That year, the day came in unusually warm, a bright winter sun scattering the leaden clouds over Petrograd, a welcome respite in what had been a brutal winter.[2] The Great War was now in its third year, and there was no one to clear the snowdrifts that had piled up on the railroad tracks, blocking trains from supplying food and fuel to the capital. Women in the city stood in line for hours, waiting for bread. Without fuel, the factories where they worked began to idle, one after another. There were more and more women with nothing to do but wait in line for bread that never came.[3]

On the morning of February 23, against the advice of all the capital's revolutionary organizations, the women working in several Petrograd textile factories went on strike.[4] As news of the strike traveled, more women walked out of their jobs. Within hours, over a hundred thousand people, men and women, were protesting in the streets. Hungry women workers marched down to the parliament. Women workers and housewives, fed up with bread lines, spontaneously joined a rally that the socialists had planned for International Women's Day. Coursing down Nevsky Prospect, the city's main artery, they carried banners that said, "If a woman is a *slave*, there will be no freedom! Long live equal rights for women!"[5]

As more workers joined the strikes in the following days, soldiers were ordered to put down the protests by force. Instead, they mutinied. Within a week, Tsar Nicholas II had abdicated the throne and a provisional government was installed. "If future historians look for the group that began the Russian Revolution, let them not create any involved theory," wrote one male revolutionary in his diary of what he saw in Petrograd during those turbulent days. "The Russian Revolution was begun by hungry women and children demanding bread and herring."[6] Leon Trotsky, who in a few months would mobilize the troops that helped the Bolsheviks seize power, wrote that Petrograd's women had "marched on the cordons of soldiers more bravely than the men, grabbed the [soldiers'] rifles and asked, almost commanded, 'Drop your guns and join us.'"

It wasn't exactly a surprise that women were so instrumental in the success of the February Revolution. In Russia's increasingly radicalized industrial labor force, women made up 40 percent of the workers. Russia also had the highest number of female radicals of any country in Europe: some 18,000 anarchist, socialist, and Communist revolutionaries, ready to fight.[7] By the turn of the twentieth century, there were so many female political prisoners in the Russian capital alone that the government had to build a new prison just to hold them.[8] "While the suffragettes or militants [in the West] smashed windows, caned politicians, and provoked arrest," wrote historian Richard Stites, "Russian revolutionary women fired at generals, plotted uprisings, and dangled from gallows."

As soon as Alexandra Kollontai got word that the Provisional Government had amnestied all political exiles, she rushed home from Norway to Petrograd, arriving on April 9, 1917. The monarchy had fallen and suddenly history was here, and she longed to mold it, to bring about the socialist revolution she had dreamt of for twenty years. Soon, Kollontai, once an opponent of the Bolsheviks, had an unexpected ally: a week after she set foot in the capital, an armored train pulled into Petrograd's Finland Station. Onboard was the famous Bolshevik Vladimir Lenin.[9]

Almost immediately, Lenin began demanding that Bolsheviks seize power and refuse to work with any of the other anti-tsarist parties. The Bolsheviks had always wanted to "telescope" the revolution described by their prophet Karl Marx. The idea was to rush Russia from its current feudal stage of development right to the socialist phase, essentially skipping over the bourgeois industrial period that Marx saw as necessary for revolution. It set them apart from the Mensheviks, the socialist gradualists. But when Lenin sought to actually make that leap, the Bolsheviks balked. They feared that if they moved too fast, their movement would be crushed. No one supported Lenin's proposals—except Kollontai. So ferocious was her proselytization of Lenin's so-called April Theses that foreign newspapers dubbed the striking forty-five-year-old the "Valkyrie of the Revolution."[10]

It was a strange molting that had transformed Kollontai from a child of privilege into a Marxist revolutionary. Born Alexandra Domontovich in St. Petersburg in 1872 into a wealthy, aristocratic family, she rebelled early, mostly against a mother that wouldn't let her take university classes or marry the man she wanted, a poor distant cousin named Vladimir Kollontai. Alexandra did both anyway. Marriage had initially seemed like a way to free herself from her mother's control and pursue her true desire, which was to study Marxist and populist philosophy. The plan worked at first. Her parents sent her and Vladimir enough money to hire a maid, but Alexandra's home life became more complicated when, at the age of twenty-two, she gave birth to her son. Being a wife and a mother, she soon realized, was extremely time-consuming. "I longed to be free," she wrote, complaining to her friends, "I hate marriage. It is an idiotic, meaningless life."[11]

Kollontai began to read widely about political theory and philosophy, searching, like many educated young people of her generation, for a meaningful way to solve Russia's myriad problems. She quickly discarded the liberalism she had grown up with, calling it "too shallow, too passive, powerless in some way." She was drawn first to Russian populism, which focused on liberating the peasants who made up the overwhelming majority of the population. She was especially captivated with the young female revolutionaries from the People's Will, the radical populist movement that killed Tsar Alexander II in 1881. One of the assassins, Sofia Perovskaya, was much like Kollontai: they were both daughters of decorated generals but had grown up to rebel against the cause their fathers served.

But, unlike Kollontai, Perovskaya had turned her beliefs into action. She had led the plot to kill the emperor and was hanged for it.

These *nigilistki*, the nihilist women of the 1860s, were deadly serious about living their convictions. They wore their hair short and their dresses dark and plain because they didn't want to be decorative objects. They studied and developed their minds and personalities and demanded respect from their male peers—often successfully. Preaching total freedom in love and sex, they wed their radical brethren in sham marriages to escape their parents' control.[12]

Eventually, though, Perovskaya and the People's Will began to seem outdated to Kollontai. She felt the populists were too preoccupied with rural peasants, whose reality was so far removed from her modern, urban life. Marxism was new and European and scientific, and it seemed to perfectly explain the grimy reality of the industrialization that she was witnessing in the capital.

At first, Kollontai tried to incorporate her newfound beliefs into her existing life. She began teaching literacy to workers, sneaking some socialist doctrine into her lessons. She had an affair with her husband's friend, a man she dubbed "the Martian." But this, too, was not enough. She was still not free.

In 1898, she handed off her four-year-old son to her parents, boarded a train for Zurich, where she aimed to join the Russian Marxist intelligentsia in exile, and sent her husband a letter saying that she was leaving him. "If she must choose between 'love and work,' [a woman] should never hesitate," she would write many years later. "It is work, her own creative work, which gives her the real satisfaction and makes life worth living."[13]

Kollontai's work made her the Russian socialists' preeminent theorist on what her contemporaries called the "woman question." Few socialist thinkers, not even Marx himself, had bothered to address the issue. (Marx did allow that women couldn't be completely ignored, since "major social transformations were impossible without ferment among women.")[14] A German socialist named August Bebel was the first to address the matter in his popular 1879 book, *Woman Under Socialism*. "She suffers both as a social and a sex entity, and it is hard to say in which of the two respects she suffers more," he wrote.[15] For Bebel, the bourgeois marriage was a clear illustration of the problem. In the capitalist system, money and property, rather than love and respect, were the cornerstones of marriage. The vast majority of women, Bebel wrote, married to find financial support, a contract "which they must enter into at any price."[16] Such an arrangement was, to him, worse than prostitution. "The prostitute has, to a certain degree, the freedom to withdraw from her disgraceful pursuit," he wrote, "but a sold married woman must submit to the embraces of her husband, even though she have a hundred reasons to hate and despise him."[17]

Most socialists agreed with Bebel but had few specific ideas about fixing the gender imbalance within the larger class struggle. Even Bebel was rather vague when it came to solutions: like most male Marxist theologians, he believed that the elimination of private property would magically resolve everything.

Friedrich Engels, Marx's collaborator, was slightly more rigorous, positing that collective labor would obviate women's traditional work inside the home. "The individual family ceases to be the economic unit of society," he wrote. "Private housekeeping is transformed into a social industry. The care and education of children becomes a public matter." Even that argument, though, was less about the woman's freedom than the man's pleasure. "Society takes care of all children equally, irrespective of whether they are born in wedlock or not," Engels explained. "Thus the anxiety about the 'consequences,' which is today the most important social factor—both moral and economic—that hinders a girl from giving herself freely to the man she loves, disappears."[18]

Just as Marx, Engels, and Bebel were traditional bourgeois married men in their private lives, they ended up being quite conventional when envisioning what a socialist society would look like for women. They agreed that marriage was paramount and that sex was for bearing children. (Bebel added that women should not opt out of having children out of convenience or to keep their figures.) Prostitution, they concurred, had to go. In a break with prevailing norms, however, they believed that married couples had to be able to separate and divorce. An adamant Lenin wrote that "one cannot be a democrat and a socialist without demanding full freedom of divorce."[19] On everything else relating to women, the great Marxist theorists were either extremely nebulous or entirely mute.

Kollontai would have bristled at being called a feminist. Like any orthodox Marxist, she saw feminists as "bourgeois equal-righters" who wanted "to drink the blood" of the revolution. She attended their meetings just to argue with them, and one prominent Russian feminist took to crossing herself whenever Kollontai entered the room.[20] Kollontai and other socialists were focused on what they saw as far bigger issues, like capitalist exploitation of the working class and the repressions of the tsarist police state. The paramount distinction for socialists was not gender or nationality or religion; it was class. Everything else was secondary.

There was arguably some truth in this analysis. Upper-class women may have suffocated in their gilded cages, but so, too, did upper-class Russian men, who lived off their estates and also had little in the way of meaningful activity to occupy their time. The peasants toiling on their land were men and women both, as were those working in the squalor of city factories. In belle époque Russia, class differences *were* more stark than those of gender, notes historian Elizabeth Wood, and Russian men and women of all classes "shared an 'equal rightlessness' under the rigid hand of the autocracy."[21]

But women in tsarist Russia suffered an additional and specific kind of rightlessness, one that began inside the family. It was embedded in the empire's legal code, which stated that "a wife must obey her husband as the head of the family, live with him in love and treat him with esteem, utmost respect, obedience and humility due to him as master of the house." A wife could not be issued a passport, travel, change her place of residence, or work without her husband's permission.[22] Marriage was a religious institution and the Russian Orthodox Church allowed divorce only in cases of adultery, impotence, criminality, or desertion. The procedure involved nine long and intensely bureaucratic stages and usually included a humiliating investigation of the wife's intimate life. To prove a husband's impotence, for instance, a wife first had to prove that she was a virgin. Proceedings quickly devolved into absurdity: upper-class spouses who wanted out of their marriages often resorted to making their servants play their fictional lovers in court.[23] What a woman said in front of a judge mattered little anyway. According to Russian law, "When two witnesses do not agree, the testimony of an adult outweighs that of a child, and the testimony of a man that of a woman."[24]

In peasant households, where girls were married off in their early teens, if not earlier, marriage was even more restrictive. It was replete with physical violence as well as the Russian tradition of *snokhachestvo*, in which the bride was forced to have sex with her father-in-law.[25] Her mother-in-law was often scarcely better, meting out physical and verbal abuse. Since there was no birth control, peasant women spent much of their lives pregnant or nursing. A 1908 study found that 25 percent of forty-five-year-old Russian peasant women had had ten or more pregnancies, one-fourth of which had ended in miscarriages. "A not atypical example," writes Stites, "is that of a fifty-five-year-old woman who had been married for thirty-five years and had been pregnant twenty-four times. Two children had lived."[26]

For women in the poor quarters of the cities, life was a blur of long hours in dangerous factories and overcrowding at home, as well as disease, abuse, alcoholism, infanticide, malnutrition, and neglect.[27] Pregnant workers were not given time off, even after the birth of a child. New mothers often had to leave babies locked alone in their tenement flats or entrust them to old women or to children scarcely older than the infants. Underground abortions and infanticide were ubiquitous, and some unwanted children were sold at birth. At work, there was sexual exploitation, both by factory owners and by pimps who recruited right on the factory floor.[28] Women were paid a fraction of what men earned, leading some to pose as men to get full wages. Factory owners explained the discrepancy by saying that men should be paid more because, unlike women, they had to provide for the whole family. In reality, the reverse was frequently the case. Historian Barbara Evans Clements writes that "many women were the sole support of their families" and "often went undernourished in order to feed their children on starvation wages."[29]

It was impossible to ignore that working women suffered in ways that set them apart from working men. A prolific writer, Kollontai gave shape to the hazy orthodoxy set down by the male theorists. On one hand, she agreed that the true source of women's oppression wasn't men but capitalism. On the other hand, as a keen observer of all the ways society failed women, she had far more developed ideas for how to fix them. Kollontai pushed for socialists to recognize that childbearing was a public good that should be supported by the state, with healthcare, maternity leave, and nurseries, regardless of whether the mother was married.[30]

Kollontai also expanded Engels's idea of a collectivized home. In the socialist future, she wrote, dozens of families would live in houses heated and lit collectively, with "common kitchens and dining rooms." (Lenin would come to espouse this idea, saying it would "relieve millions of 'domestic slaves' of the need to spend three-fourths of their lives in smelly kitchens.")[31] Child-rearing would become collectivized, too, performed by professional instructors. This, Kollontai posited, would introduce some woefully needed scientific expertise into the vital task of raising future citizens.

Like many of her contemporaries, Kollontai did not believe that marriage should disappear. Bourgeois marriage was, in her view, a man's economic and sexual enslavement of a woman. But *socialist* marriage would be a "comradely and warm union of two free and independent, laboring, equal members of communist society."[32] Nor did socialist marriage have to be a lifelong prison: simplified divorce procedures would restore freedom and dignity to both partners.

Kollontai also wrote frankly about women's sexuality. In the atomized society of the industrialized age, she observed, men and women both craved intimacy "with sick greed," trying desperately to feel less alone. Yet the only two avenues allowed to them were marriage and prostitution, which were both built on money and ownership and only deepened people's loneliness. "The normal woman seeks in sexual intercourse completeness and harmony," Kollontai wrote in

1913. "The man, reared on prostitution, overlooking the complex vibrations of love's sensations, follows on his pallid, monotone, physical inclinations, leaving sensations of incompleteness and spiritual hunger on both sides."[33]

The new socialist woman, Kollontai wrote, would actively engage her sexuality, rather than suppressing it in the ill-fitting box of monogamous marriage. "When the wave of passion sweeps over her," Kollontai wrote of this new woman, "she holds out her hand to her chosen one and goes away for several weeks to drink from the cup of love's joy, however deep it is, and to satisfy herself. When the cup is empty, she throws it away without regret or bitterness. And again to work."[34] For a liberated woman, sex and love were "only the episodes of life," Kollontai wrote. "Its real content is that 'holy cause' which the new woman serves: the social idea, science, calling, creativity ... And this cause, this goal, is often more important, more worthy, and holier for the new woman than all the joys of the heart, than all the pleasures of passion."[35]

This was a truly revolutionary view of the woman under socialism. The new woman Kollontai envisioned was the free woman that she had spent her life striving to be. This woman would be free because she worked and made her own money. Liberated from the subjugation of bourgeois marriage, she would be free to love whom and how she chose. If she decided to marry and bear children, she would be supported by the state, which would enable her to work and parent in the way a man did. For Marx, Engels, Lenin, and even Bebel, the goal was the creation of a new socialist man. The new socialist woman was a mere afterthought. For Kollontai, she was as real as her own flesh.

During the underground years, Kollontai noticed that the Russian Marxists were almost entirely overlooking working-class women. Instead, this constituency was being picked up by the loathed feminists, who were overwhelmingly from the upper classes and had little interest in overturning the existing economic order. Kollontai tried to convince the mostly male party leaders that they needed to create a special branch to target working women. At first, party officials denied her request along the usual ideological grounds: it smacked of bourgeois feminism. When they finally granted her permission to hold a meeting to discuss her idea, she and her supporters arrived at the assigned location only to find a locked door. On it was a sign. "The meeting *for women only* has been called off," it said. "Tomorrow: a meeting *for men only*."[36]

The Bolsheviks may have aimed to transform Russian society, but they were also products of that society, one that was still deeply patriarchal—and patronizing. Russian lore viewed the Russian woman as a backward and conservative workhorse, the superstitious and illogical *baba*.[37] "A chicken is not a bird," the popular saying went, "and a *baba* is not a person." The socialists simply dressed up these old canards in pseudoscientific Marxist language. Even though literacy among working women was rising rapidly, as was their participation in labor strikes, the Bolsheviks, notes Wood, saw women as "empty vessels" who needed to be "'brought up to' the level of the male workers."[38] Even Lenin, the most progressive male party leader on the subject, viewed women outside the intelligentsia with suspicion. Women were "the most backward and immobile element" of the working class, he said, an element that had served as "a brake in all previous revolutions."[39]

And it wasn't just the men who felt this way. Socialist women, too, were wary of their working-class and peasant sisters. Lenin's wife and comrade in arms, Nadezhda Krupskaya, worried that it was dangerous for a revolutionary to have a wife: uneducated in the world-historical processes unfolding around her, she would try to keep her husband at home out of fear. Even Kollontai herself was not free of this internalized bias. She referred to women as the "little sisters" of the proletariat and berated herself for crying when ordering her first arrests. It would not be the hardest thing she would have to do in forging a new socialist woman.

INESSA

ACCOMPANYING LENIN IN HIS SEALED TRAIN CAR TRAVELING FROM Zurich to Petrograd was his wife, Nadezhda Krupskaya, as well as their friend and fellow revolutionary Inessa Armand. On and off for a decade, Inessa had lived near the couple during their long exile in Paris and Krakow and was a frequent guest in their house. Inessa came over and played piano, which Lenin loved but Krupskaya had never mastered. She shared stories of her five children, who had remained with their father in Russia, and smoked and chatted with Krupskaya's elderly mother. And she went for long walks with Krupskaya and Lenin, talking revolution all the while.

There had always been rumors. In 1911, the tsarist secret police tracking Russian revolutionaries in Paris began identifying Inessa as Lenin's mistress. There was talk that Krupskaya had offered to leave Lenin that year but that Lenin refused. Forced to choose between the two women, he broke things off with Inessa—at least physically.[1] Eventually, their love seemed to mellow into friendship, and Inessa became Lenin's trusted political associate and executor. She even became close friends with Krupskaya, who kept a photo of her in her Kremlin apartment long after Inessa's death.

"Beautiful people get most of the attention, even from historians," Sheila Fitzpatrick, the great scholar of Russia, wrote of the two women. Inessa, to whom most people referred by her elegant first name, was a Bolshevik celebrity because she was "uncommonly good-looking" and Lenin's mistress, Fitzpatrick observes. Krupskaya, who was known by her last name, like a male colleague, was overlooked as "Vladimir Lenin's diligent but unglamorous wife." In truth, both have been treated unfairly by historians, most of them male, who saw their importance only insofar as their lives were intimately tied to Lenin's. Yet these women were veteran revolutionaries in their own right whose key roles in the Revolution have long gone unrecognized.

No one was particularly surprised that Lenin had fallen for the beautiful, sophisticated Inessa. She was born in a working-class neighborhood of Paris in 1874 to a French father who sang opera and a French-English mother who acted and gave voice lessons. By the time Inessa was six, both of her parents were dead, so her aunt took her to Russia to live with the large Armand family, who had hired Inessa's aunt as a governess.[2] The Armands raised Inessa as one of their own, and when she was nineteen, she married the eldest Armand son, Alexander.

Well educated and energetic, Inessa wilted in the hothouse of the Armand estate. She was a young mother with lots of help, a busy husband, and not much to occupy her. She "felt very lonely," she would recall many years later.[3] This was not an unusual predicament for a woman of her socioeconomic status: an overeducated, elaborately feathered bird, preening and chirping in a gilded cage.

Still, upper-class Russian women had more latitude than their Western counterparts. They could inherit and own property; they ran their family estates and could manage their own inheritances.[4] Moreover, if they belonged to the urban intelligentsia, as Inessa did, they were part of a milieu that had, since the mid-nineteenth century, become increasingly egalitarian when it came to questions of gender. In the salons and journals of the era, progressives grappled with "the woman question." What was to be done about the ways in which the patriarchal order of the day, enforced by the tsars and the Orthodox Church, constricted and punished women?

The non-radicals among the liberal intelligentsia began to focus on their own actions and behaviors, an approach known as the philosophy of small deeds. Upper-class men like Alexander Armand "now assumed that it was their duty to 'liberate' the women in their own immediate circles and give them their freedom if they fell in love outside the bonds of marriage," wrote Wood.[5] Love triangles became common, both in literature and in life.

Inessa's quest for changing Russia through small deeds brought her to philanthropy. She joined the Moscow Society for Improving the Lot of Women and tried to open schools to promote women's education. But the authorities, fearing that they would spread radical ideas, would not allow it.[6]

Undeterred, in 1902, Inessa opened the Shelter for Downtrodden Women—that is, prostitutes.[7] Prostitution had become a true scourge in the rapidly industrializing cities of the Russian Empire.[8] At train stations, agents of brothels intercepted young peasant women arriving in the cities looking for factory jobs. Tens of thousands of prostitutes now worked in Moscow and Petrograd. According to tsarist statistics, nearly half of Russian prostitutes were peasant girls, and 87 percent were orphans. Two-thirds had entered the profession between the ages of fifteen and nineteen.[9] The government tried in vain to control prostitution by legalizing and regulating it, issuing prostitutes licenses and subjecting them to weekly health inspections. In practice, however, regulation only fed corruption among the police while failing to reduce prostitution.

It wasn't just the well-being of the fallen young girls that the fashionable ladies of Inessa's set worried about. One study at the time found that some 70 percent of urban Russian men used their services.[10] Sixty percent of prostitutes had syphilis, which meant venereal disease was brought home to many a proper, bourgeois wife. A 1907 study of male Moscow university students found that a quarter of them had some form of sexually transmitted disease, mostly gonorrhea and syphilis, and of the nearly 70 percent of students who had already had their first sexual encounter, 41 percent had had it with a prostitute.[11]

It didn't take Inessa long to realize that her efforts to rehabilitate prostitutes were indeed a small act. Condescending lectures from society ladies about chastity were not helpful, nor were the attempts to redeem these girls through drab domestic labor, the very thing many of them were trying to escape.[12] Recidivism rates were near total. Inessa reached a breaking point when one of her colleagues in the shelter reached out for spiritual guidance to their collective idol, Leo Tolstoy. "Nothing will come of your work," the great sage of the day wrote to the ladies. "It was thus before Moses. It was thus after Moses. Thus it was, thus it will be."[13]

That was the end of bourgeois philanthropy for Inessa. In fact, the experience seems to have radicalized her. In 1903, a decade after marrying Alexander and almost immediately after giving birth to their fifth child, Inessa left him for her two great new loves: his younger brother Vladimir and Communism.

Inessa and Vladimir Armand moved to Moscow, apparently with the approval of her husband. Inessa and Alexander never divorced. He continued to support her financially, and the estranged couple corresponded warmly for the rest of her life. Alexander even became a useful ally and bankroller of the Bolshevik underground. His parents also didn't seem to mind their daughter-in-law trading one of their sons for another. Long after the fraternal swap, the elder Armands allowed Inessa to use their home as a place to operate an underground Marxist printing press and to hold illegal meetings. Whenever she got in trouble with the authorities, they used their connections to spring her from jail.[14] The Armands were an enlightened Russian intelligentsia family par excellence.

In Moscow, Inessa joined the Social Democratic Party, as the Marxists then called themselves. She was an active participant in the Russian Revolution of 1905, which had forced Tsar Nicholas II to allow some liberal reforms, like the formation of a parliament. When the inevitable crackdown came, her involvement quickly landed her in prison. After three more arrests and government-imposed exile beyond the Arctic Circle, Inessa slipped across the Finnish border in 1909 and absconded to the French Riviera, where Vladimir Armand's fragile health was failing him. Inessa reached him two weeks before he died of tuberculosis. Grief-stricken, she wandered France aimlessly for nearly a year before she found herself living in Paris. There, she met another Vladimir she could love: Lenin.

Inessa met Lenin through his wife, Nadezhda Krupskaya, who had recruited her to help organize women workers in Paris. Krupskaya had been working with Russian workers in the city but had no way of communicating with the local ones. Conveniently, French was Inessa's native tongue.

Krupskaya was well-born but raised poor, the inverse of Inessa. Her father was a Russian army officer and her mother an educated woman from an impoverished aristocratic family. When she was born, in 1869, they named their only child Nadezhda—"Hope." Whereas Inessa grew up in a big, happy family on a large estate, Krupskaya never knew much of a home or family. Her parents moved around a lot, especially after her father died and her mother had to work as a governess to support them. Krupskaya found refuge in religion and the poetry of Nikolay Nekrasov, who often romanticized the strength and struggles of rural Russian women. One now oft-quoted poem declared that a Russian woman "can stop a galloping steed and enter a burning hut," an expectation of superhuman resilience that haunts Russian women to this day.

Like Inessa, Krupskaya also idolized Tolstoy. The famous novelist had become a radical, working in the fields alongside the peasants of his ancestral estate. While attending a gymnasium for well-bred girls, Krupskaya read Tolstoy's essay "On Labor and Luxury" and decided to forgo whatever small extravagances she and her mother could afford and do her own housework. She would adhere to this Tolstoyan asceticism for the rest of her life.[15] The teenaged Krupskaya was also captivated by his essays on liberalizing the tsarist education system. Stirred by the same theory of small deeds that had inspired Inessa, Krupskaya wrote to Tolstoy about his project, the Intermediary. Its goal was to reissue popular books cheaply to make them widely available for the masses. Tolstoy was looking for volunteer editors, and Krupskaya was ready to join the effort. She began translating books for the Intermediary, her first foray into the work of educating the Russian people.

As a young woman living in St. Petersburg, Krupskaya gave lessons at a school for the workers of a porcelain factory. Three nights a week she taught basic literacy. To those who were already literate, she taught arithmetic, history, and Russian literature. There were over six hundred students in the school, and Krupskaya recalled that the students treated her and the other teachers "with boundless trust."

Krupskaya was converted from Tolstoyism to Marxism when someone gave her a copy of Marx's seminal work, *Capital*. "I literally drank the water of life," she wrote of the experience of reading it.[16] Marx gave her a new way to see her students, while her work gave her access to a world that socialist intellectuals often talked and wrote about but that very few had ever experienced. The school, Krupskaya recalled later, was "an excellent way to really get to know the everyday life, the working conditions, and the mood of the working masses."

She began attending illegal Marxist gatherings, where, in February 1894, she met Vladimir Lenin. He made a terrible first impression. Krupskaya noticed how condescending and dismissive he was of a group member who suggested forming a committee to combat illiteracy—the very work she did. "Well, whoever wants to save the Fatherland through a literacy committee," she recalled him scoffing, "we won't stand in their way!" He spent the rest of the evening mutely glowering at everyone.

Afterward, as Krupskaya and her friends walked home in the dark along the frozen Okhta River, someone explained why Lenin was so cutting and suspicious. His eldest brother Alexander had been hanged just a few years earlier at the age of twenty-one for his role in a foiled plot to assassinate the tsar. After the execution, friends and family—all of them ostensible liberals—began avoiding Lenin's mother for fear that they too would get in trouble. "This universal cowardice made . . . a big impression on him," Krupskaya wrote later. "He learned the price of liberal talk early on." This story seemed to unlock something for the twenty-four-year-old Krupskaya. Lenin was not just some petty contrarian; he was a bruised and vulnerable young man with a tumultuous inner world.

After that evening, Krupskaya and Lenin saw a lot more of each other. He gave illegal lectures on Marx in the same thicket of Petersburg factories where she taught. Every Sunday after they finished teaching, Lenin walked Krupskaya home and came up to the apartment she shared with her mother to chat. Krupskaya lived and breathed the school—"Don't feed me bread, just let me talk about the school, the students, the factory," she once wrote—and her work fascinated Lenin. Like other Marxists at the time, he showed up, talked at the workers, and left. But Krupskaya, he realized, really knew them. "Vladimir Ilyich wanted to know about every little detail that could give him a fuller picture of the workers' lives," Krupskaya recalled. She became his teacher, guiding him into the world of the people he claimed to lead.

Krupskaya went deeper and deeper into the socialist underground, learning how to evade surveillance, write in code, and develop invisible ink. She helped print Lenin's propagandistic screeds and socialist newspapers. She took a job as a clerk at the railroad office in St. Petersburg, which she used to help the revolutionaries stay in touch, a skill that would come in handy when she ran Lenin's party apparatus from abroad.

When Lenin was arrested in 1895, he wrote frequently to Krupskaya. The tsarist authorities were remarkably humane in jailing their political opponents, something Lenin and his disciples would correct as soon as they came to power. Prisoners were allowed visits from relatives, including fiancées, who could bring them food, books, and letters. Revolutionaries naturally took advantage of this loophole and began sending fake fiancées who brought coded messages into prison and took coded messages out. One revolutionary recalled being in jail with a man who had three such fiancées.[17]

In 1896, a wave of arrests of radicals snared Krupskaya. Lacking Inessa's connections, she languished in jail for months. A few months later, another female prisoner set herself on fire in protest at her imprisonment and the rattled government decided to free all women inmates. Lenin, who had by then been sentenced to three years' exile in a remote Siberian village, officially requested that his "fiancée" join him there. Tsarist officials, likely tired of revolutionaries and their fake fiancées, agreed to send Krupskaya on the condition that they actually get married. "Well," Krupskaya is said to have sighed when she learned of this stipulation, "if it must be as a wife, then I'll go as a wife." (The original Russian is even less enthusiastic: *nu chtozh, zhenoy, tak zhenoy.*)[18] In 1898, Krupskaya tied her fate to the two most important things in her life: she officially joined the Social Democratic Party, and she married Vladimir Lenin.

Despite being reduced to "Lenin's women" by historians, Inessa and Krupskaya were instrumental in implementing his vision of a socialist revolution. Inessa became a skilled agent of the Bolshevik underground and a master propagandist with a deep knowledge of Marxism. In the long years of exile abroad, "even more than Trotsky... she became Lenin's 'cudgel'—someone to beat wavering Bolsheviks back into line, to deliver uncompromising messages to his political opponents, to carry out uncomfortable missions, which Lenin himself preferred to avoid," wrote historian R. C. Elwood in his biography of Inessa.[19]

She was one of the few women in the party who had a university diploma, which she had earned in Brussels, since Russian universities did not admit women. She knew that for the party men to take her seriously, she had to be good at what they respected most: not the organizational work typically done by women, but the theorizing. During her French exile, she taught Marxist history at Lenin's Bolshevik academy in a tiny town near Paris. She was the only female lecturer. She also founded and ran *Rabotnitsa*, an illegal Marxist newspaper to agitate among the female workers for which it was named.[20] When a wave of workers' strikes seized Russia in 1912, it was Inessa whom Lenin sent back from Europe to take control of the party and make sure the Social Democrats back home toed his line and no one else's. They both knew she faced certain arrest on her return, but Lenin also knew that she would carry out her mission and not break. (She was indeed arrested and behaved stoically throughout.)

Historians have been especially unkind to Krupskaya. One Russian scholar wrote that Krupskaya lived in Lenin's "shadow, her life having meaning only because she was linked to him." Another Russian historian wrote that "she was not good at anything, not even at housekeeping."[21] This is a theme picked up by other, mostly male historians. "Her willingness to act as Lenin's revolutionary helpmate and comrade," wrote Richard Stites, "was no doubt fortified by her confessed distaste for housework."[22] The one Western biography dedicated exclusively to her, by Robert McNeal, is called, tellingly, *Bride of the Revolution*. McNeal lingers on her looks, writing that while "writers probably would not have called her a rare beauty," someone meeting a young Krupskaya would have noted "her slightly over-full lips, presuming them sensuous," as well as "her arched eyebrows, fine, high cheekbones and firm jaw—all conveying a sense of feminine challenge."[23] Then Krupskaya came down with a type of hyperthyroidism and her eyes bulged, her neck swelled, and she put on weight. McNeal describes all this in great detail but never once mentions Lenin's baldness.

Given the kind of man Lenin was—domineering, aggressive, difficult—Krupskaya was surely overshadowed by him to some extent. But it would be grossly inaccurate to underestimate her influence on him and on the Revolution. The two of them translated important socialist texts together and edited each other's writing. When Lenin theorized on the need for a small vanguard of professional revolutionaries, it was Krupskaya who actually built it, managing the party's finances, passing orders to hundreds of socialist agents with regularly changing addresses around Europe and Russia, all in constantly changing code.[24] While Lenin fought internecine ideological battles within the Social Democratic Party, it was Krupskaya, the secretary of the main party newspaper, *Iskra*, who made sure it was Lenin's line, and no one else's, that was distributed to the party rank and file. When Krupskaya and Lenin were based abroad, Trotsky wrote that Krupskaya

> was at the very center of all the organizational work; she received comrades when they arrived, instructed them when they left, established connections, supplied secret addresses, wrote letters, and coded and decoded correspondence. In her room there was always the smell of burned paper from the secret letters she heated over the fire to [develop invisible ink and] read. She often complained, in her gently insistent way, that people did not write enough, or that they got the code all mixed up, or wrote in chemical ink in such a way that one line covered another, and so forth.[25]

McNeal, who felt "there is no point in trying to inflate her independent role," nevertheless conceded that "her contribution to the development of the organization that became Bolshevism required not genius but inexhaustible devotion, and on this basis, it is no exaggeration to say that her role was essential."[26] Even this grudging admission, though, reduces her role to that of a particularly dedicated secretary. In reality, her most important contribution was to deepen Lenin's understanding of working-class life. She was his teacher, his entrée into the world of the very proletariat he professed to lead.

A FAIRY-TALE COUNTRY

LATE AT NIGHT ON OCTOBER 10, 1917, ALEXANDRA KOLLONTAI FOUND her way to a secret meeting of the twelve-person Central Committee of the Social Democratic Party. After Nicholas II abdicated his throne, the situation in Russia—and on the eastern front, where Russia was fighting Germany in the Great War—was rapidly getting worse. Soldiers, hearing from their wives and mothers that there was nothing to eat back home, were deserting in droves to go help their families. The Provisional Government hadn't been able to alleviate the food and fuel shortages, nor did it ease up on the revolutionaries. Lenin had gone underground to avoid arrest. Krupskaya had retreated from party activity and spent her time organizing soldiers' wives. Inessa had gone home to Moscow to organize the Bolsheviks there. But Kollontai stayed in Petrograd, in the thick of the political maneuvering. Lenin had called the October 10 meeting to propose a motion: it was time to overthrow the Provisional Government and seize power on behalf of the workers of the world.

After hours of heated argument, the Central Committee voted. Kollontai and eight other members sided with Lenin and his plan for a coup. The resolution passed. "The tension broke immediately," Kollontai recalled. "We felt hungry. A hot samovar was brought out, we fell upon the cheese and sausage." Sated and resolved, they dispersed in the early hours of the morning and Kollontai walked home, tired and a little nervous, but also tingling with premonition. "It will strike," she wrote later, "the end of the old world."[1]

After nearly twenty years of thankless, dangerous work, Kollontai witnessed what she thought she would never see in her lifetime: a socialist revolution. It was, she would later write, "the greatest, most memorable hour of my life." Four days later, Lenin, the undisputed head of the new revolutionary state, appointed her the commissar for social welfare, making her the first woman in the world to hold a cabinet position.

Almost immediately, Kollontai realized that the Bolsheviks' seizure of power had changed little in Russia. When she showed up for work at the building occupied by her agency's predecessor, the Provisional Government's Ministry of Social Welfare, the security guard wouldn't even let her in. She returned with an entourage and the guard relented, only for her to find that the building was deserted: all the ministry's employees were on strike. After much agonizing, she ordered the arrest of the officials who had the keys to the safe containing ministry funds. They gave up the treasure only after a few nights in jail.

Kollontai was constantly swarmed by petitioners who had taken the Bolsheviks' utopian promises of peace, land, and bread literally. Wounded soldiers came asking for food and shelter, threatening a massive demonstration if she didn't comply. Another day brought a group of tattered and hungry orphans begging for sustenance. Flustered, Kollontai gave them each twenty kopeks from her own pocket and ordered the Petrograd militia to feed them. A peasant whose horse had been requisitioned by the tsar's army showed up at Kollontai's apartment and said Lenin had authorized her to pay him.[2] Still, by the time the new year rolled in, Kollontai was able to get the bureaucracy under her control and finally start implementing her vision of how women would live under socialism.

On January 20, 1918, she issued her first decrees. Maternity hospitals would now be free and open to any woman who needed their services. Obstetricians became government employees and were banned from conducting experiments on their poorer patients, a common practice in tsarist times.[3] Eleven days later, Kollontai abolished the old regime's laws regulating maternal and child welfare. From now on, everything was to go through her commissariat—and through her.[4]

Kollontai also began work on the Palace of Motherhood, which was to be the model of what she wanted to implement across the new country: clean, safe, free places for women to give birth, regardless of marital status or social station. She occupied an old orphanage from the days of Catherine the Great where women used to drop off unwanted babies at a side window. The old nurses were horrified—they felt that pregnant but unmarried women deserved to be shamed—but had to comply.

Kollontai also requisitioned the local Alexander Nevsky Monastery, one of Russia's most sacred sites, and turned it into a home for Russia's growing population of wounded war veterans. This sparked a riot of monks and religious citizens and infuriated Lenin, who had wanted to challenge the powerful Russian Orthodox Church on his own terms. Nevertheless, the party seized the moment and issued a decree (drafted by another woman) that officially separated church and state, cutting off one of the Church's main streams of revenue and power. Now the state, rather than the Church, would control family institutions.

It was just the beginning. The Bolsheviks had made a promise to eliminate bourgeois marriage and the bourgeois family, and they intended to keep it. The Provisional Government had already given women the right to vote in July 1917, making Russia the first large country in the world to do so. The Bolsheviks went further, mandating equal voting rights irrespective of gender, nationality, or religion. Children born out of wedlock now had the same legal rights and status as their legitimate counterparts. If a woman registered a man as the father of her child and the man did not contest it, he was obligated to pay child support, starting even before the child was born.

Kollontai's writings became the blueprint for Soviet family policy. Maternity leave for eight weeks before and after childbirth became standard. The new government also abolished religious marriage. The only unions the state recognized were those concluded in the Office for the Registration of Acts of Civil Status (ZAGS). The legal age of marriage was raised to sixteen for girls and eighteen for boys. New laws established the equality of husband and wife in marriage, divorce, and property ownership. No longer did the wife have to take her husband's name or follow him if he moved. Moreover, the two citizens were no longer called husband or wife but were each referred to by the gender-neutral "spouse," both in legal documents and in life. Divorce was legalized and simplified. In a decree, the Bolsheviks decried the old system in which "people alien to each other were chained together like prisoners in a wheelbarrow." Now, simply wanting to end a marriage provided sufficient grounds for its annulment, and either spouse could request alimony. These measures made Russia the first and only country in the world with full freedom of divorce.[5] The new code, one Menshevik legal scholar proclaimed, was "almost completely free of male egoism."

Rights that women in Russia had sought for decades were granted to them seemingly overnight. Universities now had to accept women, and all educational institutions had to remove any specification of gender from their titles.[6] The 1918 constitution stipulated that every citizen was required to work and to receive the same minimum wage, regardless of gender.

These reforms weren't undertaken only for the benefit of the residents of the world's first socialist state. The Bolsheviks' goal had always been to spark world revolution, and Kollontai's policies were a very good advertisement. A 1921 Soviet manifesto directed to "Women Workers of All Countries" announced that Soviet Russian women were no longer exploited. When it came to working women, the pamphlet claimed, Soviet Russia was now "a fairy-tale country."[7]

In March 1918, Lenin struck a deal with Germany and pulled Russia out of the Great War. Incensed, Kollontai resigned her commissarial post in protest, only months after taking it. She had warned Lenin that withdrawing would plunge the country into civil war: all the forces that opposed Bolshevik power would now be free to attack the young socialist order. Almost immediately, her predictions came to pass. Fighting broke out between the Red Army and the many factions that wanted to unseat the new Bolshevik government.

But there was an unexpected boon for Kollontai's mission. Although women were important to the Bolshevik war effort, most stayed home. In the absence of their men, they tended their farms and worked in the factories, where they now made up half the workforce. Convincing these women to support the Bolshevik cause, and not the enemy's, was now a matter of life and death.

Party leadership finally acknowledged that they could not assume that women would naturally find their way to Communism. In September 1919, the party created the Zhenotdel, or the Women's Section of the Central Committee of the Communist Party, headquartered right across the street from the Kremlin. The Zhenotdel was tasked with turning the backward, slumbering *baba*s of the hinterlands into modern citizens of the first socialist state on earth. It was, historian Barbara Evans Clements wrote, "one of the most ambitious attempts to emancipate women ever undertaken by a government."[8]

Thousands of eager young women working for the Zhenotdel fanned out across the country, their heads covered in their signature red kerchiefs. The Zhenotdel organized propaganda expeditions, sending trains and river boats deep into the countryside to explain to skeptical Russian women why Bolshevism would be their salvation. (Distributing propaganda was deemed pointless, since most women couldn't read.) No more slaving away in the kitchen or over the washtub. No more dying in childbirth; no more toddlers swollen with disease. No more illiteracy, domestic abuse, or being trapped in bad marriages for economic reasons. The new Bolshevik state promised to solve all of this. "The task of [the Zhenotdel] is the propaganda of communism not only in words but also in deeds," Kollontai announced in *Pravda*. "The woman worker must find out why she should become a communist . . . not only from orators' speeches but also from living examples."[9]

Kollontai suggested that Zhenotdel agitators broach these ideas with their target audience gently. "The only correct form is to approach her by asking her about her sick cow," she advised, returning to the idea of the ignorant *baba*. "Then from the cow you can go further and lead her to the idea of world revolution."[10]

The Zhenotdel had been Kollontai's idea, but it was Inessa who was tapped to be its first head. Inessa had Lenin's ear and he saw her as more politically loyal and less flamboyant than Kollontai. Still, Inessa was not a bad choice. Like Kollontai and Lenin, she believed in the need to change the elementary building blocks of society. "Until the old forms of the family, domestic life, education, and child-rearing are abolished," Inessa wrote in 1919, "it is impossible to obliterate exploitation and enslavement, it is impossible to create the new person, impossible to build socialism."[11]

Before the two revolutions of 1917, the Bolshevik Party was the most egalitarian of the many anti-tsarist parties when it came to allowing women into its ranks and giving them high-level jobs. Once the Revolution became a reality, however, much of that egalitarianism evaporated. Most of the women who had had storied careers in the socialist underground shied away from official posts, in part because they, too, held on to certain stereotypes about themselves as women. Nor were many offers forthcoming from the men in charge. The stakes were now too high and too real to entrust such important matters to the women.

In April 1917, Inessa and Krupskaya were nominated to be Central Committee functionaries, but, despite their key roles as Lenin's loyal lieutenants, neither was elected. While Kollontai had gotten a cabinet-level position in October 1917, men in the Central Committee saw her work with women and children as far less important than the serious matters they dealt with. The only other woman to get a senior post was the Bolshevik stalwart Elena Stasova. She became the technical secretary under the Central Committee member who made decisions regarding personnel and party financing. Ultimately, the Bolsheviks never questioned the traditional division of political labor: men made the policy and women administered it.[12]

And so, despite her early successes, Kollontai quickly receded from the front lines of party politics. The party men were not her only impediment. One January night in 1918, coming home after a long day, she got a call. The Palace of Motherhood, the first free maternity hospital in Soviet Russia and her cherished pilot project, was on fire—the work of an arsonist. Kollontai rushed to the site, but it was too late. As she watched the palace burn, the old nurses from the hospital shouted at her that the fire was the manifestation of God's wrath against her, the Antichrist.¹³

Nor did Kollontai get any shelter in the Central Committee, where the men gossiped constantly about her relationship with Pavel Dybenko, a handsome swashbuckling sailor sixteen years her junior who had risen from a desperately poor peasant family to become commissar of the navy. Even after they married (at Dybenko's insistence), the gossip didn't stop. Lenin, disregarding his own dalliance with Inessa, said of Kollontai, "I will not vouch for the reliability of women whose love affair is intertwined with politics."¹⁴ After her resignation from the Commissariat, Kollontai went into seclusion and Dybenko went to war, whence stories of his philandering reached his new wife.

Inessa was able to navigate intraparty conflicts better than Kollontai, but she was trying to run the Zhenotdel while the country was at war with itself and on the brink of famine. She worked long hours, chain-smoked, had little to eat, and was so haggard by the summer of 1920 that Lenin insisted she take a rest in the south.

The Zhenotdel, meanwhile, faced massive resistance in the regions. Peasant women were often horrified by the erroneous idea that the Communists were trying to separate them from their children. Their husbands did not appreciate these strange city women trying to teach their wives strange city things. In one Ukrainian village, a Zhenotdel organizer gathered local women in a hut to teach them to read. The village men surrounded the hut and shouted, "We'll beat you up if you touch our wives!" In a nearby district, three Zhenotdel workers were killed in one year.¹⁵ Even men in the Party banned their wives from joining the Zhenotdel, fearing they would become infected with dangerous notions of liberation, sexual and otherwise. It was one thing to theorize about such things when they had been powerless in the underground but another thing entirely when their women put these ideas into practice. Zhenotdel delegates complained that party men were not taking women peasants and workers seriously, dismissing them and their "*baba* brains."¹⁶ "The business of emancipating women workers and peasants is far more complicated," Inessa wrote before her death, "far more difficult, and demands much more time that it had seemed to us at first."¹⁷

Just before 10 p.m. on August 30, 1918, Lenin arrived at Moscow's Mikhelson armaments factory to give a speech to its workers.[18] That January, Russia had held what would be its last free elections until the collapse of the Soviet Union in 1991.[19] After the parliamentary contest was won by the populist Socialist Revolutionaries (SRs), Bolshevik guards dissolved the Constituent Assembly by force. When tens of thousands of people marched in protest, Bolshevik guards shot into the crowd, killing many.[20] Soon the Bolsheviks began banning rival political parties and arresting their members. That summer, SRs were rounded up by the hundreds. The mood was tense: the morning of Lenin's speech at the factory, the Petrograd head of the new Bolshevik secret police, the Cheka, had been assassinated. Without any evidence, the Bolsheviks immediately blamed the SRs.

At the factory, Lenin delivered a long speech justifying this "proletarian dictatorship." Workers had submitted questions in writing, but, after a one-hour rant, Lenin said he had run out of time. As he left the factory, a woman approached to complain that police were confiscating bread at railroad stations.[21] Lenin, his foot already on the running board of his car, reassured her that he had given an order to stop the practice and moved to get inside. Suddenly, three shots rang out and Lenin crumpled to the ground. Two of the bullets had hit him: one broke his shoulder, the other passed through one of his lungs and lodged in his neck.[22] As he was rushed back to the Kremlin, police seized a young woman fleeing the scene with a Browning pistol in her bag. Her name was Fanny Kaplan.

Born in a western Ukrainian shtetl, Fanny was radicalized at the age of fifteen by the failed Revolution of 1905. Two years later she was with a group of anarchists in Kiev planning the assassination of the local tsarist governor general when the bomb they were building went off prematurely.[23] Partially blinded by the blast, Fanny was arrested, tried, and sentenced to death. Her sentence was commuted to a lifetime of hard labor in a Siberian penal colony. There, her sight flickering on and off, she became friends with Maria Spiridonova, a legendary Socialist Revolutionary, who converted her to the leftist cause. When the Provisional Government amnestied political prisoners in 1917, Kaplan returned to Ukraine, where surgery partially restored her eyesight. At twenty-seven years old, she was alone in the world: while she was in jail, her family had emigrated to the United States without her.[24] She eventually made her way to Moscow, the new revolutionary capital. Kaplan was infuriated by the dissolution of the Constituent Assembly and the arrests of hundreds of her fellow party members, so she joined an SR plot to kill Lenin. When a male assassin lost his nerve, Kaplan volunteered, declaring that she would turn herself in after the act was done.

She did just that. "I shot Lenin because I believe him to be a traitor," she told her interrogator. "By living long, he postpones the idea of socialism for decades to come."[25] Despite hours of interrogation, she refused to give up the names of her co-conspirators.

Lenin, in the meantime, lay bleeding on the tsar's old plush pillows. The Bolshevik leadership decided he would not be safe in a hospital, so he was treated in his Kremlin apartment. As he slipped closer to death, his staff ran up and down Tverskaya Street, trying to rent an oxygen tank from one of the pharmacies. Krupskaya, who had been at a political meeting across town, was whisked to the Kremlin without being told what was going on. But when Lenin came to, the first person he asked to see was Inessa.[26] While they talked, Krupskaya waited outside and entertained Inessa's daughter. It was the last time Lenin and Inessa would see each other.

Despite his pierced lung, Lenin recovered remarkably quickly from the shooting, which only helped fuel the semireligious cult that was already forming around him. How else could a man so critically wounded be pulled back from the antechamber of death?

That fall, as Krupskaya was tending to her recovering husband, she worried about Fanny Kaplan. What was to become of her? Was she going to be executed? Lenin demurred, saying the Central Committee would decide, but Krupskaya wouldn't let it rest. She and Lenin had grown up venerating the martyrdom of Sofia Perovskaya, the young woman who was hanged for helping to assassinate the tsar. Her execution, as well as that of other political prisoners, was proof to the revolutionaries that the monarchy was immoral and had to be overthrown.[27] Krupskaya buttonholed Lenin's visitors, asking if they knew what would happen to Kaplan. When one old acquaintance called on Lenin, Krupskaya threw herself on the woman's neck and began to sob. "A revolutionary executed in a revolutionary country!" she wailed. "Never!"

But Fanny Kaplan was long dead. On September 3, 1918, she had been taken out of her cell and brought down to a cul-de-sac behind one of the Kremlin's gates. A cluster of automobiles waited. The Cheka officers started their engines and ordered Kaplan to walk forward. One of the Kremlin's commandants drew his revolver and fired. The commandants were far better shots than Kaplan. Her body was stuffed into a steel oil drum, doused with gasoline, and set alight. Smelling the char of burning human flesh, the Soviet poet-propagandist Demian Bedny, who had been brought in to document her execution, fainted.

The next day the Bolsheviks issued a decree initiating the Red Terror, the first of several waves of mass political murders. Invoking Kaplan's attempt on Lenin's life, the order called for the arrest of all SRs and "not the slightest indecisiveness in the application of terror." Grigory Zinoviev, a member of the Central Committee and one of Krupskaya's closest friends, called for the regime's enemies to "drown themselves in their own blood." The chair of the new Revolutionary Tribunal, Nikolai Krylenko, declared, "We must execute not only the guilty. Execution of the innocent will impress the masses even more."[28]

Despite her concern for Fanny Kaplan's fate, Krupskaya did nothing to stop the Red Terror short of successfully intervening on behalf of a few acquaintances. In the campaign's first two months, there were at least 6,185 executions, almost as many death sentences as the tsarist courts had handed down in over ninety years.[29] As for Fanny Kaplan, Krupskaya never did say if she knew that in this "fairy-tale country" a revolutionary had been executed without a trial. Even the tsarist government had granted Sofia Perovskaya that much.

RIVA

MY GREAT-GRANDMOTHER RIVKA WEISSER WAS BORN IN 1901 IN SAL-nitsa, in west-central Ukraine. She was the fourth of seven children, six of them girls. Her parents owned a small shop dedicated to keeping the women of the shtetl dressed in the finest fashion they could afford. Twice a year, her mother, Ethel, went to Warsaw—the Jewish Paris—to stock up on fashion magazines and hats and gloves and ribbons with lovely French names for the colors, like *pervenche* and *fraise*.

Riva's parents provided a nice life for their daughters, but, past a certain point, they did not much feel like wasting their money on their educations. Too much schooling was a pointless luxury for girls whose destiny was to be wives and mothers. Rivka—or Riva, as she was known in the family—took matters into her own hands. As a teenager, she began tutoring Yiddish-speaking students in Russian grammar, putting her earnings in a tin that she hid behind a loose brick in the stove. If her parents wouldn't send her to the gymnasium in glamorous, cosmopolitan Odessa, Riva was determined to send herself.

But her plans were foiled by the needs of another woman in the house: the cook, who stole the money but was kind enough to replace the emptied tin in its hiding place. Riva swooned when she saw the naked bottom of the tin staring up at her. She would remember that feeling of impotent, bitter fury till the end of her days. Still, measured against the rest of her life, this would be the least of Riva's setbacks. The twentieth century in Russia was just getting started.

The Revolution and the Civil War were the stuff of my great-grandmothers' youth, the banging overture to the Soviet experiment crashing into their young lives. All four of them were born within a couple years of each other, at the exact turn of the twentieth century. When the Revolution came, it would ensure that their lives would be nothing like those of their mothers and grandmothers, the four of them entering the world as young women just as it was being turned upside down, as a new Soviet government set out to radically remake society. My four great-grandmothers, along with their children and grandchildren, would all get to live in Kollontai's fairy-tale country, a utopia whose breathtaking ambition was matched only by the tragedy it wrought in their lives.

All four were born deep in the Pale of Settlement, the theater for some of the twentieth century's greatest calamities. Created by Catherine the Great in 1794, the Pale stretched from the Baltics in the north, through eastern Poland and western Belarus, into western and central Ukraine, and south to Odessa on the Black Sea. By the end of the nineteenth century, it was the only place in the vast Russian Empire where millions of Jews were allowed to live, under an increasingly restrictive set of rules. These strictures, such as a ban on owning certain land or engaging in various professions, produced terrible poverty. The hardship of daily life was punctuated with regular explosions of anti-Jewish violence—*pogroms*, one of the few Russian words to have been absorbed into the English language.

At the turn of the twentieth century, nearly two million Jews left the Pale for the United States, Canada, South Africa, and South America. Most American Jews can trace their ancestry back to this imperial Jewish zoo. But after the Revolution, after the borders closed and their ties were severed, they and their descendants heard little of what happened to the parents, siblings, and cousins left behind. My family is descended from the Jews who stayed. The ones who, wittingly or unwittingly, remained to see what the experiment would yield, the very distant cousins of what my family calls the "smart Jews," people who must have sensed in their bones that this part of the world would never be good to their kind. It would take another three generations for our branches of those families to reach the same conclusion.

When the Great War came in the stifling summer of 1914, its eastern front aligned neatly with the territories of the Pale. Tsarist authorities drafted about half a million Jews to serve in the imperial army. Those who stayed home were persecuted savagely.¹ Russian troops stationed in the area robbed and killed them, and some half a million Jews were either deported or fled the war zones.

The Jewish population of the Pale exhaled with relief when the Bolsheviks seized power and pulled Russia out of the Great War. But no sooner had the eastern front receded than the shtetls of the Pale again found history galloping through their ancient, muddy streets. This time it was the Civil War, which brought new waves of pogroms, far more savage than the ones the Jews had come to expect. "Before the advent of Hitler, the greatest modern mass murder of Jews occurred in the Ukraine, in the course of the Civil War," wrote historian Peter Kenez, himself a Holocaust survivor.² Though the Bolsheviks did some of the looting and killing in Ukraine, the vast majority of it was executed by the so-called Whites: the Volunteer Army of General Anton Denikin, who wanted to restore the monarchy, and the armies of the Ukrainian nationalist Symon Petliura. The pogroms were carried out mostly by their shared foot soldiers, the Cossacks. "Methods of murder varied greatly," wrote Kenez. "There were instances of hanging, burning, drowning in wells, and live burials. There are recorded instances of men buried in the sand up to their necks and then killed by having horses driven over them."³ Rape was a common weapon. "They raped young girls and seventy-year-old women," wrote historian Oleg Budnitskii. "Often, the rapes were gang rapes; sometimes, women were raped in front of their husbands and children."

Almost as soon as the Bolsheviks came to power, they abolished the Pale of Settlement and its strictures, including the quota system that had kept Jewish students out of universities and large cities. These moves won the Bolsheviks many Jewish sympathizers and followers— and made the Jews even bigger targets for the Whites. Meanwhile, the Orthodox Church built support for the pogroms among the Christian population of the Pale.

The result was surreal horror. When writer Isaac Babel traveled through the area as a Red Army commissar, he and the Bolshevik troops often arrived just after the White marauders had been driven out.⁴ "They cut beards, that's standard, gathered forty-five Jews in the market, took them to the slaughterhouse, torture, they cut tongues, screams heard across the whole town square," he wrote of Zhitomir in 1920. In Dubno, "everything is smashed."[5] In Komarov, he finds "a naked, barely breathing old man-prophet, an old woman hacked to death, a child with hacked-off fingers, many of them are barely breathing, the foul stench of blood, everything ransacked, chaos, a mother standing over her hacked-to-death son." ("Our guys," he notes of his Red Army comrades, "are strolling around indifferently, stealing where they can, ripping things off the hacked-up victims.")[6]

When the war finally ended in 1921, it was impossible to count the Jewish dead. Estimates have found a queasy equilibrium at fifty thousand, though some estimates put the toll in Ukraine closer to one hundred and fifty thousand, with another twenty-five thousand killed in Belarus.

My paternal great-grandmother, Khana-Batya Ring, lived through a Red pogrom in Ostropol, Ukraine. Afterward, her two eldest siblings departed for America, leaving Khana-Batya and their other siblings locked inside a newly created Soviet Ukraine. Khana-Batya soon married a man named Moisei Tartakovsky. "The years of the Civil War in Ukraine (1919–21) imprinted themselves in my memory," Moisei's little brother Wolf recalled in his memoirs some eighty years later. Wolf was seven when the Civil War began. He could not understand which marauder belonged to which army, nor do we know if he saw what happened next with his own eyes or if he heard about it later, from the adults. "One day, right in the synagogue," Wolf wrote, "the bandits killed six men and one woman."

The woman Wolf was referring to was Ethel Weisser, my maternal great-great-grandmother and Riva's mother. All that remains of Ethel now are memories of the lovely silk ribbons with the lovely French names and the variations of how she met her end, the many deaths Ethel Weisser has endured in the retelling, all of them elaborately cruel and entirely plausible.

Wolf said Ethel was murdered in the synagogue, but I heard several other versions growing up. On the first day of the pogrom, Riva's father, Gersh, ordered his family to hide in the attic. Then he locked up the house and stood inside, just behind the door, waiting for the danger to pass. Instead, it arrived in the form of Cossacks riding through the town, whooping and shooting into the air. One of their bullets pierced the door and Gersh's body, killing him. My mother, Olga, Ethel's great-granddaughter, tells a different story. She's sure the Cossacks tied Gersh and Ethel to a wagon and dragged them to their deaths, forcing the Weisser children to watch.

According to the version my grandmother, Riva's daughter, told me, after Gersh was shot and killed through the door, Ethel was hanged the next day in the town square. Her children were lined up and forced to watch. In a more recent retelling, my grandmother contended that Ethel died when the Reds came through town and lined everyone up, shooting every tenth person. Ethel had the bad luck of being tenth, and Riva and her siblings were forced to watch.

A century later, I have no evidence for any one of these versions of Ethel's death. On one point, however, the entire family is in agreement: when Ethel was killed, her children were forced to watch, and six-year-old Eva went mad.

That was the end of their life in Salnitsa. Riva was eighteen. She took her two younger sisters, Leah and little Eva, now teetering on the edge of sanity, and her teenage brother, and moved in with their oldest sister, Hannah Weisser. Hannah lived with her husband and their two small daughters in a town sixty miles away. It, too, had been swept by a White pogrom. Then Riva's little brother came down with the Spanish flu and died. Even without the threat of a fatal virus, the chaos of a civil war was hardly amenable to feeding more in-laws. Riva overheard Hannah's husband say as much. When Riva confronted him, he didn't deny it. "Every family should live for itself," he told her.

And so Riva packed her bags and did what so many young Jews did now that the Bolsheviks had eliminated any restrictions on where they could live: she left. She went first to Odessa, where she passed her high school exams after years of lonely study—she never did get to go to that gymnasium—and then north to Moscow, the new Soviet capital, flung open to young, ambitious Jews hungry to live in the big Russian cities and attend the universities that had been closed to them for over a century.

Riva rented a tiny room in a communal apartment in one of Moscow's old side streets with two of her sisters, Leah and Dora. Her sisters went to nursing school while Riva enrolled in the pedology department at the Moscow State Pedagogical Institute. Pedology was a nineteenth-century science that blended child psychology with the study of child development.[7] In Europe it had gone out of fashion, but in Soviet Russia, which was busy experimenting with how to build the new Soviet man, pedology was all the rage. To Riva, all of it was so wonderfully new, this unstoppable propulsion toward the blindingly bright Soviet future. It no longer even mattered that the family cook had stolen her tuition money; in the world's first socialist state, education was free.

Still, those were years of hunger and cold and chaos. The Bolsheviks had inherited a state bankrupted by four years of fighting a world war and three years of fighting a civil war. Then, in 1921, just as the Civil War was ending, the economy collapsed.[8] To deal with the crisis, the Bolsheviks implemented a policy known as War Communism, seizing control of all industry and trade and suspending monetary transactions to deal with runaway inflation. Lenin ordered his troops to seize grain from the peasants to feed hungry city dwellers, unleashing a famine in the countryside that claimed some five million lives. Soon the cities were overrun with as many as seven million orphans: the *besprizorniki*—literally, the ones who have no one to watch over them.

Riva and her sisters had so little money that Riva, who was short and compact, slept on a trunk. She had to cover Moscow's great expanses on foot because she couldn't afford the fare for the trolleybus. She was often hungry, only allowing herself one little bun of bread per day. Yet, in the evenings, she somehow found the energy to volunteer as a teacher of adult literacy to members of Moscow's growing working class.

In pre-Revolution Russia, "illiteracy," wrote historian Richard Stites, "was essentially a woman's problem."[9] When the Bolsheviks took over, out of the 17 million illiterate people in the Russian Empire, 14 million were women. In 1920, Krupskaya dreamt up an adult education program much like the one she had run in the factories of Petrograd, called the Extraordinary Commission for the Liquidation of Illiteracy, or LikBez. Most of the teachers were women, either Zhenotdel staffers or enthusiastic volunteers like Riva. The campaign, writes Stites, was "the largest of its kind ever mounted by a government up to that time."[10] By 1926, government figures showed that 42 percent of Soviet women could read. By 1939, that number was well above 80 percent. By the time my mother went to university in 1976, virtually all women in the Soviet Union could read. It was the highest female literacy rate in the world.

I once saw a photo of Riva with her students. There they were, workers and peasants frozen in creamy grays on a piece of cardboard, laughing and grinning as if the camera weren't there, everyone bundled up in peacoats and shearlings and hats even though they were inside—because who could afford heat? The walls of the requisitioned old building are festooned with red flags and revolutionary slogans. And there, standing at the very edge of the photo, serious and wide-eyed, is tiny Riva Weisser in her black winter coat, surrounded by hardy men and women who were her height when she stood and they sat at the big table covered in paper exercises, all of them new Soviet people.

THE FIRST FIRST LADY

IN 1919, TWO YEARS AFTER LENIN SEIZED POWER, A BRITISH JOURNALIST interviewed Nadezhda Krupskaya and referred to her as Soviet Russia's "First Lady." The Brit hadn't known what to call the wife of the first leader of the first socialist government in the world, so he reached for a familiar Western analogue. Lenin and Krupskaya found this so amusing that Lenin began jokingly addressing Krupskaya as "First Lady" at home, in English.[1]

The first Soviet first lady did not act like one. She and Lenin lived in a third-floor walk-up in the Kremlin, which they shared with Lenin's sister Maria. The family had some servants—a bodyguard who doubled as a driver for Lenin, a secretary for Krupskaya—but when guests stopped by, it was Krupskaya and Maria who served them tea. Krupskaya never hosted a state banquet and rarely appeared with her husband at public events. She dressed modestly; Lenin was known to sew his own buttons.[2] Their austerity was appropriate for the lean times over which the couple presided.

Krupskaya also worked. She wrote copiously about her favorite subject, education, and delivered speeches at important Party congresses. In the summer of 1919, while the country was still rent by civil war, Krupskaya boarded an "agitation steamboat" (*agit-parokhod*) and steamed down the Volga River and back up the Kama on the Asian side of the Ural Mountains, bringing the Bolshevik gospel to workers and Red Army soldiers in the depths of the Russian hinterlands. She gave dozens of speeches without any sound amplification, the crowds straining to hear her. She pushed herself so hard that summer that she had a heart attack at the age of fifty and had to dial back her labors. "My heart refuses to do its job," she wrote disapprovingly to a friend. "These days, I am a lady all the time."³

Krupskaya also became the deputy commissar at the People's Commissariat for Popular Enlightenment, the Narkompros, the government's propaganda arm. She showed up early every morning and left only when Lenin called to demand she come home because he refused to eat dinner without her. The staff had to trick her into not attending "voluntary" weekend cleaning sessions of the offices. While she waged futile intra-Party battles to make Narkompros responsible for all political propaganda, Krupskaya also fought to make the new Soviet school system less centralized so communities could decide how to educate their children. Citing Horace Mann, she wrote that "the new Russia needs schools of the American type."⁴ Krupskaya successfully pushed for coeducational schools where girls wouldn't be split off from the boys to be taught how to keep house. If women were to be equal, she argued, their early education had to be equal, too. Not all attempts to encode the equality of women into Soviet government policy, however, would proceed so smoothly.

In 1920, the Soviet government instituted full labor conscription to deal with the acute labor shortage created by unending war. All women now had to work. This requirement was squarely in line with Marxist theory, but Kollontai saw another benefit. "There is no more of the old dependence of women either on the capitalist boss or on the breadwinner husband," she wrote.⁵ Another woman Communist declared that "labor conscription will deal the final and decisive blow to domestic slavery."⁶

As promised, the government pitched in to relieve some of the burdens on working women. The state opened cafeterias, laundries, and nurseries for small children, an effort popularized by the Zhenotdel. There weren't nearly enough of these facilities, and the bankrupt new government could not begin to keep up with serving such a vast country, but it was a start. By 1920, 1,500 maternity and childcare centers had opened across the country, which also gave shelter to the growing population of orphans. By 1921, 93 percent of Muscovites were eating in public cafeterias.[7] Still, for many Soviets, eating their food and laundering their clothing in government facilities was hardly an act of liberation but one of dire necessity: the Civil War had rendered millions of them hungry and homeless.[8]

In November 1920, the Soviet Union introduced another radical reform, becoming the first country in the world to legalize abortion. Although abortion had been illegal under the tsars, it flourished nonetheless. Between 1897 and 1912, the number of illegal abortions rose tenfold in Moscow alone.[9] That year, a congress of Russian gynecologists seriously considered a proposal to legalize the procedure to deal with the crisis. Lenin started pushing for this in 1913.[10] The following year, a group of criminologists, lawyers, and police officers in St. Petersburg voted in favor of legalizing abortion by a margin of three to one, arguing that the ban was unfair to poor women. The tsarist government, citing moral and religious arguments, shot down the proposal.[11]

Despite his pronouncements, Lenin and his comrades were deeply ambivalent about birth control and family planning, denouncing them as an unnatural way to undermine population growth. The male commissar of health said women had a "moral obligation" to have children. Although Lenin believed abortion should be legal, he nevertheless denounced the procedure as "a tendency of the egotistical and unfeeling bourgeois couple."[12] Some prominent Bolshevik women saw things differently. Krupskaya argued that destroying cells that were still part of the mother's body was not a crime, and Inessa went as far as proposing an official slogan. "Under the Communist order," it would say, "it is unthinkable that childbirth should be a form of labor conscription."[13]

The issue of abortion exposed a central contradiction in how the new Bolshevik government thought about the role of women. On the one hand, socialist women were to be emancipated. On the other hand, in a socialist utopia, there should be no need for women to limit their childbearing, because the state would care for all children. There was an implicit tension in Bolshevik policy over the ultimate benefit of emancipating women. Was it for the women's own freedom, or was it to enable them to work more and birth more Soviet citizens? More and more, the evidence pointed to the latter, which raised yet another dilemma: How could women work more without family planning, and how could they have more children with it? This paradox would bedevil Soviet leaders for generations.

Still, the overwhelmingly male Party leadership recognized that women were getting abortions anyway, turning to village wisewomen instead of professionals, often with dire consequences. They saw legalizing abortion as a necessary evil and hoped that, with enough anti-abortion propaganda, the "instinct of motherhood . . . would triumph."

The new state legalized abortion in 1920, becoming the first country in the world to do so.[14] In a move that would determine the fate of Soviet women for decades to come, the Soviet Union did not get around to legalizing birth control until 1923.

When Inessa's body arrived by train in the capital in September 1920, Lenin, grief-stricken, insisted on walking behind the coffin for two miles as it made its way through the streets of old Moscow toward Red Square.[15] Some said he blamed himself for Inessa's death. She had worked so hard in the first years after the Revolution that Lenin demanded she take a rest cure in the Caucasus. Worried about her health, he flooded her with letters—more letters than he sent to anyone other than his mother.[16] It was the height of the Civil War, and suddenly the resort where Inessa was recuperating on Lenin's insistence fell squarely in the path of the advancing White Army. Lenin panicked and gave orders to have Inessa immediately evacuated, which only got her stranded in a series of filthy train stations crowded with refugees. The White advance never came, but Inessa caught the cholera burning through Russia's south and was dead within two days.

At Inessa's funeral, Lenin was inconsolable. "I never saw such torment," one attendee wrote.[17] "Not only his face but his whole body expressed so much sorrow that I dared not greet him . . . It was clear that he wanted to be alone with his grief. He seemed to have shrunk . . . his eyes seemed drowned in tears held back with effort."

Kollontai was afraid he would completely lose control and embarrass Krupskaya, who was also in attendance.[18] Alexander Armand, Inessa's estranged husband, was there as well, solemnly watching his wife being interred in the Kremlin walls.

After Inessa was buried, Lenin offered Kollontai his former lover's old job leading the Zhenotdel. Kollontai emerged from her seclusion and accepted, hoping to work her way back into the Party's good graces.

But the Zhenotdel's work in the villages never got any easier. Kollontai's budget was still paltry, the staff still too inexperienced, and many key people in the Party still resistant to the very premise of the Zhenotdel's work. The bureaucracy bristled at her demands that women be better represented in the Party and the government. As Kollontai complained at a Zehntodel meeting in 1921, "many comrades already look at us as an unnecessary appendage."

And Kollontai herself felt she had bigger fights to wage. In 1917, she had backed Lenin's call to build a dictatorship of the proletariat. Now she realized that Lenin had simply built a dictatorship. Party officials, Kollontai felt, were increasingly cut off from the very working class they were supposed to represent. Worse, the trade unions, or soviets, often sided with government enterprises against workers. Kollontai felt that Lenin was betraying the ideals of the Revolution. "Comrades, there should be a guarantee that if in fact we are going to criticize ... what is wrong with us," Kollontai said at a 1920 Party congress, taking a jab at Lenin's proclivity for muzzling and exiling dissenters, "then one who criticizes should not be sent off to a nice sunny place to eat peaches."[19]

Ahead of the Tenth Party Congress, in 1921, Kollontai teamed up with Alexander Shlyapnikov, her former lover and conspirator on post-Revolutionary social reforms. Together, they headed up a faction called the Workers' Opposition, which demanded "Party democracy" and trade unions that would actually defend workers' rights.[20] Kollontai wrote out their platform in a pamphlet and passed out 1,500 copies at the congress.

Lenin was livid. He refused to acknowledge Kollontai when he passed her in the hall outside the main auditorium. When Kollontai addressed the delegates, she noted that she and Shlyapnikov were of the same mind: "Class united and class conscious." Then she directly challenged the way Lenin was leading the Party and accused the Communist Party elite of feeling "a secret distrust of the broad masses."

Lenin responded by proposing a new rule to outlaw "factionalism" within the Party and took direct aim at Kollontai. "Well, thank God, we know that Comrade Kollontai and Comrade Shlyapnikov are 'class united and class conscious,'" he said, throwing Kollontai's phrasing back at her. It was a barb designed to remind the delegates that Kollontai, who was now married to another man, had once been Shlyapnikov's lover. The remark had its intended effect: nearly a thousand delegates were now giggling at Kollontai's private life.[21] The resolution to end factionalism passed overwhelmingly. In the very near future, Lenin's new general secretary, a Georgian named Joseph Stalin, would weaponize it to make dissent within the Party a capital offense.

In 1921, Lenin also introduced a New Economic Policy (NEP) to revive an economy demolished by war. It loosened government restrictions on trade and industry and allowed the semblance of a free market. Orthodox Marxists like Kollontai were furious. They saw it as a galling concession to the bourgeois-leaning peasantry and a rollback of the Communism they had fought so hard for. Once again, Kollontai refused to remain quiet. That summer she once again spoke out against Lenin's NEP and his stifling of intra-Party dissent, but this time she did it abroad, at the Third Communist International (Comintern) Congress in Berlin, with Lenin sitting on the stage behind her. She distributed her Workers' Opposition pamphlet to the international delegates. Soon it was being reprinted and praised in socialist newspapers worldwide, including in the United States.[22]

But it was all for naught. A few months after she returned to Moscow, Kollontai was dismissed from her position at the Zhenotdel. Her husband, Pavel Dybenko, the former commissar of the navy, had found himself a younger woman. If being married to Kollontai had once helped his career, being associated with her was now clearly hindering it. In 1922, Kollontai was sent to represent the Soviet Union in a trade delegation to Norway. And though this made her one of the first women in the modern world to serve as an ambassador, this was no honor. She had begged the Party not to send dissenters "to a nice sunny place to eat peaches," and the Party obliged. Norway was far too cold to grow peaches.

On March 9, 1923, Lenin suffered his third stroke. After the first one, in May 1922, Krupskaya had quit all her government posts to care for her husband. Lenin partially recovered and was even able to return to work for a couple of months before suffering another.[23] But the third stroke had rendered him an invalid. He completely lost his ability to speak as well as the use of his right side, and his doctors reported that he was easily confused.[24] Lenin begged Krupskaya for cyanide and she relayed her husband's request to Joseph Stalin.

A month before Lenin's first stroke, in April 1922, he had appointed Stalin the Party's general secretary. This had put Stalin in charge of the Party's growing bureaucracy and membership, its personnel files and its information flows. Stalin quickly proved to be an adroit administrator. He deftly wielded the levers of power Lenin had placed in his hands, all the while inventing new ones.[25]

Naturally, Stalin was put in charge of enforcing the doctors' orders that Lenin refrain from working. The leader of the Revolution was to have no news and no information about the succession struggle that immediately broke out when he took ill. But Lenin was an obstreperous patient and demanded news anyway, which Krupskaya happily provided. She also got word out about what Lenin thought of the policies that Party leaders were trying to implement in his absence. It was a reprisal of the time when Lenin was in jail in St. Petersburg and Krupskaya, his fake fiancée, was his link to the outside world. Even in this state, Lenin did not want to relinquish his control of the Party that he and Krupskaya had spent decades building.

Stalin deeply resented not only Krupskaya's proximity to Lenin but also what he correctly saw as her enabling of Lenin's machinations. Krupskaya was ultimately no match for Stalin, but, after decades in the underground, she was a wily, seasoned conspirator who managed to throw a lot of sand in Stalin's gears. How she infuriated him! Once, after Stalin screamed at Krupskaya over the phone, she complained to Lenin's deputies. Lenin demanded Stalin apologize to her in writing. Modern scholars, however, believe that the instruction actually came from Krupskaya herself—an exquisite humiliation of her thin-skinned enemy. "Why should I get up on my hind legs for her? To sleep with Lenin does not necessarily mean to understand Leninism!" Stalin ranted to a friend. "Just because she uses the same bathroom as Lenin, do I have to appreciate and respect her as if she were Lenin?"[26]

In late May 1923, Krupskaya landed a body blow, one that Stalin would feel for the rest of his life. She said she had a new dictation from Lenin, a document in which he evaluated six of his potential successors, including Stalin. "Comrade Stalin, having become general secretary, has concentrated boundless power in his hands," this dictation read. "I am not sure whether he will always be able to use that power with sufficient caution."[27] The dictation was most complimentary (and least critical) of Leon Trotsky, Stalin's archrival. A couple of weeks later, Krupskaya produced another dictation of Lenin's words and wishes. This one was far more explicit. "Stalin is rude and this defect, although quite tolerable in our midst and in relations among us Communists, becomes intolerable in a general secretary," Lenin said. "That is why I suggest the comrades think about a way of removing Stalin."[28]

Stalin later suppressed these two documents, together called Lenin's Testament. But what was known about their contents fed alternative-history fantasies for decades. What if Lenin's wishes had been carried out and Stalin had been removed from his post as general secretary? What if Trotsky had instead succeeded Lenin at the helm? Would the Soviet Union have been spared Stalin's extravagantly bloody reign? And—most importantly for fellow travelers in the West—would socialism have been proven to work?

All those questions are predicated on the notion that the Testament was a faithful representation of what Lenin said. But recent scholarship by Stephen Kotkin, the world's preeminent Stalin historian, shows that there was no way that Lenin could have dictated it. By May 1923, Lenin was paralyzed and suffered from a bouquet of other ailments, including insomnia and memory loss. "He was desperately trying to regain the power of speech, mostly by reciting the alphabet and singing the 'Internationale,'" Kotkin writes. "But his speech was limited to a handful of words—'congress,' 'peasant,' 'worker'—and when he repeated the words Krupskaya said to him, it was not clear he understood their meaning... It was abundantly clear that he would never again play any role in political life."[29]

To preempt these criticisms, Krupskaya claimed to have taken the dictations after Lenin's second stroke, in December 1922. But he was in terrible shape even then, confusing objects and forgetting words; his right side was already completely paralyzed. Even if the Testament were a projection of what she *thought* Lenin was thinking, it was clearly Krupskaya's work.

But though the Testament seemed to tip things in Trotsky's favor, Krupskaya didn't do much to actually ensure Trotsky took over from her husband. She failed to read the Testament at a Party Congress when it could have made a difference and wound up siding with another faction against both Stalin *and* Trotsky.

Whatever her motivations, Krupskaya created a cloud of doubt that hung over Stalin's dictatorship for decades, including in Stalin's own mind. In order to dispel that doubt, Stalin would kill not only Trotsky and any perceived potential rivals to his throne but millions of Soviets who in any way questioned his legitimacy. "The document gravely threatened Stalin's embryonic personal dictatorship, and became an enduring, haunting aspect of his rule," writes Kotkin. "The Testament helped bring out his demons, his sense of persecution and victimhood, his mistrust of all and sundry, but also his sense of personal destiny and iron determination."[30]

When Lenin finally died on January 22, 1924, Krupskaya accompanied her husband's body on the train to the capital, where it was to lie in state. Stalin and the other members of the Politburo met her and the casket at the train station. Krupskaya was the only one of them who didn't cry.[31] Stalin, who had been reading reports from the secret police all over the country, was afraid that political unrest would break out and that foreign powers would invade now that the Revolution had lost its leader. Instead, so many people streamed into the capital to pay their respects to Lenin—by some counts, up to a million—that Stalin had to extend the viewing period. One of them was my great-grandmother Riva, who waited for hours on a day so cold—35 degrees below zero—that people in the line lit bonfires to stay warm and Riva's only coat caught on fire.

From exile in Norway in the 1920s, Kollontai continued to write about women's emancipation and sexuality. In 1912 she had written that, if a woman were to fall in love, she could "drink from the cup of love's joy, however deep it is, and satisfy herself. When the cup is empty, she throws it away without regret or bitterness." Party intellectuals now twisted Kollontai's metaphor of satisfaction into what they called the "glass-of-water" theory, accusing her of believing that sex should be nothing more serious than drinking a glass of water.[32] Her goal had been to destigmatize sex, not to promote irresponsible promiscuity—but it didn't matter. The men in charge had never fully bought into Kollontai's ideas and loved to gossip about her love life. Now that she had been banished by the regime and made politically toxic, she was no longer around to defend herself. The glass-of-water theory became yet another way to discredit Kollontai as a loose, sex-obsessed woman.

Her ideas, meanwhile, were proving to be much messier in practice than they had been in theory. Much to the chagrin of Bolsheviks, who had preached that prostitution would vanish as soon as the working class seized power, it was now back to pre-1917 levels. Popular literature of the Soviet 1920s described young women, Soviet flappers, who went to bed with NEP men for a pair of silk stockings or a bottle of perfume. But the reality was far grimmer. Now the ranks of prostitutes were filled with women from groups that Bolsheviks had labeled "former people": the merchant classes, the bourgeoisie, and the gentry, women of means and status who had been reduced to selling their bodies for survival. The rest were peasants and girls from the swarms of orphans, the *besprizorniki*. The 1918 Family Code had neglected to legalize adoption, and state orphanages were full to overflowing. The boys often turned to petty street crime to feed themselves; the girls chose other means.

The Bolsheviks had set out to destroy the traditional, bourgeois family, and at first their success was dizzying. Divorce rates in the mid-1920s rose threefold.[33] While many of these were unhappy couples finally breaking free of their pre-Revolution matrimonial prisons, women all over the country began to report that men were abusing the laws and abandoning them without providing legally mandated financial assistance. Alimony and child support proved much harder to collect in practice than in theory, especially at a time when millions had been displaced and impoverished by war and famine. Then there were the women who had been in common-law marriages unrecognized by the state, who found it even harder to get money from men who had never been registered as their husbands.[34] Many women were unable to care for their children and abandoned them, further swelling the ranks of the *besprizorniki*.

Young Communists, on the other hand, seemed to embrace the new, sexually liberated spirit of the decade. They had more sex and had it at a younger age than their parents' generation. When answering government survey questions about their personal lives, they said that family and marriage would only hold them back. Many lived in coed dormitories, where they shared the proverbial glass of water left and right. But not all young people liked this arrangement, especially not the young women who found themselves pregnant and their lovers uninterested in supporting them. The result, wrote Stites, "was 'liberty, equality, and maternity'—equality for the sexes, liberty for the man, and maternity for the woman."[35]

The youth were also out of step with the older Communists, including the more prudish Bolshevik women who had always been suspicious of what they saw as Kollontai's libertinism. Eventually, it was a man who applied the brakes. In 1925, Aron Zalkind, one of the preeminent philosophers of Soviet pedology, penned a treatise on the "twelve sexual commandments of the revolutionary proletariat." He warped Kollontai's ideas of mutually respectful, enlightened, and unpossessive love into a thoroughly conservative framework.[36] The first commandment banned premarital sex; the second stipulated that marriage could not happen before the ages of twenty to twenty-five. Zalkind, who theorized that prostitutes were incurable because they had a certain "clitoris type," developed a theory, based on Freud, of revolutionary sublimation. It stipulated that people had finite amounts of energy and if too much of it were wasted on matters of love and sex, there would be less left over to power the proletarian revolution. To prevent this waste of energy, Zalkind wrote, sex should be infrequent and without too much variety. Love should be monogamous and between one man and one woman. Monogamy, Zalkind concluded, was the natural state for a woman anyway. When having sex, partners needed to be fully cognizant of the possibility of pregnancy as well as of the potential harm of contraception and abortion. Partners should be chosen along class lines and members of their class should intervene in the romantic affairs of its members in cases of perceived wrongdoing. The commandments soon became state dogma.

The following year, the government updated the family code. The revised version was a far more conservative and bourgeois document than the one Kollontai had helped craft just eight years earlier. Banished to a land where she couldn't eat peaches, she was powerless to intervene.

BUZYA

IT WAS A STERN SENSE OF DUTY THAT, IN SEPTEMBER 1933, MOVED Brokha Zuckerman, my other maternal great-grandmother, to leave her six-year-old son in Moscow and take her sister Eva to Batiliman, in Crimea, to breathe the salt-whipped Black Sea air.[1] Eva had been sick again, her heart valves fluttering incorrectly ever since a bout of rheumatic fever she had when they were children. She was often bedridden for days in their communal apartment right off Moscow's Garden Ring.

The years had spun a thick web of responsibility around Brokha—or Buzya, as she was known in the family. Almost the whole family had followed Buzya from Ukraine's Medzhybyzh to Moscow, where they became her charges. Her mother, a kind but useless woman, couldn't seem to manage the particulars of daily existence after her husband died. The oldest daughter, Tsinusya, had been equally useless after the end of the Great War, when a German officer had shot her husband in the head at a café. He had done this right in front of their small daughter, now nearly twenty, and the family whispered that the shot that had killed her father had also shattered her sanity. Then there was Eva, Evochka, now in her late twenties but still the baby of the family, with delicate features, a weak heart, and a frigid husband.

Buzya, a regal woman with large brown eyes and the fine bones of a bird, supported them all, along with her young son, Yura. She was a chemist, the director of a lab at the Central Scientific Research Institute of Leather Footwear Industry, where she created organic chemical compounds for dyeing leather at an industrial scale. She wrote scientific papers and books, and, at home in the evenings, translated articles from German and English to earn extra money to buy Yura chocolate and oranges. She was a modern Soviet woman, with the kind of career that only men had before the Revolution, able to work and raise a child with the state's help. And yet it wasn't quite the fairy tale that Kollontai had imagined.

Buzya had come to Moscow two years before with her husband, Pavel, an engineer she had met at university in Kiev. At first, it was a happy, comfortable life. Pavel's work was well compensated, and they didn't feel the privations of the early Soviet years the way many did. But within a year of moving to Moscow, Buzya found herself in a doctor's office, hearing him explain that Pavel had only days to live. Sure enough, within days, Pavel was dead of lymphoma and Buzya had become the third widow in her family.

Felled by grief, Buzya couldn't leave her bed. Two days after his father's death, little Yura climbed into bed with her. He was so little and she didn't know what to say to him. "Mom, get up," Yura told her. "Why do you smell different?" So Buzya bathed and dressed and perfumed herself and took her son for a walk. Yura's world would not change, she decided then, and she never spoke to him of his father again.

Buzya was just thirty-four that September in Batiliman, but she already felt impossibly old, worn down by grief and worry. When she ran into an old university classmate named Shura, he seemed like a person from another lifetime. Sixteen years had passed since they had met in Kiev in 1917, enough time for Shura to get married, have a son, and become Alexander Umansky, an up-and-coming young professor at the Ukrainian Academy of Sciences, and for a brand-new country to emerge around them all. And now here, suddenly, was redheaded, blue-eyed Shura, sick with pleuritis, recovering in the same modernist little cubic apartments as she and Eva.

At Batiliman, Buzya and Shura talked for hours as she embroidered her handkerchiefs. They hiked into the hills beneath the bleached, white cliffs. They swam out to the lighthouse and wandered in the vineyards. Eva, sensing what was happening, told them their fortune by plucking the petals of a daisy. Buzya warned Shura not to listen to her flirt of a little sister. But even with his terrible black jacket and the

Central Asian skullcap he insisted on wearing, there was something about Shura, his kindness, his wit, the way he looked at her with those blue eyes.

They kissed.

They fell in love.

And then it was time for Shura to go home.

"The morning of the 29th at Batiliman when we met in the morning, you looked at me," Buzya would write to him later. "Your normally cheerful and lively eyes changed completely. In them was longing, joy, and a question. It's like you were trying to look inside me and you succeeded. It's possible you didn't notice it. I remember it often and vividly." Buzya had an answer to the question in his eyes: their affair had to end here, in Batiliman. Shura had a wife and son in Kiev; Buzya had a son, a sister, and two widows to take care of in Moscow. She had a respectable suitor (Pavel's cousin) who wrote her letters. Yes, they were pompous and self-important, boring letters, but this was a vacation romance, nothing more. Old people with responsibilities do not mistake such things for real love.

Shura departed for Kiev the next day.

Buzya and Eva would take the train home to the cold and rain and dirt of Moscow a few days later, entertained the whole way by passengers with a gramophone playing foxtrots and old Gypsy ballads. By the time Buzya arrived at the communal apartment, her son Yura was already asleep. "When I saw his little head in his little bed, my heart contracted," she recalled later. Suddenly she was so very, very tired again. "How little he still is, and how much responsibility I still have ahead of me for his tiny life," she thought. "Worst of all is the knowledge that I have to continue to live—and live actively—for his sake."

When she came home from work the next day, there was a letter from Shura. She sat down on the couch and opened it. "My love," he called her, and in the warmth that flooded her then, all her resolve melted.

"Completely unexpectedly for me, I really want to write to you," she wrote on October 8, 1933. It was late on a Sunday night, and Buzya was sitting alone in the lab at work after a weekend spent wrangling a defiant Yura to get their picture taken. Yura had refused to eat his lunch and threatened to show his hungry mood in the photograph, at which point Buzya had to bribe him with a bar of chocolate. At the photo studio, surrounded by the chic Moscow ladies having their portraits taken, Buzya felt like a homely, frazzled widow. Then the studio manager made her feel even worse by asking why she looked so sad. "I think the photo will turn out very poorly," she wrote to Shura. "Whatever it looks like, I'll send it to you." (Some ninety years later, the photo sits on my mother's dresser in America. Yura, a little boy in a little boy tie and a torn cotton sweater, presses his blond head into Buzya's milky cheek, her dark hair pulled back, a white strand of beads on her still-tan chest. Her eyes are dark pools of liquid melancholy. The studio manager had been right: she did look sad.)

She wrote in a scraggly script in ink that has turned purple with time, launching the yearlong correspondence that Shura would come to call their "epistolary epic":

> *My dear friend, in the rush of my emotional rebellion, I decided that we should put a period here, mercilessly cut the threads now stretching between us; that there should be no more letters, no more meetings. I couldn't understand why so much pain has been allotted to my luckless female life. Maybe this would have been right and better for both of us. But now, it's clear to me that I can't and, more importantly, don't want to lose our friendship. It's so light and easy to write to you, in a way that I have never written to anyone. Something has firmly rooted itself in my soul and it would be so hard for me to part with this. And I have no confidence that doing so would be necessary. It is, after all, much harder for you than for me.*
>
> *In the last two years, I have learned not to want anything for myself. But now I really want to receive a letter from you, one that will have a few tender words for me. I really want to chat with you and tell you many nice and warm things. And I really, really want to see you sometime... I think I've started wanting too much. I don't quite understand all of this myself. I was always so demanding—of life, of myself, of others. Your tenderness has melted me, and I've become a stupid little woman.*

Then she notices the time. It's late, her work isn't done, and she hasn't been home yet to see her son. She wraps up her letter with a flourish. "I regret nothing," she writes. "B."

After that the letters flew, a whole growing world tucked inside envelopes advertising collective farms and fire extinguishers, passing each other, sometimes daily, on the railroads stretching between Moscow and Kiev. Waiting for them, always, was a pair of hands shaking with anticipation. "My gentle little sun!" Shura wrote to Buzya on December 12, using that Russian term of endearment—*solnyshko*—for which the closest English equivalent is "sunshine."

> *Can you imagine the feelings of a person overcome by a warm wave? That's what I experienced when I ran up the staircase, read your little letter, written the evening of the 3rd. The human mechanism is a strange thing: large volumes of blood can, under the influence of reading a small piece of paper, shift from part of the body to another.*

These were the verbal caresses of lovers separated by distance and familial obligation. Shura asks Buzya to keep all their letters. By April, she needs a second box to store them.

During their courtship, Buzya and Shura bring each other into the worlds they are slowly abandoning. She writes to him from her communal apartment, her many dependents sleeping, her desk crowded with papers and dictionaries and scientific journals. He writes to her from under his green lamp in the Construction Institute, where he designs pontoon bridges that will aid the Red Army when the Germans invade a few years later. Once, Shura sends Buzya a postcard with a photo of the institute. Half the letters she's received from him, he explains, were written from behind the window he has marked with a little purple arrow.

Buzya writes from the lab and from factories where she supervises the dyeing process, from train stations and seedy hotels on exhausting business trips. She writes after delivering lectures at conferences or steals a moment between sets of math problems: she is learning calculus while rushing to turn her book in to the publisher. He starts attending lectures on chemistry to understand her world and sends her some of his own scientific work, a milestone for him. "I have never shown my work to a woman," he confesses.

He tells her about the blackouts in Kiev, where it can be hard to find firewood or decent shoes. She describes Moscow with the wonder of a bystander, its life flowing around her while she remains wrapped in the cocoon of his letters. On May Day, the workers' holiday, "there is a mass of lights and people in the streets, the radio is blaring in every square," she writes. "The window is open, from the street I can hear noise, singing, a guitar, and occasionally drunken voices." But she is inside, at her desk, writing to Shura.

Shura revels in Buzya's copious intellect and accomplishments—and why shouldn't he? He is a thoroughly modern Soviet man. He asks about her work and tells her about his because she is a fellow scientist, an equal and a peer. There is nothing about this that threatens him or makes her less appealing in his eyes. "Buzenka, I've wanted to tell you for a long time that I am endlessly happy that I met you, a wonderful little woman with such a modern construction of the brain," he wrote to her one day. "Listening to you or reading you, I can always sense, like the ticking of a clock, the work of your intellect, which seems both close and unreachable (look at those dialectics!). After reading your letter, I again feel that you went up one more step, and I again have to stretch to reach you."

He marvels at all she manages to balance on her slender back. "I often think, how can a little woman handle two real, manly, Moscow-style work shifts," he writes in March. "All I can do is suspect you of having the kind of talents and organizational ability that I can only dimly imagine. Though sitting next to you on the grass in Crimea, I always had the sense that there is an extraordinary piece of machinery hidden inside you. I don't have such qualities."

But Buzya is less charmed by her own existence. "I can't fit everything into myself," she writes to Shura at the end of 1933. She suffers from exhaustion, frequent migraines, and spikes of intense anxiety. Her work is stressful and requires far more politicking than her PhD prepared her for. The country is five years into Stalin's rule and at the end of his brutal, breakneck industrialization program known as the first Five-Year Plan. People are being sent to the Gulag for alleged industrial sabotage, and meetings at the institute have become rife with recriminations and suspicion.

The most demanding commissar, however, lives inside her. Buzya's fastidious perfectionism—which she will hand down entirely intact to her granddaughter, my mother—puts her "in a tortured state," she complains to Shura. "It's so hard to be a conveyor belt of creativity. The worst part is that I am rarely pleased with myself and my work. My demands of myself are greater than my abilities. It is bad to be an average person and to demand perfection. This is, I think, my personal tragedy."

At the end of each workday, she would like nothing more than to be able to lie down. Instead, she begins her second shift: ironing, sewing, cooking—all without the aid of modern appliances or the communal help the state had promised—then playing with Yura and reading to him from the books and magazines Shura has sent. "It's very hard to be both father and mother," she wrote, "and I'm not very good at either." After everyone is asleep, she sits down to do the translation work that allows her to support her family and occasionally spoil her son. If the Soviet authorities call a *subbotnik*—a Saturday when people have to work for the state for free—this wipes out her only day off in weeks. When the winter's flu passes her by, she is despondent: she had hoped to be forced to stay in bed for a few days.

The depths of Buzya's fatigue, the crushing weight of her responsibilities, make her long for something far more traditional than a modern, Soviet relationship. She had not asked to be the subject of a grand social experiment. In March 1934, Buzya is at the train station after a work trip and takes the opportunity to write to Shura in fading gray pencil.

I am very tired, I want to sleep and my head hurts unbearably . . . Sometimes, I get so sick of being a busy and important woman with authority and the need to engage in diplomacy. In such moments, I'm especially happy that I have you and that, with you, I can just be a woman, without any authority.

As she waits for the train, an elderly woman sits down next to her. She is from the countryside, a *baba* from the old world of pastoral Russia. Likely, this woman had been touched by the bloody drive to collectivize the farms, when the state's shock troops requisitioned grain and livestock and arrested and deported hundreds of thousands of peasants who refused to cooperate. Likely, she had seen death up close as it swept away millions in the resulting famine. The peasant woman began to tell Buzya the story of her life, "a life that is such that she is jealous of the happy ones who get to die." Buzya does not recount for Shura the horrors the woman describes, but she is clearly shaken. "Life can be so terrifying sometimes," she writes. There they sat, two newly minted Soviet women—one a collectivized peasant, the other an emancipated city dweller with a career and a married lover—both of them utterly exhausted.

The lovers' problems begin almost immediately. "I turned out to be a very bad actor," Shura writes in his second letter to Buzya, in October 1933. Lida, his wife, immediately sensed that the husband who had gone to Crimea for treatment had returned to Kiev a stranger. They move into separate bedrooms. Both Buzya and Shura keep the correspondence a secret. When Shura sends Yura some toy instruments he has made at his institute—an impossible luxury in such lean times—Buzya is to tell her son they come from "an acquaintance in Kiev." As freewheeling as Soviet society had become in the 1920s, it is still an affair.

Shura's marriage begins to unravel when Lida gets sick over the November holidays. She is too proud to ask him for help and he no longer cares enough to volunteer it. "I couldn't think about her and what she needed," he writes to Buzya. "It ended with her scolding me for being inattentive now and over the course of our entire life together." He suggests that Lida visit her sister in Leningrad, something she's long wanted to do, but the more she thinks he wants her to go, the less she wants to leave. He begins to wonder if he's sharing too much. "Should I be telling you about all these sad things?" he writes.

In late November, Shura convinces his bosses to let him travel to Moscow for work, though the purpose of the trip is really to see Buzya for the first time since Batiliman. When he returns home, Lida and his mother are waiting for him.

> *My clairvoyant wife looked at me with eyes that understood everything. We barely spoke, then she lay down and turned to the wall. I sat down next to her and said that it's hard for me, too, that I have fallen for another woman. She said she knew and asked me to describe [you]. I just said that she's just as modest as you and is half a head taller than me intellectually (I feel this). We talked the whole rest of the night, she rose to an unprecedented level of understanding of her life and mine. By the end, she asked me to take our son, not feeling that she had enough strength to raise him, and really wanted to meet you. This was genuine. I told her that there is no man and no woman who would deprive a child of his own mother for the sake of their own happiness.*

Shura asked Lida for an open marriage, which had become common among the Soviet intelligentsia in the first decades after the Revolution. A mix of guilt and grief flood Buzya on reading this, especially the part about Shura's son, who is exactly Yura's age. She begins to think obsessively about another young boy who will be deprived of his father—not because of death but because of her. In her sleep, she sees Pavel returning for her. She hears Shura telling her it's not worth the fight, that he is giving up on their love. Her sisters are worried. She's losing weight and they've never seen her this exhausted. "I sometimes get scared that all of this will be too much for me," she writes.

The stress is also taking a toll on Shura. He oscillates between delirious happiness and *toska*, that all-encompassing Russian mix of longing, nostalgia, and melancholy. "I break off the *toska* by repeating two formulas to myself," he writes. "'Everything good happens unexpectedly if you prepare for it ahead of time' and 'every revolution has a destructive and a constructive period.'"

Their love is still in its destructive stage: the arrangement with

Lida collapses after a month. As Shura sees her off to Leningrad, she breaks down in tears. "She knows well (senses it) how deeply I love you and says that she can't bear a life in which I'm physically here but my thoughts are somewhere over there, and we have to think of something," Shura writes in December. He's not sure if he's handling this well but can't bear to censor himself. "I feel I am really torturing you with my life process, and maybe a discriminating mind would have concluded that such things need to be decided immediately instead of stretching them out, let alone telling his beloved. I'm wondering if this wouldn't also be better for my wife... Why am I writing all this to you?"

"I have to confess—and you must know yourself—that I had a very hard time with your letter," Buzya responds. "Now that this has been moved aside somewhat, I'm calmer again, if you discount the *toska* that periodically becomes quite acute, and the internal tension. You write that maybe you shouldn't be torturing me with your life process, but our life processes, even at such a distance, have become integral to each other. And I need to know it just as much as you need to write it."

The new year brought more suffering. Lida complained that Shura wasn't paying enough attention to their son, Andrey, who, sensing the tension at home, has developed an awful stutter. Then Shura makes a fateful stumble. He has been sitting at his desk at home and, violating all the rules of their correspondence, writing a letter to Buzya. In the end, he decides to tear it up rather than send it: he has burdened her enough with his decomposing family life. That night, Lida tells him that she restored the torn-up letter. She found that its words were a worse betrayal than the affair itself. Nothing is too sacred, it seems, for Shura to lay down at this other woman's feet. By February, it's over. Shura announces that, come summer, he is leaving his wife. "I don't want to torture you anymore with my 'life process,'" he writes to Buzya triumphantly. "It has been simplified in the extreme."

But the decision to divorce Lida does not provide the release he imagined. Lida is despondent and talks of killing herself. His mother takes Lida's side, declaring that she, too, will die of grief. Shura shares all this with Buzya, who responds with icy fury: How can it be that, in addition to all the responsibilities she already shoulders, she also has to carry them for her man? "You really are a big child," she seethes.

Surely you must understand that it is infinitely painful for me to know that I am the indirect cause of another person's tragedy...
I know, my darling, that it is infinitely hard for you, but how can I help? My life is hard and joyless and turbulent. I'm exhausted from all the little details of it, and I will remember this winter for the rest of my life. If you come to me full of doubt, nothing good will come of it for us, and I don't want this...

Please explain to me why I can't shake the feeling, bordering on certainty, that sometimes you are waiting for me to say to you that I am done with you, which would free you of having to make the choice.

To twist the knife, she makes sure to tell him again about the seriousness of her suitors. She had always told Shura of the men pursuing her, portraying them as either hysterical or pathetic. This time it is clearly a reminder that if he isn't man enough to decide, she is free to choose someone else.

The letter does the trick. Shura responds with an abject apology—and a marriage proposal.

There will be more difficulty to come. Shura will cut off his mother for gossiping about his divorce, and Buzya, hearing that she has been called a home-wrecker, will temporarily lose her resolve and beg him not to leave his family. Her heart feels so stretched that she can't climb the stairs to her office. "I am a woman with 'willpower' but all this has cost me infinitely dearly," she writes.

But Shura has made his choice. On September 18, 1934, he will marry Buzya in Moscow, one year to the day they met in Batiliman. "I love you anew every day like it's the first day," he writes in one of his last letters. Soon he will move to Moscow and there will be no more need for this correspondence. "It's summer already; don't you want to fall in love all over again from the beginning? This whole awful winter will be our dowry and my huge debt to you for the rest of my life."

NADYA

ON THE EVENING OF NOVEMBER 8, 1932, NADEZHDA ALLILUYEVA PUT on a black dress embroidered with red roses and tucked a matching red rose in her hair. The previous day, she had marched in the Revolution Day parade, the fifteenth anniversary of the Bolshevik seizure of power. As she made her way past Lenin's mausoleum on Red Square, she turned to her comrade, Nikita Khrushchev, pointed to the Party leadership lined up on the viewing stand, and said, "Look at mine: he did not bring his scarf, he'll catch a cold and be sick."[1] They looked at the man she was talking about, "hers," the one standing on a hidden platform to make up for his shortness, "hers," the one with the thick black mustache who was rapidly turning the young country into his personal, terrifying fiefdom: her husband, Joseph Stalin.

Stalin had known Nadya's parents since before she was born. Her father, an early socialist, often sheltered the young Stalin when he was on the run from the tsarist secret police before the Revolution. Nadya grew up with Stalin a frequent presence in their house. She called him Soso, like everyone he was close to, and he had a nickname for her, too: Tatka. He read Nadya and her older sister, Anna, stories by Chekhov and regaled them with tales of his Siberian exile.[2] According to family lore, when Nadya was a toddler, he saved her from drowning.[3]

By the hectic summer of 1917, Nadya was a sixteen-year-old student and Stalin was a thirty-eight-year-old widower. After his first wife, Kato Svanidze, gave birth to their son, Yakov, in 1907, she and Stalin had to flee imminent arrest by the tsarist authorities. While they were hiding in Baku, Kato caught typhus. She was twenty-two when she died; Yakov was still an infant. Stalin was so distraught, he jumped after his wife's coffin into the freshly dug grave.[4] "This creature softened my stony heart," Stalin is said to have moaned. "She is dead and with her died my last warm feelings for all human beings."[5] He deposited

Yakov with his in-laws and didn't see his son for well over a decade. (In 1943, after Yakov was taken prisoner by the Nazis, Stalin refused to trade him, a lowly soldier, for a German field marshal. Learning that his father had refused the exchange, Yakov is said to have killed himself by throwing himself on the electrified barbed wire fence of a concentration camp.)

After the tsar abdicated in 1917, Stalin returned to Petrograd and went straight to the Alliluyev house. He and the teenage Nadya began a clandestine courtship. He absconded with her to the front, where socialists were trying to organize frustrated Russian soldiers. Discovering that she was gone, Sergei Alliluyev flew screaming into a neighbor's apartment: Stalin had stolen his daughter![6]

By 1918 they were married.

Though she did not claim power for herself, Nadezhda Krupskaya—the first first lady of the Soviet Union—had been Lenin's peer, advisor, and colleague. Theirs was, to a large extent, a partnership of equals. Nadya Alliluyeva never had this kind of relationship with Stalin. She was twenty-two years younger than her power-obsessed husband. He addressed her in the informal *ty*, while she used the deferential *vy*.[7] After they wed, she went to work in his traveling "secretariat" and, later, as Lenin's secretary.[8]

Nadya learned she was pregnant in 1920, the year of full labor mobilization. For women like her from socialist families, work was how you measured your self-worth, your contribution to society, your dignity. But even though Stalin was a veteran Bolshevik, he wanted Nadya to be a homemaker and a wife, someone to tend to their Kremlin apartment and to host their many important guests. His contemporaries contemptuously ascribed this to his roots in the macho culture of provincial Georgia. When Nadya refused to quit her job, the fighting escalated to the point that Lenin was dragged into the conflict. Stalin, the master bureaucrat, had his wife expelled from the Party. Lenin intervened on Nadya's behalf and reinstated her by personal fiat. "Asiatic," he is said to have scoffed at Stalin's sexism.[9]

Even after Lenin's death, Nadya insisted on working. She worked secretarial jobs in the *Pravda* publishing empire and then went back to school to study industrial dyes. Although she now lived in the Kremlin with a man who was the head of the Soviet Union, she refused to take her husband's last name, like all good revolutionary women. This soon became standard Soviet practice, especially among the intelligentsia. But for Nadya it was more than just good Bolshevik form. She hid behind her maiden name, hoping that people wouldn't realize who she was married to. She had her chauffeur drop her off a few blocks from the institute, but classmates—like Khrushchev—quickly figured her out.[10] (It was Nadya who introduced Stalin to the man who would succeed him.)[11] Hers was an isolating and isolated way to live. "I decidedly have nothing to do with anyone in Moscow," a despondent Nadya wrote to a friend.

Under Stalin, the state bureaucracy and the security agencies ballooned. The men at the top of the political and security structures—and they were now all men—controlled the distribution of the Soviet Union's scant resources. They and their wives became the new elite, the *nomenklatura*, occupying the grand old apartments of the capital and the abandoned aristocratic dachas on its perimeter. They had nice clothes and access to good food at a time when the country was convulsed with a deadly famine entirely of Stalin's making. Nadya's life, with its nannies, cooks, and chauffeurs, was increasingly out of step with the terrorized and impoverished lives of most of her husband's subjects.

It's unclear how much she fought the reproduction of the traditional stratification of Russian society by the very people who had sought to eliminate it. But others noticed how uncomfortable Nadya was in the role of elite wife—especially other elite wives, who could barely contain their contempt for a woman who wouldn't take full advantage of her status. The wife of one of Stalin's top lieutenants assumed Nadya must be mentally ill for complaining about her situation and her tumultuous relationship with her husband, especially given how frequently the men at the top changed their wives for younger, more adoring women.[12] "We spoke among ourselves, and many times to Nadya, that she was not a match for [Stalin]," recalled the wife of a high-ranking Soviet official. "He needed a different wife!"[13]

Still, Nadya was a worthy sparring partner for her husband. "She argued with Stalin, made objections," her daughter, Svetlana, recalled in her memoirs decades later. "She considered herself his *equal* and this went against his purely Oriental approach to women and to a wife."[14] "A woman of very strong character," Stalin's notorious bodyguard Karl Pauker recalled. "She is like flint. The Master is very rough with her, but even he is afraid of her sometimes. Especially when the smile disappears from her face."[15]

They fought frequently and from the very beginning. "She never knew what was next, what explosion [was coming]," Irina Gogua, a Kremlin employee, recalled in an interview decades later.[16] In 1926, after yet another fight, Nadya grabbed the kids—Svetlana was an infant, their son Vasily was five—and took off for her parents' home in Leningrad. "She was intent on starting to work there and to gradually build an independent life for herself," Svetlana wrote. Eventually, though, Stalin called. Nadya gave in and returned to the Kremlin.

As Stalin's power grew, Nadya's isolation deepened. Nadya's older sister, Anna, told Svetlana that "in the last few years of her life, mom was thinking more and more frequently about leaving father," Svetlana recalled, referring to her aunt by her patronymic. "Anna Sergeyevna always repeats that this was mom's insistent thought, that she wanted to free herself from her 'high station,' which only oppressed her." The nanny would later recall that, shortly before her death, Nadya became uncommonly sad and irritable. Once, she overheard Nadya talking with a friend, using phrases like "sick of everything," "it's all gone mad," and "nothing makes me happy."[17]

The last time Svetlana saw her mother was when Nadya sat her on the old Georgian ottoman in her bedroom and lectured the six-year-old girl about the perils of drinking. She and Stalin had fought the night before because he was giving the children wine, an old Georgian tradition. "Don't drink wine!" she lectured Svetlana. "Never drink wine!"

And so, on the evening of November 8, 1932, Nadezhda Alliluyeva put on a black dress embroidered with red roses and tucked a matching red rose in her dark hair. The dress was made from fabric that her brother had sent from Berlin. He had also given her a Walther pistol so tiny it could fit into her evening purse.[18] She and Stalin were going to a holiday banquet, and while Nadya was getting ready, Stalin was in his office, deepening the famine in Ukraine by ordering local officials to cut off all consumer goods to the region until it started producing grain again.[19]

At the dinner, Nadya sat across from Stalin. The tension between them rose palpably. It finally broke when Stalin saw Nadya raise a glass of wine to her lips.

"Hey, you!" he commanded. "Drink!"

"I'm not 'hey'!" she said. Then she stormed out.

That's the version Svetlana heard. Gogua heard a different story.

At the dinner, Nadya sat across from Stalin. The tension between them rose palpably. Stalin split open a cigarette and stuffed the tobacco into his pipe. Then he balled up the leftover paper and launched it across the table, right into Nadya's eye. Furious, Nadya taunted him about his "Asiatic" jokes. Then it was Stalin's turn to explode. He cursed her with his characteristic flair and then called for a car and went, apparently, to the home of a woman Nadya suspected of being his mistress.

Here, the stories converge. Nadya's face went dark and she fled. She was followed by her close friend Polina Zhemchuzhina, the wife of one of Stalin's key lieutenants. Zhemchuzhina took Nadya on a few laps around the Kremlin grounds. She knew how hard Nadya's life had become, but she was sure her friend had felt better after a walk in the bracing night air. The two women bid each other good night and went to their respective homes.[20]

In the morning, one of the nannies went to wake Nadya. She found her lying on the floor by the bed, still in her black dress with the red roses, covered in blood, a tiny Walther pistol by her side. She had shot herself in the heart.

Svetlana was allowed to glimpse her mother's body in the casket as it lay in the Party offices in the GUM department store, on Red Square. Stalin, to the amazement of his inner circle, wept openly. He could not understand why Nadya had punished him. Was it because he hadn't taken her to the theater enough? He walked behind her casket along Moscow's streets, lined by mourners (plainclothes agents of the Soviet secret police, the NKVD), all the way to the cemetery of the Soviet elite.[21] Many of those who attended Nadya's private funeral weren't as fortunate. They would soon find their eternal rest in the common graves of Kommunarka, Sukhanovka, Butovo, and the Donskoy Monastery.

Stalin never remarried after Nadya's death, which was officially attributed to appendicitis. "Whatever pleasures Stalin occasionally took," historian Stephen Kotkin writes, "he was married to Soviet state power."[22] The violence of Nadya's death presaged the destruction her husband would soon wreak upon the entire country. "In the Soviet Union, the fate of the woman at the top reflected the fate of the country," Nina Khrushcheva, Nikita's great-granddaughter, once told me. "Lenin and Krupskaya were partners. Nadezhda's fate was a reflection of the country's fate because Stalin's power was unshareable. She had to go. And, of course, she would go in the most violent way."

TRAITORS TO THE MOTHERLAND

"ONCE UPON A TIME, THERE LIVED A STUPID LITTLE GIRL," WROTE Vladimira "Mira" Uborevich in 1963. "She lived at 11 Bolshoy Rzhevsky Lane until she was thirteen and went to School No. 110 until the fifth grade. She had many wonderful friends, a good mom and a good dad, her own room with a canary, all kinds of activities and games, and she didn't understand that, for the rest of her life, she would remember this ordinary childhood as a fairy tale about her own life."[1]

Mira's childhood wasn't exactly ordinary. She lived in a grand and sunny apartment in the very center of Moscow. She had a nanny who sewed Mira blue satin pantaloons for gym class. Her mother, Nina, was a beautiful, fashionable woman, friends with the country's most famous poets and writers and artists. Nina wore lipstick and smoked and, when she was stationed with her husband in Chita, insisted on wearing heels even during the Siberian winters. Mira's father was a Red Army commander and a hero of the Civil War, which was why Mira was named after Vladimir Lenin and lived in a luxurious building with other families of the Soviet high command. She had her own bedroom, its walls constantly reupholstered by her mother with chic new fabric, with a little writing desk and a canary and a turtle and a hamster and some fish.

It was this high station that made Mira's family so vulnerable, and why their fall was so precipitous.

On May 31, 1937, Mira's best friend Viktoria "Veta" Gamarnik's father committed suicide. The Gamarniks lived in the apartment above Mira's. Veta's father, Yan, was also a famous Civil War veteran and the deputy commissar of defense. He suffered from diabetes and had been working from home that week. According to the nurse taking care of him, the day before his death he received a phone call just as she was about to give him an insulin injection. Syringe in hand, she waited patiently as a man's voice, heavily accented with the strong notes of the Caucasus, poured venom and curses on Veta's father, who seemed distressed by the conversation. The following day, two men came to the Gamarniks' apartment. They went into Yan's office and, after a short while, walked out, closing the door behind them. Then they sat down outside the room and waited. In a few minutes a shot rang out. One of the men got up and looked inside. Then he turned on his heel and left the apartment, the second man following close behind. Veta's mother sat in the living room, stunned and muttering, "Finally. It's all over."

What came to be known as the Great Terror began with the death of Sergey Kirov, who was shot as he entered his office on December 1, 1934.[2] The Leningrad Party boss was a genuinely popular leader, and Stalin feared he might become a rival for his throne.[3] Kirov's assassination was carried out on Stalin's orders but portrayed by state propaganda as a plot aimed at Stalin himself. It became the pretext Stalin wanted to purge the Party and the country of any conceivable opposition.

The killings began in earnest in 1936 with the arrests, show trials, and executions of Lenin's former lieutenants, the men who could have legitimately claimed to be his heirs. (Krupskaya intervened for her old friends and comrades until Stalin "said that, if necessary, we would proclaim another woman Lenin's widow," one of his lieutenants recalled.)[4] By 1937 the purges had spread to the rest of the Party and then to the rest of the country. Hundreds of thousands of people disappeared into the prisons and execution cellars of Stalin's feared commissar of internal affairs, Nikolai Yezhov. The Gulag, a network of "corrective labor" camps in Russia's least hospitable regions that had been set up under Lenin, exploded in size and population.

The sweeps quickly lost any semblance of logic. At first, Party members who had been opposed to Stalin in any way were annihilated. But soon, even being a militant Stalinist offered little protection. Having worked with or been in any way affiliated with a person who had been arrested made one immediately suspect. Almost everyone who held Party leadership posts was arrested, as were their replacements and their replacements' replacements. Buildings that housed the Party hierarchy, like the one in which Mira Uborevich and Veta Gamarnik lived, became the focal points of the purges. The families that moved into apartments vacated by those who had been arrested soon found themselves under arrest, as did the families who moved in after them. By the time the purges slowed in 1939, the Party elite had been wiped out. Only 2 percent of the delegates who had attended the Party Congress in 1934 were still alive.[5] Nearly half of the Central Committee had been purged.[6]

This pattern repeated itself in every realm of professional life. The Terror decapitated the Red Army, claiming three of its five marshals, thirteen out of fifteen army commanders, eight out of nine admirals, and so on down the line.[7] The arts and sciences were decimated, as were academia, medicine, and engineering. The Gulag camps of the Magadan region, in the moonscapes of the distant Russian northeast, writes Kotkin, "acquired enough performers to form a local symphony and a musical comedy troupe." Magadan, he notes, "could claim a higher concentration not just of musicians and actors, but of doctors, scholars, poets, novelists, photographers and painters than any urban center east of the Urals, and many to the west."[8] The diplomatic corps and the ranks of foreign Communists were also purged as their members were falsely accused of espionage and increasingly fantastic plots against the Soviet Union. Stalin killed so many of his own foreign intelligence agents that, for 127 consecutive days in 1938, he did not receive any foreign intelligence briefings.[9]

Even members of the NKVD, the secret police who made the arrests, pulled the triggers, and oversaw the camps, got caught in the human wood chipper. Periodically, Stalin would cleanse their ranks by the tens of thousands. A year into Yezhov's administration of Stalin's bloody campaign, he, too, was shot, whimpering and begging for mercy.

Millions of ordinary Soviet citizens were swept up in this bloodletting. Ratting on someone became a common way to settle a score or to acquire a coveted apartment or spouse, although this could backfire, since the denouncers were often also rounded up for good measure. The sight of the NKVD's signature car, known as a Black Maria, was like an apparition of the Grim Reaper. People began to sleep with their bags packed for prison. Jokes became mortal sins. Talk became dangerous, as did silence. People with foreign connections disappeared and the rest cut off contact with relatives abroad.

The scale of the Great Terror stills the mind. At its height in 1937 and 1938, there were an average of 2,200 arrests and 1,000 executions per day.[10] By the time Stalin died in 1953, nearly a million Soviet citizens had been executed and over 28 million more had passed through the Gulag, where nearly 3 million of them perished from disease, starvation, exposure, or violence.[11] "World history had never before seen such carnage by a regime against itself, as well as its own people," wrote Kotkin.[12]

Most of the victims of Stalin's terror were men. They made up the bulk of those executed and most of those sent to the camps. The female prisoner population rarely topped 20 percent of the Gulag's total population. The vast majority of Soviet women affected by the purges suffered on the outside. After their loved ones disappeared, they knew precious little about what had happened to them or whether they were even alive. Still, Soviet women tapped into their vast resourcefulness, using whatever connections they had to find out what prisons or camps their family members had been sent to and send any food or warm clothing they could.

The low proportion of women executed and sent to the camps was due in part to the fact that the purges were heavily aimed at the Soviet elite, and by this point men held nearly all positions of power. Ninety percent of the top ranks of the Red Army was purged, for instance, but 100 percent of the top ranks of the Red Army had been male.[13] But once their husbands and fathers were led away at dawn, children like Mira and Veta, as well as their mothers, were at the mercy of Stalin's terror.

As Veta's dead father lay in his office, prepared for burial, she and Mira sat in the Gamarniks' living room, looking through a photo album of their fathers' Red Army colleagues. They used a black pencil to cross out the ones who had already disappeared. The two thirteen-year-old girls were repeating a ritual happening all over the country, the names and images of the arrested expunged from newsreels, books, and photographs as if they had never existed.

Mira didn't know that her own father had been arrested two days before Veta's father had shot himself. Before the Terror, whenever her father's army train arrived from Smolensk, where he was posted, Nina would greet him at the station. This time she arrived to find his train car surrounded by NKVD troops. Pushing past them, she found her husband dressed in civilian clothes and deathly pale. "Don't worry, Ninok, everything will be fine," he managed. Then NKVD officers led him away and locked her in a separate compartment for four hours.

When they released her, Nina raced to NKVD headquarters and stormed into the office of one high-ranking friend, demanding to know what was going on. The officer assured Nina that he would sort everything out immediately. Instead, shortly after Nina arrived at home, the NKVD showed up with a search warrant. Nina did her best to take control of the situation. She sent Mira and her nanny Masha to see *The Princess Turandot* at a nearby theater while she set out an elaborate spread for the officers and tried to flirt and cajole them into stopping this foolishness. The officers, while impressed with her beauty and her charm, did no such thing.

Less than two weeks later, Mira, her mother, and Masha would be forced to leave Moscow under NKVD guard. They soon found themselves on a train bound for Astrakhan, a shabby gem of a city on the Caspian that would be their place of exile. Mira would never set foot in her beautiful bedroom again.

Veta Gamarnik and her mother were on the train to Astrakhan, too, as were many other wives and children of the Red Army commanders who had lived at 11 Bolshoy Rzhevsky Lane. Mira was largely oblivious to what was happening. She was busy with the pets Nina had allowed her to bring: a kitten, a turtle, some goldfish, and a canary. She didn't realize what a deeply delirious act of kindness it was for her mother, who had spent the previous two weeks trying to pack their entire lives into a few suitcases, to allow Mira to bring her animals on this voyage to nowhere.

Four days after Mira started school in Astrakhan, the NKVD arrested Nina.

Tens of thousands of Soviet women were arrested simply for being the wives of men who had been arrested. Their children fared scarcely better. The Soviet penal code, as amended by Stalin in 1937, stipulated that family members—parents, spouses, children, and siblings—of someone who had betrayed the Motherland were criminally liable for aiding them, not alerting the authorities, or just living with them.[14] (According to the new law, even former spouses were subject to arrest if they had not alerted the authorities to their ex-husbands' nefarious plans.)[15] They even had a special category in the Gulag with its own acronym: *ChSIR*, for "family members of traitors to the Motherland." A special camp was set up in Kazakhstan for spouses: the infamous Akmolinsk Camp for Wives of Traitors to the Motherland. Some 20,000 women eventually passed through it. Tens of thousands of women who managed to escape an executioner's bullet worked and died in this and other camps in the vast and brutal network of the Gulag.

Formally, this was why Nadya Alliluyeva's sister Anna Sergeyevna was arrested in 1938. Her husband, who had headed the NKVD in eastern Ukraine, had been executed as an enemy of the people, making her a family member of a traitor to the Motherland, a ChSIR. Many wives did not get even the procedural courtesy of an arrest. While avant-garde theater director Vsevolod Meyerhold was being tortured under arrest, his wife, the actress Zinaida Reikh, was stabbed to death in their apartment, her eyes cut out.[16] Other women were used as hostages. According to one historian, Stanislav Kossior, an Old Bolshevik and member of the Politburo, withstood torture for months but finally broke when his sixteen-year-old daughter was raped in front of him.[17] For all the Bolshevik rhetoric on the equality of women, Stalin saw these women as nothing but extensions of their husbands and fathers, his enemies.

Mere hours after the NKVD had led Nina away, they returned for thirteen-year-old Mira, who was also arrested as a ChSIR and taken to a local orphanage. Her nanny managed to find her there and tried to adopt her, but the authorities refused her request. For a while, Mira received letters from Nina, who tried hard to be cheerful. Then the letters stopped. Mira was told that her mother had been convicted of being a ChSIR and given a sentence of ten years without the right to correspondence.

Mira was eventually transferred to a distant orphanage in Perm, on the Siberian side of the Ural Mountains. After the first year, she learned to stop crying herself to sleep. It helped that she was surrounded by her childhood friends from 11 Bolshoy Rzhevsky Lane. Veta Gamarnik was there, as was Svetlana Tukhachevskaya, daughter of the famous—and famously brutal—Marshal Mikhail Tukhachevsky. So was Pyotr Yakir, son of the Civil War hero and Red Army commander Iona Yakir. The children did not know it but, except for Veta's father, who had shot himself rather than undergo arrest, their fathers had all been executed on the same day.

Not coincidentally, most chroniclers of the Gulag were men writing about the men who surrounded them in the camps, which were strictly segregated by gender.[18] It was Aleksandr Solzhenitsyn's *The Gulag Archipelago* that shaped the West's understanding of the Terror by showing the world what Stalin did to millions of Soviet men. But three years before Solzhenitsyn was awarded the Nobel Prize for Literature in 1970, a memoir by the history professor and journalist Eugenia Ginzburg was first published in the United States. *Journey into the Whirlwind* is an account of the eighteen years Ginzburg spent in jails, camps, and exile for invented political crimes. Her memoir, and those of other lesser-known female writers, document a different Gulag, on the women's side of the fence.

Ginzburg, a Party member since her teens, was arrested in Kazan in early 1937. She realized very quickly that to survive she would have to trust the other women in her cell. She would have to be accepted into their all-female family, for it was the only one she would have for years to come.

During each step of her journey through the Gulag, Ginzburg lovingly catalogued these women who accompanied her into hell and relied on each other to stay alive. There is the German Communist arrested at a black-tie gala who, months later, is still in her evening gown and heels when she's thrown in the hole and doused with icy water. There are idealistic young university students and seasoned revolutionaries who know from tsarist times how to conduct themselves in prison. There are young peasant women imprisoned for stealing stray strands of wheat to survive Stalin's famine. There are terrified Baltic women who barely speak Russian and arrive in droves after Stalin occupied their countries. There are the true believers, like Ginzburg, forced to do penance for building the very system that devoured them. There is the woman traveling next to Ginzburg in the cattle car who is in the final stages of syphilis, her nose steadily caving into her face. For a month, as their train rolled east to Vladivostok and the barrenness of Kolyma, Ginzburg was bathed in the scent wafting off the woman's collapsing nose, a smell of flesh that was both living and dying.

In Ginzburg's telling, the women are more than their invented crimes. They have names and professions and hometowns. They have families and imperfect personalities, their capacities for generosity and meanness brought out by the horror of their lives. They suffer and die, but they also joke and sing and recite poetry and save up sugar and bread for a New Year's celebration. Secretly circulated decades later as samizdat when it was forbidden to speak of what Stalin had done to his people, Ginzburg's memoir provided a kind of catalogue of the women who had disappeared into the Terror's faceless mass of victims.

The women in Ginzburg's memoir live in a mostly female world, but whenever they encounter their male counterparts, traditional Russian gender norms come roaring back. The men try to help the women with the physical work, and the women regard them "with a maternal pity," knowing that men are frailer than them, steely Russian women who can stop a galloping steed and enter a burning hut. Ginzburg recalls how she and the other women once watched a silent convoy of male political prisoners.

> They seem to us to be even more defenseless than we are. After all, they are so bad at tolerating pain (this was our shared opinion!), not one of them will find a way to wash his undergarments unnoticed the way we know how to do it, or to fix something... These were our husbands and brothers, deprived of our care in this terrifying situation. "Poor thing, no one to sew on a button for him," someone says...[19]

And yet while some women may have felt themselves better equipped to handle the hunger, disease, and violence that tormented all residents of the Gulag, female prisoners experienced an entire dimension of horror that their male counterparts did not. They had to contend with the added pressures of pregnancy and motherhood, of trying to nurture life in a place designed to grind it down.

The camps and jails were full of pregnant women and children. By April 1941, there were 2,500 women with small children in NKVD jails and 9,400 children under four in the camps. Between the camps and the prisons, there were 8,500 pregnant women. By the time Stalin died in 1953, there were nearly half a million women in the Gulag. Over 35,000 of them had children and nearly 63,000 were pregnant.[20]

Some of these children were born en route, as Anne Applebaum chronicles in her harrowing book *Gulag*.[21] (She is the rare historian of the period who devotes significant space to women caught in the Great Terror.) A letter from a group of workers in Vologda to the chairman of the Central Executive Committee, Mikhail Kalinin, complained of the conditions:

> They sent them in awful frosts—infants and pregnant women who were transported in cattle cars, lying one on top of the other, and the women gave birth to their children right

there (is this not torture); then they threw them out of the train like dogs.²²

Some children were born in the camps, products of rape or love or something in between. Surrounded by horror, people still managed to fall in love and nurture relationships in the few places where the two sexes commingled. Most of the sexual contact in the camps, however, was decidedly non-consensual. The men's camps were policed by "non-political" male prisoners—that is, actual criminals—who used rape to humiliate and discipline the men doing time for political crimes.

But sexual violence looked different on the female side of the fence. Male criminal authorities had women who were essentially their slaves, women that they bartered and traded. Sex was extorted out of women by overseers or taken by force by male non-political prisoners. For the most defenseless female political prisoners, sex simply became a survival strategy, to be traded for extra food or easier work.

When women discovered they were pregnant, some were desperate to abort despite the lack of proper medical care to safely do so. Applebaum interviewed a woman who described seeing a fellow inmate stuff nails into herself and then return to work at her sewing machine until she began to bleed.²³ Another recalled how her mother performed her own abortion, crushing the expelled fetus with her own hands.²⁴

Those who did give birth had to hand their children over to the camp orphanage, the *detkombinat*—quite literally, the child plant. Ginzburg worked in one briefly at the remote camp at Elgen, and when she first walked in, she collapsed into sobs.²⁵ She saw a mass of babies in wall-to-wall cribs, "wet and mildewy, emaciated, exhausted from screaming." It was forbidden to pick them up except to change or feed them. Every three hours, the mothers were brought in to nurse them under heavy guard. "You can't tell what they fear more," Ginzburg wrote of these mothers, "that the infant born at Elgen survives or that he'll die."²⁶

After the children were weaned, their mothers rarely got to see them, if ever.²⁷ Whether they did or not seemed to make little difference in the children's development. At the Elgen *detkombinat*, Ginzburg realized that most of the two dozen four-year-olds in her care still hadn't learned to speak. Those who could had vocabularies limited to the only reality they had ever experienced. When Ginzburg drew a house and asked the children what they saw, the verbal ones happily responded with, "A barrack!"

Children born in the camps often didn't survive long. In one camp, near Norilsk, nearly a fifth of the infants died in one year.[28] In another, in the wilds past the Arctic Circle, three hundred children died every year. Those who survived were sent to orphanages and given new names, severing any threads tying them to their mothers. Legions of Soviets grew up this way, knowing that the state had willfully stolen them from their parents.

The most excruciating story I've encountered, though, is that of Hava Volovich. She was a Jewish woman from Ukraine who was arrested in 1937 at the age of twenty-one and sentenced to fifteen years, an entire youth spent in the Gulag. "I wanted love, tenderness, and affection to the point of madness, to the point of beating your head against the wall, to the point of death," Volovich wrote in her memoirs. "And I wanted a child, a creature that is closest and dearest to you, for whom it wouldn't be a pity to give up my life."[29] She resists the urge for a long time, given the conditions of the camp. Eventually, though, she gives in. "It is a marvelous and terrifying thing, the instinct of childbearing," she wrote.

She gives birth in 1942 to Eleonora, a little girl with blond curls and blue eyes. Volovich and two other mothers are assigned a hut where bedbugs rain down like sand from the ceiling; Volovich spends all her time plucking them off her daughter's little body. All night she stands by her crib, begging a God she never believed in to let her child survive. This hut will come to seem like paradise after Volovich and Eleonora are transferred to a "mothers' camp." There, Volovich is sent to fell timber and Eleonora is put in a nursery much like the one Ginzburg described. Soon, Eleonora goes from a pudgy, breastfed cherub to "a pale shadow with blue circles under her eyes and crusted lips."

Volovich figures out how to smuggle extra firewood to the

women who run the *detkombinat* so that she can see her daughter more frequently. She sees how the staff wake the children in the morning with punches to their little backs. On beds where they have slept in the cold without blankets, the staff wash the waste off them with icy water. One woman brings in steaming hot porridge from the kitchen, ties the children's arms behind their backs, and pours the scorching sludge down their throats. "And the little ones didn't even dare cry," Volovich remembers. "They just grunted like old men and crowed. All day, this awful crowing rose from the children's beds. Children who should already be sitting and crawling, just lay on their backs, their legs folded into their bellies, and emitted these strange sounds, which sounded like the muted moans of pigeons."

Eleonora, Volovich soon discovers, is covered in bruises. Now a toddler, she begs to go back to that hut where it rained bedbugs, the only home she ever knew. But despite Volovich's bribes and complaints to the *detkombinat* staff, Eleonora "begins to melt even faster." She stops asking to go home to the bedbug hut. When Volovich comes to visit, Eleonora bites her lip hard enough to draw blood and turns away, asking for nothing.

> Only on the last day of her life when I picked her up (I was allowed to breast feed her) she looked off to the side somewhere with her widened eyes and started pounding my face with her weak little fists, pinching and biting my breast. And then she pointed down to her little bed.
>
> In the evening, when I came by with an armful of firewood, her bed was already empty. I found her in the morgue, naked, among the adult prisoners.

Volovich wasn't allowed to bury her, so she bribed a guard to do so. Afterward he brought her the branches of a pine, tied together in the shape of a cross. She would never find out where her daughter was buried. Concluding her chapter about Eleonora, Volovich writes, "And that's the whole story of how I committed the worst imaginable crime, having become a mother for the only time in my life."

In 1944, Mira, now twenty years old, finally free after years in an orphanage, was an architecture student in Moscow. In the orphanage, she had learned to push her grief deep into an inaccessible part of herself and even to imitate happiness. She could not, however, teach herself to stop waiting for her parents to appear and rescue her. One day, on a road near the orphanage, she was sure she saw her father walking toward her.

During the chaos of World War II, she had finished school and managed to enroll in the Moscow Architectural Institute, which had been evacuated from the path of the Nazi invasion to Tashkent, in Uzbekistan. There, she ran into Kira Alliluyeva, Nadya's niece, who told her that *her* family had also been decimated and scattered around the Gulag. Mira also found her mother's old friend and neighbor Elena Sergeyevna Bulgakova, whose late husband was the writer Mikhail Bulgakov. Elena Sergeyevna saved Mira from the sour-smelling shack that doubled as the institute's dormitory and offered her a bed in her own small space. Soon the institute returned to its home in Moscow, and Mira followed suit, spending a happy year as a young college student. It was the first time she had experienced anything like normalcy in seven years.

On September 11, 1944, she was arrested again.

This time Mira was charged with "anti-Soviet activity." After months of interrogations in a Moscow prison, she was sentenced to five years in the Gulag, which she served in the notorious camp at Vorkuta, north of the Arctic Circle, where Hava Volovich had given birth to Eleonora.

There was a strict division in the camps between the criminals, who were in for murder, theft, and prostitution, and the political prisoners, who had longer sentences, tougher work conditions, fewer privileges, and less food, and who suffered more abuse. Mira heard that the criminals called the residents of one notorious barrack of political prisoners the "fascists." She soon learned that they were referring to the ChSIRs, the wives of the Old Bolsheviks, the family members of traitors to the Motherland.

When the women in the "fascist" barrack saw Mira, they burst into tears. "They were in the camps, but they were calm about their children's fates," Mira told an interviewer many decades later.[30] The women believed that "their children were living with their relatives, all of them were in college, everything was fine. And here came the moment where they find out that they were starting to arrest the kids." It was true. In prison, the interrogators were trying to extract a confession from Mira by pitting her against her childhood friends from 11 Bolshoy Rzhevsky Lane, Pyotr and Svetlana, who were in neighboring cells. Veta Gamarnik, Mira's best friend from childhood, got a fresh sentence as well: ten years of exile.

By the time Mira was freed and made her way back to Moscow in 1947, she had married a man she met in the camp and together they had a daughter, now three years old. But on the train ride, the little girl lost consciousness. She was dead of meningitis within days of arriving in the capital. Mira buried her and returned to Vorkuta to work as a free woman while waiting for the release of her husband.

In 1956, three years after Stalin's death, his successor and accomplice in the purges, Nikita Khrushchev, delivered his so-called Secret Speech, revealing the full extent of the Great Terror. Mira and her late father were officially rehabilitated a year later, their sentences expunged and their standing as Soviet citizens reinstated. But Mira still could not find her mother. "My whole life," Mira would later write, "I waited to be reunited with Mom."

Only in 1957 did Mira discover what had happened to Nina. After three years as a ChSIR in the camps, where she had contracted scurvy and night blindness from severe malnutrition, Nina was brought back to Moscow to be retried for the more serious crime of anti-Soviet activity. She was shot on July 13, 1941, along with the mothers of Veta Gamarnik and Svetlana Tukhachevskaya.

At the age of sixty-four, Mira received a letter from a woman who had known Nina in the camps. It was 1988, the age of glasnost, and Soviets were beginning to speak more openly about what they had survived. For decades, this woman had been too afraid to contact her. Now she wanted Mira to know how her mother had lived her last years.

"I don't know if your mother wrote to you that she worked as a water carrier?" the woman wrote.

Wearing huge shoe covers and a quilted jacket, her head tied with a kerchief, she pulled a stubborn bull that was harnessed to a cart or a sled that held big barrels. Filling them up with water was part of Nina Vladimirovna's responsibilities. The water was needed to supply the cafeteria, the bakery, and other services.

The well was on a knoll by our barrack. It was very deep and getting water out of it was very difficult, but Nina Vladimirovna never complained of fatigue.

When the frosts came, I was put in charge of clearing the path to the well, sprinkling it with ash. During this time, I got to see Nina Vladimirovna especially frequently. One of the winter nights imprinted itself especially brightly in my memory. It was frosty and clear, the moon shone brightly. The well, covered in ice, was illuminated by the moon's light against the dark silhouettes of the barracks, as was the figure of Nina Vladimirovna, who was also covered in a crust of ice, ice that seemed to ripple with rainbows. She was tenaciously pulling a slippery bucket that wouldn't budge and expressively reciting Verlaine's poems in French. It was a fantastical moment. She was glorious in the strength of her spirit, her immense will overcoming the darkness of our situation, of our existence.

It was then that I felt that she could not be broken, that no humiliation or hardship would kill the great power of her soul.

REQUIEM

ONE SPRING AFTERNOON WHEN I WAS STILL IN HIGH SCHOOL IN SUBurban Maryland, my mother took me downstairs, where the books we'd managed to bring from Moscow were nestled around the upright piano I loathed. We sat on the piano bench and my mother opened up a volume of poetry by Anna Akhmatova, a woman I had never heard of. Despite the weekly Russian lessons, I was a thoroughly Americanized teenager, and the purges were a secret into which I had yet to be initiated.

Akhmatova had been born into an aristocratic family, my mother explained, educated in the royal schools of Tsarskoe Selo, outside St. Petersburg. A striking, oft-painted woman with black bangs and an aquiline nose, she became a star poet of the Silver Age, the explosion of poetry and literature during the waning years of the Russian belle époque. My mother read me some of her poetry from the pre-Revolutionary days, in which the melancholy, coquettish Akhmatova pines over oysters and an unrequited love. They were beautiful poems, in Russian simple enough for me to understand, the emotions painfully familiar to a teenage girl.

Then my mother flipped forward to "Requiem," Akhmatova's epic poem about the purges. My mother filled in the basic details of the Great Terror for me and explained what it had meant for Akhmatova. Stalin was too scared and too cruel to arrest the great poet herself. Instead, he arrested her only child, Lev, from her first marriage to the famous poet Nikolai Gumilev. In August 1921, Gumilev was arrested, accused of participating in some shadowy counterrevolutionary conspiracy, and shot by the new Bolshevik government. Throughout the 1930s and 1940s, my mother told me, Stalin would have Lev arrested, then released, arrested, then released. Each time, she said, Akhmatova begged Stalin for mercy and mourned her son as if he had been shot, only to have him return—and be arrested again. "He played a game of cat and mouse with her," my mother explained. "It was his special way of torturing her." When Lev finally came home from the camps, he stopped speaking to his mother, convinced she hadn't done enough to save him.

My mother read me the poem, starting from the prose introduction.

> In the frightening days of Yezhov's terror, I spent seventeen months waiting in line outside the prison in Leningrad. One day, somebody in the crowd "identified" me. A woman standing behind me, her lips blue from the cold, who of course had never heard my name, woke from the stupor that had become so natural to us and asked in my ear (everyone whispered there):
> "But can you describe this?"
> And I said:
> "I can."
> Then something like a smile slipped across what had once been her face.

The Terror touched our family, too. Buzya was never a Party member and was far from its intrigues, but as the purges spread, they slowly nibbled away at her orbit. In the early 1930s, some of her colleagues at the institute received five-year sentences for shoddy dye jobs, a sentence that would soon come to seem like a mercy. Then Shura's colleagues began to disappear, one by one.

And then the Terror came home. In 1938, Alexander Beylin, the husband of Buzya's baby sister Eva, was tipped off that his arrest was imminent. By then, people knew what happened after a Black Maria picked you up: torture followed either by a quick death (a bullet to the back of the head) or a slow one (years in the camps, digging for gold or felling trees on starvation rations). Alexander did not want to find out which was the worse fate. He did what many people did when they knew their turn in the back of a Black Maria was coming: he killed himself.

Eva was now a widow like every woman in her family. She was also heavily pregnant. Given her heart defect, the doctors had advised her against having a child, but Eva had refused to get an abortion. Now she was weeks away from giving birth and suddenly husbandless. A couple of months after her son Dmitry was born, Eva was dead: the strain on her heart had proved too great. Buzya and Shura, who both found children bewildering and had difficult relationships with their own sons, adopted Dmitry so that he wouldn't end up like the millions of children of "enemies of the people," children who woke in the morning to find their parents had disappeared and who were then swept into state orphanages, where their names were changed and their origins expunged.

Later, my mother would tell me how the purges had affected her mother's family. In September 1938, Riva's brother-in-law, Efim Bruk, was arrested. Riva had left Moscow for Odessa in 1927 with her new beau, my great-grandfather Isaak Bruk. Odessa may have been the object of Riva's girlhood dreams, but after the excitement of revolutionary Moscow, it felt like going back to a larger, prettier shtetl. It was loud and hot and full of Isaak's brothers and sisters, one crazier than the other. The two oldest, Efim and Abram, were orthodox Bolsheviks who couldn't stomach their little brother's anarcho-syndicalist leanings. But her Isaak was beautiful and kind, with a generous and childlike spirit. He was the son of an alcoholic cobbler who had given Isaak to apprentice with a tinsmith at the age of eleven. Now Isaak worked in the canning factory and was taking engineering classes at night, a true proletarian man of the age.

She and Isaak did not officially marry till years later. Formal marriage, they believed, was a bourgeois relic, and they needed no piece of paper or religious ceremony to affirm what they felt for each other. They lived together happily, as man and wife, in a rented room in a communal apartment just past Moldovanka, the city's massive Jewish slum. Her pedology degree complete, Riva found work at a sanatorium for developmentally challenged children.

In 1927, officers from the secret police arrived to search Isaak's belongings, looking for Trotskyist literature. Riva watched the search alone: Isaak was already in a jail cell across town for talking back to a new commissar at his factory. Every day for months, Riva went to the jail to bring Isaak food or letters, sometimes passing his brothers, who crossed to the other side of the street and ignored her, a class enemy. He was eventually released because the police didn't find the Trotskyist literature they had been looking for. Those were the days when a lack of evidence could actually matter.

That had all changed by the time Efim was arrested a decade later, at the height of the Great Terror. A Party member since 1919, he had once been high up in the agricultural ministry and worked in Russia's south, helping the Soviet Union develop its tobacco industry. This work had taken him to Iran in the 1920s, which made him particularly suspect once the purges started. He would eventually be tortured into confessing that he was a spy for both the Japanese and the British, a charge that was as contradictory as it was common. He was sentenced to death, but, in the chaos of the terror, his sentence was inexplicably commuted to ten years of slave labor in Russia's endless north.

Sitting in Riva's kitchen after serving his sentence, Efim would recount awaiting his fate in an overcrowded cell. Between bloody interrogations, he and his fellow prisoners speculated about what they could have possibly done to merit arrest. In Efim's case, it was obvious: he and his brother Abram had emigrated from Odessa to the United States in 1911. In America, Efim had married a Russian woman named Neonila and they had a son, Alexander, or Sasha. After the tsar abdicated in 1917, Efim grabbed Neonila and Sasha and sailed back to Russia, eager to get in on building the world's first workers' utopia. Riva would forever recall with contempt how Efim had described tossing Sasha's diapers overboard, on the logic that there would be endless diapers in the new proletarian paradise. Efim's fellow prisoners were similarly incredulous when they heard this story—not at the waste of diapers but that he had been foolish enough to return to Russia. "The rest of us are in here for no reason," Efim recalled one of his cellmates saying, "but you're in here for being an idiot!"

After Efim's arrest, Sasha, a promising student with a passion for flying, formally disowned his father, an enemy of the people, in order to be accepted to a prestigious flight school. Less than two years later he was killed in a flying accident, and Neonila was trapped and alone in Stalin's Moscow. She blamed her husband and his crazy family for bringing her such irredeemably bad luck and decided she wanted nothing more to do with them. No one in the family ever saw her again.

We were lucky by comparison. There were some families that the purges wiped clean, like that of my mother's aunt Anya. She had married Riva's son and hailed from a well-known clan of Mensheviks, the losers of the post-Revolution power grab, many of whom happened to have been Jewish. Most of the men in Anya's family—fathers, grandfathers, uncles—had been shot, and the women had all served long sentences in the camps.

Now, ninety years later, there blinks a flicker of doubt that verges on guilt that members of our family survived when so many didn't. It is the irrational fear that a relative's survival may have been secured by some dishonorable act. Did one of our own escape the Gulag by sending someone else in his or her place? Buzya's husband, Shura, came from a wealthy Kiev family and had studied in Switzerland before the Revolution. He was rising fast in the sciences while many of his colleagues were arrested and shot. Did he turn someone in to save himself? After the Great Terror, there are few things more shameful in Russian culture than snitching, so whenever my mother wondered about what Shura may or may not have done to avoid prison, this would trigger a bitter fight with her mother, Emma, who posthumously defended her father-in-law's honor. In reality, there were people marked for arrest whom the angel of death missed and plenty who had never traveled abroad or made a joke at Stalin's expense who ended up in the camps. The unguessable logic of the slaughter was the point: to inflict trauma even on those it didn't touch.

Sitting on the piano bench in Maryland, surrounded by all these ghosts, my mother read on, tears rolling down her cheeks.

> The stars of death hovered above us,
> And innocent Russia grimaced
> Under bloodied boots
> And the tires of Black Marias.
>
> They led you away at dawn,
> I followed you like a coffin,

> Children cried in the dark room
> The holy candle sputtered
> On your lips, the cold of the icon.
> A deathly sweat on your brow... How can I forget!
> Like the wives of the sharpshooters,
> I will wail beneath the Kremlin towers.

In Russian, the verse rhymes. The lines are deceptively simple and taut, their grief and horror unadorned, scorching. Then come the simple couplets, a nursery rhyme of pain.

> Quietly flows the quiet Don,
> The yellow moon enters my home,
>
> Enters with his hat askew,
> Yellow moon sees a shadow.
> This woman is sick,
> This woman is alone.
> Husband in the grave, son in jail,
> Pray for me.

My Russian then was the Russian I had brought with me as a seven-year-old who was a month away from finishing first grade. I didn't know what Black Marias were or who Yezhov was. I didn't know the Russian word for "askew." I would learn all that later. But those couplets, coupled with my mother's tears, broke me open. I cried with her as she read.

The mind-numbing facts would come in college and in the decades that followed, in obsessive, breathless dives into memoirs and histories and photographs of the period. Everything I gathered on those dives would hold up the central structure, the pulsating heart of the history: pain.

That afternoon I set sail on the dark and churning seas of Soviet history—my history. Neither my mother nor I had lived the story of the purges. But my mother had found illegal self-published samizdat in her mother's underwear drawer when she was in second grade. Samizdat was the only way "Requiem" was available till long after Akhmatova died. My mother also got a hold of an illegal copy of Solzhenitsyn's *The Gulag Archipelago* and read till it made her sick. And now she was passing it down to me, the rightful inheritance of any child born in the Soviet Union: the pain of what our history did to all of us, and the obligation to feel it.

Two decades later I would discover this pulsating heart again in Svetlana Alexievich's oral histories of the Soviet Union. One of her interviewees had been a toddler when her mother was arrested, and her mother's best friend, a childless middle-aged woman, took the little girl in. This woman raised the girl as her own, thus keeping her out of orphanages. By the time her mother returned from the camps, the girl was all grown up and her biological mother was a stranger. When the NKVD archives were opened after the Soviet collapse, the girl's mother went to look up her own case file. She had always wanted to know who had doomed her to decades in the Gulag, away from her child. The file revealed that it was her best friend who had turned her in. She couldn't have children, so she had set her eyes on her best friend's daughter. The woman closed the file, went home, and hanged herself.

Alexievich, who won the Nobel Prize for Literature in 2015, has said that her task was to show how "little people" experience the political currents wrought by big people, to document "emotional history," the experience of living and feeling through historical cataclysm. To document the emotional history of the Soviet Union, Alexievich listened for one thing in particular. "I listen to the pain," she wrote. "Pain as evidence of a life gone by. There is no other proof, I don't trust any other evidence. Words have led us away from the truth many a time. I think about suffering as the highest form of information having a direct connection to the mysterious, to the mystery of life. All of Russian literature is about this. It is more about suffering than about love."

Let others write the terse narratives of the great Soviet leaders and the wide, bloody swaths they cut through their own people. But if you read Anna Akhmatova—or Eugenia Ginzburg or Hava Volovich or Mira Uborevich—if you talk to anyone who survived it, how can you write about anything other than the pain?

This is how Akhmatova's "Requiem" concludes, a verse I have returned to time and time again since that afternoon on the piano bench. It stuns me still.

And if they squeeze shut my tortured mouth,
Through which one hundred million people scream,

Let them remember me thus
On the eve of my remembrance day.

And if in this country someday
They decide to erect a monument to me,

I give my consent to this honor,
But with one condition: that it stand

Not by the sea, where I was born:
My last ties to the sea are torn,

Not in the tsar's garden by my cherished stump,
Where an inconsolable shadow looks for me,

But here, where I stood for three hundred hours
And where they didn't unlock the gates.

For the fact that even in blissful death I'm afraid
To forget the thundering of Black Marias,

To forget how the cursed door slammed
And the old woman howled like a wounded beast.

And may melted snow stream like tears
From the bronze, motionless lids,

May the prison's pigeon coo in the distance,
And the ships on the Neva sail quietly on.

WAR

IDA SEGAL HAD JUST FINISHED HER FRESHMAN YEAR AT KIEV UNIVERsity when the war came.[1] Sunday, June 22, 1941, began with blaring sirens and announcements across the vast country. The Germans had invaded, swarming in like iron ants along the long Soviet border in the west. As German planes started bombing the airfield near the university campus, a terrified Ida made her way into the city center on foot.

At 1:15 in the afternoon, Soviet foreign minister Vyacheslav Molotov addressed the nation. Plaintively, he laid out all the ways that the USSR had abided by the Nazi-Soviet nonaggression pact signed two years prior, which Hitler had just broken. Now, Molotov announced, the Soviet nation had no choice but to beat back the German intruder. "Our entire people must be united as never before," Molotov said, his speech booming from loudspeakers across the country, addressing its *grazhdani* and *grazhdanki*, male citizens and female citizens. "Each one of us has to demand for ourselves and others the discipline, organization, self-sacrifice worthy of a real Soviet patriot in order to provide for all the needs of the Red Army, navy, and air force in order to provide victory over the enemy."

On hearing the speech, eighteen-year-old Ida and her classmates, young men and women both, ran to the closest military recruitment post.

There was nothing exceptional about Ida. She was only doing what tens of thousands of young Soviet women did that hot and hectic summer: they flooded recruitment offices en masse and demanded to join the fight to defend their Motherland. During the first week of the war, 20,000 young Moscow women petitioned their local Communist Youth

League (Komsomol) cells to be sent to the front. In Leningrad, 27,000 women did the same. And those were just the numbers for Komsomol members; many other young women who were not part of the Communist Party's youth wing also went to war. In smaller cities, thousands of young women wrote formal petitions to local military commissariats, in some cases making up nearly half of the volunteers.[2] Some simply slipped into the formations of soldiers marching by their villages.[3] Many who were deemed too young or too small to join were hidden by older female friends under tarps on the trains going to the front.[4] Others, like my grandmother Emma's beloved older cousin Tsilya, were accepted at recruitment offices but then found themselves on military trains going east, away from the front. Incensed, they jumped off their assigned trains and onto the ones headed west, toward the action.

For most of these young women, it was an easy choice. "I didn't think about it for a second, didn't vacillate," one woman veteran recalled decades later.[5] Another wrote, "It was inconceivable not to go. Everyone went. Other thoughts did not exist."[6]

Most of the women who volunteered were between seventeen and twenty-five—at least officially. Many lied about their ages, and girls as young as fourteen found their way into combat. Virtually all of them were born after the Revolution and were its unique creations, the first generation of the newly minted Soviet woman. Born under the guiding stars of Nadezhda Krupskaya, Inessa Armand, and Alexandra Kollontai, they had come of age in a country where women made up 45 percent of the workforce, including in heavy industry; where most women were now literate; and where all universities were open to them. They were fervent believers in the revolutionary project, despite the purges: the country had been invaded and they had to protect their homes and families. Naturally, it was as much their job as it was the men's.

Although Stalin was taking the country in a more parochial direction—the Family Law of 1936 made abortion largely illegal and divorce harder to obtain—there were some areas of Soviet life where the early egalitarianism of the Bolshevik Revolution still thrived—in particular, the schools these young women attended. Basic schooling for all children was free, compulsory, and, thanks to Krupskaya, no longer segregated by gender.[7] Home economics for girls had been eliminated, lest the first Soviet generation "inherit the wrong view of the woman." Instead of learning to cook or sew, girls took classes in "socially useful labor." "We sawed and planed, we learned the difference between a bastard file and a velvet file," the Soviet dissident Raisa Orlova wrote of her schooling in the 1920s and '30s. "Who needs home economics in the era of wars and proletarian revolutions!"[8] Girls also took classes in subjects needed by the rapidly industrializing state, like science and technology.

And in a decade of rising tensions with Japan and Germany, girls were taught the skills that would soon be required by its citizen soldiers. A 1932 decree spelled out the schedule on which Soviet girls would have to learn to defend the Motherland. Between the ages of eight and twelve, they learned Russian military history and met with Civil War veterans and Red Army officers. They learned to use gas masks and the basics of air and chemical defense. At age thirteen, they learned to shoot. By fifteen, girls would study how to aid the injured and to distinguish between different types of bombs. All of this was done alongside the boys.

After primary school, if young women wanted to continue their educations in technical colleges or in universities, they also had to advance their military training. In 1934, the Komsomol, which had 10 million members and would soon become mandatory for college students, introduced a "military minimum" for new members. To join, a young Soviet woman had to pass exams showing that she could shoot a rifle, throw a grenade, jump off a parachute stand, read a topographical map, and demonstrate basic knowledge of a plane, car, tractor, or tank engine.[9] (Even Riva, as a middle-aged mother of two in medical school, had to pass classes in air and chemical defense to become a pediatrician in 1939.)

The paramilitary training that the Soviets instituted for their youth was not unique. The new totalitarian state to its west, Nazi Germany, developed similar programs during the 1930s. Unlike the Soviets, however, the Germans rigidly preserved their conservative view of the woman as a mother and keeper of the hearth. Even though 140,000 German women would eventually join the Nazi armed forces, they served exclusively in noncombatant administrative positions, far from the front.[10] For the Nazis, maintaining the gender divide was part of the ideological foundation on which the society of the Third Reich was to be built.

In the Soviet Union, the military recruitment of women carried a similarly symbolic weight, but in service of a very different ideology. The point was not just to create more soldiers but to build a society based on a Marxist theory of egalitarianism. "The fewer purely female or purely male responsibilities in human society," *Pravda* declared in 1919, "the fewer will be the bases to talk about inequality between the sexes."[11]

After the Revolution, the new Bolshevik government started to experiment with a unisex army almost immediately. The constitution of 1918 said that all citizens had an obligation to defend the new Soviet state, but the only ones who would have the privilege of doing so with "weapons in hand" were "laborers." Given that the constitution insisted on using other gender-neutral terminology—like "spouse" rather than "husband" or "wife"—and that women were required to work, it stood to reason that the role of soldier applied to women, too.

All citizens between the ages of eighteen and forty were required to take an eight-week military training program, though female citizens had to give their consent.[12] In 1920, Nikolai Podvoisky, the head of the Universal Military Training program (Vsevobuch), which was to train the first generation of young Soviets, argued that all women under thirty should participate. He also pushed for their inclusion in the armed forces. "The woman worker must know how to use a rifle, revolver, and machine gun, must know how to defend her city, her village, her children, [and] herself from the attacks of the White Guard bands," Podvoisky said. "She can easily learn to work a machine gun, for example, since it is no heavier than a sewing machine."[13] Not only would this free more men up to work or fight, he argued, it would also demonstrate to the world what the Bolsheviks were trying to do: "create a workers' government where every citizen is a warrior and every warrior is a citizen." Women did their military and athletic training alongside men, and, aside from exercises deemed to be "harmful to the female organism," followed the same curriculum.[14] In October 1920, women were permitted to enter the schools for lower military command staff.

Though Russian women had participated in war as nurses and clerks since the mid-nineteenth century (much as they had in the West), they joined the new Red Army in far higher numbers. Two years into the Civil War, there were some 66,000 women serving in the Soviet army, about 2 percent of its force. And while most did the traditionally female work of nursing and administration, many performed more dangerous—and typically male—roles, such as working in reconnaissance behind enemy lines.[15] They proved to be so good at it that Lenin opened a special academy in Moscow to train female spies.[16] Many women worked in the police on the home front as well as in the Cheka, the predecessor of the NKVD and KGB. For a time in 1918, a woman named Olga Ravich ran the Cheka in Petrograd after the male chief was assassinated.

Other women took on combat roles. They were machine gunners, sappers, cavalry officers, and snipers. The women snipers in Siberia were particularly effective, not least because conservative White commanders were deeply rattled by the knowledge that they were being shot at by women. One White colonel wrote in 1919 that he would personally take a birch switch to any Red woman combatant he caught. "I am more than confident that this domestic remedy will have the proper influence on this imbecile element, who by the rights of their destiny belong with the pots in the kitchen, not in politics, which is absolutely alien to their understanding."[17] When Whites caught Bolshevik women, they treated them with particular barbarity, even those who hadn't violated traditional gender norms. Near Petrograd, for instance, they strung up three Red Army nurses by their bandages and stuck their Komsomol pins through their tongues.[18]

The women fighting in the Red Army became a feature in the propaganda of both sides of the Civil War, a symbol of everything right or wrong with the Bolsheviks, depending on your political sympathies. White propaganda demonized the Red Army as full of unsexed Amazons and lesbian savages. *Pravda* praised women's "boldness, decisiveness, resourcefulness, and devotion to the revolutionary cause."

A rare few women rose to become Red Army commanders. Rozalia Zemlyachka, a Jewish woman from Belarus, prowled the officers' quarters in pants, boots, a leather trench coat, a short bob, and a pince-nez, an outfit that left men perplexed about her gender. She became an infamously ruthless commander who cheerfully ordered the executions of surrendering Whites and disobedient Reds alike.[19] In the winter of 1920–21, she was one of a troika of commanders that oversaw the killing of thousands of White officers and other suspected enemy class elements in Crimea. Another woman, the Old Bolshevik Evgenia Bosh, was, according to the Bolshevik historian Victor Serge, one of "the most capable military leaders to emerge at this early stage" of the war, helping to force Ukraine under Soviet rule.[20] She, too, didn't flinch when ordering executions. What others may have seen as cruelty, Bosh and Zemlyachka saw as proof of their revolutionary resolve. "What do you take me for?" Zemlyachka once snapped at a condescending male commander. "A bread-and-butter miss?"[21]

Many more women were political officers. They made up some 15 percent of Red Army commissars, tasked with keeping the men in their units ideologically in line. This was a more familiar role for Russian women. Not only did the Bolsheviks have senior women in their ranks during the underground years, the nature of this work fit a much older Russian stereotype: women had the sharp eyes and strong wills necessary to steel the spines of their dissolute and feckless men. This deeply held belief was why, in 1917, the Provisional Government sent the infamous Women's Battalion of Death into the trenches of World War I, to shame dispirited male soldiers into putting up more of a fight on the eastern front.[22] Under Bolshevik rule, the state would deploy this warped image of maternal discipline to put thousands of women in anti-profiteering brigades, loathed by the peasantry during the Civil War. For similar reasons, it made them the monitors of the food supply in state cafeterias and stores in times of famine and hunger.[23]

Bolshevik propaganda during the Civil War was not unanimously radical in the way it showed women at the front. Alongside stories of swashbuckling women soldiers, there were also appeals to women to prove themselves "the worthy wives and sisters of the heroic Red Army soldier."[24] Even Kollontai tried to exhort the men at the front with that most tired trope of bourgeois chivalry. "May the thoughts of your wives, mothers, and sisters enflame your manly courage, your preparedness to defend the cause so dear to us to the end," she wrote.[25]

Still, this was the first time that Russian women had breached the inner sanctum of traditional masculinity. During the Civil War, Russian women showed that they could be just as effective in a trench as a man and that women could also be natural warriors, delighting in the bloody business of fighting for a country or a cause. "Happiness in those years was understood not as a pretty dress, a successful marriage, or a cozy flat with a gramophone," recalled one Civil War nurse. "Happiness was working at the front among the wounded, the dying, the stricken."[26] It was these women's daughters who would flood military recruitment offices twenty years later, clamoring to do even more.

To Ida's surprise, she was turned away by the older men manning the recruitment offices. It was a scene repeated across the country: older men rejecting the young women who had shown up ready to fight.[27] The young women were baffled, and not just because Molotov had called on men and women both to do their utmost for victory. They had been training for this moment for their entire lives. When one group of young women tried repeatedly to sign up for the front lines, a middle-aged officer raged at them. "Where do you want me to send you?" he shouted at the young women every time they showed up. "What are you going to do there? There they need soldiers! Do you understand? Soldiers!" The young woman leading the pack of volunteers replied, "And this is exactly who we are: soldiers!"[28]

The older men manning the recruitment points had not grown up shooting rifles in a coed setting. For them, the traditional lines separating women and men were still firmly etched. Eventually, though, Ida, like tens of thousands of her countrywomen, prevailed.

When she was in school, Ida had tried to join the flying club of Osoaviakhim, the volunteer reservist organization that also trained Soviet youth in skills like riflery, flying, and chemical defense. She was turned away then because she was cross-eyed. On June 22, 1941,

Ida's father was drafted, but she was again rejected at the Red Army recruitment post and sent to dig anti-tank ditches outside Kiev instead. The next day a commissar arrived at one of her Komsomol meetings and said he needed a Komsomol officer for his battalion. Ida volunteered. Before long, she was a paratrooper, jumping out of planes behind enemy lines.

In June 1938, at the age of twenty-six, Marina Raskova and two other women pilots had set a record, flying nonstop for four thousand miles east from Moscow to open up Siberian air routes. They became the first women to be awarded the gold star of the Hero of the Soviet Union, the country's highest military honor. All summer after the German invasion, Raskova received letters from young women begging her to help them volunteer for the war. She packed these letters into several suitcases and lugged them over to the Kremlin, beseeching Stalin and the high command to accept these highly motivated women in a more organized fashion than the chaotic storming of recruitment points by teenage girls.[29]

On October 8, 1941, Stalin relented and issued Order 0099, forming three all-female air combat regiments: one fighter regiment, one short-range bomber regiment, and one night bomber regiment. Competition for the initial three hundred slots was fierce. Raskova, who now had the rank of major, was a tough commander. She made the new recruits chop off their long, lush braids, the traditional Slavic symbol of virgin femininity. As hungry as they were for combat, the young women wept and mourned this loss. One veteran of Raskova's regiment would recall that when two planes crashed during training, killing four trainees, Raskova told them, "Friends, wipe away your tears. These are our first losses. There will be a lot of them. Squeeze your hearts into fists." After that, the veteran recalled, there were many more funerals but no more tears.[30]

By war's end, women made up 8 percent of all Soviet military personnel.[31] There were the nurses, cooks, clerks, radio operators, and laundresses—the traditional female roles at the front. But hundreds of thousands of Soviet women also served in active combat. A women's machine gun battalion defended Odessa before it fell in 1941. Another fought in vain for Kiev.[32] Two hundred thousand women eventually followed Raskova into the Soviet air force.[33] Her three regiments presaged several more mobilizations of Soviet women, and by May 1945 nearly 1 million Soviet women had fought in the Red Army, including as machine gunners, fighter pilots, antiaircraft gunners, infantry officers, rifle division commanders, reconnaissance agents, and snipers. Some of the Soviet Union's best snipers, in fact, were women. In December 1942, the government opened a school in an old factory outside of Moscow to train women snipers. It graduated nearly two thousand of them.[34] Between them, they had some twelve thousand recorded kills.[35]

The most famous of them all was Lyudmila Pavlichenko. When the Germans invaded, she was in Odessa, researching her history thesis. A week shy of her twenty-fifth birthday, Pavlichenko put on her crêpe-de-chine dress and her white summer heels and marched over to the enlistment office. The enlistment officer took one look at her and told her medics wouldn't be drafted till the following day. Puzzled, Pavlichenko told him she intended to be a sniper, producing her sniper's certificate from Osoaviakhim. As the daughter of an NKVD officer and Civil War veteran, she had spent her teenage years learning the physics and mechanics of shooting. She was an excellent shot and could disassemble and reassemble a rifle with her eyes closed. The grizzled old Civil War sniper who had trained her had told her that women—patient, detail oriented, hardy—made far better snipers than men. So Pavlichenko was surprised that these Red Army personnel weren't interested in her services and came back the following day. This time they took her, but only after asking if her husband approved.

Pavlichenko was immediately sent into battle in Bessarabia without a rifle. She was given a sapper's spade and a grenade and, like so many Soviet soldiers in the war's disastrous early days, was told to find a weapon among the enemy dead. She fought like that for weeks. When she was finally issued a sniper's rifle, still sticky with factory grease, she modified it for battle with metal files and began picking off Romanian and German soldiers in the battles for Odessa and Sevastopol. Waiting for hours in the shrubbery of no-man's-land, she learned to put the bullet right between her enemy's eyes. When she was feeling more vindictive, she shot them in the stomach, knowing she was inflicting a lethal wound that wouldn't bring death for hours. Within a year, she had 309 recorded kills.

The Soviet propaganda machine seized on Pavlichenko: a woman warrior who could inspire—or shame—men to do great deeds. Her face was printed on thousands of leaflets rained down on Soviet troops. In August 1942, Stalin sent her and another celebrity sniper, named Vladimir Pchelintsev, on a tour of the United States and Britain to help lobby for aid to the Red Army and to push the Western allies to open a second front against Germany. (Pchelintsev had just 154 kills to Pavlichenko's 309.) In the United Kingdom, Pavlichenko met with Winston Churchill and his wife, and in the United States she was received by the Roosevelts at the White House. The first lady took a liking to Pavlichenko and invited her for a weeklong stay at the family estate in Hyde Park. Always watched by her Soviet minders, Pavlichenko met Henry Ford as well as the workers at his plants, whom she unsuccessfully tried to rile up with a fiery socialist speech. In Los Angeles, she met Charlie Chaplin, who walked over to her on his hands while carrying a bottle of champagne in his teeth. Woody Guthrie wrote a song about her. According to her memoirs, one stop on the trip raised $800,000 for the Soviet war effort, a huge amount for those years.

At the time, the West was far more conservative than Russia when it came to allowing women into the armed forces. The U.S. Congress capped the number of women serving in clerical and communications positions in the Women's Army Auxiliary Corps at 25,000. In the United Kingdom, the closest women got to combat was to work as searchlight operators in antiaircraft units. However, they were not allowed to shoot when attacked by German planes. Apparently, the need to maintain the image of women as passive innocents was more important than their physical safety.[36]

For Pavlichenko, who had never been outside the Soviet Union, the attitudes she encountered, particularly in the United States, were bewildering. At a press conference, she was asked if she was allowed to wear lipstick at the front or if she cared that her uniform made her look fat. When another (male) journalist asked her what color underwear she preferred, Pavlichenko lost her composure. "In Russia, you would get a slap in the face for asking a question like that," she snapped. "That kind of question is usually only asked of a wife or a mistress. You and I do not have that relationship. So I will be happy to give you a slap. Come a bit closer..."

There were other indignities. A freshly widowed American metals magnate stalked Pavlichenko on her tour across the country, begging her to marry him. When she rebuffed him repeatedly, he wrote an official marriage proposal to the Soviet embassy. (According to Pavlichenko's memoir, Eleanor Roosevelt tried to talk her into accepting.) Even Charlie Chaplin, who was active in collecting wartime aid for the Soviet population, made her uncomfortable. He got down on his knees and kissed every one of her fingers as thanks for killing 309 fascists.

In battle, these women produced an even more powerful effect just by their very existence. Much like the Whites during the Civil War, Germans found women's presence on the front so unnatural as to be unhinging. The all-female 588th Night Bomber Regiment flew nearly 24,000 combat missions over the course of 1,100 nights, bombing German airfields, supply points, field headquarters, rail lines, and bridges. The Germans called them the Nachthexen, or the Night Witches.[37] After rumors spread that Germans didn't take women soldiers captive but paraded them in front of their soldiers as freaks and then executed them, women in the Red Army began carrying two extra bullets in case of capture.[38] When one German officer was taken prisoner, he asked to see the sniper who had taken out so many of his soldiers with one bullet to the exact same spot in the head. Soviet soldiers informed him that this lethally precise shooter was a woman. "He was stunned, he didn't know how to react," recalled a fellow female sniper. "He was silent for a long time. During his last interrogation before he was sent to Moscow... he admitted, 'I never had to fight against women. You're all beautiful... Our propaganda insists that the Red Army is full of hermaphrodites, not women.' In the end, he didn't understand anything at all."[39]

There are many accounts of female soldiers who were mistaken for teenage boys. When the first wave of women joined the Red Army, they had their hair cut and were issued men's uniforms, underwear, and boots far too big for their feet.[40] They had nothing for their periods, which often disappeared anyway because of stress and malnutrition. It wasn't until 1943 that the Red Army finally issued women soldiers pants with a removable flap at the crotch. While women like Pavlichenko bristled at the notion of lipstick in the trenches, others advertised their femininity. One woman sewed herself a wedding dress out of bandages for her marriage to a fellow soldier, performed in a dugout. Lidia Litvyak, one of Raskova's fighter pilots who initially refused to cut off her braid, was later punished for taking the fur from her flight boots and using it to make a fashionable collar for her bomber jacket. (Raskova gave her a night in solitary confinement for the infraction.) Litvyak also stole hydrogen peroxide from the medics to bleach her hair and made necklaces out of pieces of parachute.[41] Yet she was one of the best fighter pilots in Raskova's force. In less than a year, she downed nearly two dozen enemy planes.

For these women, there was nothing unnatural in what they were doing. Soviet women veterans "did not represent themselves as women enacting male roles," wrote historian Anna Krylova. "On the contrary, they were women realizing their 'hidden female talents'... The right to participate in combat violence and to acquire the specialized and technical knowledge of the war was seen by young women as an expression of their new liberated Soviet womanhood." As one woman veteran explained to Krylova, "We are a generation not from this universe."[42]

Asma Gindina was just three years older than my paternal grandmother Khinya and grew up only thirty miles away from her, but, in the violent kaleidoscope of a world war, those three years and thirty miles proved life-altering. Asma was a Jewish girl from the tiny shtetl of Volodarsk-Volynsk in western Ukraine.[43] Her father was a math teacher and the cantor in the little town synagogue. Her family kept kosher and the Sabbath, and, like Khinya, she grew up speaking Yiddish. After finishing seventh grade, Asma enrolled in a technical college in the city of Zhitomir, where she was studying to be a paramedic and midwife.

In the summer of 1941, two years into her studies and ten days after her sixteenth birthday, Asma was traveling home for summer vacation when she ran into a column of retreating Soviet soldiers. She would be wise to follow them, they told her: there would be nothing left of her town but earth and sky. Asma ran toward the shtetl anyway, where she found her parents and sister and German troops shouting about the *Juden*. Somehow she escaped, losing her family in the chaos. She would never set foot in Volodarsk-Volynsk again.

As soon as she got to the nearest town, Asma found a recruitment office and demanded to join the Red Army.

By the spring of 1942, Asma was the youngest of a team of medics pulling wounded soldiers from the battlefield outside Stalingrad as German forces closed in on the city. The others called her their little sister, and she in turn envied them their age. Surrounded by death, she could not imagine that people could live to be so old: twenty, even twenty-five years old.

Asma didn't fight, but her war was just as bloody and muddy and cruel as that of the men she rescued. Her bag of equipment strapped to her body, Asma crawled under fire to search for the men who were still alive—on the ground, in tanks, in demolished buildings—their hearts still keeping time inside their mangled bodies. She tied off the remnants of limbs with tourniquets and dragged the wounded back to the relative safety of a medical dugout. The men often weighed double what she did, and their guns and bullets and grenades had to be pulled off the battlefield with them to be counted as a rescue. Asma would strap the soldier and his weapons to her military-issued poncho and drag him on her hundred-pound frame. Sometimes she had to carry them for miles.

Once, in Stalingrad, the shelling became so heavy that she was trapped in a shallow dugout. For two days she couldn't so much as lift her head. She lay pinned to the ground, sucking on chunks of dirty snow for sustenance. Another time, her fellow medic, a young man she maybe even liked a little, was hit right in front of her eyes, his stomach slashed open by a piece of shrapnel. She saw a lot of wounds like that, men disemboweled like goats. Some were Soviet; some were German. They all asked for a woman's tenderness, she remembers, for a hug or a kiss. Out of mercy, she obliged, even with the Germans, whom she treated and dragged into a special dugout for prisoners of war. Sometimes she even brought them extra scraps of food, this Jewish girl who knew what they must have done to her family back in Volodarsk-Volynsk.

On June 25, 1942, she crawled onto a tank that had been hit, a burning metal coffin. Her fellow medic shouted for her to get down; the men in there were dead and it was pointless to endanger herself. She looked into the hull of the tank and saw the charred remnant of a young man. He was still breathing, a black husk with a pulse. Asma pulled him up through the tank's hatch. She and the other medic tied him to a stretcher and began to carry him. Suddenly she realized her hand was hot and wet. She looked down and saw that a shell fragment had hit her wrist. She managed to help carry the stretcher with the burned man for two more miles to a place where horses could relieve them. Before she was taken away to the hospital, the burned man looked up at her with his good eye and said, "If I survive, I'll come find you."

It was her seventeenth birthday.

In March 1942, a bullet pierced Ida Segal's calf. A month earlier, her unit was supposed to parachute behind enemy lines where Soviet forces were trying to encircle the 16th German Field Army. Instead, it was the Soviet troops who found themselves surrounded. Ida's unit was tasked with parachuting in to bring them supplies, but on the assigned day it was too cloudy for the planes to take off. So they put on their skis and snuck across enemy lines. When they came under fire, Ida was injured and three of her comrades spent six days trying to get her, shoeless in the late winter freeze, back to Soviet territory for treatment. The field hospital they brought her to was bombed, as was the operating room of the next one.

By June, after a few months in the hospital, she was deemed sufficiently well to be sent back into battle. She soon found herself a political officer assigned to a unit of medics in Stalingrad. Since she had no medical training, she was put in charge of organizing the evacuation of the wounded. There were so many of them in Stalingrad, casualties of the battle that would turn the tide of the war. In the months before the Germans surrendered the city on February 2, 1943, some 600,000 Soviets would be wounded in vicious house-to-house fighting, and another half million would be killed.[44]

One day Ida found herself in an inflatable boat on the Volga, the ancient, endless Russian river cutting through the city. The boat was full of heavily wounded sappers. She recognized one of them: he had been in the hospital with her that spring. His legs had been mostly blown off. None of the sappers in the boat had been given first aid, and there he sat without any tourniquets, his legs hanging by strips of skin. He looked at Ida and said, "Remember this: Sasha Dokukin, our company commander, has been killed." She remembered Sasha. He had been with her in the hospital that spring, too. "Write to his family and tell them," the legless sapper told Ida, "because there is no one left to tell them."

She would think about this moment for weeks after the battle for Stalingrad had ended, when all that was left of the city was fragments of walls sticking up from the ground like brick teeth, when she was on her way to the next famous battle of the war at Kursk and she finally heard from her mother and two sisters. For nearly two years she had jumped from planes into enemy territory, terrified the whole time not for her life but for her family's. What had become of them? Had they made it out of Kiev or were they living under German occupation? Were they even alive, given the rumors of what Germans were doing to Jews living in the cities and towns they captured?

And now, finally, she knew. A letter from her sister Asya arrived with a return address. They were alive, deep in the Soviet rear, in the Uzbek city of Bukhara. "My dears, you cannot imagine the happiness I am experiencing these days," Ida wrote to her mother and sisters on February 21, 1943.[45] Her handwriting travels wildly over the page, her thoughts cutting loops faster than her hand can capture them. Her words are those of a person quaking with a joy that, at twenty years old, she never expected to experience again. "I have acquired my family anew," she wrote. "I am defending my near and dear ones from the German scum. Germans aren't torturing my dear Mommy. Nelya

[Ida's baby sister] is experiencing some hardship, but still, she is alive and well. Asya hasn't fallen into the hands of these cursed monsters. Life seems wonderful to me these days. I had harbored a lot of grief in the depths of my soul. I thought that I would never see my mother or father again, nor my near and dear ones. But happiness smiled on me . . . I am so happy. I have someone to write letters to. I will receive letters." Ida asks her mother's forgiveness for the worry she must have caused her when she went off to war in June 1941. "War demands sacrifice," she writes. "Let the twenty months not knowing what had become of your daughter be the sacrifice our family makes."

But even in her joyous delirium, she notices an omission in her sister's letter. "Mommy, write to me about Daddy," she pleads. "I am very worried about him."

THE HOME FRONT

THE WAR FOUND KHINYA FIRST. MY PATERNAL GRANDMOTHER, THEN twelve years old, lived in Zhitomir in western Ukraine, close to the border with Romania and Poland. By nightfall of June 22, 1941, the first day of the war, German planes were already flying over the city's suburbs, bombing the munitions and fuel depots and the nearby military posts. All night, the blasts rumbled through the darkness.

In the morning, Khinya's parents, Khana-Batya and Moisei, tried to figure out what to do. Soviet propaganda had reassured them that even if there was a war, it would be over in a couple of weeks. The Soviet Union, Stalin had told his people, would never be invaded. Yet here they were, Luftwaffe planes circling Zhitomir. And so it was decided: the countryside would be safer. Nothing to bomb out there but cows and haystacks.

This decision set off a series of separations. Moisei's mother decided to stay just outside of the city with her pregnant daughter and her toddler. Moisei's cousin Isaak sent his wife and two children to rural Salnitsa, Riva's hometown. Khana-Batya hired a wagon and sent her visiting elderly father back to his home in Ostropol. Moisei wanted to send Khinya and her brother with him, but at the last minute Khana-Batya changed her mind. She would not be separated from her children and insisted that they remain together in Zhitomir.

And then they waited.

On July 4, twelve days after the invasion, German planes hit Zhitomir proper, strafing terrified civilians with machine guns. They flew so low that Khinya could see the pilots' faces before she dove into the bushes.

Moisei's younger brother Wolf knew someone who knew someone who could get the family on a truck going east to Kiev: Moisei, Khana-Batya, their children, Khinya and Grisha, along with Wolf, his wife, Rakhil, and their two-year-old son. "We'll be back before the summer is out," Moisei kept telling Khana-Batya when she tried to pack anything more than bread, the family's silver spoons, and a cut of silk for a dress for Khinya. They took just two woven baskets on the truck out of Zhitomir. They wouldn't be back for another three years.

When the truck let them out on the outskirts of Kiev, they already knew they couldn't stay. If the Germans were on the verge of taking Zhitomir, a big straight road would soon lead them right to the Ukrainian capital. There were cargo trains evacuating people east, but first Khana-Batya and Moisei set out for the city to find Khana-Batya's little sister, Sonya. As their tram approached, they saw a great column of smoke and fire rising from a factory that had been bombed by German planes. Their path to the center was blocked.

Terrified, Moisei and Khana-Batya rushed back to their family. By nightfall they were piled into a cattle car with the wounded, heading east to Kharkov. My grandmother Khinya clambered up onto a bunk, from where she could see a man with a shattered spine who moaned through the night.

In Kharkov, Moisei had intended for them to stay with his uncle. But his uncle's house was already crowded with refugees, and so they had to stay with the neighbors instead. Somehow the draft notice found Moisei there. "Don't go," Khana-Batya advised her husband, a forty-one-year-old store manager, short and balding. "You're too old; you have two children." But Moisei was a faithful *Pravda* subscriber (though not a Party member) and remained grateful to the Bolsheviks for letting him out of the Pale of Settlement. He still believed in the government that had given him his freedom and his dignity as a Jew. "If we won't defend our country," he asked Khana-Batya, "who will?"

So Moisei joined the Red Army. He went southeast for training as an artillery gunner. Wolf and Rakhil went northeast with their son, where they would end up in Molotov (formerly Perm) on the eastern edge of the

Urals. And as the Germans closed in on Kharkov, Khana-Batya took her children and got on a train again, this time escaping five hundred miles east to Stalingrad.

Despite the tens of thousands of young women who stormed the recruitment posts that summer, the vast majority of the tens of millions of Soviet soldiers were men. When they left for the front, they left behind mothers and wives and small children. And because the war effort needed everyone, fathers often joined up alongside their sons. As a result, most Soviet households became barren of men, and millions of female-led households were now on the run, part of a herculean government evacuation plan that moved whole factories and universities and millions of people past the Ural Mountains and into the great Soviet hinterland. For those in the Gulag, Russian geography was a curse. For tens of millions more, it was their salvation.

In the West, the war was a turning point for women, who stepped in to fill jobs left vacant by men, giving many their first, addictive taste of economic independence. Soviet women, however, had been at these jobs for over two decades. Now they found themselves not just working in the factories but rebuilding them in their new locations from the ground up, at dizzying speeds and in inhospitable terrain. They had to meet surreal wartime quotas while subsisting on meager rations. On top of that, they were suddenly single mothers, working superhuman shifts while also caring for their children at a time when food was painfully scarce, adequate housing in catastrophically low supply, and disease rampant. Both my grandmothers remember the years of the war as ones of dull and constant hunger as they moved from one drafty shack or barrack to another.

For American women, despite the agony of separation from their loved ones, the war was thousands of miles from their own towns and cities. But for the Soviet woman, even the home front was an obstacle course of horrors.

It was cold at dawn when my paternal great-grandmother Brokha-Pesya Komskaya—known to everyone as Bronya—went to the train station to see off her firstborn, Samuel Ioffe, or Monya as the family called him. Bronya had recently finished medical school and the government had sent her to practice in a little village a hundred miles west of Moscow. It was called Pogoreloe Gorodishche—literally, the big, burnt town. Bronya had brought her sons Monya and Yasha, my paternal grandfather, to live there with her. Her husband, Natan Ioffe, stayed behind in Moscow.

Monya was eighteen years old when the war came. School had just ended. Like so many boys his age, he had been at the prom the night the Germans were quietly cutting barbed wire and stacking shells on the border. And, like so many boys his age, he wanted to volunteer for the army the day the war began.

Bronya roared at him. She was not about to lose her firstborn to a two-week war. She decided to send Monya back to Moscow, where his father could put him to good use. At dawn, Bronya and twelve-year-old Yasha stood on the train platform, waving to Monya as he hung out the door of the train and pumped his arm goodbye. She would sear this date into her memory until the end of her life: June 23, 1941.

In August, the army took Monya anyway. He had received a draft notice. Nota, as everyone called my great-grandfather Natan, accompanied his son to the assembly point, where his son was driven off in an army truck in an unknown direction. At fifty-five, poor Nota was already an old man by the standards of those days, a barely literate driver, writing to tell his young wife that the son she had worked so hard to protect had been whisked away for a war that was clearly going to last longer than two weeks. "My dear I telegrammed you the 11th Monya has left," he wrote, skipping any and all punctuation. "I'm writing my dear that on the 11th by 8 o'clock in the morning Mon'ka had to present himself at the assembly point with his things I accompanied him as far as the assembly point at 9 in the morning in a truck Mon'ka left from the assembly point."

Nota was fifteen years older than Bronya, a fierce little bull of a woman with bulging eyes whom many feared but Nota worshipped. They had met in their hometown of Rechitsa, in Byelorussia. Bronya was just out of her teenage years and he was an awkward middle-aged man with a long upper lip and a good singing voice that she alone could coax from him. They married, had Monya, and then Yasha six years later. After Bronya graduated from medical school in Smolensk, they settled in the working-class outskirts of Moscow. Then Bronya was posted to the big, burnt town.

Nota knew that Bronya would be beside herself when she realized that she hadn't been the one to prepare her son for this dangerous trip. In his letter, he listed for her everything he had stuffed into Monya's bag, down to the gram—so much canned meat and cookies and sugar that the backpack wouldn't close. "Bronechka, don't worry that Mon'ka went to the army," he wrote. He had heard another boy's father say that their sons were being taken for training in the engineering corps. If that were true, Nota wrote, it would be less dangerous than being on constant antiaircraft watch duty at home.

"Bronechka," he went on, "I am very lonely without him the first day when I came home from work in the evening the absence had a strong effect on me and without wanting to I cried for a long time until I calmed down."

Moscow was always going to be safe from German invasion; everybody knew that. No matter how far into the western heartland the Germans got, the thinking went, they would never take the capital. But by mid-October 1941, the unthinkable had happened: the Panzer Army was racing for Moscow. Leningrad, the northern capital, had already been encircled, beginning an 872-day siege in which over a million of its residents would starve to death. Soon the Germans would be so close to Red Square that a Wehrmacht motorcyclist was able to drive onto its cobblestones and back.[1]

That fall, the NKVD had sent Riva a draft notice, which mortified her. What could this loathed and terrifying agency possibly need her for? It was just the latest in a string of professional setbacks. In July 1936, nine years into Riva's practice as a pedologist, the Central Committee outlawed the discipline for its "reactionary" and "fatalistic" tendencies. If it were true that a child's entire life was predetermined by biology and environment, then how could the Communist Party build a new Soviet person? It was the end of the experiments in education of the 1920s—and of Riva's career.

A thirty-five-year-old mother of two very small children, Riva had to find a new line of work. In the fall of 1936, she entered medical school in Moscow, where she and her family had been living. Because of her previous work, she was allowed to skip ahead to the fourth year. She muddled through the remaining two, getting more C's than she cared to admit and graduating in the summer of 1939. Riva was still learning her new trade—pediatrics—when the war broke out.

Her first NKVD assignment, at a military hospital just outside of the capital, seemed tolerable enough. She would be treating wounded soldiers, not resetting bones broken during torture sessions. So Riva went ahead, leaving Isaak to follow by train with their children: seven-year-old Emma, my grandmother, and ten-year-old Tolya.

But Isaak was not the kind of husband you could trust to pack two children for a wartime evacuation during the cold of a Moscow fall. He wasn't even the kind of husband you could send to get the kids some winter hats. Earlier that year, Isaak had taken Emma and her brother to the state department store on Red Square and let his children pick the hats they liked best. My equally impractical grandmother chose a straw hat wreathed with giant paper flowers. Tolya lit on a *pilotka*, the cloth side cap worn by Red Army soldiers. Beaming and clueless, the three returned home, where they were ambushed by Riva's wrath.

Apparently, Isaak had learned nothing from this episode, because he packed both the *pilotka* and the straw hat, along with some light fall clothing, and off they went in a taxi to the train station. On the way, Isaak ranted about the incompetence of the Soviet authorities after the German invasion. What had happened to the glorious Red Army? Why was it beating a retreat up and down the length of the front?

In fact, the Red Army had been eviscerated by Stalin during the Great Terror. After killing 90 percent of its top officers, Stalin replaced them with young, inexperienced men whose primary qualification was loyalty to him. A significant contingent had had no military education whatsoever.[2] In the days leading up to the June 1941 invasion, Stalin received—and dismissed as provocation—a flurry of intelligence reports that German forces were massing on the border. Luftwaffe planes were flying regular reconnaissance missions deep into Soviet territory. The German embassy in the Russian capital was evacuating personnel and burning documents. By the time Stalin relented and allowed his generals to put the Red Army on high alert after 10 p.m. on June 21, many of his commanders didn't receive the message: German soldiers wearing Red Army uniforms had snuck into Soviet territory and cut their communication lines.[3] Six hours later, the Germans attacked.

Stalin was paralyzed by Hitler's betrayal. When Molotov called Stalin and asked what to do, he heard only heavy breathing on the line.[4] For hours, as German troops streamed into Soviet territory, Stalin couldn't bring himself to give orders to fight back, and after the purges, few in the Red Army were brave enough to take the initiative. For a week, Stalin sat alone in his dacha, bewildered, as the Soviet air force was destroyed without ever taking off and whole infantry divisions were killed or captured. Troops were sent into battle without weapons, mere flesh to get stuck in German treads. Three weeks into the war, one in five Soviet soldiers was gone.[5] In another four months, four million Soviet soldiers would be dead or captured and another million wounded.[6]

On and on Isaak Bruk ranted about this calamity to the stone-faced taxi driver while his children, dressed in their absurd hats, watched in awe. What a brave father they had! He had a brother in the camps, he himself had been arrested for daring to contradict a commissar, and yet here he was, boldly shitting on the Father of the Nation.

It was already dark when they made it to the train station. Perhaps, in the gathering gloom, it was hard for a child to tell bravery from foolishness.

By October 1941, Bronya and Yasha had to evacuate the big, burnt town. It was now burning in earnest, set alight by German bombs. They ended up outside of Novosibirsk, where Monya's letters finally reached them. He was about to be sent to learn how to operate a tank. "We tank guys are indestructible," Monya wrote to Bronya cheerfully from basic training.

The letters from Monya, a large, masculine child away from his mother for the first time in his life, are chipper and plain. He tells Bronya not to send any more food ("They're feeding us well") and not to send any more money ("There's nothing to buy in the commissary anyway"). He saves any mention of hardship for his letters to Nota, who was evacuated from Moscow and for months couldn't find his wife and younger son in the confusion.

Bronya leaves some things out of her letters, too. She doesn't tell Monya that she has given his beloved little brother Yasha an old rifle and has him stand guard over their small potato patch so they don't die of hunger during that annihilatingly cold first winter of the war. She doesn't tell him that, when a starving woman with her starving child tried to dig some potatoes out of the frozen earth with a shiv tied to the end of a wooden stick, Yasha told the woman he would shoot her if she didn't stop. She doesn't tell him that this woman, frenzied with hunger, swung her sharp-tipped stick at Yasha and slashed his face, nearly costing him an eye.

On January 25, 1942, Monya wrote to tell his family, now reunited outside the Siberian city of Kirov, that he was being deployed west, to push the Germans out of Ukraine. "I really miss you, my dears, just like in the first days after I was drafted, when I couldn't get used to not being with my family," he wrote. "It's a good thing that I have Mommy's photographs. Sometimes I take them out and look at them and I feel better."

He writes again, on February 17, 1942, shortly before his first battle. It had been eight months since he'd seen his mother. "Mommy!" he wrote. "Remember when the train was pulling out [of the station] and I was standing on the step of the train and waving to you? And now, when will we see each other again?"

The Germans didn't take Moscow, nor did they manage to take the Soviet Union as they had taken France, Czechoslovakia, Poland, the

Low Countries, Norway, and the Balkans. They paused long enough for the Russian winter to freeze them in their gray felt coats and their thin leather boots outside Moscow's gates. Besides, Russia could give up France after France after France and still have plenty of land to retreat to. But with the thaw of spring in 1942, the Germans restarted their march, and in the south they made for Stalingrad.

My grandmother Khinya, now thirteen, was in their path once more. Khana-Batya grabbed her kids again and they set off still farther east. They would not be staying for the biggest battle of the war, for which Stalin and Hitler would sacrifice millions of men because of the city's name alone. Khana-Batya wrote to her husband at the front: "We're going to Alma-Ata, in Kazakhstan."

They never did make it to Alma-Ata. Packed like herring on a cargo train with other fleeing families, fourteen-year-old Grisha promptly fell deep into the delirium of scarlet fever. "Smell my feet," he muttered over and over. "The Germans are hiding there. Smell my feet . . ."

Khana-Batya pulled them off at Dzhambul, a city on the eastern edge of the Kazakh Soviet Socialist Republic. A woman pharmacist on the train had poured some medicine down Grisha's throat, which broke his fever, but he still couldn't walk and his skin was peeling. A stranger helped Khana-Batya carry him to the doctor. In the city, she met a woman who took pity on her. The woman brought them home and let Grisha sleep on the old Russian stove for a few days until he recovered. Then she sent them on their way.

They found a collective farm that would take them, near the border with China. It was there that they finally received a letter from Moisei. He had been wounded almost as soon as he went into battle, just outside of Kharkov. A shell had blown off the toes of one foot, then the winter frost took off another chunk as he lay on the battlefield, waiting for rescue. He had lost a lot of blood. While he was recuperating in Georgia, the fighting got too close and the army hospital had to be evacuated. Moisei was discharged with an open wound.

By the time the letter reached her, Khana-Batya had come down with jaundice. She was able to barter for some milk to make clabber, the soured milk that was the only thing that made her feel better. She scraped the cream off the top, spread it on the local flatbread, and gave it to her teenage children, who worked in the collective farm's sugar beet fields. The hunger of those years could still make my grandmother Khinya's eyes swim eight decades later—as could the memory of that flatbread with the cream, how it bloomed warm behind her solar plexus.

A few weeks later, Khinya had just come in from the fields when a telegram arrived. Moisei would be at the local train station that very afternoon. Immediately, Khana-Batya started cooking a borscht made of sugar beets, and Khinya set off on foot for the train station two miles away. On the way, she met another woman who was going to greet a passenger on the same train.

When they arrived, the platform was empty. The train had come and gone and left no human evidence of its passage. Khinya walked back and forth looking for Moisei. Was the telegram wrong? Did he miss his stop? The other woman's guest wasn't there, either. *Might as well get a haircut since we're in town*, the woman suggested to my grandmother, and they set off together for the nearby salon.

As the hairdresser got to work, the woman told her what had happened. Funny, the hairdresser said. There was a man just in here who had been on the train. Said no one had come to meet him. Short. On crutches. Bandaged leg.

Khinya flew out the door. She ran and ran, around and around, but Moisei was nowhere. Then she saw an emaciated old man with crutches and a bandaged foot. Her father. She hadn't recognized her father.

Riva's time at the military hospital didn't last long. Isaak, who had managed to weld his apprenticeship and his unfinished stint at night school into a career as a metals specialist for airplanes, was being deployed. After the Soviet air force had been obliterated in the first days of the war, the Soviets needed to churn out more planes or cede the air to the Germans for good. And so, with fall turning to winter, the Bruks went to Novosibirsk, in Siberia, where the evacuated plane factories were being relocated, out of range of the Luftwaffe. There was no time to build walls or roofs before production started, so Isaak worked and slept in the same open field in which they made the planes.

In Novosibirsk, Riva hoped that the NKVD would lose her scent. The pace of production was so frantic that Isaak didn't come home much, which left Riva alone with the children. During the hungry winter of 1941–42, she worked informally, bartering her medical services for food. She stretched Isaak's paycheck and gave her children most of the little food she rustled up. By spring, she was regularly fainting from hunger.

"I'm going to turn myself in," she finally said, and walked to the local NKVD office.

The NKVD assigned her to a local *detpriemnik*, a processing facility for children before they were sent on to orphanages or the camps. Some were ChSIRs, the children of traitors to the Motherland. Others had lost their parents in the madness of the German invasion. They were all eyes, these children, in gray uniforms, the girls with gray kerchiefs covering their shaved heads.

At first, Riva let Emma come to play with the children in the *detpriemnik*. Emma was seven, with Riva's button nose and her father's blue eyes and red cheeks, her hair clipped short like a boy's. She was stunned by the sadness in those rooms. Eventually, though, the children relaxed back into being children. Emma, who hadn't been around others her age since the war began, was relieved to play the Russian versions of dodgeball and red rover with them. They sang old songs from the Revolution and the Civil War, glorifying the very thing that had destroyed their families.

One day, one of the cooks called Emma into the kitchen and gave her hot cocoa and white bread, delicacies Emma hadn't laid eyes on in years. She fell on the bread and hot chocolate as the women in the kitchen cooed over her.

Suddenly, Riva appeared in the doorway, a tiny boulder of pure fury.

"Come here," she commanded, and led her daughter outside.

"You've let me down," she growled. Her daughter, already fortunate enough to have two living parents, was eating food allotted for playmates who had lost theirs. Riva was beside herself.

"That was the last time you set foot here," she told Emma.

For a while she sent Emma to the school for children of NKVD employees, where imprisoned intellectuals taught the offspring of their jailors while separated from their own. Emma's favorite was a political prisoner from Leningrad who instructed her on how to trace tricky Russian letters in an elegant cursive.

Emma's best friend at this school was Ada, whose father was a big man in the NKVD. Emma knew that her uncle Efim was in a camp like this one. Every night, under Riva's supervision, she and Tolya would thread a portion of their bread ration onto strings and pin them high up under the ceiling of their barrack room. Riva sent the garlands of dried croutons to Efim, now somewhere in Kolyma, bending to the will of a man just like Ada's father.

But Emma and Ada were still little girls, only dimly aware of the dark doings of the adults around them. One day, Ada invited Emma over to her apartment for lunch. Emma's widening eyes took in the fine wooden furniture polished to a warm luster. And for lunch, Ada's mother, who stayed at home in accordance with her status as the elite wife of an elite man, served a clear and golden chicken stock that smelled of warmth and plenty. Meat! During the war! How long it had been!

Emma came back to the barracks raving about the meal, and Riva's face turned to stone again. Riva had done everything she could think of to keep her son and daughter fed. She had gone hungry rather than work for the NKVD, only to eat her pride and surrender. And still her foolish daughter couldn't do her mother this small courtesy of at least signaling that Riva was not one of these hangmen who separated parents from their children for imaginary crimes, that she was just a civilian passing through and trying to keep her conscience intact as best she could.

Monya's letters became more infrequent after his baptism in battle, his tone more distant: Bronya's big child had become a man. By April 1942 he had been in some Ukrainian villages the Soviets had temporarily liberated from the Germans. "Nothing's new with me," he wrote on

April 9. "Actually, I misspoke. It's new every time you enter a liberated village and the residents greet you with tears in their eyes."

Bronya, a pediatrician, had been working in a local hospital, struggling to treat hundreds of children turned to bent twigs by hunger and rickets, their ranks culled further by the fires of typhus and diphtheria. All the while, she waited for Monya's letters from the front. He was the child she most wanted to save.

One letter to his mother, written during a break in the fighting on April 29, includes a chilling postscript. It seemed to confirm what Bronya had been hearing about the family that didn't make it out before the Germans came. "I spoke to one officer from Rechitsa," Monya wrote of the shtetl where he and Yasha, Nota, and Bronya had all been born. "He said that it's been destroyed down to its foundations."

In the barracks of Novosibirsk, my grandmother Emma found a book called *The Hell of Treblinka*, a July 1944 dispatch by Vasily Grossman, a Soviet Jewish writer. Grossman was traveling with the Red Army and writing combat reports for *Krasnaya Zvezda*, or *Red Star*. His dispatch from the liberation of the Nazi death camp in Poland was one of the first ways in which Soviet Jews found out about the Holocaust. Reading it, Emma slowly realized that, as a Jewish girl, she could have easily ended up in the gas chambers.

Emma didn't know it, but Grossman had also documented entering Soviet villages emptied of their Jews. Before he witnessed the liberation of the death camps in Poland, Grossman, like Babel before him, first crossed the old Pale of Settlement, ravaged anew by an army far more ruthless than either the Whites or the Reds.

In November 1943, Grossman entered Kiev soon after it had been retaken by the Red Army. He had heard rumors that the Nazis had killed many of the city's Jews, but he did not realize the scale until he got there. In fact, the Nazis had killed all the Jews who had not been able to flee, shooting nearly 34,000 of them in the forest on the city's outskirts in the span of just two days. Learning this, Grossman feared the worst for the Jews of nearby Berdichev, the famous Jewish shtetl in Ukraine where he had been born and where, as far as he knew, his mother, Ekaterina Grossman, the most important woman in his life, still lived.

Berdichev was liberated on January 5, 1944. When Grossman arrived soon afterward, he found that the Nazis, with the cooperation of some of the Ukrainian population, had completely emptied his birthplace of its Jews, who had made up half of the town's population of 60,000. Many of them were women and children and the elderly; most of the young men had already gone off to fight in the Red Army.

By interviewing survivors and witnesses, Grossman was able to reconstruct what had happened. The Germans entered the town just before sunset on July 7, 1941, shouting *"Jude kaputt!"*[7] Six days later they rounded up some Jews who lived near the leather tannery and forced them to jump into the vats of astringent. "The Germans thought this execution was funny," Grossman wrote. "They were tanning Jewish skin." On another day the Germans forced old men to hold a service in a local synagogue to atone for Jewish sins. Then they locked the synagogue and set it on fire.

On September 4, Germans gathered the few young Jewish men left in the town—about 1,500 of them—and told them they were being taken to do farm work and could bring back some potatoes for their families. They were all shot. This, Grossman wrote, removed "almost all the young men who were capable of resistance."

On September 14, an SS unit forced the remaining Jews to gather in the market square. Those who couldn't—the elderly, the sick, the babies—were killed in their homes. The Germans selected four hundred specialists they needed to run the town—doctors, craftsmen, electricians—and allowed them to take their families away. Everyone else was herded into sheds at the airfield, where they awaited their turn to stand on the edge of a mass grave and be shot.

> This slaughter of the innocent and helpless went on all day.
> Their blood poured on to the yellow clay ground. The pits
> filled with blood, the clay soil was unable to absorb it, blood
> overflowed the pits and there were huge puddles of it on the

ground. Rivulets of it flowed, accumulating in depressions...
The executioners' boots were soaked with blood.[8]

And that, it turned out, was how Grossman's mother had met her death. He would write letters to her for the rest of his life.

In trying to find out what had happened to his mother, Grossman had discovered the first Holocaust, the Holocaust of the East, the Holocaust by bullets, which paved the way for the Holocaust he saw later, the one of Majdanek and Treblinka and Auschwitz. As the German army advanced into the Soviet-occupied Baltics and Poland in the summer and fall of 1941, and then into the Soviet republics of Byelorussia and Ukraine, special units of the SS "pacified" the local residents. "Pacification" meant eradicating the dense Jewish populations of these areas. The SS was assisted by the Order Police, made up mostly of middle-aged German reservists as well as units formed from non-Jewish locals eager to pitch in: Lithuanians, Latvians, Ukrainians.

The "Shoah by bullets" doesn't occupy the same place in the Western narrative of the Holocaust, in part because it did not have the macabre modern flair of the assembly-line killings at places like Auschwitz, a twisted apotheosis of the industrial era. The Holocaust of Soviet Jewry was more primal. Jews in a village were rounded up, marched out into a forest, and shot. Sometimes they were told to stand on the edge of a ditch they had dug and then shot, collapsing into the pit. Sometimes they were forced to lie down on top of the people who had been shot right before them and then shot at close range. Sometimes they were just buried alive and left to suffocate. In all of these scenarios, the earth moved for days afterward.

The killings were intimate and gruesome. The executioners had to spend hours with their victims, who were often women and children, as they pleaded for mercy, tried to escape, wept, and screamed. When they were shot at close range, their bone fragments and brain tissue stuck to the Germans' uniforms. Some of the reservists were not very good shots and grotesquely wounded their victims instead of killing them. Shooting women and children, in the words of one of the German soldiers tasked with it, proved especially "repugnant."[9] "Even in the face of death," one of the German soldiers recalled later, "the Jewish mothers did not separate from their children."

Many, especially those men who were not from the SS, cracked psychologically. Some tried to get out of the killings and begged for transfers.[10] Even Heinrich Himmler, the head of the SS, who frequently toured the killing fields and wrote to his wife about them with gusto, couldn't stop vomiting during one visit.[11] This is why the Nazis switched to death camps. "A method different from the firing squad operations used against Russian Jewry was deemed essential for the murder of European Jews," wrote historian Christopher Browning, "one that was more efficient, less public, and less psychologically burdensome for the killers."[12]

Still, the Germans completed their mission in the east efficiently enough. Within months, Germans and their local collaborators had killed 1.35 million Soviet Jews. "There are no Jews in Ukraine," Grossman wrote. "A whole people has been brutally murdered."[13]

The articles Grossman wrote about what he had discovered were not published anywhere in the Soviet press. (The lone exception ran in *Einigkeit*, a Soviet Yiddish periodical.) The Soviet authorities, true to their Marxist philosophy—and Stalin to his anti-Semitism—did not want to separate out Jews from the larger mass of the Soviet people as victims of Nazi aggression. They would stick to this line for decades, suppressing any discussion of how the Holocaust had burned through their territory.

In part because of this censorship, hundreds of thousands of Jews who had fled or been evacuated had little idea what had happened to the families they left behind at the beginning of the war. The grim reality would hit them all at once when they returned home.

Perhaps the first person in our family to discover what had happened was Moisei's cousin Isaak, who had sent his wife and two children to the shtetl of Salnitsa to escape the bombing of Zhitomir. In the meantime, he had been drafted and sent to the front. According to family lore, as Ukraine was being liberated by Soviet troops, he got word that all the Jews in that village had been killed, including his wife and children. Distraught, he wrote to Moisei. He had nothing to live for but revenge, he said. After that, his letters from the front detailed how many Germans he had killed each day, a running tally that could never come close to equaling what he had lost. Then the letters stopped.

Khinya and her family returned to Zhitomir in the spring of 1944 to find that everyone who had stayed behind to shelter in the countryside had been killed. Khana-Batya's father, whom she had sent back to his home in Ostropol, had been killed, along with his wife. What must Khana-Batya have felt when she discovered that she had unwittingly sent her father to his death?

Only one of Khinya's dozen cousins survived. A young woman with blond hair and blue eyes, she successfully passed as a Ukrainian by pretending she was mute: she was unable to roll her *r*'s, a speech impediment stereotypically associated with Jews in the Russian-speaking world and one that would have betrayed her instantly.

Moisei's uncle in Kharkov had stayed behind with his wife to guard his son's furniture, while his daughter-in-law and grandchild fled. The uncle and his wife were killed and the furniture was confiscated anyway. Moisei's mother, who had gone to stay with her pregnant daughter and toddler grandchild in another part of Zhitomir, was also killed. Some Ukrainian neighbors later told Moisei that when the Germans started rounding up the Jews for the slaughter, his sister went into labor from the stress. She and her child were shot.

One man survived the shootings in the forests outside Zhitomir as a child when his mother covered him and he fell uninjured into the pit. Nearby villagers told him that the ground, "almost liquid with blood, moved in waves after the killings."[14] A family friend told me of her aunt, Rayechka, who managed to survive such a killing field in Ukraine as an eleven-year-old. She had walked to the forest holding her mother's hand. Her mother was shot and fell, toppling Rayechka into the pit. The bullets had missed Rayechka, and when the shooting finally stopped, she managed to climb out of the blood-soaked earth and find shelter in a neighboring town. Today she is an old woman cloaked in the thick fog of dementia from which she cries and searches desperately for her mother.

It was the same up and down the old Pale. In late August 1941, as soon as the Germans occupied Rechitsa—the birthplace of Bronya, Yasha, Monya, and Nota Ioffe—they organized a ghetto. By December, all but one of Nota Ioffe's many siblings had been killed, along with all of Rechitsa's Jews.

On November 18, 1941, the Germans registered all of the Jews in Simferopol, Crimea, including Nota Ioffe's brother and sister and their spouses and children. Their property was confiscated and they were forced to wear a white armband with a star of David. This humiliation didn't last long. By December 13, most of Simferopol's 12,000 Jews were dead. It had taken Sonderkommando 10a of the German death squad Einsatzgruppe D just four days to shoot them all.[15]

Most of the people who didn't manage to flee Kiev before the Germans occupied the city were women, children, the sick, and the elderly, people like Shura's mother and sister. Before the war, Shura had made peace with his mother, whom he had cut off for opposing his relationship with Buzya. In 1941, Buzya and Shura had been evacuated from Moscow to Sverdlovsk, an industrial city on the eastern slope of the mountain range where Europe ends. There, Shura would continue his work developing mobile pontoon bridges for the Red Army. They took Buzya's son Yura and his newly adopted brother Dmitry, as well as Buzya's still-feckless mother. Shura managed to pull his ex-wife, Lida, and their son Andrey out of Kiev before it fell to the Nazis in September, settling them on the same street where he and Buzya lived in Sverdlovsk. But Shura's mother didn't join them. Shura's sister was developmentally challenged and couldn't be moved, so she stayed with their mother in Kiev.

Shura's handicapped sister is said to have been shot in the hospital. His mother was killed a few days later along with nearly 34,000 other Jews in the ravines outside of Kiev, at Babi Yar, in just two days.

Only twenty-nine people survived. The massacre would become the symbol of the eastern Holocaust, its Auschwitz.

In September 1942, the 3,000 Jews in the ghetto of Medzhybyzh, Ukraine, were cleared out and shot not far outside of town. At the end of the war, Riva would discover that her older sister Lena and her three daughters had been among them. Till her dying day, my grandmother Emma believed that her cousins were buried alive, though she had no way of knowing whether that is what actually happened. I sometimes asked her why it mattered how they died, but to Emma, who vividly remembered her cousins—Polina, who at the time of her death was seventeen, Lyuba, fifteen, and Zhenya, five—it mattered a lot.

The speed with which these relatives disappeared is a chilling illustration of the capricious sluice gate that separated death and survival in the Soviet Union during the war. Khinya fled with her parents from Zhitomir on July 4, 1941. By July 9, escape was no longer possible. By October, the vast majority of the Jews who hadn't evacuated Zhitomir—nearly 10,000 of them—were dead.[16] Five more days of trying to guess which move was safest—an impossible algorithm in the summer of 1941—and my grandmother would have been killed around the time of her thirteenth birthday. Five days are why I exist in the world today.

VICTORY

IN MAY 1943, SOME NINE MONTHS AFTER KHINYA FOUND THE DESICcated shell of her father at the train station, her little sister Inna was born. Reunited, the family had traveled until they reached the shores of Lake Issyk-Kul, a prehistoric thumbprint in the Tien Shan mountain range, in the Kyrgyz SSR. Khinya doesn't remember the lake's beauty as they churned across its ancient turquoise waters in a steamship. She was hungry and cold and seasick, and her parents didn't quite know where they were going. On the ship, Khana-Batya met an old Jew from Odessa who suggested they try a tiny village on the Soviet side of the border with China. The family followed his advice and got a room in a hut that was half sky until Grisha covered the gaping hole with branches: a roof.

It was there that Khana-Batya gave birth to a healthy baby girl. She should have seen it as a miracle. Instead, she was mortified. Grisha was already sixteen. What would people say?

As the Red Army pushed the Germans back across eastern Europe, Khana-Batya wondered what had happened to her own little sister, Sonya, after their attempted rescue of her had been foiled by the bombing of Kiev. The newspapers were writing about the massacre of Kiev's Jews at Babi Yar. Was Sonya Ring buried in that ravine?

Then Moisei ran into Sonya's in-laws in Frunze, and, through them, tracked her down in Astrakhan, where her university had been evacuated. When she heard from her sister and brother-in-law, she decided to join them. Sonya's husband had been drafted two days after the Nazi invasion and was soon reported missing in action. Sonya had been unable to have children and she had nothing to remember her husband by except his photo. She would never remarry. And even if she could have stopped mourning her husband of just three sweet years, there were no men her age left to court her.

Decades later, she and Khana-Batya would end their days together, two sister-widows sharing an apartment in a leafy American suburb, where Sonya kept a photo of her husband by her bed until the day she died.

In July 1943, Bronya gave birth to another son, her third, and named him Mikhail. But the disappearance of her firstborn in battle had broken something fundamental in her. Monya's last letter was written on May 10, 1942. "I'll be going back to the fighting soon," he wrote. "They're sending us in this very moment." A few months later, Bronya got a slip of paper notifying her that Monya was missing in action. A tank man, it turned out, was not indestructible. If anything, the opposite was true. A tank man spent his days living in a metal coffin on metal treads, plowing through fire, living until the day the fire got inside. When it did, his flammable suit quickly caught fire. The heat of the flames made the tankers' eyes pop and ooze from their sockets. If medics like Asma managed to find them alive, they were often blind and burned over so much of their bodies that they didn't survive long.

It's unclear when, exactly, the fire melted Monya's blue eyes. One army record lists his disappearance in July. Another, in August. There were so many mothers' sons disappearing in those days, the fields blooming thick with their ruined young bodies, that there was barely time to bury them, let alone keep up with the paperwork.

Bronya had been a woman of faith. She had observed the Sabbath and kept kosher decades into the Soviet campaign to eliminate religion. Yet, after all the children she had saved from disease and hunger, her god could not save even one for her, the boy who had made her a mother in the first place. And so, in the summer of 1942, Bronya and her god parted ways. Even after she and Nota were reunited and had their third child, born to Bronya at the unspeakably old age of forty-two, she did not forgive Him.

Mikhail grew up to be so tall that his nickname became "Bolshoi," the big guy. Bronya spoiled him well into his adulthood. She would never let him grow up into anything more than a lanky man-child. But she never gave up on Monya, even when the rest of the family did.

"I think that you, my little son, are alive," she wrote in her journal in 1968. She still searched for him in homes for the disabled and injured, long after Stalin cleared them out of Moscow. As far as the state or Bronya knew, her son's body had never been found. She imagined that he was now a limbless trunk, a man without enough memory to remember his own name, lying in an institution somewhere, unable to get home. This thought gave her hope and tortured her because she did not know how to find such a man. And yet, for years after the end of the war, the newspapers and radio programs were full of notices placed by people still searching for loved ones. There were happy stories among them, too—not many, but some—stories in which people found each other against impossible odds: by recognizing a birthmark, by happening across an old neighbor. Bronya was nearing the end of her life—she knew that—but still she hoped her firstborn might somehow outlive her. "If you, my little son, answer my call and I'm no longer here, Yasha will help you with everything," she wrote in her journal, referring to my grandfather. "That is my bequest to him."

Every day until she died of a stroke in her office in 1973, she waited for her Monya to come home. He never did.

During the war's last winter, the NKVD transferred Riva to work in a penal colony for juvenile delinquents on the outskirts of Moscow. Isaak and Tolya remained in Novosibirsk; Emma went with her mother.

Riva had thought the colony would be like the *detpriemnik*: full of children who had been arrested for stealing a potato or for being the child of an enemy of the people. But this place was full of the angry, violent children born of the constant upheaval of the first two decades of Soviet rule, years that had devoured their parents and left these children capable, whether for survival or entertainment, of great savagery. They slipped notes under Riva's office door threatening to rape and kill her ten-year-old daughter. Every morning, before Riva went into the camp, she locked Emma inside their bare and drafty room, leaving her to stoke the stove and pee in a pot and do not much else until her mother's return at nightfall.

There was a veteran who lived down the hall, a man who had returned from the front without a leg. One day that spring, the boys in the camp beat him, left him for dead, and burned his crutches. He survived and warned Riva to take her daughter: this was no place for a woman and her child.

Riva secured a transfer to a POW camp outside of Moscow, full of German soldiers who hissed *"Jude!"* at her when she passed them on the other side of the fence. But she also met an Austrian POW who had been a baker before the war and was allowed to work in the kitchen. He taught Riva how to make what became her famous strudel. She and Emma lived in what was once a morgue, but the wife of an NKVD officer fed Emma sandwiches she made from Lend-Lease bacon and powdered eggs as thanks for babysitting their child.

One day Riva went to the NKVD offices to ask for her release, leaving Emma sitting in the lobby next to two old ladies to whom she quickly confided how her mom really felt about the organization. By nightfall they had been locked out of their quarters, their meager belongings scattered on the ground. Riva, swallowing her fury at her daughter, took Emma into the city where her oldest sister Hannah was now living. Hannah's daughters took them in and made beds for them on the floor. Hannah herself was bedridden. In January 1945, she had gotten the fateful knock on the door. Her only son had been killed in a friendly-fire incident at a base just outside of Moscow. That day Hannah lay down, turned to the wall, and never got up again.

By spring 1945, Tolya and Isaak had found their way back to the capital. On the night of May 8, Emma and her brother, now ten and fourteen, refused to go to bed. They had spent the last few months listening to the sharp tenor of Yury Levitan, a Jewish boy with a provincial Jewish twang who had grown up to become Stalin's trusted radio announcer, broadcasting the fall of German city after German city, until Berlin fell at last to Soviet forces on May 2, 1945. By the evening of May 8, Emma and Tolya knew the end of the war was imminent. All they needed to hear was the announcement of Germany's unconditional surrender. It was signed an hour before midnight

German time, which was already early morning on May 9 in Moscow. But Riva allowed Emma and Tolya to stay up past their bedtime to hear that familiar voice say the words they would remember for the rest of their lives: the war was over.

When daylight finally came, they walked toward Red Square. Tagging along was their uncle Grisha, who had come back from the front with one leg, Grisha's wife, and the baby they made immediately on his return. They crushed into the Square, where Stalin's placid, mustachioed face was beamed onto the side of the department store where Isaak had bought Emma and Tolya their useless hats an entire world ago.

People danced and sang and played harmonicas. Emma had never been so happy in her life. On this day everything they had suffered was behind them. Soon she would start school for the first time in three years. Life would begin again.

Victory found Khinya at five in the morning. Now sixteen, she was back in her old house in Zhitomir. The family they had left that summer day in 1941 were all in the earth now. The valuables the town's fleeing Jews had entrusted to two sisters of German descent were gone, along with the sisters, who had spent the war carousing with German officers and then retreated with them.

So little remained of the world that Khinya's family had known. Perhaps that was why, when a neighbor ran over to tell them at five in the morning that the war had been won, Khinya dropped to her knees and started scrubbing the floor of their house, still standing unlike so many other houses in Zhitomir. It was the only sturdy thing left beneath her feet.

Asma the medic was outside Berlin when it fell. After May 9, she was taken to tour the destroyed and pockmarked city, the burnt-out Reichstag adorned with a red Soviet flag. She was given an envelope with her army record and told to show it to the authorities wherever she ended up so she could get assistance and a job from the government.

As she had marched with the Red Army westward across Byelorussia, Asma had seen what the Germans had done to the Jews in the shtetls, empty now of anyone who knew the language she had grown up speaking. Eventually, she got the same news from home. The Soviet soldiers who had tried to stop her from going back to Volodarsk-Volynsk in June 1941 had been right: there was nothing left of her hometown but earth and sky. Her parents, like all the Jews in town, had been shot. Their house had been torched. She had nowhere to go and show her envelope. She was twenty years old.

By the time the lieutenant general laid eyes on paratrooper Ida Segal in the spring of 1944, she was a decorated soldier, a veteran of some of the war's most brutal battles. She had just helped liberate Zhitomir and Rechitsa, where she had a Red Banner medal pinned to her chest. She received the Red Star for evacuating the wounded at Kursk, the biggest tank battle in history, in which the Soviets lost nearly 1 million soldiers. Most men in the Red Army didn't have such medals.

And so she didn't know what to say when the lieutenant general looked at her and said, "What is this little girl doing here?" Her commander explained that she had just returned from the front line. The lieutenant general noted her name and said, "Get this little girl off the front line." And just like that, Ida was reassigned to the rear, to work in the communications division with sixty other women, some of whom were her mother's age.

Despite her constant lobbying to be sent back to the front, she never saw combat again. On the night the war ended, Ida was on call in a hospital in the town of Stoki, just on the Polish side of the German border. Illness had landed her there as a patient, and when she was better, she stayed, helping to evacuate and identify the wounded, sorting them into separate quarters for officers and enlisted men. One day she heard that her father had been listed missing in action somewhere on the southwestern front. He had been called up on the first morning of the first day of the war and had disappeared soon after. War demands sacrifices, Ida had once written her mother, and it was her father who had been put on the bier.

Marina Raskova, the commander of the all-female bomber divisions, got lost in the clouds over Saratov and crashed to her death on January 4, 1943. She was thirty years old. Lidia Litvyak, the young recruit Raskova had put in solitary for sewing fur onto her jacket, went on to become one of the most accomplished fighter pilots of the war. She was shot down and killed on August 1, 1943, weeks shy of her twenty-second birthday. In 1990, she was posthumously made a Hero of the Soviet Union.[1] Lyudmila Pavlichenko, the star sniper, was not allowed to go back into the fight when she returned from her tour of the United States, unlike the less accomplished male sniper who accompanied her. Instead, Stalin personally ordered her to train snipers in the rear, to pass on her skills to others instead of using her talents herself.

After the war was won and millions of soldiers were demobilized, Soviet women would never again see active combat.[2] By the time the country went to war in Korea in 1950 and in Afghanistan in 1979, Soviet women did what women in bourgeois armies did: they cooked and cleaned and clerked and ministered to the men who did the fighting.

Victory was the end of the most radical phase of the experiment in building the new Soviet woman. While Raskova and Pavlichenko were off fighting the Germans, Stalin resegregated Soviet schools by gender and reintroduced home economics for girls.[3] The military training these women received in grade school, the flying clubs and shooting practice, would become a relic of the 1930s. After the war, it would only be offered to the boys. In being the first, this generation from another universe had also become the last.

Women veterans would come home to find a different society than the one they had left, one that would quickly forget everything they had done to defeat Hitler. Writing about the great generals and the great mechanized battles of this war unlike any other, historians, most of them male, largely omitted the other element that made this war so unique: 800,000 Soviet women fighting alongside the men. The stories that the women tried to tell about their time at the front were also largely ignored, their memoirs forgotten or left unpublished.[4]

Instead, women veterans were viewed with suspicion. What had they been doing in those trenches, in such intimate proximity to men? Some did have relationships with fellow soldiers, either out of love or for protection.[5] Top-level commanders, including the famous Marshal Georgy Zhukov and future Soviet premier Leonid Brezhnev, had so-called field wives.[6] After the war, the commanders went home to their lawful wives and the field wives, many of whom had children with their field husbands, returned to civilian life as single mothers.[7] But even women who didn't have frontline affairs were suspect. One woman veteran told Svetlana Alexievich how, after the war, women in her communal apartment poured vinegar into her potatoes and called her a whore.

In the end, the women veterans fell silent. "We were as mute as fish," one woman veteran told Alexievich. "Men were the victors, heroes, suitors, they had been at war, but they looked at us with completely different eyes... They took away our victory."[8]

Soviet soldiers surged into battle with the same standard battle cry: "For Stalin! For the Motherland!" Yet, somehow, the Second World War became known to Russians as the Great Fatherland War. It capped three decades of bloodletting on Soviet territory, starting with World War I, followed by the Revolution, Civil War, famine, collectivization, and mass political repressions. Taken together, the forty years before Victory Day carried off more than 50 million Soviets.[9] In the years between the Nazi invasion and the Soviet counteroffensive that drove them out, some 27 million Soviets were killed. By some estimates, the Soviet Union lost 15 percent of its population in just four years.[10]

Most of the dead were men. In 1939, on the eve of the Great Fatherland War, there were eight million more Soviet women than men.[11] The war only exaggerated that imbalance. In some places, the gender ratio was so skewed after 1945 that there were only nineteen men for every hundred women.[12]

And yet, as one of the victors, the Soviet Union had emerged a superpower on the world stage. Stalin and his lieutenants knew that the contradiction was untenable. A powerful country needed a large and expanding population. It needed people to rebuild all that was ruined, to run massive factories and till the soil of giant mechanized farms, and, perhaps, to fight once again the kind of war it had just won.

Even before the war was over, Stalin understood that the Soviet Union would need to solve this demographic crisis; it would need to replace its dead.[13] There is an apocryphal story that, when he was warned about the catastrophic losses the Red Army would suffer while taking this or that city, he replied, "It's fine. Russian women will have more." He probably never actually said this, but he didn't have to. It was his unspoken strategy for everything. For Stalin, great achievements in industry, in politics, and in war required proportionally vast human sacrifice. And no matter how many Soviet citizens he laid down on these altars of modernity, Soviet women would always step into the breach. They would pick up guns and climb into the cockpits of planes in which they burned like matchsticks. They would give up their sons for the country, pretend their children were heroes rather than cannon fodder, and when those sons fell in battle, they would have more.

Yet it was not clear how the state could squeeze tens of millions of new Soviets out of its weary, shattered female population. Many women had stopped menstruating during the war. Venereal disease reached epidemic proportions among both men and women, which also posed problems for their fertility. Families had been torn apart by four years of constant dislocation, severed lines of communication, and violence. After the war, millions of Soviets were homeless, living in earthen dugouts. The entire country subsisted on ration cards for years, with reports of cannibalism emerging during the postwar famine. Posters and newspaper editorials weren't going to convince women to create another mouth to feed. The state would soon need to take more drastic measures.

What did this mean in practice when 21 million men didn't come home? What did it mean when many of those who did return had been disfigured by battle, both physically and psychologically? What did it mean for the women whom the war had made into young widows? What did it mean for the millions of Soviet women who were just reaching reproductive age, eager to be mothers, when the entire generation of their male counterparts had been wiped out?

They made do with what they had. There are many stories of villages where, of all the men who went to the front in 1941, only one returned, crippled and traumatized. He would father children with all the women in the village who wanted one. They did not care about society's opprobrium.

Or, like Asma, they married what was left. In 1948, the young man Asma had pulled from a tank, Mikhail Gindin, found her working as a nurse in a hospital in Tashkent, Uzbekistan. He had lived and he had promised to find her, and it may have taken him two years, but there he was, ready to marry her. Asma looked at him. His left eyelid drooped over his pupil, a memento of the eye-melting heat she had saved him from six years before. His face was one smooth scar. He had had countless operations, skin grafts from his buttocks to cover his raw stomach. "I accepted him," Asma recalled many years later. "Love, not love. For two years he looked for me, this *yid*." They married and she spent the next decade working full-time and bearing him eight children. She buried three of them. Thinking of this brutal arithmetic decades later, when her husband was also long in the ground, she shrugged and said, "That's life."

In the case of Emma's cousin Tsilya, widowed during the war, she married an army surgeon who had lost his wife. But the army surgeon died two years into their new marriage, leaving her with a toddler son, Grisha, a young man who would grow up in the shadow of his lonely mother and his two spinster aunts, Tsilya's sisters, who had never been able to find husbands or have children after the war. They trembled over him, their little Grisha, one child for three ravenous women. That was their victory.

PART II

Her lamp never goes out at night.
—"WOMAN OF VALOR," PROVERBS 31:18

SVETLANA

SHE WAS AT A FRENCH LESSON WHEN THEY SUMMONED HER.[1] NEVER before had anyone except her father invited her to his dacha. When she arrived, Nikita Khrushchev, one of her father's loyal lieutenants, greeted her at the gates, his broad peasant face stained with tears. That's when Svetlana understood that her father was going to die. It was March 2, 1953.

In her father's study, she saw doctors and nurses taking EKGs and planting leeches on the back of his head and neck. Some young doctors had arrived with a new ventilator borrowed from one of the scientific institutes. Vladimir Vinogradov, her father's personal physician, was in jail, but it was obvious that this man was beyond help. Like Lenin before him, Joseph Stalin had had a massive, catastrophic stroke.

Svetlana sat down next to her father and took his hand. Sometimes he opened his eyes and looked at her, but she doubted he really saw her. She was his youngest child, his only daughter, the one person to whom he had shown any love and affection, at least as far as he was capable. He had abandoned his first son, Yakov, first in infancy and again in war. His other son, Vasily, was a constant disappointment. Svetlana was different. Her red hair reminded him of his own mother, the only woman he had truly worshipped. Svetlana had gotten good grades and adored her father, and he was sufficiently proud of her to introduce her to Churchill when the British prime minister visited Moscow during the war. She was Stalin's proof that he was human.

In 1932, when Svetlana was six, her mother, Nadezhda Alliluyeva, died—from appendicitis, as far as Svetlana knew. Stalin grew more distant from his children after that, but he still kissed Svetlana good night as she slept and called her his "little sparrow," his *khozyaushka*, his "little mistress of the house." They wrote each other playful notes in the only language he seemed to understand: bureaucratic diktat.

21 OCTOBER 1934
TO: COM. J. V. STALIN, SECRETARY N. 1
ORDER N. 4

I order you to take me with you.

Signed: Setanka, mistress of the house.
Stamp.
Signed by Secretary N 1: I submit. J. Stalin

Stalin took Svetlana with him on his interminable working vacations to the south, where she tried in vain to adapt to his nocturnal schedule and sat at the dinner table listening to the men who surrounded him. When she had to return to school in the fall, he sent her crates of pomegranates and peaches from the Soviet subtropics as her peers around the country starved.

But it was a lonely childhood. She grew up in the Kremlin, cared for mostly by governesses and nannies, cooks and Stalin's bodyguard, all of whom worked for the NKVD. The men at her father's table began to disappear one by one, as did her aunts and uncles. When a classmate passed Svetlana a letter for her father—the classmate's father had been arrested and the boy's mother pleaded with Stalin for her husband's life—Stalin released the man but admonished Svetlana. "You're not a mailman," he yelled.[2] She never brought him another appeal again.[3]

Stalin assigned an NKVD man to trail Svetlana everywhere she went. The control was her father's way of loving her, part of what she called his "purely Oriental approach to women."[4] Stalin came from a far more provincial background than many of the urban intellectuals in the revolutionary movement. He had attended a Christian Orthodox seminary in Tbilisi and, before that, had grown up in rural Georgia, infamous for its ostentatious machismo, where brides were kidnapped and women didn't sit at the table with men. His view of women was conservative, possessive, and had little in common with official Soviet ideology on the woman question.

When she was twelve, Svetlana sent her father a photograph of herself, smiling and wearing the red Pioneer's scarf, for his birthday. He sent it back to her, marked up in the same blue pencil he used to sign execution lists. "You have an insolent expression on your face," he wrote. "Before, there used to be modesty there and that was attractive."[5] Stalin raged when Svetlana's dresses hit above the knee or when she wore socks in the summer instead of stockings. Her legs, he shouted, were completely "naked." "Only later did I learn that old men in Georgia can't stand short dresses, short sleeves, and socks," Svetlana wrote. "Even when I was an adult, I always had to consider if I was dressed too flamboyantly when I went to visit my father, as I would immediately get a reprimand from him." Once, as a teenager, Svetlana overheard her father reproach the sexually precocious Vasily for saying he was attracted to women "with ideas." "Look at him, so he wants a woman with ideas! Hah!" Stalin guffawed. "We have known that kind: herrings with ideas—skin and bones!" Svetlana understood that he was talking about her dead mother, and she would remember it, bitterly, for the rest of her life.[6]

When it was time to apply to university, Stalin vetoed her desire to study literature. If she was going to pursue something useless like the humanities, he reasoned, she may as well choose a more serious discipline, like history. Khrushchev, Stalin's future successor, saw Stalin's increasingly harsh treatment of his daughter as the explanation for what eventually happened to Svetlana, for her shattered, broken life. And despite her high station, her fate mirrored that of other Soviet women during the postwar years, their aspirations stifled, their fortunes warped by the will of an increasingly patriarchal state. But it was more than that. After Nadya Alliluyeva's death, Stalin never remarried. It was Svetlana, his only daughter, the woman he felt he had a right to mold as he pleased, who filled the role of Stalin's subordinate first lady, his little mistress of the house. Like the other Soviet first ladies, her fate reflected the fate of the entire country, broken irreparably by one man's possessive, paranoid love. "His was the tenderness of a cat for a mouse," Khrushchev wrote decades later of Stalin's love for his daughter. "He broke the heart first of a child, then a young girl, then of a woman and a mother."[7]

On November 6, 1942, the twenty-fifth anniversary of the Bolshevik Revolution, sixteen-year-old Svetlana put on her first adult dress and pinned her mother's garnet brooch on her chest. It had been exactly ten years since Nadya had stormed out of a Revolution Day party and shot herself in the heart. Nadya's son, Vasily, a fighter pilot, was throwing a party for the occasion of Revolution Day at one of the many family dachas. It was the middle of the war. Yakov, the dutiful eldest son, had left his wife and daughter and gone to the front to fight the day after the Germans invaded. But Vasily was a womanizer and a blossoming alcoholic, known less for his piloting skills than for his parties. He had surrounded himself with what was left of the loyal Soviet intelligentsia after his father had decimated it in the late 1930s.

That November evening, as the battle for Stalingrad grew fiercer, Vasily's guests included writers and poets and actresses as well as Aleksei Kapler, a well-known Soviet film director. Kapler invited the coltish Svetlana for a foxtrot. Svetlana had met Kapler a few times before at Vasily's private film screenings. Now he was trying to make a film about Soviet fighter pilots, so he was frequently in her brother's company. But that night Svetlana fell in love with this charming middle-aged man. He was famous, surrounded by beautiful, famous women, but he noticed her; he *saw* her. Even in the din of the party, he listened as she told him about her loneliness and her boredom. He listened as she told him how she had only recently learned that her mother hadn't really died of appendicitis, after coming across an American magazine that casually mentioned Nadya Alliluyeva's suicide.

After that night, they saw each other every day. He would wait by her school and, when classes were over, they would walk together through snowy wartime Moscow. He took her to the theater and to the movies. He gave her books that were impossible to find—novels by Hemingway, the poetry of Akhmatova and Gumilev—and discussed them with her. He treated her like an adult, listened to her with all the seriousness and respect and warmth she'd lacked at home.

When Kapler went to film the battle in Stalingrad, he published his report in *Pravda* in the form of a letter to the woman he loved. He did not name Svetlana, but he might as well have: the dispatch depicted his beloved watching the snow falling from behind her Kremlin window. Svetlana was horrified. Her NKVD tail had already reported her strolls with Kapler to her father. She knew Stalin would see the love letter in the newspaper and dreaded his reaction.

When Kapler returned to Moscow in January 1943, Svetlana tried to break things off with him. It didn't take, nor did a suggestion by one of Stalin's bodyguards to Kapler that he take an extended work trip somewhere far, far away. Soon the two of them were in one of the empty Moscow apartments Vasily kept for his trysts, kissing passionately as Svetlana's tail sat in the next room, pretending to read the newspaper. It was February 28, Svetlana's seventeenth birthday.

Till the end of her days, Svetlana would insist that she did not have sex with Kapler.[8] But Stalin had heard differently from his spies. The morning after her birthday, Stalin stormed into her bedroom, slapped her twice across the face, and accused her of whoring around while a war was raging. Svetlana fought back.

"But I love him!" she yelled.

"Look at yourself!" Stalin snorted. "Who would want you? He's surrounded by women, you fool!" Moreover, Stalin announced, Kapler was a British spy who was now under arrest. He demanded Svetlana hand over their entire correspondence. Wounded and stunned, Svetlana complied.

Later that day, Stalin summoned his daughter again. He was still furious, taking his rage out on Kapler's letters and photographs, which he was manually shredding into the wastebasket. It wasn't just that she was debasing herself with an older man who was also a notorious womanizer. The fact that Kapler was a Jew made his daughter's fall that much more galling. "You couldn't have found yourself a Russian?" Stalin spat. For his dalliance with Svetlana, Kapler would be sentenced to five years of exile in a town beyond the Arctic Circle and then five more years in a labor camp.

When she turned eighteen in 1944, Svetlana, desperate to flee her father's grip, married her university classmate Grigory Morozov, who was also Jewish. Stalin made his disgust with her choice known to everyone, including his Politburo, who immediately encouraged their own children to divorce any Jews they were married to.⁹ Stalin didn't arrest his daughter's husband, but he made clear that he would never meet Morozov, not even after the couple had a son in 1945, whom they named Joseph in his honor.

In 1947, Svetlana and Grigory divorced, and Svetlana quickly remarried, this time to the son of Andrey Zhdanov, one of Stalin's favorite lieutenants. In 1950, she gave birth to her daughter Katya prematurely and after a difficult pregnancy. "The state needs people," Stalin wrote to Svetlana in the hospital, "even those who are born prematurely."

It was a loveless marriage and Svetlana had several abortions after Katya's birth.¹⁰ Even though her father was pleased with her choice of husband, it wasn't enough to heal the rupture that had opened up between them on that day in March 1943. "From that day on, my father and I became strangers to each other for a long time," Svetlana wrote twenty years later. "I was no longer the beloved daughter I had been before."¹¹

Stalin had done everything in his study: work, sleep, eat long, late meals with his Politburo. It was where he had celebrated the last New Year of his life, putting a record on the Radiola and making the members of the Politburo dance for him, drunk grown men stumbling around like circus bears, desperate to please their implacable master. Then he forced Svetlana to dance, dragging her by the hair until she obeyed, her face hot with tears, the circus bears watching in terrified silence. "Go on, Svetlana, dance!" Stalin had bellowed at his daughter, by that point a twice-divorced mother of two. "You're the mistress of the house, so dance!"¹²

And now he would die in this room, a weak old man who had been found on the floor by his servants, his pants stained with urine. Svetlana looked around, past the petrified medical staff, past her father's scheming successors, to the walls behind his desk, which her father had inexplicably decorated with enlarged photographs of random children he didn't know—a boy on skis, another beneath a blooming cherry tree. He had been so distant from his own children, so indifferent to his eight grandchildren, five of whom he had never bothered to meet. And yet he had these strange photos of strangers' children on the wall. As she sat there, watching her father slowly suffocate and his lips turn black, she was surprised to feel such tenderness and pity for what she realized had been his own loneliness. She felt again that this man, who had caused her and her country so much suffering, had, however crookedly and imperfectly, loved her.

Suddenly, Stalin raised his left hand, the one he could still move after the stroke, and pointed. Everyone in the room froze. They didn't know what the gesture meant but they all understood the threat in it. Even at the moment of his death, he terrorized them. It was why, Svetlana realized, his death was so slow and horrifying. "God gives an easy death only to the righteous," she would write later.

His hand dropped and his breathing stopped. It was over. Midnight came and went. Svetlana had sat with her dying father for three days and she was in no rush to leave now, not even when the medics came to take him away for the autopsy. Dawn had come, the cold gray light filtering in through the room's big rectangular windows, and she began to shake. The man who had given her life was now just a corpse.

At six that morning, March 6, 1953, came the official radio announcement that Stalin was dead. Even in her grief, Svetlana knew what this moment meant—for her, for everyone in that room, for everyone in the country.

"Petrified and mute," she wrote, "I understood that a certain liberation had come."[13]

BERIA'S HOUSE

MANY YEARS AGO, ON A GRAY AND MUGGY DAY, I WAS WALKING WITH my grandmother Emma in Moscow. I don't remember where we were going, but we had just come up the hill from the Metro stop by the zoo and were turning left onto Moscow's Garden Ring, a road that girds the city center like a belt. It was humid, the hill was steep, and Emma, whose heart had been slowly failing for two decades, was walking too quickly and pretending to not be winded.

"That's Beria's house," she said, pointing across the many lanes of busy traffic on the Garden Ring to a beautiful two-story building where the quiet shade of Malaya Nikitskaya Street suddenly opened up onto the smog and clamor of the ring road. I had passed the house Emma was pointing to countless times. It was a lovely old mansion from the nineteenth century, its walls a pale blue with white reliefs and cornices, dressed in frilly pastels with tall windows. Now it housed the Tunisian embassy.

"How do you know it was Beria's house?" I asked Emma.

Emma looked at me like I was the last fool on earth.

"Everyone knew it was Beria's house," she said. "When I was young, all us girls knew to take the long way around."

"Why?" I asked, still not following.

"Because Beria snatched pretty girls off the street," Emma said. "Then he took them back to his house and raped them."

Three months after Stalin's death, Nikita Khrushchev, a member of the Presidium, one of the ruling bodies of the USSR, pulled off a coup that no one suspected him capable of: he arrested Lavrentiy Beria, Stalin's sadistic former chief of the secret police, the man who oversaw the

Gulag, the master manipulator and intrigue-weaving courtier. Soon, Beria would be tried and executed in secret for treason and, implausibly, spying for the British. Khrushchev was giddy. In the months after Stalin's death, it had seemed that Beria, a fellow Georgian, would be his natural successor. But now Beria was on his way to one of the miserable prisons he had once overseen, and in the wake of his arrest, a whole other dimension of his cruelty would be exposed.

On the afternoon of June 26, 1953, a bodyguard approached Khrushchev after a meeting. "I have only just heard that Beria has been arrested," the bodyguard said, as Khrushchev recalled in his memoirs. "I want to inform you that he raped my stepdaughter, a seventh grader."[1] Khrushchev, betraying no emotion, told this man that he would have to repeat the details to the prosecutor in charge of Beria's case.

"Later, we were given a list of more than a hundred girls and women who had been raped by Beria," Khrushchev wrote dispassionately. "He had used the same routine on all of them. He gave them some dinner and offered them wine with a sleeping potion in it."

On January 13, 1950, a young actress named Valentina Chizhova was invited to a party thrown by an acquaintance, Mark Michurin-Raver, a retired Ministry of State Security (MGB) officer from Georgia.[2] (The NKVD had recently been rebranded as the MGB.) Chizhova was reluctant, but her friend encouraged her to go. Chizhova hoped to break into serious theater, and Michurin-Raver's wife was a famous actress at one of the best theaters in the country. At the very least, her friend told her, it would be an interesting evening. Chizhova relented and agreed to go.

When she arrived at nine that evening, the party was crowded and she didn't know anyone there. After the host, Michurin-Raver, greeted her, he spoke briefly on the phone with someone and soon a man arrived who was introduced to her as Rafael Sarkisov. Michurin-Raver told Chizhova that a very important person wanted to see her about a pressing matter and that Sarkisov would accompany her. A car was waiting for them in the courtyard.

The car took her to a pale blue mansion, where Sarkisov showed her into a library and told her to wait. After a few minutes, a bald and doughy man wearing a pince-nez walked in. Chizhova immediately recognized Beria, the Politburo member who oversaw the Ministry of the Interior (MVD) and the secret police. At the time, he was also managing the Soviet nuclear program. He was one of the most powerful people in the Soviet Union, second only to Stalin.

Beria rattled off a series of questions: What was her name? When was she born? Who were her parents? Where did she go to school? Chizhova thought the tsar of the secret police must be sizing her up for some kind of secret mission. Satisfied with her answers, Beria led Chizhova and Sarkisov deeper into the house, to a dining room where a sumptuous table was set for three. At a time when food was still scarce, the sight of a table groaning with such plenty was intimidating. Beria offered Chizhova wine, but she politely declined. He insisted, saying the wine wasn't very strong since he had diluted it with lemonade, and once again Chizhova relented. After three or four glasses, she lost consciousness.

She woke up in the morning in a bedroom, Beria asleep next to her. "I was covered in blood because, before that night, I had never been intimately close with anyone and Beria robbed me of my virginity," Chizhova later testified.

Deeply shaken, Chizhova demanded to go home. She told Beria that she would write a letter to Stalin and tell him everything. Beria replied that her letter would only end up on his own desk. "Beria told me that I risked not ever leaving his house [alive] and that he would send my mother to the farthest possible labor camp," Chizhova later recalled. "I was afraid of his threats and decided to get out of the mansion as soon as possible so as to never return there again."

But that night Sarkisov showed up at her apartment and demanded she return. Chizhova gave him a letter for Beria in which she begged to be left alone and promised that she would never tell anyone what had happened. It didn't work. The next day Sarkisov showed up again and insisted she come to the mansion, where Beria "again used threats to force me to have sexual intercourse with him."

For the next few weeks Chizhova tried to stay away from her

apartment, but Sarkisov found out where she worked and had a car waiting for her there instead. When Beria left the city on business, Chizhova was finally left alone—only to discover she was pregnant. She found a doctor who would perform an abortion, which were then illegal, but she suffered complications and required treatment, including several blood transfusions, for weeks.

That spring, Chizhova met and married a man who worked in the interior ministry. In July, Sarkisov appeared at the couple's apartment. This time Chizhova refused to go with Sarkisov and declared that she would tell her husband everything. Sarkisov told her she would only get him arrested and sent to the far north. Terrified, Chizhova went inside and confessed to her husband, who was so enraged that he wrote a letter of protest to Stalin. He didn't include his own name but he named his wife. Before long, he was demoted and then fired. When he asked his boss why, he was told, "The master is not happy with you."[3]

Moscow had whispered about Beria's predilections for years. After Beria's arrest in June 1953, the prosecutor in charge of the case showed particular interest in a twenty-year-old woman named Valentina Drozdova, known to her friends as Lyalya. She became one of the twelve witnesses in Beria's secret trial because she had been a minor when Beria first spotted her walking down Kachalov Street, as Malaya Nikitskaya was known in Soviet times. I couldn't help but notice that her story had contours similar to the one told to Khrushchev by the bodyguard.

In the only publicly available photo of Lyalya, she is a pastoral vision, a young woman in a flowered dress with wisps of white-blond hair around her impassive freckled face. In 1949, Lyalya was sixteen and in the seventh grade, having missed years of schooling during the war. That spring, her grandmother died suddenly. Then her mother fell ill and was consigned to a hospital on the outskirts of Moscow, far from their communal apartment. Lyalya was left on her own.

On May 6, Lyalya went out to buy some bread. "That's when a car stopped and an old man wearing a hat and a pince-nez got out," she recalled in her official statement to the prosecutor. The pince-nez was

Beria's signature accessory, but Lyalya did not recognize him. She did, however, immediately recognize the other man's secret police uniform. "There was a colonel in an MGB uniform," Lyalya continued. "The old man stopped and began carefully inspecting me. I got scared and ran away, but I noticed that a man in civilian clothing followed me all the way home."[4]

The next day, when Lyalya got home from school, her neighbors in the communal apartment told her that a strange man had come by several times, asking for her. He returned at three that afternoon, and Lyalya recognized him as the man who had trailed her. He asked her to come outside with him for a moment. They went into the courtyard, where she saw the colonel in the MGB uniform and a waiting car. She would later learn that this was Rafael Sarkisov, Beria's chief bodyguard.

> It turned out that Sarkisov was up to speed on all our family affairs, knew that my mother was in the hospital, that she had a cot in the hallway, that she was in very serious condition. [Sarkisov] said that we have to go and get a certain professor who could help her and transfer her to her own room. He wanted to arrange all this. I believed him, went home and locked the door, and then went with him in the car. I couldn't not believe him since everything he said about our family and my mother was correct, and she really was in very bad shape at the time. The car took me right away to a mansion that I later learned belonged to Beria.
>
> There [Sarkisov] told me that his comrade would help me, a very responsible worker who helps everyone and who also decided to help us when he found out about my family's predicament.
>
> At around 5 or 6 in the evening, the old man who saw me in the street came into the room where I was sitting with Sarkisov. He greeted me very affectionately and told me not to cry, that they'll cure my mom and that everything will be fine. Then he invited me to have lunch with him and, despite my refusals, sat me down at the table anyway. He was very kind and treated me to wine, but I didn't drink. Sarkisov was at the lunch, too. Then

Beria offered to take me on a tour of the house, but I refused and asked him to go see the professor as soon as possible so we could bring him to my mom.

Then Beria grabbed me, notwithstanding the fact that Sarkisov was in the room, and dragged me to the bedroom. Despite my screams and resistance, Beria raped me. No one came in response to my screams. Then they didn't let me out of the house for three days. I was in very bad shape; I was crying the whole time. Beria kept saying to me, 'What's the big deal, nothing major happened, otherwise some snot-nose who wouldn't appreciate it would have gotten it.'

Before letting me out of the house, Beria and Sarkisov told me not breathe a word of this to anyone or else both my mother and I would perish.

When Lyalya was finally allowed to return home, she locked herself in her room, saying nothing to the neighbors. Alone and frightened, she fell ill and stopped going to school. Before long, Sarkisov showed up and demanded that she return to Beria's house. This time he had a gun and told Lyalya that if she refused, she and her sick mother would be sent to the Gulag. When she arrived at the pale blue mansion, Lyalya finally realized who her rapist was: the omnipotent Lavrentiy Beria, a man whose name was synonymous with the repressions of the vast and brutal Soviet system. If she ever told anyone what he had done, Beria warned her, he would "wipe [me] from the face of the earth."

To Stalin, physically destroying a political enemy was not enough; he insisted on destroying his reputation, too. Using an elaborate simulacrum of investigations, witness testimony, confessions, and carefully choreographed trials, Stalin gave his retribution a patina of justice. The confessions convinced many in the West that the charges were legitimate, even though they had been procured through elaborate torture, which Beria sometimes took part in personally.[5]

In eliminating Beria, Khrushchev and the other party leaders vying to succeed Stalin followed the Stalinist playbook. They did not charge Beria with torturing innocent people: The men of the Presidium were all implicated in the Great Terror, and so they could not try Beria for something of which they, too, were guilty. Instead, they turned the most basic facts of Beria's life and work over the past two decades against him. His operations running spies inside and beyond the Soviet Union became proof that, actually, *Beria* had been the spy—for the Soviet Union's enemies. His torture of prisoners became a charge of terrorism. And Beria's systematic rape and intimidation of women and young girls suddenly became central to the prosecutor's case as evidence of Beria's "moral decay."

Khrushchev and the other victorious Presidium members had long known about Beria's predations. They had simply chosen to ignore them until it became politically expedient to notice them. They included Lyalya Drozdova's testimony in the case not because they wanted justice for her but because she was a useful weapon in the men's struggle for the throne.

Still, the main focus of Beria's secret trial was his alleged spying for the British, not what he had done to the two Valentinas, and, aside from the testimony in his case, not much documentary evidence of Beria's rapes remains. As a result, Beria's use of the state machinery of terror to rape scores of women remains but a footnote or a prurient aside in most histories of the era. The men of the Presidium were intrigued by the lists Sarkisov and Beria's other lieutenants said they had kept of their boss's exploits. However, Stephen Kotkin, the Stalin historian, told me that no one has ever seen those lists. After Beria's arrest and execution, his personal files were destroyed and many members of his staff—the drivers, housekeepers, and cooks who could have been witnesses—were also arrested and executed. Testimony was often obtained under coercion, and it's hard to know what's true and what isn't. Any surviving documents would likely be in the KGB archives, and it's hard to imagine any critically minded scholars having access to them anytime soon.

But close scrutiny of Beria's cultural imprint reveals plenty of damning details. Beria was widely known in Moscow as a sexual predator, not least in the whisper networks of Soviet women who, like

Emma, came of age after the war, when Beria's appetite seems to have peaked. People talked about the Soviet film star Tatiana Okunevskaya and the other actresses whom Beria had raped. Both my parents have childhood memories of learning about Beria's crimes. My mother discovered some of the stories of Beria's victims in the samizdat hidden in Emma's underwear drawer. My father remembers his father pointing out the blue house to him when he was a young boy and telling him what went on there in Stalin's time. If they, average Soviet children, knew, then the men at the top certainly knew. In her memoirs, Svetlana Stalina described how her father never allowed her to dally at the Beria residence. "I don't trust Beria!" Stalin screamed into the phone, demanding that Svetlana return home immediately.[6]

Most of the men of the Presidium had harems of young women whom they rewarded with apartments, food, and other basic goods that were impossible to find in a war-ravaged country with a command economy. They used their power and access to scarce resources to, essentially, purchase sex—and this was, in turn, a measure of their power and status. Yet none were known for drugging and raping scores of women. Beria did not just use perks and sweeteners to buy women. His chief resource was the immense coercive power of the Soviet state, and he used it for his personal pleasure.

Like many serial sexual predators, Beria seems to have had a routine for finding and attacking his victims and then procuring their silence. The women's stories—both in the official testimony and in the women's memoirs—are strikingly similar. Beria found them through friends and subordinates who served as pimps, plucking them from screens and stages or while slowly cruising the streets of Moscow in his black Packard. He would then dispatch his bodyguards to bring the women to his house, where they were treated to an elaborate feast, usually drugged, raped, and then cowed into silence with threats of execution or the prospect of their families being sent to the Gulag.

Most women knew not to call his bluff. One, the wife of Beria's jailed subordinate, testified that she sent Beria a birthday telegram after her husband was freed. Beria immediately sent Sarkisov to fetch her to his mansion, where he raped her. Fearing that her husband would be rearrested if she resisted, she kept returning without protest to the blue mansion every time Sarkisov came for her.[7] Beria drugged Chizhova by offering toasts—for Stalin, for the Motherland—that were impossible to turn down. What kind of person wouldn't drink to Stalin's health? Tens of thousands of people had disappeared for less. One Soviet starlet, the beloved Zoya Fyodorova, dared to reject Beria's advances and called him an "ugly monkey" before storming out of the mansion.[8] On her way out, a bodyguard handed her a bouquet of roses, which, he clarified, was a wreath for her grave. A couple of years later, Fyodorova was arrested and given a death sentence, which was commuted to eight years of hard labor, for her affair with an American admiral stationed in Moscow during the war. Okunevskaya, the film star, was raped by Beria twice but did not complain because her father and grandmother had been arrested and she feared angering the man who held their fate in his hands. (She later discovered that by the time Beria took a shine to her, they were long dead.) In 1948, she, too, was arrested and sent to the Gulag.[9]

Beria used his position in other unique ways. Under interrogation, Sarkisov revealed that he was responsible for tracking down the names, addresses, and personal details of women that had caught his boss's eye.[10] Sarkisov, who had the state's vast surveillance powers at his disposal, also tracked down women who wrote to Beria asking for favors, usually involving loved ones who had disappeared into the penal system Beria oversaw. If the women proved attractive, his men would arrange for them to visit the blue house.[11] "We invited some woman to spend the night with him almost every day," Sarkisov's subordinate Sardion Nadaraia testified. He and Sarkisov kept long lists of Beria's victims and nine such tallies were included in the case materials.[12] When some of the women inevitably became pregnant, Beria used his power to arrange abortions (which remained illegal until 1955). In at least one case, the woman gave birth, and Beria took the baby and put it in an orphanage.[13]

In the 1990s, after the fall of the Soviet Union, the KGB archives were opened and two Russian historians were able to get Beria's case file and publish it. It is from their books that I have drawn the witness testimony of both Valentinas, Chizhova and Drozdova. But there are other sources. There was a time when the women who survived Beria were still alive and spoke about their experiences openly. Fyodorova did not hide what had happened to her. She told her friends in the art world and the story spread from there. After she was mysteriously killed in 1981, her daughter told her story—including to foreign journalists and in English—until she died in 2012. Okunevskaya wrote about being raped by Beria in her memoirs in great detail and did not shy away from speaking about it in media interviews until her death in 2002.[14] After 1991, still more women came forward. One told a British journalist that, when she informed Beria she couldn't sleep with him because she was married, Beria had her husband arrested. She never saw him again and was forced to become Beria's mistress for the next year and a half.[15]

The one Western historian who has attempted to seriously address Beria's assaults is a woman, Amy Knight. In her biography of Beria, she noted that the Americans who lived in a diplomatic residence on the same street as Beria's baby-blue mansion also heard tales of Beria's hunts and often saw limousines bringing girls to the house on Kachalov Street late at night.[16] Knight argues that we should operate from a place of assuming that these stories are based in fact, not just political smears. "I don't doubt that the many rumors about Beria raping women were true," Knight told me. "The fact that Stalin and the other leaders turned a blind eye to Beria's violence against women reflected the depravity of the Stalinist regime that went beyond even the mass executions of Stalin's perceived enemies."

As soon as her mother returned home from the hospital, Lyalya told her what had happened. After Beria's arrest, Lyalya's mother also filed the following statement with the prosecutor. I include it at such length because it has not been published in English before, and the (mostly male) historians of this period have largely glossed over Beria's sexual crimes, treating them either as a salacious footnote or not worthy of serious scholarly inquiry.

I went with Sarkisov and my daughter in his car. Beria met us at the mansion and introduced himself. He said not to worry, that all will be well, and began inviting us to the table, which was laid with food and wine. I refused and said to him, "So it was you who raped my daughter?" Then he turned to my daughter and said, "Is that really what happened, Lyalya? . . . I told you that you're not to upset your mother. You obviously don't love her." He said this in a seemingly affectionate tone, but his eyes sparkled with anger. My daughter was crying during this time. Then he said to me that he loves her and that he couldn't control himself. When I asked him, "Well then, you invited me here to tell me that you're marrying her?" . . . I, of course, didn't even consider marrying her off to him even in these circumstances—this rapist, this elderly pervert—but I wanted to understand his intentions. Then, when I started yelling at him, he declared that I shouldn't forget where I am and who I'm speaking to. Then I was unable to contain myself and began cursing him in all sorts of ways and slapped him on the cheek. He went pale and jumped up in a rage and began screaming at me [to the point of] losing his breath. That's when I screamed, "Just kill us both, here and now, in your mansion, and let them take two corpses out of here! That would be the best thing that you could do for us now."

Then he sat down and began repenting, saying, "You're right, I feel like a villain, a criminal," etc. At that moment, I felt like I was having a heart attack. When it passed, my daughter and I left. When we left, Beria told us not to tell anyone about what happened, that he'll talk to us again, otherwise things will turn out very badly for us.

I wrote Beria a letter in which I cursed him and said that I would write about all of this to comrade Stalin. That same night, Sarkisov summoned me to Beria's. Beria began telling me that I'm acting recklessly, that, now that things have turned out this way, I shouldn't further traumatize my daughter and that I would be finishing her off. . . . He said that no matter where I wrote, all the complaints would end up with him. That's how my daughter became a slave-hostage of his harem, for, as far as I know, he had many women . . .

In her statement, Lyalya described what happened next.

They didn't bother us for some time. We were afraid to send complaints anywhere about what had happened. Then Sarkisov started coming to get me, but we hid, turned off the lights, locked the door, but Sarkisov, threatening me with a weapon, forced me to visit Beria, with whom I had to live. In 1950, I became pregnant from him. Beria demanded that I have an abortion. Sarkisov demanded this of my mother, but she slapped him. He gave her money for an abortion, but I didn't get an abortion and my mother said that if they tried to force me, then she would write to Stalin or go and scream in the streets and they could do what they wanted with her. Afterward, Beria demanded that I send the child off to some village but I refused.

Having raped me, Beria crippled my entire life.

To investigate, interrogate, and prosecute a man of Beria's stature, the Presidium brought in a storied prosecutor. Roman Rudenko had represented Russia at the Nuremberg trials. He personally questioned Beria and the wooden transcriptions of these interrogations covered much ground, including Beria's many "cohabitants" and "intimate connections" with multiple women, which one witness described as "live goods" supplied to the mansion on Kachalov Street.[17] Or, as Beria puts it, "delivered to me." At one point Rudenko forced Beria to admit that he had been treated for syphilis in 1943. He asked Beria why his office was stocked with expensive imported lingerie. Beria said they were gifts for his wife, sister, and Lyalya Drozdova.

Rudenko also questioned Beria specifically about his many victims. After reading Chizhova's statement into the record, Rudenko asked Beria if he had raped her. "I deny the testimony of the rape of Chizhova by me, and that I made her drunk," Beria responded. "I do not deny that she was in my mansion more than once and that I had an intimate connection with her."

Beria responded similarly to Rudenko's questions about the testimony of Lyalya Drozdova.

> QUESTION: Was the old man in the pince-nez you?
> ANSWER: Yes, that was me.
> QUESTION: Do you admit that you raped the minor Drozdova?
> ANSWER: No, I do not admit it. Drozdova and I had the best possible relationship. When she was delivered to me for the first time, I cannot confirm if she had come of age or not, but I knew that she was a student of the 7 [sic] grade ... What she describes in her testimony, how she was delivered to me, how Sarkisov talked her into it—I don't know about this, but I allow that she is telling the truth. I don't remember if there was a conversation about my helping in the medical treatment of her mother, but I allow that there could have been talk of this, but Valentina Drozdova did not cry.

Valentina Drozdova died in 2014 at the age of eighty-one. Many years later I learned that, when she was seventeen, she gave birth to a child, a girl, whom she named after Beria's mother. When she was in labor, Beria offered her a gift, anything she wanted. Lyalya, still a child herself, asked for a bicycle. Her mother learned to accept her daughter's status: elite apartments from the state, where she and Lyalya moved from their communal apartment, blunted her rage. After Beria's downfall, Lyalya married a black marketeer who was later arrested and also executed. A former lover of Lyalya's told me that this earned her the nickname "Lyalya the Coffin," as if it were she who had brought these men their bad luck.

Lyalya was still alive when I was living in Moscow and working there as a correspondent and I wish I had known who she was and tried to interview her. But at the time I, too, was trying to write about serious things—that is, topics that men took seriously. It never occurred to me to pull on the string that Emma had held out to me on that muggy walk through Moscow: What had happened in that frilly blue house where Beria raped girls like my grandmother?

HERO MOTHERS

ONE FEBRUARY EVENING IN 1956, NEARLY THREE YEARS AFTER HER father's death, Svetlana Stalina was summoned again, this time by Anastas Mikoyan, another member of the Presidium.[1] A black car took her to his mansion in Lenin Hills, overlooking the lights of Moscow. Mikoyan, an old comrade of her father, had known Svetlana since her birth, and she had always been drawn to his warm and maternal wife, Ashkhen, who had been friends with her mother, Nadya.

When she arrived, Svetlana later recalled, Mikoyan took her into his library. "Read this," he said, handing her a thick sheaf of papers. "Afterward, we'll discuss it if necessary." It was an indictment of her father's long reign that Mikoyan said would be read at the Twentieth Party Congress, which had just started in Moscow. He did not want her to learn about it from the newspapers, and so he was letting Svetlana learn the truth about her father before it was revealed to everyone else.

Svetlana sat for hours in the Mikoyans' library, reading about her father's many sins. She read how Lenin and Krupskaya had tried to warn the party about Stalin and how he had orchestrated the arrest and execution of loyal veterans of the Revolution on fabricated charges. She read about the torture her father's henchmen had used against the party's best and brightest and how her father's decisions nearly lost the war. She read about the incalculable suffering caused by the man who once called her his little mistress of the house.

She felt as though she should try to defend her father, but she knew it was all true. She had seen enough herself. And she knew, too, that it was good he was gone. Her father's death had freed her, and she could see that it had freed the country as well. The Soviet Union was changing all around her, slowly but irreversibly. Survivors were starting to trickle home from the camps; conversation flowed a little more freely.

Svetlana finished reading. The Mikoyans and dinner were waiting. In a few days, on February 25, Nikita Khrushchev, Stalin's heir to the throne, would read a version of what she had just absorbed at a closed session at the Twentieth Party Congress. Khrushchev's "Secret Speech" detailed how Stalin had monopolized the party, arrested and shot millions of innocent people, and built a cult of personality around himself.[2] That era, Khrushchev would declare, was finally over.

"There was no halting the progress," Svetlana wrote later, recalling this moment. "Progress pushed its way through, like bright grass among the flagstones. The same slow, unyielding process of inner liberation from the past went on in my soul: a liberation from my country's past and my own."[3]

The following year, she would change her last name from Stalina to her mother's: Alliluyeva.

Nina Petrovna Khrushcheva learned about her husband's decision to de-Stalinize the party from a brochure that was given to her at her neighborhood party meeting in central Moscow at the end of February 1956. Nina Petrovna was not pleased—not because her husband hadn't consulted with her but because he had framed the reign of Stalin as a betrayal of socialism. Khrushchev, the new premier of the Soviet Union, had vowed to correct Stalin's mistakes. But Nina Petrovna believed that the Communist Party didn't make mistakes, which meant that what Stalin had done as its leader could not have been a mistake, either. And even if it were, Nina Petrovna believed that publicly discrediting the man who had headed the party for nearly thirty years would only damage its legitimacy.

But as a doctrinaire Communist, Nina Petrovna did not protest her husband's decision. If steering the country away from Stalinism was now the party line, then her personal thoughts on the matter were irrelevant. She would continue to loyally serve the Party, just as she had for decades.

Indeed, it was Nina Petrovna who had taught the future general secretary of the Communist Party his Marxist theology, not the other way around. In 1922, just five years after the Revolution, she was teaching the history of Marxist thought and political economy in the Ukrainian coal-mining town of Yuzovka (later known as Donetsk).[4] One of her students was Nikita Khrushchev. "He was told to fall in love with strong women and so he did," their great-granddaughter, also named Nina Khrushcheva, told me. "She was his professor and he was totally in love with her. She was bright and interesting and was just really a very impressive person."[5]

Nina Petrovna idolized Nadezhda Krupskaya and Alexandra Kollontai, but she came from far more humble origins than those two pioneers of Bolshevik feminism. She was born Nina Kukharchuk in 1900 to two Ukrainian peasants in Vasilyov, a poor village in what was then Russian-occupied Poland. Still, her parents were comparatively well-off. They owned land, a house with an orchard, and some trees in the forest, while the rest of Vasilyov's residents worked for the local landowner for wages and, as Nina Petrovna remembered until the end of her days, the women made half as much as the men. As for Nikita, he came from a poor peasant family and worked as a shepherd until his parents moved to Yuzovka to take jobs in the coal mines.[6] "We were doing better than the Khrushchevs in Russia!" Nina Petrovna used to tell her granddaughter.[7]

Nina went to the country school, where she and the other Ukrainian children were forced to learn Russian. The teacher quickly recognized little Nina's intelligence and convinced her father that the girl would have better educational opportunities in the city. In 1912, her father sent her off to Lublin, Poland, to study in the gymnasium.

When World War I broke out two years later, it seemed to spell the end of Nina's education at the age of fourteen. But her father told his commander about how bright his daughter was and the commander helped arrange for her to attend an elite school for wellborn girls in Odessa. The year after her graduation in 1919, she joined the Bolshevik Party in Odessa. "She was poor," her granddaughter explained. "She was a very bright young woman for whom the future was only through Communism because otherwise she would be cleaning other people's houses."

As the Civil War raged, the party sent Nina to the front in western Ukraine and eastern Poland to work as a political agitator attached to a Red Army unit. Since she knew the area and spoke its three languages—Russian, Polish, and Ukrainian—she was assigned to sell locals on the Bolsheviks' utopian vision. She soon became head of the local Zhenotdel, the women's section of the party created by Kollontai. She was a gifted propagandist and her work earned her notice in Moscow.

When she met Nikita Sergeyevich Khrushchev in 1922, he was noticeably below her in social standing, even among the egalitarian Bolsheviks. He was a divorced and widowed Civil War veteran with two young children and a fourth-grade education and would mangle Ukrainian so badly that Nina Petrovna wanted "to fall through the floor."[8] Still, there was something about him she couldn't resist. He was mercurial and charming, full of energy and revolutionary zeal. Despite his lack of formal education, he was a talented organizer rising rapidly in the Party apparatus overseeing the mines of Yuzovka. And he was completely smitten by Nina Petrovna. In 1924, they were married and began working together at the Petrovka mine.

In a picture of the couple from this time, Khrushchev is a strong-jawed young man in a high-necked white linen peasant shirt, his hair buzzed close to his scalp. Nina Petrovna is in a sailor's top, her dark hair cropped short, her fleshy, bulbous nose sitting atop thin lips curled into a subtle smile. They are in the full blossom of youth and clearly very happy. Khrushchev was then working as a deputy director of the mine and half-heartedly taking classes at the *rabfak*, or workers' training program. Nina Petrovna helped to care for his two children, Yulia and Leonid, whose mother had died of typhus. She also worked full-time, teaching political literacy classes to the miners and lecturing on politics at the workers' club. "Many women came when I delivered lectures at the club," Nina Petrovna wrote. "It turned out that they were interested in seeing the wife that their friend Nikita Khrushchev had found somewhere else, not at the mine." Sometimes the women trailed her home, haranguing her for working—two jobs in one family, when there was still so much unemployment. Though she felt badly for the women, Nina Petrovna did not take these complaints seriously, seeing them as a sign of their poor political development, which it was her job to fix.

Nina Petrovna would continue to work as a propagandist long after her husband rose from mine manager to Moscow party boss in the mid-1930s and the family moved into a spacious apartment in the prestigious House on the Embankment. She continued to go by her maiden name and did not advertise her status as an elite wife. Even after the birth of her own three children (a fourth died in infancy), she was at work every morning at eight, after an hour-long trolleybus ride to the massive electrical equipment factory on Elektrozavodskaya Street, where she organized meetings and taught political classes. She spent her commute reading new books to further her political enlightenment and maximize her usefulness to the party.

The factory never idled, and Nina Petrovna's workday rarely ended before ten in the evening. Though Khrushchev's parents lived with them and helped care for their five children, when one fell ill, as happened often, it was Nina Petrovna's responsibility to shuttle between work and the hospital. She was perpetually exhausted, but she took pride in her work, and in the fact, as she wrote some six decades later, years after Nikita Sergeyevich's death, that "at one time, I was paid more than N.S."

After her husband's secret speech, things finally began to change. Millions of Soviets came home from the camps, most of which were shut down. The vast majority of political prisoners were rehabilitated. "Now those who were arrested will return," wrote poet Anna Akhmatova, "and two Russias will look each other in the eye: the one that sat in the camps and the one that put them there."[9] The secret police was reformed and held somewhat in check. There was a loosening of censorship and a flowering of the arts, which Khrushchev tried to simultaneously encourage and ham-fistedly control.[10] It was still a totalitarian system, one that now had colonies in Eastern Europe it held by brute force. But Svetlana had been right: the blades of grass were coming up thicker now. The Khrushchev thaw was real.

This was still the Soviet Union, however, and its leadership remained intent on reengineering society from the top down.[11] In January 1955, a year before the secret speech, Khrushchev delivered an address aimed at the party's young people. The audience was made up mainly of college students who had volunteered to tame the so-called Virgin Lands of Central Asia, one of Khrushchev's many agricultural fantasies.[12] But he digressed during the speech, as he often did, this time veering into another pet project of his: population growth. "Whoever gets himself a family, that's a good citizen!" Khrushchev declared.

> We have people who neither marry, nor have children after marriage. For the moment, we will not discuss why they don't. In any case, such people exist in our society, and they are taking advantage of all of our public weal. They will get old. We might ask, "who will take care of them when they can no longer work?" Of course, the answer is, those very young people who are being raised by our marvelous mothers with many children. That is why Comrade Stalin proposed to provide support for large families. At whose expense? At the expense of those who live without thinking about tomorrow.[13]

If it was not clear why Khrushchev thought the Soviet Union needed more large families, he spelled it out. "Our country will be stronger the more people it has," he said. "If we could add another 100 million to our 200 million, that would still be too little!"

Khrushchev's aspirational arithmetic often earned him ridicule. In 1957, he pledged that Soviet agriculture, still stunted by the war and the disaster of collectivization, would miraculously surpass American production of meat, butter, and milk in three years.[14] It never did, but his call to "catch and overtake" the Americans—*dognat' i peregnat'*—would become his signature expression of Soviet maximalism, much as Stalin's Five-Year Plans only ever officially took four to complete. And now that the Americans were having a baby boom, Khrushchev was intent on catching and overtaking them in baby production, too.

A decade earlier, in July 1944, the Presidium had issued a new family law, developed by Khrushchev, that was purportedly designed to increase government aid to pregnant women and mothers.[15] The law delineated the exact amount of monetary support a mother was to receive, including a onetime payment at the time of a child's birth, followed by a monthly stipend per child, to be paid between the child's second and fifth birthdays. It increased maternity leave and allotted pregnant women extra rations, a real boon during those hungry years. It called for building more nurseries and kindergartens as well as rest homes for needy women who were pregnant or nursing. Single mothers who felt unable to care for their children could hand them off to a state orphanage, which would look after their offspring free of charge until the mother felt she was capable of caring for them again.

The government framed the law as an act of generosity, but its real goal was quite different. In 2006, the historian Mie Nakachi discovered the original draft in the Soviet archives, along with Khrushchev's explanatory memorandum. Neither had been previously published. In both documents, Khrushchev was clear on the purpose of the law. He titled the memo "On Measures for Increasing the Population of the USSR."[16] In his mind, whether a woman wanted children was irrelevant. New children were needed for the future good of society, and so all members of that society had a responsibility to help its fertile citizens procreate. After the catastrophic bloodletting in the first three decades of Soviet rule, writes Nakachi, he felt "that all citizens must participate in the state project to replace the dead."

In November 1941, shortly after the Nazis invaded, Khrushchev convinced Stalin to introduce a tax on the childless, which he expanded in 1944.[17] After that, active-duty soldiers and officers, students (up to the age of twenty-three if they were women, twenty-five if they were men), and the elderly and disabled were the only people who didn't have to pay the tax. And because women were largely excluded from the military after the war, the brunt of the tax fell on women, who now had two fewer years than men to get an education before being pressed into reproductive service for the state.

Khrushchev also expanded the tax to include not just the childless, who had 6 percent of their paychecks garnered, but people who he felt did not have enough kids. He wanted to make abundantly clear the disapproval of both society and the government for the one-child family. Parents with one child had to pay a 1 percent tax, while those with two children had to turn over half a percent of their wages. The taxes only stopped once a woman had three children—that is, after she had replaced herself and the father of the children and added an additional person to the country's human coffers.[18]

For those who went above and beyond, there would be new, military-style honors. Medals of Motherhood were to be awarded to women who had five or six children. The Medal of Maternal Glory went to women with seven, eight, or nine children. The highest honor, that of Hero Mother, went to women who had ten or more children. The idea for bestowing state honors on women for having astounding numbers of children came directly from Nazi Germany, a deeply ironic twist given that the Soviet law stipulated that "the count is to include children killed or missing in action in the Great Fatherland War."[19]

The law kept in place Stalin's 1936 ban on abortion but did not go as far as Khrushchev had originally wanted: criminal punishment for those who made contraceptives without a license and increased jail terms both for abortion providers and the women who sought them out. He got his way in other realms. The rest homes for needy pregnant and nursing women were not created for women's welfare; rather, they were intended to monitor and control mothers so as to "'remove such phenomena' as abortion, infanticide, and/or abandonment," Nakachi wrote, quoting Khrushchev's secret memorandum. They were not rest homes but, essentially, reproductive prisons.

But Khrushchev's biggest innovation—the one that would change Soviet and then Russian society for decades to come—was the creation of the legal concept of the single mother, or *odinokaya mat'*. He drew a clear line between legitimate and illegitimate offspring and between official and common-law marriages. The former would be recognized by the state; the latter would not. This was a stunning reversal of one of the Bolsheviks' earliest and most progressive reforms. Nor would the state recognize children born of common-law unions as legitimate, another dramatic regression. Khrushchev's decree stipulated that only a marriage officially registered with the state "generates rights and obligations between spouses." And only children born inside such an officially registered union could take the father's last name and be considered his legal offspring. A mother who bore a child outside of wedlock would no longer be allowed to name the child's father in the birth certificate and her child would automatically get her last name. She also lost her right to take the father to court to seek child support, undoing yet another of the Bolsheviks' first feminist measures. Now, as far as the law was concerned, a man who provided the genetic material for the creation of a child was in no way responsible for that child unless he had been legally married to the mother at the time of the birth.

What all of this meant in practice was that the law implicitly sanctioned and even encouraged male adultery.[20] With the carrot of direct payments and the stick of taxes, women were encouraged to have more and more children, yet there were far fewer men with whom to have them. In the meantime, men were incentivized to marry and stay in their marriages, since the law also made divorce far more difficult to obtain. With so few men of reproductive age available after the war, it was not statistically possible for all women to have children if children could only be had within the parameters of a legally registered marriage. Some women would *have* to have children out of wedlock, including with men who were married to other women. Therefore, Soviet men's duty to the Motherland was to impregnate not just their wives but also women who were not their wives, without needing to worry about supporting the children they conceived out of wedlock. The state would take care of that. The state would be the father.[21]

The measures had their intended effect. From 1945 to 1955, Soviet authorities registered 8.7 million illegitimate births.[22] At the height of this phenomenon, one third of Soviet children were born out of wedlock.[23] Meanwhile, by 1959, only half of Soviet women of childbearing age were married, down from a peak of over 80 percent twenty years earlier.[24] The millions of children born to these millions of unmarried women began their lives with birth certificates that had a blank space where the father's name would normally be recorded. State propaganda encouraged citizens not to judge single mothers, who now became a common sight.[25]

When the 1944 law was first announced, Soviet papers crowed that it would "force certain women to take marriage and family more seriously," as if the cause of the Soviet Union's demographic collapse were loose women rather than two men starting a disastrous war.[26] Instead, Khrushchev's reforms institutionalized male irresponsibility. As the state began to replace absent fathers, the very idea of fatherhood began to dissolve. Parenthood became synonymous with motherhood. Even children who had legal fathers saw little more of them than the names on their birth certificates. Mie Nakachi also discovered a secret study, conducted in 1948 by a female party functionary, that revealed how quickly the law changed the interactions between men and women. "Male partners were abandoning women as soon as they found out about their pregnancy and beginning to go out with other women," Nakachi writes of the study's conclusions. (Single mothers interviewed for the study referred to these men as "male butterflies.")[27] Underground abortions spiked, as did the number of women who died from their complications.[28]

Thanks to the greater freedom of speech during the thaw, a wave of letters soon flooded in to newspapers from despondent women complaining about these "male butterflies." Some pointed out that the state had essentially legalized polygamy and called for "fugitive fathers" to be punished.[29] One article quoted the letter of a man dismissing the pleas of a woman with whom he'd had a child. "According to Article 29 of KZOBS [Code of Laws on Custody, Marriage, and Family], since the child was born in a non-registered marriage, I owe nothing to you or your child," the man sneered. "Extricate yourself as you wish. You are now an adult. No one asked you to bear children. Our socialist Fatherland will direct and raise the boy in the Communist spirit."

Soviet propaganda was trying to advance two contradictory messages: nuclear families were the best families, but men could do as they pleased and single mothers should not be judged. Not surprisingly, this created a hierarchy among Soviet women, with married women at the top, followed by single mothers.³⁰ Below them both were childless, unmarried women, who were largely objects of pity. The same hierarchy translated to children as well. Despite government efforts to normalize single mothers, their children still suffered discrimination.

In 1956, a group of prominent male cultural figures, including the composer Dmitri Shostakovich, pleaded with Khrushchev in the pages of the state literary weekly to repeal the law.

> As a result [of the blanks on birth certificates], thousands of tragedies have been created, ruining the lives of women who are now labeled "single mothers" and those of their children, whom people view as "illegitimate." We're not going to contest the purpose of the law ... but now, when 12 years have passed since the law, there's enough evidence to judge how it has been applied in reality. A preponderance of evidence speaks to the obvious, to the difficult and ambiguous situation in which the women and children to whom the law applies find themselves. [The law] splits motherhood into legitimate and illegitimate. The law contradicts our morality, the Soviet legal system, which has always protected the interests of mothers and children, and, finally, the very Constitution of the USSR, which affirms the equality of men and women, and the equality of everyone before the law. V. I. Lenin saw the full equalization of children born in and out of wedlock as one of the main victories of the revolution.³¹

But Khrushchev stood firm. Though his brief rule is typically seen as creating a spell of modest political liberalization for the country, for more than half of the Soviet Union, its women, his policies were a giant step backward. He not only embraced Stalin's parochial and conservative sexual and family norms; he codified and enforced them. The result was neither a socialist approach nor a bourgeois one; it was the worst of both rolled into one monstrous law.

The law also exposed the limits of Khrushchev's desire to return to "Leninist norms," which he had voiced in his secret speech. Lenin had famously called for the bourgeois family to end up a museum relic, displayed alongside Neolithic tools. The Bolshevik feminists—the ones Nina Petrovna so admired—wanted to liberate women from the drudgery of the home and enable them to plan their marriages and families—or to be free of them if they so wished. Her husband turned these Bolshevik ideals on their heads.

Lenin had once declared that "one cannot be a democrat and a socialist without demanding full freedom of divorce," but the thrice-married Khrushchev personally abhorred it.[32] His children recalled that, "for him, there was no greater tragedy than a marital rupture or divorce."[33] His law, which required divorcing couples to announce their split in the newspaper, pay a hefty fee, and go through mediation, was an echo of the Orthodox Christian laws the Bolsheviks had repealed. By the time Kollontai died in 1952, her ideas that love should be free and that sex should be destigmatized had long been abandoned by the Soviet system she had helped build. The party's official tone had become so puritanical and sexophobic that it would, in the words of one Russian demographer, "make Victorian England jealous."[34]

Yet the reality her husband wrought did not affect Nina Petrovna the way it did other Soviet women. She and her husband never officially registered their marriage.[35] ("In the 1920s, Krupskaya said not to," her great-granddaughter explained, "so it never occurred to them.") According to her husband's law, therefore, Nikita Sergeyevich had no legal obligations to Nina Petrovna or to their three children, who were rendered illegitimate by their father's diktat. Of course, as the first lady of the Soviet Union, she did not have to worry about this: her husband was too high-ranking for his law to apply to his own children. Nor did it seem to alter Nina Petrovna and Khrushchev's actual thinking on the matter. They told their adult children that marriage was gauche and bourgeois and did not attend their daughter Rada's marriage ceremony in 1949. As Rada's husband observed, "The idea of a wedding ceremony was absolutely alien to the Khrushchevs."[36]

Although Khrushchev wanted an American-style baby boom, he did nothing to make sure that Soviet women had anything approximating the time-saving conveniences that American women enjoyed. After the war, when returning G.I.'s filled the labor market, most American women went back into the home and became full-time mothers and housewives, an ideal that was heavily reinforced in popular culture. Soviet women had no choice but to keep working after they had children. To ensure that they did, food, healthcare, and spots in nurseries and kindergartens were still tied to a woman's workplace. Yet many of these services were either in short supply or totally lacking and the financial assistance that the government had promised single mothers rarely materialized.[37]

When Khrushchev became premier, he overruled the recommendation of fellow Presidium member Georgy Malenkov that Soviet industry should be shifted more toward light industry—that is, producing consumer goods. This move could have made women's lives significantly easier.[38] But because Khrushchev banked everything on heavy industry and the defense sector, food and clothing were chronically scarce. When Soviet women were not at their jobs, they had to spend hours waiting in lines, working personal connections, tilling dacha gardens, and even foraging for food in the forests to make up for these shortages. Nor did they have any of the appliances—refrigerators, washing machines, vacuum cleaners—that made running a household more manageable for their American counterparts. Soviet women had to buy or find food daily, since it could not be refrigerated. They had to cook it from scratch because they could not purchase TV dinners or cake mix. They had to wash the laundry, the dishes, and the floors by hand, often in crowded communal apartments.[39] America's postwar housing boom had created space for the expansion of new families. In the Soviet Union, despite Khrushchev's plans to construct fast, cheap prefabricated apartment blocks, housing remained exceedingly limited. There was hardly any room for all the new children and families Khrushchev had dreamt into being.

Nina Petrovna, of course, had none of these problems. With Nikita Sergeyevich's increasingly demanding job, she found it too hard to work and care for five children, including the two from her husband's first marriage. In 1937, after having her third child, she retired. The next year, her husband was promoted to party boss of Ukraine and the family moved to Kiev, where they lived in an elegant pre-Revolutionary mansion staffed with cooks, nannies, and drivers. Though Nina Petrovna tried to live as ascetically as possible, she did not have to strain under what sociologists would come to call the Soviet woman's "double burden." She worked neither inside nor outside of the home. Her husband continued his inexorable rise toward the apex of Soviet state power, and the ascent brought ever larger houses, ever fatter provisions, ever bigger armies of staff. "There were nannies, good medical provision," she wrote in her diary shortly before her death in 1984. "Bringing up the children was easy."

Nina Petrovna did have one job, however, and it was rather important. She was the first real and public first lady the Soviet Union ever had. If Krupskaya had refused to embrace this role, and Nadya Alliluyeva was too young and hardheaded to do so (or if Stalin had let her), Nina Petrovna was happy to play the part if that was what the Party required. Her job was to keep her husband's social schedule, to temper his drinking, and to rein him in when his chatter became embarrassing. And, most importantly, it was to show the world a friendlier side of the Soviet Union. In Khrushchev's avuncular embodiment, the Soviet Union professed to want world peace, not nuclear war, and Nina Petrovna was a key prop in this theater.

When Khrushchev made his first trip to the United States in 1959, Nina Petrovna accompanied him. This was not standard practice. "Stalin was very suspicious of anyone who took his wife on a trip with him," Khrushchev wrote. He recalled that in the Presidium it was seen as "unbusinesslike—and a petty-bourgeois luxury—to travel with our wives."[40] But Khrushchev wanted the world to believe that the Soviet Union had shed the darkness of its Stalinist legacy. His family was his proof. And so, on the Khrushchevs' tour of the United States, the American public saw the matronly, modestly dressed Nina Petrovna greet Mamie Eisenhower, who wore a voluminous ball gown and long white satin gloves. They saw her talking to farmers' wives in Iowa and riding through the streets of proletarian Pittsburgh, her simple face radiating calm and gently smiling.[41] The trip was such a success that Nina Petrovna began to accompany her husband all over the world—to France, Hungary, Poland, East Germany, Egypt, and Syria.[42]

When she returned to the United States in 1961 to meet with the dashing new president, John F. Kennedy, and his wife, Jackie, an international style icon, Nina Petrovna wore a floral robe that looked more like a muumuu, which did nothing to flatter her figure. (Her great-granddaughter describes her as "built like a bit of a dumpling.") With her greasy hair haphazardly brushed back and held away from her face by randomly arranged bobby pins, she looked like a Soviet grandmother who had just stepped away from stirring a pot of cabbage soup. "What I understood from her is that that was also a decision," her great-granddaughter recalls. "It was to show that we are homey, that we are kind, to change this illusion that Soviet power is unbendable. It showed the domestic front of Communists, that there was human life outside of this enthusiastic building of Communism."

After the visit, Nina Petrovna addressed Americans from the studios of Radio Moscow, in her lilting, heavily accented English. (She had taken English classes in the late 1930s and was determined to speak to the American people in their own tongue. Her husband always addressed the Americans in Russian, through a translator.) In the speech, which aired in the United States in February 1962, Nina Petrovna showed her old skills as a Bolshevik propagandist, deftly explaining Soviet nuclear policy. She also did something that Krupskaya and Kollontai would have never contemplated: she spoke first as a woman, not a Communist. If the party needed her to set aside Marxist doctrine and appeal to female, maternal solidarity in order to advance Soviet power, Nina Petrovna would do it.

In her high and pleasant voice, she declared that women the world over had a common interest: avoiding the wars that men make. "We Soviet women vividly remember the horrors of the last war," she intoned. "It came into the home of every Soviet family. Mine was no exception. That is why we in the Soviet Union fervently desire a life of peace and quiet . . . Let us sink atom bombs along with the other weapons in the deepest part of the ocean and live without weapons as good neighbors going about our peaceful affairs. Only then can every mother's heart be at rest about the health and life of her children."[43] Nine months later, her husband nearly triggered nuclear war by placing nuclear missiles in Cuba, ninety miles from the United States.

Decades after his ouster, Khrushchev is often portrayed as a joke, a fat and blathering simpleton who drank to excess and beat the UN rostrum with a shoe. But this obscures the fact that Khrushchev was a deft and wily administrator who just as often succeeded in making Soviet fantasies a reality. Unlike Stalin, he relished understanding an issue thoroughly, visiting the farms, factories, and battle fronts he oversaw. In the 1930s, he was in charge of building the Moscow Metro, an underground rail system whose speed and splendor continue to dazzle tourists to this day. He oversaw the launch of Sputnik, and though the Americans were the first to put a man on the moon, Khrushchev helped put the first woman, Valentina Tereshkova, into space decades before Sally Ride.

Khrushchev brought the full force of his bureaucratic and policy-making prowess to the problem of repopulating the Soviet Union. In the end, he didn't get the astronomical number of births he wanted, but he did incentivize a real Soviet baby boom. The measures he implemented demolished much of what was left of the legacy of Nina's idol, Alexandra Kollontai, and they radically transformed society once again, creating cultural changes that would outlive the Soviet Union itself and persist in Russia to this day. These reforms would make my grandmothers' lives and marriages in the postwar years vastly different than those of their mothers.

KHINYA AND EMMA

WHEN KHINYA ARRIVED IN KIEV TO APPLY TO THE POLYTECHNIC Institute in the summer of 1947, the Kreshchatik, the city's main avenue, was still in ruins. Two years after the victory, the grand boulevard, wide and tree-lined in the old European style, was nothing more than a long, dusty path winding through dunes of brick pierced by twigs of wretched metal.

There had been no school in the three years Khinya had spent outrunning the Nazis. Those years had to be made up once Khinya's family returned to Zhitomir in 1944. By the time Khinya finished the required ten years of grade school in 1947, she was not sixteen, like high school graduates were supposed to be, but nineteen. She had reached an age when strong young women were now being encouraged by the state to make new soldiers to replace the millions who had been killed in the war.

And yet the state still needed women to get an education and work. The Soviet Union was now in direct economic and geopolitical competition with the United States, which had seen no fighting on its soil after the attack on Pearl Harbor. The Soviet Union, in contrast, was entering the Cold War still ravaged by the world war, most of which had happened on its territory. In the three years between the Nazi invasion and the Soviet counteroffensive, 70,000 Soviet villages had been razed, nearly 2,000 towns and 100,000 collective farms destroyed. Thirty-two thousand factories and 52,000 miles of railroad track had been blown up.[1] All of it had to be rebuilt, and quickly, despite the fact that the Soviet Union had lost 15 percent of its population in just four years of war, including 21 million able-bodied men.[2] In the countryside, noted historian Tony Judt, this absence was especially pronounced. "The Soviet rural economy now depended heavily on women for labour of every kind," he wrote, "not only were there no men, there were almost no horses."[3] If the country was to recover, women could not stay at home as full-time mothers. But if it was to repopulate, they could not put all their lifeblood into work. To catch and overtake America, the state needed Soviet women to do the impossible: be full-time laborers *and* full-time mothers.

And so, despite the official pressure to procreate, higher education, even for girls, was usually a given in the lower-middle-class world around Khinya. Most of the girls she knew went on to university or technical college after school. There was one aunt who wondered why Khinya needed to learn anything other than sewing, and her father Moisei was skeptical about educating either of his daughters, but in the end he supported Khinya. (It helped, of course, that higher education was free.) Even Khana-Batya, who had never gotten much schooling and remained a housewife all her life, encouraged Khinya to get an education before settling down. Since women were still required to work, Khana-Batya figured her daughter might as well secure a better job by getting a "profession," as it was called at the time.

As for Khinya, she did not intend to let the chance of an education slip through her hands. She was good at math and science and she wanted to make a career of it in one form or another. The war had nearly derailed this for her.

When she entered the Polytechnic Institute in 1947, Khinya was surrounded by women. Most of her classmates in the chemical engineering department were women, though their professors were mostly men. She lived in the female dorms, in a crowded room with five other girls. One was even older than Khinya, a *frontovichka*, a girl who had fought at the front and commanded her new roommates as if they were her troops.

The pressure to marry was inescapable. There were dances with the boys who dominated the more technical and prestigious departments at the institute, and one of them began to court Khinya. With her curly light chestnut hair, round face, and rosy complexion—what Russians admiringly call "blood with milk"—she was pretty in a plain way. But she wasn't interested in anything but her studies. Soon, one of the girls in Khinya's crowded room got married, but, because of the postwar housing shortage, she had to stay in her six-bed dorm and her new husband had to stay in his. Sometimes, coming home from class, Khinya found the door locked. Her naïveté bordering on ignorance, she would stand there and knock until her flustered roommate and her new husband let her in.

Another one of her roommates, a Jewish girl named Sonya Ioffe, would become the nearest thing Khinya ever had to a close female friend. A tall brunette from Crimea, she was as charismatic and effusive as Khinya was stoic and self-effacing, and yet they became inseparable.

Sonya had been through her own share of tragedy. She and her parents had fled Simferopol at the end of the summer of 1941 as the Germans closed in on Crimea. They took an overcrowded motorboat across the Kerch Strait, where they caught a train to Makhachkala, in Dagestan, hiding under the treads of tanks and heavy machinery damaged in battle. Sonya's father, Mendel, was a sick man with bad lungs, so her mother, Bluma, worked to support the family while Sonya stayed with her father in a chicken coop, the only place they could find shelter. That fall, the cold, wet wind blowing off the Caspian made Mendel sicker and sicker. Twelve-year-old Sonya did her best to comfort him, but she was too weak with hunger to do much other than drift in and out of sleep, listening to her father's rattling breath. One evening, Bluma's scream roused Sonya. Her mother had returned from work to discover that her husband had died in the chicken coop with Sonya obliviously curled up on his lap. When the war ended, Sonya would learn that the family who had stayed behind in Simferopol—aunts, uncles, little cousins—had all been murdered by the Germans.

After Khinya and Sonya graduated in 1952, the government assigned them to jobs in chemical factories 1,600 miles apart. Sonya would be sent to Kemerovo, a dreary Siberian backwater, and Khinya lucked out with Kuybyshev, a historically Tatar city in the warm south. Sonya cried; Khinya was embarrassed by her friend's tears. But she did not protest when Sonya appealed to the authorities, who agreed to place both women in Kemerovo, puzzled why anyone would choose it over sunny Kuybyshev.

The summer after their graduation, the two friends packed their suitcases and boarded a train going north to Moscow, where they would stay with Sonya's aunt Bronya for a couple of weeks before heading east to Kemerovo. It was a visit that would change Khinya's life.

In the Ioffe family's modest apartment in the Moscow suburbs, Khinya met Sonya's cousin Yasha Ioffe, Bronya's oldest surviving son. Khinya's first impression was not a good one.

Yasha did not have a job. He had been let go from an overstaffed engineering post and it was hard for a Jewish boy to find employment in Stalin's Moscow. He lived with his parents because there was still nowhere to live, certainly not for single people without work. But he didn't seem to mind. He loved his mother and her fierce affection for him. He was tall and extremely well-fed, Bronya's culinary care depositing itself on his front and his sides and around his chin. He was garrulous to a point Khinya found pathological. He seemed to have an endless supply of girlfriends, whose flaws his mother confidently dissected right in front of him.

Khinya learned that Bronya had lost her oldest son, Monya, in the war. Now Bronya seemed determined not to lose her remaining sons to anything or anyone. Grief had turned her love for Yasha and his little brother into something possessive and permissive. Her husband, the much older Nota, was Bronya's shadow, hardly relevant.

Khinya was stupefied by the clamor of this family, so unlike the quiet introversion of her parents' home. There was something emasculating about how Bronya talked to her middle son: about him and at him at the same time, judging, berating, doting, constantly emoting. Khinya could not understand how a grown man could live under a stream of criticism and adoration so pressured that it would strip the bark off anyone's soul. She was relieved when it was time for her and Sonya to board a train going east to their new jobs in Kemerovo.

After eight months of working at the chemical plant, Khinya received a telegram: her father, Moisei, had suffered a massive heart attack. Khinya was able to get permission to go see him, but her parents had just moved to the far western edge of Ukraine, which the Soviet Union annexed after the war. She could only get there by switching trains in Moscow, where she would once again have to stay with the Ioffes.

While they were in Kemerovo, Sonya had turned her advertising talents on her aunt Bronya, telling her in countless letters what a nice Jewish girl Khinya was and what a nice family she came from. By the time my grandmother made her brief layover in Moscow, Bronya saw the mortifyingly shy young woman with curly brown hair and legs bowed from childhood rickets in a new and promising light. She encouraged Yasha to take their young guest for walks, to ply her with his raucous attention. When Khinya stopped back in Moscow again after visiting Moisei in Ukraine, Yasha's courtship continued.

Little by little, Khinya found that when the beam of his intensity was focused on her, it was not completely unpleasant. It's not that she fell in love with Yasha. Rather, she was twenty-five, which meant the time to find a husband and start having children was quickly running out. Yasha was Jewish, seemingly a decent, educated man, and men didn't grow on trees in Russia, especially after the war.

Khinya returned to Kemerovo and, after a few months' correspondence, Yasha proposed. Doing her part, Bronya had found Khinya a new job at a nearby Moscow water plant. On July 1, 1954, Khinya and Yasha went down to the local city council and registered their marriage. On the way home from the registrar's office, they passed some young boys playing soccer. When the ball went astray and landed at Yasha's feet, he decided to show off for his bride and kick the ball back onto the field. Instead, he launched it confidently and squarely into Khinya's back.

After the war, Emma finally had a chance to breathe. As she finished her high school years, she shared the hope she felt all around her: that a people victorious would be a people rewarded—with food, with housing, with freedom, or, at the very least, a lifting of the blanket of fear that had suffocated every human interaction. Now eighteen, Emma was proud of herself. She had survived the war and she was determined to live a good life, an interesting life, a life of the mind. She would hobnob with the actors and artists of the Moscow intelligentsia and enjoy what she was coming to recognize as her extravagant beauty. She was in no rush to marry.

Many of Emma's friends had decided to study literature at Moscow State University, and Emma wanted to join them—a dream her pragmatic mother Riva promptly quashed. Her daughter, Riva decided, would be a doctor and have a good, steady job, just as she did. Although Emma cried and fought her mother, she discovered that she liked medical school more than she expected. She loved the beautiful drawings of the flayed human body, the coral-colored muscles tethered to bones by the white ribbons of tendons. The Latin names slotted themselves easily into her memory, and she imagined she was studying a kind of ancient literature. She found an unexpected happiness as she sat in the Lenin Library, its severe and angular gray columns staring down the frilly red walls of the Kremlin across the street.

January 13, 1953, sent her careening back to earth. It was the winter break in Emma's first year of medical school, a chance for her to spend time with her literary friends. One of them handed her a copy of that day's *Pravda*. "Dastardly Spies and Murderers Under the Masks of Professor-Doctors," a front-page headline blared. The article announced the arrest of nine doctors, most with obviously Jewish last names. Even Stalin's personal doctor was thrown in jail, though he wasn't actually Jewish. They all stood accused of having killed two of Stalin's deputies. Stunned, Emma skimmed the rest of the article. It was all delirious nonsense—allegations that the doctors had been "contract killers" hired by American and British intelligence agencies through a "Jewish bourgeois" charity to poison the Soviet high command. The article ended with a call to the Soviet people to "squash" these Jewish doctors "like disgusting snakes."

Emma's friends tried to reassure her. They were a humanistic, independent bunch and told her it couldn't be true, even if—*especially if*—it had been on the front page of *Pravda*. But Emma knew that this was how the Terror had started in 1936: arrests and condemnations in the press followed by a call for the Soviet people to vigilantly root out enemies of the people. And it had ended with millions of people disappearing forever. One wave had crested and ebbed with the war, leaving the Bruk family largely unscathed. Another, smaller one caught people like her uncle Efim just as they were finishing their ten-year sentences in 1948. Was this the beginning of yet another wave? Was this what awaited them now: a Black Maria, then a bullet in the head or a cattle car to the Gulag?

For Soviet Jews like Emma and her family, the postwar years were especially precarious. During the war, Stalin had turned Hitler's anti-Semitism to his advantage. He formed the Jewish Anti-Fascist Committee and enlisted prominent Soviet Jewish cultural figures to raise money from American Jews. The committee helped raise some $45 million for the war effort. But when the fighting was over, Stalin no longer needed their assistance. And although he supported the creation of the Jewish state in Palestine—mostly because it was a way to rob the British of another colony—Israel's existence made Soviet Jews, in Stalin's paranoid mind, a potential vehicle for foreign influence.[4] His suspicions were only confirmed by the excitement with which traumatized Soviet Jews celebrated Israel's independence and embraced their rediscovered Jewishness in the wake of the Holocaust.

The final straw seemed to be the arrival of Israel's first ambassador to the Soviet Union in September 1948. Golda Meyerson—she would soon shorten her last name to Meir—had been born in the Pale of Settlement before her family emigrated to the United States. Shortly after her arrival in Moscow, she attended Shabbat services at the old Choral Synagogue, not far from the Kremlin. Tens of thousands of Moscow's Jews spontaneously gathered outside, chanting her name. They gathered again on Rosh Hashanah, and again on Yom Kippur, when they followed Meir and her embassy entourage down the streets of the capital chanting, "Next year in Jerusalem!"[5]

On November 7, 1948, the Russian Foreign Ministry invited foreign ambassadors to a reception marking the anniversary of the Bolshevik Revolution. Polina Zhemchuzhina, the wife of Foreign Minister

Vyacheslav Molotov, buttonholed Meir and began speaking to her in fluent Yiddish. Surprised, Meir asked Zhemchuzhina how she knew the language. "*Ich bin a Yiddishe Tochter!*" Zhemchuzhina replied.[6] "I am a Jewish daughter!"

Born Pearl Karpovskaya ("Zhemchuzhina" means "pearl" in Russian) to a Jewish tailor in eastern Ukraine, Zhemchuzhina's siblings had left the Pale for Palestine and America, but she stayed and joined the Bolsheviks in 1918. During the Russian Civil War, she served as a political commissar in the Red Army. Her husband became one of Stalin's key adjutants, but Zhemchuzhina was a powerful figure in her own right—at least as much as a woman could be during Stalin's time. At one point she ran Soviet fisheries and oversaw Soviet perfume production and was one of the few visible women functionaries at the top. She was also close with Nadezhda Alliluyeva, Stalin's second wife, having tried, unsuccessfully, to soothe her on the night of her suicide.[7]

Zhemchuzhina was a committed Communist, yet the Holocaust and the founding of Israel had moved something in her as it had for many Soviet Jews. Communism and assimilation had promised an end to the anti-Semitism to which their forefathers had been subjected, but the Holocaust, in which many of them lost dozens of family members, reminded them that the world would never see them as anything but Jews. Meir recalled in her memoirs that when Zhemchuzhina bid her goodbye at the reception, she had tears in her eyes. "If everything goes well with you," she said, "it will go well for all Jews everywhere."

This shift among Soviet Jews was not lost on Stalin. He instantly shot down Israel's request that his government allow Soviet Jews to emigrate. He disbanded the Jewish Anti-Fascist Committee and the secret police began rounding up its remaining members.[8] In January 1949, less than two months after that fateful reception, Zhemchuzhina was arrested and charged with promiscuity, debauchery, and harboring Zionist sympathies. (Two men who worked for her "confessed" to having sex with her.)[9] Her husband kept silent, not knowing if he should be loyal to Stalin or to the wife he loved to distraction.

Soon, attacks surfaced in the press against "rootless cosmopolitans"—updated Soviet-speak for "wandering Jew." Stalin encouraged the purging of Jews from the sciences, the arts, and many other fields and demanded the institution of strict Jewish quotas.[10] Scores of Jewish scientists, writers, musicians, cultural critics, journalists, actors, playwrights, and poets—as well as Party functionaries—were arrested, tortured, and killed. In the summer of 1952, a dozen members of the Jewish Anti-Fascist Committee were tried in secret and condemned to death.

One of them was Boris Shimeliovich, the chief doctor of Moscow's hallowed Botkin Hospital. Six months later, the *Pravda* article announcing the arrests of the "doctor-murderers" said that Shimeliovich had been their ringleader, a modern twist on the centuries-old blood libel. The state was building a chain of guilt by association, and there was only one way to deal with the guilty, as the newspaper had said: crush them like disgusting snakes.

The arrests of prominent Jews terrified Riva, and by 1953, the walls started closing in. Riva worked at a school in the suburbs of Moscow and moonlighted at an infectious diseases unit at the nearby pediatric clinic. Formerly grateful parents began pulling their children from Riva's care, convinced this Jewish doctor was poisoning them. By the end of January, she was out of a job. In early February, she visited her best friend from medical school, an ethnic Russian woman named Alexandra Kuzmina, and spilled out her sorrows. "But you know, Riva," Alexandra finally said, "there's no smoke without fire."

There it was. For so many years, Riva had thought there was no difference between them. They were both doctors, modern Soviet women of science, but now the government had drawn a line between them and her friend had quickly accepted it. Alexandra had known her for decades, but if Riva were arrested and accused of poisoning her patients, would Alexandra believe there had been fire there, too? Did she believe it now?

Riva got up and left the room. Somehow she made it home, resolving en route that she would never speak to Alexandra again. At home, she collapsed into bed. Isaak took one look at her and called his kids. They were to watch her around the clock lest their mother kill herself.

At the time, Emma was still in her first year of medical school at Moscow State University. That winter the new semester began with a meeting of the Komsomol. Like most college students, Emma was a member. She sat in the amphitheater as one by one, Komsomol functionaries took to the podium to denounce the doctor-murderers who had stained their white coats with the blood of innocents. "We don't need doctors like Shpinel or Bruk," said one, listing Emma and a few other Jewish students in the class by name. "We need doctors like Vanya Smirnov!"

Emma looked around the auditorium. No one looked at her or at Nora Shpinel or at poor Vanya Smirnov, who had been singled out not for his scholarly aptitude—he had come back shattered from the front and was unable to remember much of the medical Latin—but for his most Russian of names. "It felt like the end of the world," Emma would remember decades later. There were rumors now that the Jewish doctors arrested in January would be hanged in Red Square, that Stalin was getting ready to deport all the Soviet Union's Jews to camps in Siberia.[11]

There was no refuge at home, either. Riva wasn't eating or drinking. She wouldn't get out of bed. The pogroms hadn't broken her, the war hadn't broken her, the NKVD hadn't broken her, but Alexandra Kuzmina had. Emma's bright new world had withered and blackened. Yet, as she sat in that auditorium, no one said anything. They had all come of age under Stalin and knew how to make their faces betray none of what was in their thoughts.

When Stalin died in March 1953, Emma's life changed in an instant. The Jewish doctors were quickly released, Riva came back to life and went back to work, and most everyone pretended that nothing had happened. The Khrushchev thaw soon followed.

By the summer of 1956, Emma was a twenty-one-year-old medical student. She had inherited her father's good looks and looked like a

Hollywood starlet, her thick auburn hair framing her perfectly symmetrical face with its big blue eyes, tiny nose, and full, red lips. Her curviness managed to be trim and athletic because she spent her vacations in the mountains, climbing the icy peaks of the Caucasus and Central Asia. Alpinism was all the rage among a certain subset of intelligentsia youth. They were *shestidesyatniki*, the generation of the sixties, the blades of bright green grass coming up in the warmth of the thaw. They passed around samizdat and discussed books long banned by the authorities. They went on extended camping trips in the mountains to get away from government spies and their snitches, away from crowded and filthy communal apartments, to breathe the open air and to feel the only kind of freedom they could feel in their country, the freedom of its vastness. They sat around campfires singing subversive, poignant poetry to the strum of a guitar. The young men who wrote and sang these musical poems were known as bards. They were the giants of these circles, the troubadours of the times. Emma had gotten her interesting life after all.

One summer day in 1956, Emma was in charge of picking up her cousin Dmitry—Dima—from the train station, where he'd just arrived from summer camp, and bringing him to Buzya's apartment. It was an academician's apartment, commensurate with her husband Shura's standing in the academy, with a grand piano and many rooms with elegant furniture. When Emma arrived with a suntanned Dima in tow, one of Buzya's nieces invited her to sit down for tea. Buzya's china was so fine that if you looked in as you drained your cup, you could see the sunlight through it. As they sat drinking tea, Yura emerged from his room.

Emma had first met Yura, a distant cousin by marriage, when she was eleven. It was right after the war, at a birthday party for Dima, who had been adopted by Buzya after his father was swept up in the Terror and his mother, Buzya's sister Eva, died shortly after giving birth. Yura was Buzya's only biological child and an eighteen-year-old college student at the time. His brown eyes sparkling behind his round, wire-rimmed glasses, he had recited reams of poetry while Emma sat there, slack-jawed. She had seen him again at Dima's birthday parties over the years, but he had never seemed to notice her.

Now Yura was nearing thirty, a brooding graduate student in chemistry with a long face, thick glasses, and dark hair parted neatly to the side. Emma again reveled in his wit, the quickness of his mind, his encyclopedic memory for poetry. Not only that, he was a scientist—the second most fashionable profession after being a bard. This time he noticed the beautiful, blossoming Emma, who sat smiling at him with her straight white teeth.

After that day, Yura and Emma started going to the movies and the theater. On long walks through Moscow, he recited poetry to her. It was the ideal romance in those days of lofty prudishness and lack of personal living space. "Our romances were mainly the promenading and conversational kind," the poet Joseph Brodsky wrote of the era. "An astronomical sum could have been accrued if we had been charged by the kilometer."[12] Emma fell in love with Yura and everything he represented. For this ambitious, curious girl from a simple family, he offered an entrée into the rarefied circles of the Soviet scientific elite.

In July 1957, Emma put on her one good dress, a light gray checkered frock with red buttons, and married Yura at the ZAGS, the government authority set up by the Bolsheviks to register marriages and other milestones. She hadn't wanted a wedding—her parents still dismissed the ritual as a bourgeois atavism—but this was the minimum now required by law. Aside from the Communist saccharine of the newly invented ceremony, it was a sweet and happy day. Yura was pleased with himself for snaring such a beautiful woman, and Emma looked forward to being the muse of a famous scientist. In an age of desperate women settling for what they could get, she appeared to have beaten all the odds. She had found true love.

LONELY MOTHERS

AS FAR AS HUSBANDS WENT, KHINYA KNEW YASHA WAS MUCH BETTER than most. He was a loyal family man. He didn't drink, didn't cheat, didn't hit her. He brought home his entire salary from his job as an aviation engineer in Moscow. And after they got married, he even tried to help Khinya around the house, which was not something Soviet men did at that time. The newlyweds lived in Rublevo, a working-class suburb of Moscow, where they rented one quarter of a wooden-walled room from a single mother named Marusya, who had just come home from the camps. The dividing wall between them didn't reach the ceiling. Despite the grand promises of Khrushchev's family law, eleven years later there still weren't nearly enough nurseries, and so while Yasha and Khinya were at work, Marusya watched their baby, my aunt Bella, for an additional fee. Then Bronya found out that her Yasha was doing housework and intervened. If she ever heard of her boy doing women's work again, Bronya threatened Khinya, she would make him leave her, kids or no kids. After that, Bronya started openly mocking Khinya's bowed legs and Yasha stopped helping.

Eventually, they moved into a new apartment in one of the cheap, five-story paneled buildings called *khrushchevki* after their mastermind began erecting them all over the country to alleviate the acute housing shortage. In 1959, they had a second child, my father Mikhail, or Misha, named after Khinya's father, Moisei, who had died just weeks before the birth. Khinya rose to become the head of the chemical department at the water plant, where she had anywhere from twelve to fifteen people working for her, all women. The lab worked around the clock, and until Khinya was able to get a phone connected in their apartment, one of the women had to run to fetch her whenever there was an emergency.

For a while, Khinya made more money than her husband and had a job with more responsibility than his. This meant very little at home, where her second job began. It was the balancing act performed by tens of millions of Soviet women who shouldered the "double burden." After dropping the children off at the nursery or at school, Khinya was at the lab by eight in the morning. She had an hour and a half for lunch, which she often used to forage for mushrooms in the woods near the plant. At five, her workday ended and Khinya raced to pick Bella and Misha up from school, where they had been waiting for her in an extended-day program. The three of them would then go to the store and wait in line to see what food was available, then wait in another line to pay for it. At home, Khinya cooked dinner every night. Yasha would arrive around half past seven and eat the children's leftovers while Khinya helped them with their homework.

Yasha's life was very different. He worked in the city and took the bus to the office. On the way home, he got off a couple stops early and strolled back through the fresh forest air around Rublevo to clear his mind. After he ate, he would sit on the couch and read the newspaper or watch soccer on television while Khinya cleaned up dinner and got the children ready for bed. Occasionally he would do the kinds of chores around the home that his mother deemed sufficiently masculine. He put a hole through the wall between the kitchen and the bathroom and hooked a hose from the boiler to the kitchen, which had no hot water. He pitched in with the potato harvesting and cabbage brining and with the garden in the small plot that supplemented the uneven supplies in the grocery stores. Sometimes he helped Khinya bring the laundry down to the neighborhood laundromat, though he did it rarely enough that Khinya and her mother, Khana-Batya, couldn't fathom what Khana-Batya's sister meant when she wrote from her new home in America and mentioned that her husband did the laundry after work. They couldn't imagine that, in America, there were washing machines in individual homes or that men might choose to operate them.

Khinya was always tired. She went to bed after everyone in the family so she could finish ironing and folding the laundry and rose before them so she could start breakfast. Sleep, she always hungered for sleep, but Khinya also knew she was lucky. She had a husband and two healthy children. She had married into a Moscow family, which gave her permission to live in the capital, while her best friend, Sonya, remained in Kemerovo. Sonya had met and married a nice Jewish man out there, but she had so many miscarriages over the years that she lost track after six. She figured it was because the chlorine plant where she worked had frequent accidents and the protective gear was so leaky. When Sonya finally managed to have a son, it was a welcome relief in more ways than one. After that, she had to pay only 1 percent of her salary—rather than the previous 6 percent—to the government.

Still, Khinya's life wasn't easy, and Yasha rarely made it easier. Once, when Khinya was washing the floor, she tripped and knocked over the bucket of soapy water. Yasha laughed and laughed but didn't get up to help. Sometimes he hit the children or said nasty, hurtful things to them. But he also took them for walks in the woods or pulled them on a sled through the snow or took them mushroom picking on the weekends, leaving Khinya to the drudgery of cleaning, boiling, and pickling the mountains of mushrooms they gathered. He managed to find the kids a bike and helped my father make a hockey stick and soccer cleats at a time when recreational sports equipment was impossible to find. He loved his children fiercely, sometimes too fiercely, but he was in their lives, which was more than many of the other kids in the neighborhood could say.

So many women were raising children alone. So many had husbands who were a legal technicality, ghosts in their own homes, fictions to their children. Even stooping under the double burden, Khinya enjoyed the privileged social status that having a husband conferred in the age of the *odinokaya mat'*, the single mother.

Most scholars of the era translate the term *odinokaya mat'* as literally that: a single mother. Others have rendered it as "lone mother," like a wolf. But I hear something else in the word *odinokaya*. In its less literal but more common use, the word means not single but lonely. These were women who, in the words of historian Greta Bucher, "had to perform each of her roles—worker, mother, and homemaker—as if it were her only occupation."[1] And as if it were her occupation alone. The state had promised to support them, but that promise had largely proven hollow. Meanwhile, the men became incidental members of their families, large children who needed just as much attention and feeding and washing as the small ones, their only distinction being that they occasionally brought home some money. My grandmothers had husbands, my parents had fathers, but Khinya and Emma were each in her own way an *odinokaya mat'*, a lonely mother.

Emma's troubles started on her honeymoon. After a celebratory dinner at her parents' house, Emma and Yura boarded a train that took them on their wedding adventure. En route, she said something that upset Yura, who turned to the wall of his bunk in the sleeper car and refused to speak to his bride for the next two days. When they disembarked at the newly annexed Carpathian Mountains and went for a hike, Yura lost his new wide-film camera, a wedding present from Emma. They had stopped to rest and Yura had hung it on a tree branch, where he promptly forgot it. When he realized it was gone, he was inconsolable, unable to focus on anything but his catastrophic loss. (They eventually found the camera.)

Upon their return to Moscow, Buzya moved her mother and Dima to her grand flat and gave Yura and Emma her mother's room in the communal apartment on the Garden Ring. After all, Buzya reasoned, a newlywed couple needed privacy. But their neighbors in the apartment were a noisy, nosy Jewish couple. The wife was a film censor who supported her husband's full-time occupation of lying around on the couch. Yura fought with them constantly because they interrupted his work. They, on the other hand, didn't see why they should have to walk around on eggshells in their own home. Emma, pregnant and finishing her last year of medical school, constantly played peacemaker.

In November 1958, their only child, my mother, Olga, was born. Yura used his wedding camera to take endless photos of her, experimenting with lighting and exposure. That seemed to be as far as his love for his child went. Like his mother, he suffered from debilitating migraines and could not understand why the baby insisted on crying and eating in the middle of the night, interrupting his sleep and condemning him to a foggy mind in the laboratory the next day. Did nobody care that he had a dissertation to write? He demanded that Emma postpone the feedings until morning. Emma cried and worried how she could possibly convince an infant to wait for its feeding, and eventually her milk stopped coming. At this point Riva commanded Emma to take the baby and move in with her and Isaak in the family house in Ilyinka, outside the city.

A relieved Emma took my infant mother and settled in with her parents. Riva fed Emma and washed Olga's cloth diapers on an old metal washboard while Emma slept and took Olga on walks around the village. Gradually her milk came back. But after that, Yura was firmly against having more children. Thanks to Khrushchev's policies, contraceptives were not really produced in the Soviet Union, so Emma had to have several abortions, which had been made legal again in 1955.

Shura had found his stepson a job at a scientific institute attached to a ceramics factory an hour and a half outside of Moscow. It manufactured toilet bowls. The work was comically beneath Yura, but after Stalin's anti-cosmopolitan campaign, this was as good a position as Yura, a Jew, was going to get. He tolerated the job, but every evening he went across town to the new Moscow State University campus on Lenin Hills to take night courses in the mathematics department. Emma was proud of her intellectually insatiable husband, even as he became less accessible to her and their child, whose care fell entirely on her. She tried to put Olga in a nursery, but the little girl got sick seemingly every time she set foot in the building. With no other childcare options, Riva retired from her job to take care of Olga full-time.

By the time Olga was a toddler, the only way Emma could get her into a crowded preschool was to take a job as a doctor at one of them, a low-paying position that was also beneath Emma's ambitions. She was now part of the Soviet Union's vast dispensary-based healthcare system, where a clinic and its doctors were attached to a neighborhood for routine care. It was dominated by women, who did the unglamorous work of tending to fevers and sore throats while the men performed surgery, did research, and ran the big hospitals.

Emma was at work every morning at eight, when she would start making house calls to any of the 1,500 patients assigned to her polyclinic. In the afternoon she saw patients who had made appointments. Her day ended at six, at which point she rushed home to feed and bathe Olga. Her salary was 700 rubles a month, which, after Khrushchev's 1960 monetary reform, was converted to 70 rubles a month. When Emma realized that a pair of winter boots now cost 74 rubles, she burst into tears.

In 1963, Emma completed her residency in cardiology at Moscow's prestigious Botkin Hospital. The government assigned her to a heart clinic on the other side of the city, where the Metro had yet to reach. She and Yura had just bought an apartment with help from Buzya, and the commute to her new job was two hours each way. After two months Emma quit. For a year she worked for free at the cardiac diagnostic center at Botkin and the family lived off of Yura's 90-ruble salary and the food Riva brought them. Emma mainly saved it for Olga and Yura, while she subsisted on pickled cabbage.

It was not the glamorous life of the mind she had envisioned, and her dream of being the muse to a great scientist was also coming apart, first slowly, then all at once. Yura's job at the toilet factory ended in scandal. He felt the job was degrading and that the plant was run by uneducated barbarians, who returned the favor by hating this impertinent Jew. When he figured out a more efficient way to fire the ceramics, his bosses rejected it. Then they fired him. As payback, Yura went to the lab in the middle of the night and broke every glass beaker and test tube on his bench with his hands. (In his fury, he left behind his papers—which the barbarians submitted without his name for the Lenin Prize and won, a slight that Emma would remember to the end of her days.)

After that, Yura was offered a job at the Academy of Sciences, the very apogee of Soviet science, but he turned it down because he wanted absolute freedom to do his work his way. Emma and Buzya pleaded with him, reminding him that, in their country, no one had any freedom of any kind; surely he could at least enjoy the prestige and perks the academy provided. Their entreaties proved useless. Yura took a position at another obscure scientific institute far outside the city, where he had no lab assistant and no resources. The staff found him demanding and obsessive, and the administration wanted to send him to a country lab in the Urals and give his plum Moscow position to an ethnic Russian. But Yura ignored them all and set up a cot in his lab so he could work through the night, powering through on tea and amphetamines. He sank into a depression. A stint in a sanatorium that treated the condition by subjecting patients to long fasts helped, but not for long. Emma tried desperately to dredge him up from the depths, but she also had a child to care for and her own job to do.

In the meantime, Olga was growing up, raised in part by her grandparents but mostly alone. She took the trolleybus and the Metro to school alone, came home alone, and made her after-school meals alone before descending into the comfort of homework and the books she devoured by the shelf, as well as the samizdat she found in Emma's underwear drawer. Her mother worked long hours and her father lived in his own galaxy of grievance, depression, and worsening migraines. Periodically he emerged to tell Emma that she was not a very good muse for a scientist or to berate Olga, who resembled him, for not looking more like her dazzling mother. Many years later Emma found some of my mother's childhood scribbles: stories and drawings, homemade birthday cards, and notes to her father. "Dad," she wrote in one of many like it, "I'm going outside to play. Lunch is on the stove." She was five.

After the war, "a heavy burden fell on mothers' shoulders: to raise children without a father," wrote Boris Urlanis, a prominent Soviet demographer and economist, in *Literaturnaya gazeta* in January 1970.[2] The state literary weekly had become the main forum for public discussion—or what passed for it in the Soviet Union—on issues of gender, family, and the country's anemic postwar population growth. Urlanis, who specialized in such matters, believed he had come up with an answer.

In his view, the people who most needed the state's support were not these overworked, underpaid mothers. After all, Urlanis wrote, "the whole country helped them." The real cause for concern was what Urlanis called *bezotzovshchina*, or fatherlessness. "No one can deny that the care of the government and public organizations are incapable of replacing a father," Urlanis said.

Fatherlessness, Urlanis warned in this essay, was a grave social ill. Children who grew up with only their mothers' income had fewer resources than the offspring of what Soviet society called "complete families." Children from "incomplete families" were also cognitively underdeveloped, Urlanis claimed. A disproportionate number of smokers and drunks and juvenile delinquents, Urlanis wrote, had been fatherless. "No one disputes the massive role a mother plays in raising a child," Urlanis argued, "but it is obvious that she is busy at work and consumed with worries about the household, she is in no condition to give the children enough attention." Fathers had to be part of their children's lives and they should do so by getting married and having children at a young age to maximize the time they spent with them. This was of utmost importance, Urlanis wrote, because "a man's time on earth is shorter" than a woman's.

Though Soviet propaganda still gave lip service to the old Bolshevik ideals of egalitarianism, the postwar Soviet woman was nothing like what Kollontai or Krupskaya—or even Lenin—had envisioned. Her revolutionary duty was no longer to become an active participant in a workers' society; it was to fulfil her destiny as a mother. Even though Soviet women formed the majority of the postwar Soviet workforce, their family responsibilities were seen—by their bosses and by women themselves—as more important.[3] Reinforcing this division, in 1974, the Soviet government introduced a list of several hundred professions that would now be closed to women.[4] Most of the jobs on the list—like loading a factory furnace or rolling hot metal—had been deemed too dangerous because they required heavy lifting, which was believed to cause miscarriage and infertility. But these were also well-paying jobs, and locking women out of them kept them earning less than men.

In the late Soviet period, according to Greta Bucher, women were rarely considered for advancement by the men who were increasingly in charge of factories, hospitals, schools, and universities. They were seen as preoccupied with home life, spending too much time at home with sick children or vanishing for months of maternity leave or simply too exhausted by the double burden to have real careers. Besides, really, careers were for men.

In the postwar years, however, it became increasingly difficult for men to self-actualize in the workplace. With the onset of stagnation in the 1970s, social mobility declined and salaries became leaner. After work, most men were marginalized figures in their families, like my grandfather Yura. They came home from work mainly to eat and sleep while their wives and children had entire lives without them. Now that the state had promised to take on the role of the father, fatherhood became, at best, an abstract concept.[5]

Left without purpose once the workday ended, Bucher wrote, men "studied, drank, or slept." Alcohol consumption took off in the postwar era, in part because the state, which had a monopoly on alcohol, needed the funds, and in part because, as Russian demographer Mikhail Denisenko explained to me once, it was the only antidepressant available. After the trauma of a horrific war, with few constructive opportunities or responsibilities, men turned to drink.

Paradoxically, in an increasingly patriarchal society, men had become nearly irrelevant. This became the overwhelming worry in the government papers: the women would manage—they always did—but what was to be done about the men?

In October 1969, a woman who identified herself as A. Ronina wrote in to *Literaturnaya gazeta* from her home in Leningrad. A retired teacher, Ronina was curious about a modern phenomenon that seemed to be reaching epidemic proportions: the feminization of young Soviet boys. She was very worried about her grandson Andryusha, whom she was helping her daughter raise. "I don't see in my grandson the signs of that precious boyish spirit," Ronina wrote. Andryusha, she felt, cared too much about his friends' opinions. He was too attached to his long, curly hair, which his grandmother wanted to "rip off along with his skin." He was too scared to visit Ronina when she was briefly hospitalized. Her letter was full of contempt for this sensitive boy, "so lacking in everything." "I read somewhere that a child is an idol sculpted out of his parents' disappointments," Ronina wrote. "How I wish that my grandson would help me part with mine, rather than providing fresh ones."[6]

In response, the editorial staff of *Literaturnaya gazeta* convened a roundtable to discuss this most pressing matter: the alarming erosion of Soviet masculinity. They summoned all kinds of experts, men and women, teachers and sociologists, psychologists and demographers, who found many reasons for this disturbing trend. For one thing, the teaching profession had become almost entirely female, and female teachers were guilty of two somewhat contradictory sins. Saddled with the double burden like all Soviet women, they didn't have enough time to devote to their students. But, like all women, they were also emotional creatures who couldn't separate their maternal instincts from their professional duties. "A mother is always a mother," the experts noted, "always a bit of a broody hen."

At home, the roundtable participants observed, the traditional roles—father-provider, mother-nurturer—had been upended. Women writing letters to *Literaturnaya gazeta* insisted that the idea of "a master of the house" was anachronistic; after all, while they were giving more of themselves at work they were also almost solely responsible for the home. This was no good at all, according to the roundtable, especially for their young sons.

Meanwhile, the men, overwhelmed by this reality, escaped into the easy-to-understand structures of the workplace. All too often these days, the experts remarked, one encountered the phenomenon of the "absent father," or *bezotzovshchina*. This phenomenon included instances when a child actually lacked a father "and those when the child has a father, but his presence in the house isn't felt." Whatever form it took, they wrote, "it is always a serious tragedy for a young boy." In part, the experts concluded, this was because a boy will always seek out some kind of male influence, and, in a time of *bezotzovshchina*, he was likeliest to find it among his peers in the street. There he would learn a perverted, ersatz version of masculinity: "strength, but the kind that is blind to the evil it does; bravery but without the bridle of morality; independence without responsibility."

This was what concerned the editors of *Literaturnaya gazeta* and their government bosses: not the plight of women but of men. Likewise, no one seemed to express any worry for girls growing up without fathers because they were seen as more resilient. "It has been reliably established that boys who are raised without fathers are significantly more prone to emotional instability," the young sociologist Igor Kon wrote in *Literaturnaya gazeta*, "and it is more difficult for them to master specific male roles and their corresponding style of behavior."[7]

It was clear who was at fault. No one could blame state policy in a state newspaper run by a totalitarian government. Others were reluctant to blame men, even those "male butterflies" who shirked their paternal duties; they were pathetic enough, and berating them would only emasculate them further. The problem, of course, was the women. There were too many little boys being raised by a mother and a grandmother rather than a mother and a father, and all that feminine influence was damaging. "It may be that in the personality of a boy who has grown up totally surrounded by women," concluded the roundtable charged with the dilemma of A. Ronina from Leningrad, "there really do appear cracks and fissures that are unnatural for boys."[8]

In 1968, as the sexual revolution exploded across the West, Urlanis published another essay in *Literaturnaya gazeta*. This one was titled "Save the Men!"[9] "Since ancient times, women have been called the 'weaker sex,'" Urlanis began. "If one considers their physical strength, this is accurate... But if you consider the question from a demographic point of view, then there is ample reason to call men the 'weaker sex.'"[10] Men's weakness, Urlanis went on, begins at birth. He noted that, even though 6 percent more boys than girls are born in every population, Soviet boys had a much shorter lifespan than Soviet girls. By the time they were fifteen, Soviet boys were twice as likely to die as girls. By twenty-five, their standardized mortality ratio had grown by another 25 percent. In 1968, life expectancy for a Soviet man was sixty-six; for a Soviet woman, it was seventy-four.

Many Soviets, Urlanis noted, erroneously attributed this to the war. But by 1968, all men under forty-two would have been too young to have fought and still their mortality spiked. "It means that the problem isn't the war and its consequences," Urlanis declared. "The problem is that, compared to women, we pay far less attention to preserving men's health." Since 1960, Urlanis pointed out, the growth of alcohol consumption had increased far out of proportion to the growth of the population. Not unrelated, he noted, men were far likelier to die in "unfortunate events" in the neighborhood. They also smoked far more than women, and boys were picking up the habit at younger ages.

Urlanis had a ready solution: pivoting the Soviet medical system to focus more on men. He called for Soviet men to receive regular consultations with their neighborhood doctors, to which they'd be summoned by government notice. This would be yet another responsibility for Soviet women to shoulder, since, as Urlanis noted, "the overwhelming majority of our doctors (four-fifths to be exact) are women. Consequently, the health of our men is in the hands of our women."

The Revolution, Urlanis concluded, had done "a colossal amount for women . . . providing them with special attention and care." Now it was time for the men to be nurtured by the state. "Women, take care of the men," Urlanis signed off, "for they are just as wonderful a half of the human race."

NOMENKLATURA

NINA PETROVNA FOUND OUT ABOUT HER HUSBAND'S DETHRONING after the fact and completely by accident. On October 14, 1964, she was vacationing in Karlovy Vary, the Czech town famous for its hot springs, with her good friend Viktoria Brezhneva, wife of Leonid Brezhnev, a member of the Presidium and Khrushchev's mentee.[1] Neither woman knew that, as they enjoyed the thermal spas, Viktoria's husband was leading a conservative coup against Nina Petrovna's. The Presidium, which had long chafed at his erratic style and his increasingly phantasmagorical ideas for reforms, had decided that Khrushchev would be replaced as the leader of the country by Brezhnev, the charming, thick-browed pragmatist from Ukraine. When the phone rang in the sanatorium room where the two elite wives were staying, Nina Petrovna picked up the receiver and heard the Soviet ambassador to Czechoslovakia gleefully recounting what had just happened at the meeting of the Central Committee and how overjoyed he was that that idiot Khrushchev had finally been ousted.

That phone call changed everything in Nina Petrovna's life. After rushing back to Moscow, she and her politically castrated husband were forced to move to a dacha outside the city where they were closely monitored by the KGB. Nikita Sergeyevich would spend his days gardening aggressively, listening to the Voice of America, reading the samizdat his children and grandchildren brought him, and meeting with the occasional dissident author. His successor rehabilitated Stalin and unleashed the government censors, stamping out the bright blades of grass that had come up during the thaw. The young dissidents who visited Nikita Sergeyevich told him what he desperately needed to hear: that he had been right to democratize the Soviet Union and that the usurpers were wrong.

But Nina Petrovna could not abide subversive books in her house.

Her great-granddaughter recalls her giving back the samizdat copy of Eugenia Ginzburg's *Journey into the Whirlwind*, her face pinched with disgust, holding the pages between her thumb and index finger "like a dead rat."[2] Even after her husband had been all but imprisoned at this leafy dacha where she hid her own agony and humiliation for his sake; even after many of his old friends and colleagues failed to send their condolences when he died seven years later; even after watching her son argue with KGB agents to be allowed to say something as his father's body was lowered into the ground—even when *Pravda* failed to write so much as an obituary for him—for the remaining thirteen years of her life, she still believed in the primacy of the Party. If it had been decided that this was to be her fate, then she must live it.[3] It was the conviction that had been the rudder of her entire conscious life, just as it was on that day in October 1964 when, after silently listening to the Soviet ambassador deliver his devastating news on the phone, she calmly turned to her friend Viktoria and said, "I think it's for you."[4]

For years, Soviets had no idea that the general secretary of the Communist Party and leader of the Soviet Union Leonid Brezhnev had a wife named Viktoria. The first family lived in a different layer of the Moscow atmosphere, along with the other *nomenklatura* families, much like the tsarist aristocracy had a century before them. Their lives rarely intersected with those of the people they ruled and at whose expense they existed. They shopped in their own stores and were treated in their own hospitals; they lived in their own apartment complexes and rested in their own resorts and secluded dacha communities. They ate in restaurants and special cafeterias where the Soviet public couldn't dream of going. They did not take the Metro or the trolleybuses but were instead chauffeured around in private cars. Their children went to their own schools and grew up to marry each other.

During Brezhnev's eighteen-year reign, the country settled into a long and musty period of stagflation: a stultifying combination of stagnant economic growth and rising inflation. Its hallmark was increasing deficits of consumer goods, and the brunt of these shortages fell on women. In addition to working, keeping house, and raising the children, the average Soviet woman now spent hours of her day waiting in lines, sometimes to purchase items she didn't even need but which could be sold on the black market or bartered for something that was actually useful. Clothing or shoes that didn't fit were tailored and hemmed and stretched and adjusted. Other goods were acquired by pulling on a thread in a tangle of one's connections—*blat*—a carefully calibrated game of personal politics. Some items could be purchased on the black market, but it was both expensive and dangerous, since private commerce was against the law.

Viktoria and the other *nomenklatura* wives never had to go on scavenger hunts to feed and clothe their families. The *nomenklatura* grocery stores had impossible-to-find goods at absurdly discounted prices. Their husbands, who had the exclusive privilege of traveling abroad, brought back Western clothes and electronics. It was said that the gold and gemstone jewelry seized from criminals and black marketeers were rerouted directly to the *nomenklatura* wives, who swanned around town in diamonds and furs.[5] They shopped at Berezka stores that took only foreign currency, which was illegal for average Soviets to possess. "The wives of top officials, for the most part, were as lacking in culture as the masses, but they had tasted the fruits of leisure, which gave them an incredibly smug sense of superiority," Brezhnev's niece Luba wrote of the *nomenklatura* wives of her uncle's stuffy reign.

> They had their manicures, massages, and hair done at home, and the only clothing problem they had was *l'embarras du choix*. They did of course worry about how to get rid of the blubber easily accumulated at state expense. Their narrow minds were, by and large, curious only about other people's lives, and their special joy was gathering in small groups to sip tea and dish out the latest dirt.
>
> It was traditional for them to take an interest in their husband's business and even participate in it. The little beehive buzzing around the Kremlin, with its passionate intrigues, included former wives, present wives, and future wives along with legitimate and illegitimate children alike.[6]

The queen bee of this hive was Viktoria Brezhneva, a train engineer's daughter from a village in western Russia. She was studying to be a midwife in the local medical technical college, a homely girl with short, dark hair, slightly bulging dark eyes, a fleshy nose, and an overbite that pushed her lips out unevenly. For much of her life, people would mistakenly think she was Jewish, which was not a compliment in the late Soviet era. When Leonid Brezhnev, a handsome, swarthy peasant boy from Ukraine studying at the agronomic institute, met her at a dance in 1925, he noticed Viktoria's pretty friend first. But she rejected him repeatedly, so Brezhnev reluctantly picked Viktoria, clomping all over her feet as they danced. Viktoria, on the other hand, was smitten with the good-looking, slick-talking Brezhnev. "He had thick, charcoal black eyebrows," she told an American journalist at the end of her life about what she first saw in her husband. "I could recognize him from far away by his eyebrows."[7] Eventually, he came to like Viktoria. He loved women, all kinds of women, and they were drawn to him, too, but Viktoria was devoted and patient and had lovely hands—swan wings, he called them. In 1928, they married, and a year later their daughter Galina was born.

Viktoria did not return to work after Galina's birth. She devoted herself instead to running the household and raising the children while her ambitious, gregarious husband advanced in the party in Ukraine, a path made smoother because its ranks had been so radically culled during the Terror. When the Germans invaded, Brezhnev was sent to work as a political commissar on the southern front. It was there that he ran into the beautiful Tamara Laverchenko, a nurse from his hometown who became his field wife. Brezhnev was by all accounts besotted with Tamara, who was nearly two decades younger than him. For a time, he considered divorcing Viktoria, but, in the end, family loyalty and the party's traditionalist line prevailed.

But Tamara was not his last mistress.[8] As his career took him across the Soviet Union to serve in high-ranking party posts in Moldova, Kazakhstan, and Ukraine, rumors of women—and sometimes illegitimate children—followed. In this, he was like the other *nomenklatura* men, who conducted business in *banyas* and at dachas, surrounded by beautiful young women. Many of them were given apartments, cars, and jewelry for their time and attention, expensive courtesans and mistresses kept at the proletariat's expense. In her memoirs, Luba Brezhneva recalled an evening in 1964 when her father, Yakov, Leonid's brother, brought her to a party at the dacha of Nikolay Ignatov, a member of the Presidium who had just helped oust Khrushchev.

> Next to Ignatov sat two young women, a blonde and a brunette, both remarkable. With her dark complexion, green eyes, slender, aristocratic wrists, and emerald earrings, the brunette bore a striking resemblance to a serpent. She wore a skimpy white dress, obviously from Christian Dior. I looked her up and down... She was so gorgeous that I truly found it hard to take my eyes off her. Knowing that I was Yakov Brezhnev's daughter, she smiled condescendingly.
> "Do you like her?" Ignatov asked across the table.
> "She's lovely," I answered.
> "That's what money and power can buy," he said. "You know what they say—the pretty girls go where the banknotes are."[9]

Because there were virtually no women at the top of Brezhnev's government, this was one of the few ways Soviet women could access the resources that came with state power. Women could not hold the posts the men held, but they could be their servants, their wives, or their mistresses, and they could profit off that.

Viktoria, like the other *nomenklatura* wives, tolerated her husband's womanizing in silence.[10] This was the way of all men, the women believed. Like tomcats, they wandered until they sated themselves, but they always returned home. They needed home. And home was Viktoria's specialty. Unlike her friend Nina Petrovna, she hated going on foreign trips or playing first lady at official functions.[11] She preferred to be at the dacha or in the family apartment on the grand Kutuzovsky Avenue that her husband had converted to take up an entire floor of the building. Viktoria managed its staff and sternly supervised the cooks in addition to doing her own cooking, forever pickling, canning, kneading, stewing, braising, and making her famous gooseberry jam, sitting for hours with a tiny pair of scissors and cutting off the gooseberries' little beards.[12]

On October 9, 1963, Svetlana Alliluyeva was recuperating in a *nomenklatura* hospital after having her tonsils out. She was thirty-seven, with two nearly grown children and two divorces behind her. Svetlana may have hated the system that suffocated her and wanted nothing to do with the *nomenklatura* elite, but she still enjoyed all its privileges. She had a four-room apartment in the city center, a dacha, a car, and access to a good state cafeteria and the best medical care in Moscow.

Wandering the hospital's halls, she spotted a slight old man strolling around in his pajamas and a robe, with thick glasses perched on his nose and cotton plugs sticking out of his nostrils. She couldn't quite place him. He was clearly foreign—there were many guests from "brotherly countries" in Moscow during the Khrushchev era—and she heard him speak various languages, including English, to the other international patients at the hospital. He looked to her "like an elderly Italian or a quiet, sorrowful Jew."[13] Something drew her to this frail man, but she wasn't sure how to approach him. Although she had studied English, she had never really had the chance to speak it, except the one phrase she was allowed to mutter to Winston Churchill when he visited in 1942: "How do you do?"[14] In her hospital room, she wrote out a couple of sentences in English and practiced them quietly.

The old man, she discovered when they did speak, was an Indian Communist named Brajesh Singh. As a prominent communist intellectual, Singh had been offered medical treatment in the USSR, which he had never visited. Thinking he'd accomplish two tasks in one trip, he set off for Moscow in the fall of 1963 to see "the Communist Mecca" and to get some nasal polyps removed.

As they sat on a couch in the hallway and talked, Svetlana realized two extremely pleasant things: that her English was quite passable, and that Brajesh Singh had no idea who she was. Unlike the Soviet inhabitants of the hospital, he laughed loudly and asked questions freely. When he inquired whether life had changed much since the death of Stalin, she could have wept. Svetlana was often plagued by what she called "'loyal-subject' effusions"—secret Stalin fans who told her in hushed tones that her father had been a great man, not knowing everything that had happened to her in the last three decades.

Meanwhile, the people whose company Svetlana actually wanted—writers and intellectuals—looked with suspicion at the daughter of the Great Murderer. When Svetlana got a job at the Institute of World Economics and International Affairs, one of her friends recalled, "every few minutes the door would open and someone would stare in with undisguised hate."[15] When they looked at her, they saw only Stalin. One evening Svetlana found herself at a dinner party sitting next to the dashing young poet David Samoilov. She was smitten, but he had other intentions. The next morning, after he had spent the night in bed with Svetlana, Samoilov called up a friend and shouted into the phone, "We fucked him!" He was talking about Svetlana's father. ("Never in my life have I been so directly shaken and captured by the tragedy of another person," Samoilov would write after their fling ended in heartbreak and rage for Svetlana. "And never had I such an intense need to run from a person, from the circle of her unresolved and suffocating tragedy.")[16]

Now here was Brajesh Singh, seventeen years her senior, who had no idea who she was. When she finally told him in one of their now daily hospital conversations, he reacted with a simple "Oh" and never asked about her father again. He was not starstruck: he came from a family that had been close to Mahatma Gandhi and Jawaharlal Nehru. "For him, I was just a human being," Svetlana recalled.

The doctors prescribed a rest on the Black Sea for each of them, giving Svetlana and Brajesh the gift of another month. By the end of it, the couple had decided. Brajesh would go back to India, lobby for a visa, and return to marry Svetlana. Things were freer now; it seemed like a reasonable plan. Having met Svetlana's teenage children and told them of his intentions, Brajesh left in December 1963, hoping to be back in short order. "We failed to take into consideration how quickly the political climate of Moscow could change, and how Communist parties in other countries, like weathervanes in the wind, instantly turned in the same direction," Svetlana wrote. "Besides, how could we have foreseen Khrushchev's downfall at the height of his world popularity? Or that our destinies would depend on it?"[17]

It was a year and a half before Brajesh Singh was able to get an invitation to work in the USSR, which he needed to secure a visa. Under the new, conservative Brezhnev regime, such international exchanges were now far less welcome. When Brajesh finally returned, in April 1965, Svetlana immediately noticed a change. He had been suffering from chronic bronchiectasis and emphysema for decades, and the effort he had expended arguing with Indian and Soviet officials had clearly sapped him. He looked paler, he coughed constantly, and his face was puffy. Still, he was here and their life together was finally beginning.

Brajesh moved into Svetlana's spacious apartment in the House on the Embankment, a constructivist behemoth across the river from the Kremlin. She quit her job at the Gorky Institute of World Literature, which she was able to do because she received a government pension as the daughter of the late generalissimo. But less than a month after Brajesh's arrival, Svetlana was summoned to the Kremlin for a meeting with Alexei Kosygin, the chairman of the ministers' council. The Kremlin had gotten wind that Stalin's daughter was making inquiries about marrying a foreigner. Sitting in her father's old office, Kosygin chided her for not working and informed her she would not be allowed to marry Brajesh. That would give him the right to take her to India, which simply wouldn't do. If they wanted to call each other husband and wife, he couldn't stop them, but the state would not officially register any marriage between them.

In the cold of Moscow, Brajesh's health declined rapidly. In October, sensing the end was near, he begged to be taken to India to die. Desperate with grief, Svetlana wrote a letter to Brezhnev. Instead of a reply, she got a summons from Mikhail Suslov, the chief neo-Stalinist ideologue in Brezhnev's government. "How are you? How is everything, materially? Why aren't you working?" Suslov asked her when she arrived in his office.

> I allowed myself to remind him of my letter: "Will I be granted the permission I'm asking for? We are both asking for it. Is it possible that a man's last wish cannot be granted?"

Suslov moved nervously behind his desk. His pale hands, with thick sclerotic veins, weren't quiet for a moment. He was thin, tall, with the face of a fanatic. The thick lenses of his glasses did not soften the manic look with which he pierced me.

"Your father was very much against marriages with foreigners, we even used to have a law against it!" he said, relishing every word.

"So what?" I replied as politely as I could. "He was mistaken. Now such marriages are allowed to everyone but me."

Suslov's whole frame gave a jerk and he almost choked. His fingers began to twist a pencil furiously.

"We shall not let you go abroad!" he said with great precision. "As for Singh, he may go if he wants. No one is holding him back."[18]

Svetlana would not be allowed to accompany him because there would be "provocations," Suslov insisted. As the daughter of Stalin, she would be mobbed by the press. Besides, they had had enough of Soviet women marrying men from friendly Third World countries solely in order to escape the Soviet Union. They did not need Stalin's last surviving child joining this embarrassing exodus.

A week later, on the morning of October 31, 1966, Brajesh Singh died in Svetlana's bed. It was the second death she had witnessed, after her father's. "The two deaths were just as unalike as their lives had been," Svetlana wrote years later. Her father's was tortured; he had died in the darkness of night. Brajesh went peacefully with the first light of morning. Brajesh had requested that his ashes be submerged in the Ganges, in the old Hindu way. Svetlana wanted to do this herself, to take the small urn and let her husband's ashes go into the waters of that holy river. She wrote to Kosygin and Brezhnev, and the next morning she again found herself sitting in Kosygin's office. This time it was decided that Svetlana would be allowed to take Brajesh's ashes to India provided that she promised to avoid the press and return promptly with the expiration of her visa.

On December 20, Svetlana said goodbye to her children and

boarded a plane for Delhi. It was her first time leaving the Soviet Union. She was forty years old.

For all her homeliness and domesticity, Viktoria knew how to appreciate the material privileges of being the woman at the very top of the *nomenklatura* hierarchy. She reveled in her share of diamonds and clothes, which apparently mortified her husband, despite his fleet of foreign cars. Once, a delegation of Viktoria's relatives visited Moscow from Ukraine, and Viktoria took them shopping at a special *nomenklatura* store. When word got back to Brezhnev that Viktoria and her relatives had completely denuded one such store of its wares, he came home and, without saying hello to his wife, shredded all of the day's purchases. He periodically carried out such "family purges," as he called them.[19] This didn't stop Viktoria, who had a handsome wardrobe and a house full of crystal and elegant furniture. Unlike Nina Petrovna, who was so disoriented by the rugs she was given by the shah of Iran that she sent them to Moscow orphanages, Viktoria kept all the gifts that her husband received from foreign leaders, stashing them in a separate apartment retained for this very purpose. She would periodically visit the apartment to view her possessions and rearrange the tags marking them for inheritance for her children and grandchildren.[20]

Her son, Yuri, born in 1933, did well enough. He married a nice girl and got a plum job with the Ministry of Foreign Trade and they both used Yuri's position to enrich themselves. While stationed in Sweden and ostensibly working on trade deals for the Soviet Union, Yuri, according to his cousin Luba, was doing a lucrative trade of his own. He sent home entire containers of Western goods: clothes, cassette players, and other luxuries that could turn a mind-reeling profit on the black market. His mother-in-law would come to Moscow from Dnepropetrovsk on shopping trips for clothes that she then resold at home at a generous markup.[21] (After his father's death in 1982, Yuri was forced out of government service.)

But the real celebrity in the family was Galina, Brezhnev's eldest, who inherited her father's good looks. Claiming to be a creative spirit, Galina drank and caroused and danced on tables. At twenty-two, she married a circus performer twenty years her senior and then, a decade later, took up with a magician who was fourteen years her junior, leaving her daughter to be raised by her parents. Infuriated, her father had the KGB seize the eighteen-year-old magician's passport, and, nine days after he and Galina had registered their union, it was returned without any trace of the now-invalidated marriage, a vanishing act only the magicians at the secret police could pull off.[22]

In 1971, at the age of forty-two, Galina met Yuri Churbanov, a middling employee of the powerful Interior Ministry. Churbanov was married and had a child, but when the opportunity to marry the general secretary's daughter presented itself, he quickly divorced his wife, married Galina, and began his dizzying ascent, rising in less than a decade to become the interior minister's deputy.[23] In the meantime, Galina had affairs with other men who used her name and connections to enrich themselves from the corruption that blossomed under her father's watch. One of them, the Bolshoi Ballet dancer Maris Liepa, a decade her junior, strung her along for five years, always promising to leave his wife while using Galina to get an apartment on a coveted street in central Moscow. He never left his wife, but Galina didn't seem to mind. Every time she went to the Bolshoi, there was a giant bouquet of flowers waiting on her seat and the orchestra conductor would bow to Galina first.[24] She was the inversion of all those young women surrounding her father's *nomenklatura* men: the rare Soviet woman powerful enough to hand out political and material favors to the men *she* kept.

If Galina inherited her father's love of love and pleasure, she also got her mother's acquisitiveness. Her cousin Luba accused her of using insider information of an upcoming government increase in the price of gold to earn money off the difference. (In 1981, Luba writes, Galina and her friend, the interior minister's wife, went in on a deal with the director of a jewelry store to buy up the gold in his store at the old price and resell it when prices rose.)[25] Galina was famous for her diamond jewelry and some have accused her of stealing the diamonds of a lion tamer in the Moscow circus, a cinematic heist that involved her uncle's suicide, a police cover-up, and her Romany lover, the singer Boris Buryatse.[26]

In the end, though, very little of what Galina or Viktoria had actually belonged to them. After Brezhnev died in 1982, the government informed Viktoria that she would have to vacate her beloved dacha, which was state property. "Of course it had to be like this!" she shot back sarcastically, wounded by the injustice of it. "I'm the one guilty for the war in Afghanistan!"[27] She outlived her husband by thirteen years and, in 1995, at the age of eighty-six, died alone in her apartment. Her children and grandchildren never came to visit anymore, she told an American reporter in her later years, because she had no more gifts left to give them.[28]

After the ceremony in which Svetlana handed over Brajesh's remains to the river, she found peace in her husband's native village, where his family continued to rule as rajas. She spent hours meditating and chatting with his relatives. She realized that she didn't want to go back to a place where she was the government's property simply due to the accident of her birth. Her son Joseph was eighteen and married. Her daughter Katya was a teenager. They would be fine without her. They both had fathers and their fathers could take care of them for a change. For once, she wanted to live only for herself.

After her visa was extended, Svetlana lobbied Brajesh's powerful nephew, who was a cabinet minister, and even Indira Gandhi herself, to grant her asylum. They turned her down, not wanting to endanger Soviet sponsorship in the Cold War while the Americans were supporting Pakistan. Defeated, Svetlana moved into the Soviet embassy in Delhi in early March while awaiting her flight to Moscow on March 8, International Women's Day. On the evening of March 6, 1967, while the embassy staff drank to the coming holiday, Svetlana told her minders that she was going across town for one last dinner with Brajesh's family. Instead, she hailed a cab, which took her through an alley and around the corner to the American embassy. Holding a small suitcase that contained her unpublished memoir, Svetlana walked up the stairs. The Marine guarding the glass doors took one look at her burgundy Soviet passport and ushered her inside. "Like a swimmer, I had reached the opposite shore," Svetlana wrote, "had touched the bottom and could take a deep breath."[29]

OLGA

SHE DIDN'T CRY WHEN THEY BURIED HER FATHER. IT WAS HARD TO feel the loss of someone who had been so distant. Her mother, Emma, and her grandmothers, Riva and Buzya, were a vibrant, active presence in her life, but her father mostly worked, slept, and listened to music, a ghostly but exacting roommate. It was as if Yura lived somewhere else, in the suffocating depression that had expanded to fill the void left by his broken career. He died one night in his sleep in Buzya's apartment in January 1975, at the age of forty-seven. Emma was heartbroken, but Riva was relieved that her daughter was finally free of the burden of a sickly and difficult man.

Life went on without him. Olga started her final year at School No. 12, the French immersion school right off the old Arbat. She gave tours around Moscow to French tourists, who asked her where in France she had studied, seemingly forgetting about the Iron Curtain. She dreamed of attending the Institute of Foreign Languages and becoming a French translator, but everyone told her it wouldn't be possible despite her excellent grades: the institute was effectively closed to Jews.

Things had gotten a little better for Soviet Jews under Khrushchev. But after Brezhnev ousted him, the Soviet Union sided enthusiastically with the Arab countries during the Six-Day War in 1967 and broke off relations with Israel. This fueled a resurgence of both popular and state anti-Semitism.[1] Jews of Olga's generation found themselves in a tragic, deeply ironic place. Few of them knew anything about what being Jewish meant. For some, like Olga, this was the result of their revolutionary grandparents tossing their Judaism overboard in the rush to assimilate into a new internationalist utopia. They had believed in its promises that if they were less Jewish there would be less anti-Semitism. For others, like my father's grandparents, it was because the state made it impossible to practice Judaism. Even teaching Hebrew was illegal. "Jewishness," noted the writer Gal Beckerman, "was a negative identity, a reminder of avenues that were closed."[2] Stalin had begun the process of thoroughly Slavicizing the government, which set the tone for every other field considered to be prestigious or politically sensitive.[3] Not only were Jews stereotyped as politically disloyal, weak, sickly, ugly, and deeply annoying beings, but many Jews themselves came to believe that being Jewish was, in Beckerman's words, "a handicap."[4] It was hard not to loathe yourself when everyone around you did.

Emma, still beautiful at forty, began to date. There was Andrei, a handsome and tall physicist. Olga liked his wit and dynamism, but Emma soon ended things, unmoved when Andrei got on his knees before her door. Then came Jerzy, from Warsaw. He was handsome and foreign, and he had spent his teens in the Polish forests as a resistance fighter. This appealed to Emma, who romanticized scientists and dissidents above all. Jerzy invited them to Warsaw, and both Olga and Emma had to sit through political meetings at school and at work to be grudgingly issued an official letter attesting that they were "politically literate and morally stable." Only with this certification could they travel beyond the confines of the USSR, even to a Warsaw Pact country. These forms weren't freely given to Jews at a time when many were trying to emigrate—a trip abroad was the perfect opportunity to flee—but the relevant authorities took pity on a widow and her fatherless daughter. In Warsaw, Olga gorged herself on cherry cheesecake and Emma bought a set of china with little blue flowers, the kind of luxury that was so scarce at home. But soon the relationship faded into friendship and Jerzy drifted out of their lives.

In 1964, Emma had started working at the Botkin Hospital as an unpaid grunt in the cardiac diagnostics department. It was there that she met her best friend, Flora Litvinova, a biologist and the daughter-in-law of former foreign minister Maxim Litvinov. In 1968, Flora's son Pavel was arrested after going to Red Square to protest the Soviet government's crackdown on the Prague Spring, in Czechoslovakia. Flora followed her son into dissident life, and Emma, who had been exposed to this world through her brother and his friends, followed Flora. She passed around samizdat and she and her brother did what they could to help the families of jailed dissidents. Emma also provided activists with medical care. Many became her patients and then her close friends.

As she immersed herself more in dissident circles, Emma had become a salaried cardiologist at Botkin and was transferred to its cushiest department, No. 7, known as the "Kremlin wing." The Kremlin wing was for the staff of the cabinet of ministers. Emma treated the cooks, chauffeurs, waitstaff, and repairmen who served the Soviet Union's ministers, while the ministers themselves were treated somewhere else, in facilities that were entirely unimaginable if this was the incredible care provided just to their servants.

At work, she met a handsome and widowed nephrologist named Misha Mendelson. Olga dismissed him as dim-witted and thought his son Kirill was even worse. Though Emma would eventually come to agree with her, she also knew she was lucky to have male company in her widowhood. One of the village women who took care of Mendelson's dacha in the off-season told her about how she had let the other women use her husband after the war so they too could become mothers. It would have been selfish, she said, not to let them have this joy.

In the summer of 1976, at the age of seventeen, Olga applied to medical school in Moscow, hoping to follow her mother and grandmother into the medical profession. It had been just over a century since the first Russian woman, Nadezhda Suslova, became a doctor, in 1868, declaring that she was "the first but not the last." Suslova had to go to Switzerland to get her medical degree. The Swiss had never licensed a female physician but were willing to try, whereas the conservative tsarist government would not even allow women to audit university lectures. When Suslova returned to Russia, the authorities had to be convinced to recognize her Swiss degree and she had to re-defend her dissertation.[5] Yet Suslova had been right: she was not the last.

After Suslova blazed a path through Zurich, a medical doctorate became the degree of choice for hundreds of ambitious and socially conscious young women, many of whom were radical revolutionaries. (Sofia Perovskaya, the revolutionary who was hanged for killing the tsar, was trained as a medic and had worked during the Crimean War.)[6] The tsar's government soon became concerned that Zurich and its medical school had become a hub of revolutionary activity for Russian women. To lure them home, it opened up classes to women at the Military Medical-Surgical Academy in St. Petersburg, where they could study medicine under the watchful eye of the Okhrana, the tsarist secret police. The first class of ninety women, admitted in 1872, consisted mostly of the gentry, with a smattering of the middle class and a relatively high percentage of Jewish women, unusual in a system that kept Jews out of the big cities and universities.[7] When they graduated five years later, just in time for the War of 1877, twelve of the women had died, mainly from disease and exertion, as well as two by suicide. But the survivors of the grueling courses were soon distinguishing themselves in the field of battle, performing major operations without male supervision. One woman doctor organized and directed an entire military hospital in the Balkans.

In 1897, after banning women from studying medicine again, the tsar's government relented and opened the Women's Medical Institute in the capital. By 1910, 10 percent of Russian doctors were women. It would take European countries years to reach even a fraction of that number. Only the United States, where 5 percent of doctors were women, had more total female physicians. By the time Olga applied to medical school, medicine had become a thoroughly feminized profession in the Soviet Union, where 70 percent of all physicians were women.[8] It had also become a hereditary profession, with the daughters of doctors far more likely to become doctors themselves.

Yet Olga didn't get in on her first try, mostly because she had applied to a school with a strict Jewish quota. Seeing the word "Jewish" on the fifth line of her passport, the exam proctor gave her a 3 in physics and sent her away. Disappointed but not surprised, Olga took a job working at a hospital while Emma strategized. Someone told her that Smolensk had a good medical institute—it was the same one my paternal great-grandmother Bronya had attended—and that their quotas weren't as stringent, so, the following summer, Emma found some cousins in Smolensk and moved Olga in with them while she studied for her entrance exam. She passed, and Emma found her a room in the apartment of an older woman who chided Olga for showering too frequently and advised her against cleaning her nether regions with soap. She'd had a friend who had died of vulvar cancer because she, like Olga, used soap down there.

For a year, Olga thrived. She flew through the exams and managed to join as many extracurricular clubs as she could. After a year, Emma helped her transfer back to Moscow, to the Second Medical Institute.

In the summer of 1981, just after Olga had finished her fourth year of medical school, a friend invited her to a party, where she met a young man named Mikhail. He was from one of the blue-collar suburbs on the city's periphery and had just graduated from one of the few Moscow institutes that admitted Jews. He was impossibly handsome, Olga thought; he didn't even look that Jewish. She concluded that she didn't stand a chance. Olga had been one of the few Jewish girls in her school, surrounded by blond Slavic girls, svelte as antelopes. She had learned to feel ugly with her big brown eyes behind her thick glasses, her brown hair and her round cheeks. It didn't help that her going-out clothes were also her mother's and that the two of them had to share them and coordinate their schedules accordingly. Nor did it help that she was almost twenty-two and was operating on a tight deadline.[9] All Soviet women knew that there was a limited window in which to snare one of the very few men on the market—and not to set their expectations too high.

Yet here Olga was, talking to a cheerful blue-eyed man who was tan, freckled, athletic, and seemingly interested in her. Mikhail—or Monya, as everyone called him—was a vast improvement on her previous boyfriends, and she realized she would have to deploy every Russian feminine trick she knew to fool him into liking her. It was advice she would pass down to me, the intricate web a Russian woman believes she must subtly weave around an unsuspecting male victim: *Play hard to get. Be easygoing and light on your feet, up for anything. Set yourself apart from other women by emphasizing how cool and rational and male-like you are.* (Women, she taught me, are never reliable friends anyway. They will always vanish on you the second a man appears in their life.) *Give him as much freedom as he can stomach. Be accommodating: What does* he *want to do? Hide the desperate glint in your eyes and don't scare off a man by admitting how hungry you are for marriage. You're too cool for marriage, unlike those other desperate girls chasing him.*

Olga was hardly alone in approaching marriage like a hunter luring her skittish prey into a trap. In fact, the problem was that there were too many hunters stalking that critically endangered species, the Soviet man. So Olga laid her snares carefully over the course of several months, not realizing that this man had already fallen in love with her at the party.

My parents were married on January 30, 1982, she, coquettish in a cream suit with a pencil skirt, he, with wide lapels and a wide striped tie, his hair combed out into the frizzy halo that had earned him the nickname Angela Davis in high school.

The table in the living room of the bride's family's apartment on Bryanskaya Street was set with white carnations and larded with the staples of a Soviet celebration: pickled vegetables and bowls of cubed boiled vegetables slathered in mayonnaise and generously called "salads." Vodka and cognac and wine from Moldova and Georgia were passed around. In the bedroom, furniture was moved out of the way so guests could dance the old Jewish way as the groom's cousin Tanya pounded out *freylekhs* on the black upright piano. Tanya was studying in the Sverdlovsk conservatory and had come to town for the wedding, as did her grandparents, Rakhil and Wolf Tartakovsky.

When Khinya, the mother of the groom, called to invite her uncle Wolf to the wedding, she mentioned that the bride's people had also come from the small Ukrainian shtetl of Salnitsa. Khinya wondered if

Wolf remembered anyone. The following day, Wolf called Khinya back with a question: Did the bride-to-be happen to have a grandmother named Riva? He remembered a young woman named Riva Weisser, whose parents had been murdered during a pogrom.

At the wedding, some seventy years since they had last seen each other, Riva and Wolf recognized one another immediately. While the guests toasted the newlyweds and danced, the two of them sat together and cried, remembering how Wolf had chased cows down Salnitsa's streets, and how Riva's parents had been killed in the pogrom, and how so very little remained of that world.

PERESTROIKA

TATYANA ZASLAVSKAYA WAS SICK IN BED WHEN HER PHONE RANG.[1] IT was a warm Siberian summer, the gentle northern sun gilding the pines around Akademgorodok, the town just outside of Novosibirsk that was home to the local branch of the Soviet Academy of Sciences. Zaslavskaya, an economist and sociologist, was one of its few female members. She picked up the receiver and heard the voice of her boss's boss, Valentin Koptyug, the head of the local academy. He was not happy.

Zaslavskaya hadn't meant to cause trouble, or even to become an economist. Growing up in Kiev, where she was born in 1927, she and her older sister were expected to follow their grandfather, a famous physicist, into the hallowed world of science. Zaslavskaya was good at math and everyone told her she would become a professor, so, in 1943, she enrolled in the physics department of Moscow State University. But a mandatory seminar on political economy changed the course of her studies. The subject fascinated her in a way that physics no longer did, so Zaslavskaya successfully lobbied to be transferred into the economics department.

There, she got an inadvertent real-world tutorial in how the Soviet political economy worked—or failed to. Like all Soviet college students, whom the government saw as a pool of free labor, Zaslavskaya and her classmates were sent into the countryside to help with the harvests. The poverty she saw in the villages astounded her. Her father was a professor of linguistics who had come from a peasant family, and he still had siblings and cousins on the collective farms, the *kolkhozy*. Through them, Zaslavskaya had heard that the farmers on the *kolkhozy* were no better than serfs. They had no passports or state identification papers, were not allowed to move or change jobs without a vote from the collective, and were barely paid for their work.

When her aunt came to Moscow to sell potatoes, she told Zaslavskaya about the ruthlessness of the government collectors, who took not just the farm surpluses to feed the cities but a good chunk of the produce the farmers needed to survive. It had been one thing to hear stories, but seeing it all firsthand affected her deeply. She began to wonder why what she saw and heard differed so radically from what she was learning at university.

In 1953, a few months after the death of Stalin, she started her dissertation on the financial relationship between the state and collective farms but soon discovered that the data she needed were tightly restricted by the state. There was only one option, Zaslavskaya decided: to go into the *kolkhozy* and gather her own. Zaslavskaya packed up her infant daughter, her nanny, and the provisions she knew she would need because collective farms were so short on basic goods. She brought a Primus stove and the kerosene to power it, a washbasin, food, and even soap. Still, she was not prepared for just how poor the collective farms were. Nearly a decade after the war, many families in the villages between Moscow and Leningrad still lived in earthen dugouts. Others spent the winters sleeping in the same quarters as their livestock. And though Zaslavskaya had brought her own canned food so as not to be a burden on the farmers she was studying, she hadn't anticipated that no one in the village would own a can opener. They didn't even know such a device existed. Zaslavskaya resorted to whacking the cans open with an axe.

In 1961, Zaslavskaya, now a working economist, wrote a report for Khrushchev, who wanted to know how much more meat and milk American farms produced than Soviet ones. She found that American farmers churned out as much as ten times more dairy and meat than their Soviet competitors, an unbridgeable gap. Furious, Khrushchev and the Central Committee revised the number down to three and confiscated Zaslavskaya's report and all her research materials. Two years of work simply vanished into the KGB archives.

She found relative freedom in Akademgorodok, where she moved with her family in 1963. Here, she was far from the scrutiny of Moscow and her boss provided her the necessary political cover to pursue her research into the dysfunction of the Soviet economic system.[2] She also became interested in sociology, a field that had been banned by Stalin as yet another bourgeois pseudoscience. Zaslavskaya knew the real reason. Sociology was feedback, the measure of how well government policies were working—or not—and Stalin wanted none of it. The field was partly rehabilitated during the Khrushchev years, and in 1970, Zaslavskaya established the country's first institute for the study of economic sociology.

By 1980, Zaslavskaya was fifty-three years old and an established economist and sociologist, but she was not content to coast to the retirement to which women were entitled at fifty-five. She could see the Soviet system was edging closer to catastrophe. To find out why, she set off on another one of her "expeditions," as she called her fieldwork. Her idea was to look at the collective farms of the Baltic republics, which had been annexed by Stalin in 1939. These farms were set up exactly the same way as the Russian *kolkhozy* but they were far more efficient and productive. How was that possible? Zaslavskaya wondered. When she and her brigades of researchers asked the Baltic farmers this question, the Balts told them, proudly, "We don't steal," "Our people are used to working hard," and "Russians are all drunks and poor workers." Zaslavskaya knew there was an element of nationalist defiance in those statements—the Baltic republics chafed under the brutality of Soviet occupation—but what she saw on those farms proved that it wasn't all bluster. She concluded that in the factories, the people were just as important as the machinery. If you couldn't incentivize people to work well, all the machinery in the world couldn't make Soviet factories function.

In the freezing early months of 1983, Zaslavskaya worked up her findings into an academic paper called "About the Perfection of Socialist Relations of Production and Problems of Economic Sociology." The oblique title belied the report's explosive contents. The Soviet Union, Zaslavskaya wrote, was no longer what it had been in the early 1930s when Stalin put in place the current system of highly centralized economic planning. Half a century had passed and technology had radically advanced. The economy had become far more complex, and bureaucrats in faraway Moscow could no longer manage all its intricacies. Moreover, Zaslavskaya observed, the people themselves were different. If the workers who had powered the early Soviet industrial boom were displaced peasants who could be cowed into subsisting, the modern Soviet workforce was largely urban, far better educated, and more sophisticated. They demanded a higher standard of living than their forebears, and some of what they wanted was not even material: they craved a sense of purpose and satisfaction from their work.

Yet the bureaucratic management of the economy, driven by fear and inertia, warped any and all incentives for people to be innovative or efficient. Soviet people, as Zaslavskaya later told an interviewer, had "no reason to work well, do not want to work well, do not know how to work well." Their only job was to meet arbitrary quotas set in Moscow, even if what they actually produced was defective or useless. Jokes abounded of factories filling their quota of, say, 10,000 kilograms of ball bearings by making one 10,000-kilogram ball bearing. It was not far from the truth and this system, Zaslavskaya wrote, was approaching collapse. To survive, it would need to incorporate elements of capitalism and undergo a massive overhaul, a wholesale restructuring—and here she coined a new term to capture what she meant: a *perestroika*.

The government censors were livid. How could a member of the Soviet Academy of Sciences, the world's premier socialist brain trust, call for an introduction of capitalist principles into the world's first socialist economy? They immediately banned Zaslavskaya's report, but her boss and political protector, Abel Aganbegyan, found a work-around. He and Zaslavskaya called a scientific conference for April 8, 1983, to which they invited 150 scientists from Akademgorodok and around the country. Aganbegyan made one hundred photocopies of the report, just under the quota for a print run that would need approval from government censors. In an effort to closely control the self-published run, he numbered each copy and distributed them to the social scientists arriving in Novosibirsk.

Zaslavskaya's report was a sensation. Its conclusions, obvious decades later, were earth-shattering in 1983. She was the first to identify the problem underlying Soviet economic malaise. The conference attendees were ecstatic. The discussions went on for hours as the specialists talked themselves hoarse. Everything they had been thinking or saying privately was now being shared openly. Knowing they would have to return the photocopies of the report at the end of the conference, some attendees copied it out by hand. Others, who were not lucky enough to receive their own printouts, borrowed copies and took them to their hotel rooms, where they wrote Zaslavskaya's words into their notebooks late into the night. Returning to their universities and institutes, these scholars brought Zaslavskaya's ideas with them, ensuring that, in the coming years, they gained wide acceptance.

When the conference finally ended, Aganbegyan—and his minders—counted the returned copies of the report, but there were only ninety-eight. Where were the remaining two? The KGB was called in. They searched Zaslavskaya's office and her institute, she later recalled, "was turned upside-down." Failing to find the two missing copies, the KGB began searching the entire USSR. In July, Koptyug, Aganbegyan's boss and the head of the entire Novosibirsk academy, called to inform Zaslavskaya that they had finally been found. One had been translated into English and printed in the *Washington Post* under the title "Novosibirsk Manifesto." The other had made it to West Germany, where the enemies of the Soviet people were reading it on radio waves that were broadcast deep into the Soviet Union several times a day.

Zaslavskaya was horrified. "It turned out that I, completely unwillingly, had 'scored an own goal,'" she told a colleague decades later. She was an ardent socialist, but like many *shestidesyatniki*, the people who had come of age during the thaw, she believed that socialism didn't need to be abolished but reformed, made more efficient and humane. "Despite my critiques of the social structures of Soviet society, I was absolutely loyal to the socialist system and thought it necessary and possible to perfect it," she said. "I wasn't thinking at all of demolishing or undermining it." Zaslavskaya and Aganbegyan were officially reprimanded for "ideological errors," and the stress and terror of everything that had happened turned Zaslavskaya's cold into bronchitis and then a bilateral pneumonia. Sick and exhausted, she was admitted to the hospital. It would be two months before she felt well enough to go home—and just over two years before *perestroika* became the official policy of the Soviet Union.

RAISA

RAISA GORBACHEVA SAT IN THE MASSIVE MAIN HALL OF THE KREMLIN Palace of Congresses, nervously watching her husband. It was the February 1986 Twenty-Seventh Communist Party Congress and Mikhail Gorbachev's first address to the forum as the party's general secretary. Under a massive image of Lenin, Gorbachev called for "a structural *perestroika*"—or restructuring—of the economy as well as a "*perestroika* of thought."

Gorbachev had been preceded on the Soviet throne by a succession of old and actively dying men. Through a long and humiliating decline, Brezhnev could barely speak or function for years, but he remained on the party throne until he died in 1982. He was succeeded by former KGB chief Yuri Andropov, who died fifteen months later of kidney failure at the age of sixty-nine. Next came the barely mobile, largely unintelligible Konstantin Chernenko, who, at seventy-three, was already well on his way to dying, which he did in less than a year, on March 10, 1985. Within hours, the Politburo, sensitive to the optics of appointing yet another quasi-cadaver to the top post, tapped Andropov's protégé, Mikhail Gorbachev. At fifty-four, Gorbachev seemed impossibly young and sprightly by comparison. He was the first Soviet leader to have been born in the Soviet Union.

Gorbachev differed from his predecessors in other ways, too. While they carefully hid their wives from public view, he brought his wife everywhere. The slim, stylish, and smiling Raisa startled a Soviet population used to seeing exclusively elderly and grim male faces at the top. An educated and deeply cultured woman, she made a strong impression abroad, too. In London in 1984, Raisa stunned British prime minister Margaret Thatcher and her flustered and intellectually outgunned husband, Denis, when she expounded at length about David Hume and English literature. "Raisa was completely different and unlike those we habitually associated with the Soviet system," Thatcher later observed.[1] "She wanted all of us to know," recalled the British Foreign Ministry officer assigned to translate for Raisa in London, "that she wasn't just another dumpy, head-scarved wife."[2] François Mitterrand, the president of France, wrote to Gorbachev that Raisa's "presence at your side has created a new impression of your country: one of charisma and culture."[3] "Thanks to you, the image of the Soviet woman is changing, both in our country and in the world," one Soviet woman wrote to Raisa. "She is regaining her dignity."[4]

Raisa was Gorbachev's obvious equal as well as his closest aide and counselor. From the earliest days of their courtship, he consulted her about his work, and she agonized over it as if it were her own. When they moved to Moscow in 1978 so Gorbachev could take up his post as a secretary on the Central Committee, Raisa stayed up every night waiting for him so they could take their nightly walk in the woods around their government residence. Since the house was bugged and the forest was the only place they could speak privately, Gorbachev used these strolls to consult Raisa on the day's events at the Kremlin, his bodyguards trailing at a respectful distance.[5] He particularly valued her insights on his advisors, their motives, and the quality of their counsel.[6] When Tom Brokaw asked Gorbachev in 1987 if he discussed "national politics, political difficulties and so on in this country" with his wife, Gorbachev said simply, "We discuss everything."

"Including Soviet affairs at the highest level?" Brokaw pressed.

"I think that I have answered your question in total," the general secretary shot back. "We discuss everything."[7]

While Raisa tried to stay out of view of the cameras when her husband was speaking, she was always there, usually in the front row, all nerves. "In any room, he has no more sensitive an ear than hers," recalled Georgiy Pryakhin, a Soviet journalist. When listening to her husband deliver a speech, Pryakhin wrote, "She becomes a membrane."[8] And if Nina Petrovna Khrushcheva only found out about her husband's speech to the Twentieth Party Congress after the fact and through a brochure, Raisa was an active participant in crafting Gorbachev's revolutionary address to the Twenty-Seventh. For weeks that winter, Raisa worked long hours with her husband and his speechwriters to develop and polish the speech. "Raisa Maksimovna was there practically the whole time, listening to our discussions and participating in them," Gorbachev recalled in his memoirs. "Her experience in social research, her work with university youth, and simply her knowledge of everyday life and female intuition proved useful. She chided us for ignoring the subject of the position of the family and women in society in the report and suggested ways to improve it."[9]

Few of the Communist Party members listening in the grand Kremlin Hall or the Soviet citizens watching on television knew that Gorbachev's speech was, to a significant extent, the work of two women: Tatyana Zaslavskaya, the economist who had coined the term *perestroika* and had become an informal advisor to Gorbachev, and Raisa Gorbacheva, the general secretary's wife. It was, in part, their words and thoughts that he delivered to the Party Congress on that gray February day when he announced that the country needed a *perestroika* to change itself or perish.

Like her husband, Raisa Maksimovna Titarenko came from peasant stock. Without the Soviet feminist experiment, she likely would have led a life only slightly better than that of her maternal grandmother, Anastasia. "Her life," Raisa told Pryakhin in a series of interviews that became her memoir, "was hard labor. She sowed, planted, fed six children. And for her entire life, she was silent." In the 1930s, Anastasia's husband was arrested and never seen or heard from again. "My grandmother died of sorrow and hunger as the wife of an 'enemy of the people,'" Raisa recalled with disgust, an unheard-of heresy for a Soviet first lady. Only when Raisa's husband became general secretary and she asked for her grandfather's file did she discover that he had been executed in 1937.[10]

Alexandra, Raisa's mother, was illiterate. Alexandra's father, like many peasant men, saw education as a luxury reserved exclusively for his sons. After she married, Alexandra took advantage of the free educational opportunities provided by the Revolution and completed LikBez literacy classes. And though she was a housewife, tending to their temporary living quarters in barracks and huts as her husband's work for the railroads kept them moving around the country, Alexandra was intent on educating her two daughters, Raisa, born in 1932, and Lyudmila, born in 1938.

Raisa's childhood was one of hunger and poverty. Her daily meal was a bowl of watery soup. At school, four or five students shared one textbook. They wrote in homemade notebooks with homemade ink made out of soot. She managed to graduate in 1949 with a gold medal, the highest honor available to Soviet schoolchildren, which gave her the right to go to any university without taking the entrance exams. She chose the most prestigious institution in the country, Moscow State University, where she enrolled in the philosophy department.

She lived just as ascetically in Moscow. She had one thinning coat and no winter shoes and became adept at riding the city's public transport by hopping the turnstiles. Still, the university was Raisa's introduction to the worldliness that would become her trademark. Raisa studied with some of the finest minds of the Soviet academy. She learned German and how to pepper her speech with the Latin aphorisms that people of her generation considered a sign of intellectual refinement. She discovered the vast cultural life of Moscow, watching all the symphonies, operas, ballets, and plays she could from the cheap seats, voraciously making up for everything she had missed in her childhood. She got engaged to a young man from a prominent Moscow family, but it soon fell apart.[11] Her fiancé's mother would not have her son marrying a simple peasant girl.

Brokenhearted, Raisa poured out her heart to the young law student she met at a dance and who took her on long walks around the city. His name was Mikhail Gorbachev, and when he covered his creeping baldness with a hat, he really was quite dashing.[12] Mikhail, for his part, had just arrived from the farms of the Stavropol region in the south, and he was struck, in his words, by Raisa's "aristocratic bearing and sense of pride mixed with reserve."[13] Raisa was the prettiest girl in the group, she had the best figure, and she took elaborate care of her hair, which, in the conditions of a Soviet dormitory and with access only to a communal *banya* every other day, was no minor achievement.[14] They were both country people, but Raisa had lived in the capital a year longer, and she moved through the big city confidently, his knowing guide to all things sophisticated.

After a chaste courtship of strolls and theater visits, Mikhail proposed. Then he went home to the collective farm where his family lived and spent the summer working literally around the clock to pay for the wedding. He wanted his bride to look pretty because Raisa, he recalled proudly decades later, "had an inner compulsion to look good on every occasion."[15] After helping bring in the harvest that summer, Gorbachev was able to afford a suit for himself and a dress for Raisa. There wasn't enough money for shoes, so Raisa borrowed a pair from a friend. In September 1953, six months after Stalin died, they wed in a ceremony so simple that they didn't even exchange rings.[16]

Raisa, who graduated with top honors a year ahead of Gorbachev, began her graduate studies in philosophy. He spent long hours on his Komsomol duties and his thesis. For the first months of their marriage, the university rector assigned them to different rooms in different zones of the dormitories. Gorbachev had to get a special permit and show the marriage stamp in his passport to visit Raisa's room, where the phone rang at 11 p.m. on the dot, demanding that the "unauthorized visitor" who had stayed past curfew remove himself from the premises.[17] Soon after they were given their own room in the university's new building in Lenin Hills, Raisa discovered she was pregnant. A previous illness had left her with rheumatism and it flared violently with her pregnancy. Her joints swelled up and she had to be carried to the hospital, where the doctors advised her to have an abortion. Raisa agonized over the decision but in the end acceded to the doctors' counsel. When the traumatized young couple asked what they should do in the future, they were told to practice abstinence.[18]

It was a dark moment in an otherwise happy time at the university, which, in the wake of Stalin's death, had become a place of intellectual and ideological ferment. The young Gorbachevs befriended one of the international students studying there at the time, the Czech law student Zdeněk Mlynář. Like them, he exuded the optimism and desire for change emblematic of that generation of the thaw, the *shestidesyatniki*. Eventually he would take his doctrine of "socialism with a human face" back home, where, in 1968, he became the ideologue of the tragically short Prague Spring.

After Gorbachev graduated, he took a post at the prosecutor's office in his home region of Stavropol, and, to her mother's chagrin, Raisa quit graduate school and followed her husband south in 1955. It was a drastic change from cosmopolitan Moscow. Stavropol, the region's eponymous capital city, had few paved roads and little of the high culture Raisa had come to love. With her husband climbing the party ladder—he quickly abandoned the prosecutor's office for a choice job with the local Komsomol—Raisa had little to do but keep house in the tiny room they rented in a communal apartment. Like much of the city, the room had no plumbing or heat and was so small that Raisa had to cook on a kerosene stove in the hallway. In 1957, the couple had a daughter, Irina. But, without a job, Raisa felt listless. "Work wasn't simply a paycheck for me," she said. "It was also something without which I considered my life a failure."[19] She tried to get a teaching position at the local university, but all the slots were filled with well-connected locals who looked at this outsider with defensive suspicion.

In the meantime, she became increasingly fascinated with sociology. The field was in vogue among the *shestidesyatniki* who, like their intellectual predecessors a century before them, wanted to see how the real Russia lived. In the early 1960s, Raisa enrolled in the Moscow State Pedagogical Institute for a remote PhD program in sociology. She and her husband lived in an agricultural region, and she frequently visited her in-laws, who still lived on a collective farm near the city. Like Zaslavskaya, who was working farther north, Raisa decided to focus not on party-approved texts but on fieldwork among the people living this part of the Soviet experiment. Borrowing from her friend Mlynář, she called her approach "sociology with a human face."[20]

Hitchhiking on trucks and motorcycles and wooden wagons—or sometimes just tramping through the sucking spring mud in her rubber boots—Raisa covered hundreds of miles of back country roads and administered nearly three thousand questionnaires.[21] But if contact with the collective farms showed Zaslavskaya just how fundamentally broken the Soviet economy was, it revealed something else to Raisa: the women. She saw that they made up nearly three-quarters of the field hands and did the most physically demanding farmwork, but were only 2 percent of the *kolkhoz* administration. Of the families she studied, 91.2 percent of the men earned more than their wives, and nearly two-thirds of them made at least twice as much.[22] Little had changed for these peasant women since her grandmother's time, she realized. Raisa's work and relative affluence confounded them, much as it had their grandmothers when the Zhenotdel crusaders came around the village. In her memoirs, Raisa recalled how, late one evening, she knocked on the door of one hut, clutching her questionnaire. A skeptical old woman answered.

> "My dear, why are you so skinny?"
> "Why, no," I say, "I'm just average."
> She went on anyway.
> "I bet you don't have a husband, do you?"
> "I do," I say.
> She sighed again.
> "Bet he drinks, huh?"
> "No..."
> "Hits you?"
> "My goodness! Of course not."
> "Why are you lying to me, my dear? I've lived a century on this earth and I know that it's not a good life that makes a woman go door-to-door."[23]

Raisa also saw how the war was still fully present in these southern villages twenty years after its end. Many houses were occupied by single women. Some were war widows; others were slightly younger women who had never married. The aloneness of these women reared up before her. "Can you imagine it?" she asked Pryakhin.

> The home of the dispossessed woman's fate, ruined by war... I never imagined that it was so obvious, visible, and painful. But

when I surveyed the villages and every fourth or fifth house turned out to be the home of a single woman, I saw firsthand these homes and these women. Women who never knew the happiness of love, the joy of motherhood. Women living out the rest of their lives alone in old, crumbling houses.

To Raisa, who had come of age during the postwar return to conservative family values, this was the cruelest fate she could imagine. "Think about it," she demanded of her interviewer, "we're talking about people whom nature has predestined to give life and to be its locus." She couldn't understand why they did not seem broken. "What's surprising is that most of these women weren't bitter, didn't come to hate the whole wide world and didn't become locked inside themselves," Raisa marveled. "They kept the self-sacrifice and compassion for another's suffering that has lived in the souls of Russian women for eternity."[24]

Later, transcribing the interview in his study, Pryakhin was struck by the first lady's words. He remembered his own mother, who had also been a lonely mother, an *odinokaya mat'*. "How many of them were there, whose justly destined grooms the war had betrothed to itself instead," Pryakhin mused bitterly. "I want to believe that [Raisa] didn't just discover, didn't just study or even absorb the lives and fates of those like my mother. But that she now sees the world that's been thrown open to her through their watchful eyes."[25]

In Stavropol, Raisa eventually became a lecturer at the agricultural institute, and after defending her dissertation in 1967, she taught philosophy and sociology full-time. She gave lectures to undergraduates and graduate students as well as people who attended night school. Because of the wide range of students, and because it was a provincial center without large universities and narrow specialists, Raisa had to master a dizzying array of topics. In addition to the staples of Soviet philosophy, like scientific atheism and dialectical materialism, she gave lectures, by her account, on the history of philosophy,

Hegel's *Science of Logic*, Kant's antinomies, Lenin's theory of reflection, epistemology, "problems of consciousness, the role of the individual in history, the structures and forms of social consciousness, contemporary sociological concepts, philosophical currents abroad, ethics, the history of atheism and religion, etc."[26]

Raisa loved her work and made decent money, and her daughter was now married and in medical school. Raisa had even learned to love Stavropol and the severe beauty of its steppes and mountains. She also helped her husband in his career after he became the regional party boss—the equivalent of a governor—in 1970. He drew on her expertise in the sociology of collective farms and she helped him entertain visiting party dignitaries from Moscow.[27] The Gorbachevs' mountain hikes and campfire sing-alongs with Politburo members like Andropov helped Mikhail get noticed in the capital.

Her husband's position at the top of the Stavropol political hierarchy also gave her access to goods that regular Soviet women couldn't find. She had her own seamstress. It was just her neighbor in the large communal apartment, but it was still an incredible luxury. Whenever Gorbachev went on a trip—to Moscow or, say, Sochi—Raisa presented him with a list of things she needed. It was a common practice for those who had relatives in comparatively affluent Moscow or had permission to travel to the Soviet satellite states in Eastern Europe. "What's long and green and smells like sausages?" went the tired joke. "A train from Moscow."[28] But those long, green trains smelling of sausages were usually filled with women bringing food home. This was their way of patching a broken and inefficient economy. In her memoir, which was published in 1990, when shortages of basic goods were reaching their apex, Raisa was keen to show that, despite her high position, she had been just like those regular women. "We've lived our whole lives with deficits!" she recalled. "Whenever [Gorbachev had] a business trip to Moscow . . . a long list was compiled of our personal needs and those of our closest friends. The list included everything: books, a coat, curtains, underwear, shoes, stockings, pots, cleaning supplies, medicine."[29]

When Gorbachev's professional rise mandated a move to Moscow in 1978, it was the height of the Brezhnev era, and Raisa discovered that not all Party wives lived the way she did. What seemed like perks far from the capital paled in comparison to the lifestyles of Kremlin women. They ate crab and caviar and their tables were laden with fresh fruit, a fantasy for most Soviets.[30] They had state apartments and state dachas, state cars with state drivers, state allowances for state food, state vacations at state resorts, and state entertaining for state parties. (Of course, once they moved to Moscow, Raisa got all these perquisites, too, and she especially appreciated the unlimited allowance for the acquisition of books, which were also a deficit good.) When Raisa scolded a Kremlin child for nearly breaking a chandelier at a state dacha, one of the wives scolded her in return. "It's not a big deal," she said to Raisa. "It's government property, they'll write it off!"

While Raisa was now lecturing at her alma mater, the other Politburo wives did nothing much of anything. They played politics among themselves, mimicking their husbands while meticulously staying in their shadows. Occasionally they got together to play cards, gatherings that Raisa found painful. "Endless toasts to the health of their superiors, gossip about their inferiors, discussions of food and about the 'extraordinary' talents of their children and grandchildren," Raisa recalled, repelled by their pompous materialism.[31]

The Politburo wives returned the sentiment. Raisa was a generation younger, still trim and stylishly dressed, highly educated, and trying to maintain a career independent of her husband's—a man who, unlike their men, didn't drink or have a harem. They could smell the moral superiority she exuded and rarely missed a chance to remind her that she was still a newcomer. At an official reception for foreign guests in 1979, Raisa, not knowing where to stand in the receiving line, took a spot next to the wife of the very high-ranking Andrei Kirilenko, Elizaveta. Elizaveta coldly pointed to the opposite end of the room and declared, "Your place is over there, at the end of the line."[32]

Like her husband, Raisa felt more comfortable in the West. After he became general secretary, crowds greeted her when she accompanied him on overseas trips and magazines put her on their covers. Western leaders seemed more sophisticated and cultured than stodgy Soviet politicians and their nasty wives.[33] Thatcher liked her, as did the Mitterrands, the Kohls, and the Bushes.

But not every Westerner appreciated Raisa's erudition. "From the moment we met," Nancy Reagan wrote in her memoirs, "she talked and talked and *talked*—so much that I could barely get a word in, edgewise or otherwise."[34] It wasn't just the talking that bothered Nancy, though Raisa certainly did a lot of it. It was what she talked about and how. "I had assumed we would talk about personal matters: our husbands, our children, being in the limelight, or perhaps our hopes for the future," Nancy recalled. She had wanted to tell Raisa about her "Just Say No" anti-drug program, but Raisa didn't seem interested and assured her that the Soviet Union didn't have a drug problem. ("Oh, really?" Nancy quipped in her memoirs.) She lectured Nancy on everything: Russian history, American history, art history, Marxist-Leninist thought, the superiority of the Communist system, and the absence of homeless people in the Soviet Union. "I wasn't prepared for it," Nancy wrote, "and I didn't like it." At their second meeting, at the Soviet mission in Geneva in 1985, Raisa showed Nancy an exhibit of children's art and insisted on explaining exactly how the desire for world peace was expressed in every individual drawing. Nancy smiled politely and nodded along, but inside she was screaming, "Enough! I know what a missile is! I get the message!"[35]

Their husbands immediately liked each other, but while they were working on arms control agreements to end the nuclear stalemate between the two superpowers, Nancy and Raisa were fighting their own Cold War. Or, to be more precise, Nancy was fighting Raisa, who was largely blind to the irritation she caused. The Soviet first lady blithely violated all kinds of protocol. Instead of talking to the other wives at dinners with Gorbachev, Reagan, and their advisors, Raisa inserted herself into conversations with the men, starting up discussions with people at distant ends of the table. She flew to Reykjavik for their husbands' summit in 1986 even though wives weren't invited and Nancy had dutifully stayed home. ("We missed you in Reykjavik!" Raisa chirped obliviously when she saw Nancy in Washington the following year. Nancy fumed.)[36] Raisa also occasionally sat in on important meetings, which Nancy felt was the height of impropriety for first ladies.[37] Raisa made insulting comments to the press about how the White House was too cold and museum-like to be fit for human habitation. In retaliation, Nancy joked with the American press about that droning Mrs. Gorbachev, only to then coyly deny that anything was amiss between them.

Gorbachev saw the conflict as one of personalities. "Nancy is an actress, Raisa is an academic," Gorbachev wrote in his memoirs, maintaining that his wife "did a lot for mutual understanding and good will."[38] But it was more than that. These two women were exemplars of their respective societies, which expected very different things of women and girls. Naturally, this led to a clash of what they expected of each other in their roles as wives and women.

Nancy was the embodiment of America's postwar parochialism. She had been raised in the home of her very conservative stepfather, a wealthy surgeon, and she imparted those political views to her previously liberal husband Ronald.[39] When they met, Nancy, a graduate of the all-female Smith College, was making a living in the most American of industries: Hollywood. After they married in 1952, she stopped working; she was a wife and a mother first. For the most part, she was a very traditional first lady. She had a project focused on the welfare of children, she looked glamorous on her husband's arm, and she was a gracious and untaxing hostess of official teas and state dinners.[40]

Nancy was also a true cold warrior like her husband. One of her fondest memories from her eight years as First Lady was hearing "The Star-Spangled Banner" burst from the orchestra pit of the Bolshoi Theater. "This is really happening," she thought. "Here we are in *Moscow* and they're playing *our* anthem."[41] Everything about the Soviet system was anathema to her. And in Raisa's didactic manner she perceived a desire to demean her—and the American way of life. She catalogued every slight, real or imagined. When the Gorbachevs visited Washington in 1987, for instance, Nancy was stung that Raisa didn't ask about her recent breast cancer surgery. "The Soviets know everything, so I can't believe she didn't know what I had gone through only a few weeks earlier," Nancy complained in her memoirs.[42] Much like her husband's administration, Nancy vastly overestimated the Soviets. She did not consider the possibility that this intelligence had not reached Raisa or that, if it had, asking a woman she'd met only once about something so personal might seem prying and vulgar.

Raisa might as well have come from a different planet. She was both the product of her country's radical social experiment and its great patriot. Her people had come from the grinding poverty of the Russian countryside and she had risen to become a professor of philosophy and sociology, married to the leader of one of the two most powerful countries on earth. Of course she was proud of herself. When she spoke to Pryakhin, Raisa allowed herself some casual immodesty—and a shot at Nancy, who had since left the White House. "I will say this without flattering myself: often my interlocutors, and for some reason, it is mostly women, are surprised at how I know this or that piece of scientific knowledge, sometimes from spheres that are very far from each other," she said. "But this, very simply, was given to me by my profession, which entails a wide sphere of knowledge."[43]

Yet Raisa also had the insecurity of every sophisticated Soviet when encountering a Westerner. Westerners were fraught figures. They were carriers of the culture that Soviets like Raisa idealized and studied and tried to emulate. But Westerners also believed themselves superior to Russians—and Russians always feared they might be right. Raisa's brilliant confidence was shot through with the unsteadiness of a woman who was performing a high-stakes public role while making it up along the way. "She prepared for these trips, sometimes maybe even too much, because she wanted to show that she knows this culture, that she knows this, and knows that," Gorbachev's translator Pavel Palazhchenko explained. "And that irritated some people."[44]

In the end, Nancy told the press, which delighted in chronicling the drama between the two first ladies, that they had reached a "Mexican stand-off."[45] It was the best they could do. Soon, Raisa would have far bigger things to worry about.

RECKONING

ON FEBRUARY 25, 1986, AS GORBACHEV MOUNTED THE DAIS AT THE Twenty-Seventh Party Congress to preach *perestroika*, Svetlana Alliluyeva was across town, storming the American embassy in Moscow. Once again, she wanted to flee the Soviet Union, and had planned on doing what had worked nearly two decades earlier, when she had walked into the American embassy in Delhi and defected to the United States. This time, she wasn't as lucky. Soviet police officers intercepted her and dragged her away.

Svetlana was now sixty years old, a grandmother. What had she done? Why had she come back? Twenty years and a whole life in America later, she was exactly where she had started, in the cold, gray Soviet capital. It was thirty years to the day that Khrushchev had delivered his secret speech denouncing her father and Svetlana had spent every one of them running from Stalin and his legacy. She had arrived in Moscow just as the entire country, under Gorbachev's policy of glasnost, was embarking on a journey similar to her own, grappling with what her father had done to it.

Once the Americans at the U.S. embassy in Delhi realized who had just walked through their doors on that March day in 1967, they knew they had to get Svetlana out of the country before the Soviets realized where she was. That night, accompanied by a CIA officer, she flew to Rome and then on to Switzerland, where, for a time, she hid in a remote convent. When she finally arrived in the United States in April, the U.S. government summoned George Kennan out of retirement to help navigate the political ramifications of Joseph Stalin's last surviving child crossing over to the enemy on the fiftieth anniversary of the

Nadezhda Krupskaya. *Public domain, sourced from Wikimedia Commons*

Alexandra Kollontai. *Public domain, sourced from Wikimedia Commons*

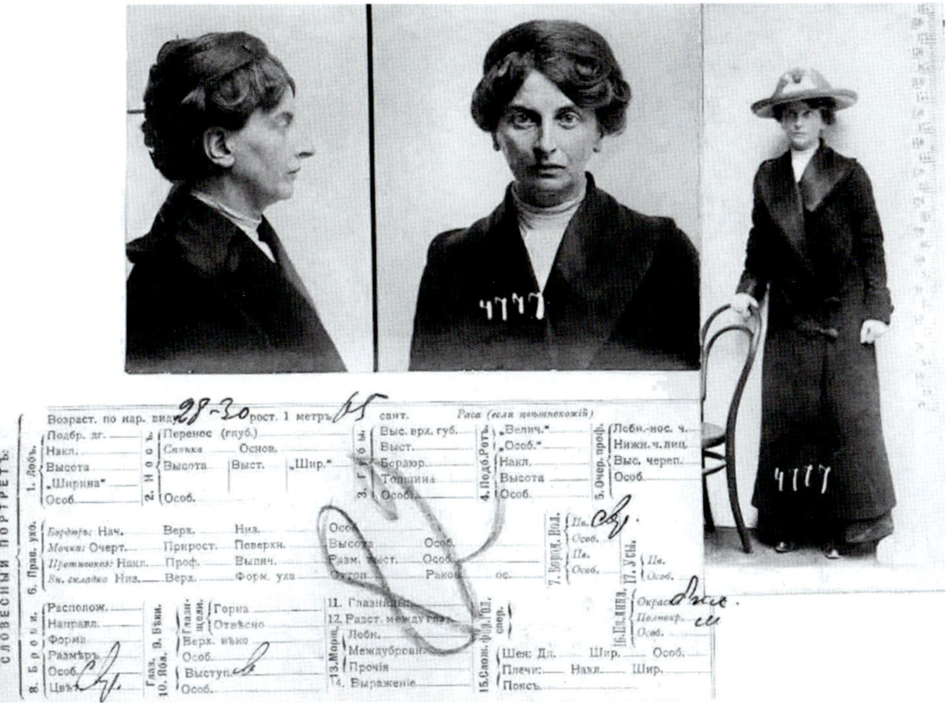

Part of Inessa Armand's police file, 1912. *Public domain, sourced from Wikimedia Commons*

My maternal great-grandmother Riva Weisser (*far left*) teaching an adult literacy (LikBez) class, 1920s. *Courtesy of the author*

Riva Weisser with her husband, my maternal great-grandfather Isaak Bruk. *Courtesy of the author*

My maternal great-grandmother Brokha "Buzya" Zuckerman with her first husband, my great-grandfather Pavel Barsky. *Courtesy of the author*

Buzya with her son, my maternal grandfather, Yuri (Yura) Barsky, shortly after her return from Batiliman, Crimea, 1934. *Courtesy of the author*

Buzya and her second husband, Alexander (Shura) Umansky, in Crimea, 1950s or '60s. *Courtesy of the author*

Nadezhda Alliluyeva. *Public domain, sourced from Wikimedia Commons*

Mira Uborevich, 1937, shortly before her father's arrest. *Public domain, sourced from Wikimedia Commons*

Hava Volovich. *Public domain, sourced from Wikimedia Commons*

Fighter pilot Marina Raskova. *Public domain, sourced from Wikimedia Commons*

Fighter pilot Lidia Litvyak. *Public domain, sourced from Wikimedia Commons*

Sniper Lyudmila Pavlichenko. *Public domain, sourced from Wikimedia Commons*

The Tartakovsky-Ring family, 1930s. Top row (*left to right*): My paternal great-grandparents Moisei Tartakovsky and Khana-Batya Ring; her younger sister, Sonya Ring; and her husband, Zalman Tubis, who was killed in the first days of the war. Bottom row (*left to right*): Grisha Tartakovsky; Khana-Batya and Sonya's father, Shmuel Ring; and my paternal grandmother, Khinya. *Courtesy of the author*

Rakhil and Wolf Tartakovsky.
Courtesy of the author

My paternal great-grandparents Moisei Tartakovsky and Khana-Batya Ring.
Courtesy of the author

The Ioffe-Komsky family, 1935. *Clockwise from the top*: My paternal great-grandmother Brokha "Bronya" Komskaya; her husband, Natan "Nota" Ioffe; my paternal grandfather, Yankel "Yasha" Ioffe; and his older brother, Samuel "Monya," who was killed in the war. *Courtesy of the author*

The Bruk-Weisser family, late 1930s. *Clockwise from top left*: Isaak Bruk, Riva Weisser, my maternal grandmother, Emma Bruk, and her brother, Anatoly (Tolya). *Courtesy of the author*

Joseph Stalin with his daughter, Svetlana, 1935. *Public domain, sourced from Wikimedia Commons*

Svetlana sits uncomfortably on the lap of Secret Police Chief Lavrentiy Beria, while Stalin works in the background. *Public domain, sourced from Wikimedia Commons*

The young couple: Nikita Khrushchev and Nina Petrovna Kukharchuk. *Public domain, sourced from Wikimedia Commons*

Soviet first lady Nina Petrovna Khrushcheva (*far left*) standing next to Mamie Eisenhower at a state dinner at the White House, 1959. *Public domain, sourced from Wikimedia Commons*

My paternal grandmother, Khinya Tartakovskaya (*left*), and her best friend, Sonya Ioffe. *Courtesy of the author*

Khinya in the lab. *Courtesy of the author*

My paternal grandparents, Yasha Ioffe and Khinya Tartakovskaya. *Courtesy of the author*

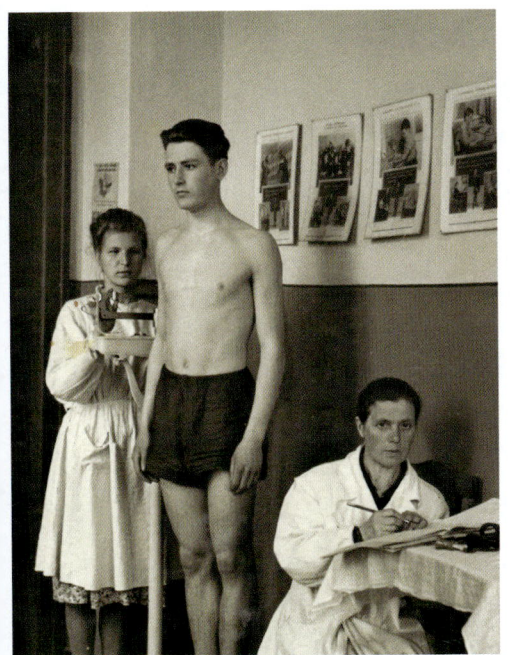

Riva (*front*) at work at a clinic in Moscow, 1950.
Courtesy of the author

My maternal grandmother, Emma Bruk.
Courtesy of the author

The Bruk family in 1953, the year of the Doctors' Plot—and Stalin's death. *From left to right*: Riva Weisser, Tolya Bruk, Emma Bruk, and Isaak Bruk. *Courtesy of the author*

Emma on Mount Elbrus, 1954. *Courtesy of the author*

My maternal grandfather, Yura Barsky, in the lab. *Courtesy of the author*

Emma at Ullu Tau, 1955. *Courtesy of the author*

Emma holding my mother, Olga.
Courtesy of the author

Viktoria and Leonid Brezhnev. *Public domain, sourced from Wikimedia Commons*

Svetlana Alliluyeva on her arrival in the United States, April 1967. *Public domain, sourced from Wikimedia Commons*

My mother, Olga Barskaya. *Courtesy of the author*

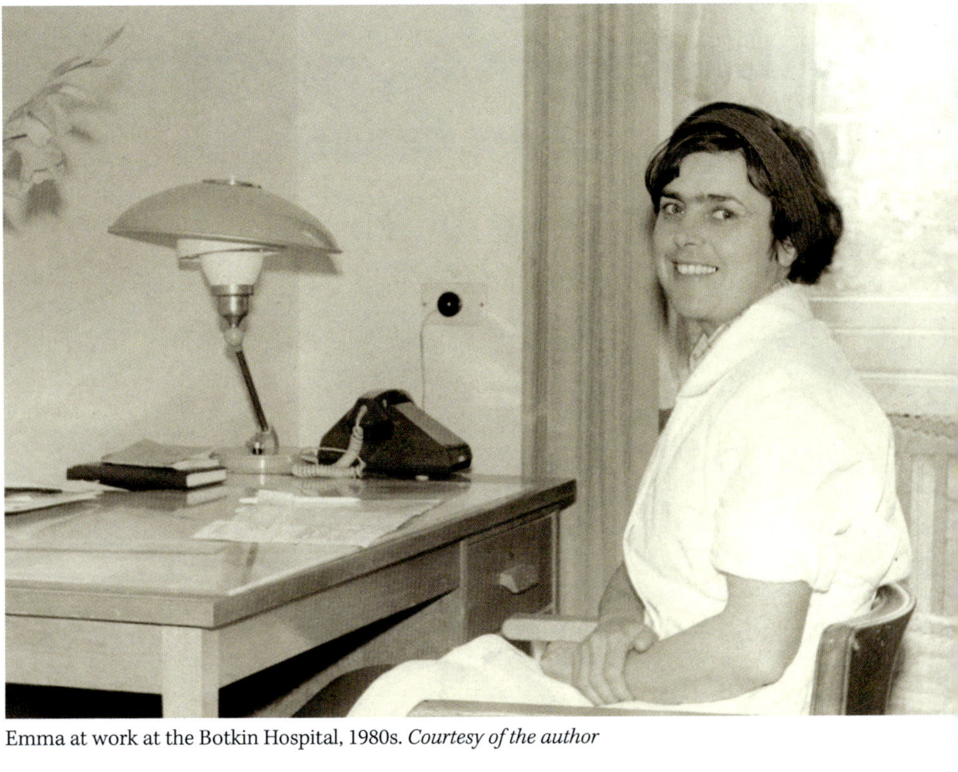

Emma at work at the Botkin Hospital, 1980s. *Courtesy of the author*

My parents' wedding,
Moscow, January 1982.
Courtesy of the author

Raisa and Mikhail
Gorbachev departing
Moscow for Reykjavik,
October 1986. *Courtesy
of the Gorbachev
Foundation*

My sister, Dina (*right*), graduating from medical school, becoming the fourth generation of women doctors in my family. My mother (*left*) is the third—and a professor of medicine. *Courtesy of the author*

My parents on the iconic rooftop terrace of the Hotel Washington, 1990. *Courtesy of the author*

My family, shortly after our arrival in the United States. *Courtesy of the author*

Bolshevik Revolution. The Soviets were convinced her flight was a CIA ploy to humiliate them, and her decision threatened to derail the delicate diplomacy Washington was trying to weave with Moscow at the height of the Cold War.

For this reason Kennan advised Svetlana to apply for a tourist visa, which he thought would make her decision seem less political than seeking asylum. She could be presented as an author coming to the United States to write, not a fugitive aligning herself with Moscow's archrival. Kennan found a publisher willing to pay Svetlana $1.5 million—a fantastic sum in those days—for her memoirs. Far from being mollified, the Soviets saw this as an American bribe for a high-value target.

When Svetlana touched down in New York, she gave a press conference, which she used to talk about God and freedom. The Soviet response was unsparing. Alexei Kosygin, the Politburo functionary who had refused to let her marry Brajesh, used his own press conference at the United Nations to call Svetlana "unstable" and "sick."[1] *Izvestia* claimed the CIA had written her memoirs.[2] The Kremlin even had the Moscow bishop of the Russian Orthodox Church condemn Svetlana, who had been baptized in the faith in 1962, when it was still illegal. "A woman who has had several husbands, who abandoned her children, who betrayed her people and stripped bare the nakedness of her father is now trying to say something about religion and faith in God," the bishop wrote. "The moral character of this woman, who has sold everything sacred for a few dollars, can only engender disgust and rage."[3]

Svetlana was distraught. She had agonized over the decision to leave her children, and the Soviet government knew that this would be the most powerful way to discredit her in the eyes of a population that believed that a woman's first duty was motherhood. She understood the tactic, but it still stung keenly. It was summer, and she was staying with Kennan's daughter Joan in rural Pennsylvania, hiding from both the press and the KGB. Sitting on the veranda, Svetlana noticed a small charcoal grill. She asked Joan's teenage brother, Christopher, to fetch some lighter fluid. "You are all present here to witness a solemn moment!" she proclaimed. (Since Joan was out, Svetlana's audience consisted only of Christopher, Joan's children, and their babysitter.) "I am burning my Soviet passport in answer to lies and calumny!" Then she tossed the passport into the flames.[4]

But Svetlana only had a vague understanding of what freedom meant in the West, and she was not prepared when she encountered its fullness. "I had idealized America and the American way of life in my fantasies, which were mainly built on old films," she wrote. "It wasn't easy for me to make peace with its stupidity and tactlessness."[5] Her fantasies hadn't included a press that hounded her car from JFK Airport and hid in the shrubbery of the private homes where she was a guest during her first months in the United States. They wrote about her copyright battles and her charitable donations, her shopping trips and the price she paid for a pair of slacks. They even wrote about things that didn't exist, like her Moscow orgies and a cache of riches that her father had stashed away for her in Switzerland. They followed her trail through the Indian countryside. They tracked down her niece and ex-husbands in Moscow.

The leftist European press, meanwhile, ran with the Soviet line: Svetlana was a "nymphomaniac" afflicted with "hysteria."[6] The Indian papers wrote that she had once been consigned to an insane asylum. An Italian journalist found Kapler, the dashing film director who had been her first love, who speculated that "something terrible, something abnormal must have happened to Svetlana, perhaps an illness of some kind."[7] The Soviets gladly fed that lie. The KGB's new code name for Svetlana was *kukushka*, Russian for a cuckoo bird—and an insane woman.

Most painful of all, the Western media had discovered that her children had denounced her, first privately, in a letter, and then openly in the Soviet press.[8] ("I consider that by your action you have cut yourself off from us," her son Joseph wrote in April, reducing her to tears.) One American reporter went to her old apartment in Moscow and photographed her children, who looked heartbroken and scared, and Svetlana was furious that their grief had been put on public display. Another journalist interviewed the twenty-two-year-old Joseph in Moscow. In the story, which ran in the German magazine *Stern* under the headline "Mother Is a Bit Confused," Joseph described his mother as a "wobbly" and "unstable being."[9]

Svetlana began work on another memoir, this one about the events of 1967, the whirlwind year of her life. She wanted to reclaim the truth of her own story, but already she knew it was a futile effort. "I knew and I felt that lies spread about me . . . would be believed sooner than anything I might say or write," she admitted. "My father's name is too odious, and I am living under its shadow."[10]

With the money she'd made from her first memoir, Svetlana set up the Brajesh Singh Hospital in his ancestral village in India and bought herself a house in Princeton, New Jersey, not far from George Kennan, who had become a close friend. She got a car, hired a gardener, and bought every modern kitchen gadget she'd seen advertised on television. She was invited to cocktail parties and dinners in the well-appointed homes of Princeton academics. After spending time in a poor Indian village and her gilded existence at the top of the Soviet hierarchy, she found life as an American woman more than a little funny. "The American housewife is the most spoiled woman in the world," she mused."[11]

For her first few years in America, Svetlana was a Cold War celebrity. Every day she received a flood of letters, not all of them kind. "Go back home, Red dog!" one American wrote. "Our cat is better than you. She takes care of her children!"[12] But there were also letters from interesting people who wanted to meet her, like Isaiah Berlin, Tolstoy's exiled daughter, a banished Georgian countess, and Olgivanna Wright, the widow of the architect Frank Lloyd Wright, who invited her to Taliesin, the architectural commune her husband had founded outside of Scottsdale, Arizona.

Olgivanna's letters sparked something in Svetlana. She knew that Olgivanna was from the old kingdom of Montenegro, which had become part of Yugoslavia, and that she had spent her youth in Georgia, the land of Svetlana's ancestors. Olgivanna had named her daughter Svetlana, an uncommon name at the time. After mother and daughter moved to the United States and Olgivanna married Wright, the teenage Svetlana eloped with one of Wright's architects, Wesley Peters. But in 1946 tragedy struck when Svetlana Peters and one of her young sons drowned in a car accident. Svetlana Alliluyeva saw in Olgivanna a mirror of her own tragedy: Olgivanna had lost a daughter named Svetlana, and Svetlana had lost a mother from Georgia. She imagined that in Olgivanna she would find echoes of her own mother, Nadya. Instead, she found something much more sinister.

When Svetlana arrived at Taliesin in March 1970, Olgivanna Wright was holding court with a black Great Dane slumbering at her feet. "She was a small, rail-thin woman with a wrinkled face that was yellow, like parchment, with quick, intelligent eyes," Svetlana remembered. "There was nothing of the soft and dreamy beauty of my mother, of her shyness, her velvet gaze. Before me sat the regal widow of a famous architect, the president and heir to his legacy, with a quick, feline gaze in her light brown eyes, which reminded me far more of the quick gaze of my father."[13]

She chased away the thought and allowed herself to be swept up in the fantasy of the low-slung buildings blending into the stark beauty of the Sonoran Desert. She reveled in the attention of Wes Peters, Olgivanna's son-in-law and chief architect of the Wright Foundation, who seemed as bereaved and lonesome as if a quarter century hadn't passed since the deaths of his young wife and child. Within three weeks of her arrival, they were married and Olgivanna was introducing her as her daughter, the new Svetlana Peters. Svetlana couldn't believe her luck. "Marriage, the most commonplace marriage, family, children—everything that I had so wanted since my youth and could never achieve," she wrote. "I was afraid to let myself dream of this."[14]

As soon as Svetlana was married, however, she realized that she had bound herself not to Wes but to the Wright Foundation—and to something eerily similar to what she had escaped in the Soviet Union. The newlyweds were expected to continue eating all their meals communally with the rest of the architects, the apprentices, and their wives. Olgivanna expected them to share details of their private lives, which she then used to manipulate them. Those who were honored with an invitation to eat at her table had to anticipate and applaud her thoughts—"just like at my father's table," Svetlana thought. Olgivanna knew how to throw her interlocutor off balance with sudden questions or a penetrating look. "My father had this habit of asking unexpected questions, and it was frightening," Svetlana recalled. "Under his point-blank glare, people would back out of the room, paralyzed."[15]

There were other unpleasant reminders of her father's home. Olgivanna had rewritten her dead husband's history, recasting herself as the muse who had allowed Frank Lloyd Wright's genius to flourish—though he had been sixty and already a world-famous architect when they met. She cut out anyone whose claims could undermine her legitimacy as Wright's sole spiritual heir. Svetlana knew this playbook only too well: her father had used it when he crowned himself Lenin's successor and annihilated his old comrades. "I asked myself, 'How did I end up in this strange place? This primitive communism under a dictator!'" Svetlana wrote in her memoirs. "It seems I will never outrun this. What fate!"[16]

She didn't understand until later that Olgivanna wasn't trying to dominate Svetlana for power's sake. She was after Svetlana's money. Olgivanna had seen the press reports about Svetlana's book and her charitable donations, the tabloid claims about Stalin's secret treasure in Switzerland. The commune had two campuses and dozens of residents; their maintenance cost a tremendous amount of money. Soon after the wedding, Svetlana got a call from her lawyers: Olgivanna's Frank Lloyd Wright Foundation had sent Svetlana's Alliluyeva Charitable Trust a request for an annual donation of $30,000.[17] Svetlana's trustees declined, so Olgivanna presented her with a bill for her time at Taliesin—totaling $30,000. And it wasn't as if Svetlana hadn't worked for her keep. In addition to helping in the kitchen, she was expected to entertain potential donors at black-tie events. Every day, paying tourists came to the campus, coming up to her room to see Stalin's only living child.[18] She was Olgivanna's cash cow.

And Wes, it turned out, was Olgivanna's willing coconspirator. Before the wedding, Olgivanna had informed Svetlana that her soon-to-be husband had a shopping addiction and had run up quite a credit card debt. A lovestruck Svetlana happily paid off the debts, which totaled half a million dollars.[19] But Wes kept spending. He bought jewelry and cars and expensive clothes—for her, for himself, for the people at Taliesin, for everybody. "I'd never seen a man who loved shops as much as women do," Svetlana marveled.[20] She didn't know that on the day of the wedding, Wes had transferred the Wisconsin farm he had bought with his inheritance to the Frank Lloyd Wright Foundation, putting it out of his new wife's reach.[21] He introduced Svetlana to his surviving son, now approaching thirty, who had abandoned a career as a classical cellist and was turning the farm into a cattle ranch. Delighted at the prospect of a new family to replace the one she'd abandoned in Moscow, Svetlana poured another half million into the farm, only to have her stepson tell her she was not welcome there. Now over two-thirds of her money was gone.[22]

A couple months after the wedding, Svetlana discovered that she was pregnant. She believed it was a blessing: cut off from her two grown children, shut out by Wes's son, here was the family she craved. But not everyone was happy with the news. Olgivanna demanded that she get an abortion and pushed Wes to insist on it. "Women of Svetlana's age don't give birth in America," she told him.[23] Wes dutifully carried the message to his wife, but Svetlana refused to terminate the pregnancy. In May 1971, at the age of forty-five, she gave birth to a girl, whom she named Olga, in honor of her grandmother. A few days later, Wes arrived at the hospital with a TV film crew. Before long, Svetlana began getting letters from Americans scolding her for having a child at such a disgracefully late age—or for procreating at all. "America does not need Stalin's heirs," one person wrote.[24]

Svetlana's daughter was a salve for the wound Svetlana had inflicted on herself by leaving her first two children. She refused to raise her child inside Olgivanna's cult and moved out over Christmas. In February, the Frank Lloyd Wright Foundation announced that Wes Peters was seeking a divorce. Once again, Olgivanna had outmaneuvered her, portraying her to the press as capricious, spoiled, and unable to abide by Taliesin's democratic ethos. *The New York Times* ran with this interpretation, calling Svetlana a "Soviet princess." Olgivanna's other child told the press that Svetlana did not deserve anyone's sympathy: "She was a murderer's daughter."[25]

So began what Svetlana called "my descent down the social ladder of American society."[26] Growing up, she had never needed money and never been taught its meaning or its value. Now she lived in a society where everyone seemed obsessed with it—where it determined how well you lived, how your children were educated, and what kind of healthcare you received. She had arrived in America as Svetlana Alliluyeva, millionaire, but she departed Taliesin as Lana Peters, a forty-six-year-old divorcee with a toddler and cobwebs in her bank account. Hoping to keep Wes in little Olga's life, Svetlana decided not to fight him for child support or to make her stepson buy her out of the Wisconsin farm. But Svetlana miscalculated again: Wes didn't care to develop a relationship with his daughter, and now she had no money. She moved back to Princeton, bought a small house, and began a lonely, frenetic existence.

Although she had received American citizenship in 1978, her adopted country began to bewilder and embitter her. "When I returned to Princeton as a single mother," Svetlana wrote, using that old Khrushchev-era term *odinokaya mat'*, "I discovered that a divorced woman is not a sympathetic figure in this society. Having twice gotten divorced in the Soviet Union, I never felt myself humiliated in any way. But here I understood that I was a 'sinner' in everyone's understanding. I was no longer invited to those homes where I had been so welcome before my marriage and divorce. The injustice of this hurt."[27]

She threw herself into motherhood, insisting that Olga attend only private schools, which further deepened her financial problems. There were months when she couldn't pay the bills and took out ever more loans. She sold her house in Princeton and moved to California, where she bounced from city to city—Carlsbad, La Jolla, Oceanside—before returning again to New Jersey. She was periodically rejected as a renter when landlords discovered she had a child, which struck her as another bitter point of irony in this ostensibly conservative, family-loving nation.

Svetlana was coming apart. She was drinking. She was volatile and believed the KGB was testing new microwave weapons on her.[28] But more than anything, she was disillusioned. This country that had promised so much—freedom, dignity—had shown itself to be a greedy, small-hearted place, full of hypocrisy and materialism. Was it really any better than what she'd left behind? Had this been worth losing her children? In 1982, Svetlana moved with Olga to Cambridge in the United Kingdom, believing that she would have more privacy there. But the paparazzi soon found her, confronting the eleven-year-old Olga outside her school to ask what she thought about her murderous grandfather. Svetlana hadn't yet told Olga about her lineage and was now forced to have the conversation.

By then she was out of money. She needed an income, but what could she do? She wanted to write, but no publishers were interested unless it was about Stalin. The occasional academic invited her to their university, but people wanted to draw her into their political activism or to speak about her father. There was occasional translation work and an Indian publisher published her third memoir, this one about her disastrous marriage to Wes and her life in America, but it was hardly enough to pay rent and Olga's tuition. The only way she could make money, it seemed, was to cash in on a father who had caused her and her country so much suffering. Everyone wanted to know more about Stalin, the man. No one was interested in Lana Peters, the woman. "If I ever defect back to Moscow, no one should be surprised," she wrote to a friend. "What I confronted in this so-called Free World was enough to kill the enthusiasm of even a strong man."[29] On September 11, 1984, she took the train to London to present the Soviet embassy there with a letter requesting to go home. By October, she was in Moscow, her Soviet citizenship reinstated. At a press conference at the Soviet Women's National Committee headquarters, she complained of the "lawyers, businessmen, politicos and publishers who turned the name of my father, my own name and life into a sensational commodity."[30]

When Svetlana returned to Moscow, she hadn't seen her children in seventeen years. Joseph had divorced and remarried, had become a surgeon and an alcoholic, and was bitterly resentful of his mother. Katya was a widowed vulcanologist on Kamchatka and refused to see her, eviscerating Svetlana in a letter as a traitor to the Motherland. Nor would Katya let her meet her granddaughter, while Joseph's ex-wife was reluctant for her teenage son to see his defector grandmother. And, worst of all, here there was no Lana Peters or even Svetlana Alliluyeva. There was only Svetlana Stalina, a propaganda tool of the Soviet Union, just as she had been in the United States.

So she fled again, to Tbilisi, the land of her mother and grandmothers. In Georgia, as in Moscow, the state again built a gilded cage around her: state apartments and cars and chauffeurs and Olympic swimming coaches and horseback riding lessons for Olga. On the streets, people stared at her—in admiration or in loathing—but never did they see her, only her father. The one person who truly saw her was her nephew Alexander, her brother Vasily's son, who had made a life in the theater under his mother's maiden name, Burdonsky. (Vasily had drunk himself to death in 1962.) "Princesses or daughters of some leaders, all of their attempts to be more human, to simply be a woman, to simply be a mother, to simply be a citizen—they are all doomed," he said of his tortured aunt, though he could have been speaking of the entire nation's fate after decades of Stalin's torture, launching itself into the arms of the West only to recoil into the grievance of being misunderstood. "Her whole search for some spiritual shelter ... I understood that she would never find it, even though she thought she would. She is one of the most tragic figures that I know." Svetlana put it even more bluntly. "You are Stalin's daughter," she said of herself. "Actually, you are dead. Your life is already finished. You can't live any life. You exist only in reference to a name."[31]

Almost six weeks after the Twenty-Seventh Party Congress, Gorbachev finally agreed to her request and let Svetlana out. He had just announced his policy of glasnost, and now the whole country had joined Svetlana in processing what Stalin had done to them. Every week seemed to bring another gruesome revelation of his crimes. At such a fraught time, Gorbachev didn't need Svetlana around to complicate the narrative. On April 6, 1986, Svetlana was summoned one last time to the Kremlin. Gorbachev didn't address her himself. Instead, he sent a trusted lieutenant, Yegor Ligachev, who told Svetlana she would be allowed to depart but that she would be expected to "behave." A few days later, she and Olga would surrender their Soviet passports and board a plane for Wisconsin. But before they did, Ligachev wanted to leave Svetlana with a parting kernel. "The Motherland will survive without you," he told her. "The question is, will you survive without the Motherland?"[32]

END OF THE
FAIRY TALE

IT WAS A WARM JUNE DAY—TOO WARM FOR HER GRAY SUIT AND HIGH-necked pink blouse. Raisa nervously rooted around in her clutch for a white handkerchief to dab her face, tense as she listened to the translation of Barbara Bush's cheerful address to Wellesley's class of 1990.[1] The American first lady had been asked to speak at commencement after playwright Alice Walker, the graduating women's first choice, declined the invitation. But Bush wasn't everyone's second choice. She may have gone to Smith College, Wellesley's sister school, but she had dropped out after her freshman year to get married, then bore her patrician husband six children as he climbed to the top of American politics. What kind of role model was she for ambitious young Wellesley women entering the workforce, the daughters of second-wave feminism? One hundred and fifty women, a quarter of the graduating class, wrote a letter of objection to Dr. Nannerl Keohane, the college president. "To honor Barbara Bush as a commencement speaker is to honor a woman who has gained recognition through the achievements of her husband, which contravenes what we have been taught over the last four years at Wellesley," the letter read.[2]

The protest became a national political story. Even the American president had to publicly defend his wife. At a White House lunch, reporters asked Mrs. Bush about the controversy. "They're twenty-one years old and they're looking at life from that perspective," she said calmly. "In my day, they probably would have been considered different. In their day, I'm considered different. *Vive la différence.*"

The White House soon found a work-around. Wellesley's graduation coincided with a Washington summit between Bush and Gorbachev. Raisa was planning to accompany her husband on the trip, and it was decided that she would also deliver a commencement address: with her doctorate and teaching career, she would provide a fitting contrast to the homebound Mrs. Bush.

At the ceremony, the two first ladies held hands and smiled encouragingly at each other. Barbara Bush was no Nancy Reagan. A deeply secure woman, Mrs. Bush liked Raisa and didn't find her overbearing. "I feel enormously comfortable with Mrs. Gorbachev," she told reporters that day.[3] But Raisa was nervous. She sat onstage with her feet primly folded under her, the way all proper Soviet girls were taught to sit. Her suit and leather clutch, impossibly chic in the impoverished Soviet Union, looked cheap next to Barbara's pearls and flowing black graduation robe. Raisa listened as the class speaker, the leader of the protest, delivered a speech about the solidarity of womankind, one that crossed all divisions, including class. Raisa's predecessors would never have stomached this heresy, but Raisa merely nodded along. In her speech, Mrs. Bush noted how times had changed. In decades past, the winner of Wellesley's annual hoop race was said to be destined to be the first of the class to get married. These days, Mrs. Bush noted, the winner was bound to become the next CEO.[4]

When Dr. Keohane introduced Raisa, she praised her "intelligence, wit, style, and sophistication" and highlighted her professional achievements: her dissertation and "highly original" methodology, her work as a "pioneering sociologist." "Mrs. Gorbachev," she declared, "has brought new prominence to the role of First Lady of the Soviet Union, and is often compared in this respect to Nadezhda Krupskaya, Lenin's wife."

When it was her turn to speak, Raisa delivered a series of platitudes in Russian about youth, hope, and women's innate talents as peacemakers. "Always, even in the most cruel and troubled times, women have had the mission of peacemaking, humanism, mercy, and kindness," she said in her thin, officious voice, using flat, officious Sovietese. She also alluded to the politics back home, "the land of *perestroika*." "This vast and difficult task is a top challenge," she said, "but we are confident that *perestroika* will succeed."

The crowd was primed to love her, and they did. Raisa got a standing ovation. The mission was a success. As Mrs. Bush recalled later, "She saved me."[5]

The Wellesley commencement took place on June 1, 1990. The Berlin Wall had fallen just seven months prior, and a few months before that the USSR had withdrawn from Afghanistan in humiliation after a decade of brutal, pointless war. The people of Hungary and Poland had swept their Communist parties out of parliament in their first free elections since the Soviet takeover. The Baltic republics had just unilaterally declared their independence, and Belarus and Ukraine were edging toward the same. Ethnic conflicts and miners' strikes were increasingly common all over the Soviet Union, as were protests in the Soviet capital.

Perestroika, the policy to which Raisa's husband had tied his political success, was running aground. Gorbachev's reforms—like making factories balance their budgets or get rid of extraneous workers—were too little, too late for the Soviet economy. The increasingly broke government printed more money at home while running out of hard currency to buy food abroad. It was far more expensive to buy grain in the West than to grow it, but inefficient Soviet *kolkhozy* just couldn't keep up with the demands of feeding their own country. Incomes continued to rise, but there was nothing to buy. Soviet factories made consumer products that were of terrible quality but wildly expensive. Tens of billions of rubles' worth of these goods sat unwanted on store shelves. Meanwhile, the things Soviets actually needed—meat, fruits and vegetables, sugar, toothpaste, soap, detergent, batteries, notebooks for schoolchildren—were nearly impossible to find. Anywhere between a quarter and a third of fruits and vegetables spoiled in unventilated warehouses; 40 percent of harvested potatoes met a similar fate, while the rest rotted in the fields.[6] "On any given day, only 23 of 211 basic food items were available in state stores," wrote historian William Taubman.[7]

"Deficit" became the watchword of *perestroika*, as did *dostat'*, a typically ample but precise Russian verb that meant to obtain something valuable through great difficulty and still greater wit. People took pride in being able to snare unicorn items such as stereos and bananas. When trickery failed, they hoarded, buying up as much of any "deficit good" they came across as they could for fear that it would never appear again, which only exacerbated the shortages. The cooperatives—small private businesses that Gorbachev had legalized as part of the *perestroika* reforms—tried to fill the gaps, but they relied on the same broken supply chains as the state enterprises with which they competed. The Soviet economy was failing faster than it could be restructured, and soon Gorbachev would be asking Mrs. Bush's husband for aid to prop up the bankrupt state. Gorbachev, Raisa recalled, "lived in a state of incredible tension" and she was now constantly worried about his health.[8]

Raisa, meanwhile, had come to Wellesley to be Barbara Bush's foil, a Russian working woman to offset the American first lady's total commitment to family. The college president, herself a prominent political scientist, had emphasized how Raisa had balanced the demands of motherhood and career and how she represented the new Soviet woman.

But did she? The new Soviet woman couldn't even access basic menstrual products, resorting to wads of cotton that leaked and stuck painfully to her body when they dried. When cotton was not available, which was often, the new Soviet woman tucked rags between her legs.[9] She carried around an *avos'ka*, an expandable "just-in-case" bag made of cheap netting, in case she came across something—anything—worth buying. She shopped at several stores for basic supplies because there were few supermarkets, and in each store she waited in three different lines to order, pay for, and pick up whatever hadn't already rotted or been taken home by store employees. The new Soviet woman often got into fights with the clerks and other shoppers, fellow new Soviet women who were just as angry, hopeless, and exhausted as she was.[10] Through it all, she worked full-time, usually in a "feminized" and therefore less prestigious profession, making about 30 percent less than her generally less educated male colleagues.[11] After work, the new Soviet woman spent an additional forty hours a week on housework, which wasn't bad considering that the rural Soviet woman spent fifty-five hours doing the same. Her husband, if she was lucky enough to have one, on average did six.

And the housework had to get done.[12] But Soviet appliances were expensive, heavy, and of overwhelmingly poor quality. Women did the laundry in steaming pots on crowded stoves and on washboards, dried it on clothing lines in crowded apartments, and then ironed every piece of it. The new Soviet woman may have had a PhD, but she still spent her evenings darning and patching, knitting and sewing and crocheting, because there was so little clothing available to purchase. A 1989 survey found that "a woman with young children has seven hours and 36 minutes a day for herself—this includes the time she is supposed to sleep. After paid employment and domestic chores end, there is 17 minutes a day for family 'quality time.'"[13]

When Raisa spoke to the young American feminists at Wellesley, it had been nearly seventy years since Alexandra Kollontai had published a brochure for the world's workingwomen, a piece of propaganda proclaiming that Soviet women lived in "a fairy-tale country." Since then, three generations of Soviet women had carried this fairy-tale country on their backs, rebuilding and repopulating it as the men in charge repeatedly laid waste to it. Three generations after Krupskaya and Kollontai, the new Soviet woman was utterly and totally exhausted. "We still apply the old stereotype of the all-capable and resilient [Soviet] woman," one woman wrote in the *Moscow News* during the height of *perestroika*. "Yes, she *can* do everything, but she *doesn't want to anymore.*"[14]

In February 1982, Olga returned to Moscow from her honeymoon to discover she was pregnant. This was not in her plans. She was still in medical school, she had only met my father six months before their wedding, and, having only ever lived under her mother's roof, wanted to live with her new husband, on their own, before they had children. There wasn't much she could have done to prevent the pregnancy, however. Although contraception had been legalized in the Soviet Union in 1923, it was notoriously scarce and shoddy. A Soviet birth control pill, known mostly for its side effects, was actually banned by the Ministry of Health, while imported pills were nonexistent.[15] IUDs were so poorly made that they frequently caused damage to the uterus and cervix; diaphragms were rudimentary and condoms, or "galoshes," broke frequently.[16] (In the words of historian Stephen Kotkin, Soviet condoms were "ludicrously thick, rarely lubricated, and thus despised by men."[17]) The remaining options were the rhythm method, the pullout method, and douching—either with lemon juice or vinegar, or by running to the bathroom after sex, frantically twisting the showerhead off the hand shower, and directing as strong a stream inward as you could muster.

When those methods failed, which they regularly did, Soviet women turned to abortion.[18] It was, in the words of public health scholar Amy Rankin-Williams, "the only absolute form of family planning."[19] More than 80 percent of Soviet women had had at least one abortion. Before the end of the average Soviet woman's childbearing years, she could be expected to have between three and seven of them—a rate 6.5 times higher than that of the United States. By 1989, the Soviet Union had 6 percent of the world's population but accounted for 20 percent of the world's abortions.[20] This worried Soviet demographers—every live birth was offset by two abortions—but there was little they could do about it.

Because abortion was so common, it was not a taboo topic. Olga knew that her mother, Emma, had had several abortions and that her grandmother Riva had nearly died of complications from one. Still, she was despondent. Like the entire Soviet medical establishment, she believed incorrectly that terminating the first pregnancy doomed a woman to a life of infertility.[21] It was why the vast majority of women seeking abortions were married with children. Desperate, Olga did everything doctors, midwives, and friends recommended to induce a miscarriage. She drank wine, she carried heavy suitcases, she jumped from anything that seemed high enough. Emma found her an anesthesiologist who did acupuncture on the side. When the doctor stuck the needles in, Olga fainted, so she tried having a specialist tap her sacrum with spiky metal hammers instead. Nothing worked. The pregnancy stuck. In October, I was born.

It had not been a pleasant pregnancy. In the third trimester, when the Braxton-Hicks contractions kicked in, a doctor prescribed bed rest. My mother spent a month alone in a maternity hospital, attached, with a long metal needle, to an IV drip for hours on end. No one was allowed to visit her, not my father, not my grandmother, despite being a doctor whose connections had gotten Olga a bed in one of the most prestigious maternity hospitals in Moscow. My mother cried for a month straight. When it came time to give birth, she found herself naked and alone on a birthing bed in a room with a half dozen other naked women who were screaming in pain and fear.

My mother and I came home after a week in the maternity hospital—the standard stay, which was when my father first saw me. I was colicky and didn't eat. Because there were no breast pumps, my mother manually expressed her breast milk, which I had refused, and passed it on to a family friend whose wife had also just given birth but was not producing enough milk: formula was also a deficit good. My father washed my cloth diapers—disposable diapers were unheard-of, quite literally. Since detergent was also hard to obtain, he grated soap on a box grater, and after he'd finished rinsing, boiling, and wringing the diapers and swaddles, he festooned the kitchen with them before ironing them on both sides. For this, and for helping with the shopping, cooking, and cleaning, his father mocked him for being hopelessly henpecked.

After a year's maternity leave, my mother went back to school. She lived in constant fear of getting pregnant again, so every period was cause for celebration. But like her girlfriends, my mother ultimately had several abortions, which were never a secret in our family. "If you didn't want twenty kids, then you had twenty abortions," she once told me. Unlike most Soviet women, who went to free public clinics where several women were operated on in the same room, my mother was lucky: she got anesthesia for her abortions. Anesthesia was yet another deficit good and had to be administered in the presence of an anesthesiologist. The impoverished Soviet healthcare system couldn't afford to waste such precious resources on women, who, it was believed, were strong enough to handle the pain anyway.

The level of care provided during a typical abortion was minimal. Women lined up in a clinic hallway, entered a blood-spattered room, and perched on an orange rubber mat to have their cervixes dilated and their uteruses scraped without any analgesic, staggering out just as the next set of women was ushered in, a gory assembly line one observer described as reminiscent of a slaughterhouse.²² Even with the extra care my grandmother's connections provided, my mother's experience was hardly pain-free. During one abortion, she remembers feeling like she was being taken down long white corridors toward a white light. She woke up to realize that she had bitten through the heel of her hand.

On the fifth day after giving birth, Yevgenia Albats was filthy and fed up. When the doctor came around to check on her and the other freshly postpartum women in her room, she demanded a prescription—for a shower. Almost apologetically, the doctor replied, "But you know that we don't have a shower in our wing."

Albats was a special correspondent for the *Moscow News*, a popular, *perestroika*-era newspaper that catered to a liberal, urban audience. She had made her name as a journalist writing about the KGB. Taking full advantage of Gorbachev's policy of glasnost, Albats tracked down the NKVD agents who had tortured and killed the leading lights of the Soviet intelligentsia in the late 1930s. She showed up in their spacious apartments and interviewed these old but still unrepentant men. But in the spring of 1988, at the age of twenty-nine, she got a different kind of assignment: she was to chronicle her pregnancy and the birth of her first child.²³ Exactly seventy years after Kollontai opened her Palace of Motherhood to show the people what the new Bolshevik government would do for women and their infants, Albats showed her readers what had become of Kollontai's dream.

Her reports began with humor and irony, about how male traffic cops were more accommodating of her "condition" than female clerks in overcrowded stores. She jokes about how in "Stork"—the specialty shop for expecting mothers where women can only shop with a special pass issued by their doctor at twenty-five weeks—maternity underwear exists in only one elephantine size. "Take it, take it," the clerk urges her. "It's rare that we even have this. Just shorten the straps, replace the back with elastic. Plus, it'll shrink in the wash." ("As for maternity clothing, no one has tasked us with this problem—and you can write that," says the male bureaucrat in charge of maternity health at the Health Ministry.) She wonders why, at thirty-two weeks, when the fetus would be viable outside her body, the government is still deducting the tax for childlessness from her salary. She notices that the informational stand warning of the dangers of the growing AIDS epidemic is placed across the hall from where a phlebotomist takes blood samples with a multiuse needle. "I'm sure she's heard of disposable syringes, but I'm not sure she's ever seen one," Albats muses.

By the time Albats gives birth, the jokes give way to alarm. Splayed out alone on a birthing table covered in an orange mat and a tattered bedsheet patterned with faded bloodstains, Albats labored for twelve hours, screaming herself hoarse not because it hurt—though it did—but in the desperate hope that someone would check in on her. Finally, one nurse did: "Stop screaming!" she screamed. "Perhaps the most horrible thing I experienced in those twelve hours was the feeling that everyone has abandoned you, forgotten you, and that you will have to face this entire ordeal on your own," Albats wrote. "It is a feeling that literally paralyzes your will."

Albats was, of course, not entirely alone. She was in a room with seven other women, all in equally desperate stages of active labor. One, "a mere teenager," was told by the doctor that, given the "peculiarities of her physique," the birth would be difficult for both her and the child. The doctors and nurses then proceeded to ignore her for hours. Later, Albats would learn that, after such a difficult labor, they told the young woman that they could not guarantee that her child would be "normal."

Albats was lucky. She gave birth to a healthy baby girl. A nurse was dispatched to fetch the obstetrician or pediatrician but soon returned alone. "Neither one is here," she said, shrugging. Exhausted and famished, Albats asked for something to eat. "Dinner ended a while ago," she was told. She was transferred to a room with four other women and they were given old robes to wear, orange plastic men's slippers, and ancient nightgowns split down to the belly button. Periodically, a doctor came by to ask the women if they had any complaints, which he summarily dismissed as "insignificant."

LENA: My stomach hurts.
DOCTOR: That's insignificant.
GALYA: My sutures hurt.
DOCTOR: That's insignificant.

The women had no choice but to laugh and to remember the wisdom passed around by Soviet women of childbearing age. Don't give birth in the summer: half the maternity hospitals are closed for "prophylaxis," which means the other half is so overcrowded that the nurses can't keep up with the patient load. Don't give birth on Fridays: the pediatrician who examines the newborns won't be in till Monday. And yet, they hadn't listened: it was July 1988 in a bankrupt, crumbling empire that spent only 4 percent of its budget on its citizens' health.[24]

Albats counted seventy women in her wing, and yet there wasn't a single shower. There was one bathtub, which was reserved for washing bedpans and those ubiquitous orange mats. The only bidet in the maternity hospital was taped shut because it was broken. "I've worked here for twenty years," one of the nurses told Albats, "and it's always been broken." The only bathroom in the entire wing had two toilets in it, side by side, one of which was also reliably broken. Albats's fellow patients hadn't been able to clean themselves after giving birth and their old sheets quickly became stained with blood. In the laundry room, they were told that there were no clean linens available. There weren't even diapers and swaddles for the newborns, who were left to lie in their own filth and changed only three times a day.

Albats and her roommates were not permitted to bring in anything from the outside: not their own bathrobes or towels or cotton or even disinfectant. Everything from the outside world—people, linen, medicine—was, according to the authorities, full of germs. After twenty-four hours, during which Albats did not see her child, the little girl was brought into the room and placed on the bloodstained sheets. Albats was petrified, not just of AIDS but "of every imaginable streptococcus, staphylococcus, gram-negative infection." Sure enough, after bringing her daughter home, Albats discovered that the baby had picked up a staph infection in the hospital. No wonder, Albats marveled, the Soviet Union was in fiftieth place—"After Barbados!"—in infant mortality.

Months after giving birth, Albats remained enraged by the experience. She was a well-known journalist, with connections, in one of the best maternity hospitals in Moscow and therefore the whole country. What happened to women who couldn't pull the right strings, who lived in the even more impoverished provinces? "How many more years will we be ruled by the thesis 'Everyone gives birth—you're not the first, and you won't be the last'?" Albats wrote. "Sure, never mind the women. They unload trains and put down asphalt, they'll manage with this, too. But what about the children?"

In June 1987, Mikhail Gorbachev addressed the World Congress of Women in Moscow. Delegates from friendly nations had come to the capital of the world's first socialist state to see the wonder that was the state-mandated emancipation of women. The Soviet premier reiterated the fiction that the Soviet government propagated at home and abroad. "Not one government, not one democratic legal code that existed before 1917, had done even half of what the Soviet state had done for women in just the first months of its existence," Gorbachev bragged. "Women in the USSR really do have rights equal to men—and, in some cases, even more." Of course, Gorbachev conceded, Soviet women's emancipation "hasn't always been accompanied by relieving her in carrying out her ancient functions—as mothers, wives, and child-rearers." This mostly had to do with "shortcomings" in the service sector and "trade." Because of this, Gorbachev said, "the social burden on women has grown."[25]

That same year, Tatyana Zaslavskaya moved to Moscow to head up the All-Union Center for the Study of Public Opinion, the Soviet Union's first public polling agency. Her team of sociologists surveyed people across the entire Soviet Union, both male and female, to find out what life was really like for working women. Essentially, Zaslavskaya and her team were asking if the Revolution had fulfilled the promises it had made to Soviet women.

They found that, seventy years into an ostensibly radical and emancipating experiment, patriarchal gender roles were once again the norm in the vast majority of families. The only significant change that *had* endured was the obligation of women to work full-time. "As a result," the study's authors noted, "the phenomenon known as the 'double burden' leads to women's physical and psychological strain and has a significant negative impact on their professional engagement, the degree of realizing their creative potential, the quality of their children's upbringing, family relationships, and so on."[26]

In other words, just as American women were starting to learn about juggling career and family, Soviet women, who had been doing this for three generations, had reached the point of exhaustion. They felt like bad workers *and* bad mothers. Two-thirds of Soviet women complained that they didn't have enough time for their children—or, really, anything at all. Soviet men didn't disagree. "According to a significant proportion of those [men] polled, women have fewer opportunities compared to men not only to advance their educational or professional level, [to engage in] leisure activities, vacation, and even restore their physical and emotional strength after the workday." But there was nobody else to fall back on at home. "In most families, the man either does none of the housework, or does the minority of it," the study found.

And so Soviet women had adjusted their priorities. A second study overseen by Zaslavskaya found that married women now saw their "productive labor through the prism of family interest."[27] Besides, they didn't have time for the supplemental work and study that could advance their careers or increase their pay. Here again, the essentialism that had come to dominate Soviets' thinking about gender made itself known. When Zaslavskaya's team asked people to account for women's absence in the managerial class, only half of Soviets agreed that women *should* be equally represented there. Over a third said women were naturally unfit for leadership roles.

Indeed, Zaslavskaya herself was one of just three women who were full members of the Soviet Academy of Sciences, even though women had flooded into the sciences during the Soviet era. By the mid-1960s, 80 percent of biology students, two-thirds of chemistry students, half of math students, and a quarter of physics students were women.[28] And yet, over the six decades of the academy's existence, only seven women, including Zaslavskaya, had ascended to full membership, out of 835 members.

This paltry ratio was reflected across most fields. Women made up over half the Soviet workforce but were a vanishing fraction of its management. Seventy percent of Soviet doctors were women, but over 90 percent of them worked in poorly paid primary care, while men made up the vast majorities of tertiary care specialists, surgeons, researchers, and hospital administrators.[29] Nearly a third of Communist Party members were women, but women held only 7 percent of the chairs of district Party committees.[30] There had been no women on the Central Committee or in the Politburo since Khrushchev's time. (There had been none during Stalin's.) By the *perestroika* era, among men who had some higher education, every second one held a managerial position—48 percent. For women with the same educational level, it was 7 percent. Women had once again become the draft horses of the economy, the very fate that Kollontai and her Zhenotdel had tried to free them from.

Zaslavskaya's subjects believed the government's main priority should be to rescue Soviet women from the exhaustion of the home front—something Lenin had advocated nearly a century prior—and they had different ideas of how this could be done. Majorities of respondents supported proposals like correcting the deficit of essential goods, making home appliances available and affordable, and improving housing, childcare, and public transport (since women spent hours in transit between home, work, and the many stores they had to visit to feed and clothe their families). And yet a mere 13 percent believed that men should be reeducated to view housework as a shared responsibility.

Instead, two-thirds of Soviets now felt that women should be able to choose whether to stay at home as full-time mothers or to balance motherhood with work. This choice had been unavailable to Soviet women since 1920, when the Soviet constitution mandated that all able-bodied women work, but now only 15 percent of Zaslavskaya's respondents agreed with that fundamental Bolshevik tenet. Zaslavskaya's researchers called for a "fundamental improvement of conditions at work and at home" so that a woman could be free to pursue a career and have a family "without detriment to herself, her family and her work." It was something that could have been written by Armand or Kollontai or Lenin, as if the intervening century had never happened.

If at the beginning of the Revolution, young, educated people had embraced the ideas of radical egalitarianism and an abolition of bourgeois family norms, Zaslavskaya's team discovered that young people were now moving in the opposite direction. Urban and highly educated Soviets, especially men under thirty, were becoming far more conservative and traditional in their outlook. They tended to think that women did not have the innate talents to be decision-makers in the workplace and that family was of paramount importance for them. Strong pluralities of young Soviets supported allowing women to work only part-time and to take up to three years of maternity leave. Forty percent of Soviets felt that men's salaries should be raised so that women could "dedicate themselves fully to the family." The lowest ranking of the survey options, garnering just 1 percent each, went to what the authors called the "feminist positions": that a woman should work while the man stayed home or that a woman could choose to put her career above everything else and not have a family at all.

Once upon a time, the Bolshevik experiment had been so successful at challenging traditional gender norms that it produced hundreds of thousands of young women who volunteered for active combat. Their education instilled in them the idea that soldiers, traditionally the most masculine of the professions, were not inherently male or female. As the Bolshevik experiment neared its end, however, young women believed that their primary role was to bear and rear children and that it was men's duty to provide for them.

In Gorbachev's speech to the World Congress of Women in 1987, he did not mention what his government was preparing for Soviet women as *perestroika* continued. Because, to truly restructure the economy, the government, as the only employer in the USSR, would have to make its enterprises more efficient. Every entity, from factories to mines to universities, would have to balance their books, and that meant they would have to consider their bloated employment rolls. Gorbachev didn't mention that, under these reforms, 6 million women were about to lose their jobs in industry and agriculture alone.³¹ In a complete reversal of the early Bolshevik reforms, he was about to embrace a policy encouraging women to "return to their purely womanly mission," as he put it, while saving the jobs for the men.³² "Why should we employ women when we employ men?" Russia's minister of labor would declare several years later. "It is better if men work and women take care of the children and do housework."³³

MOTHERLAND

ON JUNE 10, 1988, RAISA ATTENDED AN EVENT AT THE BOLSHOI THEatre, celebrating the day 1,000 years ago when Prince Vladimir had ordered the citizens of Kiev to be baptized into Orthodox Christianity. It was a spectacular evening, with famous Russian actors and operatic prima donnas and a rotating set of orchestras and church choirs. The event was opened by the patriarch of the Russian Orthodox Church, who extolled the virtues of *perestroika* and the democratization of Soviet society.

This was a stunning about-face for the Communist regime. Lenin had despised the Church. He cut it off from government support and banned it from playing any role in regulating family life or educating Soviet youth. The Bolsheviks dynamited churches across the Soviet Union, then melted down the gold and silver ritual objects and sold them abroad to fund their industrialization drive. Some of the first concentration camps of the Gulag had been for imprisoned priests. Stalin, himself a former seminary student, had tens of thousands of clergymen arrested and shot. And while the Soviet constitution guaranteed citizens' freedom of conscience, most religious activity was banned. Scientific atheism became official state dogma and taught in schools. When Yuri Gagarin became the first man to go to space in 1961, he came back and, in a moment of priceless Soviet propaganda, declared that even that far up in the sky, he hadn't seen God.

For seventy years the Church had existed only as a withered appendage of the state, its ruling clergy forced to cooperate with the KGB. But now the Soviet first lady was attending an official state celebration of the Church, which was being feted on the government's most prestigious stage, the Bolshoi. The Church was being returned to its pre-Soviet social status—by a Soviet government.[1] History had to be, once again, rewritten.

The celebrations, which lasted for months, felt different for the tens of millions of Soviets who were not Orthodox Christians. Fifty million Soviets were Muslims. The Armenian, Georgian, and Lithuanian Republics all had their own national churches unrelated to the Russian Orthodox Church. There was a significant Buddhist minority. Millions of Soviet Jews remembered the role the Church had played in fomenting and condoning pogroms. The promise of an internationalist utopia where ethnicity and religion were irrelevant was one reason so many of the Russian empire's minorities, including young Jews from the Pale of Settlement, had joined the socialist movement in the first place.

Instead, after the war and the Holocaust, the country that this movement created had institutionalized anti-Semitism. The USSR had essentially forbidden the practice of Judaism, which it had not done for either Christianity or Islam. Going to a synagogue could get one expelled from work or university. The state prohibited opening any rabbinical schools to replenish the stock of aging rabbis, something it did not do for Orthodox Christian clerics. "More than any other faith," wrote historian Geoffrey Hosking, "the Jewish religion was being slowly stifled by administrative action."[2]

Now, as millions of Jews were attempting to flee the Soviet Union because of these discriminatory policies, the country was harking back to an even more ancient hatred. The official language around the thousandth anniversary wasn't just about Christianity and the Church but about Russianness. Andrei Gromyko, the chairman of the Presidium, talked about Russia's "ancient Slavic roots." The closing act of the Bolshoi celebration was a piece from Russian composer Mikhail Glinka's opera "Ivan Susanin," which the official Soviet wire service, TASS, called "a hymn to the great Russian people, its glorious history and its luminous future."[3] The term it used was telling. It did not refer to the Soviet people, or even the people who lived in the Russian Soviet Federative Socialist Republic, *rossiyane*. It used the words *russkii narod*, the Russian *Volk*.

It was not an accidental turn of phrase. The late 1980s were a time of rising nationalism all over the USSR. As the national republics like Georgia and Lithuania called for independence, they looked to their pre-Soviet identities. The Russian republic was the biggest and most important in the Soviet Union. And though its culture and language were the Soviet lingua franca, imposed on the other republics by force, an increasing number of ethnic Russians felt left out by the nationalist upswell. They, too, wanted a republic for themselves and their national, Christian culture.

As part of glasnost, Gorbachev allowed the formation of nongovernmental civic organizations. Soon, a group called Pamyat, or "memory," emerged. It was a Russian nationalist collective that wanted to restore the Orthodox Christian monarchy. Their singular obsession, however, was not Russian history and heritage but the Jews. The group blamed Jews—or "yid-freemasons"—for every tragedy that had befallen the *russkii narod*, the Russian people, from the Bolshevik Revolution to the economic struggles of *perestroika*. Their boisterous rallies in the center of Moscow drew hundreds of people (not a bad showing for Soviet times) and the group seemed to have the support of conservative elements in the Soviet government who didn't like Gorbachev's reforms.[4] In 1987, the leaders of Pamyat were even invited to meet with Moscow's Communist Party leader, Boris Yeltsin.

As Moscow celebrated its Christian roots at the Bolshoi Theatre, Olga was at the family dacha at Ilyinka, about an hour's train ride from Moscow. It was the house that Isaak and Riva had built after the war, when their Moscow apartment had been redistributed to another family and they had tired of sleeping on Riva's sister's floor. Now, many years later, Isaak and Riva's children and grandchildren lived in the city. The grandchildren would stay at Ilyinka for the summer months, watched by Riva, while the adults came out from the city on weekends, when they would tend the small garden plot and grow and pickle the provisions that would last them through the winter.

That year, Olga planned to spend the entire summer at Ilyinka. She was on maternity leave. My sister, Dina, had been born that winter, a child my mother had wanted badly.

After graduating medical school at the top of her class, my mother had applied for graduate school. She was rejected—again because of that fifth line in her passport. Olga soon learned that cardiology, her mother's specialty, was closed to her for the same reason; Emma had gotten into the prestigious field just under the wire. Instead, the government sent my mother to train in otolaryngology, regarded as the lowliest of medical specialties. Doctors who treated the ears, nose, and throat were called *dyrochniki*, hole specialists. She would be making 100 rubles a month, less than a bus driver, but standard for the medical roles into which Soviet women were segregated. After crying bitterly about her assignment, my mother quickly came to love the field. Though she had to perform gruesome tonsillectomies on children without anesthesia, she mastered the delicate operation that could restore a person's hearing. This miraculous but simple procedure could have saved Beethoven's ears, a fact that delighted my mother, who practically lived at the Moscow Conservatory.

My father chafed under the totalitarian dysfunction and anti-Semitism of the Soviet system. He yearned to leave, for his children's sake but also for his own. My mother, on the other hand, was happy. She and my father had taken over Emma and Yura's apartment on Bryanskaya. (Emma had moved down to the third-floor flat that Buzya had occupied after Shura's death until she succumbed to a stroke in 1984.) Few couples Olga and Mikhail knew lived alone in such a spacious apartment in the center of the capital.

As far as Olga could tell, she had a good life. She had a husband and two children, the second of whom seemed to be a miracle. Dina was a healthy, easy baby who looked like a blond doll. My young and handsome father would take her with him to tug on every heartstring of the older women waiting in store lines, who would immediately wave him to the front. Olga had a good job. Thanks again to Emma's connections, my mother worked at an elite ENT polyclinic that treated well-known cultural figures and happened to be a block from home, an unthinkable convenience. She had her family and her husband's family nearby and ready to help. She had many friends as well as the high culture of Moscow, with its countless theaters, museums, and concert halls. Life was poor and clothing and food were scarce, but somehow things always worked out. Except for that one short trip to Warsaw with Emma when she was a teenager, she had never seen a world that was much better than the one she inhabited, and she found it hard to imagine. She wasn't willing to trade her happy life for an unknown country that wouldn't recognize her medical diploma.

But Ilyinka that summer wasn't the same. Riva, who had largely raised her, had died four years earlier. Her absence filled the house like a fog. My mother watched over us and tended to the garden plot and greenhouse that Riva and Isaak, now dead a decade, had built. She swung in the hammock near the gooseberry bushes that they had planted. Dina babbled in the playpen, dappled by the shade of their apple trees. My father worked in the city, and my mother spent the long and mild June weekdays with her two children and the ghosts of her grandparents. That's where the rumors of the pogroms reached her.

She heard them first from one friend, then another: There would be pogroms that year to celebrate the thousandth anniversary of the Christianization of Russia, and the police were already handing out names and addresses of Jews. The idea sounded fantastical to Olga but also entirely possible, even in Moscow, in 1988. Soon the rumors were so prevalent and persistent that my father even went to the KGB's office for dealing with civilians to ask what, exactly, was going on. They told him they hadn't heard about any pogroms.

And yet the rumors continued to reach my mother in Ilyinka. She was alone in the countryside with two children, completely unprotected and at the mercy of anyone who might decide to barge in through the old wooden gate. She had no phone and no car. The train station was a long walk away. Would the neighbors come to her aid? She thought of Riva, who had been a young woman when a White pogrom came to her village; how Riva's father had been shot and the children lined up the next day and forced to watch their mother's execution; how the youngest went mad and how Riva never spoke about it; and how, to this day, my mother didn't know her great-grandmother's name. And now here she was, alone in Riva's house in a small village, with a pogrom gathering somewhere on the horizon like an ominous cloud.

"Something serious has happened, maybe even terrible," Mikhail Sergeyevich Gorbachev said, bursting into his wife's room at 5 p.m. on August 18, 1991.[5] The day had started off like all the others during their two-week vacation at Zarya, the presidential dacha at Foros, in southern Crimea. Raisa and her granddaughters had gone swimming and worked assiduously on their tans while their son-in-law Anatoly scanned the horizon with his binoculars, his strange and contemplative hobby. They had lunch on the veranda facing the mountains, after which Mikhail Sergeyevich withdrew into his office.

It was a working vacation but a vacation nonetheless, one that Raisa had lobbied hard for. The last year had been grinding, her husband pleading fruitlessly with the West for economic aid as he tried to keep the Soviet Union from coming wholly undone. The Baltics were gone and, after a series of reforms meant to democratize the union, he was no longer the general secretary but the president of the USSR, a far less powerful position. He spent months negotiating desperately with the heads of the union's constituent republics on a treaty that would keep what was left of the country from disintegrating. One day on a walk at Zarya, Mikhail Sergeyevich told Raisa he was thinking of writing something, a book or an article, in which he wanted to address the questions now nagging at him: "Was *perestroika* necessary?" he mused. "Are we headed for catastrophe?"

He, too, was unraveling. His calm, confident, cheerful bearing had given way to angry outbursts and scattered digressions. One of his advisors had long ago noticed that "it was as if everything was too much for him," but now world leaders and ambassadors were also seeing the strain.[6] When James Baker, the American secretary of state, visited him in Moscow, he found Gorbachev to be "positively neuralgic." And because Raisa was his closest advisor, she was also suffering. That July, the British ambassador noted that Raisa, her husband's "emotional shock absorber," looked "gray and badly run down."[7]

By summer, negotiations had been completed for an agreement in which the remaining Soviet republics would enter into a new and less centralized relationship with Moscow; the USSR would be a confederation, rather than a union. Its signing was set for August 20, and Gorbachev agreed with his wife that it was finally time to rest. On August 4, they arrived in Crimea along with their daughter, Irina, her husband, Anatoly, and their two granddaughters, Ksenia, eleven, and Nastya, four. They stayed as always at Zarya, a luxurious compound carved into the side of a cliff. Every afternoon Raisa read the newspapers and the anxiety came roaring back; the political situation in the capital was as poisonous as ever. Still, she believed that her husband could afford to relax. Ever the teacher, Raisa set a schedule for the group, one that involved lots of swimming, hiking, and a "cultural program": a movie, TV, or guests. Her priority was that everyone, especially Mikhail Sergeyevich, catch up on sleep.

August 18 was to be their last day at Zarya before they flew back to Moscow for the treaty signing. But now her husband was in her room, vibrating with nerves, announcing the arrival of uninvited guests: his chief of staff, two members of the Central Committee, a general, and the head of the KGB directorate charged with the president's safety. They demanded a meeting with Gorbachev. Mikhail Sergeyevich told his wife that he picked up the phone to get some kind of explanation, only to find the line cut. One after another, he picked up the different receivers in his office—all dead. "You understand?!" he shouted at Raisa. "This is isolation! Which means, a conspiracy? Arrest?"[8] He didn't know what the visitors wanted, but whatever it was, he would not give in. "I will not go along with any of these shady adventures, I won't cut any deals. I will not give in to any threats or blackmail," he told his wife. He paused and looked at her, as if remembering what country he was in. "But this may cost us dearly," he managed. "All of us, the whole family. We have to be ready for anything."

"Whatever you decide," Raisa replied, "I'll be with you, no matter what."[9]

They called in the "children"—Irina and Anatoly—and explained the situation. Raisa ordered tea, though she couldn't quite explain why. Nobody so much as touched it. Irina and Anatoly informed them that the television and radio connections had also gone dead, and they agreed they, too, would stand with Mikhail Sergeyevich and Raisa.

When the visitors were finally called in, Raisa and the children waited in the hallway, trying to overhear what was being said and to catch a glimpse of Mikhail Sergeyevich if he were to be arrested. In the end, the visitors left alone. One extended his hand to Raisa, who proudly turned away.

"Why did you come?" she said dryly. "What's going on?"

"Forced by circumstances," he answered, and walked out of the house.[10]

The visitors had some news for Gorbachev. Because, in their view, the country was hurtling toward the abyss, they had formed the State Committee on the State of Emergency, which they wanted him to declare by formally transferring his powers to his vice president. Or to resign. When Gorbachev refused, the delegation left, taking Zarya's head bodyguard with them. A coup had begun.

Anatoly's binoculars finally proved useful: the entrance to the bay was now guarded by a military ship and all civilian traffic had vanished. Periodically, the ship's telescope pivoted, watching Zarya with its big, glassy eye. They were prisoners. The family discussed fleeing but quickly decided against it. The road to Yalta was closed. Trucks and street-cleaning machines were parked on the helipad and in front of the gate. Soldiers with automatic rifles, young men whose faces Raisa didn't recognize, appeared around Zarya's perimeter, three rings deep. No one was allowed in or out, not even the dacha staff, now also trapped at Zarya. Among them, Raisa noted with anguish, were women who had children at home. Understanding that the house was bugged, she insisted that sensitive conversations happen exclusively outdoors.

Then a chink appeared in the enclosure. Anatoly discovered that his pocket Sony radio was still working, feebly transmitting news from the BBC about what was happening in Moscow, where a state of emergency had been declared. The committee had promised Soviets free land and announced that, in light of Gorbachev's grave illness, his vice president was now in charge.

The family immediately understood: this was not just a lie but a prophecy. The committee knew that Gorbachev was not ill, but they could certainly make him so, and the public would never know the difference. Raisa and the cook decided that the family would only eat food that had been brought into Zarya before the seventeenth. Everything they ate from then on had to be boiled. Raisa and Irina, a doctor, hid any medicine they might need. They would touch nothing else.

Every day, Mikhail Sergeyevich sent his demands to Moscow through a KGB chaperone—*reconnect the phones, open the gates, send a plane to take me to Moscow, tell the people I'm not sick*—and every day, they were met with silence. One of the secretaries was in despair: back in Moscow, her child had fallen ill. Raisa tried to get the captors to let the young woman return to her son—and bring news to the capital that Mikhail Sergeyevich was alive and well. The KGB chaperone refused. So every day Raisa took Mikhail Sergeyevich for a walk on the beach and around the land of Zarya, in full view of the ship. "They all need to see—both 'our people' and those who are watching us from the cliffs and the sea—that Mikhail Sergeyevich is healthy and in a normal state," Raisa wrote in her diary, committed to keeping a detailed record of their imprisonment.[11]

At night, only Ksenia and Nastya slept. The adults dedicated themselves to maintaining the girls' blissful ignorance. Anatoly found a camcorder, which they used to tape an address from Mikhail Sergeyevich to the nation. All night, Anatoly and Irina cut the tape with manicure scissors, rolled up the fragments in tissue paper, and hid the little nuggets of tape around the house. The bodyguards who had been at Zarya all month said they would stand with Mikhail Sergeyevich "till the end." Maybe someone could smuggle the tape out, or, if the worst happened, perhaps someone would find the fragments and discover the truth.

During their demonstrative walks on the beach, Raisa made sure everyone stayed together. "Anything could happen," she wrote on August 20, the day on which her grandfather had been executed by the NKVD in 1937.[12] The guards had advised them not to venture too far along the shore.

Through the Sony and another transistor radio that Anatoly and one of the groundskeepers managed to rig up, they learned that Yeltsin was back in Moscow and condemning the putsch. The committee had promised to arrest him, but he had managed to evade their grasp. Raisa was shocked: her husband's greatest political rival was standing up for Mikhail Sergeyevich. Yeltsin, the BBC informed the family, had holed up in the White House, the seat of the new Soviet parliament. Several thousand Muscovites had joined him, throwing up barricades and preparing for the committee, which included the interior minister and KGB chief, to storm the building. The committee sent tanks into Moscow, a city that was now openly up in arms over the coup. "The feeling: something could happen at any moment," Raisa jotted in her diary. Some of the guards were brought into the house, and Irina brought the girls into her bed. Anatoly slept on the floor, and all of Zarya waited.

They woke to bad news on the twenty-first. There had been casualties at the White House: three young men were crushed under the tank treads. Raisa was shaken. "Has the worst really begun?" She shuddered.

They could see more battleships on the horizon now. At 10 in the morning, three landing craft raced toward the shore but at the last moment turned back. "What are they trying to demonstrate?" Raisa wondered. "A blockade? Their ability to arrest us? Save us? I have no doubt that they know: the president is alive and well."[13]

The guards loyal to Mikhail Sergeyevich advised the family not to leave the house lest they get caught in any crossfire their captors might try to provoke. At 3 p.m., the Sony brought grim news. The BBC reported that Vladimir Kryuchkov, head of the KGB and a member of the committee, was sending a delegation to Foros, where Zarya was located, to confirm that Gorbachev really was gravely ill and incapacitated. "We understood it to be a signal of the worst," Raisa wrote. "In the coming hours, actions might be undertaken so that the vile lie becomes reality."

Mikhail Sergeyevich gave out orders: guards were to be ready for battle and to block the driveway and entrance to the house. No one was to be allowed in without his permission. In case of necessity, deploy deadly force. Guards with machine guns lined up on Zarya's front steps. Irina and Anatoly locked the girls and a maid in a room deep inside the house, away from any windows.

Raisa was seized by the feeling of imminent, terrible danger. One thought beat wildly in her head, like a panicked bird slamming against its cage: *Hide Mikhail Sergeyevich*. But where? The dacha had never seemed so open to the world, so vulnerable.

Suddenly her arm went numb, hanging loosely by her side. She tried to speak, but nothing came out. *A stroke*, she thought as someone laid her down on a bed.

By evening, it was over. Raisa regained consciousness to the sound of jubilant voices. The committee had inexplicably folded. They had sent a delegation to Zarya to apologize to Mikhail Sergeyevich, who had them detained and refused to see them. Communications had finally been restored, and Gorbachev immediately called Yeltsin and the other presidents of the Soviet republics, as well as the Bushes, who were nervously watching the news from Kennebunkport. Yeltsin had sent his own people to try to rescue Gorbachev. When Yeltsin's men arrived, Raisa rose from her sickbed to meet them. The Zarya doctors told her that she had probably not had a stroke after all, just a spike of blood pressure. Still, she looked like a ghost, wobbling down the stairs to greet the heroes who had come to liberate her family, determined to kiss each one of them in gratitude.[14] Raisa's health would never fully recover.

A plane arrived to take the Gorbachev family back to Moscow, where they landed at 2 in the morning and were immediately swarmed by journalists. In the city, thousands of protesters were still on the barricades, celebrating their victory. They had stood up for democracy and for the man who had brought them to the brink of a new era, who had shown them that they could defy the tanks and win. Now they demanded to see their president, Mikhail Sergeyevich Gorbachev. But in a mistake that would haunt him for years, he didn't join them to share in their joy and to thank them for what they had done for him. Instead, he got into the car waiting planeside, sank into the seat beside his shattered wife, and took her home.[15] He chose Raisa over his country.

Somewhere on those barricades was Emma. She was approaching sixty, but the excitement of the political moment made her feel impossibly young. She had just remarried, to Oleg Larichev, a well-to-do scientist, and moved into his sprawling apartment behind the American embassy, where her daughter and son-in-law had spent hours in line waiting for their American visas, their documents pressed neatly into plastic sleeves.

The pogroms had never happened that summer three years earlier. But their absolute plausibility was enough for my mother, the idea that she and her children could meet the same fate her great-grandmother and Riva had seventy years prior. The country of her birth had been pushing her out from the moment she was born and she realized she no longer wanted to fight it. She chose herself and her children. She gave my father, who had always wanted to leave, permission to start the process of applying for exit visas and refugee status.

Emma was crushed. She loved her daughter and her granddaughters, but she was still young. She had a prestigious and satisfying career, a rich social life, and her romance with Oleg had only just begun. She could not, at the age of fifty-five, give up everything and become a homebound grandmother in a country where she knew no one and didn't speak the language. And she couldn't leave Russia when it was finally becoming the country she had always known it could be. It was what she and her generation, the *shestidesyatniki*, had hoped and worked for all their lives. She had to see that dream through. She chose herself and her country over her family.

But Emma felt betrayed that her daughter was leaving and taking her granddaughters with her. People who left the Soviet Union were considered traitors, never allowed to return. Émigrés were as good as dead to those who stayed. Emma could not fathom what it would mean to never see her daughter and grandchildren again. So she threw herself into the political moment and into her new relationship.

Olga, too, felt betrayed. For her whole life, her beautiful mother had always chosen her friends and her men over her. My mother felt like she was just one of the many people competing for Emma's attention instead of being the only person who could hold her gaze by doing nothing other than breathing, by simply being her child.

I understood little of what was happening, though my parents must have explained it to me. I took a couple of lessons with an English tutor and learned how to say "apple" and "elephant." I learned the chorus of "Don't Worry, Be Happy," which played endlessly on Soviet TV, a foreign anthem for *perestroika*. When the lights were turned off at night, I hosted what I thought was an American television talk show from my bed, speaking gibberish into my hairbrush and offering it for commentary to my invisible guests. I continued going to school, where my first-grade teacher continued to torture me for reasons I couldn't understand, but likely because I was one of the few Jewish kids in the class. There was the time she didn't excuse me to go to the bathroom until I wet myself in the first row, which earned me a very public tongue-lashing. Like many children in one of the world's most polluted cities, I suffered from eczema and gastric issues and had to bring a special "dietetic" lunch from home. Because I was not allowed to eat cafeteria food, my teacher decided that I should not be allowed to eat in the cafeteria at all, so most days I spent the lunch hour alone with my dietetic lunch in a big, empty classroom lit with the thin, metallic light of the endless Moscow winter.

I can't remember the teacher's name now, but I remember the last day I was in her classroom. It was April 1990, and we were about to leave for America. I brought in Khinya's oatmeal cookies for the class. The teacher, her face sour and her voice condescending, handed me a book, which I have since misplaced. It was her farewell gift. When I got home, I opened it to the page she had inscribed for me. "Don't forget, Yulia," she had written in her sharp black script, as if I had been the one making the decision to emigrate, "Russia will always be your Motherland."

PART III

**Virgin Mary,
Mother of God,
Become a feminist!
Become a feminist!**
—PUSSY RIOT

JULIA

ON APRIL 28, 2010, EXACTLY TWENTY YEARS TO THE DAY SINCE WE LEFT 12 Bryanskaya Street for America, I woke up at 12 Bryanskaya Street, on the third floor, in apartment 89, which had once belonged to my great-grandmother Buzya and was now my home in Moscow. I had come to Moscow in 2009 on a Fulbright, intending to stay for a couple of months, and would stay instead for three years, reporting on the country of my birth and living with Emma in my great-grandmother's apartment all the while. From where I slept on a foldout couch in the living room, I could see the armoire that held the remnants of Buzya's affluence and good taste: the teacups of china so fine that they caught and gently filtered the light, the green crystal goblets, the big-bellied orange teapot spangled with blossoms.

I had grown up four floors above, in apartment 100, the co-op Emma and Yura had managed to buy in 1965, as they were tired of living in a communal apartment and of waiting for the state to bestow an apartment on them. When my parents got married, Emma moved in with Misha Mendelson and my parents moved into apartment 100. After Buzya died in 1984, Emma ended things with Mendelson and moved back into apartment 89, which she had inherited. Death moved much faster than the government housing authorities.

Khinya and Yasha, my paternal grandparents, lived in the city's suburbs a good hour away when I was growing up. Emma lived four stories below me, and we understood each other better than Khinya and I ever did. Khinya was quiet and practical, focused on the earthly demands of a Soviet existence. Emma, on the other hand, was my fellow cosmonaut. During my childhood summers at Ilyinka, she helped me compose poems to the lilac tree whispering at the attic window. She took me on overnight train rides to the Estonian coast, tramping through the dark pines and over white dunes to the cold, gray waters of the Baltic. And in Moscow, on evenings when Emma was home, I would trot down the stairs to her apartment and we would read stories and write and fantasize. She was my prince, and I, her Cinderella, loved her madly.

While my parents prepared to emigrate, Emma was too distracted by love and sorrow to stoop to the pragmatic and agree to that most sacred of Soviet operations, the extrajudicial apartment swap. Instead, we ended up selling apartment 100 for $5,000 to a friend of a friend who was running a cooperative and had lots of cash to spare. We didn't get to keep much of the profit, since the Soviet Union demanded reimbursement from exiting émigrés for the free education and healthcare we had received. In reality, this was little more than a way to punish us and keep hard currency inside the country.

The man who bought our apartment would go on to found Yandex, the homegrown Russian search engine, and become a billionaire. For years after we left, Emma would go back up to apartment 100 to try to recover the curtains and the books we had left behind and which she had forgotten to collect in her distraction. He was a rich man now, she figured. He could buy new curtains, ones that didn't have sentimental value for her. But his wife, the new mistress of apartment 100, never let Emma back in and the curtains stayed where they were.

The Soviet Union surprised everyone by disintegrating a year and a half after we left it. When Gorbachev returned from Crimea on August 22, 1991, he found it even harder to convince anyone that the Soviet Union should continue to exist, even in the amended, more federative form he proposed. A referendum on independence in Georgia earlier that year had returned overwhelming results—99.6 percent of Georgians said they wanted out of the USSR—and Ukraine was well on its way to a similar showing. Still, Gorbachev persisted, and by late fall he believed that he had enough support for a new USSR that would be a loose embrace of autonomous republics. Then, on December 8, Yeltsin and the leaders of Soviet Ukraine and Belarus met at a hunting lodge deep in the nature preserve between Belarus and Poland. Here they declared that the USSR no longer existed and would be replaced by a Commonwealth of Independent States. On Christmas Day 1991, the red Soviet flag came down over the Kremlin and the Russian red, white, and blue tricolor went up. A new country was born, and the one I had been born in ceased to exist.

Even before its final collapse, the regime had loosened its grip, granting my family a stream of visitors who, on April 28, 1990, had essentially buried us when they said goodbye at Sheremetyevo Airport. Now they were all free to visit. The friend who introduced my parents witnessed the August 1991 putsch from our living room floor in suburban Maryland. He happened to have arrived for a visit from Moscow not long before the Emergency Committee's tanks rolled into the Soviet capital. For those three days in August, his cross-legged figure seemed to grow out of the beige carpet in front of the used television donated to us by a family from the local Reform synagogue. And in May 1992, my father and I drove up to JFK to welcome my paternal grandparents, Khinya and Yasha; my father's sister Bella; her husband and her two kids. They had all decided to emigrate.

But the first to visit was Emma, in the spring of 1991. She stayed with us at Bentana, the 1970s-era brown apartment complex that was our new home in the United States. Within a couple of weeks of our arrival, my father had found a used Datsun and a job programming at a small consulting company. When we wanted a treat, we walked to Safeway in the evenings when the day's donuts went on sale.

My mother, to her great chagrin, arrived in America pregnant. We were picked up from Dulles International Airport by Emma's friends, who had immigrated to America years earlier, and they took us to their house for a rest. With its two floors and many rooms, the house seemed palatial. The heat, the humidity, and the green lushness of the Maryland suburbs made me wonder if we had actually been diverted to the tropics. A few weeks after our arrival, our hosts took my parents for a quick tour of Washington, DC. They stopped for a drink at the rooftop bar of the Hotel Washington, with its iconic view of the White House, the Washington Monument, and all the splendor of their new country's capital. It was a fine spring day and the breeze off the National Mall tousled my mother's permed hair, but all she could think about was how queasy she felt sitting high above the seat of American power.

It was a bad time to be pregnant. My mother did not know what she would do in America. She had packed her medical instruments just in case, though she knew the United States wouldn't honor her medical degree. The American ladies from the synagogue tried to introduce her to a local otolaryngologist—they thought perhaps my mother could work in her office—but the doctor had no use for her. She took a typing test but was too slow in her third language to be a secretary. She had taken some classes to learn how to do nails, figuring that if all else failed, she could buff and paint American fingers and toes.

Eventually she learned about a yearlong course for foreign medical graduates at Kaplan, the test prep company, that would prepare her to take the medical school board exam. If she passed, she could continue on to residency without having to repeat medical school at age thirty. It would be hard—taking a days-long exam in a language she had yet to master—but it was her only shot at reclaiming her career and restoring some of the social status she had lost by ripping her roots up and transplanting them to foreign soil. She had to study and work, all while raising two small and very confused children, one of whom, my sister, kept crying and asking to go home to her toys. This was no time to birth another child, one she might not be able to support.

So my mother asked the synagogue ladies where she could get an abortion, casually, the way she would have asked where the library was, and could not understand the ladies' shock. My mother figured that they were women; they should know. All the women back home were fluent in such matters, having themselves been through the procedure many times. But these were the wives of American lawyers and doctors and dentists. They had not worked since they married and had taken their husbands' names. They had planned their families as carefully as they balanced their checkbooks, and they never had need of something so tragic as an abortion. Abortions were for wild teens and women outside their socioeconomic class. Of course, they were enlightened, liberal people who supported a woman's right to choose, but they had never had to make that choice, and they had certainly never met a woman who spoke of it so matter-of-factly, as if she needed to have a tooth pulled.

Still, the ladies found a gynecologist among the synagogue's members and drove my mother to and from the appointments. They handled her gingerly, as if she were a delicate egg. She sensed their hesitation, however inexplicable, but she was grateful, both to the ladies and to the doctor, who didn't charge her for anything, not even the hospital fee or the anesthesia, which was included automatically, without any special favors, and didn't make her bite through the heel of her hand.

Emma arrived while my mother was studying at Kaplan for the boards, surrounded by other Soviet émigré doctors, many on their second or third attempt. My mother was convinced that she would soon become one of them, doomed to years of Kaplan purgatory. While my father worked and my mother went to classes, they discovered that combining work and childcare in America was difficult in an entirely new way. In America, there was no free government day care, and our grandmothers were all back in the Soviet Union. Emma came just in time, landing in Maryland a few months before the exam and freeing up my mother to study long into the night.

Oblivious to these dynamics, I was simply relieved to be reunited with Emma. She was the person I had missed the most, and I had carefully preserved her parting gift to me, a cardboard box in robin's-egg blue, cradling, in small compartments padded with wisps of cotton, part of Yura's extensive mineral collection. I wrote her letters from America, where I was sent to summer camp to learn to swim and speak English, which I did, eventually, after floating through that summer like a barely tethered balloon. When Emma arrived, we read *The Lord of the Rings* in Russian and went on walks on which she stopped to photograph every squirrel. My sister and I spent most of our days after school with Emma, who got more and more restless as the weeks stretched on. Unable to drive, she was trapped in the silent, cultureless American suburbs, with no sidewalks or public transport. Children—even her own grandchildren—were far less interesting to her than the news coming out of Moscow, a city seized once again by history, history she was missing in this lifeless backwater. In the evenings, my parents tried to convince her to join them in America forever. Cornered in their rental kitchen, she put off giving an answer.

Her husband, Oleg, who had a bad heart, did not appreciate his new wife being away for so long. Emma was both his companion and his cardiologist, and he sent her increasingly anguished missives, begging her to come home. He would go to Sheremetyevo Airport, he wrote. He would sit down on a bench in the arrivals hall, and he would wait there for as long as it took for Emma to walk through those mirrored, bronzed doors.

That last letter broke her. Emma packed her bags and changed her flight, leaving just a week before my mother's exams.

In the summer of 2002, we walked through those mirrored doors at Sheremetyevo once again—our first trip back to Moscow since we'd left twelve years earlier. Until that point, my parents had refused to waste scarce time and money on travel to a place that had rejected them. They had grown up behind the Iron Curtain and now had an entire world to discover. As soon as they got their green cards, my father took my mother to Paris, and she got to wander the city she thought she'd never set foot in. Finally, after a decade in the United States, my parents relented and agreed to visit their friends back in Russia. We got our Russian visas and made a visit to Moscow, a familiar city that had changed utterly.

After seven decades of an increasingly ineffective planned economy, the Russia that emerged from the Soviet Union in 1991 was completely bankrupt. Food shortages were so bad that our friends in Moscow thought famine was imminent. It was around this time that my father's sister and parents decided to leave. "Moscow in December 1991 is one of my most painful memories," a young reformer named Yegor Gaidar wrote of this time. "Grim food lines, even without their usual squabbles and scenes. Pristinely empty shelves. Women rushing about in search of food, any food, for sale. Expectations of disaster were in the air."[1]

Gaidar was one of the young men Yeltsin, the new Russian president, had hired to revive the economy. Urged on by their American expert advisors, they embraced a strategy of "shock therapy," releasing the supports of central planning all at once. By freeing prices, they unleashed inflation that ran as high as 25 percent per month and vaporized the life savings of most Russians. Industry came to a standstill; millions of Russians learned to live with monthslong wage arrears. Others took advantage of the gangland free-market economy and flaunted their instant fortunes—only to have them snatched away by brasher, more violent rivals.

Russia was wild in those years, unshackled after hundreds of years of autocracy, the new rules still in the process of being written. There was a vibrant press, an art scene that exuberantly ripped up every Soviet taboo, and a competitive political system that could not control the chaos or violence released by the Soviet collapse. The country careened from crisis to crisis, war to war, but it felt perilously, gloriously free.

By the time we arrived, Russia was no longer using the ruble but the "conditional unit," the equivalent of a sum in dollars, a remnant of the cataclysmic 1998 financial crisis. But Moscow was full of new restaurants, bars, and shops, all of them packed. It was nothing like the gray, monotone city we had left. Our family and friends had moved on without us, adjusting to the twin whirlwinds of capitalism and democracy. My mother's grade-school friend who had studied French at the Institute of Foreign Languages was now a bank executive. Another, who had studied programming with my father, was a successful businessman. Only my grandmother, it seemed, remained in her old job, still working at the Botkin Hospital, which crumbled, often quite literally, without the largesse of the long-deceased Central Committee.

My mother was different now, too. She had passed her exams and was now a pathologist. Otolaryngology, so lowly in the Soviet Union, was one of the most competitive specialties in American medicine and therefore closed to foreign graduates. My mother had mourned the loss of her expertise, but she learned to love the new one, too, the beauty of the pink and purple plumes of cells blooming like paisley on the slides under her microscope. Women like her had been a dime a dozen in the Soviet Union, physicians who also ran households after coming home from their clinics. But in America, where most doctors were men, my mother was a rarity. Many of the children I knew in school had mothers who they said were homemakers, pronouncing the word as if it were a skilled profession. It puzzled me. *My* mother did everything their mothers did, but she was also a doctor. She had a real job.

It wasn't anything my mother said; it was what she and my father did. She was a warm and involved mother as well as a phenomenal cook, but she was the one with the career, and my father, who also worked full-time, was the one for whom family was paramount. The way he spoke to my sister and me about school and work was founded on the assumption that we girls would be the breadwinners, an assumption so obvious that it didn't need to be stated or explained. Women married, had children, and worked. That was what my mother did, and her mother did, and her mother did. It was what my father's sister did and what his mother did and what his grandmother did. It was what all the Soviet women I knew in America did. Not working was for American women, and I grew up believing that there was something pathetic about it, as if they were incapable of being real women. Often my mother and my aunt would roll their eyes at American women who didn't work but didn't cook, either. What kept them so busy that they would poison their children and husbands with frozen dinners and takeout? It never occurred to me that the Soviet immigrant women I knew in America worked not because they were superior but because they had to. What I perceived as privilege was its opposite. And it wasn't until we returned to Moscow that I learned that not all Soviet women were like my mother.

Toward the end of our visit in 2002, Irina, my mother's best friend from medical school, invited us to her apartment, along with Natasha Gapchenko, another friend from Second Med, as they called it. Irina had married and taken her husband's name, which was unusual. My mother had only taken my father's last name a few years after we moved to America, where no one could pronounce or spell her maiden name or understand why she'd kept it. Neither Khinya nor Emma had taken their husbands' names, nor had their mothers, but America seemed to demand it. And, apparently, Russia now did, too. Irina had become a Petrova and her husband was a big businessman who owned a chain of car dealerships all over Moscow. I remember having tea in their sweeping apartment just off the Garden Ring and the look on my mother's face when Irina and Natasha proudly told her they hadn't practiced medicine in over a decade. They, too, were now homemakers.

In America, I had become Julia. The name on my refugee card offered a cluttered transliteration of my given name—Yuliya—and another of my last name—Ioffe—that would confuse every American who encountered it. (The last name, somewhat common among Soviet Jews, should have been spelled with a *Y* or maybe a *J*, but probably not an *I*, which, though it was the closest analogue to the Russian letter И, is easily mistaken for a lowercase *L* in English.) Thirty-some years later, my English name still rings foreign in my ear—a clashing *J*, a deaf, blunt *L*—a formal, multisyllabic equivalent of the name I had at home, all vowels and an *L* so light and lilting that it could hardly be a consonant. "Julia" never quite fit, but it sounded better than an American mouth mangling "Yulia," so I wore it, donning it every morning like a suit.

I didn't really fit, either. Even after my accent disappeared, I was reminded constantly by my schoolmates that I was the weird Russian girl and I should go back to where I came from. It was impossible to explain to an American that, although my parents and I were born in Moscow, no one would ever call us Russian. In the Soviet Union, Russian was strictly a Slavic ethnicity to which we Jews could never belong. "Right, but you were born in *Russia*," they'd say, "so you're Russian." It was pointless to argue. Besides, I loved being different from these provincial people in the suburbs. They looked down on me, and I looked down on them. I was an immigrant, yes, but I was from the capital city of a great world power. I had good table manners, and my parents took me to Europe and to the opera and the symphony, not to Florida or Broadway musicals and shopping in New York. I was the cultural heir to Pushkin and Tolstoy and Akhmatova, all of whom I was now reading in the original with my Russian tutor on Fridays after school. And I was the descendant of women who were doctors and scientists and engineers, women who kept their names, the product of what I thought to be the greatest feminist experiment on earth.

This was why I found myself baffled when I moved to New York as an adult and became friends with women who were steeped in American feminism. As far as I could tell, American women believed they had invented feminism, but their feminism seemed to encompass only sex and reproduction. If they wanted to be seen as more than human incubators, I wondered, why did they talk only about reproductive rights? My mother had always been open with me about her abortions. I knew that she had tried unsuccessfully to trigger a miscarriage when she was pregnant with me, and even at a relatively young age I fully understood why she had been so scared to have a child. It was something I never took personally. This was nearly two decades ago, when the question of abortion access in the United States looked far more settled, but the language of shame and urgency around the procedure was alien to me. So was the way that educated, progressive American women talked about sex and men and marriage, agonizing over whether they could "have it all," when their boyfriends would propose, and what their wedding dresses would look like.

So when I moved back to Moscow on a Fulbright, in September 2009, I expected to find a city full of women I recognized. They had, after all, been raised by the same system and the same culture. In Moscow, I thought, I would find women just like my mother and my grandmother, women just like me.

THE HUNT

I MET ALINA ROTENBERG IN THE SUMMER OF 2012 THROUGH GIAcomo, my Sicilian friend in Moscow. Despite his humble origins as the son of a small-town used car salesman, he had successfully infiltrated Moscow's beau monde, enamored as it was of anything European. Impeccably dressed, he became the willing plaything of the wealthy wives and ex-wives of oligarchs, discarded women that, to him, were beautiful and fascinating creatures. "These men trade in their old Porsche for a new Maserati," he told me once. "But, to me, there is nothing more beautiful than an antique car."

This was Alina: an antique Porsche traded in for something trendier, shinier, and, most importantly, younger. There were a lot of women like her in Moscow. They were beautiful, their laser-toned skin and ostentatiously expensive clothing advertising their wealth. But to the city around them, they were only beautiful *despite*: despite having been cast off, despite being old at thirty-five, despite having a "character," the Russian analogue of "difficult."

At thirty-six, Alina was no longer married, but her last name spoke volumes in Moscow: her ex-husband, Igor, was the son of Arkady Rotenberg, one of Vladimir Putin's childhood friends and judo buddies. After Putin was elected president in 2000, he made it clear that the oligarchs who had made their fortunes under Yeltsin would be able to keep their wealth only if they played by his new rules. Those who didn't were quickly forced to sell their assets, driven out of the country, or arrested. Putin then went about creating a new oligarchic class, one that consisted either of childhood friends, like the Rotenberg brothers, or members of the government hierarchy. The new oligarchs received plum no-bid contracts from the state. This was how Arkady Rotenberg, Alina's former father-in-law, became a billionaire. Civil servants, especially the *siloviki*, the strongmen of the FSB and other security structures, used their positions to extract tribute, extort protection money, or to expropriate businesses that caught their eye.

This post-Soviet *nomenklatura* was not that different from the Brezhnev-era one it replaced—and that was intentional. Putin had joined the KGB during Brezhnev's tenure, and, having used its power structure to reach Soviet society's upper rungs, he was all too happy to reproduce it. Back were the villas and apartments, the chauffeurs and the mistresses swaddled in foreign luxury. This time, however, it was on an entirely different scale. Now Russia had access to world markets—both for its exports and for its elites' insatiable appetites for foreign real estate and high-end goods. Among Russian women, this created a desperate desire to launch oneself into that gilded stratosphere, which could only be accomplished by snaring a man who flew up there.

In the constellation of the Putinist aristocracy, Alina's last name was a measure of how high she had risen and how far she had fallen. She arrived for our meeting in a white Audi convertible—her summer car, she told me. (A Range Rover Sport was her chariot of choice for the winter.) She was a striking woman, with dark, expertly curled hair spilling over her shoulders and the kind of delicate skin you could get only at the best Moscow spas. Her wrist was adorned with a Rolex, her neck and earlobes in diamonds and pearls. It was a steamy late summer weekday afternoon, but for a former duchess of the new Russian empire, there was no easing up on her grooming regimen.

In some ways, Alina's story could have been mine. Born to a Jewish family in Soviet Ukraine, her parents sent her away when she was fifteen to live with her grandparents, who had already emigrated to Israel. It was 1990 and they wanted to get her out of her native Lvov, which, as the Soviet Union disintegrated, was quickly becoming the domain of "racketeers and foreign-currency prostitutes," as Alina put it. In Israel, she finished high school and earned a degree in psychology from Tel Aviv University. At twenty-one, she moved to England and studied organizational psychology at the London School of Economics. In London, she ran with a crew of women just like herself: smart, educated twenty-somethings who worked in the financial sector as investment bankers and consultants.

In 2001, she followed a Russian boyfriend to Moscow. After coming of age around the hard women of Israel and the emancipated ladies of London, she was amazed by what floors most Western visitors to Moscow: Russian women. "I see them a lot in the gym, these very obvious one-day butterflies," Alina told me. "Long, styled hair; very, very thin. These are physically very attractive girls, usually without any real education, and usually from out of town. You see them one day suddenly drive up in a Bentley, and you think, 'Okay, she made it.'" These were the girls to whom Alina would find herself losing, time and time again, in the city's fierce battle for men.

She eventually left the boyfriend, started working in finance, and, in 2003, married spectacularly well, to Igor Rotenberg. As his father's wealth grew, Igor was also handed state contracts and groomed as his heir. But Alina couldn't seem to get the hang of the marital dynamic. "We had a very good relationship for a long time, until I started working again and I started competing with him," she said. She had quit her finance job and, like so many elite wives, started an interior decorating business. She figured there were now two entrepreneurs in the family, but her husband didn't see it that way. Even as Igor's fortune grew, Alina told me she kept pointing out her achievements and his lack of them. She had been educated abroad at prestigious universities; he had gone to St. Petersburg's State University of Physical Education. She was sophisticated; he was a jock. "Everyone was looking at him adoringly, and I was constantly haranguing him," she said. "At some point, he just got sick of it." They divorced in 2008. Igor left her an apartment and her parents the dacha he had built for them. That was it. She went from being the wife of a multimillionaire to someone with a nice apartment and not much else.

"It was my fault," Alina concluded. If she could do it all over again, she would change everything. "I understood that you have to protect the male ego very, very carefully," she explained. "It's delusional to think that a man needs some kind of exceptional woman. He needs a woman with whom *he* feels exceptional." Igor had since married his secretary, a woman Alina considered to be "of average appearance and dubious internal composition." And yet, "with her, he feels like a great man. I didn't understand this before. I always thought that I'd be this extremely exceptional woman, and he'd say, 'This is my dog. I'm very proud of it. I am its owner.' But it's not like that at all."

In fact, she noted, none of the ultra-wealthy men in her circle had married educated, Westernized women like her. They married women like Igor's second wife. Two years after Alina and Igor got married, Igor's father, Arkady, married a twenty-four-year-old peroxide blonde named Natalia. She was a dance teacher from Kurgan, an impoverished backwater just past the Urals. Natalia had gone from a shabby apartment building to the Moscow and London mansions of one of the most powerful men in Russia and one of the richest in the world. To Alina's amazement, Natalia, who was five years younger than her, never seemed self-conscious about her origins. "She's absolutely confident in the fact that she deserves everything," Alina said. "Someone once asked her if she could have ever imagined that she'd have a three-hundred-foot yacht, and she says, 'Yes.' How? How did she imagine it? She's from a family with many, many kids, and they all lived in one room without a bathroom." Whenever Natalia called her husband, Alina told me, Arkady always answered the phone, even when he was in a meeting with Putin.

Alina became convinced that these women had a special, subconscious talent. It was the Russian woman's innate ability to understand men for the animals that they are and to use her feminine wiles to manipulate their simple instincts. A trained observer of psychology, Alina made careful note of the strategies that seemed to work for the gazelle-like young women who became the lovers of her friends' husbands.

She identified several key strategies. A man, Alina posited, needs a good fight once in a while, preferably in public, to prevent boredom. After the squabble, the woman had to disappear into the appearance of nonchalant busyness, "even if she's never worked a day in her life." Another lesson: "A man values a woman a lot more if she is constantly dragging presents out of him, and he values her a lot more than the woman who says, 'No, no, no, I don't need anything.'" In Alina's calculation, a woman's value was proportional to the effort and resources a man had invested in her.

"They get everything this way," Alina said, half-rueful, half-awestruck, as she compared these canny young women to supposedly smarter women like the two of us. "But we're emancipated, we want to do everything honestly, and we'll insist on our truth. It doesn't work." She went on, cradling her teacup in her elegant hands: "I think that these things should be explained to girls in childhood. It's a very important thing. And it doesn't matter if the girl is smart or not, because you can have a girl who goes to university and gets a PhD and is tremendously accomplished but then loses to these pretty young things who will take away her husband before she can count to three."

As for those pretty young things, Alina warned me that feeling superior to them is a fool's comfort. "Everyone makes fun of these women because they're walking around with designer bags with diamond clasps, but they're all set: things are working out just fine for them," she said, shaking her head. "They're geniuses. Absolute geniuses."

"A man doesn't go where he is nagged, he doesn't go where he is put down, but where he is told that he is exceptional, that he is the god-emperor, the light in the window, that he is the very best," said Olga Kopylova.[1] It was a cool evening in September 2012, and about a dozen women sat cross-legged on the floor at an open house at the Life Academy, just off Aleksandr Solzhenitsyn Street, as Kopylova and the other instructors explained how they could help these busy Moscow women find happiness in their personal lives.

It was no small task. Several generations after World War II, there was still a sense, bordering on panic, that good men—the ones with well-paying jobs and without drinking problems—were essentially an endangered species. Even my Moscow girlfriends constantly blamed the war for what they called the "depletion of the gene pool," though when it came to men of marrying age, the male population had long since recovered, at least on paper, for the simple reason that boys and girls are born at essentially equal rates.

Still, this didn't *feel* true to Russian women. Single, decent men seemed to them a deficit good. As one Russian girlfriend told me, "Men are like public toilets: either taken or shat in." And so Russian women felt time keenly, as if knowing down to the second how long they had until their physical beauty—their main *aktiv*, their chief asset—would cease to be competitive in a cutthroat market. Until then, they capitalized on what nature had given them, investing as much as they could in clothing, makeup, and beauty procedures. (I was often asked by women in Moscow why American women "didn't take care of themselves.") During the financial crisis of 2008, Russia was the G20 country hit hardest by the economic collapse, and yet cosmetics sales didn't budge. Russian politicians, usually male, frequently touted Russian women as the most beautiful in the world, as if they were, like oil and gas, another natural resource to be exploited in Russia's march back to superpower status.

Among themselves, Russian women competed fiercely for male attention and male commitment—a commodity even rarer than the actual men. Expecting a man's sexual fidelity in a marriage was seen as puritanical and unrealistic, even by the women they were cheating on.[2] Infidelity was just men's nature, they said, implying that, in this country that had once diverted wild rivers and dried up whole seas, a man's nature was absolutely immutable. If anything, having mistresses was a status symbol for successful men: How many women (and love children) could he afford to maintain? One Moscow banker I knew, on his third marriage at thirty-six, told me about a real estate project his bank was financing: an elite gated community with $10 million homes in the center for the wives and the legitimate children, surrounded by a ring of smaller, humbler homes, around $2 million each, for the mistresses and their illegitimate children. This was much more convenient for everybody, explained the banker, who always vacationed with his wife, two ex-wives, and all their children, even though each successive wife had started out as a mistress.

And yet, despite the paltry, tentative prize at the end of it, this was a race Russian women never stopped running: first to snare a husband, then to fend off the other women who were surely scheming to take him from her. (As the sociologist Lyubov Borusyak explained to me, Russian women see men as "veal calves on a rope that a crafty woman can lead away.") When I moved to Russia in 2009, I felt this competition everywhere—in the hostile looks from other women in the Metro, in cafés, even in the checkout line at the little shop on the ground floor of our building, where the middle-aged, gold-toothed cashier growled at me only to coo flirtatiously at the old man in an *ushanka* buying cigarettes and single-serving-sized bottles of cognac.

The Life Academy was created to serve this demand for men, which was itself an outgrowth of the failure of the Soviet feminist experiment. By 1991, Russian women were exhausted from all the things that the previous decades of Soviet rule had required of them. But the collapse of the Soviet Union did not allow women to return to their womanly mission, as Gorbachev had proposed. Faced with hunger, instability, and salaries that weren't paid for months, millions of Russian men lay down on the couch and took to drink.

Again, it was women who stepped into the breach. School principals washed toilets; physicists became cashiers. As their men fell away—and divorce rates surged—it was, once again, on the women to feed their families. And because there was no longer a paternalistic state that promised to be their child's father, they had to assume that role, too, unless a grandmother moved in to help. All of this had left them pining for a romantic, Western ideal of a stay-at-home wife supported and protected by a rich and masculine man. As Elena Zdravomyslova, a sociologist and feminist scholar in St. Petersburg, argued, "The liberation of women from at least part of the double burden can be seen, at least in part, as a liberation of women."

This new ideal, which Zdravomyslova called "civilized patriarchy," offered Russian women many benefits, the chief one being choice. She can, theoretically, stay at home or she can work for her own pleasure and self-actualization. She can call the reproductive shots while her husband works, shielding her from the harsh reality of the Russian workplace. A family with one breadwinner is "all people dream of here, because they never had it," explained Zdravomyslova. One hundred years after Kollontai and Lenin railed against traditional, economically motivated marriage as a prison for Russian women, it had become their ultimate fantasy.

The Life Academy fed on that desperate longing, telling women that they could unlearn all the behaviors society had forced them to master—or at least mask them well enough to fool a man. Every woman, Kopylova explained, cycled through four states of being: the little girl, the seductress, the queen, and the *khozayka*, the mistress of the house, "who," Kopylova clarified, "has the most expensive things and all the very best men." Like the four humors, these four states of femininity could explain absolutely everything that went wrong in a woman's life. What did it mean, Kopylova asked her rapt students, if a man stopped giving you gifts? "It means the state of the little girl is suffering, that the girl isn't present enough," she declared, striking the satisfyingly didactic chord of a teacher in front of a chalkboard. "Because the girl moves the man to action, to feats of chivalry. He wants to take care of the girl, he wants to give her presents, because she doesn't say, 'You're doing everything wrong.' She doesn't nag him, so he wants to do things for her. A man feels big with a girl like this, and the girl for him is small." Or, let's say, Kopylova posited, you were able to attract a man but not keep him. What was to blame for that? This was obviously the weakening of your internal *khozayka*—which was, of course, fixable with the right procedures taught exclusively at the Life Academy.

"This is a man," Kopylova said, holding up a dry-erase marker to signify a phallus. She wrapped her manicured hand tightly around it. "When we interact with him, we take him in, squeeze him, and surround him. And this is natural, because a woman receives, squeezes, and surrounds, and a man is a vector. A man even has a special little device that shows his vector, his direction. So if he suddenly finds some woman attractive, his little device immediately shows him what direction to move in." If a woman fails to hold his interest, Kopylova said, "his device goes down," he starts saying he's busy at work, "and we'll never see him again."

There was another way, Kopylova explained, to confuse a man's little device. "When we keep saying, 'I'll do it myself,' or when we give him advice—stupid advice, let's be honest—a man interprets it as you taking a sickle to his balls. Tell me, will he have any potency left after you've cut everything off down there?" And if a woman was too focused on her career, too headstrong, Kopylova warned, she risked having her feminine energy turn into an invisible phallus made of masculine energy. "A man can see, on an intuitive level, that you have a member and he has a member," Kopylova pressed on. "Can you have sex with him? He's a normal, traditional guy, right? You can't!" What would he do with a woman like you, she wondered: Get into a measuring contest?

But all was not lost. The expert teachers of the academy were happy to guide women back to a true feminine balance. A successful enterprise with several national outposts, the Life Academy had a large syllabus of classes: "How to Find Love," "Flirtation from A to Z," "The Art of Walking Beautifully," "Mysteries of the Jade Cave: How to Use Your Intimate Muscles," "How to Play the Magic Flute: The Art of Fellatio." (These last two offerings aroused the most interest during the open house.) The academy's all-time most popular class, however, was "How to Not Be a Mother to Your Man."

The academy's teachings were an awkward pastiche, combining Eastern Orthodox Christianity, Hinduism, Slavic paganism, Siberian shamanism, South American spiritual practices, as well as those from the Daoist, Sufi, and Tibetan traditions—spiked with elements of Jungian and American pop psychology. After explaining the four feminine humors, Kopylova revealed that an imbalance could be corrected only by reopening and realigning one's chakras, an ancient Hindu concept. "I had one young woman who really wanted to give her boyfriend an expensive new car," Kopylova said to illustrate how badly a backward-spinning chakra could mislead a woman. "Of course, it's your choice, but if you give a man expensive presents, then you are definitely not his girlfriend. You are his mommy, and men don't want to sleep with their mothers." By the end of the open house, she was selling the women on a very handy dildo—a *falloimitator* in Russian—which was for sale at the academy for just 2,200 rubles, perfect for practice in the Magic Flute class.

One evening not long after the open house, I stopped by the Life Academy to interview its founder. Larisa Renar was soft-spoken and deliberately dainty. She had dyed bright copper hair, round cheeks, and big blue eyes. She wore a long, diaphanous dress and the Medallion of Women's Strength, a round, filigreed pendant with four gemstones representing those four states of femininity: the little girl, the seductress, the queen, and the mistress of the house. The medallion, worn by all the academy's instructors, was, according to the website, connected to antiquity and "the cult of Aphrodite." You could earn one by taking at least six seminars and demonstrating that you understood Renar's core teachings.

As Renar poured me tea, I asked why she had opened the academy back in 2000. "I think the real problem is that modern society, and not just in Russia but in the whole world, forces women to live according to male standards: to be like a man, to act like a man, to look like a man," she began, her lilting soprano unhurried and thoughtful.[3] In Russia, this problem was especially acute. "Women carry all the responsibility," she explained. "A woman makes all the decisions. She makes the money. And in Russia a lot of women are too active, too independent. It's related to historical events, to wars and revolutions when men were killed and women had no choice but to take on leadership roles. Our mothers are very active; they don't acknowledge male authority or respect men. My generation of women, the ones born in the sixties, who are now somewhere between thirty-five and forty-five—it really is easier for us to do everything ourselves and not depend on the men."

I told Renar that I had to agree with her. By that point, I'd been living in Russia for three years and dating a Russian man for one of them. This particular man gave me flowers and paid me poignant compliments, he held the door and pulled out my chair in restaurants. By all outward appearances he was successful and handsome, but with me, he was a needy and manipulative child. His inability to make hard decisions or abstain from becoming a maudlin, clingy drunk had transformed me from his girlfriend and lover into his mother and disciplinarian. As much as I had come to find him pathetic, I hated myself far more because of what I had become with him: a scold, a jealous girlfriend who waited for him to fall asleep so I could read through his phone, a woman angry and bitter beyond my years.

And yet I knew for certain that, in Moscow, he was the very best that I could get. Every woman I knew (and some I'd never met) made sure to remind me of this fact. Other women openly pined for him; one tried to kiss him in public. "Men don't grow on trees," my grandmother chided whenever I would lose my mind with rage and despair at his behavior. Plus, as she and my Russian girlfriends pointed out, he really loved me. What did it matter than I no longer loved him? What a foolish idea! Many of those Russian girlfriends believed my problems would vanish if I simply married him and had a child. "Just give birth!" they would all say. Emma agreed with this assessment, pointing out that you didn't need a perfect man to have a baby. Having a baby was paramount and I didn't need a perfect man for *that*. "You can always get divorced!" she said by way of reassurance. After all, I was nearing thirty and, apparently, the end of my life.

"Yes, men have been ground down," Renar said, as if reading my thoughts. "This situation when a woman is strong, and not in a feminine way but a masculine one, and a man is weak, this role reversal is what has led to women's unhappiness. Because after all, she is a woman. Her head is wired differently, she manifests differently in the world, and she has different functions. Taking on these male functions destroys her. They destroy her psychologically and, unfortunately, physically. This is what leads to diseases like breast cancer, uterine cancer—because of this lack of acceptance of her own femininity." Renar believed that the problem for women—her wildly inaccurate ideas about the etiology of gynecological cancers notwithstanding—wasn't that they were still working the double shift; it was that they were too much like the men they had had to replace out of sheer necessity.

Russian men, Renar posited, had abandoned their three core functions. The most important of these was making decisions. This dereliction, however, was the fault of their women. "This ability to relinquish authority to a man is very difficult for Russian women," she explained. A man's second function was to protect his woman, which is hard to do if the woman he is supposed to protect has become *his* protector—or his mother. A man's third function was to provide—for his woman and for his family. And yet, for many years now, Renar said she'd been hearing shocking stories from the women who came through her doors, like the wife who spent her salary on the family's rent, groceries, and their children's education while the husband, who also made a decent bit of money, contributed nothing. "I don't know what he spent it on. Himself, I guess!" she exclaimed, flustered at the sacrilege of it. "But the wife of course still sleeps with him, still cooks for him. I see these kinds of stories and I think, 'Then what is the point of living with a man like that?'"

The solution, as Renar outlined in her 2015 book, *Make Your Husband a Millionaire*, is to channel your feminine energy into inspiring your man to become wealthy and successful. Renar, who is herself a successful businesswoman, told me she thinks it is wonderful for women to have careers. But she also defined feminism as an extreme ideology because it destroyed the natural equilibrium between men and women. "A man gives us women a home, physical protection, and a woman gives him pleasure, enjoyment of sex, beauty," she explained. "And so we should be ready to listen to and follow our man, to say, 'You're the man, you're the boss, you're right.'"

Eleonora and Leyla never attended the Life Academy, but they understood its teachings instinctively. Like me, they were both born in 1982; Leyla in Ufa, the capital of the Soviet Republic of Bashkhorostan, Eleonora in what was then Leningrad. Like me, both came from the Soviet middle class, from families of engineers and accountants who, in the stagnation of the 1980s, found themselves to be, practically, rather poor.

Both women had provincial upbringings until they met men significantly older than themselves. Leyla's Frenchman, an art collector twice her age, picked her up in one of Moscow's posh nightclubs and began to educate her intensively. There were days in Parisian galleries and museums, quizzes at night. "Like Pygmalion," Leyla told me. Eleonora met the scion of a celebrity Moscow family in St. Petersburg. He taught her about luxury hotels, about fine dining and silk napkins. "Like *Pretty Woman*," Eleonora recalled.

After Leyla and the Frenchman eventually parted ways, she made use of that education and became an interior designer, the universal profession of a glamorous Russian *devushka*. But although she loved her work, she craved the economic security of marriage—and she proceeded to make it happen in record time. After meeting her future husband through a friend, she quickly determined that he ticked most of her boxes. Ten days later, he proposed. How did she do it? "I think that my abilities helped me: conviction, marketing, management," Leyla said. "I successfully advertised myself and was able to show myself in a positive light." If it had been love with the Frenchman, this relationship, Leyla admitted, was "cold calculation."

When we met, she showed me around the well-decorated apartment she shared with her husband, who was also her boss in the design business they ran together. He wasn't home, and he'd been gone all summer. Sometimes he called to say something sweet, but mostly he called to tell her he didn't owe her anything.

Recounting this, Leyla, who had told me she strived to be "a flinty woman" like Margaret Thatcher, began to cry. "When I got married, I was hoping for solid ground under my feet, a husband as my shoulder, and I've got nothing," she said, her face going blotchy. "We've been married for two years, and for the last six months I've been realizing that there's only me, my work, my head, my strength, my brains, my ambition, and that's it. That there is absolutely nothing around me."

She wasn't sure that she was ready for divorce. The women in her circle who had found rich husbands "will absolutely stay with them," she said, even if these husbands openly cheated or had parallel families with their lovers. Her friends took lovers, too, usually men over whom they had some power: bodyguards, drivers, or *hachiki*, a racial slur for men from the Muslim North Caucasus. Leyla's friend Mahmoud, a Dagestani, used to sleep with one of her friends and said he looked for these kinds of women: rich, married, and neglected. They were perfectly low-maintenance, he said, and they wanted only one thing from him. Alina Rotenberg also remarked that several of her friends, even those married to *Forbes*-listed billionaires, liked to play around with the occasional Mahmoud.

When I met Eleonora at a Moscow restaurant, she at first appeared to be an anomaly in that she was still unmarried at the advanced age of twenty-nine. A pink-cheeked, pug-nosed blonde who looked like she'd walked off the pages of a Russian folktale, Eleonora had spent the morning examining an out-of-town warehouse in heels and an elegant cashmere sweater. She was a real estate broker, a business that, in Moscow, is as vicious as it is lucrative.

Her parents did not approve of her high-grossing career. "The ideal picture for my parents is to give me away to some wealthy guy so that I am taken care of, so that he earns all the money, and so that I would take care of the house," Eleonora explained. She was in no rush to get married, but when the time came, Eleonora said, she wanted a man who was "stronger," by which she meant a man who earned more money than she did. "It is the nature of Russian women to be behind a man's back no matter how successful they are," she reasoned. "If there's a man, then the woman will always prefer to be number two."

This was so strange to hear. Eleonora reminded me of my girlfriends back in New York: She was a beautiful, intelligent, well-educated woman who loved her career and made a fabulously good living doing it. But, unlike them, she would gladly give it all up in an instant. Renar would have approved, I thought.

But when I met Renar again, in 2015, I discovered that she hadn't managed to successfully apply her teachings to her own life. She had a marriage that most Russian women only dream of. Her husband was a handsome and intelligent older man who was a pioneer in the post-Soviet advertising market. He had helped her achieve her dream of getting into a psychology PhD program, and after he became a millionaire, he bought her a building in St. Petersburg to house the business that eventually became the Life Academy.

And yet she wasn't happy. On the scale of love that she had developed, the fifth and highest level was when two people love each other so completely that their hearts block their bodies from lusting after anyone else. Most love in the world falls short of that ideal, she told me. Renar and her husband's love, for instance, was on the second level, when you choose your mate not with your heart but with your head. At this level, Renar explained, your desire for others does not disappear. And so he had affairs, she had affairs, and in this way they were just like so many other Russian couples "who are always searching for someone better, constantly scanning the options," Renar said. As much as Russian society insisted on traditional marriage, she observed, "the value of faithfulness isn't supported in our society; it's laughed at. Like, 'What, you're faithful to your wife? Is everything okay? Are you having issues?'"

As the academy flourished, Renar increasingly questioned her own marriage. "I thought, 'My God, how is this happening?'" she recalled. "'I'm smart, I'm beautiful, I'm sexy, I've learned every sexual technique I can think of. I'm trying to develop myself, I'm doing everything for our family.'" When she asked her husband for a divorce, in 2010, he thought it was foolishness. This was as close to happiness as any married couple could get in Russia. Asking for more could lead only to being alone, a far worse fate for a Russian woman than being unhappy. But he complied.

Five years later, Renar was dating a man a decade her junior, which clearly delighted her. "I think I will get married again, absolutely," she told me. "And I will only marry a man not because he loves me, or because he checks the boxes on some checklist, but only when, inside of myself, I will have that knowledge that this man is the best man for me."

After three years in Moscow, I knew that I simply did not want to be a woman in Russia. In all that time, I had not managed to find those Russian women who were just like me. Meanwhile, Russian men hardly saw me as a woman. I didn't dress or behave like a cartoon of femininity and I had ideas about equality and work that they found either threatening or comical. Most treated me as if I were some kind of neutered, third-gender *it*.

In 2012, I turned thirty and my biological clock was roaring in my ears, as was the advice of my grandmother and every Russian woman I knew when I tried, over and over again, to break up with the Russian man. The chorus was deafening: "But he really loves you!" they all said. Deep in my most Soviet of souls, I feared they were right. Could I really do better? I was, after all, old. I had a "character." I was reminded of my mother's advice: "If you're looking for perfect," she would say, "you'll end up alone." My mother, too, I realized, was not that different from these Russian women, always on the hunt. And neither, it seemed, was I. Over and over again, I went back to the Russian man, only to get frustrated, break up with him, become paralyzed with the realization that I'd never do better, go back to him, and start the cycle over again. In the fall of 2012, I moved back to the United States, but that just stretched the torture across eight time zones. After three years, and as many breakups, the Russian man followed me to Washington, over my repeated objections, understandably not believing that I had finally made up my mind and broken up with him one sixth and final time. "You don't know what you want," he told me. "I do."

My time in Russia had left me confounded: How had Russian women gone from Lyudmila Pavlichenko, the legendary Soviet sniper, to the academy's man-hungry client base? How had the stereotype of the Russian woman gone from a superhuman figure who could stop a galloping steed and enter a burning hut to a one-day butterfly or an accomplished woman whose highest aspiration was to be a number two to her husband? The answer lay not with Russian women but with Russian men—and explained the rise of one Russian man in particular.

LYUDMILA

"LYUDA, I CONGRATULATE YOU!" ONE OF HER GIRLFRIENDS EXclaimed, using the familiar version of her name when Lyudmila picked up the phone. It was New Year's Eve 1999, and she thought this was yet another of the many New Year's greetings pinging around Moscow that day.[1]

"And I you!" she responded automatically.

Her friend was baffled.

"Haven't you heard?" she asked.

"No," Lyuda stuttered. "What happened?"[2]

What happened was that at noon, Boris Yeltsin, the Russian president, had announced on national television that he was resigning his post and handing it over to a caretaker until the presidential elections in March.[3]

It was a wonder that Yeltsin had held on for that long—or that he even won a second term in 1996. As his first term neared its end, his approval ratings were in the single digits while the Communist Gennady Zyuganov surged in the polls. The oligarchs who had accumulated so much wealth under Yeltsin's rule, as well as much of the Russian intelligentsia, were petrified: What if Zyuganov won and reinstated the Soviet system just five years after its collapse? Unwilling to take the chance, the oligarchs teamed up with American political consultants, domestic spin doctors, and Russian journalists to reelect Yeltsin. In July 1996, after a runoff, Yeltsin was elected to a second term with 54 percent of the vote.

But the victory proved Pyrrhic. A few months after his reelection, Yeltsin barely survived quintuple bypass surgery. Just when he had recovered, he caught a nasty virus and again disappeared from view. Yeltsin, a charismatic giant who had faced down tanks in 1991 and again during a standoff with the Duma in 1993, was now a shadow of himself. He slurred his speech; his attention wandered. Increasingly, Russia was ruled in his stead by regents in the Kremlin, the oligarchs, and Yeltsin's daughter and son-in-law.

At the end of Yeltsin's second term—the last permitted by the Russian constitution—his minders decided to pick an interim president they could control rather than risk an open election with a newcomer in the presidential election of March 2000. Yeltsin's minders wanted a younger, more vigorous man to contrast with Yeltsin, who could now barely speak. They also needed this person to feel indebted to the consortium of oligarchs and Yeltsin's family members who had made him king—and allow them to keep their often ill-gotten gains. They settled on Yeltsin's newly appointed prime minister and Lyuda's husband: Vladimir Vladimirovich Putin.

Lyuda and Volodya had discussed this possibility once, months ago, but she had thought it was all theoretical. It turned out that Yeltsin had anointed her husband as his successor nearly three weeks before springing it on the country, but Volodya hadn't bothered to tell her. She didn't even find out when her countrymen did. Since she hadn't known that she should turn on the TV, she missed her husband informing the entire country that he was now their president. The full understanding of what her husband had just done, without any consultation, overwhelmed her. "I understood that my personal life ended with this," she confessed a few weeks later. "For three months at least, until the presidential election, and at most for four years." She cried the rest of the day.

In reality, her personal life had ended long before. It happened in Leningrad over the International Women's Day holiday weekend in 1980, when the twenty-two-year-old Lyuda met the friend of a friend of a friend on the steps of the Lensovet Theatre. He was a bleak and unremarkable young man named Volodya Putin.[4] "He was very modestly dressed," Lyuda recalled years later. "I would even say, shabbily. He was so nondescript, I wouldn't have even noticed him on the street."[5] Lyuda herself was hardly a great beauty. It was mostly her youth that made her pretty. It amplified her thick blond hair and big blue eyes set low and wide on her face; it distracted from her tiny mouth with its slightly buck teeth.

Lyuda had grown up in Kaliningrad, a new Soviet outpost nestled on the northern coast of Poland, part of the spoils of 1945. The daughter of a factory worker and a cashier, she had dropped out of technical college for the much more glamorous work of being an Aeroflot flight attendant.[6] This is what had brought her and her coworker Galina on a short trip to Leningrad in March 1980. A local young man had invited Galina to the theater and she asked Lyuda to come with her, which prompted the young man to invite his friend. It was Volodya who, through his connections, was able to produce the tickets for this popular and hard-to-see show. Growing bold during the intermission, Lyuda asked him if he could get tickets for the next night's show at the Leningrad Music Hall. Volodya managed to procure those, too, as well as more tickets for the following night. When it was time for Lyuda to fly back to Kaliningrad, Volodya gave her his telephone number. This surprised his friend: Volodya didn't readily give out his personal information.

When Lyuda got home to Kaliningrad, she called him. Soon she was cobbling together four-day weekends and flying to Leningrad to visit.[7] By July she had decided: "This is exactly the person that I very much needed."[8] She moved to Leningrad and applied to Leningrad State University, Volodya's alma mater. Volodya helped her find a room to rent in a communal apartment and a job to cover the rent.[9]

But Volodya proved a hard man to love. He was stubborn and silent, closed and bristly. He was gratuitously late for every date. By the time he arrived an hour and a half late (his standard), Lyuda felt too defeated to register her discontent. And yet she always showed up on time, hoping that this would be the day he would be as punctual for her as he was for his work. Remembering her long waits decades later, she chided herself for not bringing a book.[10]

Lyuda's decision in July 1980 to love Volodya Putin proved to be her last in the relationship. Going forward, it was Volodya who made all the decisions, big and small. She was his obedient subject, his first before he acquired 143 million more.

In 1981, Volodya decided they would take up downhill skiing. He didn't ask Lyuda's opinion. "For Vladimir Vladimirovich, it was self-evident that we would just start skiing," she recalled.[11] This was not an obvious hobby in a city that was built on a flat marsh, and the ski jump took nearly two hours to reach on public transport. But Volodya insisted on going every weekend.[12] Every Sunday night, exhausted and freezing in the commuter train back to the city, all Lyuda wanted was to be home in her room. Skiing now took up all her free time as well as her resources.

That was how their relationship unfolded. Nadya Alliluyeva had fought for her autonomy despite Stalin's suffocating traditionalism, and even Viktoria Brezhnev had managed to carve out her own fiefdom under her husband's staid rule, but Volodya Putin did not want or need a woman to have goals or thoughts of her own. He required only mute obedience. In the summer of 1981, while on vacation in Crimea, Volodya insisted on going out to the end of a wild peninsula that was accessible only by trekking over treacherous cliffs or swimming around the shoreline. Lyuda didn't know how to swim, but Volodya decided to take the sea route anyway. Since not going was not an option, she paddled along on a raft in the open water and got so badly sunburned that her skin sloughed off for days afterward. When they finally reached the spot he had in mind, Volodya spent an hour sitting underwater with a spear gun, which he made her carry on the return journey, since he had decided to trek back over the cliffs. Lyuda was left to paddle back alone and was so panicked during this ordeal that she couldn't remember how she made it back to their room.[13]

This was, she felt, his way of testing her. "I always had the feeling that he was constantly observing me," she remembered. "What decision will I make? Will it be the right one or not?"[14] Once, early in their courtship, she made the wrong decision. During one of her visits to Leningrad, they went to a party where Lyuda danced and laughed and enjoyed herself. "Vladimir Vladimirovich didn't like this, and I was told extremely clearly that a continuation of our relationship was impossible," she said. "I didn't even argue since everything was said quite definitively." Heartbroken, she returned to Kaliningrad.

Two weeks later, she saw a note from him pinned to her apartment door. The note, which addressed her as *druzhochek*, or tiny little friend, included his number at the hotel. Lyuda raced over and, when they met, she wept and confessed her love. Volodya, however, was very clear that Lyuda was not the reason for the trip: he was in town for work. The hour of his flight back to Leningrad approached, and he still hadn't taken her back. Lyuda followed him to the airport, where, at the departure gate, in the last moments before boarding the plane, "he decided to continue our relationship."[15]

Lyuda was nearing her mid-twenties. It was high time to get married, and Volodya had an inner strength that pulled her to him like a magnet. In a country where masculinity was in crisis, he exuded a "masculine dependability," she told an interviewer decades later. He didn't drink or lose control of himself. He was always trim and active and took his health seriously. Unlike the driftwood that passed for men in those days, Volodya had goals and ambitions and focus.

He was the third and only surviving son of two parents hardened by life. His father, Vladimir, had been gravely injured in World War II in a battle just outside Leningrad. His mother, Maria, had nearly died of starvation during the city's 872-day siege. Volodya's two eldest brothers died of disease, the first shortly after his birth, the second of typhus in an orphanage in besieged Leningrad. Volodya was born when Maria was forty-one, part of the postwar baby boom. His barely literate mother worked menial jobs and his crippled father worked long hours, a cold and distant presence. Volodya's world was largely devoid of girls. What he saw in popular culture, especially in *The Sword and the Shield*, the popular spy films that inspired him to join the KGB, reinforced the notion that women were not real people. In the films' romanticized view, men ran the world and women were there to help them. They were to be treated politely, but they were not equals, nor were they for falling in love with. They were tools, vessels.

This rigid division of the sexes was familiar, even reassuring, to Lyuda, as it was to most Soviet women born into the traditionalism of the postwar era. If anything, it appealed to her that her wishes were always subservient to Volodya's. It took the pressure off her. In a hard Soviet life, he offered the rare promise of stability and comfort.

Lyuda didn't understand exactly what Volodya did, but she knew he had a very good job. He told her he worked as a detective in the police department, though he always deflected her questions with jokes.[16] His salary and connections allowed him to get goods others couldn't—like those theater tickets at their first meeting—to drive her around in his own car, and to take her on vacation to the Black Sea, where they stayed in the guardhouse of Brezhnev's seaside villa and played tennis.

It was a year and a half into their relationship when she learned he was working for the KGB. In the office one day, her coworker, the girlfriend of one of Volodya's friends, revealed the truth out of nowhere. "You know, Lyuda, that Volodya..." She hesitated. "I don't think he works in criminal investigations," she finished, adding that Lyuda's boyfriend was in fact an officer of the feared secret police.[17]

The news hurt Lyuda deeply. She had always wanted to know more about what Volodya did all day, not because she was nosy but because she wanted to be his confidante, his support. But no matter how much she tried to create this kind of partnership, he never told her anything, and now she knew why. A year and a half into a courtship she hoped would end in marriage, he still did not trust her.[18] After all those tests, she was still hovering on the perimeter of his life, waiting to be allowed in.

It occurred to Lyuda that perhaps Volodya had asked this coworker to tell her on his behalf. But she couldn't be sure. There was suddenly a lot she couldn't be sure of. She remembered an incident when she went outside to the pay phone to call Volodya at an agreed-upon time—her apartment in Leningrad didn't have a phone—but he didn't pick up. As she turned to go back inside, she saw a young man walking briskly behind her. When she started running, he did, too. Then he called out to her—from the depths of his heart, Lyuda felt. "*Devushka*, young lady!" he exclaimed when he finally caught up to her. "It's fate. It's fate! I would so like to get to know you!" She waved him off. He begged for her telephone number; she said she didn't have one. He asked her to take down his; she refused and went home. Lyuda hadn't thought anything of it at the time, but now she wondered: Had Volodya sent that young man to test her? She asked him about it again and again, and each time he deftly evaded the question. Speaking to an interviewer twenty years later, she said, "I still don't know what it was, a test or just some young man who wanted to get my number."[19]

Lyuda may have decided fairly quickly that she wanted to marry Volodya, but it took him three years to decide the same about her. It was an unheard-of delay for a generation more accustomed to shotgun weddings than long engagements. But Volodya was in no rush. He had been engaged before, to a young doctor also named Lyuda, but broke things off just before the wedding. At Lyuda's first meeting with his mother, Maria told her that she had liked the first Lyuda better.

Volodya's friends liked the second Lyuda well enough. Though his friend Sergei Roldugin described her as occasionally "suffocating," he appreciated that his friend was with "a real woman." As Roldugin recalled approvingly, she "can not sleep all night and have fun, but in the morning, will tidy the apartment and cook everything."[20]

Volodya himself would have been perfectly happy living a life independent of attachment to another human were it not for his socially conservative employer.[21] There was something dangerously nonconformist about men who didn't marry, and in the KGB it made them susceptible to blackmail and honeypot traps. Volodya's career had been puttering along for nine years, and he seemed no closer to his dream of spying for the Soviet Union abroad, the most elite tier of KGB work.

Eventually, he seemed to have decided that he needed Lyuda for his career, and his proposal one spring evening in 1983 was as romantic as his calculations. "*Druzhochek*," he began, addressing her again as his tiny little friend, his buddy. "Now you know what I'm like. I'm not a very easy person."[22] Then he laid out his many faults: he was prone to long silences, he could be quite harsh, he was adept at hurting her feelings.

"In three years, you've probably made up your mind?" he asked.

"Actually, I have," Lyuda offered, sensing that he was breaking up with her.

"Really?" he asked skeptically, then added, to Lyuda's utter surprise, "Well, if that is the case, then I love you and I propose we get married on this date."

They married three months later. They had a small reception for family and friends on a boat in one of Leningrad's many canals. Lyuda had a wonderful time celebrating her hard-won marriage. Later, she would remember how loved she felt by those who had come to toast them, but she couldn't remember if she and her new husband had kissed to the traditional shouts of "*Gor'ko!*"[23] The following day, they had a second reception, in a private dining room of the Moscow Hotel. This one was for Volodya's KGB colleagues, who could not risk being unmasked to the bride and groom's relatives.[24]

A year later, Volodya was finally selected for training at the Red Banner Institute in Moscow, the exclusive KGB academy that molded agents into foreign spies. When he set off for the academy in September 1984, a pregnant Lyuda stayed in Leningrad, where she now lived with Volodya's parents. Once a month she made her way to the capital to see her husband. He rarely made the return visit.[25]

On April 27, 1985, Lyuda went into labor. By this point she had moved out of the elder Putins' apartment and rented a small room near the aerodrome. Although Volodya was very touching in his concern for her health, she had been alone for virtually her entire pregnancy. When the contractions started, she spent the day cleaning, doing laundry, and preparing the apartment for her return. At 10 p.m., she caught a taxi and went to the hospital. At 2:30 in the morning, her daughter was born. Volodya arrived the next day, but since men weren't allowed into maternity hospitals, Lyuda had to call him to discuss the girl's name.

Lyuda had one picked out: Natasha. She had a friend named Natasha and she felt it had a lovely ring to it. "No," her husband told her over the phone. "She will be Masha," like his mother. Lyuda burst into tears. "But I understood that I had no choice, and my little daughter would be Masha regardless."[26]

Three days after Lyuda and little Masha came home, Volodya left again for Moscow. Lyuda found it hard to be alone with an infant while trying to keep up with her university studies, but she tried to see her husband's departure in a positive light. "Because he didn't change diapers, get groceries, or cook breakfast, lunch, and dinner, it became easier after he left," she told herself. "Because before, I had to take care of the two of them—my husband and my child—but now I was left with just Masha."[27]

In the summer of 1985, Lyuda was summoned to the personnel department of the university. When she arrived at the office, she was told that she had passed the KGB's background check, which she hadn't known was happening.[28] She also discovered that another decision had been made about her life: her husband was being transferred abroad. He had hoped to go to Berlin, the hub of Cold War espionage, but he was posted instead to Dresden in East Germany, a backwater in a Soviet satellite where the small KGB staff operated almost in the open.[29] Still, Lyuda was happy. A posting abroad meant access to precious goods—food, electronics, clothing. When, in the fall of 1985, Lyuda arrived in Germany with little Masha in tow, she found that Volodya, who had gone ahead of them, had lovingly prepared their new apartment for their arrival. There were fresh flowers and a bowl of fruit on the kitchen table. Lyuda was deeply touched to see a bunch of bananas, their waxy yellow skins so unfamiliar and enticing.

Volodya had also set aside some money for Lyuda's arrival, expecting her to do what every Soviet woman dreamed of: shop for clothes and jewelry. Instead, she spent it on pots and pans and things for her new domestic domain. The wives of KGB officers were discouraged from working outside the home. "There was an unspoken rule: the wife has to stay at home and to create the right conditions for her husband's work," Lyuda recalled.[30] Not that she minded. She had a toddler and was seven months pregnant with her second child: her husband had wanted two children close in age.

Life for Lyuda wasn't exactly easy. Their apartment was on the sixth floor and the building, which also housed the families of Stasi officers, had no elevator. One day, a KGB neighbor saw Lyuda, heavily pregnant, Masha on one arm, a big bag of groceries in the other, huffing up the stairs. Horrified, he grabbed Masha and the groceries and carried them up to the Putins' apartment. Afterward he scolded Lyuda's husband. "Volodya, you have to help out. You have to help out, Volodya!"[31]

The intervention produced no discernible results. "Vladimir Vladimirovich had a rule: a woman must do everything at home by herself," Lyuda explained.[32] This didn't necessarily upset Lyuda. She knew how to manage a household and it would only be more work to teach her husband. When she was briefly hospitalized during her pregnancy, she left Volodya at home with Masha and came home to find the apartment a disaster and Masha dressed in clothing she had long outgrown. "Before that moment, my husband never really thought much about a woman's labor in the home: what's the big deal, a housewife,"[33] she observed.

There was a natural order to their life. Every morning she made her husband a hot breakfast before he left for work and to take Masha to the nursery. "A hot breakfast, lunch, and dinner were the norm for the whole group [of KGB officers' wives], and the wife of [Volodya's] boss, Evgenia Timofeevna, kept careful track of this," Lyuda remembered.[34] After Volodya and Masha left, Lyuda tried to get in a quick nap before buying groceries, feeding Katya, the new baby, and beginning the day's chores. At half past noon, Volodya came home for his hour-long freshly cooked lunch. By three, Masha was home. Somewhere in there, Lyuda had her German lessons. At seven, Volodya finished work and came home again. "Then, for an hour and a half, slowly and unrushed, he ate dinner in front of the television," Lyuda recalled.

"I, of course, was bringing plates back and forth, pouring tea." Evgenia Timofeevna, who kept watch over the KGB wives, was an excellent cook, much better than Lyuda, who spent hours studying cookbooks, trying to please her husband. "Vladimir Vladimirovich is capricious when it comes to food," she told his biographer.

> If a dish doesn't measure up to his expectations of a repast, he prefers to reject it entirely. So he won't eat just anything, let alone shower it with praise. There's a type of man who eats plate after plate with such gusto, constantly praising it: how delicious, how wonderful! And they ask for seconds. I always wanted my husband to be just like this, so that he would eat while talking all the while: how tasty, how great! I always envied women who had this kind of husband.
>
> In our family, it was very different. Volodya comes home for, say, lunch. I, of course, set the table for him. He starts eating. With bated breath, I wait for his reaction. There isn't any.
>
> "How's the meat?" I ask, unable to restrain myself.
>
> "A little dry."
>
> For me, it was like a knife to the heart. I had tried so hard, went to a special butcher's shop for the meat, then prepared it. You could say I put my whole soul into it. And—a little dry!
>
> And so I gradually began to experience a revulsion toward the kitchen, in part because no matter how long I waited for a compliment, none was ever forthcoming. If something was truly delicious, then his conclusion was as follows: not bad.
>
> On the other hand, there is this famous saying: don't praise a woman lest you spoil her. I guess you could say Vladimir Vladimirovich was always keeping me on my toes.

Many years later, the biographer tracked down Evgenia Timofeevna and asked her what she thought of Putin. "Volodya didn't drink and didn't smoke," she said. "He was a very good family man. After work, he always went home, not out somewhere with friends. A woman must feel very secure behind this kind of man."[35]

In February 1990, Lyuda and her family returned to Leningrad. Life in Dresden had flowed pleasantly along for four and a half years until the Berlin Wall fell and the Soviet puppet regime in East Germany fell with it. Lyudmila was saddened by the events. Her babies had become little girls who spoke German. She, too, had learned the language and made some local friends. During the harvest season she would pick peaches and currants with some of the Soviet military wives. She and Volodya had saved up for a cassette player, a VCR, and a car that they took on day trips during the weekends, enjoying beer and sausages. (Those were the only days she didn't have to cook, since her husband did not like eating outside the home.) And in Dresden, unlike in Leningrad, Volodya came home in the evenings and spent time with his daughters. He never put them to bed, of course, but he always played with them after dinner. So when it was time to go home, Lyuda felt wistful.

Leningrad in 1990 was another planet. With the Soviet economy on the brink of collapse, this was a city of angry women jostling each other in lines in their hunt for scant supplies, getting into shouting matches and physical fights with the women behind the counter, who were just as angry as they were. In Leningrad, Volodya and Lyuda moved in with his stern parents, who had managed to trade their small apartment for a three-room flat that fit all of them but was in disrepair. They had no furniture and no money to renovate it, and Volodya was not around to help. "As soon as we returned to Leningrad, my husband immediately immersed himself in work," Lyuda recalled. "It seemed as if my husband had disappeared from home, escaped."[36]

There were thousands of KGB officers returning home as the Soviet empire crumbled, and the agency didn't know what to do with them all. For a while, Volodya was the KGB's representative at the university, but these were desperate times. There was a stretch when he wasn't paid for three months and the family nearly ran out of money. So Lyuda got a job, likely through her husband, teaching German at the university. Volodya eventually found a stable position as the deputy to the city's first democratically elected mayor, Anatoly Sobchak. Volodya helped Sobchak navigate the city's transition from Leningrad to St. Petersburg, from a totalitarian system to democracy, from a command economy to a free-market one. It was a daunting task for men who had never experienced any form of political or economic freedom. Volodya left early in the morning and came home after midnight.

There were rumors and investigations surrounding his work in the mayor's office, like a shadowy deal in which $120 million of precious exports were to be traded for food that the city desperately needed but which never materialized. If Lyuda heard about these scandals, she never let on.[37] She avoided going to social events with her husband. She found politics boring and the people on the political circuit fake and suspect. It was not for her.[38] Her life was in the university and at home, where she was raising two young girls according to their father's strict standards. He insisted that Katya and Masha attend all manner of extracurricular activities: dance, music lessons, and language classes. It was Lyuda's job to make sure the girls got to them all.

During these years, Lyuda finally got a taste of what it was like to be a real Soviet woman. Four times a week, after dropping one daughter off at school and the other at kindergarten, she went to teach at the university. She got off work just in time to scoop them up from school and ferry them to ballet and violin lessons, then scrounge for groceries. "No one gave me a pass on doing the housework," she remembered. At least Lyuda had a car, unlike the average Soviet woman. It made her life as a working mother far easier—she didn't have to manage heavy bags of groceries and unruly children on crowded public transport—until it almost ended it. One day in October 1993, she was taking Katya to school when a driver ran a red light and slammed into the side of Lyuda's car.[39] Katya was unharmed, but Lyuda woke up naked in the hospital. Later, it would turn out that she had fractured some vertebrae in her neck as well as the base of her skull. Someone contacted Volodya Putin, now the second man in the city, who arrived at the hospital and was reassured that Lyuda was fine. He took the doctor's word for it and went back to work without seeing his wife.[40]

THE WEAKER SEX

THE VILLAGE OF MEDVEDEVO, IN THE KOSTROMA REGION, IS FOUR hundred miles northeast of Moscow. It sits on a hill overlooking a perfect Russian vista: sweeping fields dappled with wildflowers, a wide, slow river, and, behind it, the dark blue of a thick pine forest. A few decades ago, Medvedevo and two neighboring villages had a booming collective farm, and Medvedevo had over two hundred residents. When I visited in the summer of 2012, it had seven. Five of them were women. Of the two men, one was away in Moscow, working. The other had given up.

The latter was named Alexey, or Lesha. At forty-four he still lived with his mother in a traditional wooden home decorated, like all the other houses in the village, with carved window frames that looked like lace. Lesha used to be a truck driver, but that work had dried up. Sometimes he worked on a crew repairing local roads, but the work was seasonal and at best he only made about 2,000 rubles a month, $60 at the time. Considering that unemployment benefits were about 850 rubles a month (about $25) and that the pay for the road work didn't include the cost of the round trip to the city to pick up the money, Lesha decided it was better to simply live with his seventy-three-year-old mother, Tonia, a retired milkmaid from the collective farm. Her pension, by comparison, was luxurious: 11,000 rubles, or $300 every month.

It was a Friday evening in June when I visited Lesha and Tonia. Lesha was in slippers and a dirty flannel shirt tucked into black polyester track pants, and he sat in the corner watching television as his mother and I talked. His face was red, and when he joined the conversation, he had a difficult time speaking: he was drunk. When I asked him about work, he scoffed. "What can I do but drink gin and tonic?" he slurred, showing me a can of the premixed drink and a smile that was short a few teeth. "There's isn't fuck all left to do."

I asked how he will get by after his mother dies.

"I'll survive. What else can I do?" he said, shrugging.

"Maybe he'll drink less," his mother said. "Won't have anything to buy it with!" She laughed loudly and good-naturedly, and Lesha went back to watching television.

Four decades after Urlanis sounded the alarm about the crisis of Russian male mortality, things had only gotten worse. During the tumultuous years after the Soviet collapse, average male life expectancy crashed from sixty-five to fifty-eight by 1994. And while it was no longer true that Russian men were in scarce supply at the age of marriage, it was a bleak actuarial fact, visible to everyone, that they started dying in rapidly increasing numbers in their fourth decade. In Urlanis's day, the gap in life expectancy between men and women had been eight years. By the time I first visited Medvedevo in 2012, it was thirteen years, with only 60 percent of Russian men surviving to the age of sixty. Urlanis had wanted to see more great-grandfathers in Soviet society, but now even grandfathers had become a rarity.

This had a lot to do with how much Russian men drank. At the time, in 2012, Russia had "one of the riskiest patterns of drinking in the world," according to the WHO.[1] Russians consumed twice the annual dose of alcohol recommended by the organization and were the world's top consumers of hard liquor. Russian men drank four times as much alcohol as Russian women. Not only did this lead to heart, liver, and lung disease, it also drastically increased the chances of deadly car accidents and other mishaps, as well as of murder and suicide. (Nearly half of male suicides in Russia involved alcohol.) "Our country is split into two distinct groups," said Mikhail Denisenko, a demographer at Moscow's Higher School of Economics. "One dies young, drinks a lot, and has unstable employment. This is a mostly male segment of the population."

Denisenko was part of a group of demographers, sociologists, and cartographers who studied "shrinking villages" like Medvedevo. "What's always amazed me is that even here there are single men," he told me as we sipped tea in his office. The men in these villages, Denisenko went on, have never been married and "are usually in their mid-thirties, but they look fifty, fifty-five.... And all of them live with their mothers." He added, "In Russia, there's a huge population of people who can't find themselves, and the majority of them are men."

The statistical canyon that opens up between men and women after the age of sixty "deformed society," Denisenko said. Elena Zdravomyslova, the sociologist and feminist scholar, observed that the Russian cultural obsession with early death among men "formats our gender consciousness to such an extent" that the discourse that we should be advancing the rights of women seems ludicrous, she explained. "Why do you keep talking about women? We have a problem with the men!" "Feminism" had, once again, become a dirty word in Russia. This time it was not because it conflicted with a larger worldview of class struggle but because it was seen as man hatred, and men needed to be protected and preserved.

But the decline of feminism had also diminished the Russian man. Infinite forgiveness and coddling had emasculated him, both physically and culturally. When I lived in Moscow, Russian television ads seemed to alternate exclusively between commercials for diapers and cures for erectile dysfunction. "Despite the talk of them all being prostitutes, Russian women are a positive cultural brand. It's not shameful to be associated with it," Zdravomyslova said. "But a Russian man is a different story. It's better not to be a Russian man."

After visiting Tonia and Lesha, I went to the house of another elderly woman in Medvedevo, also named Tonia, short for Antonina. Her husband had been a tractor driver on the collective farm, and soon after their marriage, he began to drink. Then he started drinking at work. Then he started crashing his tractor. In the summer of 1983, after one particularly bad accident, he was ordered to stay in bed. While their three children were in the yard playing and Tonia was out getting bread, he hanged himself. He hadn't been able to find anything to drink to make the shakes stop.

When millions of Russians faced financial ruin amid the collapse of the Soviet Union in 1991, Russian sociologists found a curious trend in how families responded. "The typical reaction of the man was waiting for work to appear," said sociologist Alexey Levinson. Many enterprises didn't close outright but kept their workers on for a pittance while the factory or mine idled. Except for the entrepreneurial few who went into the semi-legal and often violent world of business, most male employees simply waited for the plants to fire back up again or to find something in the same sector, which rarely panned out.

Why does a Russian man behave like this in times of economic crisis? If a man loses his job and "goes to unload train cars, or he goes to sweep the streets, he can feed his child and not let his family starve," Levinson explained. "But he understands that, having once become a street cleaner, he won't return to his former status." The social status of a Russian woman, on the other hand, is far more flexible. "If you're a woman, you have this supra-value—your child—which a man doesn't have," Levinson explained. "So a woman is willing to do any work." Thus, most of the *chelnaki*—the petty merchants so common in Russia in the 1990s who traveled to Turkey and China and brought back cheap goods for resale, often literally on their backs—were women.

For a time, Lyuda Bugaychenko was one of these *chelnaki*. A cook from the small southern town of Krasnoarmeisk, Lyuda found herself responsible for her husband and her infant daughter when, one by one, the factories in the area shut down. Her husband, an engineer, waited for the work to come in and drank. She began ferrying cheap clothing and shoes from Ukraine, carrying loads so heavy that she would often vomit bile from the strain.

I met Lyuda when I lived in Moscow with my grandmother. Lyuda had been hired by a Jewish charity to help elderly Jewish people in the city. I loved Lyuda, and so did my grandmother. She was a chipper fifty-six-year-old with several gold teeth and awkwardly dyed black hair, and she regularly offered me folksy advice, like telling me that I could get rid of pimples by putting sperm on my face.

When I asked Lyuda if I could interview her for this book, she told me about her life from a cheerful distance, as if its continuously unfurling tragedy were something amusing she had seen on TV. "I lived in the shadow of my family," she said of her childhood. Her brother was "allowed everything," her mother had a fifth-grade education and worked around the clock, and her father, raised in an orphanage, was an engineer in a local factory. He drank and hit her mother, and he cheated. "There weren't a lot of men in town then," Lyuda recalled. This was the early 1960s. As she aged, she had come to understand her father's infidelity. "Before I thought I would never forgive cheating," she explained. "But if a man provides enough for his family—money, attention to the kids—if a man does everything for his family, and he needs something else on the side, who am I to deny him?" As if racing the demographic trend, her father died weeks before his sixty-first birthday.

Her parents foiled her various attempts to improve her life—dance school, university in Leningrad, emigration—and pushed her to marry an ensign who worked on the nuclear-test site in Kazakhstan where Lyuda spent her early twenties as a pastry chef. When he got his first paycheck after their wedding, he disappeared for five days. She found him drunk and with his arm around an ex-girlfriend. "I decided to go for a jaunt," he told her, "to remember."

Lyuda divorced him and returned home, where she began to experience strange health problems. She had horrible abdominal pain, her teeth fell out—the souvenirs, she believed, of her years working around all that radiation.

One day, Lyuda's father invited a young man who was courting her to drink moonshine with him and forced a proposal. "I didn't love him," she says. "But he wasn't bad. At least, I thought, I wouldn't be ashamed to go somewhere with him." So she accepted. For years, she couldn't get pregnant. Finally, the doctor told her of a local woman who had come in with a botched late-term abortion. The fetus had somehow survived and the hospital was looking for someone to adopt the baby. Lyuda took the baby in, named her Dasha, and nursed her to health. "You can't imagine how badly I wanted kids," Lyuda explained, tearing up for the first time as we talked in Emma's tiny kitchen. "I thought that, since no one has ever loved me, maybe my kids will love me. And I would do anything for them. Anything."

When Dasha came into their lives, Lyuda's husband started to cheat, often flagrantly. At one point he had an affair with her brother's wife. When he drank, which he did often and heavily, he would hit her. "But he helped, he washed the cloth diapers, and Dasha loved him," Lyuda said. "And I was strong and proud. I thought I could conquer any tragedy, any grief."

In the meantime, while her husband's wages often went unpaid, Lyuda managed to turn her small retail business into a store, then two. When the financial crisis of 1998 wiped her out, she chopped chicken parts at the local market until she could repay her debts and start another store. When it failed again—her employees were stealing from her—she decided to go to the big city, first to nearby Saratov, then to Moscow. "I was sick of not having any money," she says. Her husband, who had been laid off, was nonplussed. "He said, 'You're the one who needs it, so you go.'"

She found work in Moscow at the Jewish charity, earning money on the side as a cleaning lady. That was how my grandmother and I met her, and she'd spend half of each visit to the apartment sipping tea and gossiping with my grandmother.

Every two months, Lyuda went home for a month to see her family. Her husband still didn't work. He had recently been diagnosed with lung cancer, and she took time off, paid for his medical care, and saw him through to remission. Her daughter, now twenty-two, quit her government job and broke up with the boyfriend who had impregnated her, so now Lyuda was supporting her, too. She was both hungrily anticipating the arrival of a grandchild and worried that Dasha, who had all kinds of health problems because of the way she had entered the world, wouldn't survive the pregnancy. "I'm the one who has to sort all this out," Lyuda said, laughing. But she was proud of the lesson Dasha had learned from her first, failed relationship. "She says, 'Mom, I'm not looking for love anymore. I need a man who will feed and clothe me, who will put shoes on my feet.'"

Finally, as if realizing the sorrow of her life for the first time, Lyuda started to cry. Surprised, she tried to laugh to stop the tears, as if, once unleashed, they would erode the fragile buttresses holding up the entire family. "That's my life!" she exclaimed with a smile, quickly recovering her composure. "Maybe I shouldn't have listened to my parents so much. Maybe I should have done what I wanted to do. Oh, well!"

I asked her why, in all those loveless, abusive years, she had never left her husband. "I tried," she said. "He wouldn't let me go." Once, Lyuda tried to sneak out of the house at night with Dasha. He chased them down with a knife.

A couple days after we talked, Lyuda called me. She had been thinking.

"You asked me why I never left my husband," she said. "I'll tell you why. Because he never once said anything to me about the fact that we couldn't have our own kids. Not once. And he never tried to leave. Even when he was drinking and fooling around, he always came home. That's a really manly act. As my old grandmother once said to me, 'Lyuda, he's a real *muzhik*'"—a manly man. "'So he drinks and fools around, so what? They all drink and fool around, these Russian men.'"

In February 2019, I returned to Medvedevo. The tall hills above the river were now drifts of perfect, untouched snow. It lit the leaden sky from below and hung heavy on the indigo pines. It lay on the folded-in roofs of the old wooden houses, their lace-trimmed windows blank with darkness. The snow was hip-deep in places where it hadn't been cleared, and it swaddled the semi-abandoned town in a hollow silence. A taxi took me from the nearby town of Manturovo, where the train from Moscow stops, as far toward Medvedevo as the old car could go. I had to walk the rest of the way, following someone else's footsteps, putting my feet in the cylindrical holes leading to the village.

Denisenko had warned me that winter was no time to go to Medvedevo. In the past decade, he and other intellectual Muscovites from the Higher School of Economics had bought several dachas in the village. They had hoped to establish a base that would be part laboratory, part scholars' colony, to help them understand the emptying of the Russian countryside. But there was not enough infrastructure to support them. An infusion of urban intellectuals wasn't enough to revive a village that had been slowly, inexorably fading back into the hills. Still, the empty houses waited.

"Sure, it's pretty, but when it's like this for several months..." Misha Sazonov replied to my compliment as we sat in his living room. It was centered around an ancient Russian *pech'*, a whitewashed brick hearth that takes up half the room. Slices of white bread were toasting on one of its outcroppings. His wife, Zhenya, offered us tea with "sand"—sugar in the local slang—and homemade raspberry jam. By November, Sazonov said, the snow would be firmly in place and it would stick around until April or May. A truck that was essentially a mini grocery store came by twice a week. If anything went wrong—like the time Zhenya got appendicitis—you first had to go get the *feldsher*, a field medic, and then wait for an ambulance to drive in from nearby Manturovo and hope it had the tires to get close enough to your house. "You can die very quickly here," Sazonov warned.

Sazonov, who was going to turn fifty-six in the spring, didn't have high hopes for his own longevity. The Kremlin had just rammed through a deeply unpopular pension reform that crashed Putin's approval rating and raised the retirement age from fifty-five to sixty for women and for sixty to sixty-five for men. Protests erupted across the country, with older men carrying signs pointing out that, given the actuarial odds for Russian men, most of them would die before collecting their pensions. Sazonov would now have to wait not four years until retirement but nine, a retreating horizon he feared he'd never reach.

During my earlier visit to Medvedevo, Sazonov had been working elsewhere. Now that he had returned, the number of men in the village was still two. Lesha was still here; the other man had moved away. Sazonov, who was born in 1963, used to work as a sailor out of Sakhalin, in the Russian Far East. In the late 1980s, he found himself in Alaska, where he was offered a well-paying job as a fisherman, but he felt he couldn't stay. "I had all this KGB brainwashing," he said regretfully, "that you can't abandon the Motherland." So he went home. When the Soviet Union collapsed and the paychecks dried up,

Sazonov found his way to Medvedevo, where he bought a house and fished in the river to feed himself. In Manturovo, he met Zhenya, who was four years younger than him, had two adult children, and, like so many people around here, a fondness for the bottle.

Sazonov had a big tattoo of Lenin's head on the back of his hand and a nose that had been broken at least once. His skin was red and leathery and he looked far older than he actually was. "People say, 'Oh, in the villages people drink,'" Sazonov railed. "Of course people are going to drink! They have no pay, no benefits, terrible living conditions, nothing, but they have to work from dawn to dusk! Of course people are going to drink if your whole life is this hopeless nonsense!"

The verb he used was *spivat'sya*, which doesn't mean merely to drink but to drink oneself to death. It's why Sazonov encouraged me repeatedly to visit the local cemetery. "They keep hammering us hicks over the head with this, that our life expectancy is going up, but you go and see who's been buried there in the last ten, twenty years," he growled. Mostly it was young men, he said. "The best ages. They should've kept living and living, but they're all there. It's from all the villages around here, and you know how many young men there were around? All younger than me, and now they're all dead. Every time I go away for a while, I come back and someone's missing. Then it turns out they've been dead a long time."

I asked what had happened to the other residents of Medvedevo I had met in 2012, the two Tonias and Lesha. The Tonia whose husband had hanged himself had gone to live with her son in St. Petersburg. The other Tonia, Lesha's mom, had recently had a stroke but was still hanging on. And Lesha had gotten married to Zhenya's thirty-four-year-old daughter Nastia. There still wasn't any work—or anything to do at all, really—so the newlyweds lived with Tonia, subsisting on her pension, and drank. Sure, Zhenya conceded, she drank, too, but never like this. "I called them this morning," she told me. "They're already sauced."

She offered to walk me over, so we bundled up and set out through the white drifts, the dogs bounding alongside us, sinking and then exploding from the snow. As we got closer to Tonia's house, Zhenya told me something else: the old woman was also a drinker. "Oh, yes! She's been drinking all her life!" she said conspiratorially. "Spent twenty years milking cows!" None of this was surprising. This region, according to a Kremlin project called "Sober Russia," was one of the most alcoholic in the country, where, according to the WHO, a full fifth of the population had some sort of alcohol dependency. In the previous year, Kostroma had fallen to seventy-first place on the "Sober Russia" rankings—out of eighty-five regions.[2]

Tonia met us in her kitchen. The paralysis from her stroke had abated somewhat, but she couldn't cook anymore and her legs hurt. She didn't mind that her son and new daughter-in-law lived on her pension, now about $260. They cooked for her and washed her in a big metal basin. They also made *samogon*, or moonshine. Before, she used to do it, setting the still before heading off to work at the collective farm. Her husband had died fourteen years prior—dropped dead while chopping wood. "He had a bad heart," Tonia explained. "He wasn't supposed to drink, but he did." After she found him dead by the woodpile, she had to slaughter all their chickens and cows: there was no one left to care for them.

We sat at the kitchen table, which was covered in an old yellow oilcloth. Tonia was getting tired of talking, losing her train of thought and forgetting words. But she didn't want to go back into the living room where Nastia lay on the couch under a pile of blankets—she had spent all night vomiting—and her son sat in an armchair. They both stared blankly at the television. "I don't like the TV," Tonia said and stayed in the kitchen as Zhenya and I moved into the living room.

Lesha greeted me with a shy, toothless smile. "Middle of nowhere," he gestured vaguely when I asked how he was doing. His face was red, like last time. He hadn't worked in two years. He had no money of his own. Now he spent his days caring for his mother and waiting for the grocery truck to come by. Lesha perked up when I asked him to tell me about his wedding last summer. He took out a photo album and flipped through the glossy pictures: his mother, Nastia, Zhenya, Sazonov, all of them carousing around a table. There was a man with an accordion. It had clearly been the highlight of everyone's lives in many, many years.

But it was hard to talk to Lesha. He kept stopping mid-sentence as his watery gaze drifted back to the television. Sunshine poured in through the dusty windowpanes, its glare amplified by the snow. Time seemed to stop here and speed up all at once. I don't know how long we sat there like that, watching the soap opera on the old television set. It had a tragic ending, of course. A young home health aide had fallen in love with her charge, a paraplegic man in a wheelchair. When she went home to her village to tell her mother about her newfound happiness, her beloved, briefly out of her care, went on a fishing trip and drowned. Without her, he had been truly helpless.

"When you come back here in ten years," Sazonov had told me when I had left his house, "there will be no one left."

A MANLY MAN

VLADIMIR PUTIN DOES NOT DRINK, AT LEAST NOT BY RUSSIAN STANdards. He has been known to raise a glass of champagne with a visiting dignitary or to tip back a shot of vodka to demonstrate that he is a real *muzhik*. When he was posted to Dresden, he developed a fondness for beer and sausages, but the habit added twenty-five pounds to his short frame.[1] Which is why, he told reporters on his sixty-eighth birthday, in 2020, he tries not to drink much beer. "Makes your belly grow," he said.[2]

The significance of this pronouncement was obvious: few men of Putin's generation made it to their late sixties, let alone in such good shape. For all the Kremlin's focus on improving life expectancy, recent statistics had revealed no meaningful improvement in male mortality. According to the Russian Health Ministry, the death rate for Russian men ages thirty-five to forty is double that of their female peers.[3] Eighty percent of the Russians who die between the ages of eighteen and sixty are men.[4] In 2023, the ministry reported that 52 percent of Russian males died before sixty-five, the new retirement age for men. The vast majority, the ministry's expert noted, died suddenly in their place of work.[5] Sazonov's conviction that he wouldn't live to collect his pension was based in fact: the odds were certainly against him.

And yet, here was Putin, healthy and spry, well on his way to seventy and positioning himself to run in 2024 for a fifth presidential term. This Russian man, it seemed, would live forever.

Russian men have weak hearts.[6] The rate of heart disease in Russia has nearly doubled during Putin's two decades in power and it is the reason behind a full half of all deaths in Russia, most of them men.[7] It is by far their leading killer. Some invoke this to offer an easy explanation for Russia's discrepancy in male and female life expectancy, which has settled at around ten years.[8] Women's hearts, these people argue, are stronger because they are naturally protected by estrogen, at least until they hit menopause. In fact, biological and genetic differences between the sexes account for only a couple years of the life expectancy gap, according to Yulia Zinkina and Andrey Korotaev of Moscow's Higher School of Economics. The far bigger contributor, the two scholars concluded, was bad habits born of traditional gender roles: "the denial of weakness or vulnerability, emotional and physical control, exhibiting strength and stamina, refusal of any help, constant interest in sex, exhibiting aggressive behavior and physical dominance."[9]

These powerful notions of what makes a man manly determine how Russian men take care of themselves—or fail to. They go to the doctor less frequently than women. Their diets are richer in saturated fat and cholesterol and poorer in fiber, fruits, and vegetables. They exercise less. As a result, they are more likely to develop health issues like heart disease, less likely to discover them in time, or to take appropriate measures to mitigate them. "In showing or embodying the hegemonic ideals of masculinity in behavior as it relates to health," write Zinkina and Korotaev, men reinforce the cultural conviction that "the most influential people among men are those for whom health and safety are not important."

That is true for men in most cultures, America's included. But according to various studies cited by Zinkina and Korotaev, the more rigid a society's gender norms, the deadlier the outcome. In the years after the Soviet collapse, even as Russia craved acceptance by the West, its people and government lionized ideas about gender that were fast becoming passé in Europe and the United States. In Russia, men were men, Russians told me smugly, and women were women. This division of genders had deepened under Putin, and it was, quite literally, killing the nation's men. Eager to prove their manhood, they smoked, they drank, they drove while drinking, they refused to wear seat belts while driving. They sought out violence, both to participate in and be entertained by. And the more a man drank, the more he became a champion of his gender. Women, on the other hand, were expected to moderate their drinking or to not drink at all. A woman who drinks, Zinkina and Korotaev noted, was compromising both her sexual integrity and her ability to perform her maternal duties.

Yet, the more a Russian man drinks, the closer he inches toward the grave. The second leading cause of death among Russian men, after heart disease, is what demographers call "external causes of death": car accidents, murder, suicide, alcohol poisoning.[10] When alcoholism took off again in the 1990s, alcohol-related suicides surged along with it. As Elena Zdravomyslova had told me, Russian men pay a high price for their masculinity: an early death.

In 2012, speaking to a recreational hockey club for middle-aged men, Putin alluded to this crisis among men, which was, once again, the emergency du jour. "The average life expectancy is lower because men of middle age leave this life in large numbers," he said. "Why? Drinking, drugs, tobacco, all kinds of road accidents, and unfortunate incidents in the workplace. That's why we're losing people. That's why attention—and here I don't want to offend the women—[must be paid] to the men of our, your age, getting them into sports, the creation of the right conditions [for them to play sports]—this is an extremely important thing, and a national task."[11]

Putin loves sports. As a scrawny boy, he studied judo to conquer the other boys in the schoolyard; it took him off the streets and set him on the path to success.[12] He came of age when sports were central to the Soviet Union's global prestige. In world championships and the Olympics, Soviet athletes' dominance was intended to prove the Communist regime's superiority. As president of Russia, Putin adopted the same approach, building the country's sports complex back up from the ruins of the 1990s. He competed fiercely to host the winter Olympics in 2014. He built judo training centers in his hometown of St. Petersburg and across the country. His motivation was not only to beat the West but to promote a healthy lifestyle at home.

A "healthy lifestyle" was one of Putin's chief policy obsessions, even as it became yet another wooden Kremlin slogan: *zdorovyy obraz zhizni*, or "ZOZh" in its slightly mocking abbreviated form. In 2012, Putin announced that he wanted at least 40 percent of the Russian population to participate in ZOZh by 2020.[13] And when Putin tried to rein in his people's drinking, he appealed constantly to ZOZh.

Putin himself is ZOZh's most potent mascot. Not only is he a teetotaler (at least by Russian standards), he also doesn't smoke. He is constantly exercising and talking about exercising. He told the American film director Oliver Stone that he works out every day. He told an interviewer from Chinese state TV that staying in physical shape was important for his stamina as the leader of a great country. "Workouts aren't the goal in and of themselves," he explained. "It's a means of accomplishing important, really important goals, which is the opportunity to work intensively, in a way that allows you to get the results you need."[14] It was just over a week after his seventy-first birthday.

In 2015 he worked out for the cameras in Sochi. Wearing lifting gloves and sweats, he made his way deliberately through the gym, building his calves, working his abs.[15] Afterward he and then prime minister Dmitry Medvedev grilled some kabobs, *shashlik*, an activity synonymous with a Russian man's leisure and usually accompanied by large volumes of beer and vodka. But when Putin and Medvedev sat down to eat, there was not a drop of alcohol on the table, only tea.

These days Putin doesn't even drink tea. Instead, he steeps herbs from the mountainous Altai region in Siberia into an invigorating elixir. Putin has vacationed in Altai many times with Sergei Shoigu, his friend and, until recently, long-serving defense minister. Together they go hiking and mushroom picking. They forage for herbs and have picnics, sometimes in matching shearling coats. They bump around the taiga in all-terrain vehicles and fiddle with wood in Shoigu's workshop, always with a Kremlin photographer on hand. Once, Putin told reporters, he and Shoigu were nearly knocked over by some stampeding elk, the Altai wapiti. It was little wonder the animals were running: according to an investigation by the independent media outlet *Proekt*, Putin regularly takes baths made from the wapiti's young horns, a practice he learned from Shoigu. The spongy, immature horns are cut from their heads while the elk are alive and screaming.

Literal bloodbaths are prepared by extracting the blood and boiling the horns. Supposedly rejuvenating, these baths are now reportedly popular among members of the Kremlin elite.[16]

Putin lives ZOZh every day and he makes sure his subjects see it. He practices judo. He skis. He taught himself to skate so that he could play ice hockey. In every match, he scores many goals and bristles if anyone dares to suggest that the other side lets him win. He goes spear fishing in remote Tuva. He tags tigers.[17] He shoots whales with a crossbow (to get a biopsy) and leads expeditions to save polar bears.[18] He guides endangered Siberian cranes south for the winter in a motorized glider.[19] He dives to the bottom of the Black Sea to find ancient amphorae.[20] He fly-fishes, sometimes shirtless, his hairless torso gleaming in the sun like an uncooked turkey. He rides horses, also shirtless, infamously so. When cameras caught Putin topless on horseback in 2009, the headline in a state news wire was "Putin Vacations Like a Real Man."[21]

In the West, images of a shirtless Putin on horseback have become a staple of jokes and countless memes, including one where a giant bear was photoshopped in for the horse. A Russian reporter even dared to ask Putin about it. "I haven't ridden a bear yet," he quipped, adding that there were plenty of photos of him, fully dressed, "in my office, with papers, but that's not interesting to anyone."[22] In the West, the photos neutered Putin, made him seem less dangerous. What kind of serious world leader engaged in stunts like that? The Russian opposition laughed at the photos, too. But among the Russians the photos were aimed at, they had exactly the desired effect.

One evening when I was covering the 2014 Winter Olympics in Sochi, I found myself on the brand-new electric shuttle train built specially for the event. Sitting across the aisle from me were two Russian women. One was in her twenties, the other one was a pensioner, likely in her early sixties. They were strangers to each other but soon got to chatting. The older woman reached into her bag and took out a few souvenir magnets she had purchased, one of which had the iconic image of Putin shirtless, on horseback. To my surprise, the women cooed over the magnets. "Look at him," the younger woman marveled. "Where can you find another leader like him? Athletic, decisive. And who do they have? Obama." Here, she put her hands behind her ears to make them stick out and added, "He just stands there and does nothing."[23]

The photos, I realized, were for these women. With his ZOZh campaign, Putin seemed to be insisting that the realest men didn't have to become physical wrecks and die young. Real men were sporty, outdoorsy teetotalers. Real men were sober, focused, and disciplined.

But most Russian women didn't know men like Putin. The men they knew, their fathers, their brothers, their husbands and boyfriends, were all heavy drinkers who ate mayonnaise-slathered salads and *shashlik*. They smoked like steam engines; they didn't exercise. They were spendthrifts who could barely be trusted to bring their salaries home. They were both reckless and helpless. And then they died. By the time Russian women turned sixty, there were some 1,300 women for every 1,000 men. By the time they turned seventy, they outnumbered their male peers by more than two to one.[24]

Women were left behind by their men just as they were becoming grandmothers. In that role, they became sexless old ladies, responsible, as always, for caring for someone other than themselves. They were invisible and there were millions of them. Yet the state still needed them. Putin needed them to make sure election results went according to plan: the school principals and teachers and mid-level bureaucrats who ran election precincts were almost all middle-aged women. He needed them to stuff the ballot boxes at night and push through fake voter rolls during the day. He needed their votes, too. Even if the results were predetermined, he wanted the turnout to show just how much the people loved him. He needed judges, most of them women, to rule according to his interests. Russian women were the foot soldiers of Putin's autocracy, and they enforced it jealously. They did so not just because the government jobs they held were stable and paid relatively well. They did it because Putin was the man they never had.

It was why Lia Volyanskaya idolized the Russian president. Volyanskaya, who once went by the name Sexy Lia, was, two decades ago, the front woman in a Russian pop group called White Chocolate. They were popular in the early, oil-fueled days of Putin's reign. "He is strong, reserved; I love his way of talking to people, his subtle humor," Volyanska explained when we met in a restaurant in Moscow's poshest suburb. "He speaks rarely and he doesn't say much when he does, but it's always on point. He has so much charisma that, okay, maybe he's not Alain Delon, but there's just something about him, because he has this inner strength, and for a woman, that's the most important thing." She was just a couple years older than me, but all the injections in her cheekbones, her chin, and her lips made her seem older. I asked if she personally found Putin attractive. She leaned forward and smirked knowingly. "He's a man that 70 percent of women dream of in their moistest fantasies," she confessed. "Including me. Leaders like him are appointed by God."

PUSSY RIOT

AT ELEVEN IN THE MORNING OF FEBRUARY 21, 2012, FIVE WOMEN walked into the Cathedral of Christ the Savior, just down the Moscow River embankment from the Kremlin. The cathedral's giant onion domes glowed a dull gold under a gray winter sky. They were gaudy replicas, built during the 1990s, when the Soviet Union's scientific atheism gave way to a muscular Christian Orthodox revival. The USSR had fallen and the state, now bereft of a unifying ideology, gladly welcomed the Church in that role, much as it had in tsarist times. And, much like in tsarist times, the new Russian state began to fuse with the Church.

This cathedral, commissioned by Alexander I to commemorate the victory over Napoleon in 1812, was built on the site of a centuries-old convent. Legend has it that when the convent was razed, its chief nun, Claudia, cursed the new cathedral. *It will be a puddle*, she swore. Undeterred, the tsar's architects went ahead, completing the grand edifice in 1883. Less than fifty years later, the Soviet government stripped the gold off the domes, took the gold, silver, and gemstones from inside, and confiscated its heavy bronze doors. What the state could not sell to fund its breakneck industrialization, it melted down. In 1931, the cathedral was dynamited.

In its stead, the Soviets decided to build a new home for the Supreme Soviet, the USSR's top governing body. The building was to be a kind of futurist ziggurat, nearly 1,500 feet high and topped with a giant statue of Lenin. But construction stopped with the Nazi invasion, and the empty foundation began to flood with water from the Moscow River. After the war, the government abandoned the project and turned the place into a massive heated outdoor swimming pool. My mother used to go swimming there. In old videos, it looks like a giant cup of soup steaming in the freezing Moscow winters. Claudia's curse had come to pass.

In the fall of 1999, the new Russian state finished building an exact replica of the old tsarist cathedral on the site, just in time for the new millennium. When it was completed, the Cathedral of Christ the Savior was once again a state church. It was where Dmitry Medvedev went for Easter services with his wife when he was the placeholder president from 2008 to 2012. Next to him were Putin and Lyuda, in one of her rare public appearances. The Easter services, led by the Patriarch of Moscow and All Russia, were broadcast live on state television; identifying who stood with Putin in the gallery became a little like watching who had stood atop Lenin's Mausoleum in Soviet times. It was the cathedral of the new Russian Empire, and yet, after that February morning in 2012, it would forever be known as the Pussy Riot Church.

The five young women met that morning at the Metro stop closest to the cathedral.[1] They went to a café and drank ice-cold Coke and café glacé despite the weather.[2] Then they donned their church-appropriate headscarves and approached the hulking white cathedral. They knew the guards wouldn't let them in with a guitar case, so they gave it to Petya Verzilov, the token man in their group. A guard stopped them at the metal detector. He asked Petya about the contents of his guitar case, and Petya, who had spent part of his childhood in Canada, answered in perfect North American English: "Nothing special!" The guard waved him through.[3] Then he searched the women's backpacks, addressing them, as most everyone would for the next two years, as "girls."

Once inside, two of the women distracted a church attendant by asking how to properly light a candle. This gave a third woman, Katya, just enough time to pull on her red balaclava, grab the guitar from its case, and start climbing the green-carpeted steps to the soleas, a raised platform leading to the Holy Gates. Katya's mission was to plug the guitar into an amp, but before she could do so, a security guard blocked her and hustled her out of the cathedral.[4]

In the next forty seconds, the other four women dropped their kerchiefs and coats to reveal colorful dresses and tights, put on their neon balaclavas, hopped onto the soleas, and performed what they called their "punk prayer." Without Katya and her guitar, it would be screamed a cappella.

> *Virgin Mary, Mother of God, chase Putin out,*
> *Chase Putin out, chase Putin out!*
> *... Head of the KGB, their chief saint,*
> *Leads protesters to jail under guard.*
> *So as to not offend His Holiness,*
> *Women must give birth and love.*
> *Shit, shit, holy shit!*
> *Shit, shit, holy shit!*
> *Virgin Mary, Mother of God, become a feminist,*
> *Become a feminist, become a feminist!*

The unquestionable leader of Pussy Riot was its founder, Nadezhda Tolokonnikova, who was born on Revolution Day, November 7, 1989, just as the empire that the Bolshevik Revolution had built was collapsing. In her own telling, she likes to note that she entered this world "a few days before the fall of the Berlin Wall."[5] She was born in Norilsk, the world's northernmost big city, built by inmates of the Gulag, and one of the most polluted on the planet. Her parents were young and peripatetic, and for a long time, like so many Soviet children, she was raised by her grandmother, who was in Krasnoyarsk, another part of Siberia famous for its Soviet penal colonies.

When Nadya was five, her parents divorced. Her father, Andrei, popped in and out of her life, periodically pulling her out of the grayness of Siberia to show her the wonders of Moscow. "I am a holiday," Andrei told writer Masha Gessen, author of a book about Pussy Riot. "I was always highly prized—both because girls always privilege men and because I provide a contrast to women's strict ways."[6] Andrei had wanted to be a philosopher and an artist but studied medicine to avoid conscription. His enthusiasm for philosophy infected Nadya, who idolized her dad. When I told her I had met him at her trial, her face lit up immediately. "And what did you think of Dad?" she asked, beaming and suddenly shy. "Dad's great, right?" When she was ten, Dad took away her fashion magazines and gave her political newspapers. "I didn't understand much of what I was reading, but because I looked up to my dad, I still wanted to read it," she told me.

When she got to high school, she began to supplement her homework with Schopenhauer, Kierkegaard, Hegel, and Sartre. Andrei bought her books by the hot young iconoclasts of the turn of the millennium, Russian novelists like Victor Pelevin and Vladimir Sorokin, as well as the Moscow Conceptualists and the classic rebels, like Eduard Limonov and Venedikt Erofeev. All of it instilled in her an appreciation of radical, political art. "When your teen crush is Vladimir Mayakovsky, the revolutionary poet," she wrote, "you're fucked."[7]

Nadya was also in awe of her mom, Ekaterina, on whose bookshelf she happened to find a book by Maria Arbatova, a Soviet feminist and the godmother of contemporary Russian feminism. The book made a huge impression on Nadya, although she doesn't know how much it influenced her mom. "For her, like for a large number of people from the Soviet era, it was obvious anyway that a woman is equal to a man," Nadya explained. "Plus, she has this strong matriarchal attitude. She believes a man should be completely under her thumb." That kind of female power appealed to young Nadya.

As soon as Nadya could get out of Norilsk, she did. In 2006, she set off for Moscow, where she'd been admitted to Moscow State University's prestigious philosophy department. But she was sorely disappointed, finding both the department and its students pedantic and boring. The one bright spot was Petya Verzilov, a wiry and hyperactive philosophy student. Petya was drawn to Nadya's passion for radical art but mostly to her spectacular looks. They quickly became a couple.

She and Petya joined an art collective with Petya's best friend, Oleg Vorotnikov, and Vorotnikov's wife, Nastia Sokol, known as "Baby Goat." They called themselves Voina, "War," and they lived a life of romantic poverty, moving from apartment to apartment and stealing food from booming Moscow grocery stores. "At some point, I was holding master classes in shoplifting in Moscow," Nadya wrote proudly in her book before outlining her technique in great detail.[8]

Most importantly, they staged guerrilla performances, or "actions," all over the city, seeking to highlight the absurdity, hypocrisy, and emptiness of Russia's new gilded era. They mock-hanged five people representing migrant laborers from Central Asia, in Auchan, a popular French grocery chain. They threw live cats into a McDonald's. They projected a massive Jolly Roger onto the Russian White House. They welded shut the doors of a posh Moscow restaurant named for Ivan the Terrible's secret police. They flipped cop cars onto their roofs. They sent Vorotnikov into a grocery store dressed in a priest's black cassock, and he breezed out with a cart full of food without paying for any of it. They sent one of Voina's women into a St. Petersburg grocery store and photographed her pushing a frozen chicken into her vagina. (The focus on grocery stores was not accidental. After the privations and humiliations of the Soviet era, the laden shelves of the new capitalist Russia held an almost religious significance for all survivors of the Soviet regime, myself included.) One summer night in St. Petersburg, Voina drew a giant phallus in white paint on half of one of the city's famous drawbridges. When the bridge was opened to allow ship traffic through, the cartoon penis was raised with it, and, for a brief and perfect moment, there was a massive erect phallus facing the local headquarters of the FSB.

In December 2007, Putin, whose second and last constitutionally allowed presidential term was coming to a close, declared that he had picked a successor, just as Yeltsin had picked him. Dmitry Medvedev, a lawyer Putin knew from St. Petersburg, would become president, and Putin would stay on as prime minister. As the Kremlin prepared for the election that would make it official, Putin swatted away Western criticism. "They're always trying to teach someone something," Putin snarled. "They should teach their wives to cook cabbage soup instead."[9]

On February 29, 2008, just three days before a presidential election would install Medvedev as Putin's heir, Voina staged an action inside the capital's natural history museum. Two men held a giant sign that said "Fuck for the Heir Puppy Bear!"—a play on Medvedev's name (*medved* means "bear" in Russian). As Masha Alyokhina, a member of

Pussy Riot, would later explain to me, it was also a commentary on the government's "aggressive demographic agenda." Putin had introduced a policy in which Russian women would be paid by the state for having children, an obvious throwback to Khrushchev's postwar reforms.

The members of Voina stripped off their clothes and began fucking among the museum's displays, the men holding their women from behind. Ironically, on that night in the museum, Nadya was already extremely pregnant. Four days later she gave birth to a little girl. She named her Gera, Russian for Hera, the chief goddess of the Greek pantheon.

In March 2011, Voina devised another action to protest police corruption and brutality. They would run around the Metro and smother the ubiquitous cops there with kisses. It was to be like kissing a frog, Nadya told me later, "to turn them from bad cops into good ones." Voina had by then splintered, bitterly, into two factions, the Moscow and St. Petersburg cells. Nadya and Petya, now married young parents, were the heads of the Moscow section and had planned the cop-kissing action. But when it was decided that all the cop kisses would be same-sex, Nadya told me, "Petya simply pissed himself. He said, 'Man, what if they beat me up?' And I said, 'So what? If it's for the action, that's not a big deal!'" Uncomfortable with kissing another man, Petya bowed out.

And yet, when they published the video of the kissing assaults, everyone kept referring to Petya Verzilov as Voina's Moscow leader. Nadya was livid. Growing up, she didn't know much about feminism beyond that book on her mother's shelf, but the concept had been reinforced by certain life experiences. In elementary school, she once told a boy that she was a feminist. "It's okay," he responded magnanimously. "When you grow up and start liking boys, you'll stop with all this man-hatred." At university, Nadya had disgusted her advisor when she told him she wanted to write about queer theory, which hadn't yet made it to Russia. "Why don't you write about how you sleep with your husband and what your favorite positions are," he snarked.

After high school, Nadya discovered Nadezhda Krupskaya, Inessa Armand, and Alexandra Kollontai. She was stunned at how ahead of her time Kollontai was. "She managed to be a second-wave feminist five dozen years before the actual second wave," Nadya wrote later, "a kind of seeing that can only occur in highly sensitive and intuitive thinkers and artists who feel the air of an epoch before the epoch is born."[10] She also noted how Kollontai was dismissed by her male peers.

As Nadya worked her way through the Bolshevik and Western feminist canons, she discovered that, in Voina, neither was welcome. Vorotnikov, Nadya told me, was "a legendary sexist," not to mention "a fantastic asshole." He marginalized his wife and photoshopped Nadya out of every picture, including the White House action, even though Nadya was its mastermind. "He was constantly insisting that women are incapable of making art and that Leni Riefenstahl was the only woman who had produced any real art," Nadya recalled. "He ate through my brain with all that." In retrospect, though, she was grateful. "I thank him for the development of my feminist orientation," she told me, her voice still crackling with anger over a decade later. "Without him, it never would have exploded in this way."

By this point Voina had recruited dozens of young new members, primarily from the new Rodchenko Art School. One was a short, awkward young woman with dark hair named Katya Samutsevich.[11] Katya was raised in a strict and miserable family. Her father, a Moscow intellectual, was embarrassed by his Ukrainian peasant wife, who in turn felt suffocated by her husband's domestic authoritarianism. "My mother really did work at home her whole life," Katya told Gessen. "Always cooking, cleaning. My father never did a thing, from what I understand. And she was always resenting him for that . . . In the summers, we lived at the dacha, and I would see it: the summer, the heat, and she and my aunt are always cooking. Making preserves, too, and other strange things. I didn't understand what it was all for. But she told me, 'Your life is going to be like this. You'll spend it in the kitchen.' I looked at it all in horror." In the end, Katya's mom dropped dead of a massive heart attack while standing at the dacha stove.[12]

Katya's father pushed her into a computer programming degree.

After quitting her job at a government research center that was developing nuclear submarines, she found the Rodchenko school and then Voina. In 2009, she met Nadya and they became close. When Nadya, sick of Voina's patriarchy, decided that she wanted to start something new and with a feminist direction, Katya agreed. Petya didn't. "Petya is always for super-inclusivity," Nadya explained, "but we understood that we need *militant* feminism, that's it, nothing less." Petya tried another tack. "Okay, fine," Nadya remembers him saying. "But you understand that this is not a very viable topic right now, right? No one is going to be interested in what you're doing."

Nadya and Katya didn't quite know what their new project was, nor did it have a name, but it started with a song called "Kill the Sexist." They tried to record it in Katya's apartment, but her dad kicked them out: it was three in the morning and they were screaming their hastily written lyrics into a Dictaphone:[13]

> *Don't forget to scratch your ass while you're at it,*
> *Burp, spit, drink, shit,*
> *While we happily become lesbians!*
> *Envy your own stupid penis*
> *Or your drinking buddy's huge dick,*
> *Or the guy on TV's huge dick,*
> *While shit piles up and rises to the ceiling.*[14]

They continued their recording session in a playhouse in a nearby park, alarming the junkies outside, who peeked in to ask if the girls were okay.

Around that time, in October 2011, Katya and Nadya were invited to give a lecture at a festival organized by the Russian opposition. "We told the organizers the subject would be 'Punk Feminism in Russia,'" Nadya recalled later. "We started preparing the lecture the night before and suddenly discovered that Russian punk feminism did not exist . . . There was only one solution: invent punk feminism so we would have something to talk about."[15] So Nadya and Katya gave the audience a crash course in Bikini Kill, Niki de Saint Phalle, Shulamith Firestone, Guerrilla Girls, Martha Rosler's *Semiotics of the Kitchen*, Marcel Duchamp's gender-bending *Mona Lisa*, Diane Arbus's portrait of a transvestite, and on and on.[16] They also mentioned a new group on the Moscow scene, Pussy Riot. No one had ever heard of it, but that would soon change.

Nadya and Katya lured over Nastia, an old friend who actually knew something about music. Another friend became their videographer. Katya took up the bass. A few other women joined and Pussy Riot started staging their guerrilla actions around Moscow. They wore balaclavas to protect their anonymity—colorful ones because, as Nadya explained, "we didn't want to be taken for terrorists."[17] Their brand of anti-Putinist performance art was clearly and loudly feminist. And while Voina's actions were one-off events, Pussy Riot filmed performances of each new song in several locations, editing the footage into a music video and releasing it on YouTube. Like commandos preparing for a raid, they rehearsed fastidiously to make sure they could climb whatever structure they needed to occupy, unpack the guitar and the microphones, sing the song, dance the dance, and run away before the police could nab them.

For their first action, they climbed onto the scaffolding and into the arches in various Moscow Metro stations and onto the roofs of Moscow's trolleybuses. From there they screamed a song invoking the Arab Spring and calling for a feminist revolution. The song also took aim at the Kremlin's constant urging of women to birth more babies, and before every performance Nadya stuffed a down pillow under her green minidress. As they sang and thrashed, she would go into paroxysms of mock labor, pull out the pillow, and, ripping it open, unleash a shower of feathers onto puzzled onlookers.[18]

The song was terrible, the music even worse, but that was precisely the point. "The essence of punk is an explosion," Nadya wrote later. "It is the maximal discharge of creative energy, which does not require any particular technique."[19] And yet each performance drew a crowd—as well as plainclothes operatives from the government's feared Center Against Extremism. After the first video went viral, Petya realized that feminism actually *was* a viable and interesting idea. He joined up to help with logistics, and was soon making television appearances alongside Nadya to discuss Pussy Riot.[20]

A few weeks later, the women burst into the luxury boutiques of Stoleshnikov Lane and climbed onto the roof of a trendy Moscow nightclub to perform a song titled "Sexists Are Fucked, Fucking Conformists Are Fucked!"[21] For the video, they crashed an invitation-only fashion show and tossed flour over the catwalk. The idea "was to riff on new bits of everyday life," Nadya later explained, "things women encounter every day."[22] What they hadn't counted on was that flour is highly flammable and there were lit candles ringing the runway. The flour burst into flame, singeing the terrified models' clothes. Somehow, no one was hurt and Pussy Riot managed to escape.

In December 2011, Moscow erupted into protest. I had been in the press gallery that September at the United Russia convention where Putin had announced that he and Medvedev would be switching places: Putin would again become president for a third, nonconsecutive term, and Medvedev would become prime minister. Now, however, each presidential term was six years rather than four, and everyone immediately understood that they were going to be ruled by Putin for another twelve years, if not longer. By December, the sense of despair had hardened into anger when the sheer brazenness of the fraud in the parliamentary election was captured by Russians with smartphones. That winter, I witnessed the heady upheaval that followed. Five thousand furious people came out in central Moscow on December 5. Five days later, 50,000 protested in Bolotnaya Square, just outside of the Kremlin. On December 24, nearly 80,000 did. In February, over 100,000 marched through the center of Moscow, which hadn't seen protests like this since just before the fall of the Soviet Union.

Masha Alyokhina never forgot the magic of the Snow Revolution, or what she called the "magical winter of 2011."[23] Small and fierce, she seemed made for this moment. She was born in Moscow in 1988 to an unmarried thirty-five-year-old woman who got pregnant by a mathematician who wanted nothing to do with fatherhood, or with Masha. Like so many Russians, she was raised by her mother and grandmother, but her mother was no match for her strong-willed daughter. "I wasn't an unproblematic child; let's just put it that way," Masha told me.[24] In her late teens, she gravitated toward the wanderers on the Arbat, a picturesque pedestrian street in central Moscow. That was where she met Nikita, an itinerant and alcoholic young man five years her senior. Soon, in 2007, their son Fillip was born.[25] Masha was nineteen and took him to live with her mother. For the first years of his life, he, too, was raised by a mother and a grandmother, the classic Russian nuclear family.

After Fillip's birth, Masha went to college classes on weekends and found her way into environmental activism. She met Nadya and Petya through their mutual friend Nastia, whose apartment was a central gathering spot for Pussy Riot. Masha started living there and wound up joining the group.

In January 2012, the protest movement was heating up. More than a thousand protesters had already been arrested, including Petya. Nadya and Katya were getting tired of bringing him care packages and waiting outside the prison walls like the women of Anna Akhmatova's generation. So they decided to stage another action. This time they popped up on the roof of a garage behind the jail where Petya was sharing a cell with an up-and-coming opposition activist named Alexey Navalny. When Pussy Riot lit flares and screamed for the freedom to protest, the action quickly became a call-and-response between the women and the prisoners, who started cheering through the barred windows.[26]

Pussy Riot's members—Nadya, Katya, Masha, Nastia, and four other women—were just getting started. Their next action was right in Red Square, at a stone pedestal in front of St. Basil's Cathedral, whence the tsar's edicts had been read to the population. This was also where eight activists had been arrested for protesting the Soviet Union's violent quashing of the Prague Spring in 1968. "There were eight of us, like the eight dissidents of 1968," Masha noted.[27]

On January 20, it was minus 12 Fahrenheit when the women of Pussy Riot climbed onto the icy stone wall, dropped their coats, and released purple smoke bombs. It wasn't their song "Putin Pissed Himself!"—which took aim at the "Orthodox religion of a hard penis"—that made them famous.[28] It was the image of eight women rioting in dresses of motley colors and bright balaclavas in front of the equally Technicolor St. Basil's, the traditional symbol of Russia. The cops who detained them were nonplussed. At the station, they offered them hot coffee and chided them. "Silly girls, you must be frozen!" they clucked.[29] The girls gave fake names pulled from an old government database—a tactic they had developed to deal with their accumulating arrests—and went home to plot the next action.

On February 8, with the presidential election approaching, Putin met with the head of the Russian Orthodox Church, Patriarch Kirill, who offered his full-throated endorsement of Putin's proposed leadership swap with Medvedev. The only thing that had saved Russia from the "chaos" of the 1990s—which the patriarch compared improbably to World War II and the Russian Civil War—was a "miracle of God," by which he meant Putin's rule.[30] A few days earlier, the patriarch had declared, pointedly, that the Orthodox faithful don't protest; they pray.[31]

That decided it. The next Pussy Riot action would take place inside the main symbol of the Russian Orthodox Church and its unconstitutional fusion with the state: the Cathedral of Christ the Savior. Nadya and Masha venerated Jesus Christ as a radical and a revolutionary and saw the patriarch as a perversion of his message. Kirill fraternized with the Kremlin elite, who pledged government funds to build him more churches. He wore luxury watches and had a fleet of luxury cars. He allegedly owned a yacht. He lived in giant villas surrounded by unscalable walls. His mistress, posing as his third cousin, was ensconced in a luxury apartment just across the river from the cathedral.

Petya, who was more politically ambitious than the women, was the lone dissenter. "He said, 'Navalny won't like this action,'" Nadya recalled. "He argued, why knock out so much potential political support? He was very, very against it." Nadya couldn't care less. They threw chairs at each other, but she and Pussy Riot won. The next performance would be in the Cathedral of Christ the Savior.

Nadya, Katya, and Masha went on trial on July 30 of that year, nearly six months after they had called on the Virgin Mary to become a feminist and chase Putin off the throne. On February 26, warrants had been issued for their arrest on charges of hooliganism motivated by religious hatred, with a potential sentence of two to seven years. The women moved from apartment to apartment, trying to outrun the authorities. They were finally apprehended on March 3, the day before Putin was elected president for the third time.

Since then, Katya, Masha, and Nadya had been held in pretrial detention. (The two other women who performed with them in the cathedral managed to remain anonymous and at large. Petya was briefly questioned and released.) To protest their arrest, Masha and Nadya went on a hunger strike.

Petya may not have been an early or enthusiastic supporter of Pussy Riot, but he was fully invested now. In leading the campaign for the women's freedom, he discovered his natural talents in political PR. By the time their trial began, Amnesty International had declared them "prisoners of conscience." Famous Western musicians, believing, apparently, that Pussy Riot was a band, would demand their release: the Red Hot Chili Peppers, Sting, Franz Ferdinand, Peter Gabriel, Paul McCartney, Yoko Ono.[32]

None of this made any difference because Putin, unsurprisingly, did not take kindly to the punk prayer. It was a direct assault on what he was trying to build, an authoritarian state with traditional social mores. And while he could not go after each one of the tens of thousands of protesters in Moscow, he could make an example of some of them. The massive crackdown on the protest movement would come several months later, but its first victims were Pussy Riot.

Four days after the women's arrest, Putin's mustachioed spokesman, Dmitry Peskov, made clear his boss's attitude toward the performance: "negative." Later that day, Putin apologized to "all the faithful and members of the clergy" for certain unnamed people "violating the order established in a church." "It won't happen again," he added ominously.[33] The signal had been given.

The Russian elite obediently piled on. The patriarch, who was rumored to have called Putin to demand a harsh sentence, said the punk prayer was "blasphemy."[34] A famous archconservative priest said Orthodox Christians had to stand up for Russia's holy sites, even if it meant killing people.[35] A television host said Pussy Riot had "spit in the souls" of believers. Vladimir Kolokoltsev, a former Soviet *silovik* and the head of the Moscow police, now identified himself as an "Orthodox person" and said Pussy Riot had "spat in my soul." (Soon afterward he would be named minister of the interior.)

Few Russians supported what Pussy Riot had done. Russians were not a religious or churchgoing people—less than 3 percent attended church weekly—but, under Putin's increasingly nationalistic rule, nearly 80 percent identified as Russian Orthodox. It had become a national identity more than a religious one, and Pussy Riot had attacked its core. Just after they were arrested, a poll by the independent Levada Center found that nearly half of Russians felt that two to seven years in prison for dancing in a church was an "adequate punishment."[36] Among those who had heard about the punk prayer, 42 percent said that the state was prosecuting Pussy Riot for offending the faithful; only 17 percent said it was because they had called for Putin to step down. Half of those who had heard of Pussy Riot thought the harsh charge was justified because the women had "grossly violated the norms of social morality." By the end of their trial, which only one-third of Russians thought fair and independent, 51 percent had a negative opinion of Pussy Riot.[37]

Even in the growing opposition, many hesitated. After Pussy Riot was arrested, one woman I knew, a prominent journalist and human rights defender who also happened to be a pious Orthodox Christian, told me, "Good. Lock them up." (She eventually turned into a fervent defender of the group.) Most in the opposition found Pussy Riot's performance silly at best; its feminist message had gone completely over their heads. The opposition's priorities were free and fair elections, an end to corruption, and a release of political prisoners. They wanted Putin to step down so Russia could finally become "normal," a favorite watchword among the educated urban elite in those days. "Normal" meant a classic European liberal democracy and market economy. What did feminism have to do with it? (That feminism *was* now part of Western normalcy seemed irrelevant in the Russian context, where women, unlike men, were believed to be doing just fine.) Most of the opposition came to support Pussy Riot only when the extent of Putin's retribution became clear. They were political prisoners who now fit squarely into what the opposition was fighting for.

Petya had been right about another thing: Navalny didn't like the action, at all. The young Moscow lawyer had gained prominence as the author of a wildly popular blog about government corruption, but the protests had turned him into one of the main leaders of the Russian opposition. Yet while Navalny was a liberal democrat, he was also a traditional Russian *muzhik* who liked to show that he was a pious Christian. When I was writing a profile of him the previous year, he drove me to the Moscow bedroom community where his family lived. Every time we passed a church, he crossed himself three times.[38]

Four days after Nadya, Katya, and Masha were arrested, Navalny wrote a post on his LiveJournal page called "About Pussy Riots," calling for the women's release on legal grounds.[39] Their detention was "senseless and disgustingly cruel," he declared. They were too poor to be a flight risk, they were not a danger to society, and, most importantly, they had small children. (In the Russian criminal code, having minor children was supposed to result in a lighter sentence, or one postponed until the children turned fourteen.)

But Navalny hated what they had done. Pussy Riot, he wrote, were "stupid women" who had "committed an act of petty hooliganism for the sake of publicity." "The best thing that the Russian Orthodox Church could do right now is to show mercy and forgive these silly girls," he concluded, "and to conduct an educational conversation with them once they are free and have returned to their underage children."[40]

A century had passed but one fact remained the same. Whether you were a Bolshevik or a liberal democrat, opposing a conservative, patriarchal autocrat who was using the Church to buttress his rule in no way meant that you were a feminist.

The trial, when it finally came, was a travesty.

Nadya, Katya, and Masha were led into a tiny, hot courtroom in handcuffs, pale from five months of detention. They were parked inside a giant plexiglass cube called an "aquarium." Inside, it was very hard for the women to hear the proceedings—and very hard for those of us in the courtroom to hear them. The small courtroom was where the second trial of oil tycoon Mikhail Khodorkovsky had taken place in December 2010. The Kremlin preferred to hold politically charged trials in venues that couldn't fit many journalists, and we fought each other to muscle into the room.[41]

The roles the women would play during the trial quickly became clear. Nadya, somehow still beautiful and sultry in the stuffy aquarium, was the revolutionary theorist. Masha, defiant with her mane of dull blond frizz, was the brain, inventing novel legal tactics on the fly and yelling back at Judge Marina Syrova, a sour middle-aged woman. And then there was Katya, the awkward, shy one, who had little to say at all. She had obviously been far more comfortable behind a balaclava.

Nadya, Katya, and Masha all apologized for causing unintentional emotional harm to Orthodox believers, though Masha expressed dismay at the lack of Christian forgiveness. "I thought the Church loved all its children," she said in her written statement. "But it turns out it only loves those children who love Putin."[42] None of the seven "victims" in the case, mostly cathedral attendants and security guards, would accept the women's apologies when they took the stand, saying they were insincere or had come too late. "A spoon is useful at lunchtime," one scoffed.

When the prosecutor read the charges, I can vividly remember sitting on the hard brown bench in the courtroom and starting to laugh, mostly out of shock. The prosecutor was a representative of a state that, as mandated by the Russian constitution, was secular. Yet here he was, alleging that Nadya, Katya, and Masha were motivated by "religious hatred" and "trying to devalue centuries of revered and protected dogmas." The young women of Pussy Riot had apparently shaken "the spiritual foundations" of the Russian Federation.[43] These "girls" were that strong and the state that weak.

No one, myself included, had expected this to be a fair trial, but I did not anticipate what we got instead, which was a trial as performance art. As a political action that exposed the new direction Putin was pushing the country—toward an increasingly authoritarian system governed by parochial, patriarchal norms—it far exceeded anything Pussy Riot could have staged on their own.

The first witness, Lyubov Sokologorskaya, set the tone. She took care of the candles in the cathedral. Sokologorskaya was vicious when I tried to speak to her in the women's bathroom, but on the stand she could have been one half of the Pietà. She had been suffering terribly from the harm Pussy Riot inflicted on her in their forty-second performance, she said. The prosecutor asked a series of rapid-fire questions. Was she an Orthodox believer? Did she celebrate all the holidays and keep all the fasts of the Russian Orthodox Church? What is God? What were the girls wearing? Was their clothing tight?[44]

Yes, Sokologorskaya said, the girls' clothing was mostly tight, bright, and extremely inappropriate for a holy place. She may have even seen a bra strap. What was worse, she said, they had climbed onto the soleas, where women were not allowed. There, they commenced their "devilish jerking."

One of Pussy Riot's lawyers, Violetta Volkova, jumped in. "Have you ever seen any devils?"

The judge struck the question. (She would do that for most of the defense's questions and did not allow the defense to call a single witness.)

"I just wanted to clarify, how does she know how devils jerk themselves around?" Volkova yelled.

That, too, was struck.

It wasn't just that these girls had invaded a holy space. It was what they had done up there, kicking their legs in the air, revealing what lay beneath their dresses. "They raised their legs so high that everything past their waists, you could see," Sokologorskaya lamented. (Later the church treasurer, another victim, would sob as she recalled how one of the women had prostrated herself on the soleas. "And her butt was raised high and this butt was facing the altar," she wailed.)

Because Sokologorskaya was claiming "moral damage," one of the defense lawyers, Nikolai Polozov, asked her if she had sought help from a doctor or a psychologist.

"The gracious power of the Holy Spirit," Sokologorskaya shot back, "is a million times stronger than any psychologist!"

"Then why didn't the gracious power of the Holy Spirit assuage your moral suffering?"

"The question is struck!" snapped the judge.

"Have you seen the video of the punk prayer?" Polozov asked.

"Yes."

"If the performance caused you such moral suffering, why did you decide to poison your soul again?"

That question, too, was struck. Sokologorskaya would spend the rest of the trial sitting in the gallery, loudly sighing and crossing herself.

The defendants were given a chance to ask questions through the small opening in the aquarium. When it was Nadya's turn, she asked how Sokologorskaya could determine that Nadya and her friends had a hatred for Russian Orthodoxy.

"Because you disturbed the peace in the cathedral," Sokologorskaya said. "You used curse words."

"Do you remember what I personally said on February 21?"

"I don't want to repeat these words."

"Do you remember what I said?"

Struck.

"Is 'feminist' a bad word?" Nadya pressed on, referring to the part of the punk prayer in which they implored the Virgin to become one.

"In a church," Sokologorskaya replied, "yes."

Over the coming days, the trial devolved into full comic farce. "Do you think they could have been possessed?" one of the defense lawyers asked another one of the victims, an altar boy. "The question is struck!"

said the judge. "He is not a medical expert!" There were moments when the whole room erupted in laughter—even the defendants, slowly wilting in the aquarium. The women weren't being regularly fed and were getting fewer than four hours of sleep every night. At one point, an ambulance had to be called for Masha. She hadn't seen Fillip in months, nor had Nadya seen Gera. And yet none of that obscured how morbidly funny this trial had become. "Is this funny to you!" the judge screamed at Masha at one point. "No," Masha responded, barely stifling her giggles. "It's quite sad." Eventually, the judge attempted to ban laughter in the courtroom and the burly bailiffs prowled the gallery, threatening to toss out anyone who so much as smiled.

It didn't work. One expert witness, a sweaty middle-aged man with a dirty shirt stretched over his belly, brought the house down with his testimony on the etymology of the group's English-language name. He was declared an expert witness because he had seen the clip of the punk prayer and an interview with the group on YouTube. Perhaps Russian speakers didn't understand the perfidy hidden in the English words, he said. "Do you even know what 'pussy' means?" he asked the court. "I do. I brought a dictionary." "Riot" was simple enough. It meant a revolt, an uprising, he explained. But "pussy" was harder. The audience—and we were an audience now—waited with bated breath. "Pussy," the expert witness explained, came from the English word for "pus," the viscous yellow fluid that oozes from an infected wound. Far from being feminists, he concluded, they were a rotten rebellion.

Outside the courtroom, pressure was mounting on Putin, who was still in a stance of uneasy cooperation with the West. When Putin traveled to London for the summer Olympics, Prime Minister David Cameron confronted him about Pussy Riot. Madonna, performing in Moscow, had called for their freedom, pulling on a black balaclava and stripping off her top to reveal "PUSSY RIOT" scrawled on her back.[45] Alicia Silverstone petitioned the Kremlin to allow Masha, a vegetarian, to get vegan meals in prison.[46] Ukrainian *Playboy* invited Nadya to pose on its cover. One day, as Nadya was being led out of the courtroom under armed guard, Petya yelled to her: *Björk said hi!*

On the fourth day of the trial, Putin denied that Cameron had pressed him on the issue, but he did have a message for the court. "I don't think that they should be judged so harshly for it," he said. "I hope that [the defendants] will learn their lessons."[47] Until then, the concern had been that Nadya, Katya, and Masha would get the full seven years requested by the prosecutor. But now the tsar had called for Christian mercy and the prosecutor quickly revised his request to three years.

In the end, on August 17, Judge Syrova gave Nadya, Katya, and Masha two years each in minimum-security penal colonies. This was not a harsh sentence from the Kremlin's point of view, although the opposition didn't see it that way. Navalny, by now totally on Pussy Riot's side, called the three-week trial "medieval" and said he was "too angry to comment on the verdict."

After the three women were led out of the courtroom under guard, Petya was surrounded by a scrum of reporters.

"What will happen to your wife and daughter?" one journalist asked. "Who will take care of them?"

"My daughter, wife, and everyone else will be saved by the revolution," he said blithely. "Only the revolution. And we're going to make it happen."[48]

But there would be no revolution. Things would only get worse.

WOMEN'S ZONE

IN PUTIN'S RUSSIA, WHEN A CRIMINAL CASE MAKES IT TO COURT, IT results in a conviction 99 percent of the time. If a judge hands down a not-guilty verdict, everyone down the chain—investigators, police, prosecutors—will be punished. So all a judge needs to do is take an indictment and reformat it into a verdict. "A not-guilty verdict is harder to write," explained Kirill Titaev, a sociologist who studies the Russian criminal justice system. A judge thinks, "Instead of copying and pasting, I have to write two hundred pages." Who is best suited for this? Women. "Diligence, thoroughness, being detail-oriented are seen as female qualities," Titaev told me.

During the past three decades, as Russian courts have become increasingly subservient to the Kremlin, they have also been steadily feminized. This is no coincidence: the less independent and powerful the courts became under Putin, the less attractive they became to men as a career option. But there was another dynamic at play. As the older male judges who survived the Soviet period retired, many of them promoted their clerks and secretaries to replace them. These younger women, the reasoning went, were not independent thinkers. They could be trusted to rubber-stamp the ready-made decision the system presented to them. On a few (relatively) more independent or prestigious courts, like the arbitrage court and the Constitutional Court, the judiciary is still predominantly male. By contrast, judges on local courts are up to 90 percent female and, overall, two-thirds of Russia's judges are women. They are the ones who implement decisions made by the more powerful men behind the scenes. Which is why, during Pussy Riot's trial, no real decisions had been made in that courtroom, not even by Judge Syrova.

Katya didn't know any of this. The thought of a year and a half in what was, in essence, a lightly modified Gulag, terrified her. According to Gessen, a provocateur may have been placed in Katya's cell after the verdict: a woman who talked loudly to the other inmates about how bad things were in the colony where Katya might end up.[1] After a few days of this, Katya fired her lawyer. Under the mistaken impression that her trial had actually been a trial, she was convinced that she had been given a two-year jail term not because of the political nature of the case but because Pussy Riot's attorneys had spent too much of the proceedings tweeting.

Masha and Nadya tried to talk her out of it. Bizarrely, the one place they were allowed to be reunited outside court was in the jail's salon, where they were taken under armed guard to get their hair and nails done—not because they had requested a manicure or a blowout but because the system thought it appropriate for women in their position to look nice for the kangaroo court. But Katya insisted.

During Pussy Riot's appeal hearing, her new lawyer successfully argued that Katya was stopped before she could even get on the soleas, let alone undermine the spiritual foundations of the Russian Federation. In October, Katya was freed and largely disappeared from public view.

A few days before her release, Putin was asked about the Pussy Riot verdict. "The court was right in making this decision," he said in a television interview. "Because you can't undermine the foundations of morality and destroy the country. What will we be left with then?"[2]

On December 12, 2012, four months after the verdict, Putin announced a new direction for the country in a speech to the federal assembly. "You know, respected colleagues, it is painful for me to speak about this, but I am obligated to say something," he said. "Today, Russian society is experiencing an obvious deficit of spiritual bindings." The word he used for these bindings, *skrepy*, would become the byword for the onslaught of conservative policies that Putin unleashed in response to the protest movement. *Skrepy* were a return to a Russian traditionalism untouched by the West—or the Bolsheviks. And for Putin, they were the perfect foundation on which to build his new Russian Empire.

"We need to wholly support institutions that are the bearers of traditional values, that have historically proven their ability to transmit them from generation to generation," Putin explained in his speech.[3]

Six months later, he signed a law that criminalized "offending the feelings of religious believers." It had been introduced in the Duma just weeks after the Pussy Riot verdict. The sin those three young women had committed would now be punishable by up to three years in prison—exactly what the prosecutor in their case had asked for. Inspired by the latest signal from the boss, the Duma started proposing all kinds of legislation. These included a ban on homosexual propaganda and initiatives to make it more difficult to obtain a divorce, to cap the number of times Russian citizens could get remarried, and to remove free abortions from the national healthcare system.

The Russian Orthodox Church, flexing its new power, teamed up with American evangelical organizations to push for abortion bans. Priests began showing up in state-run clinics to dissuade women from getting the procedure and to convince doctors that abortion was sinful.[4] They also appeared as experts on Duma committees, especially those dealing with the family. In 2016, Anna Kuznetsova, a priest's wife, was named the president's ombudswoman for the rights of children. Kuznetsova, who birthed her seventh child for the Motherland while in office, was the ideal woman in the government's eyes. Her church-based values were shellacked with a coat of pseudoscience. "Basing ourselves in the relatively new science of telegony, we can speak about the cells of a uterus having wave-informational memory," she explained in an interview, though she later denied having said this. "Let's say a woman had previous partners, then there is a high likelihood that she will have a weakened child because of the mixing of information. This fact has a special influence on the moral foundations of the future child."[5] By 2023, Kuznetsova would be bragging that private clinics in a half dozen regions of Russia were no longer providing abortions.

In his 2012 *skrepy* speech, Putin had declared that "a government's attempts to intrude into the sphere of people's convictions and views" is "a manifestation of totalitarianism." "That is completely unacceptable to us," he stressed. "We will not go down that path." But it was exactly where he was headed. It was getting harder to come out as gay, harder to protest, harder to organize, to speak out, to make art, to practice journalism. More people were being arrested on politically motivated charges. More activists and reporters were being branded as foreign agents for disagreeing with the official line. Elections were becoming so tightly managed that not even the municipal level escaped the Kremlin's control. *Skrepy* weren't just the ties that would hold the new Russian Empire together; they were a straitjacket to control Russian society. It was the final unwinding of the Bolshevik feminist experiment. Pussy Riot had been the beginning of the end.

Their appeals rejected, Masha and Nadya were put on train cars going to two different penal colonies. As in Soviet times, neither they, their families, nor their lawyers knew where they were during the weeks-long journey. As in Soviet times, they traveled in Stolypin cars, crowded into compartments with metal bunks and taken to the bathroom twice every twenty-four hours. (The women relieved themselves in empty mayonnaise tubs in the meantime.)

Nadia was sent to Mordovia, a region with the highest concentration of prisons in the world. Masha ended up on the other side of the Urals, in Berezniki, just north of Perm, a place once dotted with the camps of the Gulag. In the months they had spent in jail awaiting trial, the women had already learned things that political prisoners in Russia have known for generations. They learned how to deal with the bone-withering cold. (Masha, for instance, discovered that women used sanitary napkins to seal drafty cell windows.)[6] They learned how to sleep on beds that left bruises on their bodies. They learned how to talk to interrogators. They learned how to survive solitary. They learned the value of cigarettes. They learned how to communicate with prisoners in other parts of the jail: by knocking or sending notes on improvised ropes strung between cell windows. They learned how to cook and sew with the nothing that they were allowed. (A simulacrum of soup, for instance, could be made with a hot water coil.) They learned how to stay clean when what passed for a bath was available only once a week. ("There is no hot water in our barracks," Masha wrote of a similar struggle in the penal colony. "You wash yourself every day over the toilet bowl, pouring water from a plastic bucket over your cunt, the water warmed beforehand in a large vat.")[7] They learned how to form alliances with cellmates and how to spot moles placed there by the prison authorities. They learned how to deal with prison guards, like the ones who, on the first morning of Masha's arrest, made her do ten squats while naked to make sure she wasn't hiding anything "in there." That memory, Masha wrote, "stayed with me throughout my sentence."[8]

Inside this system, very little had changed since the days of Eugenia Ginzburg. The penal system was one of the main institutional "bearers of traditional values," to use Putin's phrase, and it had maintained and protected those values from tsarism to Communism to Putinism. There were still special units in some camps, for instance, for the children of imprisoned women. They were allowed to receive visits from their mothers until they were three. After that, they were transferred to a state orphanage and, as in Ginzburg's time, often lost to their mothers.

There were other holdovers, too, like slave labor. Women were no longer required to fell giant trees or dig in the permafrost for gold, but both Nadya and Masha were put to work sewing uniforms for the police and federal penitentiary service. In Masha's camp, the factory worked around the clock, and women did twelve-hour shifts. For all this, the women were paid 150 to 200 rubles a month, less than $3. Unless family sent more money, as well as the necessities in care packages that took a full day to drop off, that was all the women had to buy pads, lotion, shampoo, cigarettes, and food to supplement the gray slop served in the canteen. Vitamin deficiency was common, just as in Soviet times. So were dental issues; often there was only one dentist for a colony of 1,000 people, and the visit wasn't free. Many women suffered from HIV, venereal disease, and drug withdrawal, but the prison doctors were more interested in getting the women back to the factory to sew uniforms.

Corporal punishment, which was common, was often specifically designed to humiliate female prisoners. Masha was regularly subjected to "body searches," allegedly to check for contraband documents, because she had once managed to smuggle an account of her imprisonment out through her lawyer, to be published in a magazine. "Outside, we'd call these searches a gynecological exam," Masha wrote in her book after she got out. "In January [2013], I had four of these exams a week, with no medical instruments or an examining table. It was a blatant means of causing pain in revenge for my magazine article . . . I'd managed to smuggle it past the guard, so they searched me 'in full' before and after every lawyer's visit."[9]

There were other things unique to the women's *zona*, or zone, slang for penal colony. Male prisoners build strict hierarchies and help each other, and they have contraband cell phones. The women are too scared to break such a big rule, explained Katya Shutova, who worked for Russia Behind Bars, an NGO that helped prisoners and their families. "Women are much more vulnerable," Shutova told me as we drank tea in her Moscow office. She was heavily pregnant. "Women have families back home. They want to get out as soon as possible. They just want to do their time quietly and not put up any resistance, not make any noise."

Shutova was a former inmate herself, arrested at twenty-three for fraud, one of the main reasons that women in Russia find themselves in prison. (Other large categories of offenders are women who killed their men while drunk or in self-defense and those convicted of drug offenses, after helping their men deal, or getting caught holding the bag, or using themselves.) Shutova had been an accountant, a predominantly female profession in Russia. (If you see a woman in the C suite of a Russian company, she is most likely the CFO.) In Russia, businesses compete by every means necessary, including bribing authorities to open criminal cases against their competitors. The men in charge of those companies typically blame the accountants, who are the ones signing off on the financial documents. "Accounting is a very dangerous profession in our country," Shutova sighed.

Shutova was young and unmarried when she went in. Her mother quit her job so she could assume another full-time job: ferrying packages to her daughter in a distant penal colony. Most women don't have that kind of support. "The husbands last one to two months," Shutova said. This was a well-known fact in the zone. "When it sinks in that their wives will be stuck behind bars for years to come, [husbands] usually abandon their women," Masha wrote. "Wives don't abandon their husbands, though. Often, women bring enormous bales of goods they've hauled thousands of miles for their husbands in prison." To make up for the loneliness, Masha told me, women form prison families. "It's considered cool" to have a girlfriend in the colony, she said. Hers was Olga, a member of the hard-left, nationalist National Bolshevik Party.

Masha and Nadya were relatively lucky. Their sentences were short, journalists kept track of them, friends and family didn't desert them. Nikita and Fillip and Petya and Gera came to visit, though the visits were upsetting. When Petya and Gera visited Nadya, Gera, who turned four on the day Nadya was arrested, acted like her mother was a stranger. The first time Fillip saw his mother behind a glass wall, he started crying, which made Masha cry, too.

Yet Masha's time in prison didn't pass in vain. She studied the criminal code and used her new knowledge to improve life in the colony, however marginally. She documented abuse and violations and began filing case after case against the camp administration. Why was there only one telephone for 1,500 inmates? What law says prisoners can't sleep during the day? Why were they not allowed milk? Some cases made it to court and sometimes the corrections officers fixed the issue after Masha's complaints made it out into the free world through her lawyers. Once, they padlocked her entire barrack and prohibited phone calls for anyone. That way all the women would know the one reason they couldn't speak to their kids: Masha Alyokhina. So Masha went on hunger strike. She wouldn't stop, she said, until the padlocks were removed. "For the half year I've been in the colony, the guards . . . have failed to understand why, when you're thrown in prison for protesting, you keep protesting," Masha wrote later.

Nadya also protested for the rights of her fellow inmates. In September 2013, she described the conditions in her penal colony in gruesome detail—women purposely starved while working sixteen-hour shifts; made to sew even as a fire began engulfing the factory; a Roma woman beaten to death; others forced to sew naked when they couldn't complete their quota—and she, too, launched a hunger strike in protest. "Sanitary conditions at the prison are calculated to make the prisoner feel like a disempowered, filthy animal," Nadya wrote in an open letter declaring her hunger strike. She described how eight hundred prisoners would be sent to wash in a room meant for five people, creating a stampede "as women with little tubs try to wash their 'breadwinners' (as they are called in Mordovia) as fast as they can." Their allotted weekly bathing day was often canceled because of plumbing problems, she went on; her barrack had sometimes been unable to wash for two or three weeks. "When the pipes are clogged, urine gushes out of the hygiene rooms and clumps of feces go flying," she wrote.

Nadya barely survived that hunger strike. She ended up in a TB hospital inside the penal system, and the authorities allowed her to serve out the rest of her term working there. Masha, on the other hand, seemed invigorated by her protest, in part because she won: the administration removed the padlocks. When she returned to her unit, she wrote, "The unit monitor gave me a birthday card. She wrote in it: 'Masha, I wish you simple woman's happiness.'"[10]

On December 13, 2013, Putin, wanting to appear magnanimous ahead of the Sochi Olympics, announced an amnesty. He closed the cases of some people who had been arrested after a police provocation turned an opposition protest violent on the day before his May 2012 inauguration. He also pardoned all women who were first-time offenders and who had small children—prisoners like Nadya and Masha. When they were finally freed, they had only two months of their sentences left.

In the fall of 2014, *Glamour* decided to honor Pussy Riot in their Women of the Year issue and asked me to write something about the group. After I filed it, the editor called from New York. She was a bit confused. Why hadn't I mentioned Pussy Riot's stance on abortion and reproductive rights? she wondered. They had kids; what about that? And what did their husbands think about their activism? I was a little stunned until I realized how perfectly perfect this moment was. What better way to illustrate the chasm between American and Russian feminism? I gave the editor a quick run-down, explaining the Bolshevik feminists; that, having had access to legal abortion for nearly a century, Russian women largely take it for granted; and that Pussy Riot, as feminists with roots in the hardest left as well as in Russian anarchism, were absolutely uninterested in what their husbands had to say. In fact, most of them weren't even married. There was an uncomfortable silence on the other end of the line. Finally, the editor said, "Maybe we should've done some more research before assigning this..."

When I related this story to Nadya a few years later, she laughed. She had spent a lot of time in the United States since her release, and had grown tired of explaining exactly this to American feminists. "Don't you understand that we were the first country in the world that allowed civil marriage? Get out of here with your shitty United States!" she said, her voice rising with indignation and laughter. But it wasn't just a problem abroad, Nadya felt. It was also how younger Russian women thought of feminism. "When we talk about feminism, we are, first and foremost, talking about Western feminism," she said of the Russian discourse. "We never think about our own past." Most young Russian women, she went on, aren't aware "that we were one of the first countries in the world to give women the right to vote, that we had civil marriage and allowed abortion at a moment when this didn't exist anywhere else."

I had spent that reporting trip, in the fall of 2018, talking to Russian feminists, journalists, and sociologists, and everything they told me confirmed this. The lexicon of American feminism had made its way to Moscow and, from there, percolated out to other big Russian cities. The young and in-the-know spoke about white heterosexual, cis-gendered men, a distinction largely without a difference in a country where some 80 percent of the population was Slavic and therefore white. People used terms like *toksichnaya maskulinnost'*, which was just "toxic masculinity" dressed up as Russian, but which nevertheless sprouted a new Russian verb: *toksichit'*, "to be toxic." There was a vigorous debate about "feminitives": Should people add feminine endings to nouns describing a profession? Should a female film director be *direktor* or *direktorka*? Should one's female partner be just a partner, *partnyor*, or a feminized *partnyorka*? A popular feminist blogger explained to me that she had descended from the Komi people and that, for her, Moscow was rife with "microaggressions" from "white Russians," Slavs. Except that the Komi are a Finno-Ugric tribe from the northern Urals and so, though perhaps subject to ethnic discrimination, are not discriminated against on the basis of race: they, too, are lily white.

I went to a women's conference in Perm where two young men were the sole speakers on a panel on toxic masculinity. One told a story about how he and his girlfriend had gotten into a fight that escalated so badly that he ended up tearing out one of her dreadlocks. He recounted standing there, holding his girlfriend's dreadlock in his hand, realizing that it would never reattach itself to her head and that he, a liberal, vegetarian, feminist man, was now the embodiment of *toksichnaya maskulinnost'*. That was when he decided to go to therapy, also very trendy at the time. It was like watching French culture come to Russia in the eighteenth century: something that made sense in an American context refracted itself through the Russian lens to become a comically warped derivative.

I mentioned this to Julia Taratuta, a Russian journalist I'd known for years who had left what she ironically referred to as serious male topics to become the editor in chief of Wonderzine, an online feminist publication. She had observed the same trend. The majority of her readers were young and had grown up online. They spoke English and could understand what their peers were doing abroad, even if they hadn't traveled there. Those who started discussions on Wonderzine's website belonged to an even more specific category. "Often, these are young women who have been admitted to Western universities," Taratuta explained. "These are women who have taken courses on gender and then, *from there*, are telling everyone here about what they learned. Some of it obviously has local, national roots, but how to *name* these things came from abroad, yes."[11]

And yet, that, too, was quintessentially Russian. For the previous two centuries, educated young Russians had been going to Europe and coming back with exciting new ideas to make their big, backward country "normal." Often, these ideas, like socialism or constitutional democracy, became garbled in translation while also meeting resistance from a deeply agrarian and conservative population that was violently uninterested in, say, Communism or abandoning wooden spoons for European forks. Sometimes the resistance was even broader. The #MeToo movement, for instance, was met with intense negativity in Russia, even among liberal Moscow intellectuals enamored of Western culture. They associated #MeToo with the same lack of due process and presumption of guilt that Russians encountered in their own criminal justice system. They also viewed it as a puritanical imposition on the sexual freedom they had finally won in the post-Soviet era.

And so despite the trendiness of feminism among a small and extremely online sliver of the Russian population and the falling away of certain gender norms—it was becoming increasingly popular, for example, for the father to be present at the birth of his child—in a country of over 140 million people, Wonderzine still only attracted 2 million unique viewers a month. "You would think that with this state push toward traditionalism, there would be a liberal wave that should only grow and grow," Taratuta told me. "I thought that all of [the people who protested in the winter of 2011–12] should be coming to us. But, when it comes to questions of gender, the liberal crowd has been quite traditionalist."

Nadya wanted to see Russian women embrace a feminism that proudly reflected their own national history. She wished that the history of Russian and Soviet feminism were taught in schools and that people knew what Russian revolutionaries like Kollontai, Armand, and Krupskaya had contributed to the cause of feminism, both in Russia and abroad. That time of bold, daring feminist reform was her favorite period in Russian history. "I live in the early twentieth century," she said, her big, dark eyes lighting up. "I think it's the coolest time for Russia, when it set the tone not just in feminism but in philosophy and in political theory, in the arts and the avant-garde. Sometimes, when I talk to my friends, I say, yes, Russia needs to conquer the world, but it needs to conquer it through ideas, like it did in the beginning of the twentieth century. There was nothing derivative about it then, because there were original artistic movements developing in Russia in that moment. When Picasso was painting his *Demoiselles d'Avignon*, Russia was creating the [Malevich's] Black Square. No one was talking about falling behind, that you have to catch up to some other country. And it was so recent! I don't understand how, in one century, we became a so-called superpower that is constantly chasing someone else. Everyone just needs to return to the beginning of the twentieth century, where I've been living for a long time."

We were sitting in a sunny café in a quiet residential neighborhood of Moscow. We met there because it was close to Petya's mother's apartment, which was where Gera lived most of the time. Today, Nadya was going to take Gera to a nearby park. Nadya loved Petya's mother, a strong woman with, as Nadya put it, a man in every port of call, but she was more than a little frustrated with Petya, whom she had divorced two years ago. Petya's new girlfriend, Veronika, looked like a model and immediately joined Pussy Riot, though she refused to allow Petya to be anywhere near Nadya, Pussy Riot's founder. That summer, when Russia had hosted the World Cup, Petya, Veronika, and two other women dressed up in police uniforms and ran out onto the pitch during a match between France and Croatia. Although Petya had advertised it as a Pussy Riot action, there was nothing feminist about it. The joke in Moscow became that the action was performed by "Petya and his girls."

I asked Nadya how she felt about this. She had suggested to Petya that the action should be done under Voina's name since it was making a more general statement about the Russian state, rather than a feminist one. "But then we came to the conclusion that I don't have any right to tell him, 'No, you can't be Pussy Riot,'" Nadya said. As Masha once explained to me, Pussy Riot was a leaderless organization: "Anyone can be Pussy Riot, just like anyone can be a feminist, man or woman."

Nadya said she preferred this "all-inclusive approach," but it didn't sound convincing. From jail, she and Masha had published a letter saying Petya had, in her words, "seized power in the group." "It was a completely disgusting letter and Petya's feelings were really hurt," Nadya conceded. But she repeated the critique to me again that day. Yes, Petya had been the one constantly agitating for their release, but she and Masha resented that the press still called him Pussy Riot's producer. "What is a producer?" Nadya said, her voice rising. "It's a person who, at least in the Russian understanding, is a manager. It's a person who determines the direction of the work, the ideology of the group; he is in charge of the financial and organizational roles. And Petya isn't in charge of any of the above."

After Nadya and Masha got out of prison, they, along with Petya, founded a journalistic project that covered the Russian criminal justice and penal systems, called Mediazona, a play on the slang *zona*, or penal colony. Petya helped run Mediazona, which was funded, in part, by honoraria and concert fees from Masha's theater projects and Nadya's music. It would quickly become one of the pillars of independent journalism in Russia. But Mediazona became yet another one of the group's projects where Petya had inserted himself and made himself the indispensable man.

"I'm not trying to minimize all he's done, but the constant elevation of the male figure is irritating, of course," Nadya went on. She was angry now. "I asked him many times; I said, 'Listen, can you just make a public statement that you're not anyone's producer, that you're just a member of the group?' And he said, 'They call me that themselves!' And I said, '*Of course* they do! And they will *always* call you that because you're a man, so you will always be the leader, the producer, so just correct them and tell them that's not the case.' But he doesn't do that. Because Petya is sneaky. He knows that all the inequalities benefit his side. So he's not really doing anything bad proactively, but he's also not really fighting it."

Would it have been easier if Pussy Riot had just been all female? I asked.

"It was," Nadya said. "But when we went to jail, Petya became a part of it by himself." She paused, not sure if she wanted to say the next sentence. "He took over our legacy," she finally managed. "Before that, it was all female." Her voice was low, laced with regret and hurt. "I'm very angry at all these inequalities. Because Petya is, of course, my dearest friend and it's a shame that all this fuckery, at least in part, destroyed us as a couple."

GASOLINE

ON DECEMBER 11, 2017, MARGARITA GRACHEVA WOKE UP AT SIX IN THE morning, just as she always did. She turned on some music and made herself coffee. Soon her sons were up and her oldest, Dima, was asking yet again when his fifth birthday was. "In three days," she told him. At ten to eight, Margarita shooed the boys out the door and into the waiting car of their father, her estranged husband, Dmitry Grachev.[1]

She had known Dmitry since their school days in Serpukhov, a small town sixty miles south of Moscow. After his mandatory military service, they reconnected and married in August 2012. They released doves in the forest and Dmitry carried her around like a queen. They were so young and so happy. Soon their first child was born, named Dmitry after his father, followed a year and a half later by his little brother, Danila.

It was a happy life at first, though Dmitry could be a difficult man. He was thin-skinned and splenetic, not given to compromise. He held grudges, nursing them almost lovingly. He had a streak of pride so stubborn, it sometimes dumbfounded Rita, as she was known to friends and family. Once, picking him up from work, she pulled up to a spot he deemed too far from where he was standing on the curb. Infuriated, he refused to get in her car and took the bus home instead. Dmitry sometimes told Rita that he'd kill her if she ever had an affair, but she never took those warnings seriously because she had no intention of cheating on him. "To live with Dima, you need to really love him," his grandmother used to tell Rita. "You have to accommodate his personality, forgive him."[2]

But by the fall of 2017 their marriage was coming undone. Rita felt that they were two strangers sharing a tiny one-bedroom apartment. When she told Dmitry she wanted a divorce, he didn't believe her. Reality sunk in a few days later when Rita presented him with the paperwork. Dmitry couldn't fathom why she would want to leave him—unless she were having an affair.

Dmitry began checking her phone, where he discovered text messages from Alexander, one of Rita's colleagues, a divorced middle-aged man with a young daughter around the same age as Dmitry and Rita's sons. Dmitry didn't believe Rita's explanations that Alexander was just a coworker and a friend and that their children liked playing together. Alexander, Dmitry decided, must be the reason Rita was leaving him. Dmitry stopped going to work and would lie on the couch imagining vivid scenes of his wife having sex with Alexander—and boil over.

But it was Rita, not Alexander, who became the focus of Dmitry's rage. He started doing spot checks of Rita's underwear: if her bra matched her underwear, it meant she was cheating. If she had shaved or waxed, she was cheating. If she baked muffins for more than four people, she was cheating. He began surveilling her movements using GPS trackers. He showed up at Rita's office, a local newspaper where she was the head of the marketing team, and screamed about his wife's phantom infidelities. Once, he checked her phone in the middle of the night and saw that Rita had deleted texts from Alexander, likely to avoid angering her husband. Furious, he kicked Rita awake, leaving bruises on her thighs. Her screams woke up their sons in the next room, who ran in and saw their mother in tears. After that, Rita demanded that Dmitry move out. Before he left, he slashed Rita's coat and squeezed out every tube of her makeup into the sink. He destroyed the dishwasher and took her laptop, along with every cord and charger in the house. He ripped up her passport so she couldn't file for divorce, then ripped up the paperwork required to obtain a new copy.

On November 10, two days before Rita's twenty-fifth birthday, Dmitry offered to drive Rita to her regular manicure appointment and then to work. Back then, Rita still hoped they could have an amicable divorce despite Dmitry's increasingly brutal threats: to throw acid in her face, to drive her and the kids into a brick wall at two hundred kilometers per hour. In the car that morning, all her illusions vanished. Dmitry grabbed her phone, then turned off the road and into the woods. There, he pulled out a knife and put it to her throat, then her belly, and demanded she confess. Rita pleaded: there was nothing to confess, no secret trysts, not with Alexander, not with anybody else. Finally, Dmitry relented and drove her to the nail salon, warned her not to call the police, and waited outside. Rita told everything to her manicurist Yulia, whom Dmitry kept calling to ask what was taking so long.

Terrified, Rita didn't call the police that day, but her mother, Inna, convinced her to file a report the next morning, November 11. The police made clear their distaste for getting dragged into a family matter. They did not question Dmitry or Rita or the manicurist. It took nearly three weeks for someone from the local precinct to finally call Rita. A few days later, a neighborhood cop had a chat with Dmitry, who smugly told Rita about their friendly conversation, "man-to-man." When she and Inna followed up weeks later, the police tried to dissuade them from pressing charges. Rita had two young boys at home. What if they grew up and wanted to join the FSB? Would they really want such a stain on their records? One of the officers told Rita that Dmitry's outbursts were a "manifestation of love."[3] Despite Inna's insistence that she wanted the police to take action, the neighborhood police officer closed the case and went on vacation. It was December 7.

The previous year, on July 4, 2016, Vladimir Putin signed legislation that changed how the Russian state treated domestic violence. Before this date, all kinds of battery were wrapped into one statute of the criminal code, and its prosecution depended on the victim essentially proving their own abuse had occurred. The new law created two legal categories, two types of battery. One was the kind that occurred out in the open between strangers; the other was the more intimate kind that occurred inside the home, between family members. The former became part of the civil code, punishable by a fine, a brief arrest of two weeks, or community service for first-time offenders. (Repeat offenders would be sent to prison.) Battery between family members, however, remained under the aegis of the criminal code, and the onus was now on the police to investigate and gather evidence.

Almost as soon as the law passed, however, two powerful female members of the Russian parliament, Elena Mizulina and Olga Batalina, decided that it had gone too far. They belonged to different political parties, but this had been a distinction without a difference for over a decade. After becoming president, Putin had rooted out any real political competition while explaining to an increasingly concerned West that Russia had to settle for a uniquely Russian form of democracy—"sovereign" or "managed democracy"—because the Russian people were not yet ready for the real thing. By the beginning of his third presidential term in 2012, the two chambers of the Russian parliament, the Duma and the Federation Council, were little more than rubber stamps for the Kremlin. The political parties represented in parliament were either United Russia, the party created around Putin and to which Batalina belonged, or the "loyal opposition," like the Communists or Mizulina's party, A Just Russia. These were also funded by the Kremlin and existed to create the illusion of political choice.

Mizulina and Batalina had often banded together to advance a conservative social agenda on the Kremlin's behalf. Mizulina had been one of the main architects of the 2013 law banning "homosexual propaganda" to minors. She also vocally championed Russia's law that prohibited gay couples, in Russia or abroad, from adopting Russian children, while Batalina cowrote the law that banned any Americans from doing so.[4]

In November 2013, the two women traveled to Germany to attend a conference of European ultraconservatives. They spoke alongside right-wing activists who opposed same-sex marriage and bemoaned the low birth rate among white, native-born Europeans. When LGBT activists accosted them outside the meeting, Batalina and Mizulina spun this into proof of liberal Europe's undemocratic intolerance. It was why, Mizulina said, Europe was becoming increasingly alien to Russians, who "are going from passive to active defenders of traditional family values."

In the fall of 2016, Mizulina and Batalina went into battle to decriminalize domestic abuse. They felt that it should be grouped with the other offenses that the government had recently moved to the civil code, at Putin's request. He had deemed they were not a "significant social danger" and were sending too many young people to jail, ruining their future. Batalina contended that domestic violence belonged in this category. "We're talking about abrasions, bruises, scratches, small hematomas," she told the press. Besides, if real physical injury did occur in a domestic altercation, the Russian criminal code already had a provision for that, she said, the statute prohibiting the "conscious inflicting of light physical harm."[5] Mizulina, a generation older, argued that the law undermined the government's policies to "strengthen, support, and protect the family." Both women concluded that the new law had bungled Putin's true intent. It needed to be amended to save all those young people—mostly men—from jail. It needed to be *skrepy*-friendly. A Duma study group quickly agreed.

Mizulina and Batalina made formidable advocates for this cause. It wasn't the men in the Kremlin telling the country that hitting your wife was no big deal. In fact, the powerful men in charge of the Investigative Committee and the Interior Ministry, which runs Russia's police, were begging the Duma *not* to change the law. But when a mother and a grandmother tacitly invoked the traditions of the *Domostroy*—a draconian sixteenth-century domestic codex that named the father the lord and master of the household—who were the men to resist? Women in the villages had once consoled each other with the old adage *"Byot—znachit lyubit"*: "If he hits you, it means he loves you." Now two blond women, looking every bit the traditional Slavic Russian stereotype, wanted to make it government policy.

It didn't matter, of course, that thousands of women in Moscow took to the streets to oppose Mizulina and Batalina's proposals. It was clear from the beginning that their opinion had the backing of the most important man in Russia. On February 7, 2017, Vladimir Putin signed their legislation into law.[6] Domestic abuse that did not result in anything more than a scratch or a bruise had been officially decriminalized in the Russian Federation.

Russians learned about Margarita Gracheva ten months later, on December 11, 2017. That morning, after dropping the kids off at day care, Dmitry was supposed to drive Rita to work. Instead, he grabbed her phone, locked the car doors, and headed back into the woods. When Dmitry finally stopped the car, he ordered her to get out and zip-tied her hands together. Then he used tourniquets to tie each arm above the elbow and at the shoulder. Ranting about Alexander and how she had destroyed their family, he grabbed an axe from his trunk.

Dmitry made Rita march deeper into the woods until they reached a clearing with a tree stump. He forced her to kneel and put her hands on the stump. "You wanted a new car?" He laughed. "You'll never have a car or a man, you won't even be able to pet the kids, and you so loved doing that!"[7] Rita begged him to believe that she had never betrayed him.

For a moment, Dmitry seemed to relent and started to pull her back toward the car. But then he realized that it was too late. If he let Rita go now, she would immediately turn him in to the police. Then he might go to jail and she would get off scot-free without having learned her lesson. That wouldn't do at all. So he dragged Rita back to the stump. He made her put her hands on it again. Then he took a swing and the axe landed just above Rita's wrist, severing her hand. He swung again, and the other hand came off, too. He chopped at the hands on the stump, over and over again. In shock, Rita tried to crawl away, but Dmitry landed a couple blows of the axe on her thigh. For days afterward she remembered the feeling of its blade slicing into her leg like fire scorching her flesh. At that point Dmitry abandoned the glass jar with clear liquid in it he had brought with him—acid, Rita assumed. "Fine," he said, "we won't ruin your beauty."[8]

He ordered her to stand and walk back to the car, but she kept stumbling, so he dragged her the rest of the way, pushed her onto the floor in the back, and sped to the hospital, where he deposited Rita in the emergency room, barking at the shocked personnel to "look alive." On the way there, as Rita lay bleeding in the car, fruitlessly willing herself to lose consciousness, Dmitry had opened the windows to the bracing December air and whooped, "The adrenaline!"

Dmitry went straight from the hospital to turn himself in at the local police station. At first, the police didn't believe his account and tried to send him on his way. But Dmitry insisted on being arrested: he had this all planned out.

Dmitry had researched how and where to tie the tourniquets so Rita wouldn't bleed to death. He had also consulted legal textbooks and an aunt in the profession on how to get the shortest possible sentence. Because he had not killed Rita and had two small children, he could expect to spend less time in jail. Turning himself in and cooperating with the police would also shorten his imprisonment, which was why he led officers to the stump in the woods to show them where he had left Rita's severed hands. They had been out there for nearly four hours. The police rushed the hands to the hospital and surgeons decided to attempt to attach the left one, which was only in three pieces. The right looked like a pile of raw ground meat with a pinky finger barely hanging on by a flap of skin.

In the weeks that Rita spent recovering in the hospital, Inna became obsessed with the thought that her daughter might have remained whole if not for Mizulina and Batalina's law. Inna had carefully documented the bruises Dmitry had left on her daughter's thighs in October 2017, but by then it had been eight months since the Russian legal system had stopped considering bruises to be real physical harm for which criminal charges could be brought. The Russian police had never taken spousal abuse seriously, but now they had a signal from the very top that they could essentially ignore it. It was why local police officers hadn't bothered to investigate the report that Dmitry had kidnapped Rita and threatened her with a knife. This meant that when Dmitry turned himself in, he had no criminal record. With time off for good behavior, he could be out in just four years, all without losing custody of his sons.

Inna, a local journalist, realized that she had to make as much noise around her daughter's case as possible. Thanks to her efforts, the story quickly reached the national media. The state-controlled TV channels interviewed Rita in her hospital bed. Still groggy from anesthesia, her voice shook with fear. "I am afraid of what will happen next, if he leaves jail," she told one interviewer. "Because he said he would find me and kill me."

In September 2019, I was back in Moscow on a research trip for this book when my friend Irina Shikhman called me about a documentary she was making on domestic violence. I had met Ira in 2010, shortly after I first moved back to Moscow, when she interviewed me for a short segment on state TV about people born in the Soviet Union who were returning to live and work in Russia.

Like all the most ambitious Muscovites, Ira was actually not from Moscow. She grew up in Tomsk, a small Siberian city, where she had worked at one of the last local television stations in the country to lose its editorial independence, before following her dreams to Moscow. The capital was where over 10 percent of the population and most of the country's wealth were concentrated; it was Russia's New York, D.C., LA, and San Francisco, all rolled into one sprawling megalopolis.

When Ira started working in Moscow, television was already fully controlled by the Kremlin or owned by it outright, and anything relating to politics was tightly censored. So, like many journalists who worked there, Ira focused on cultural topics that were comparatively free from the soul-corroding influence of the censors: interviewing movie stars, hosting cooking shows. We became friends, but, during the tumultuous winter of 2011–12, we didn't see each other much. I was reporting on the protests for American publications and, like Emma twenty years before me, consumed by the foolish hope that Russia would finally change for the better. Emma, now in her late seventies, had never abanonded that hope and accompanied me to many of the protests that winter and spring. I went with my press credentials, while she went to demand a democratic Russia. Meanwhile, my Russian boyfriend had become the golden boy of opposition journalism and was both covering the political tumult and helping to organize it. It was all I could talk about, but Ira wasn't that interested. Like so many Russians, she saw politics as dirty, dangerous, and futile.

But in the following decade, as Putin's authoritarianism grew harsher at home and more militaristic abroad, politics burst into the lives of people like Ira with shocking and violent regularity. It wasn't just enemies of the regime or the professional opposition that the Kremlin went after now. Actors were being thrown in jail; journalists were being framed. When I had dinner with Ira during my trips back to Moscow, she no longer talked about cooking shows and celebrities. She railed against the corruption and cruelty of the regime.

It was during these years that YouTube took off in Russia. On YouTube, people could broadcast their own content to millions of people, free of state control. Navalny, who had turned the momentum of the 2012 protests into a national grassroots political organization, had his own YouTube channel, which became a full-fledged media arm of his Anti-Corruption Foundation. More and more Russian YouTubers were becoming celebrities. Ira was then working at a TV station owned by the Moscow mayor's office that decided to get in on the phenomenon. It launched a new long-form interview show on YouTube called *A pogovorit'?*—which translates loosely to *Let's Talk*—with Ira as its host. As its audience quickly grew, the government censors started paying closer attention and vetoing interview subjects.

Ira had had enough. Politics was now what she wanted to talk about most and it was clearly what her viewers wanted to watch. She bought out the mayor's office and relaunched *Let's Talk* as her own YouTube channel, which soon became one of the most popular such shows in Russia. She began making documentaries that picked up prizes at film festivals. People now stopped her in the street to thank her for her work. In early 2019, Ira took me to the *banya* in Moscow. We were standing in the space between the sauna and the cold dipping pool, completely naked, rubbing ourselves down with the coffee grounds Ira had brought—an excellent natural body scrub, she explained—and woman after woman, all of them also completely naked, raved to Ira about how much they loved her show.

Her next documentary topic, she decided, would be the Kremlin's decriminalization of domestic violence. In 2016, a Ukrainian woman had started a hashtag, #YaNeBoyusSkazat (#ImNotAfraidToTell) that went viral on the Ukrainian and Russian-language internet. On Instagram and Facebook, young women shared the kinds of stories—of physical abuse, rape, harassment, and assault—that their mothers and grandmothers had only whispered about. Another viral campaign, #IDidntWanttoDie, publicized the stories of women who had been murdered by their partners or who had gone to jail for fighting back against their abusers. Then Margarita Gracheva's husband took an axe to her hands.

Suddenly the news was awash with stories of domestic violence, such as that of the Khachaturyan sisters. In the summer of 2018, half a year after Dmitry cut off Rita's hands, three teenage sisters stabbed their father, Mikhail, to death. Mikhail had turned his daughters—Krestina, nineteen, Angelina, eighteen, and Maria, seventeen—into slaves. They regularly missed school to iron his shirts or cook for him. He summoned them with a special bell and once pistol-whipped Krestina when she didn't respond quickly enough. He raped them regularly; one sister attempted suicide after Mikhail forced her to perform oral sex on him.[9] Their mother, whom Mikhail had beaten for two decades before banishing her from the house, repeatedly reported Mikhail to the police, as did the neighbors and the girls' teachers, but Mikhail seemed to be linked to the criminal world as well as to law enforcement, and his friends in the precinct made the complaints disappear. Eventually, the girls stopped going to school altogether. Meanwhile, Mikhail went to church every Sunday, spangled the apartment with icons, and made frequent pilgrimages to the Christian holy sites in Israel.

On July 27, Mikhail came home from a hospital stay to find that the girls had spent 14,000 rubles (about $200) more than he had budgeted for them. Enraged, he blasted each of them in the face with pepper spray. Krestina, who had asthma, fainted. His rage sated, Mikhail nodded off in his chair, and his daughters, who had at last reached their limit, attacked him with knives and a hammer. And yet, despite all the grotesque details the investigation uncovered, the Khachaturyan sisters were charged with murder and faced up to twenty years in prison.

Russian liberals rallied to their cause, while conservative organizations, like the new radical men's rights group Male State, demanded that the sisters face the harshest possible penalty.

When Ira called me, the sisters were still in jail, awaiting trial. But their case, as well as Rita's, had turned domestic violence into one of the few issues into which Russian women could safely channel their growing frustration with the regime. Ira told me she had landed an interview with Margarita Gracheva. Did I want to come along and interview her, too? Ira asked me. Of course I did.

"You'll never believe where she wants us to film her," Ira said.

"Where?" I asked.

"At her nail salon."

Margarita Gracheva's story stunned Russia. Notes of support flooded in, as did donations. Someone sent her a tablet, which made it easier to dictate text and type, which she now did with her elbow. An engineer showed up at her bedside with an electronic prosthesis that operated by sending signals from electrodes on Rita's forearm to her robotic hand.

Soon after she was discharged from the hospital, she appeared on Andrey Malakhov's eponymous talk show, Russia's most popular daytime program. She wore a short black skirt and a white short-sleeved shirt with cartoon dogs on it, looking much younger than her twenty-five years. Her left, reattached hand was still swaddled in gauze and she hid the stump of her right in her lap. And yet she looked radiant. Malakhov marveled at his guest, who somehow seemed psychologically untouched by what had befallen her. "Looking at how you are living through everything happening in your life, with such a smile, with such a sunny disposition, you've become a symbol for many for how to face the most difficult situation with a smile," Malakhov gushed. "Where did you learn this?"

"They don't teach this anywhere," Rita replied cheerfully. "If I sit here and cry, my hands won't grow back and I won't heal any faster. I'm focused on my health and on my inner world." The studio audience applauded.

Malakhov asked if she was angry at her ex-husband, who was then in pretrial detention. "It's strange for a lot of people, but if I wish him ill, it will just eat me from the inside," she said. "I just hope that he realizes what he's done and lives with it for the rest of his life." More applause. After that, Inna came out and argued loudly with the other guests, Dmitry's mother cried backstage, while Rita mostly listened and smiled.

But it wasn't the smile of a person who was overwhelmed or simple. When she spoke, she did so with clarity and strength. She would not, she said, allow her children to spend time with Dmitry's family because she had heard them make excuses for him and she refused to expose her sons to that. When a male guest, a lawyer, grilled Rita about why she didn't try to run away from Dmitry, she calmly pointed out that jumping out of a moving vehicle is dangerous. Besides, how could she have fathomed what Dmitry planned to do? How could anyone? The guest pressed her on what she could have done to provoke Dmitry. When she went to the movies with Alexander, was it during the day or at night? Rita didn't take the bait, letting others explain why chopping off her hands was not a justifiable response to a trip to the movies.

She said her experience had made her aware of two issues she had never really contemplated: the struggles of people with disabilities, and domestic violence in Russia. She planned to advocate for people struggling with these issues. Meanwhile, Dmitry was sending her notes from jail. "I will never let anyone have you," he wrote in one. The courts were still refusing to strip Dmitry of his parental rights over their two young sons. She was scared, she said, that Dmitry would get out of prison and make good on his promise to kill her. But she didn't look scared. She seemed to have enough bravery not just for herself and her children but for all the women who were writing to her from across the country, sending pictures of their bruises and cuts and recounting their own horror stories.

One of the panelists onstage, an activist named Alyona Popova, was stunned. "I realize I'm just covered in goose bumps because I just can't imagine how strong this person must be," Popova told me later.[10] She had been working for an opposition member of parliament when, in 2014, her pregnant friend confided to Popova that her partner was beating her. But when Popova called the police, she learned there wasn't much she could do. Her friend would have to come forward and gather all the evidence herself, which she was far too frightened to contemplate. Popova decided that domestic violence would be the cause of her life.

At that time, people still believed that the system could be changed from the inside, so she took night classes to earn a law degree and became a well-known activist. She was the person who had come up with the #IDidntWanttoDie campaign. Now she and her allies were agitating the Duma to change the decriminalization law.

"You know what shocked people about Margarita's case?" Popova recalled. "It was that she looked—how can I explain this? She wasn't meek and cowed, which is how our society has learned to see the victims of violence, but she also wasn't aggressive. She behaved not as if someone had chopped her hands off but as if they'd just had a misunderstanding. And she was very focused on society at large . . . She's sitting there and she's saying, 'Yes, domestic violence is a problem and I'm going to help people.' It just takes incredible strength. I think it's why she resonated with so many women, because when you see a person whose life will never be the same but who speaks not about herself but—" Popova stopped. "There, you see?" She showed me her forearm, which was again covered in goose bumps.

By the time Margarita went on Malakhov's show, it was clear that the decriminalization of domestic violence had been a disaster. Alexander Bastrykin, Putin's friend from their KGB days and the head of the feared Investigative Committee, offered a rare public rebuke. "A year and a half ago, legislation was introduced—it passed, even though we were against it—about domestic violence," he said at a committee-wide meeting. "So we excluded this issue from the criminal code. Well, now we're reaping the violence."[11] He urged his colleagues to "fix this."

That October, the Moscow office of Human Rights Watch announced the results of its research into the effects of the law. The consequences were "exclusively negative," said Yulia Gorbunova, the lead researcher, at a press conference. "The decriminalization created a sense of impunity for the aggressor, that they don't have to fear legal consequences," she said. "The preventative function of criminal punishment, which is so important in cases of domestic violence, has all but disappeared."[12]

Gorbunova noted that, in 2012, according to the government's own statistics, one in five Russian women had experienced some form of domestic abuse at least once and that the number of cases rose steadily year after year. Then, in 2017, the year Putin signed the decriminalization amendment into law, the number of cases suddenly dropped by half. "And that, obviously, is connected to the decriminalization," she said. At the same time, the number of civil cases against people hitting their partners had risen sharply. Proponents of the decriminalization amendment saw this as proof that the law was working. Gorbunova pointed out that most of those convicted received only a fine, and, since the fines were often paid out of the family budget, "the people who suffer here are the women themselves."

In November 2018, I went to see Mari Davtyan, Rita's lawyer and a well-known legal expert on the issue. Even before the decriminalization amendment, she told me, the statistics were abysmal. Only about 10 percent of reports to the police resulted in a criminal case, while the number of women who never call the police in the first place was huge and unknowable. But after the passage of the decriminalization law, Davtyan said, "the police have completely stopped reacting."[13] As a result, there was little she could do to help her growing roster of clients. Restraining orders don't exist in Russian law, so Davtyan's only real recourse was to file petition after petition, motion after motion, knowing none would be upheld but hoping the offender would get bogged down in legal proceedings. "We chase him so he doesn't have time to chase her," Davtyan explained. In the meantime, she and other organizations worked to hide the woman, changing her phone number, address, even her name. They weren't always successful. "The scariest category is the wives of policemen," Davtyan said. Their new names immediately popped up in police databases, along with their new phone numbers.

I told Davtyan I still couldn't understand why the Russian government went out of its way to decriminalize domestic violence. It just made no sense to me. But to Davtyan, it was quite obvious: sanctioning violence in the home helped to sanction violence by the state. "In my view, this has a very clear ideological message. Our entire society begins with the family," she explained. "So if the government wants our society to be tolerant of violence, then domestic violence serves it well. Because this way everyone knows from childhood that violence is a way to solve problems. What's the problem, right? 'Dad hit Mom, both of them hit me, what's the big deal?'" When people became used to violence in the most intimate spheres of their lives, in other words, violence everywhere else—in domestic politics, in foreign affairs—became not only tolerable but expected.

It was also, she believed, about the type of power that Putin and Russia wanted to project, both at home and abroad. "Russia is now demonstrating that they are, so to speak, the last bastion of the conservative world, one that constantly positions itself in opposition to the liberal West," Davtyan said. "And in conservative circles [in Russia], this kind of violence is very often justified; it's considered the norm in family life." In Russia's political world, she went on, "you can really feel this discourse of *power*: might makes right."

Perhaps the most chilling theory was the one advanced by Irina Prokhorova, a well-known public intellectual and the elder sister of a prominent oligarch. With the economy stagnating and political dissent off-limits, the state had once again taken away men's venues for masculinity as outlined by Renar: it was harder than ever to be a provider and, in a country where the state was gathering more and more power for itself, harder to make autonomous decisions. Men could self-destruct—or take out their frustrations on their women. "Irina Prokhorova said that this could be a way to give men in Russia a steam valve," Davtyan explained. "That is, all that negative energy has to go somewhere, and since it can't go up the chain for obvious reasons, then it has to come out this way."

Davtyan was heavily pregnant and her long black hair fell around her pale, round face and onto her belly. There was something almost ghostly about the way she calmly recounted the macabre stories of her clients. A man who beat his wife began dragging her toward the balcony of their fifteenth-story apartment. She managed to grab a knife and somehow hit her husband right in an artery. He bled out and she went to jail. A woman was picking mushrooms in the forest when a man suddenly jumped on her. She hit back and managed to kill him with one strike of her tiny mushroom-picking knife. She, too, went to jail. Almost none of Davtyan's clients got off for self-defense.

It was dark outside, though it was only early evening, and Davtyan's office was in an old building that was perched by itself on a little hill. One of her colleagues peeked into her office. "We're all going home," he said brightly, "so we're leaving you here alone." It was eerily quiet in the building; outside, the world was stifled in snow and darkness. I suddenly felt afraid. It was not a feeling I had often in Russia or anywhere else. But our conversation had revealed something primal and irrational and violent, and, for once, I felt completely exposed, unprotected.

"It's all very bleak." I shuddered.

"Nah, it's actually good," she said, smiling. "Because it can't get any worse."

Ira and her film crew barely fit into the manicurist's tiny studio on that sunny afternoon in September 2019. As burly cameramen contorted themselves around the manicurists' stations, Ira sat next to Rita as Yulia, Rita's nail lady of many years, filed the old gel nail polish off her mangled left hand. Yulia had been a witness in Dmitry's trial a year earlier. He and his defense had argued that Rita had had ample opportunity to get out of the car or otherwise stop Dmitry from chopping off her hands. But the judge rejected that argument and sentenced Dmitry to fourteen years in a penal colony. Rita had hoped for a life sentence, but it was better than the three or four years Dmitry had been counting on. And the courts had finally stripped him of his parental rights, on Rita's fifth attempt.

After months of painstaking rehabilitation and several more surgeries, Rita was thriving. She had a sophisticated robotic prosthesis from Germany, which she had purchased with the help of the government and public donations. She had purposely chosen a striking black one, rather than something flesh-colored: she wanted to fight the stigma around disability in Russia. On her popular Instagram account, she called herself "Transformer Mommy" and posted photos of herself going scuba diving and posing in lingerie and beautiful evening gowns with her black robotic arm.

But it wasn't all rosy. Even the most sophisticated prosthesis cannot feel cold or heat, softness or touch. Rita couldn't feel her children's warmth or her cat's fur, and even after months of rehab, there were so many things she still couldn't do. She couldn't do crafts with her kids. She couldn't put up her hair. Zippers and shoelaces were out of the question. Since she couldn't get her prosthesis wet, doing the dishes was hard, as was bathing two small children. The prosthesis was so heavy that her shoulder and arm felt strained at the end of the day. When she was stressed, the bionic arm's sensors could get overloaded and fritz out. She had only partial sensation in her scarred left hand and needed still more surgery and rehabilitation.

Still, Rita told me just before we went inside for her manicure, there was so much to be grateful for.[14] Dmitry had warned her that she would never drive a car or touch another man, but now she drove a new pumpkin-colored SUV with a modified steering wheel. She demurred when I asked her if the ring on her left hand was an engagement ring but, a year later, she would reveal that she had secretly married Max, a tattooed and bearded musician from St. Petersburg who had showed her the unique kindness of treating her like a regular young woman while also submitting to her scrutiny, like sending her his passport information so she could run a background check. Rita and her mother were finishing a book—*Happy Without Hands*—that would eventually be turned into a television drama, with Rita as a consultant. Two years after we met, she gave birth to a baby boy. She and her sons moved to St. Petersburg, where she and Max built and lovingly decorated a house. In 2024, she gave birth to her fourth child, a girl. And though she still feared Dmitry's return, she was insistently, stubbornly happy.

That afternoon in the fall of 2019, I had asked her if she had any symptoms of PTSD after what her ex-husband had done to her less than two years earlier. She wasn't sure what I meant.

"Nightmares, flashbacks," I explained.

She shrugged. "I haven't worked with a psychologist at all. I don't think I need it right now," she said. "Maybe in three or four years I'll fall into a depression but, no, I don't have nightmares. I also don't have any anger. This person just doesn't exist for me. Yes, I understand that this was a particular phase of my life that I can't undo, but I live in the present and in the future."

She could tell I was taken aback.

"People write to me and ask me the same things, if I cry," she tried to explain. "I cried maybe three times, including when I was in the hospital and had to miss my kids' New Year's recital. But, yes, of course I freak out sometimes, like when I can't open something. Once, I couldn't open a container and it flew into the wall."

Sure, I said, I got that, but that wasn't quite what I meant.

"Look," she said, "I have kids. That's a big motivator. I can't just sit down and fall apart and not leave the house for a week." She was not going to play the victim for anyone.

In the nail salon, she and Yulia laughed as they recalled how Rita had come to get her nails done only a couple of months after leaving the hospital. Her left hand was still covered in bandages, but she happily got a pedicure and Yulia, who had trained as a nurse, helped her care for the sutures on her leg. When I mentioned to Rita that I was surprised that she had asked Ira to film at the salon, she was perplexed. "What, do women in the West not get their nails done?" Then, thinking about it, she said, "I guess Russian women do put more effort into their appearance." Plus, she explained, the damage to her left hand had limited the blood flow to her fingers and her nails constantly broke, exposing the sensitive flesh underneath. The manicure, in addition to making her feel feminine, was a practical measure. And Rita was nothing if not practical. Yulia asked her what color she wanted and Rita smiled. "Red," she said. "With sparkles."

On July 25, 2019, Valentina Matvienko, the head of the Federation Council, the upper chamber of the puppet parliament, held a press conference. On paper at least, she was the most powerful woman in Russia—a member of Putin's political clan and technically second in line for the presidency. That day, she made a point of criticizing the way Russian police now handled domestic violence. "Law enforcement doesn't react as they should," she declared. "Essentially, it's 'he didn't kill her, right, so figure it out yourselves.' So what are you supposed to do, wait till he kills you and *then* go to the police?" She confirmed that she would be seeking to strengthen the law on domestic violence. "It's time to change this patriarchal mindset of 'so he hit her, so what,'" she added.[15]

This kicked off a flurry of legislative activity, or what passed for it in Russia. Study committees were formed in both chambers of parliament. Experts and activists, like Popova, Davtyan, and a lawyer for the Khachaturyan sisters, were invited to participate. Thousands of women marched in Moscow in support of reforms, and more than 700,000 Russians signed an online petition to advocate for their passage. A poll found that an overwhelming majority of Russians—some 70 percent—approved of doing something to fight domestic abuse. It was an unusual burst of democratic activity in a country that was rapidly closing avenues for any kind of political expression.

By that time, political protests were being met with a shocking level of violence I had never witnessed during my time in Russia. Watching from the United States, I was stunned by the videos now circulating on social media: riot police knocking a young man off a bike and pummeling him with their batons and feet; dragging away old women protesting the construction of a trash incinerator in their community; punching young men; cracking a young woman's head open. The signal was quite clear: any kind of peaceful protest would be met with unfettered and ferocious violence. And yet, somehow this talk of reforming the domestic violence laws was allowed.

As it appeared increasingly likely that the legislation would pass, the Russian Orthodox Church grew alarmed. According to the independent Russian media outlet *Verstka*, Patriarch Kirill and the reactionary Bishop Tikhon Shevkunov, rumored to be the increasingly pious Putin's personal confessor, privately lobbied the Kremlin against the legislation.[16]

In the meantime, a new domestic violence story rocked Russia. In early November, a respected sixty-three-year-old historian named Oleg Sokolov was fished out of one of St. Petersburg's canals. The police who saved him discovered that the bag he was carrying contained two female arms. They belonged to his twenty-four-year-old girlfriend, Anastasia Yeshchenko. She had been a graduate student at St. Petersburg State University, Putin's alma mater, where Sokolov was a specialist in the Napoleonic era. Police searched Sokolov's home, where they found Yeshchenko's head. Sokolov, it turned, had strangled her, then shot her in the head four times at close range with a shotgun. After dismembering her body and dropping it into the canal, he had planned to commit suicide while dressed as Napoleon.

And yet, when Matvienko published the draft of the legislative reforms online on November 29, 2019, it reflected none of the urgency, none of the horror that Sokolov's or Rita's stories aroused. Popova and Davtyan were shocked: the proposed document was vague to the point of uselessness. This was not a draft that they had ever seen, nor had it been approved by any of the various study committees. Although it introduced the idea of restraining orders, it lacked any of the details a piece of actual legislation would require.

Over 11,000 comments streamed onto the Federation Council site, most of them negative. Liberals and feminists felt the law didn't go nearly far enough. Conservatives and men's rights groups thought it went too far. Andrei Kormukhin, a religious conservative with nine children, called it a Trojan horse for European gays and liberals.[17] Tamara Pletnyova, who chaired the Duma committee on family affairs, was skeptical of the very premise. "On one hand, you shouldn't hit women," she said. "On the other hand, people in our country make up quickly. A husband might get one of these [restraining] orders or be sent to jail, God forbid, and then who [in the family] will make money?"[18]

Five days after the draft's publication, the Russian patriarch served the Sunday liturgy in the Cathedral of the Dormition, inside the Kremlin walls. During his homily, he referenced the proposed legislation against "so-called domestic violence." He wanted to be clear that he did not approve of violence in the home. But he wanted to be even clearer that he did not approve of this law, which he saw as a "dangerous" attempt to interfere in family life.

Less than a week later, on December 11, the two-year anniversary of the attack that cost Rita Gracheva her hands, Matvienko urged her colleagues "not to rush."[19] The legislation, which Matvienko had promised to bring to the floor by the end of the year, would now be pushed back until early 2020. On December 19, Putin weighed in. He said he hadn't read the law but said that his attitude toward it was "mixed."[20] He, too, called for slowing things down. Though no one said as much, it was obvious: the reform was dead.

It all felt like a terrible omen, Popova shared, like Russian society was hurtling toward something cataclysmic. "This law is a litmus test," she said of her thinking then. To her, its failure meant Russia would "arrive at some place very bad, a place of total violence. It could be a war, it could be mass political repressions." She used a Russian expression that encapsulated the sense of foreboding: "It smelled of gasoline," she said. "It all smelled of gasoline."

FIRST LADY

IT WAS 6:40 ON THE MORNING OF AUGUST 20, 2020, WHEN YULIA NAVAL-naya's phone rang. She wasn't normally up that early, but that morning she was preparing to go to the airport to meet her husband, Alexey, now the sole remaining leader of the Russian opposition. His flight from the Siberian city of Tomsk was scheduled to arrive in Moscow at eight. Yulia looked at her phone. It was Kira Yarmysh, her husband's press secretary, who was supposed to be mid-flight with Alexey. "Yulia, don't worry," Yarmysh said when she picked up. "Alexey has been poisoned, the plane landed in Omsk." Navalnaya said, "Okay," and hung up. Only then did she understand. If the plane carrying her husband had to make an emergency landing, Alexey's life must have been in imminent danger. This was it, then. She had been preparing for this moment for a decade and now it was finally here. Her children were still asleep. A thought flitted by. "The most important thing is not to relax," she felt, "to not show weakness." The thought would stay with her for weeks.

Yulia threw a random medley of clothes into a suitcase and bought a ticket to Omsk in the back of a cab. As she waited in the airport for her flight, a message from Yarmysh arrived: Alexey was in a coma and on a ventilator. Navalnaya got up, found a café, and, despite the early hour, ordered a whiskey. That was when the tears began to fall, a silent cascade. "I was unable to restrain my emotions," she would later tell an interviewer, as if justifying an embarrassing lapse.[1]

By the time she boarded the plane, Ivan Zhdanov, the director of Alexey's Anti-Corruption Foundation, had joined her. Yulia realized they would be cut off from any information about her husband for the three-and-a-half-hour flight. "Yulia is a very closed person," said the journalist Yevgenia Albats, who was close with both Navalnys. "She doesn't like to talk about herself." And yet, Yulia talked at Zhdanov for the entire length of the flight. "I think I told him all our family secrets," she would recall. "I was scared to be alone with myself and to think."

Her husband didn't die while she was in the air. At the hospital in Omsk, Navalnaya encountered a wall of doctors who seemed more scared of their civilian superiors than they were of losing their patient. They were reinforced—or kept in line—by a small battalion of plainclothes federal security officers, all intent on keeping her from seeing her husband. She would need to present a marriage certificate, they said, and secure verbal consent from Alexey, who was unconscious and on life support. She would stare them down and out-argue them, all while a gathering swarm of journalists trained their cameras and microphones and smartphones on her. She would finally break through to see him, his body sprouting tubes and cords like vines, writhing in near-constant seizures. (She wouldn't learn until days later that this was the result of his poisoning with a weapons-grade nerve agent in the Novichok family.)[2] She would have to fight with doctors and hospital administrators to see her husband's lab results, give impromptu press conferences on the hospital steps, sneak around the city to find the German physicians who had arrived with a private medevac plane and whom the authorities had barred her from seeing. She would have to demand, over and over, for the hospital to release her husband and allow him to be taken to Berlin, the only possible way, everyone knew, of saving his life. And she would never, ever lose control of her emotions again.

For two days, Russia and the world waited nervously to see if Alexey Navalny, the man who was the only halfway plausible alternative to Vladimir Putin, lived or died. While they waited, they saw Yulia. This tall, pretty blond woman in a black leather jacket who had always appeared at her husband's side was suddenly alone on the world stage, doing battle with the entire repressive machinery of the Russian state to pull her husband from the jaws of death. And what they saw astounded them.

Yulia was a revelation. The country saw her living out the worst moment of her life in real time. And yet she was strong and she was stoic, she didn't crumble under pressure, and, through the force of her will and the strength of her love, she got the dragon to release her man.

In a culture that intuitively understands redemption through suffering, a society that believes that women are by their nature maternal nurturers, Navalnaya was immediately relatable. Journalist Anna Mongayt added, "Russia has never had a queen like Yulia." But it was more than a fairy tale. Through Navalnaya, all of her husband's sins—his prickliness and perceived authoritarianism, his propensity to pick fights with his allies, his past flirtations with nationalism—were suddenly expiated. As journalist Sergey Parkhomenko, a friend of the couple, put it, "There are some people for whom she is Navalny without the downsides of Navalny."

While Navalny lay in a coma, Alexey Venediktov, the editor in chief of the liberal Ekho Moskvy radio station, went on the air and telegraphed to Navalnaya what she needed to do to save her husband. "Until Yulia makes a public declaration, until she makes a request to the Russian government to transport Alexey Navalny out of the country," Venediktov said, no transfer would be possible. "We're waiting." People close to the Navalnys understood this to be a message from the Kremlin, passed through Venediktov, who maintained a cozy relationship with the presidential administration, ostensibly to keep his station from being shuttered. It put Yulia in an impossible situation. "You know you have to bend your knee to Putin and ask for your husband to be let out, but you know that Alexey would die rather than ask Putin for anything," explained Albats, who was in touch with Yulia at the time. "And that's the only thing you can't do. Because this is a betrayal of Alexey."

The next day she issued a public letter to Putin. "I am officially addressing you," she wrote, "with a demand for permission to transport Alexey Anatolievich Navalny to the Federal Republic of Germany."[3] Within hours, she was boarding the plane alongside her husband, invisible on a gurney that was part cocoon, part coffin. Her formulation—a demand rather than a plea—was not lost on the opposition. Even at her most desperate and vulnerable, she approached the man trying to kill her husband not as a fearful supplicant but as a defiant equal.

In the following months, as Yulia and her husband documented his recovery on social media, they became the measure of decency and nobility for millions of Russians. There were Yulia TikTok memes and

Yulia Instagram flash mobs.⁴ People wondered whether they would be capable of such heroism under duress—and, of course, everyone wanted a love like theirs. "Oh, they are definitely #relationshipgoals," one friend in Moscow told me.

In a country where there hadn't been a real first lady since Raisa Gorbacheva, here was a political wife who could more than hold her own in an almost exclusively male arena. She was inevitably compared to Sviatlana Tsikhanouskaya, who, a week before Navalny was poisoned, spearheaded a revolution in neighboring Belarus after her husband, an opposition activist, was jailed. Could Yulia Navalnaya be not just the next first lady of Russia but its next leader?⁵ Yabloko, the old liberal democratic party where her husband had gotten his start, announced it was willing to support her run for the Russian parliament.⁶ Tsikhanouskaya encouraged her "to begin her political career."⁷

Yulia quickly shut down these rumors, some of which had been amplified by the Kremlin to split the opposition.⁸ "I think it's much more interesting to be the wife of a politician," she told Russian *Harper's Bazaar* in December.⁹ "Then again what I do is, to a certain extent, also politics."

Yulia Abrosimova was born in Moscow, on July 24, 1976. Her father was a government scientist, and her mother worked at Gosplan, the Soviet central economic planning agency. Her parents divorced when Yulia was in grade school, and her mother married a Gosplan colleague. They were an average Soviet family, living in a sea of high-rise apartment buildings. Yulia majored in international economics at Moscow's Plekhanov University. In the summer of 1998, while vacationing at a resort in Turkey, she met a young lawyer named Alexey Navalny. "He immediately felt that I would be his wife," she told me when I first met her in early 2011. Two years later, it came to pass. People who know her say she never had any professional ambitions of her own, so when her first child, Dasha, was born in 2001, Navalnaya became a stay-at-home mom. In 2008, a son, Zakhar, was born. They were very difficult pregnancies and the couple scrapped their wish for more children.

Albats remembers meeting Yulia at her husband's thirtieth birthday party in the summer of 2006. At the time, Navalny was a real estate lawyer who was just getting a foothold in opposition politics. He was tall, stoop-shouldered, awkward, with a bit of a beer belly—"a man-child," a fellow activist remembers.[10] He was from a simple family from a military town outside of Moscow—the boonies for any self-respecting Muscovite—and far less worldly than the refined intelligentsia that dominated opposition circles. But at his birthday party, he had Yulia in tow. She was tall and slim, blond, with big blue eyes and fine features. "She's a queen," Albats thought to herself. "And Alexey was dancing around her like a little rooster. And that's when I thought, 'This is the motivator. In addition to his personal ambition, he needs to constantly prove to this beautiful woman that he is worthy of her.'"

For years, Yulia focused on raising their children while her husband published detailed investigations of fraud in the Russian government and state-owned enterprises. At the time, most people were deeply apathetic to politics. After the poverty of the 1980s and '90s, most Russians were happy to indulge in the fruits of the thriving economy of the 2000s, which had been fueled by a commodities boom. Opposition protests attracted a couple hundred people at most. The indifference frustrated Navalnaya, who was now fully invested in her husband's political work. "People ask why he's doing this," she told me back in 2011. "Mostly they're not interested; they just want to go shopping. I can't judge them, but things would be a lot better if they cared."

We were sitting in her tiny kitchen in the tiny apartment that she and Alexey rented in a lower-middle-class Moscow residential neighborhood. With traffic, it took a good hour to get there from the city center. As Alexey stepped up his investigations, the FSB bought an apartment across the way so they could monitor the couple around the clock. ("Can you imagine it?" Albats exclaimed. "They're making love under the eye of the FSB!") Agents began trailing not just Alexey but Yulia and her children. Although it bothered her, she joked with friends that they might as well save her some time and just drive Dasha home from school.

Others began to wonder if this life really satisfied her. Navalny was a talented lawyer who had been on track to a promising corporate career until he chose to be a poor and harried opposition activist. On the rare occasions that Yulia gave interviews, she was always asked some version of this question: *Haven't you asked Alexey to stop what he's doing, for the family's sake?* It was that familiar Bolshevik sentiment: that women are not the engine but the brakes of revolution, tearfully holding their men back from the barricades. When Navalny ran for mayor of Moscow in 2013, Yulia fielded the question in her first television interview. "No, I've never in my life said anything like that to my husband, because I genuinely understand that he's not doing it for himself," she said, perfectly poised on the edge of a studio couch. Why not stop for the sake of Dasha and Zakhar? the interviewer asked her. Obviously surprised, Navalnaya exclaimed, "Because it's them he's fighting for!"

During the protests of 2011–12, Navalny became the undisputed leader of the opposition—just as Putin began to crack down on the movement in earnest. Navalny was arrested at every protest he attended and given short sentences ranging from two weeks to one month. Once he was arrested just as he was being released from jail, right at the prison gates. Another time, he went out to buy Yulia flowers for her birthday, only to be picked up in the street and slapped with a month-long sentence. In 2014, he was put under a yearlong house arrest.

Yulia had always insisted that her primary concern was the home front. "My main task is so that, in spite of everything, nothing in our family changes," she said in her December 2020 interview with *Harper's Bazaar*, "so that the children can remain children, and the house a home." But maintaining the home front as the wife of Putin's chief rival was not easy. In addition to the usual domestic tasks, it now also meant assembling packages of food, clothes, and toiletries to pass to her frequently jailed husband.

"A lot of people don't understand: they only see the glamorous side," says Albats. "But there's this everyday life where you have to maintain a household on not a lot of money and make sure the kids do their homework. Receptions and articles—that's Alexey. Her routine is packing bags for jail. It's the dirty work of being in opposition politics."

Still, Yulia did her best to maintain a sense of normalcy. Dasha, who told her kindergarten class that her father's job was going to protests, started her own popular YouTube channel as a high schooler and then moved to California to attend Stanford. Zakhar, who grew up constantly hearing that his father was on the verge of being killed, didn't even tear himself away from his video game when he was told about Navalny's poisoning.

This was the division of labor in the Navalny home: the man was the strong, public-facing provider, while the woman tended the hearth and the children, supporting her man unconditionally as he marched through the fire. As much as Navalny presented himself as a Western-style liberal, he, like many in the opposition, had come of age at a time when Bolshevik ideals of egalitarianism seemed like a moth-eaten anachronism. He and Yulia were all the things Zaslavskaya's surveys showed people wanted at the end of the Soviet feminist experiment: a traditional family where the man works and the woman is free to stay at home.

While the opposition armed itself with Western ideas, the movement was dominated by men, and feminism was one Western concept they were happy to leave out of their ideological bouquet. It seemed irrelevant for a country that felt it had solved the "woman question" decades ago. There were plenty of women in the movement, to be sure. They were activists and journalists and organizers; they, too, were strong and brave, they ran campaign offices and went to jail for their political and journalistic work, just like the men. But, as ever, they were never the public leaders.

Yet Yulia's presentation as the private, homebound half of the couple was deceiving. "Navalny the politician is two people: Yulia and Alexey," Albats told me. "She's his editor in chief; she reads everything he writes before it's published." Yulia was also a crucial sounding board. "He consults with Yulia and talks through certain ideas with her to formulate them better," said Lyubov Sobol, a lawyer who was one of Navalny's first employees at his Anti-Corruption Foundation. Before Navalny hired a press secretary, it was Yulia who would take to his blog and social media accounts to update his supporters when he was in jail. She dressed Navalny and was very attuned to his image. She also kept him humble. "It's obvious that she criticizes him when there's something to criticize him for," said economist Sergei Guriev, a friend and advisor to Navalny. "This forces Alexey to remember that he's not the greatest person in the world, and that's very important for him." Most importantly, said Vladimir Ashurkov, one of Navalny's longest-serving lieutenants, "Yulia is the rock on which Alexey stands. She's got his back."

Yulia was also an astute political observer. "She feels everything very keenly and observes everyone around her," said Albats. "I honestly think that she likes being the shadow politician." Navalny once joked that his wife was even more radical than he was. Still, she was careful to never make her positions known on the one subject that dogged him: nationalism and the problematic, even racist comments he made about migrant laborers at the start of his political career. People close to her simply said that her views aligned with her husband's, who had evolved toward a much more tolerant, egalitarian vision.

Yulia's radicalism, people close to her reported, manifested itself in a different way: She was a harsher judge of character and less forgiving of transgressions. When a Kremlin loyalist posted a doctored photo purportedly showing that she had German citizenship (she did not), she refused to accept his subsequent apology. "You are apologizing because you are a coward," she wrote on Instagram, where she had more than a million followers, and called him "an overgrown mama's boy." When Oleg Kashin, a journalist who was once close to the Navalnys, alleged that Yulia's father was actually an FSB agent living in London, she squashed the theory. Her father had never worked for the security services. Moreover, he was not currently working for the FSB in London because he had died in 1996; here was his death certificate. Kashin, who admitted that the incident was "an embarrassing failure," told me, "I have apologized several times, but I don't think these apologies are welcome." Like many people I spoke to, Kashin believed Yulia was the source of Alexey's conflicts with others in the Russian opposition. A source who had known the

Navalnys for a decade told me, "She'll be quiet, quiet, and then she'll annihilate you with one word."

Yulia had always been extremely self-contained. "She is like the consummate British lady from classic novels," said the source. "She is always extremely polite and friendly, but you'll never find out anything about her if you're not in her inner circle. You'll walk away with a pleasant impression, but you'll never get under her skin." The years of unrelenting pressure from the Kremlin transformed her introversion into steel. On top of a string of arrests and jail sentences, Navalny suffered a severe chemical burn to his right eye in 2017 when a thug, apparently hired by the government, splashed a bright green antiseptic in his face. She avoided revealing the identities of her nonpolitical friends because her friends' and family's apartments had been searched by authorities several times. "The experience has hardened her," said Ashurkov. "I think she's become tougher and more decisive," said the source, who had known the Navalnys for ten years. "Everything that's happened to this family doesn't predispose them to letting in strangers and trusting easily. It's great to be friends with everyone when they're not trying to take out your eye."

In July 2013, while Navalny was running for mayor of Moscow, he was also facing politically motivated criminal charges of embezzlement in the city of Kirov. A train car full of journalists and activists set out for the overnight trip from Moscow to hear the verdict. It was a carnival atmosphere, and everyone, including Yulia, stayed up all night drinking and laughing. They seemed sure that the Kremlin wouldn't allow a provincial court to jail Navalny while he was running for mayor of the capital—which was only happening with the Kremlin's blessing. The next morning the verdict came down. This was not the fifteen-day sentence Navalny had become accustomed to. Pyotr Ofitserov, Navalny's former associate, was sentenced to four years in a penal colony. Navalny got five, and both men were led away in handcuffs. Ofitserov's wife began to wail and clung to her husband's neck and had to be dragged away by the bailiffs. Sobol cried. Navalny's press secretary cried. The men were shell-shocked. Only Yulia kept her composure. "These bastards will never see our tears," she said.

When Navalny finally opened his eyes, he didn't recognize Yulia. For eighteen days she had waited, not knowing what it was she was waiting for. So few people had ever been exposed to Novichok and survived that the doctors at the Charité hospital in Berlin had not been sure if he would ever emerge from his coma. And so Yulia waited. She came to the hospital, adjusted his pillows. She talked to him and played him their songs, like Duran Duran's cover of "Perfect Day." Their twentieth wedding anniversary came and went. She got through each day by breaking it into survivable increments. "Right now, I'm doing this, and then I will do that, and after that—something else," she said of her mindset. "And then maybe later, I'll let myself cry." But sometimes the tears came unbidden. If they started to fall while she was on the phone with a friend, she made sure to mute herself. No one would hear her cry—not her confidants, not whoever else was listening on the line.

When doctors brought him out of his coma, it seemed that the old Alexey was gone. This new Alexey just sat there and stared. Everything was erased: Yulia, his children, what a spoon was, how to walk, how to write. At one point he tried to rip out every cord and line keeping him alive, including the tracheostomy tube in his throat. Somehow they wrestled him back down. Eventually, Dasha and Zakhar arrived. Her husband's colleagues were already there, as were Kremlin agents. RT, the Kremlin-owned propaganda network, announced a bounty for anyone who could sneak inside the hospital and get a photo of the felled opposition leader.

Inside, Alexey was relearning how to be himself. A month after his poisoning, he wished Yulia a belated happy anniversary in an Instagram post. For once, he put aside his sardonic tone and recounted how a kind and cheerful feminine presence pierced the veil of his hallucinations and pulled him from the other side. "I don't doubt for a second that this has a scientific explanation," he wrote. "Yulia, you saved me, and let them put it in all the neurobiology textbooks."

In the fall, Alexey was discharged from the hospital and the family decamped to Todtnauberg, a small German village on the Swiss border. The area was known for its thermal springs and picturesque waterfalls and was normally crowded with tourists. But that year the pandemic had left it deserted. Every morning, Yulia took her son to school and her husband to physical therapy. When the session was over, she picked him up and took him on his daily walk, a key part of his rehabilitation. Yulia and Alexey wandered the streets and the nearby hills, talking to farm animals and joking about who was the donkeys' favorite Navalny. The villagers treated the couple like celebrities.

In mid-November, Christo Grozev arrived. He worked for Bellingcat, the British investigative journalism outfit, and he was trying to figure out who had tried to kill Navalny. Grozev was surprised to discover that the Navalnys were what they had appeared to be on social media: a good-looking, cheerful couple who continuously teased each other. Sometimes Yulia joked that her husband had gotten a little slow because of the Novichok. Their private and public messages were the same: that, with work and organization, there would soon be a free and democratic Russia and Navalny would be its president. "It's a very infectious feeling," Grozev told me. "You spend twenty minutes around it and you believe it."

Soon, Grozev and Maria Pevchikh, the head of Navalny's investigations team, had a clear picture of who had poisoned Alexey: an elite team of chemists, doctors, and operatives working for a special unit of the FSB. Their boss reported directly to the head of the FSB, who, in turn, reported to Putin. They also discovered that this team had in fact made three attempts to poison Navalny. One went sideways: the assassins accidentally poisoned Yulia. On July 6, just weeks before the emergency landing in Omsk, while the Navalnys were on a short vacation on the Baltic shore, Yulia suddenly felt sick and collapsed onto a park bench. Nothing hurt, but her legs didn't respond to her commands to move, as if they had stopped working. It was a mysterious, nonspecific illness and by morning it had vanished as quickly as it had arrived.

In mid-December, Navalny and Bellingcat published the results of their investigation. The Russian authorities responded by announcing that Navalny had violated his parole for an old, politically motivated conviction: he had failed to check in in person with the Russian authorities while he was in Germany, recovering from the Kremlin's attempt to kill him. If he didn't return to Russia, he would be a fugitive from the law. If he came back, he would be arrested for violating it. For Navalny and his colleagues, the answer was obvious: he had to go home.

A stunned Grozev wondered if Yulia was privately trying to dissuade her husband from returning. "But she said, 'Yes, he should go, there's a risk, but that's his life and that's where he should be,'" Grozev recalled. "She said, 'I think there is no chance that they will let him out. He'll be in jail for a long time.'" Grozev went on, "You must understand how shocking this conversation was. I've never been in a situation like that. She's this wide-eyed, earnest, honest person. She says these things like they're the most obvious things on earth, but she's saying very non-obvious things. You have to process what she says before you realize that it's obvious only in a certain universe." That universe was the imagined future in which Russia is free and happy. For all her fierce pragmatism, Yulia obviously believed it completely. It would be impossible to survive if she didn't.

On January 14, Grozev hosted a farewell dinner. He made pasta and served local wine and gin made from the juniper harvested in the nearby forests. Several nights earlier, Grozev and Navalny had called Konstantin Kudryavtsev, the chief hit man. Navalny pretended to be one of Kudryavtsev's superiors and, in a forty-five-minute conversation, coaxed him into explaining exactly how he had tried to poison Navalny. Amazed by their luck, they listened to the call again, this time with Yulia in the room.

That evening, as they sipped their wine and gin, Grozev offered a hypothetical: If you could go back in time and make Kudryavtsev disappear so that he couldn't live to poison Navalny, would you? Everyone said yes except Yulia. Grozev was stunned. Behind her was the corkboard with pictures of her husband's would-be assassins. Why? Grozev asked. "I'm a Christian," she answered simply. "I would never harm a person."

The next day, Yulia and Alexey took a train to Berlin, and on the seventeenth, they boarded a plane for Moscow. Russian police were waiting for Alexey at passport control. He quickly kissed his wife, who then turned to fish her passport from her purse, as if her husband being led away by the police were the most natural thing in the world.

When Navalny arrived in Moscow, Western observers couldn't help but reference Vladimir Lenin's arrival at Petrograd's Finland Station in April 1917 after his long exile. The parallel seemed obvious: two men who had endured many arrests while trying to overthrow a corrupt Russian autocrat. But there was another overlap that most failed to notice: their wives. Though Yulia was not running the party's operations and developing invisible ink, she was, like Nadezhda Krupskaya, her husband's moral and ideological helpmeet.

Yulia's very presence in the political arena, even as a wife, was a stark contrast to the ruling elite. Putin was an acolyte of the Brezhnev era, when the wives of Soviet leaders had disappeared entirely from public view. The Soviet people only found out that Chernenko had a wife when she made her public debut at his funeral. Similarly, Putin swaddled his family in military-style secrecy. Lyuda was rarely seen in public, and on the rare occasions she was trotted out to stand near her husband, she often stared blankly and blinked slowly, as if she had been drugged. The biography of Putin that was written in the first years of his presidency, for which the author interviewed Lyuda at length, was taken out of circulation in Russia. Even electronic copies were scrubbed from the web. (I found a lone physical copy on Amazon for nearly $200.) Then Lyuda disappeared completely, not even making her annual appearance at the Easter service at the Cathedral of Christ the Savior. There were rumors that Putin had packed her off to a convent.[11]

Then, in June 2013, she suddenly reemerged. During the intermission of a performance of a ballet at the Kremlin Palace theater, Putin and Lyuda walked over to the state television cameras that just happened to be lurking in the hallway. The first couple had an announcement to make: they were divorcing after twenty years of marriage. Putin pinned the marital dissolution on Lyuda's dislike of the public eye, but Lyuda offered a different version. "Our marriage is finished because we barely see each other," she said. Gone was the deer-in-headlights Lyuda. She was shyly confident, almost pleased. "Vladimir Vladimirovich is completely submerged in his work," she went on. "Basically, it just turned out that we each have our own lives."

But it wasn't just that the Putins had grown apart. In 2008, a newspaper reported rumors that Putin had taken up with Alina Kabaeva, a former Olympic rhythmic gymnast who was three decades his junior and with whom he'd supposedly had several children.[12] The newspaper was immediately shut down by the authorities.[13] That year Putin was asked about Kabaeva at a joint press conference with his friend Silvio Berlusconi, then the prime minister of Italy. "In what you said, there is not one word of truth," Putin fired back. "I have always reacted negatively to those who with their snotty noses and erotic fantasies prowl into others' lives."[14] Berlusconi made his hands into pistols and playfully fired them at the offending journalist.

Then, in 2015, a number of publications reported that one of Putin's daughters, his second with Lyuda, oversaw a billion-dollar slush fund tied to Moscow State University and bankrolled by some of her father's closest associates.[15] It was the first time that anyone had seen what one of Putin's daughters looked like as an adult or even learned her name. (She went by Ekaterina Tikhonova, using Putin's mother's maiden name to disguise her lineage.) The Kremlin immediately denied the reports. True to his KGB training, Putin saw his family as a weakness that could be exploited rather than a point of pride. In a 2019 press conference, he referred to his daughters as "one woman" and "the second woman."

Navalny pounced. Putin's comment, he said, "shows that we'll never hear even a single word of truth from these people because they lie even when you would think it's too embarrassing to lie, because they're essentially disowning their own children."[16] It was a deliberate point of contrast. Everyone knew what Navalny's children looked like because Navalny proudly posted pictures of them on his Instagram. Everywhere he went, Yulia was there, holding his hand or intimately whispering in his ear. After twenty years of marriage, they still genuinely and obviously enjoyed each other's company. When Navalny ran for mayor of Moscow in 2013, Yulia made a point of comparing her family to Putin's in a speech. "I came out here to say that if those in power see families as a weakness, they are mistaken," she declared. "Family is the strength of any normal person—and especially any genuine politician."[17]

This contrast constantly reinforced itself. In October 2020, TASS, the state-owned news agency, broadcast an interview with Putin. When the Russian president mentioned his grandchildren, the interviewer lobbed a softball about which daughter's children they were. "What difference does it make?" Putin snapped. The interviewer coughed uncomfortably. "You shouldn't oink," Putin sneered. "You don't live my life, and you don't understand questions of security."[18]

The following month, more information about Putin's private life emerged. *Proekt*, an independent Russian media outlet, published an investigation into Svetlana Krivonogikh, a former hotel maid who became a major stakeholder in the giant Rossiya Bank. Krivonogikh, it seemed, had been Putin's lover just as he was ascending to the presidency in 2000. She also had a seventeen-year-old daughter who bore an uncanny resemblance to Putin.[19] Navalny, meanwhile, was posting photos of his walks with his wife in the German countryside.

Navalny's strategy was to be the opposite of Putin in everything, including this. If Putin was an autocrat who was married to Russia and lived on a plane far above his subjects, Navalny positioned himself as a man with earthly attachments like any other. He wanted to show Russians, even those who didn't support him, that it was these familial bonds that made him want to change Russia for the better. "Navalny decided that he would show Yulia," said Parkhomenko, who became close with Navalny after the two men helped organize the pro-democracy protests in 2011–12. "It was all done with the understanding that this was being done for public consumption. And she is this cinematographic, nearly perfect woman who embodies total support and agreement and solidarity with what he's doing." (Some, like Albats, believed that it wasn't just Navalny's supporters who noticed the contrast. "I think Putin really envied Alexey," Albats theorized. "No woman ever loved you like this without money. He's tall, and you're tiny. He's handsome, you're a mouse. And a woman like this loves him.")

To Parkhomenko, this was indicative of a much deeper philosophical divide. "Putin is an absolutely Soviet ruler," Parkhomenko told me.

"He sees politics as an inherently male thing, which is very convenient for a totalitarian regime. And that's the root difference between totalitarian and democratic politics. For democratic leaders, it's very important for people to see the human in them. Soviet leaders are scared for people to see the human in them."

Navalny was sentenced, on February 2, 2021, to two years and eight months in prison. He was transferred to a notoriously brutal penal colony in Ivanovo, sixty miles east of Moscow. Dasha went back to Stanford, ten time zones away, and Zakhar remained at his boarding school in Germany. Suddenly, everyone for whom Yulia was responsible was no longer under her roof.

Yulia continued packing bags of food for her husband and talking to doctors about his faltering health. She went to court hearings and visited him in prison when she could, calling them "dates" on her Instagram. In April 2021, he appeared by video link at an appeal hearing, gaunt after a twenty-four-day hunger strike. "Yulyashka," he said, using the diminutive of her name. "If you can hear me, stand up, let me get a look at you." She stood. "I am awfully happy to see you," he said, beaming.[20]

And she continued swatting away calls to become a politician in her husband's stead. Back in 2013, when he had been sentenced to five years in prison, thousands of Muscovites spontaneously appeared in the streets and the Kremlin had miraculously released him and Ofitserov. This time, tens of thousands of people across all of Russia demanded his release but the Kremlin did not relent, arresting hundreds. Yulia came out with the protesters twice, and twice she was arrested. The third time the authorities refrained. Her husband's supporters surrounded her and began chanting her name: "Yulia! Yulia! Yulia!" She held her hands to her chest and bowed, touched but overwhelmed by their attention. This was not her role. In her sole television interview until that point, in 2013, she had been asked if she saw her husband as the next president of Russia and herself as the first lady. "Yes, I can see him as president," she responded. "I don't see myself as a first lady. I see myself as his wife, no matter who he is."

BRING THE BOYS HOME

ONE MONDAY EVENING IN OCTOBER 2022, MARIA ANDREEVA'S HUSBAND, Ivan, came home from work and announced that he had been served with a draft notice. Worse, he had signed for it on the spot. Since the draft had been announced the previous month, hundreds of thousands of Russian men had fled the country, by plane or train or even on foot. Others hid at addresses where they were not registered with the authorities or hired lawyers to argue an exception or disability, anything that would allow them to avoid the grinding, bloody war in Ukraine. But Maria's man had simply signed his summons, like an obedient, stupid lamb.

Maria was stupefied with rage. They had a one-year-old daughter, after trying for nearly a decade to get pregnant, and the first year of motherhood had been hellish. Now she wondered if Ivan was actually *choosing* the war—a war in which, given the Russian casualty rates, he was quite likely to become cannon fodder. How? How could this man she had loved from her teenage years pick death over her and their daughter? And if he hadn't actively chosen it, why hadn't he fought harder? Why didn't he *think*?

She cried for two days straight; she wanted a divorce; she didn't know what to do with herself. But in the end there was nothing she could do. Early on the morning of October 12, Maria took Ivan to the mobilization point where scores of other drafted men and their families were gathering. They sat quietly and waited for his paperwork to be processed, half watching the patriotic World War II film playing on the small television in the corner. Then it was time. The men were loaded onto buses and driven off.

Maria went home to their silent apartment and decided that she would do everything in her power to get her daughter's father back.

In September 2022, Putin declared what he called a "partial mobilization" of military reservists. By that point he had been waging war on Ukraine for eight years, starting with his stealth annexation of Crimea and invasion of eastern Ukraine's Donbas region in the spring of 2014. Nearly a decade of frozen conflict had cost some 15,000 lives, as Putin attempted to do by force what he couldn't do politically: keep Ukraine from joining the West. On February 24, 2022, Putin sent nearly 200,000 Russian soldiers into Ukraine in a full-scale invasion that he believed would end the war—and Ukraine as a sovereign state—once and for all.

He had spent the previous winter pulling these troops toward the Ukrainian border, along with tanks, artillery, and field hospitals. But, somehow, most Russians didn't believe their president would be foolish enough to try to take by force Europe's largest country, populated with a brotherly Slavic people. They all thought he was bluffing, Maria included. She had never paid much mind to politics, and the background hum about Russian troops on the Ukrainian border had been drowned out by the all-consuming minutiae of caring for a colicky infant. On the morning that Putin announced his "special military operation," Maria, like most Russians and most Ukrainians, was in total shock.

Putin's war plans had been crafted in deep isolation with a small circle of his closest aides and informed by wishful thinking and faulty, sycophantic intelligence. They quickly disintegrated on contact with reality. Ukrainians, whom Putin expected to greet his troops as liberators, met them instead with deadly, paralyzing force. As the Ukrainian military ambushed columns of Russian troops, Ukrainian women gathered to make thousands of Molotov cocktails. They merrily told reporters that a real Ukrainian woman knew two recipes by heart: one for borscht and one for a Molotov cocktail. Women tossed the bottles into Russian tank treads or tried to block the metal beasts with their bodies. One woman became an instant icon when she was caught on camera telling a heavily armed Russian soldier to put sunflower seeds in his pockets. When he was inevitably killed, she informed him, his body would send up a hundred Ukrainian sunflowers.[1]

The world watched to see what Russian women would do. In the

West, people remembered the Committee of Soldiers' Mothers. During the ill-conceived Soviet invasion of Afghanistan that stretched into the 1980s, the committee had prevailed on Gorbachev to roll back a draconian draft.[2] After the Afghan war ended in failure, in 1989, the committee switched to protesting *dedovshchina*, the brutal practice of hazing that left scores of young conscripts gravely wounded and even dead. When, in 1994, the new Russian state invaded the Chechen Republic to keep it from breaking away, the mothers' committee stepped in once again.

In January 1995, after the botched and bloody Russian assault on Grozny, the Chechen capital, mothers from the committee began arriving in Chechnya to search for their sons. Many of those listed as captured or missing in action were teenage draftees with little to no training, and Dzhokhar Dudayev, leader of the Chechen rebels, had announced that he would release Russian captives only to their mothers.[3] Led by an engineer named Maria Kirbasova, the committee helped hundreds of Russian mothers make the journey to the war zone. They searched the morgues and bargained with Chechen field commanders to give them back their children.[4] Some walked right up to Russian military formations and snatched their sons back.

The mothers went even further. Starting on March 8, 1995, International Women's Day, Kirbasova led a protest tour, the March of Maternal Compassion, that, by April, had reached Sernovodsk, a town on the Chechen border. The Russian military tried to stop them, but the mothers used side streets to bypass the soldiers. As the Russian mothers walked, Chechen women emerged from their hiding places to embrace them. By the time the first Chechen war ended in defeat for Russia in 1996, the mothers of the committee had succeeded in getting dozens of their sons released from captivity and in helping scores of parents locate the bodies of their missing children and bring them home for burial.

The Committee of Soldiers' Mothers became a powerful cultural and political symbol because it showed women at their most essential and socially acceptable: as mothers. In 1987, Gorbachev had declared that women should return to "their purely womanly mission" of being wives and mothers, and the women of the committee had taken him quite literally.[5] Now, some thirty years after the first Chechen war, the world expected Russian mothers to once again show the same superhuman morality and strength. Where the men in charge had yet again fallen prey to their most destructive instincts, it would be the mothers who would save them—and their country—from themselves. They had done it before; surely they would do it again.

After the bus took Ivan away, Maria quickly tracked down his training facility in the Moscow region. She was still on maternity leave, which she had the option of stretching from one year to three, the last two unpaid, one of the very few Gorbachev reforms that Putin hadn't undone. Maria's mother had moved in to help take care of their daughter. Now, despite having a living, breathing husband, Maria was raising a child like so many Russian and Soviet women before her, in an all-female household. But the free childcare allowed her to focus obsessively on her mission.

Every weekend, Maria boarded a cold and dingy commuter train for the two-and-a-half-hour journey and then walked the rest of the way. Once she reached the base, Ivan and Maria were free to stroll near the grounds between lunch and dinner. Each meeting began with an inventory of what Ivan needed. He had been drafted in October, when snow begins to fall in Moscow, but the Ministry of Defense had issued him a summer uniform. His boots were the wrong size. He had no belt. He needed a first aid kit. Maria would write all this down and deliver bags of necessities on her next sojourn. After taking stock of Ivan's equipment, they'd talk about their now separate lives. And then, in the time left to them, they would stand in the autumn cold, their arms wrapped around each other, Maria sobbing.

This lasted about a month until Ivan caught a bad cold. During their weekly visit, Maria, a pediatrician, heard a rattle in his breathing and told him to go to the infirmary. He resisted, but when other men in his unit went with the same complaint, he tagged along. It was pneumonia. Ivan was hospitalized, then sent to a sanatorium to recover, and Maria hoped he would be released on medical grounds. But the

Russian military needed bodies, nothing more, to reinforce the lines in Ukraine. In early December, Ivan was transported to the Ukrainian border and Maria lost all contact with him.

When he resurfaced two weeks later, Ivan was in a panic. His unit would soon be going to the front lines in the occupied Luhansk region of eastern Ukraine. By then, troops with less than two weeks' training were being sent to attack heavily fortified Ukrainian positions, often without ammunition. They fared so poorly that Ukrainians called these assaults "meat waves." When Ivan was first drafted, he had told Maria that he'd be gone for only six months at most; everyone said so. Maria had always known better. "People, are you serious?" Maria told me, still incredulous and fuming nearly two years later. "Do you really think that, once the Ministry of Defense gets its paws on you, that you'll spend three months standing in formation and that'll be it? I have this feeling that many of our men, in their infantilism or stupidity, thought that they'd be in the reserves or that it would just be military drills. For some reason they didn't expect that they were being drafted specifically to fulfill the duties of a soldier." Now it had finally dawned on Ivan what he had gotten himself into, and he needed his wife to save him.

Maria was tired of thinking for her husband, of pulling him out of the holes he seemed to dive into so eagerly. But she had made a promise to herself and to her daughter, so she reminded Ivan that he had a medical background. Perhaps he should invoke that to get himself away from the constant shelling, as a medic or a nurse in the rear.

Maria and Ivan had met at a technical college in Moscow, where both were studying medicine. Soon after they began dating, Ivan confessed that maybe he had made a mistake: he was scared of blood. Maria tried to help him find a different path. She suggested something more sanitized, like scientific research. Ivan wasn't interested: a real degree at a real university sounded like too much work. Maria kept thinking. What about massage therapy? Ivan liked that idea, so Maria helped him find and enroll in a licensing program. For six months, after her full week of coursework, she would arrive at Ivan's classes at 8 a.m. on Saturday mornings to be his practice dummy, falling asleep on the massage table until the class let out six hours later.

Now, as Ivan panicked, she blamed herself for not thinking faster when he came home with the draft notice. As they texted between Moscow and Luhansk, Ivan casually mentioned that, before he left, his boss back home had actually found a bureaucratic loophole to save his male employees, by offering bogus vacation time to Ivan and the others with draft notices. The office would backdate their time off and tell the authorities that the draftees had all disappeared on ghost vacations. But Ivan had taken a principled stand, he told his wife proudly. He was a man. He was not going to run from his obligations to his country.

"It was a good thing he told me over text and not face-to-face," Maria remarked to me later, "or I think the conversation would have ended in assault."

As the draft notices arrived, mothers and wives all over the country came out to protest, especially in the ethnic enclaves of Buryatia and the North Caucasus, which had already borne the brunt of the war's casualties. Others filmed tearful videos addressed to Vladimir Vladimirovich, complaining about the misdeeds of local recruiters and appealing for help, as if Vladimir Vladimirovich weren't the person who had set it all in motion in the first place. Still more piled into their cars and followed the military trucks that had taken their sons and husbands. Caravans of angry women trailed the convoys for days until they reached their destinations in occupied Ukrainian territory, not far from the front lines. Videos of these women began circulating on social media.

In one, Svetlana Gorbatenko, pregnant with her third child, sits in the driver's seat of her car, which is filled with draftees' wives. She's filming a military truck right in front of her, which is teeming with men in camouflage and bulletproof vests. "We won't abandon them," she says firmly. She posted her demands on social media, adding that, if her husband was not released, she would stand next to him in battle, feeding bullets into his gun. Numerous commenters praised her as a "real Russian woman."[6] In another video, a group of women harangues a commander who is standing in front of their husbands, recently returned from a battle in which they suffered heavy casualties. The commander tells the women that they won't be allowed to stay with their men. "Well, we're not going to ask permission," one of the women shouts. "We already sent them off once and look how many are left!" The men shuffle their feet in silence. They look pleadingly at their women, then at the ground—as does their commander.[7]

These women began to form groups on social media and Telegram, the messaging app popular in Russia. They petitioned their local offices of the Defense Ministry and the state prosecutor's office, demanding formal, written explanations as to why their husbands and sons, inexperienced, unequipped civilians, were doing the jobs of professional soldiers. On November 7—Revolution Day in the Soviet era—they came out to protest in Moscow. In the end, Vladimir Vladimirovich had to do something.

On November 25, 2022, two months after announcing the partial mobilization, Putin invited seventeen soldiers' mothers to meet him at his residence just outside Moscow. The women, looking somber, sat around Putin at a long oval conference table. They were served tea and cookies along with dried fruit and fresh berries in little silver dessert bowls. Putin was the *tsar-batyushka* that day, the benign tsar-father. As the Kremlin cameras rolled, Putin listened to each of the seventeen mothers, some of whom had already lost their boys to the war. For over two hours he responded with warmth and compassion, even tenderness, jotting down reminders in his notepad to follow up with this or that woman. Glancing around at his guests, Putin noted that the day after tomorrow was Mother's Day. "It's not some pompous, noisy holiday," he said, smiling gently. "Rather, it's a day that is filled with a special, benevolent something and it highlights a feeling that . . . all the people in our country feel toward a mother: respect, veneration, admiration."

A week later, independent Russian journalists at Meduza published a report. Of the seventeen women who had attended tea with

Vladimir Vladimirovich, only three had sons who had been called up in the September mobilization. The sons of the others had all volunteered well before the draft or even before the February 2022 invasion. Almost all the women belonged to organizations affiliated with the Russian state or Putin's United Russia party and were therefore on the Kremlin's payroll. None of the women who had protested or recorded videos or driven down to the front had been invited, though many had petitioned to come. "You can't just have people come in to see the President off the street," one source in the presidential administration explained to Meduza. "Who knows what they'll ask, what they'll demand. There might be an unpleasant incident."[8]

Ivan was finally deployed in early February. Taking Maria's advice, he had managed to wrangle a job as an orderly at a medical station closer to the rear. But Ivan could not evade the sight of blood. His days were filled with ghastly and jagged wounds, the result of antediluvian trench warfare as both sides fought tree line to tree line, pounding each other with unfathomable amounts of artillery, dropping bombs on each other from drones that found soldiers hiding in the muddy dugouts. The casualty counts were staggering. A year into the full-scale war, some 200,000 Russian soldiers had been killed or wounded. (The Ukrainian casualty counts were estimated to be about half the Russian toll.) Often, the bodies of Russian soldiers came in days, even weeks after they had been killed. They were swollen, teeming with maggots, though there were also living soldiers who arrived with the vermin spilling from their wounds. Through the fog of his revulsion, Ivan learned that maggots provided a perverse kind of cleaning function, clearing away necrotic tissue. As he worked, something inside him began to come undone.

Back in Moscow, Maria noticed that the hunt for draft dodgers had slowed. The police had apparently given up trying to catch them in the Metro and at work. On October 28, just two weeks after she had delivered Ivan to the recruitment post, the defense ministry announced that the mobilization, having reached its goal of drafting 300,000 men, had ended. No new draft was planned.⁹ The government seemed to have realized the political dangers of terrorizing the residents of the wealthy capital. Instead, the Kremlin began recruiting volunteers with pay and perks: debt forgiveness, preferential admission to college for their children, leniency in criminal sentencing, mortgage assistance, and money, lots and lots of money. In a country where the median monthly salary in 2022 was 40,000 rubles (about $670 at the time), the Ministry of Defense was offering 210,000 rubles a month for infantry soldiers, plus a 400,000-ruble signing bonus. A soldier's home region often threw in hundreds of thousands more on top of that. In the case of injury or death, the government would pay the soldier's family 3 million and 5 million rubles, respectively.[10] Recruits, the Kremlin claimed, began streaming in by the hundreds of thousands.

It drove Maria nuts. To know that Ivan could have avoided the draft altogether—it was too much to bear at times. Sometimes she was so angry at Ivan that she wasn't sure she wanted him back. "They gathered all the fools into a little pile," Maria groused, "and whoever was a little more clever laughed at it all and went on living as before." She avoided taking her daughter on walks on the weekends. She couldn't bear to see happy, "complete" families strolling through the park.

There were constant rumors, on social media and at the front, that the men were about to be sent home on furlough to visit their families and rest. Each time, Maria would get her hopes up, only to have them dashed. By the summer of 2023, nearly a year after the mobilization, Maria began seeing groups pop up on Telegram that were created by women like her.

There was Olga Kats from Novosibirsk, whose younger brother Sasha was fighting in Ukraine. In June 2023, after failing to get any response to her complaints to the Defense Ministry, city hall, or the local prosecutor's office, Kats launched the Telegram group *Vernyom rebyat* (Let's Bring the Boys Home), as well as a number of petitions addressed to Vladimir Vladimirovich. They all echoed Putin's own language about why the war was being fought: to defend Russian territorial integrity and traditional values. Kats was no pacifist, nor did she seem to care about Ukrainian suffering. Her complaint was that the Russian men who "came to the aid of the Motherland" deserved a break and to have their service end within a reasonable time frame. The professional soldiers from the Interior Ministry and Rosgvardiya (Russian National Guard) received furloughs every three to six months. Their contracts had end dates. Even the convicted criminals that the private military company Wagner Group was recruiting from Russian prisons by the tens of thousands were sent home to freedom after six months in Ukraine. But the civilian men who were drafted, men like Sasha and Ivan, seemed to have been sentenced to serve indefinitely. They were exhausted and their families were at a breaking point. Kats's Telegram group soon had over 20,000 members.

As the one-year anniversary of the partial mobilization approached, the Russian government began pushing back. In early September 2023, the head of the Duma's armed services committee announced that the men mobilized a year earlier would return only "after the end of the special military operation. No rotation has been envisioned."[11] He added that they were about to take the first of the furloughs they were entitled to every six months, but the furloughs never happened.

By the end of September, Olga Kats collated all the versions of her petitions, which between them had more than 100,000 signatures. She included all the bureaucratic nonresponses she and the other women had received to their previous requests for furloughs or troop rotations. She also included nearly two hundred personal appeals from mothers, wives, and daughters all over the country who wanted their men back. They wrote of sleeping with their phones in their hands in case their husbands called, of the physical strain of running rural households alone, of their constant, debilitating anxiety, of children who couldn't remember their fathers or who had developed behavioral issues in their absence.

On September 30, Kats submitted her packet to the Kremlin and demanded a meeting with Putin or one of his trusted representatives. A month later, she received a written response from a faceless bureaucrat in the Kremlin's citizen reception office. In so much bureaucratese, it said that the men would go home when the war ended. She was furious. "Giving up is simply not an option," she wrote to the group on November 16.[12]

Maria had joined Kats's group, as well as another called *Put' domoi*,

The Way Home. Both were demanding a general, nationwide demobilization of *all* non-volunteer, non-professional soldiers. Maria began writing letters to the Defense Ministry, to Moscow City Hall, to the Duma, to the prosecutor's office and the office of Putin's human rights ombudswoman—everywhere she could think of. By October, she was attending one to two meetings a week at the Moscow city legislature with other wives and mothers, demanding that their men be released from military service. On November 7, she and around thirty other wives joined the Communist Party's Revolution Day rally on Pushkin Square, holding up protest signs. "We're not against the war," they told the cameras. "We're peaceful women!"

Maria was small and feisty, with big brown eyes and a tightly pursed mouth. She sounded perpetually indignant, which she was. Although she had never been politically active or received any media training, she seemed to have a knack for it all, and she was soon giving interviews to the press. After hundreds of anti-war protesters were arrested in the first days of the invasion, she knew not to publicly question the premise of the war, comparing Ukraine in one interview to "a difficult teenager" who shouldn't have been let out of the house when the Soviet Union fell apart.[13] It didn't help. When she and the other wives of The Way Home applied for a permit to protest again the following month, their request was denied.

On November 23, exactly one week after she posted the Kremlin's response to her petition, Olga Kats posted a photo of Sasha in the Bring the Boys Home Telegram group.[14] In it, he is smiling goofily at the dog and cat scooped up in his arms. "Yesterday, November 22, I found out that my brother was killed while fulfilling his military duty," Kats wrote. "He was 25 years old and he hadn't had time to get married and have kids, but all his relatives, friends, and colleagues loved and valued him very much." As for the group and the activism, Kats wrote, "my heart is broken. I'm out."

The Committee of Soldiers' Mothers had had one key advantage that Olga Kats and Maria and the other wives lacked: it didn't have to contend with Vladimir Putin. When the committee had sprung up in 1989, the Soviet Union itself was nearly dead, its vast repressive system mostly neutered by Gorbachev's reforms and the preceding decade of decay. Gorbachev applauded the creation of informal clubs, *neformaly*, which would go on to form the backbone of post-Soviet civil society. After the collapse of the USSR in 1991, when Western-style democracy was all the rage and Russia suddenly had dozens of political parties (including one for beer lovers), it didn't occur to anyone to shut down a group of mothers who were protesting conditions in the Russian army that everyone could agree were appalling. And when the committee made real trouble for Yeltsin during his war against the breakaway Chechen Republic, the central government was far too weak to do anything about it.

Putin had loathed Gorbachev and Yeltsin as naïve weaklings who sold Russia out to the West. Over the two decades of his reign, he gradually restored the cult and traditions of the Cheka, the Bolshevik secret police. That code, honed over decades as the Cheka became the NKVD, KGB, and now the FSB, stipulated that any kind of independent opposition to the central government could not be given an inch. Putin believed that even he had been too lenient by allowing a liberal thaw during the Medvedev interregnum. The more freedom he gave spoiled city dwellers, the more they wanted to emulate the West and oust him from power. And the West, as he imagined, had taken advantage of this by attempting a color revolution in his capital. He would not let another wave of protests dismantle the empire he loved.

By the time he ordered the full-scale invasion of Ukraine, Putin had mostly eviscerated Russian civil society. In the year after Navalny was arrested at Sheremetyevo Airport, scores of journalists and activists, facing bogus criminal charges, had been forced to flee the country. Many others ended up in jail. Independent media organizations and NGOs were declared "foreign agents" by the Justice Ministry, a label that choked off their advertising revenue and stifled their fundraising efforts. Putin even shut down Memorial, the most august NGO formed during the Gorbachev years, which had been dedicated to exposing the crimes of the Stalin era. Putin was instead busy rehabilitating the NKVD officers who had committed those crimes.

Meanwhile, the Committee of Soldiers' Mothers had been fully infiltrated and co-opted by the Kremlin.

When the full-scale invasion began, Putin signed a raft of censorship laws. Anyone who called the "special military operation" a war, who relied on sources other than the Defense Ministry for information about it, or who "discredited" the Russian armed forces could be punished with prison time. Russians were arrested by the thousands for posts and even likes on social media, for wearing the colors of the Ukrainian flag even accidentally. A seventy-two-year-old woman was given a five-year sentence for sharing someone else's posts condemning the war on Ukraine, where her brother had ended up under the rubble. A single father was arrested when his twelve-year-old daughter made an anti-war drawing in class and her teachers turned her in. He was eventually sentenced to two years in jail, lost his custodial rights, and his daughter was placed in an orphanage. Two ten-year-old boys and their eleven-year-old friend were caught on camera throwing snowballs at an eternal flame monument in their neighborhood and charged with "rehabilitating Nazism."[15] A fifteen-year-old boy was arrested and sentenced to five years in jail for passing out flyers against the war and against Putin. "Mom, I think I'm going to die soon," he wrote to his mother from prison, where he said he was subject to constant torture and physical abuse.[16]

Maria and the other women of The Way Home, in other words, were operating in a far more hostile environment than their ideological predecessors. The November 7 mothers' protest alongside the Communists lasted all of five minutes before the police broke it up. A couple of days later, the women of The Way Home, which now had over 30,000 members and branches all over the country, posted a furious manifesto on its channel addressed to the entire "multiethnic people of Russia." "Our government turned away from those who were the first to respond to its call for help," it read. "They fucked us over," the women warned, "and they'll fuck you over, too."[17]

Five days later, Vladimir Soloviev, the Kremlin's most powerful propagandist, aimed his firepower at the women. On his Telegram channel, where he has over 1.3 million subscribers, he accused The Way Home and others as being part of a "psyops" mounted by "foreign intelligence services."[18] On November 29, a Kremlin spoiler, a lawyer named Ilya Remeslo, who had made a name for himself hounding Navalny with spurious allegations, filed a complaint with Telegram. He alleged that there were two channels called The Way Home and that this was proof that they were astroturf organizations. (In fact, there were thirty such channels: they were regional branches of the same group.) The following day, Telegram, whose founder Pavel Durov prided himself on his free-speech absolutism, slapped a big red label on the group's flagship channel: "FAKE."[19]

All over the country, state authorities began cracking down on local chapters. Dozens of women reported being visited at home by the police for "prophylactic conversations" to discourage them from protesting. In mid-November, the women of Krasnoyarsk's The Way Home branch were discussing plans for a protest on their local channel when, suddenly, the group administrator, citing her many worries at home, passed on her duties to a woman named Irina Vorontsova, the aide to a city official. When the women insisted on going ahead with the protest, Vorontsova deleted their messages and shut down the channel.[20]

In December, a pretty young woman named Paulina appeared in the national Telegram group. The women had recently applied for another protest, which the Moscow city government had denied. Paulina, who had not signed the application, suggested that the women should go ahead and protest anyway. Maria quickly realized that Paulina was most likely a mole sent in by the Russian authorities to get members of The Way Home arrested for protesting without a permit. Maria was already on thin ice. She had been caught on camera during the November 7 protest. A few days later, Ivan was summoned by his superiors. They finally made clear to him the conditions under which he would be allowed to go home: either when the war ended or his life did, whichever came first. They also berated him for Maria's burgeoning political career. The man who couldn't navigate life without his wife's help was now being asked to control her.

LAND OF MOTHERS

ON FEBRUARY 15, 2024, I WAS LEAVING A COCKTAIL RECEPTION AT THE Munich Security Conference when, in the lobby of the Hotel Bayerischer Hof, I ran into Yulia Navalnaya. She was statuesque in a long coat, her peroxide blond hair tied into her tiny signature bun. Like so many of our mutual friends and acquaintances, Yulia had fled Russia. In June 2021, six months after Navalny had been imprisoned on a two-and-a-half-year sentence, a Russian court declared his Anti-Corruption Foundation an extremist organization on a par with Al Qaeda, ISIS, and the Taliban. The foundation, which Navalny had spent years building into a grassroots powerhouse, would have to be shut down. Almost immediately, the arrests of Navalny's colleagues began. Then, in March 2022, Navalny himself was found guilty of fraud in a separate criminal case and sentenced to another nine years. In August 2023, he was given nineteen additional years in prison, this time on charges of extremism. Soon afterward his troika of lawyers was arrested and charged with associating with extremists. The chekists were not giving an inch.

By the time I saw her, Yulia was splitting her time between London and Germany, where Zakhar, her youngest, was still in school. Dasha was finishing up at Stanford. Yulia was no longer able to communicate with her husband except through handwritten letters; returning to Russia to visit him was too dangerous, and the authorities wouldn't even allow them phone calls.

In the fall of 2023, Yulia and the Navalny team had raised the alarm: Alexey had vanished. While they knew he could have been in transit between penal colonies, there was also a much darker possibility. Navalny's health had not fully recovered from his August 2020 poisoning. He still complained of nerve pain in his legs, and he looked gaunt at every court appearance despite the extra food his lawyers brought him. His supporters began to fear the worst: Was Navalny dead?

Then, right around Christmas, Alexey reappeared. The authorities had secretly transferred him to a maximum-security penal colony in Kharp, well past the Arctic Circle, where Russia fans out in tentacles of tundra into an icy sea. Notorious for its brutality, the colony had been dubbed the Polar Wolf by its inmates. Prisoners were kept in tiny single-man cells and allowed out once a day for minimal exercise in the bitter cold. When I saw Yulia, her husband had spent nearly two months in these conditions. I asked her sheepishly how he was doing. It was a stupid question, I knew, but it was a small way of showing my concern.

"He's good!" she said, chipper and steely despite her obvious fatigue.

I looked at her, puzzled.

"Everyone asks me this all the time and I've been trying to find a concise way to say it," she relented. "But I think I've finally settled on a formulation: he's doing really well in really bad circumstances."[1]

We chatted a little longer and then said our goodbyes.

The following morning I was going through security at the conference when a friend messaged me: Navalny had died in prison. A cold wave of nausea and panic began to crest somewhere in my bowels. I sat down in the first place I could, woozy with shock. Navalny and I hadn't always agreed. We had gotten into a screaming match over the phone back in 2010 after I publicly said his speech at the nationalist Russian March was anti-Semitic. His press team had shut me out during his 2018 campaign. But I had written the first English-language profile of him back in early 2011, and we had spent a lot of time getting to know each other for it. We were friends with all the same people, and our relationship had always been cordial. Even when I didn't agree with him, I respected his ability to self-reflect and evolve, admired his curiosity and his unearthly courage.

More than that, though, I had come to believe him. I had, without even noticing it, bought his promise of a post-Putin Russia. I believed, even took for granted, that, by dint of his youth, he would simply outlive Putin. Once he'd done that, I figured, he would at least have a chance of making Russia something different, something better than what it had always been: an imperialist, bureaucratic, authoritarian system built around a cult of personality.

When I had decided to study Russia's history and literature in college, my father warned me that our homeland was a country without a future. Why would I tie my own to its lack of one, especially after my parents had given up so much to decouple the two? Every country had a future, I argued at the time. The question was what kind of future it would be. Now, sitting in an echoing hotel lobby in Germany, I felt it deeply. My father had been right. Russia's future would never be different from its present or its past.

In the fall of 2022, at the height of the draft, Russian social media brimmed with jokes and memes about men vanishing from society, leaving behind a country populated mostly by women—jokes that echoed the post–World War II fixation on *bezotzovshchina*, or fatherlessness. As the war dragged on into the next year, Putin also invoked the past, but his reference point went much further back. The "special military operation" in Ukraine was a holy war, he contended, and not just to gather together the lands of the old Russian Empire. It was to protect the country from the corrosive liberalism of the West, a necessity in his larger project to restore the true Russia, one where men were men, women were women, and the men were in charge.

This patriarchal vision had been central to his justification for the war from the outset. In his initial speech announcing the invasion on February 24, 2022, Putin ranted about NATO and the West and claimed that the residents of Crimea and the Donbas wanted to return to Russia. But he also made clear that defending "traditional values" was one of his core reasons for attacking Ukraine, which he saw as a Western puppet. "The [West's] efforts to use us in their interests, to destroy our traditional values and impose their pseudo values on us, which would have eaten away at us, at our people from within—these ideas that they aggressively impose in their own countries and that directly lead to degradation and extinction because they contradict human nature itself," Putin declared. "This will not happen."²

The West, in Putin's view, was guilty not only of threatening Russia's geopolitical interests. He had long insisted that *skrepy*, or traditional values, bound the country together and made it stronger. Now he was claiming that those values were the very quintessence of Russian sovereignty, under attack from the decadent West with, as he put it, its "faddish tendencies like dozens of genders and gay parades." "Do we really want our country, Russia, to have a 'parent number 1, number 2, number 3' instead of 'Mom' and 'Dad'?" Putin asked in an address to the Federal Assembly in September 2022.

He was speaking a week after announcing the partial draft, which he had not wanted to resort to, knowing it would spark unrest. Yet, seven months into the war, he had little choice. In March, just a month after the invasion and after suffering heavy losses, the Russian army had abandoned its quest to take the capital and Kharkiv, Ukraine's second-largest city. By November, Ukrainian troops would retake Kherson, the large—and largely Russian-speaking—city in the country's south. "Do we really want for these perversions, which lead to degradation and extinction, to be imposed in our schools from the earliest grades?" Putin went on. "So that it's drilled into them that, in addition to women and men, there are certain other *genders* and where they offer them gender-reassignment surgery? Do we really want this for our country, for our children? This is all unacceptable to us. We have our own, different future."³

In November 2022, Putin defined that future in a diktat outlining Russia's strategic and national security interests for the coming years. "Traditional values"—chiefly patriotism, collectivism, and a strong family—were "the foundation of Russian society, allowing for the defense and strengthening of Russian sovereignty," the document declared. The main enemies of this order, it went on, were terrorist organizations, unfriendly "multinational corporations," and NGOs, as well as "the United States of America." In other words, any culture that embraced feminism, gender fluidity, and homosexuality was not just perpendicular to Russian culture; it was a mortal danger to its manifest destiny. In the international arena, Putin appealed to countries in the Global South—which, he pointed out, shared similar conservative values—to join Russia in standing against the degenerate, gender-fluid West. He remained hopeful, however, that one day "the real, traditional West"—like the American evangelical organizations that had helped the Russian Orthodox Church curb abortions and gay rights in Russia and were then working to return Donald Trump to power in the United States—would gain primacy in America and Europe.[4]

In the summer of 2023, Russia outlawed gender reassignment surgery and Russians were no longer permitted to change their gender in official documents.[5] Russians who had transitioned were banned from adopting or fostering children; marriages in which one partner had changed genders were automatically annulled. That fall, Russia's Constitutional Court approved a law that classified "the global LGBT movement" as extremist, legally equating gay Russians with ISIS terrorists. Police started raiding gay clubs and parties in private homes, beating and humiliating the participants on camera and then leaking the videos to popular Telegram channels. A young woman was arrested for wearing rainbow earrings; the owners of a gay club in Orenburg were charged with creating an extremist organization, which carries a maximum prison sentence of ten years.[6] In December 2024, the head of a travel company was found dead in his cell a month after he was arrested for organizing "gay tours," which, state prosecutors alleged, constituted an extremist gathering.[7]

The Kremlin also began to police the behavior of straight Russians. In December 2023, a social media influencer named Anastasia Ivleeva threw an "almost naked" party attended by many Russian pop icons. Her risqué parties were an annual event, but this one drew the full force of the traditionalist, conservative, pro-war wing of the Russian system. The event was condemned by everyone from right-wing religious groups to masked, gun-toting Russian soldiers fighting in Ukraine. Even Maria Butina, a Duma deputy who had been deported from the United States after being convicted of spying for Russia, weighed in, appealing to the Interior Ministry to check if the party had violated Putin's "traditional values" diktat.[8] Ivleeva, once the "it" girl of Moscow, lost her lucrative corporate contracts and was eventually found guilty of "offending human dignity" and propagating a "nontraditional sexual orientation." She received a fine and managed to save herself from a harsher punishment by issuing a tearful apology and promising to vote for Putin in the upcoming presidential election. Her standing in Russia never recovered.

Meanwhile, Ivleeva's guests had to perform elaborate rituals to demonstrate their complete obeisance to the Christian, traditionalist order. Singers who had long been Kremlin favorites but found themselves on blacklists for attending Ivleeva's party tried to claw their way back to favor by performing for the troops in the occupied Donbas. The owner of the nightclub that hosted the party donated a piece of the relics of St. Nicholas the Wonderworker to the Russian Orthodox Church. (It didn't work: the club was closed for "sanitary reasons.") A young rapper named Vacio, who had come to Ivleeva's party wearing nothing but a sock on his penis, was sentenced to fifteen days in prison for "hooliganism," given a military draft notice, and ordered to pay a large fine for "LGBT propaganda."[9] "LGBT activism isn't my thing at all," the stunned twenty-five-year-old wrote on his Telegram channel. "I'm a heterosexual guy, I abide by the laws of the [Russian Federation], and I'm only interested in women."[10] Almost as soon as he was released from prison, he was sentenced to a second term, also for hooliganism.

Even when Putin's obsession with "traditional values" veered into the absurd, the Russian elite faithfully parroted him. In January 2024, Putin claimed that Russian émigrés were streaming back to Russia because in the West, there are "common bathrooms for boys and girls." "It's very hard to live in conditions like these for people with normal, traditional, human values," he explained.[11] Not long afterward the governor of St. Petersburg described visiting some wounded soldiers in the hospital. They had seen untold horrors in Ukraine, he said, chief among them "gender-neutral bathrooms." "They know well what they're fighting for," he concluded, sounding every bit like the Soviets who denounced Trotskyists and right-deviationists in a desperate bid to win favor with Stalin and avoid his execution cellars.[12]

A new Russia had dawned, and it was a lot like the old one. Every time I read the news from Russia, all I could think was: "Thank God Emma isn't here to see this."

In November 2020, at the height of the coronavirus pandemic, my grandmother's neighbors in Moscow called to tell us she had vanished. A short while later, she resurfaced in a Moscow ICU. What had begun as a bad headache had progressed to violent vomiting, and, as a doctor, Emma knew to call an ambulance. A CT scan revealed an ugly mass in her brain, a white opacity enveloping her cerebellum like an octopus. She was eighty-six, always one step away from heart failure, and despite all the calls my mother and I and our Moscow friends placed, no matter how many favors we called in, we couldn't find a surgeon who would operate on her lest she die on the operating table and spoil their numbers. The Soviet Union had fallen three decades prior, but its obsession with production statistics lived on.

The neurosurgeons at my mother's hospital, however, were willing to try for a colleague. If my mother could get Emma to Baltimore, they would give it their best shot. But it was the middle of a global pandemic, and Russia's borders were closed to non-citizens. (When we emigrated from the Soviet Union in 1990, we had been stripped of our citizenship and, since then, had refused many offers from the Russian Federation to have it restored—for a fee, of course.) Emma had been discharged from the hospital, but she couldn't fly across the Atlantic alone. How could we get to her? I messaged Maria Zakharova, the vicious spokeswoman from the Russian Foreign Ministry. We had often tangled, in private and in public. She once accused me on live TV of hating my Motherland. But I had heard that she liked to show largesse in private, even to her adversaries. I messaged her, asking if she could let my mother into the country for just a day or two so she could rescue *her* mother. Within half an hour, my mother received a call from someone at the Foreign Ministry, who took down her information and passed it to the border police.

On November 29, my mother drove from Maryland up to JFK. She arrived in Moscow the next morning, masked and terrified of getting

Emma sick, at the apartment where Buzya had once lived, and where I had lived with Emma. Emma put on a good face. She told my mom she didn't want to give up, that she wanted every treatment. But she cuddled her gray, flat-faced cat all evening and, away from my mother's ears, confessed to her caregiver that she just wanted to stay home. She was a doctor and she had seen the scan. She must have known that she was never coming back to Moscow.

On the morning of December 1, Emma and my mother boarded a plane for New York and then drove back to my parents' house in Maryland. I met them there the following day and gave Emma a big hug. I hadn't seen her in person since my last visit to Moscow, in September 2019. Her pandemic had been very different from ours. Russia had lifted its lockdown after just a few weeks, even as Putin, terrified of getting sick, retreated into deep isolation. Anyone who wanted to see him, including cabinet ministers and visiting heads of state, had to live in a hotel, alone and under presidential guard, for two weeks before being granted an in-person audience. The rest of the country, meanwhile, was encouraged to go back to work, for the sake of the economy.

Even as Covid deaths skyrocketed in Russia, my friends in Moscow went to theater openings, ate in crowded, gorgeous restaurants, and partied as hedonistically as they ever had. Emma, though decades older, was never far behind them. During our regular FaceTime calls, she would insist that she was staying in, but something would always slip out: an evening spent singing the songs of the old bards with her friends, a gallery opening, a crowded museum exhibit. During our most recent conversation, she accidentally mentioned attending a screening of Fellini's *8½* at the hipster movie theater near her apartment. In that moment I was furious with her. Two weeks later I was glad that she had had that evening of living exactly as she pleased, right up to the very end.

On the morning of December 3, my father called. My mother had a fever of 103. Emma couldn't stop coughing. My grandmother, it turned out, had caught Covid in the Moscow ICU and given it to my mother. My mother's condition deteriorated precipitously, but she recovered after qualifying for the antibody treatment. Emma fared far worse. She had to be hospitalized but nothing seemed to help. Since my mother had just recovered from the virus and was a physician at the hospital, her colleagues suited her up like a cosmonaut and let her spend the next twenty-four hours with Emma. They FaceTimed me from the hospital room. Even through the screen, I could see that she was already adrift, moving somewhere beyond us. Crying, I told her that I loved her. Emma smiled her Hollywood smile at me one last time.

"And you," she said, "are the love of my life."

Hours after learning of her husband's death, Yulia Navalnaya took the stage at the Munich Security Conference, once again facing the world on the worst day of her life. As she addressed the assembled presidents and prime ministers and generals, she didn't even know if the news was true: if her husband was really dead or if Putin was playing one of his demented games. "I thought for a long time, whether I should come out here or fly immediately to see my children," she said that February morning, her eyes still red with tears but her voice unwavering. "And then I thought, what would Alexey do in my place? I am sure that he would be here, he would be on this stage."[13]

The speech marked Yulia's official entry into Russian opposition politics, an unexpected turn after years of insisting that her most important roles were those of a wife and mother. Alexey's death seemed to demand it. But, in truth, Yulia's task was far more difficult than his had ever been. The war and the accompanying crackdown allowed Putin to consolidate power even more than he already had in the preceding two decades. The core of Navalny's base, hundreds of thousands of educated, urban Russians, had fled the country after Putin invaded Ukraine. Most of those left behind were too scared to protest. Those who did were arrested. And the government opened criminal cases against prominent journalists, activists, academics—anyone who disagreed with them—even after they had left Russia, making return impossible.

Yulia was now assuming leadership of an opposition whose most active and dedicated members were either in jail or scattered across the world, in Berlin, Tel Aviv, Tbilisi, Lisbon, New York, and London. It was unthinkable to ask those who had remained in Russia to take on the tremendous risks of active opposition from the safety of the West. Russians had always been deeply skeptical of being led from afar by people who didn't share the burdens of their daily reality; this was precisely why Navalny had returned home from Germany. The war only accentuated this divide. Squabbles between the émigrés and those who stayed behind broke out constantly on social media, while polls showed a growing suspicion by Russians at home of Russians abroad. When it came to the Russian opposition, killing Navalny was akin to unplugging a comatose patient's ventilator. In killing Yulia's husband—and with him any hope that many Russians had for their country—Putin had finally broken the movement's back.

Treading in this darkness, Yulia somehow had to find a way to revive that hope and then keep stoking it for years, even decades. And while she certainly commanded symbolic legitimacy as Navalny's saintly, stoic widow, she did not have his warmth, his charisma, or his political genius. Yet here she was, stepping once again into the breach, her own future desolate and uncertain.

For now, though, there was so much to do. She would have to do battle with Putin and his state yet again to release her husband's body, a gruesome reprisal of their clash in August 2020. She would have to fight Putin to allow a public funeral, to give Alexey's tens of thousands of supporters still in Russia the opportunity to bid him farewell. She would have to fight for information about how her husband had died, and months later, when the report from the prison finally leaked, she would learn that he had died writhing in pain, seizing and vomiting from the poison, alone, without her. She would organize a contest for a monument to adorn her husband's grave, a grave she would most likely never visit.

Back in Moscow, Maria Andreeva grappled with what Navalny's death meant for her and the other women petitioning the government to bring their men home. The previous month, she had been arrested and briefly detained at a rally to place red carnations at the Tomb of the Unknown Soldier beneath the red Kremlin walls—a conscious throwback to a protest staged by the Committee of Soldiers' Mothers in 1995.[14]

Now Navalny was dead and the presidential election was just two weeks away. Maria understood instantly what that meant: whatever vanishingly small space there had been for the women's protests, it was gone for good now. If Navalny's death had moved Yulia to abandon her position as a wife who stays out of the political spotlight, it did the opposite for Maria. "At a certain point, we bet that the system would meet us halfway," Maria recalled. "But when it became obvious that they wouldn't, it was time to pull up our fishing rods and make the switch to swimming alone." She was done with politics.

Yulia Navalnaya and Maria Andreeva were doing something quintessentially, fundamentally feminine in the most traditional Russian sense. They were the latest in a long line of women who, in Nekrasov's tired description, could stop a galloping steed or enter a burning hut if that was what their families and their country required. They were the heirs to the women who had toppled the Romanov dynasty and the women who stood in line with Akhmatova to pass bread to their imprisoned men, to the teenage girls who had volunteered to fight the Nazis and the women who rebuilt and repopulated the country when that fight was won. They were like the women who went to wash toilets and sell rags at the markets while their men lay down on the couch with a bottle. When the men in power savaged their country, these women heaved it on their backs and charged forward, heedless of their own selves. They were the women of Russian history and Russian lore, the people who held the place together in spite of itself, but they were not the kind of mothers and wives Vladimir Vladimirovich was looking for.

He needed loyalists who were happy to sacrifice their men to the Motherland, the kind of women who reveled in their status as military wives, trading tips on Telegram on how to stay attractive so their husbands would still want them when they returned from war.[15] He certainly didn't need women to fight, as they had in the Great Patriotic War and as some women were doing in Ukraine. He simply needed them to supply more soldiers. Putin had dispatched hundreds of thousands of men to the front and scared a few hundred thousand more out of the country just as Russia was going through yet another demographic dip, the result of falling birth rates during the chaos of the 1990s. The country needed more people, but there were fewer people to produce them—and Putin was reducing their number every day. But instead of killing fewer of their men, Putin asked Russian women to do exactly what Stalin had asked them to do eighty years prior: have more.

And though Putin despised Khrushchev, he copied many of his proposals to "replace the dead," which he rebranded as "promoting the prestige of motherhood." Putin's government had already restricted abortion and doled out cash payments for women who had children—*matkapital*, or "maternal capital." Now one of his cabinet ministers advised young women to forgo higher education and have children instead.[16] His speaker of parliament said the best way to prepare Russian girls for adulthood was to "teach them to make *borsch* and to care for their future husband."[17] Schools introduced a new curriculum called Family Studies, which would teach students the values of "marriage, having many children, and chastity."[18] Even Valentina Tereshkova, the first woman in space, joined in, proclaiming that "the most important thing in life is strengthening the family and raising children."[19]

But the war called for more extreme—and familiar—methods. And so, in August 2022, Putin issued a presidential order bringing back the Khrushchev-era honor of "Hero Mother," itself borrowed from the fascists of Germany. Now any woman who bore and raised ten or more children would be awarded a military-style medal (featuring a diamond solitaire) and paid one million rubles. Putin also declared that 2024 was to be the year of the family. It featured intensive propaganda, conferences, and pageants showing off the best big Russian families, usually in matching outfits. In addition to increasing the financial incentives for women to have more children, the Kremlin now began to introduce punitive measures for those who shirked their reproductive obligations. There were reports that the government was examining proposals to revive yet another Khrushchev policy: a tax on childlessness.[20] In November 2024, Putin signed into law a measure that banned "child-free propaganda"—that is, anything that could be construed as glamorizing a life without children.

In Putin's eyes, the ideal woman, the kind on which young Russian girls could model themselves, was Maria Lvova-Belova, the Kremlin's commissioner for children's rights. A century earlier, children's rights had been a key part of the portfolio of Alexandra Kollontai, who had championed the emancipatory power of a woman's work and called for unshackling love from marriage. It was also a focus for Inessa Armand, who believed that forcing women to give birth was an unacceptable form of labor conscription. Lvova-Belova would have made their blood curdle.

Lvova-Belova grew up with parents who found the Russian Orthodox Church in the years after the Communist collapse and embraced it with the zeal of the converted. When the young Maria met her future husband, Pavel, she made sure that he was serious about having a big, Orthodox family. As she liked to explain to the media, if a man wanted fewer than three children, there was no next date.[21] Pavel passed the test and they married when she was nineteen. Within the next fifteen years, the couple had five biological children and adopted four more, and Pavel left the private sector to become a priest. Lvova-Belova, meanwhile, became a gifted procurer of Kremlin grants for her various religious charities helping disabled children graduating out of orphanages. She also became the legal guardian for thirteen of them. When Putin appointed her the children's rights commissioner in October 2021, he asked, as everyone always did, how she managed to juggle everything. Lvova-Belova, who was thirty-six at the time, didn't hesitate. "That's just how moms of many kids are," she said, smiling, "multitaskers."[22]

In March 2023, the International Criminal Court issued a warrant for her arrest, accusing her of committing genocide by kidnapping Ukrainian children. Lvova-Belova had helped organize what she called the "evacuation" of over 15,000 Ukrainian children to Russia, but those children, it turned out, had been abducted by the Russian state. They were shipped to Russia, informed they were no longer Ukrainian, and given Russian citizenship. Some, including children with living parents or legal guardians, were adopted by Russian military families.

Modeling the acquisitive stance of the state, she herself had adopted a fifteen-year-old boy from Mariupol, her tenth child. She paraded him around, on stages and on television, like a pet dog. "Is this not unity?" Lvova-Belova told a state-sponsored social policy forum. "Is this not a patriotic feeling when there are no kids who aren't yours, when they are all ours?"[23]

All of these efforts should have worked. Abortions, now far harder to access even in private clinics, were falling as women were able to use safer forms of birth control. Despite strict Western sanctions, the Russian economy was roaring onward, powered by military spending. In poll after poll, vast majorities, over three-quarters of the population, said they supported the war. And yet the decisions of individual Russian women reflected a deep uncertainty about the future. In September 2024, nine months into Putin's year of the family, the birth rate dropped to its lowest point since 1999, the year Vladimir Vladimirovich came to power.[24]

I spoke to Maria that same month. Although she'd stopped attending protests in February and had never received foreign funding, the Russian Ministry of Justice had declared her to be a foreign agent in May. Three months later she was let go from her job and, with it, the ability to easily renew her medical license.[25] Maria, who complained to me that she was going gray at thirty-four, had somehow managed to get Ivan into a Moscow hospital for treatment for his PTSD. It was not a condition that the Russian military took seriously—at least, not enough to pull men from the line—but Maria had made a promise, and if she couldn't get her man back, she could at least find a way to keep him safe.

Maria and Ivan had always wanted more kids, and before he got his draft notice, they had put five embryos in storage. But when I asked her if she planned to have another child, she recoiled. "Do I look feebleminded to you?" she shot back. "No, but seriously, if I have a boy, I'm fucked." A boy would be just another body for Putin or his successors to throw on the imperial pyre. "Have you noticed that we go to war once in a generation?" she asked. "Afghanistan, Chechnya, this now. With enviable regularity!" A girl would be scarcely better. "If I have another girl, then I need to urgently start thinking about getting her an apartment," she went on. "Because a girl needs, in case of an unsuccessful marriage, to be able to turn on her heel and leave." But Maria couldn't afford to buy another apartment. Once she knew Ivan was truly safe, once he was back home and off the Defense Ministry's rolls, she planned to discard the embryos. The war had changed everything, she said. "I just don't have the strength anymore."

The war had once found Khinya in Zhytomir, where she hid in the rushes as the Luftwaffe strafed the city's streets. This new war, where one former Soviet republic invaded another, found her in America, lost somewhere in the fog of the dementia that had crept in during the pandemic. Between fleeting moments of clarity, she looked for Khana-Batya and Moisei, her long-dead parents, separated from them in some kind of chaos, trying desperately to find them, even as a ninety-four-year-old woman. The broadcasts of Russian state television in her American apartment confused her further. One day when I went to see her, I foolishly asked if she'd heard about the recent bombing of Zhytomir.

"Yes," she replied. "The Nazis are bombing it."

My aunt gestured for me to change the subject. "She doesn't understand there's a new war on," she told me afterward. "She thinks it's World War II." The wars all swam together for her. After that, they stopped allowing her to watch the news.

We never got to bury Emma. We knew she wouldn't have wanted to be put in the foreign earth of America, though she admired the country so much. She wanted to be buried where she had lived, in Moscow, near her family and friends, in the soil of a country she had believed in despite all the available evidence. We had a funeral for her outside, in December 2020, just me and my parents, her friends joining by teleconference from around the world. My mother and I decided that, when the pandemic died down, we would go to Moscow, organize a memorial with her scores of friends and admirers, and bury her ashes near Riva and Isaak, at the cemetery near their old home in Ilyinka, the dacha where my mother and I had spent our childhood summers, where Emma and I had written odes to the lilac tree whispering at the attic window.

Emma's death had spared her the shame and horror of seeing her Russia bombing her father's Odessa. But it left her remains stranded. Travel to Moscow now meant risking arrest, for me and likely even for my mother, who has made no secret of her pro-Ukraine stance on her social media accounts. Unable to visit, we couldn't sort through the apartment Emma had left in such a hurry. A neighbor had adopted her cat but all her things were still there: the paintings her friends had made, my grandfather Yura's beloved art books and tomes of poetry, his mother Buzya's fine china. In the summer of 2023, my parents' friend sold the apartment and, before handing over the keys, he rushed us through for a final visit on FaceTime, my mother and I weeping as we sorted through her belongings and saw each beloved corner for the last time. Emma's ashes now sit on my parents' bookshelf, a suburban purgatory she would have hated, as her friends in Moscow flee or get old and die, one by one. Even if we still wanted to have a memorial in Moscow for her when the war ends and Putin is gone, there would be no one left, I think, to attend it.

I dream of Moscow almost every night. The city I loved so much, the place where my grandmother, my mother, my sister, and I were born, where my great-grandmothers reinvented their post-revolutionary selves, where my grandmothers toiled and loved, where my mother snipped tonsils and listened to symphonies, is closed to all of us. None of us can return, not even Emma in her little box. In these dreams, when I arrive in the city of my birth, I cannot recognize it. I get lost in its unfamiliar streets but I don't know whom to call for help. Everyone I know and love, the many people who made the city home, have all left or died. I am a stranger in what is now a foreign place. When I wake, the loss hovers around me for hours, a shadow cast by nothing. It is doubtless the smallest tragedy of this war, but it is mine nonetheless, a Motherland that I have lost, twice in one life.

ACKNOWLEDGMENTS

This book was all my agent Gail Ross's idea. She is the one who had the vision—a book about Russian women and the women in my family—but let me wander in the wilderness until I found my way to it on my own. Thank you, Gail, for making this book happen and for patiently, firmly guiding me, from the seed of an idea through to publication. Thank you also to Howard Yoon, Gail's business partner and my friend, for helping me hone the idea. Thank you to Dan Halpern and Denise Oswald of Ecco, who first believed in the idea enough to buy it, and to Sarah Murphy for taking over the project and seeing it through to the end. Rachel Morris took what was a rough and long draft and made it shine. Thank you, Rachel, for the endless hours you spent on this book and for infusing it with your brilliance. Jenny Volvovski, whose parents were my father's very first friends in college, designed the cover and the family trees. Thank you for giving this book a beautiful skin. Nina Khrushcheva, thank you, not only for sharing your family stories but for helping me think of a title and a narrative structure. Your idea that the Soviet Union's first ladies were a reflection of the country's fate is the spine of this book. Thank you to Thomas Keenan at the Princeton University Library for always finding what I needed. Thank you to Max Avdeev for accompanying me to Medvedevo and documenting one of my last reporting trips for this book—and one of my last trips to Russia—and for making such elegant headshots. And a special thank-you to the Robert B. Silvers Foundation, the Rockefeller Foundation's Bellagio Fellowship, and to Jon Kelly, my partner at Puck, for the space and the resources to finish the damn thing.

Thank you to my beloved friends: to Miriam Elder for reading early drafts and offering wisdom, editorial direction, and encouragement. To Leon Wieseltier for being my champion always, and reading the half-formed early versions. To Milana Mazaeva for her help with research and finding people, for her love and good cheer, and for showing me a world I would have never had access to. To Linda Kinstler for sending me endless JStor articles at any and all hours. To Stephen Kotkin, for unwittingly setting me on this path, and to David Remnick, for giving me the opportunity of a lifetime. To Galina Samoiloyna Khodorkovskaya, my Russian tutor back in my grade school years, who gave me the reading and writing skills I needed to do this. To my tribe of Moscow friends, the people who knew what the hell I was talking about and were there to bounce ideas off of, and some of whose work appears in the bibliography: Susan Glasser and Peter Baker, Amie Ferris-Rotman and Lenka Kabrhelova, Yevgenia Albats and Irina Shikhman, Alex Kliment, Michael Schwirtz, Yana Lantsberg, Anna Makanju, Kate Marsh, and Chris Mewett. To Ayana Elizabeth Johnson, Franklin Leonard, and Boris Khentov for always coming through. And to Lindsay Brillson, Kathy Gilsinan, and Stacey May for their boundless friendship and sisterhood.

Thank you to my family: to Christian for the kind of love that I thought existed only in the storybooks and that I have run out of words to describe. To my in-laws, Pam and Bob, for being so welcoming and supportive. To my sister, Dina, for being my number one fan and, more importantly, the embodiment of our foremothers' most revolutionary aspirations. Thank you especially to my parents, who didn't make me study engineering like other immigrant parents did and allowed me to study Soviet history, even when you knew better and even when you really couldn't afford to fund such frivolous scholastic adventures. Thank you for pushing me, for cheering for me, for loving me in a way that humbles me every day. Thank you to my grandmothers, Khinya and Emma, for sitting with me for hours and hours, for sharing the stories of their lives, and for setting an example.

Thank you especially to Emma, to whom this book is dedicated, who was most excited about this book and who was my first and best research assistant, who went to the Odessa archives and the Moscow archives, and dug through her own; who, knowing, I think, that her time was running out, went through and, without telling me and with an increasingly wobbly hand, labeled all the family photos with the names of endless ancestors, cousins, aunts and uncles, all the people she had kept track of as the keeper of the family history. Babulya, I will try my best to keep it in your stead, to remember and pass on everything you told me. I so wish I had finished this book before you died. I wish that you were here to see it, to hold it, to read it and critique it. I wish you were here to see, too, the beauty that is my own little family, the thing that sprouted and grew while I worked on this book and delayed it, the thing you most wanted for me; that you could have met Christian and held Isaac, who is named after your father, and who will, I'm sure, be a fitting heir for all your dreams.

NOTES

INTRODUCTION
1. Anna Krylova, *Soviet Women in Combat: A History of Violence on the Eastern Front* (Cambridge University Press, 2010), 12.

VALKYRIE OF THE REVOLUTION
1. Barbara Evans Clements, *Daughters of Revolution: A History of Women in the U.S.S.R.* (Harlan Davidson, 1994), ix.
2. When World War I broke out in 1914, St. Petersburg was deemed too Germanic and was renamed to the more Slavic-sounding Petrograd. After Lenin's death in 1924, the city's name was changed to Leningrad.
3. Richard Pipes, *The Russian Revolution* (Knopf, 1990), 272–75.
4. Leon Trotsky, *The History of the Russian Revolution*, trans. by Max Eastman (University of Michigan Press, 1967), 75.
5. Richard Stites, *The Women's Liberation Movement in Russia: Feminism, Nihilism, and Bolshevism, 1860–1930* (Princeton University Press, 1978), 291; Pipes, *Russian Revolution*, 274.
6. Stites, 289–90.
7. Barbara Evans Clements, *Bolshevik Women* (Cambridge University Press, 1997), 29–30.
8. Stites, 273.
9. Clements, *Bolshevik Feminist: The Life of Aleksandra Kollontai* (Indiana University Press, 1979), 103–4.
10. Clements, *Bolshevik Feminist*, 109.
11. Clements, 16.
12. Stites, 99–114.
13. Clements, 20.
14. Stites, 235.
15. August Bebel, *Woman Under Socialism*, trans. Daniel de Leon (Schocken, 1971), 79.
16. Bebel, *Woman Under Socialism*, 87.
17. Bebel, 97.
18. Clements, *Bolshevik Feminist*, 51.
19. Stites, 263.
20. Stites, 252.
21. Elizabeth A. Wood, *The Baba and the Comrade: Gender and Politics in Revolutionary Russia* (Indiana University Press, 1997), 16–17.
22. Clements, *Bolshevik Feminist*, 31.
23. Stites, 182.
24. Clements, *Bolshevik Feminist*, 41.
25. Stites, 160.
26. Stites, 160.
27. Igor Kon, *Seksualnaya kultura v Rossii: Ocherk istorii russkoy seksualnoy kultury s dokhristianskikh vremen do sovremennosti* (Izdatelstvo AST, 2019), 93.
28. Stites, 164–65.
29. Clements, *Bolshevik Feminist*, 45.
30. Clements, 65.
31. Stites, 266.
32. Stites, 351.
33. Clements, *Bolshevik Feminist*, 70.
34. Clements, 73.
35. Stites, 350.
36. Clements, *Bolshevik Feminist*, 46.
37. Wood, *Baba and Comrade*, 16–21.
38. Wood, 38.
39. Wood, 38.

INESSA
1. Robert H. McNeal, *Bride of the Revolution: Krupskaya and Lenin*

(University of Michigan Press, 1972), 140.
2. Clements, *Bolshevik Feminist*, 14–15.
3. Ralph Carter Elwood, *Inessa Armand: Revolutionary and Feminist* (Cambridge University Press, 1992), 23.
4. Clements, *Bolshevik Feminist*, 41.
5. Wood, *Baba and the Comrade*, 20–21.
6. Elwood, *Inessa Armand*, 28–30.
7. Elwood, 30–31.
8. Kon, *Seksualnaya kultura*, 96–101.
9. Kon, 99.
10. Stites, 183.
11. Kon, *Seksualnaya kultura*, 107–8.
12. Elwood, *Inessa Armand*, 31–32.
13. McNeal, *Bride of Revolution*, 137.
14. Elwood, *Inessa Armand*, 54.
15. McNeal, *Bride of Revolution*, 16–23.
16. McNeal, 29.
17. McNeal, 52.
18. McNeal, 56.
19. Elwood, *Inessa Armand*, 125.
20. Elwood, 119.
21. Jane McDermid and Anya Hillyard, "In Lenin's Shadow: Nadezhda Krupskaya and the Bolshevik Revolution," in *Reinterpreting Revolutionary Russia: Essays in Honour of James D. White*, ed. Ian D. Thatcher (Palgrave Macmillan, 2006), 158.
22. Stites, 240.
23. McNeal, *Bride of Revolution*, 51.
24. Clements, *Bolshevik Women*, 110.
25. McDermid and Hillyard, "In Lenin's Shadow," 151.
26. McNeal, *Bride of Revolution*, 101.

A FAIRY-TALE COUNTRY
1. Clements, *Bolshevik Feminist*, 120.
2. Clements, *Bolshevik Feminist*, 122–27.
3. Clements, 129.
4. "Prikaz po Narodnomy Komissariatu gosudarstvennogo prizreniya," *Izvestia*, February 22, 1918. Princeton University Archives.
5. Stites, 369.
6. Wood, *Baba and Comrade*, 50.
7. Wood, 130.

8. Elwood, *Inessa Armand*, 240.
9. Wood, *Baba and Comrade*, 74–75.
10. Wood, 84.
11. Elwood, *Inessa Armand*, 249.
12. Clements, *Bolshevik Women*, 134–40.
13. Clements, 130.
14. Stites, 325.
15. Stites, 339.
16. Wood, *Baba and Comrade*, 138.
17. Wood, 100.
18. Stephen Kotkin, *Stalin: Paradoxes of Power, 1878–1928* (Penguin Press, 2014), 284–86.
19. Geoffrey Hosking, *First Socialist Society: A History of the Soviet Union from Within*, 2nd enlarged ed. (Harvard University Press, 1996), 54–56.
20. Kotkin, 247.
21. Pipes, *Russian Revolution*, 806.
22. McNeal, *Bride of Revolution*, 208.
23. Pipes, *Russian Revolution*, 807.
24. Pipes, 807.
25. Pipes, 807.
26. Kotkin, 285.
27. McNeal, *Bride of Revolution*, 208.
28. Pipes, *Russian Revolution*, 818–22.
29. Kotkin, 287.

RIVA
1. Oleg Budnitsky, "Rossiyskie evrei v gody voyny i revolyutsii,1914–1920," *Istoria evreyskogo naroda v Rossii: Ot revolyutsii 1917 goda do raspada Sovetskogo Soyuza*, ed. Michael Beizer (Most Kultury, 2017).
2. Peter Kenez, *Red Advance, White Defeat: Civil War in South Russia, 1919–1920* (New Academia Publishing, 2004), 166.
3. Kenez, 168–69.
4. Isaac Babel, "Dnevnik 1920 goda," in *Sobranie sochinenii v trekh tomakh*, vol. 2 (Azbuka-Atticus Press, 2012), 231.
5. Babel, "Dnevnik 1920 goda," 271.
6. Babel, 342–43.
7. E. S. Davidson and L. T. Benjamin, "A

History of the Child Study Movement in America," in J. A. Glover and R. R. Ronning, eds., *Historical Foundations of Educational Psychology: Perspectives on Individual Differences* (Springer, 1987), 41–60.
8. Hosking, *First Socialist Society*, 74.
9. Richard Stites, *The Women's Liberation Movement in Russia: Feminism, Nihilism, and Bolshevism, 1860–1930* (Princeton University Press, 1978), 397.
10. Stites, *Women's Liberation Movement*, 397.

THE FIRST FIRST LADY

1. McNeal, *Bride of Revolution*, 183–84.
2. Clements, *Bolshevik Women*, 192.
3. McNeal, *Bride of Revolution*, 207.
4. McNeal, 194.
5. Wood, *Baba and Comrade*, 104.
6. Wood, 105.
7. Elwood, *Inessa Armand*, 249.
8. Clements, *Bolshevik Feminist*, 204.
9. Stites, *Women's Liberation Movement*, 181.
10. Stites, 264.
11. Stites, 181.
12. Wood, *Baba and Comrade*, 107.
13. Wood, 108.
14. Wendy Z. Goldman, *Women, the State, and Revolution: Soviet Family Policy and Social Life, 1917–1936* (Cambridge University Press, 1993), 255–56.
15. Elwood, *Inessa Armand*, 1–2.
16. Elwood, 186.
17. Elwood, 3.
18. Clements, *Bolshevik Women*, 222.
19. Clements, *Bolshevik Feminist*, 183.
20. Kotkin, *Stalin: Paradoxes of Power*, 385.
21. Clements, *Bolshevik Feminist*, 195.
22. Clements, 216.
23. McNeal, *Bride of Revolution*, 215.
24. Kotkin, 491.
25. Kotkin, 425.
26. Kotkin, 488.
27. Kotkin, 499.
28. Kotkin, 472.
29. Kotkin, 498.
30. Kotkin, 418–19.
31. McNeal, *Bride of Revolution*, 238.
32. Eliot Borenstein, *Men Without Women: Masculinity and Revolution in Russian Fiction, 1917–1929* (Duke University Press, 2000), 7.
33. Stites, *Women's Liberation Movement*, 370.
34. Stites, 367.
35. Stites, 360.
36. Borenstein, *Men Without Women*, 13.

BUZYA

1. Not to be confused with Eva Weisser, my great-grandmother Riva Weisser's youngest sister. Apparently, Eva was a popular name among Jewish families in turn-of-the-twentieth-century Ukraine.

NADYA

1. Stephen Kotkin, *Stalin: Waiting for Hitler, 1929–1941* (Penguin Books, 2018), 110.
2. Stephen Kotkin, *Stalin: Paradoxes of Power, 1878–1928* (Penguin Press, 2014), 193.
3. Svetlana Alliluyeva, *Dvadtsat' pisem drugu*. http://lib.ru/MEMUARY/ALLILUEWA/letters.txt.
4. Kotkin, *Stalin: Paradoxes of Power*, 115.
5. Robert Conquest, *The Great Terror: A Reassessment* (Oxford University Press, 1990), 58.
6. Irina Gogua, "Semeynye istorii," *Ogonek*, March 13, 1997; Nina Khrushcheva, interview with the author, July 2018.
7. Kotkin, *Paradoxes of Power*, 264.
8. Kotkin, *Paradoxes of Power*, 301, 413.
9. Kotkin, *Paradoxes of Power*, 467.
10. Nikita Khrushchev, *Khrushchev Remembers*, trans. and ed. Strobe Talbott (Little, Brown, 1970), 43–44.
11. Gogua, "Semeynye istorii."
12. Svetlana Alliluyeva, *Dvadtsat' pisem*

drugu (1967), http://lib.ru/MEMUARY/ALLILUEWA/letters.txt.
13. Kotkin, *Stalin: Waiting*, 109.
14. Svetlana Alliluyeva, *Only One Year: A Memoir*, trans. Paul Chavchavadze (HarperCollins, 1969), vi.
15. Kotkin, *Stalin: Waiting*, 109.
16. Gogua, "Family Stories."
17. Alliluyeva, *Dvadtsat' pisem*.
18. Alliluyeva, *Dvadtsat' pisem*.
19. Kotkin, *Stalin: Waiting*, 110.
20. Alliluyeva, *Dvadtsat' pisem*.
21. Kotkin, *Stalin: Waiting*, 111.
22. Kotkin, 525.

TRAITORS TO THE MOTHERLAND

1. Vladimira Uborevich, *14 pisem Elene Sergeevne Bulgakovoy*, ed. Yuri Kantor (Vremya, 2009). Courtesy of the Sakharov Center. https://www.sakharov-center.ru/asfcd/auth/?t=page&num=13136#t26.
2. Alliluyeva, *Dvadtsat' pisem drugu*.
3. Conquest, *Great Terror*, 37–45.
4. Conquest, 73.
5. Conquest, 446.
6. Kotkin, *Stalin: Waiting*, 603.
7. Kotkin, 450.
8. Kotkin, 599.
9. Kotkin, 496.
10. Kotkin, 437.
11. Anne Applebaum, *Gulag: A History* (Anchor, 2004), 583.
12. Kotkin, *Stalin: Waiting*, 488.
13. Kotkin, 430.
14. Conquest, *Great Terror*, 68, 235.
15. "Operativnyy prikaz narodnogo komissara vnutrenikh del No. 00486 'ob operatsii po reprissirovaniu zhen i detey izmennikov rodiny, 15 avgusta 1937,'" *Deti gulaga: 1918–1956*, dokumenty, Mezhdunarodny Fond "Demokratia," Moscow (2002), 234–36.
16. Conquest, 307.
17. Conquest, 127.
18. Applebaum, *Gulag*, 310.
19. Eugenia Ginzburg, *Krutoi marshrut:* *Khronika vremyon kul'ta lichnosti* (Agenstvo FTM, 2018), 356.
20. William Taubman, *Khrushchev: The Man and His Era* (W. W. Norton, 2003), 246.
21. Applebaum, *Gulag*, 307–33.
22. *Deti Gulaga*, 81.
23. Applebaum, *Gulag*, 319.
24. M. A. Solomonik, "Zapiski raskulachenoy," *Deti gulaga*, 131.
25. Ginzburg, *Krutoi marshrut*, 432.
26. Ginzburg, 439.
27. Applebaum, *Gulag*, 323.
28. Elena Shmaraeva, "Gulag dlya samykh malen'kikh," Mediazona, September 26, 2014.
29. Khava Volovich, "Vospominaniya." https://topliba.com/books/589526.
30. Vladimira Uborevich, interviewee, "Film Two," Mira. Doch' Komandarma Uborevicha, by Vladimir Meletin, *Kultura*, January 29, 2012. http://tvkultura.ru/video/show/brand_id/37545/episode_id/229173/video_id/229173/.

WAR

1. Blavatnik Archive, http://www.bafdigital.org/viewpdf/24691/rus.
2. Krylova, *Soviet Women*, 89–90.
3. Blavatnik Archive, http://www.bafdigital.org/veteran/5255.
4. Svetlana Alexievich, *U voiny ne zhenskoe litso* (Vremya, 2016), 107.
5. Alexievich, *U voiny*, 75.
6. Krylova, *Soviet Women*, 91.
7. Stites, 397.
8. Raisa Orlova, *Vospominanie o neproshedshem* vremeni, http://avtorsha.com/text_336.html.
9. Krylova, *Soviet Women*, 51–53.
10. Krylova, 115–16.
11. Clements, *Bolshevik Women*, 177.
12. Wood, *Baba and Comrade*, 53.
13. Wood, 53–54.
14. Wood, 55.
15. Clements, *Bolshevik Women*, 172–75.

16. Stites, *Women's Liberation Movement*, 319.
17. Clements, *Bolshevik Women*, 174.
18. Stites, *Women's Liberation Movement*, 318.
19. Stites, 321.
20. Clements, *Bolshevik Women*, 149.
21. Stites, *Women's Liberation Movement*, 321.
22. Wood, *Baba and Comrade*, 52.
23. Wood, 56.
24. Clements, *Bolshevik Women*, 178.
25. Wood, *Baba and Comrade*, 52.
26. Stites, *Women's Liberation Movement*, 322.
27. Alexievich, *U Voiny*, 39, 59, 203, 231.
28. Krylova, *Soviet Women*, 95.
29. Krylova, 123; Anne Noggle, *A Dance with Death: Soviet Airwomen in World War II* (Texas A&M University Press, 1994), 15–17.
30. Alexievich, *U voiny*, 85.
31. Barbara Alperin Engel, *Women in Russia: 1700–2000* (Cambridge University Press, 2004), 215.
32. Engel, *Women in Russia*, 215.
33. Engle, 215.
34. Krylova, *Soviet Women*, 163.
35. Martin Pegler, foreword to Lyudmila Pavlichenko, *Lady Death: The Memoirs of Stalin's Sniper*, trans. David Foreman; ed. Alla Begunova (Greenhill Books, 2018).
36. Krylova, *Soviet Women*, 116–17.
37. Noggle, *Dance with Death*, 20.
38. Alexievich, *U voiny*, 148.
39. Alexievich, 45–46.
40. Alexievich, 93.
41. Krylova, *Soviet Women*, 274–75.
42. Krylova, 12.
43. Asma Gindina, full, unedited interview, 2013, Blavatnik Archive, https://www.blavatnikarchive.org/item/2173.
44. Antony Beevor, *Stalingrad* (Penguin, 2007), 591.
45. Ida Firer, letter sent to family, February 21, 1943, Blavatnik Archive,

https://www.blavatnikarchive.org/item/13026.

THE HOME FRONT

1. Hosking, *First Socialist Society*, 273.
2. Kotkin, *Stalin: Waiting*, 893.
3. Kotkin, 901.
4. Constantine Pleshakov, *Stalin's Folly: The Tragic First Ten Days of World War II on the Eastern Front* (Houghton Mifflin, 2006), 6.
5. Pleshakov, *Stalin's Folly*, 9.
6. Krylova, *Soviet Women*, 115.
7. Krylova, 256–59.
8. Vasily Grossman, *A Writer at War: A Soviet Journalist with the Red Army, 1941–1945*, edited and translated by Antony Beevor and Luba Vinogradova (Vintage Books, 2007), 259.
9. Christopher Browning, *Ordinary Men: Reserve Battalion 101 and the Final Solution in Poland*, rev. ed. (Harper Perennial, 2017), 61.
10. Browning, 58–70.
11. Yehuda Shohat and Elad Zeret, "Himmler's Letters Revealed: 'I'm Going to Auschwitz. Kisses,'" Ynetnews.com, January 26, 2014, https://www.ynetnews.com/articles/0,7340,L-4481014,00.html.
12. Browning, *Ordinary Men*, 49.
13. Grossman, *A Writer at War*, 251.
14. Leonid Kogan, "Holokost na Zhitomire," https://zwiahel.ucoz.ru/novograd/evrei/Kogan_04_01_13.pdf.
15. Yad Vashem, https://collections.yadvashem.org/en/untold-stories/killing-site/14626677.
16. "Nazis Drive Jews in Ukraine 'to Unknown Destination'; Kiev Made 'Judenrein,'" Jewish Telegraphic Agency, October 21, 1941.

VICTORY

1. Krylova, *Soviet Women*, 276.
2. Krylova, 3.
3. Stites, 391.
4. Krylova, *Soviet Women*, 12.

5. Alexievich, *U voiny*, 255.
6. *A Date with War*, series 4, https://www.youtube.com/watch?v=oDXpsR40hoU.
7. Alexievich, *U voiny*, 256.
8. Alexievich, 135.
9. Massimo Livi-Bacci, "On the Human Costs of Collectivization in the Soviet Union," *Population and Development Review* 19, no. 4 (1993): 743–66, www.jstor.org/stable/2938412; Applebaum, *Gulag*, 583.
10. Jennifer Utrata, *Women Without Men: Single Mothers and Family Change in the New Russia* (Cornell University Press, 2015), 25.
11. Boris Urlanis, *Wars and Population* (Progress Publishers, 1971), 285.
12. Mie Nakachi, "N. S. Khrushchev and the 1944 Soviet Family Law: Politics, Reproduction, and Language," *East European Politics and Societies* 20, no. 1 (February 2006): 40.
13. Nakachi, "N. S. Khrushchev."

SVETLANA

1. Alliluyeva, *Dvadzat' pisem*.
2. Rosemary Sullivan, *Stalin's Daughter: The Extraordinary and Tumultuous Life of Svetlana Alliluyeva* (Harper, 2015), 84.
3. Alliluyeva, *Only One Year*, 212.
4. Alliluyeva, vi.
5. Alliluyeva, vi.
6. Sullivan, *Stalin's Daughter*, 84.
7. Khrushchev, *Khrushchev Remembers*, 292.
8. Alliluyeva, interview with Nicholas Thompson, March 29, 2008.
9. Khrushchev, *Khrushchev Remembers*, 292.
10. Sullivan, *Stalin's Daughter*, 275.
11. Alliluyeva, *Dvadtzat' pisem*.
12. Khrushchev, *Khrushchev Remembers*, 289–90.
13. Alliluyeva, *Dvadzat' pisem*.

BERIA'S HOUSE

1. Khrushchev, *Khrushchev Remembers*, 338.
2. Oleg Mozokhin, *Politburo i delo Beria. Sbornik dokumentov* (Kuchkovo Pole, 2012), 496–500.
3. Mozokhin, 500–502.
4. Mozokhin, 101–102.
5. Kotkin, *Stalin: Waiting*, 549.
6. Alliluyeva, *Only One Year*, vi.
7. Mozokhin, 388.
8. "Life Has Been a Drama to Russian-Born Actress," *Chicago Tribune*, June 21, 1985.
9. Irina Zaichik, "Tatiana Okunevskaya: Chernye rozy moyey zhizni," *Ogonek*, May 4, 1997.
10. V. N. Haustov, ed., *Delo Beria: Prigovor obzhalovaniiu ne podlezhit* (Mezhdunarodny fond "Demokratia," 2012), 18–19.
11. Haustov, *Delo Beria*, 606.
12. Haustov, 606.
13. Haustov, 18–19, 189; Mozokhin, 34.
14. *Beria: Stalin's Creature*, directed and written by Helen Bettinson, BBC, 1994; Zaichik, "Tatiana Okunevskaya."
15. Helen Womack, "Beria's Mistress Comes Out of the Closet," *Independent*, July 25, 1993.
16. Amy Knight, *Beria: Stalin's First Lieutenant* (Princeton University Press, 1995), 97.
17. Mozokhin, 500.

HERO MOTHERS

1. Alliluyeva, *Only One Year*, 161.
2. Svetlana says she was given the speech a week before it was read at the Congress, though, at the time, the speech was still being written and rewritten. Khrushchev fiddled with the speech right up to the day he delivered it (Taubman, *Khrushchev*, 277–82). It's unclear if Svetlana was given an early draft or the internal report on which the

speech was based, if she was allowed to read the speech shortly after it was delivered or before it made it into the press—or if she made up this scene entirely.
3. Alliluyeva, *Only One Year*, 161.
4. Nina P. Khrushcheva, "Mama's Notebooks," *Memoirs of Nikita Khrushchev*, vol. 2: *Reformer (1945–1964)*, ed. Sergei Khrushchev; trans. George Shriver and Stephen Shenfield (Pennsylvania State University Press, 2006).
5. Nina Khrushcheva, interview with the author.
6. Taubman, *Khrushchev*, 19–24.
7. Nina L. Khrushcheva, *The Lost Khrushchev: A Journey into the Gulag of the Russian Mind* (Tate Publishing, 2014), 46.
8. Khrushcheva, *Lost Khrushchev*, 48.
9. Taubman, *Khrushchev*, 285.
10. Taubman, 306–10.
11. N. S. Khrushchev, "O kulte lichnosti i ego posledstviakh: Doklad Pervogo sekretarya TsK KPSS tov. Khrushcheva N. S. XX s'ezdu Kommunisticheskoi partii Sovetskogo Soyuza, 25 fevralya 1956" (Izvestia TsK KPSS, 1989), no. 3.
12. "Rech' tovarischa N. S. Khrushcheva na sobranii komsomoltsev i molodezhi g. Moskvy, iz'yavivshykh zhelanie poekhat' rabotat' na tselinnye zemli, 7 yanvarya 1955 goda," *Izvestia*, January 8, 1955.
13. Mie Nakachi, *Replacing the Dead* (Oxford University Press, 2020), 170.
14. Taubman, *Khrushchev*, 305.
15. "Ukaz Prezidiuma verkhovnogo soveta SSSR," *Pravda*, July 9, 1944.
16. Nakachi, "N. S. Khrushchev," 41.
17. Nakachi, 45.
18. Nakachi, 49.
19. "Ukaz Prezidiuma verkhovnogo soveta SSSR," *Pravda*, July 9, 1944.
20. Utrata, *Women Without Men*, 23; and Nakachi, "N. S. Khrushchev," 47.
21. Utrata, *Women Without Men*, 23.
22. Nakachi, "N. S. Khrushchev," 64.
23. Utrata, *Women Without Men*, 28.
24. Igor Kon, *Klubnichka na beryozke: Seksual'naya kul'tura v Rossii* (Vremya, 2010), 276.
25. Utrata, *Women Without Men*, 26.
26. *Pravda*, July 12, 1944.
27. Nakachi, "N. S. Khrushchev," 65.
28. Kon, *Klubnichka na beryozke*, 260–61.
29. Nakachi, "N. S. Khrushchev," 65.
30. Utrata, *Women Without Men*, 36.
31. S. Marshak et al., "Pismo v redaktsiu: Eto oprovergnuto zhiznyu," *Literaturnaya gazeta*, October 9, 1956.
32. Stites, *Women's Liberation Movement*, 263.
33. Taubman, *Khrushchev*, 59.
34. Natalia Lebina, *Muzhchina i zhenshchina: Telo, moda, kul'tura, SSSR - ottepel'*. Novoe literaturnoe obozrenie, 2018, 34.
35. Khrushcheva, *Lost Khrushchev*, 48.
36. Taubman, *Khrushchev*, 209.
37. Bucher, "Struggling to Survive: Soviet Women in the Postwar Years," *Journal of Women's History* 12, no. 1 (2000): 145.
38. Taubman, *Khrushchev*, 265.
39. Bucher, "Struggling to Survive," 149.
40. Taubman, *Khrushchev*, 421.
41. "Beyond the Doc: Khrushchev," *American Experience*, PBS, November 18, 2014, https://www.pbs.org/video/american-experience-beyond-doc-khrushchev/?continuousplayautoplay=true.
42. *Izvestia*, March 29, 1960; *Pravda*, March 24, 1960; *Pravda*, July 4, 1963; *Pravda*, May 18, 1964; *Pravda*, April 1, 1960; *Gudok*, August 29, 1964; *Pravda*, July 22, 1964; *Pravda*, April 8, 1964; and *Izvestia*, March 25, 1960.
43. "Cold War First Lady Nina Khrushcheva Sends a Message for World Peace," Annotations: The NEH Preservation Project, WNYC, May 26,

2016, https://www.wnyc.org/story/cold-war-first-lady-nina-khrushcheva-sends-message-world-peace/.

KHINYA AND EMMA

1. Taubman, *Khrushchev*, 179.
2. Utrata, *Women Without Men*, 25.
3. Tony Judt, *Postwar: A History of Europe Since 1945* (Penguin, 2005), 19.
4. Stalin had rejected a proposal brought to him in 1944 by the Jewish Anti-Fascist Committee to create a Jewish republic in Crimea, inside the Soviet Union. Among other considerations, Stalin apparently felt it would create a beachhead for Zionism and, therefore, American influence. Joshua Rubinstein, *The Last Days of Stalin* (Yale University Press, 2016), 19–25; and Khrushchev, *Khrushchev Remembers*, 261.
5. Yuri Slezkine, *The Jewish Century* (Princeton University Press, 2004), 297; Rubinstein, *Last Days*, 41.
6. Rubinstein, 46.
7. Alliluyeva, *Dvatzat' pisem*.
8. Stalin had already killed the committee's head, Solomon Mikhoels, the legendary actor of Moscow's Yiddish Theater. In January of that year, he had been lured to Belarus, where he was murdered and then run over by a truck to make it look like a hit-and-run. Khrushchev, *Khrushchev Remembers*, 261–62.
9. Khrushchev, 260; Taubman, *Khrushchev*, 217.
10. Rubinstein, *Last Days*, 94.
11. Gal Beckerman, *When They Come for Us, We'll Be Gone: The Epic Struggle to Save Soviet Jewry* (Houghton Mifflin Harcourt, 2010), 94.
12. Kon, *Klubnichka na beryozke*, 268.

LONELY MOTHERS

1. Bucher, "Struggling to Survive," 137.
2. Boris Urlanis, "Bezotzovshchina," *Literaturnaya gazeta*, January 7, 1970.
3. Bucher, "Struggling to Survive," 144.
4. Natasha Fedorenko, "Otkuda vzyalsya spisok professii, zapreshchennykh dlya zhenshchin, i chto s nim budet teper'," *Theory & Practice*, July 8, 2019.
5. Utrata, *Women Without Men*, 25.
6. "Vremya byt' muzhchinoy," *Literaturnaya gazeta*, October 15, 1969.
7. Igor Kon, "Zachem nuzhny otzy?" *Literaturnaya gazeta*, February 28, 1973.
8. "Vremya byt' muzhchinoy," *Literaturnaya gazeta*, October 15, 1969.
9. Boris Urlanis, "Beregite muzhchin!" *Literaturnaya gazeta*, July 24, 1968.
10. Urlanis, "Beregite muzhchin!"

NOMENKLATURA

1. Taubman, *Khrushchev*, 621.
2. Interview with Nina L. Khrushcheva.
3. Interview with N. L. Khrushcheva; N. P. Khrushcheva, *Mama's Notebooks*; and Taubman, *Khrushchev*, 622.
4. Interview with Nina L. Khrushcheva.
5. Larisa Vasilieva, *Kremlin Wives*, trans. Cathy Porter (Arcade Publishing), 1994.
6. Luba Brezhneva, *The World I Left Behind: Pieces of a Past*, trans. by Geoffrey Polk (Random House, 1995), 311–12.
7. James P. Gallagher, "The Sad Fall of Brezhnev's Widow," *Chicago Tribune*, April 30, 1995.
8. Yevgeni Zhirnov, "Peredal emu gazetu v kotoroy lezhali obligatsii," *Kommersant Vlast'*, December 10, 2012.
9. Brezhneva, *World I Left*, 155–56.
10. Vasilyeva, *Kremlin Wives*, 283.
11. Vasilieva, 212.
12. Vasilieva, 212, 215.
13. Alliluyeva, *Only One Year*, 51.
14. Alliluyeva, 165.

15. Sullivan, *Stalin's Daughter*, 360.
16. Sullivan, 344.
17. Sullivan, 62.
18. Alliluyeva, *Only One Year*, 85.
19. Brezhneva, *World I Left*, 314.
20. Brezhneva, 312.
21. Brezhneva, 354–58.
22. "Belaya magia dlya chernogo mersedesa," *Novy vzlgyad*, February 15, 1992.
23. Yevgeni Dodolev, *Delo Galiny Brezhnevoy: Brillianty dlya printsessy* (Algoritm, 2013), 3–5.
24. Dodolev, *Delo Galiny Brezhnevoy*, 9.
25. Brezhneva, *World I Left*, 354.
26. Vasilieva, *Kremlin Wives*, 210; Dodolev, *Delo Galiny Brezhnevoy*; and Gallagher, "Sad Fall."
27. Vasilieva, *Kremlin Wives*, 215.
28. Gallagher, "Sad Fall."
29. Alliluyeva, *Only One Year*, 261.

OLGA

1. Hosking, *First Socialist Society*, 436.
2. Beckerman, *When They Come*, 95.
3. Hosking, *First Socialist Society*, 431.
4. Beckerman, *When They Come*, 95.
5. Anna Cavalli, "Buntarka ot meditsyny: Kak Nadezhda Suslova stala pervoy zhenshchinoy-vrachom v Rossii," *Forbes Woman*, February 9, 2021.
6. Stites, *Women's Liberation Movement*, 147n.
7. Stites, 87.
8. Jeni Harden, "'Mother Russia' at Work: Gender Divisions in the Medical Profession," *European Journal of Women's Studies* 8, no. 2 (2001): 181–99.
9. By 1989, only 6 percent of Soviet women were single by the age of thirty. Utrata, *Women Without Men*, 33.

PERESTROIKA

1. Boris Doktorov, "Interview with Tatyana Zaslavskaya," *Sotsiologicheskii zhurnal* 3 (2007), https://cdclv.unlv.edu/archives/Interviews/zaslavskaya_07.html.
2. David Remnick, "Perestroika Nurtured at Siberian Think Tank," *Washington Post*, February 10, 1990.

RAISA

1. Margaret Thatcher's recollections in *Raisa Gorbacheva: Shtrikhi k portretu*, Gorbachev Foundation, https://www.gorby.ru/activity/projects/shtrihi_k_portretu/page_6/.
2. William Taubman, *Gorbachev: His Life and Times* (W. W. Norton, 2017), 253.
3. Raisa Gorbacheva, *Ya nadeyus'* . . . (Kniga, 1991), 72.
4. Gorbacheva, *Ya nadeyus'*, 72.
5. Mikhail Gorbachev, *Memoirs* (Doubleday, 1996), 165; and Taubman, *Gorbachev*, 212.
6. Taubman, *Gorbachev*, 282.
7. Felicity Barringer, "Soviet Tongues Wag over Raisa Gorbachev," *New York Times*, December 2, 1987.
8. Gorbacheva, *Ya nadeyus'*, 70–71.
9. Gorbachev, *Memoirs*, 186.
10. Gorbachev, 25–26.
11. Nina Mamardashvili's recollections in *Raisa Gorbacheva: Shtrikhi k portretu* (Fond Gorbacheva, 2009).
12. Gorbachev, *Memoirs*, 49–50.
13. Taubman, *Gorbachev*, 95.
14. Nina Mamardashvili's recollections in *Raisa Gorbacheva, Shtrikhi k portretu*.
15. Taubman, *Gorbachev*, 97.
16. Gorbacheva, *Ya nadeyus'*, 63.
17. Gorbachev, *Memoirs*, 52.
18. Taubman, *Gorbachev*, 100.
19. Gorbacheva, *Ya nadeyus'*, 85.
20. Gorbacheva, 94.
21. Gorbacheva, 93.
22. Gorbacheva, 93.
23. Gorbacheva, 96.
24. Gorbacheva, 94.
25. Gorbacheva, 95.
26. Gorbacheva, 89–90.
27. Gorbachev, *Memoirs*, 104.

28. Utrata, *Women Without Men*, 21.
29. Gorbacheva, *Ya nadeyus'*, 101.
30. Seth Mydans, "Westerners Get Rare View of Kremlin Wives," *New York Times*, March 10, 1985.
31. Gorbacheva, *Ya nadeyus'*, 119.
32. Taubman, *Gorbachev*, 215; and Gorbachev, *Memoirs*, 122.
33. Taubman, *Gorbachev*, 491.
34. Nancy Reagan with William Novak, *My Turn: The Memoirs of Nancy Reagan* (Random House, 1989), 159.
35. Reagan, *My Turn*, 161.
36. Taubman, *Gorbachev*, 514.
37. Reagan, *My Turn*, 157.
38. Gorbachev, *Memoirs*, 447.
39. Rick Perlstein, *Before the Storm: Barry Goldwater and the Unmaking of the American Consensus* (Nation Books, 2009), 122.
40. Taubman, *Gorbachev*, 364.
41. Reagan, *My Turn*, 187–88.
42. Reagan, 169.
43. Gorbacheva, *Ya nadeyus'*, 89.
44. Interview with the author, September 27, 2019.
45. Susanne M. Schafer, "Nancy, Raisa in 'Mexican Standoff,'" Associated Press, June 1, 1988.

RECKONING

1. Peter Grose, "Kosygin Calls Mrs. Alliluyeva 'Morally Unstable' and 'Sick,'" *New York Times*, June 26, 1967.
2. *Izvestia*, June 2, 1967.
3. *Izvestia*, July 1, 1967.
4. Alliluyeva, *Only One Year*, 340.
5. Svetlana Alliluyeva, *Dalekaya muzyka docheri Stalina* (Alistorus, 1983), 92.
6. Sullivan, *Stalin's Daughter*, 284; and Alliluyeva, *Only One Year*, 338.
7. Sullivan, *Stalin's Daughter*, 288.
8. "Son Says He Wrote to Mrs. Alliluyeva Denouncing Exile," *New York Times*, May 23, 1967.
9. David Binder, "Recollections on Mrs. Alliluyeva Printed in a German Magazine," *New York Times*, August 19, 1967.
10. Alliluyeva, *Only One Year*, 339.
11. Alliluyeva, *Dalekaya muzyka*, 10–11.
12. Sullivan, *Stalin's Daughter*, 278.
13. Alliluyeva, *Dalekaya muzyka*, 41.
14. Alliluyeva, *Dalekaya muzyka*, 44.
15. Alliluyeva, 44.
16. Alliluyeva, 55.
17. Sullivan, *Stalin's Daughter*, 351.
18. Alliluyeva, *Dalekaya muzyka*, 50.
19. Sullivan, *Stalin's Daughter*, 347.
20. Alliluyeva, *Dalekaya muzyka*, 48–49.
21. Sullivan, *Stalin's Daughter*, 345.
22. Sullivan, 361.
23. Sullivan, 352.
24. Sullivan, 354.
25. Sullivan, 363.
26. Alliluyeva, *Dalekaya muzyka*, 96.
27. Alliluyeva, 84.
28. Sullivan, *Stalin's Daughter*, 384–85.
29. Sullivan, 437.
30. Sullivan, 446.
31. Sullivan, 455.
32. Sullivan, 470–71.

END OF THE FAIRY TALE

1. "Wellesley College Commencement," C-SPAN, June 1, 1990, https://www.c-span.org/video/?12521-1/barbara-bush-commencement-speech-wellesley-college-1990.
2. Fox Butterfield, "At Wellesley, a Furor over Barbara Bush," *New York Times*, May 4, 1990.
3. Donnie Radcliffe, "Barbara Bush, Wowing Wellesley," *Washington Post*, June 2, 1990.
4. "Commencement Speakers: Barbara Bush, Raisa Gorbachev," Wellesley College, 1990, https://www.wellesley.edu/events/commencement/archives/1990commencement/commencementaddress.
5. Barbara Bush's recollections in *Raisa Gorbacheva: Shtrikhi k portretu*.
6. Stephen Kotkin, *Steeltown, USSR* (University of California Press, 1992), 68.

7. Taubman, *Gorbachev*, 503.
8. Taubman, *Gorbachev*, 501–2.
9. Francine du Plessix Gray, *Soviet Women: Walking the Tightrope* (Doubleday, 1990), 17.
10. Kotkin, *Steeltown, USSR*, 133.
11. Chanie Rosenberg, *Women and Perestroika: Present, Past and Future for Women in Russia* (Bookmarks, 1989), 9, 15.
12. Rosenberg, *Women and Perestroika*, 31.
13. Kerry McCuaig, "Effects of Perestroika and Glasnost on Women," *Canadian Woman Studies* 10, no. 4 (1989): 11–14.
14. Du Plessix Gray, *Soviet Women*, 37–38.
15. Amy Rankin-Williams, "Post-Soviet Contraceptive Practices and Abortion Rates in St. Petersburg, Russia," *Health Care for Women International* 22, no. 8 (2001): 699–710.
16. Rankin-Williams, "Post-Soviet Contraceptive Practices," 700; and Du Plessix Gray, *Soviet Women*, 20.
17. Kotkin, *Steeltown, USSR*, 132.
18. Anna Temkina, "The Gynaecologist's Gaze: The Inconsistent Medicalisation of Contraception in Contemporary Russia," *Europe-Asia Studies* 67, no. 10 (2015): 1527–46.
19. Rankin-Williams, "Post-Soviet Contraceptive Practices," 701.
20. Kotkin, *Steeltown, USSR*, 131.
21. Utrata, *Women Without Men*, 34.
22. Mary Buckley, "Glasnost and the Woman Question," in *Women and Society in Russia and the Soviet Union*, edited by Linda Edmondson (Cambridge University Press, 1992), 208; Kotkin, *Steeltown, USSR*, 131.
23. Yevgenia Albats, "Reporter poluchil zadanie: Rodit'!" *Moskovskie novosti*, July 17, 1988; and Yevgenia Albats, "Reporter zadanie vypolnila," *Moskovskie novosti*, January 1, 1989.
24. Kotkin, *Steeltown, USSR*, 63.
25. *Pravda* 175, June 24, 1987; *Gudok* 145, June 24, 1987.
26. T. I. Zaslavskaya, "Zhenshchina v semye," Levada Center Archives, December 20, 1989.
27. T. I. Zaslavskaya, "Obshchestvennoe mnenie o problemakh rabotayushchikh zhenshchin," Levada Center Archives, Moscow, April 17, 1990.
28. Stites, *Women's Liberation Movement*, 398.
29. Harden, "'Mother Russia,'" 182.
30. Rosenberg, *Women and Perestroika*, 20.
31. McCuaig, "Effects of Perestroika."
32. Mikhail Gorbachev, *Perestroika: New Thinking for Our Country and the World* (Harper & Row, 1988), 103.
33. Harden, "'Mother Russia,'" 187.

MOTHERLAND

1. Andrei Gromyko, "Po sluchayu istoricheskoi daty," *Izvestia*, June 11, 1987.
2. Hosking, *First Socialist Society*, 436.
3. TASS, "Torzhestvenny kontzert," *Izvestia*, June 11, 1988.
4. Beckerman, *When They Come*, 523.
5. Raisa Gorbacheva. "Foros: 73 chasa pod arestom. Iz dnevnika zheny prezidenta," Gorbachev Fund, https://www.gorby.ru/raisa/diary/.
6. Taubman, *Gorbachev*, 573.
7. Taubman, 593.
8. Gorbacheva, "Foros."
9. Taubman, *Gorbachev*, 607.
10. Gorbacheva, "Foros."
11. Gorbacheva.
12. Gorbacheva.
13. Gorbacheva.
14. Taubman, *Gorbachev*, 613.
15. Taubman, *Gorbachev*, 619.

JULIA

1. David Hoffman, *The Oligarchs: Wealth and Power in the New Russia* (Public Affairs, 2002), 183.

NOTES

THE HUNT
1. Author's visit to open house at Life Academy, September 3, 2012.
2. Julia Ioffe, "The Cheating Cheaters of Moscow: How Infidelity Has Become Accepted and Even Expected in Russia," *Slate*, December 1, 2010.
3. Author's interview with Larisa Renar, September 6, 2012.

LYUDMILA
1. Oleg Blotsky, *Doroga k vlasti: Kniga vtoraya* (Osmos Press, 2002), 417.
2. Natalia Gevorkyan et al., "Ot pervogo litsa: Razgovory s Vladimirom Putinym," http://www1.lib.ru/MEMUARY/PUTIN/razgowor.txt_with-big-pictures.html.
3. "Novogodnie obrashchenia Borisa Yeltsina i Vladimira Putina (1999)," Prezidentsky tsentr Borisa Yeltsina, https://www.youtube.com/watch?v=q0Zb8QqXo0A.
4. Blotsky, *Doroga k vlasti*, 13–14.
5. Gevorkyan et al., "Ot pervogo litsa."
6. Catherine Belton, *Putin's People: How the KGB Took Back Russia and Then Took on the West* (Farrar, Straus and Giroux, 2020), 256.
7. Blotsky, *Doroga k vlasti*, 30.
8. Blotsky, 23.
9. Blotsky, 35.
10. Blotsky, 24–25.
11. Blotsky, 39.
12. Blotsky, 40.
13. Blotsky, 45.
14. Blotsky, 39.
15. Blotsky, 34.
16. Steven Lee Myers, *The New Tsar: The Rise and Reign of Vladimir Putin* (Alfred A. Knopf, 2015), 30.
17. Blotsky, *Doroga k vlasti*, 57.
18. Blotsky, 58.
19. Blotsky, 60.
20. Gevorkyan et al., "Ot pervogo litsa."
21. Myers, *New Tsar*, 33.
22. Gevorkyan et al., "Ot pervogo litsa."
23. Blotsky, *Doroga k vlasti*, 50.
24. Myers, *New Tsar*, 32.
25. Gevorkyan et al.
26. Blotsky, *Doroga k vlasti*, 127.
27. Blotsky, 129.
28. Gevorkyan et al., "Ot pervogo litsa."
29. Myers, *New Tsar*, 38.
30. Blotsky, *Doroga k vlasti*, 222.
31. Blotsky, 241.
32. Blotsky, 241.
33. Blotsky, 243.
34. Blotsky, 249.
35. Blotsky, 213.
36. Blotsky, 273.
37. Myers, *New Tsar*, 79.
38. Blotsky, *Doroga k vlasti*, 324.
39. Blotsky, 351–53.
40. Gevorkyan et al., "Ot pervogo litsa"; and Myers, *New Tsar*, 90.

THE WEAKER SEX
1. Vladimir Poznyak and Dag Rekve, "Global Status Report on Alcohol and Health 2018," World Health Organization, 2018.
2. "Natsional'nyy reyting trezvosti subyektov Rossiiskoy Federatsii – 2017," Trezvaya Rossiya.

A MANLY MAN
1. Gevorkyan et al., "Ot pervogo litsa."
2. "Prezident rasskazal ob otkaze alkogol'nogo napitka," Lenta.ru, October 7, 2020.
3. Yulia Abugalieva, "Muzhskaya smertnost' v vozraste 35–40 let v dva raza vyshe zhenskoi," *Kommersant*, August 8, 2022.
4. Marina Sovina, "Golikova otsenila masshtaby muzhskoi smertnosti v Rossii," Lenta.ru, September 7, 2021.
5. Oleg Apolikhin, "V Rossii, 52% muzhchin ne dozhyvayut do 65 let," Interfax, March 24, 2023.
6. "Chislo umershikh v trudosposobnom vozraste po osnovnym klassam i otdel'nym prichinam smerti na 100 tys. naselenia sootvetsvuyushchego

pola i vozrasta, yanvar'–dekabr' 2019 god, predvaritel'nye dannye po date registratsii v organakh ZAGS, bez ucheta okonchatel'nykh meditsinskikh svidetel'stv o smerti," Federal'naya sluzhba gosudarstvennoy statistiki, March 4, 2020.

7. "Zabolevaemost' naselenia po osnovnym klassam boleznei v 2000–2021 gg. (zaregestrirovano zabolevaniyu u patsientov s diagnozom ustanovlennym v pervye v zhizni), Dannye Minzdrava Rossii, raschet Rosstata," Federal'naya sluzhba gosudarstvennoy statistiki, November 20, 2022; Svetlana Khlebnikova, "Tsena smerty," *Vedomosti*, December 19, 2017; "Chislo umershikh," Rosstat.

8. "Pyanstvu – boy: Pochemu zhenshchiny zhivut dol'she muzhchin," Vysshaya Shkola Ekonomiki, August 12, 2021.

9. Yulia Zinkina and Andrey Korotaev, "Razryv v ozhidaemoy prodolzhitel'nosti zhizni muzhchin i zhenshchin: Obzor geneticheskikh, sotsial'nykh i tsennostnykh faktorov," *Demograficheskoe obozrenie* 8, no. 1 (2021): 106–26.

10. "Chislo umershikh," Rosstat.

11. "Predsedatel' pravitel'stva Rossii V. V. Putin, pribyvshyy s rabochei poyezdkoy v Perm', posetil hokkeinyy match komand Rossiyskoy lyubitel'skoy hokkeynoy ligi, a takzhe pobesedoval s rukovodstvom ligi i predstavitelyami komand," Pravitel'stvo Rossiyskoy Federatsii, February 4, 2012. http://archive.government.ru/docs/18004/.

12. Gevorkyan et al., "Ot pervogo litsa."

13. "Vladimir Putin postavil tsel' priobshchit' k sportu 40 protsentov rossiyan," *Rossiyskaya gazeta*, April 13, 2012.

14. "Putin uveren, chto sport vospityvaet pravil'niye ustanovki," TASS, October 16, 2023.

15. "2015: Putin Shows Off His Muscles as He Trains with PM," *Daily Mail*, https://www.youtube.com/watch?v=UV98crU_7rU.

16. Mikhail Rubin et al., "Chem boleet Putin? Rassledovanie k 70-letiyu Vladimira Putina," *Proekt*, April 1, 2022, https://www.proekt.media/investigation/chem-boleet-putin/.

17. "Rabochaya poezdka Vladimira Putina v Ussuriyskiy zapovednik," Programma "Amurskiy tigr." http://programmes.putin.kremlin.ru/tiger/premier; "Putin, belukha, peredatchiki," Interfax, July 31, 2009.

18. Andrey Kolesnikov, "Kit sezona," *Kommersant*, August 26, 2010.

19. "Polet Vladimira Putina so sterkhami," *Kommersant*, September 6, 2012.

20. "V. Putin nashel dve amfory na dne morya," *RBK*, August 10, 2011, https://www.rbc.ru/society/10/08/2011/5703ea9e9a79477633d36618.

21. "Putin otdykhaet, kak nastoyashchiy muzhchina. Foto," Interfax, August 5, 2009.

22. "Putin prokommentiroval svoe foto slovami 'na medvede poka ne skakal,'" *RBK*, March 10, 2018. https://www.rbc.ru/rbcfreenews/5aa3a5599a79472bcf418f32.

23. Julia Ioffe, "Two Russian Women on a Sochi Train," *New Republic*, February 11, 2014, https://newrepublic.com/article/116525/two-russian-woman-sochi-train.

24. "Chislo zhenshchin na 1000 muzhchin sootvetstvuyushchey vosrastnoy gruppy," Federal'naya sluzhba gosudarstvennoy statistiki, 2024.

PUSSY RIOT

1. Maria Alyokhina, *Riot Days* (Henry Holt, 2017), 21.

2. Masha Gessen, *Words Will Break Cement: The Passion of Pussy Riot* (Penguin, 2014), 115.
3. Alyokhina, *Riot Days*, 23.
4. Gessen, *Words Will Break*, 116.
5. Nadya Tolokonnikova, *Read & Riot: A Pussy Riot Guide to Activism* (HarperOne, 2018), 2.
6. Gessen, *Words Will Break*, 19.
7. Tolokonnikova, *Read & Riot*, 18.
8. Tolokonnikova, 28.
9. "Putin o trebovaniyakh BDIPCh: Eto ikh khotelki, pust' svoyu zhenu uchat shchi varit'," Interfax, February 14, 2008.
10. Tolokonnikova, *Read & Riot*, 206.
11. Miriam Elder, "What Does Pussy Riot Mean Now?," *BuzzFeed*, February 7, 2014, https://www.buzzfeed.com/miriamelder/what-does-pussy-riot-mean-now.
12. Gessen, *Words Will Break*, 47–48.
13. Tolokonnikova, *Read & Riot*, 32.
14. Gessen, *Words Will Break*, 65.
15. Tolokonnikova, 31.
16. Elder, "What Does Pussy Riot Mean Now?"; and Gessen, *Words Will Break*, 60–63.
17. Tolokonnikova, *Read & Riot*, 36.
18. Garadzha Matveeva, "Devchonki PUSSY RIOT zakhvatyvayut transport," November 6, 2011, https://www.youtube.com/watch?v=qEiB1RYuYXw.
19. Tolokonnikova, *Read & Riot*, 35–36.
20. Gessen, *Words Will Break*, 71.
21. Garadzha Matveeva, "Gruppa Pussy Riot zhzhet putinskiy glamur," November 30, 2011, https://www.youtube.com/watch?v=CZUhkWiiv7M.
22. Tolokonnikova, *Read & Riot*, 67.
23. Alyokhina, *Riot Days*, 3.
24. Interview with the author, September 28, 2018.
25. Gessen, *Words Will Break*, 87.
26. Garadzha Matveeva, "PUSSY RIOT poyut politzekam na kryshe tyurmy," December 14, 2011, https://www.youtube.com/watch?v=mmyZbJpYV0I.
27. Alyokhina, *Riot Days*, 8.
28. Garadzha Matveeva, "Pussy Riot na Krasnoy Ploshchadi – pesnya 'Putin zassal,'" January 20, 2011, https://www.youtube.com/watch?v=7kVMADLm3js.
29. Alyokhina, *Riot Days*, 10.
30. "Vystuplenie Patriarkha na vstreche s V. V. Putinym," February 8, 2012, https://www.youtube.com/watch?v=5_CQRIQ_x4U.
31. "Patriarkh Kirill: Pravoslavnye lyudi ne vykhodyat na demonstratsii," VFM.ru, February 1, 2012, https://www.bfm.ru/news/169330.
32. Sean Michaels, "Franz Ferdinand and Red Hot Chili Peppers Voice Support for Pussy Riot," *Guardian*, July 24, 2012.
33. "V. Putin izvinilsya pered veruyushchimi za 'pank moleben' gruppy Pussy Riot," RBC.ru, March 7, 2012, https://www.rbc.ru/society/07/03/2012/5703f46f9a7947ac81a65a03.
34. "Svyateyshyy Patriarkh Kirill: U nas net budushchego, esli my nachinaem glumit'sya pered velikimi svyatynyami," Patriarchia.ru, March 24, 2012, http://www.patriarchia.ru/db/text/2101850.html.
35. "Protoierey Chaplin: V 20-e gody nravstvennym delom bylo by 'unichtozhit' kak mozhno bol'she bol'shevikov," Gazeta.ru, March 21, 2012, https://www.gazeta.ru/news/lenta/2012/03/21/n_2252589.shtml?updated.
36. "Rossiyane o dele Pussy Riot," Levada.ru, July 31, 2012, https://www.levada.ru/2012/07/31/rossiyane-o-dele-pussy-riot/.
37. "Tret' Rossiyan v chestnyy sud nad Pussy Riot," Levada.ru, August 17, 2012, https://web.archive.org/web/20120824121435/http://www

.levada.ru/17-08-2012/tret-rossiyan-verit-v-chestnyi-sud-nad-pussy-riot.
38. Julia Ioffe, "Net Impact," *New Yorker*, March 28, 2011.
39. Alexey Navalny, "Pro Pussy Riots," *LiveJournal*, March 7, 2012, https://navalny.livejournal.com/690551.html.
40. Alexey Navalny, "Pro Pussy Riots," March 7, 2012. https://navalny.livejournal.com/690551.html.
41. Most of what follows is from my reporting on the trial for *The New Republic*.
42. Julia Ioffe, "Pussy Riot v. Putin: A Front Row Seat at a Russian Dark Comedy," *New Republic*, August 6, 2012.
43. Ioffe, "Pussy Riot v. Putin."
44. Ioffe.
45. "Madonna Gives Support to Russia's Imprisoned Pussy Riot at Moscow Show Despite Threats of Violence," Associated Press, August 8, 2012.
46. Joshua Keating, "Alicia Silverstone Writes to Putin, Demands Vegan Meals for Pussy Riot Defendant," *Foreign Policy*, August 15, 2012.
47. "Putin sovetuyet ne sudit' strogo uchastnits Pussy Riot," BBC Russian Service, August 2, 2012.
48. Julia Ioffe, "How Three Young Punks Made Putin Blink," *New Republic*, August 17, 2012.

WOMEN'S ZONE

1. Gessen, *Words Will Break*, 228.
2. "Putin shchitaet pravil'nym reshenie suda po delu Pussy Riot," RIA Novosti, October 7, 2012.
3. "Poslanie prezidenta federal'nomu sobraniyu," Kremlin.ru, December 12, 2012, http://kremlin.ru/events/president/news/17118,
4. Amie Ferris-Rotman, "Putin the Pro-Choice Champion," Coda, September 20, 2018, https://www.codastory.com/disinformation/traditional-values/putin-prochoice-champion/.
5. Natalia Chernova, "Matushka vseya Rusi," *Novaya gazeta*, July 1, 2020, https://novayagazeta.ru/articles/2020/07/01/86097-matushka-vseya-rusi.
6. Alyokhina, *Riot Days*, 59.
7. Alyokhina, 157.
8. Alyokhina, 58.
9. Alyokhina, 153.
10. Alyokhina, 173,
11. Interview with the author, September 24, 2018.

GASOLINE

1. Margarita Gracheva, *Shchastliva bez ruk: Real'naya istoria lyubvi i zverstva* (Komsomol'skaya pravda, 2020), 64.
2. Gracheva, *Shchastliva bez ruk*, 20.
3. Judgment in the case of *Tunnikova v. Russia*, European Court of Human Rights, March 14, 2022, https://hudoc.echr.coe.int/eng?i=001-213869.
4. Pavel Lobkov and Anna Mongayt, "Istochniki Dozhdya: Zakon o zaprete usynovleniya pisali Vyachelav Volodin i Olga Batalina," Telekanal Dozhd, December 21, 2012, https://tvrain.ru/teleshow/here_and_now/istochniki_dozhda_zakon_o_zaprete_usynovlenija_pisali_vjacheslav_volodin_i_olga_batalina-334587/.
5. "Batalina poyasnila, pochemu domashnee nasilie—eto ne ugolovnaya statya," BMF.ru, November 15, 2016, https://www.bfm.ru/news/338807.
6. Anna Boytsova, "Putin podpisal zakon o dekriminalizatsii poboev v semye," RBC.ru, February 7, 2017, https://www.rbc.ru/politics/07/02/2017/5899de8e9a79479489b2cd98.
7. Gracheva, *Shchastliva bez ruk*, 69.
8. Gracheva, 70.
9. Pavel Kanygin, "Khachaturyan. Tantsy s pistoletom," *Novaya gazeta*, December 21, 2018.

10. Interview with author, November 17, 2022.
11. "Glava SK otmetil rost nasiliya v priemnykh semyakh posle dekriminilizatsyi poboev," TASS, February 6, 2018.
12. "V Human Rights Watch zayavili o negativnykh posledstviyakh dekriminalizatsyi poboev v RF," Interfax, October 25, 2018.
13. Interview with author, November 27, 2018.
14. Interview with author, September 16, 2019.
15. "Matvienko prizvala menyat' patriarkhal'nyi mentalitet," Lenta.ru, July 25, 2019.
16. Maria Ilyina, "'Patriarkh lichno obrashchalsya': Kto i pochemu zablokiroval zakon o domashnem nasilii," Verstka, September 7, 2022, https://verstka.media/pochemu-ne-priniali-zakon-o-domashnem-nasilii.
17. Inna Novikova, "Andrei Kormukhin: Zakonoproekt 'O semeino-bytovom nasilii' – dyavol v detalyakh," *Pravda*, December 2, 2019, https://www.pravda.ru/society/1455616-kormuhin/.
18. Svetlana Sukhova, "Tamara Pletnyova: Predstavlenie ob orderakh," *Ogonek*, October 28, 2019, https://www.kommersant.ru/doc/4117361.
19. "Matvienko prizvala ne speshit' pri dorabotke zakona o domashnem nasilii," *Izvestia*, December 11, 2019, https://iz.ru/953228/2019-12-11/matvienko-prizvala-ne-speshit-pri-dorabotke-zakona-o-domashnem-nasilii.
20. "Putin vpervye prokommentiroval zakon o domashnem nasilii," *Vedomosti*, December 19, 2019, https://www.vedomosti.ru/society/news/2019/12/19/819162-zakon-o-nasilii.

FIRST LADY

1. Yury Dud', "The Navalnys: After the Poisoning," vDud', October 6, 2020, https://www.youtube.com/watch?v=vps43rXgaZc.
2. David Steindl et al., "Novichok Nerve Agent Poisoning," *Lancet*, December 22, 2020.
3. Alexey Navalny, "Obrashchenye," August 21, 2020, https://twitter.com/navalny/status/1296769338683338754.
4. "#negrustivsyobudetkhorosho: Flashmob v podderzhku Yulii Naval'noy sobral bolee 6 tysyach postov," Wonderzine, February 4, 2021, https://www.wonderzine.com/wonderzine/life/news/254881-ne-grusti.
5. Alexander Tsypkin, Instagram, January 19, 2021, https://www.instagram.com/p/CKONCpUBMiq/?igshid=1o0yltoo54it8.
6. Aleksei Polorotov, "Navalnaya—2021. Vydvizhenie suprugi glavnogo rossiyskogo oppozitsionera v Gosdumu gotovo podderzhat' 'Yabloko,'" Dailystorm.ru, December 10, 2020, https://dailystorm.ru/vlast/navalnaya-2021-vydvizhenie-suprugi-glavnogo-rossiyskogo-oppozicionera-v-gosdumu-gotovo-podderzhat-yabloko.
7. "Tikhanovskaya ob areste Navalnogo, bor'be ego zheny Yulii, Putine, Lukashenko i khokee na krovavom l'du," DW Russian YouTube Channel, January 19, 2021, https://www.youtube.com/watch?v=Dfq8LUfdpDI.
8. Julia Taratuta, "Chto ne tak s razgovorami o politicheskom budeshchem Yulii Navalnoy?" Wonderzine, February 10, 2021, https://www.wonderzine.com/wonderzine/life/life-opinion/254971-navalnaya.
9. Dasha Veledeeva, "Yulia Navalnaya:

'Esli segodnya vse klassno, to ya uzhe schastliva. Potomu cho zavtra sovershenno mozhet vse izmenit'sya, i ya budu sil'no razocharovana," *Harper's Bazaar Russia*, February 17, 2021, https://www.thesymbol.ru/heroes/the-symbol/yuliya-navalnaya-svoyu-glavnuyu-zadachu-ya-vizhu-v-tom-chtoby-u-nas-v-seme-nichego-ne-izmenilos-deti-byli-detmi-a-dom-domom/.
10. Roman Dobrokhotov, interview with the author.
11. Adam Taylor, "Putin's Ex-Wife Returns to the Spotlight with a Dashing Young Husband and a Fancy French Villa," *Washington Post*, April 6, 2017.
12. "Putin Romance Rumors Keep Public Riveted," Radio Free Europe/Radio Liberty, April 18, 2008, https://www.rferl.org/a/1109593.html.
13. C. J. Chivers, "Putin Denies Reports of Divorce; Newspaper Suspended," *New York Times*, April 19, 2008.
14. Francesca Piscionieri, "Berlusconi Returns to World Stage with Putin Visit," Reuters, April 18, 2008.
15. Irina Reznik, Evgenia Pismennaya, and Ilya Arkhipov, "Putin's Dancing Daughter Said to Run Fund Backed by Dad's Allies," Bloomberg, January 30, 2015; Stephen Grey, Andrey Kuzmin, and Elizabeth Piper, "Putin's Daughter, a Young Billionaire and the President's Friends," Reuters, November 10, 2015; and Farida Rustamova and Mikhail Rubin, "'Ne zvezdniye deti': Chto izvestno o Katerine Tikhonovoy," RBC, December 17, 2015, https://rbc.ru/politics/17/12/2015/5672a1ba9a79471ab070fead.
16. "Putin otkazalsya ot svoikh docherei," Navalny Live YouTube, December 20, 2015, https://www.youtube.com/watch?v=S4zTPx-yY68.
17. "Yulia Navalnaya na Prospekte Sakharova (06.09.2013)," Navalny Live YouTube, September 6, 2013, https://www.youtube.com/watch?v=euy2FguOfos.
18. "Vladimir Putin: 'Zrya vy khryukaete,'" TNV, October 8, 2020, https://www.youtube.com/watch?v=j2uey_I1ajw.
19. Andrey Zakharov, Roman Badanin, and Mikhail Rubin, "Zheleznye maski, chast' 2: Rassledovanie o tom, kak blizkaya znakomaya Vladimira Putina poluchila chast' Rossii," *Proekt*, November 25, 2020, https://maski-proekt.media/tainaya-semya-putina/.
20. Anastasia Yakoreva, "Ya, konechno, skelet," Meduza, April 29, 2021, https://meduza.io/feature/2021/04/29/ya-konechno-skelet.

BRING THE BOYS HOME

1. "Ukrainian Woman Offers Seeds to Russian Soldiers So 'Sunflowers Grow When They Die'—video," *Guardian*, February 25, 2022, https://www.theguardian.com/world/video/2022/feb/25/ukrainian-woman-sunflower-seeds-russian-soldiers-video.
2. Just as it was trying to secure its hold of Afghanistan after invading in 1979, the Soviet Union hit another demographic nadir created by the Second World War. There was a sudden drop in the number of military-age men by the middle of the 1980s because there had been so few children born in the 1960s for one simple reason: not enough babies had been born in the Soviet Union during the first years of World War II to have enough babies in the early 1960s for the Soviet military to have enough young men to fill its ranks in the mid-1980s.
3. Alessandra Stanley, "Nazran Journal; Mothers Act to Save Their Sons from

War," *New York Times*, February 11, 1995.
4. Fred Hiatt, "Desperately Seeking Their Sons: Russians Go to Chechnya to Learn Children's Fate," *Washington Post*, January 15, 1995.
5. Gorbachev, *Perestroika*, 103.
6. Svetlana Gorbatenko, VKontakte, November 10, 2022, https://archive.ph/7eEFv.
7. "'Bylo mnogo ranenykh, oni prosto tam istekali krov'yu!' Kak zhena rossiiskogo mobilizovannogo pytalas' vernut' muzha s peredovoy," Nastoyashchee vremya, November 12, 2022, https://www.currenttime.tv/a/32127060.html.
8. Andrei Pertsev, "'K prezidentu lyudi s ulitsy priiti ne mogut': Pomnite, Putin nedavno vstretilsya s materyami soldat - a okozalos', chto mnogie iz nikh svyazany s vlastyami? 'Meduza' vyyasnila, kak Kreml' gotovil eto sobytie," Meduza, December 3, 2022, https://meduza.io/feature/2022/12/03/k-prezidentu-lyudi-s-ulitsy-priyti-ne-mogut.
9. Varvara Koshechkina, "Shoigu dolozhil Putinu o zavershenii mobilizatsii," Lenta.ru, October 28, 2022.
10. https://contract.gosuslugi.ru/.
11. Ekaterina Khabidulina, "'Rotatsiya ne predusmotrena': Kartapolov nazval sroki vozvrashcheniya mobilizovannykh domoy," Forbes.ru, September 15, 2023.
12. Olga Kats, "Vernyom rebyat," Telegram, November 16, 2023, https://t.me/vernemrebyat/5038.
13. "'Eto dolzhno delat'sya rukami kontraktnoy armii'. Zhena mobilizovannogo – o voyne, razocharovanii v Putine i popytkakh vernut' muzha domoy," Nastoyashchee vremya, November 24, 2023, https://www.currenttime.tv/a/32697107.html.
14. Olga Kats, "Vernyom rebyat."
15. "Troe podrostkov zakidali snegom Vechnyi ogon' v Kingiseppe. Vozbuzhdeno delo o reabilitatsii natsizma," Fontanka.ru, January 1, 2025, https://www.fontanka.ru/2025/01/01/74951426/.
16. "Mama, ya, navernoe, skoro umru," *Meduza*, October 8, 2024, https://meduza.io/feature/2024/10/08/mama-ya-navernoe-skoro-umru.
17. "Put' domoy," Telegram, November 11, 2023, https://t.me/PYTY_DOMOY/398.
18. Vladimir Soloviev, "Soloviev," Telegram, November 16, 2023. https://t.me/SolovievLive/221887.
19. "Telegram-kanal zhen mobilizovannykh poluchil plashku Fake posle ataki propagandista Solovieva i provlastnogo yurista Remeslo," Agentstvo, December 1, 2023, https://www.agents.media/telegram-kanal-zhen-mobilizovannyh-poluchil-plashku-fake-posle-ataki-propagandista-soloveva-i-provlastnogo-yurista-remeslo/.
20. "Pomoshchnitsa deputata iz Krasnoyarska poluchila prava admina v chate zhen mobilizovannykh i udalila ego iz-za prizivov k mitingu," Mediazona, November 15, 2023, https://zona.media/news/2023/11/15/wayhome.

LAND OF MOTHERS

1. Julia Ioffe, "The Tragedy of Navalny," *Puck*, February 19, 2024, https://puck.news/the-tragedy-of-navalny/.
2. "Obrashchenie Prezidenta Rossiiskoy Federatsii," Kremlin.ru, February 24, 2022, http://kremlin.ru/events/president/news/67843.
3. "Putin: Dlya Rossii nepriyemlemo chtoby detyam navyazyvali izvrashcheniya," TASS, September 30, 2022. https://tass.ru/politika/15921455.
4. "Vladimir Putin prinyal uchastie

v XIX Yezhegodnom zasedanii Mezhdunarodnogo diskussionnogo kluba 'Valdai.' Stenogramma plenarnoy sessii," October 27, 2022, https://ru.valdaiclub.com/events/posts/articles/vladimir-putin-prinyal-uchastie-v-xix-zasedanii-kluba-valdai/.
5. Matt Murphy, "Russian Parliament Bans Gender Reassignment Surgery for Trans People," BBC News, July 14, 2023.
6. "V Rossii zaveli pervoe ugolovnoe delo ob 'LGBT-ekstremizme'," RBC.ru, March 18, 2024, https://www.rbc.ru/politics/18/03/2024/65f877509a794776142bd004.
7. Daria Egorova, "'Na nego zhestochayshim obrazom davili.' V SIZO pogib direktor turfirmy 'Men Trevel,'" Radio Svoboda, January 4, 2025, https://www.svoboda.org/a/na-nego-zhestochayshim-obrazom-davili-v-sizo-pogib-direktor-turfirmy-men-trevel-/33263010.html.
8. Polina Motyzlevskaya, "Deputat Butina poprosila proverit' vecherinku Ivleevoy na LGBT-propagandu," *Kommersant*, December 21, 2023, https://www.kommersant.ru/doc/6413694.
9. "Jailed Russian Rapper Summoned to Recruitment Center," RFE/RL Russian Service, January 8, 2024, https://www.rferl.org/a/russia-rapper-vacio-party-jail-draft/32765966.html.
10. Lyubov Borisenko, "Parad izvineniy," *Novaya Gazeta Europe*, December 26, 2023, https://novayagazeta.eu/articles/2023/12/26/filipp-kirkorov-kseniia-sobchak-i-lolita-izvinilis-za-uchastie-v-pochti-goloi-vecherinke-nasti-ivleevoi.
11. "Putin rasskazal, chto emigranty iz Rossii vozvrashchayutsya na rodinu iz-za 'obshchikh tualetov dlya mal'chikov i devochek' v drugikh stranakh," MediaZona, January 16, 2024, https://zona.media/news/2024/01/16/toilets.
12. Alexander Beglov, Telegram, January 13, 2024, https://t.me/a_beglov/5869.
13. "Srochno: Yulia Navalnaya vystupila v Myunkhene posle soobshcheniy FSIN Rossii o gibeli Alekseya Navalnogo," *DW na russkom*, February 16, 2024, https://www.youtube.com/watch?v=F325WG-TpPw.
14. "White Scarves and Flowers: Wives and Mothers of Mobilized Soldiers Take Resentment to the Kremlin," *Moscow Times*, January 16, 2024, https://www.themoscowtimes.com/2024/01/16/white-scarves-and-flowers-wives-and-mothers-of-mobilized-soldiers-take-resentment-to-the-kremlin-a83720.
15. Robyn Dixon, Francesca Ebel, and Natalia Abbakumova, "Have Babies for Russia: Putin Presses Women to Embrace Patriotism over Feminism," *Washington Post*, June 30, 2024.
16. "Tatyana Golikova vystupaet na VMF-2024: Pryamaya translyatsiya," *Komsomol'skaya Pravda*, March 6, 2024, https://www.youtube.com/watch?v=r43jKpOHngs.
17. "Volodin prizval devochek varit' borsch. Video," RBC.ru, December 6, 2023, https://www.rbc.ru/politics/06/12/2023/657059179a794725e38f705d,
18. "Shkolnikam na zanyatiakh po 'Semyevedeniyu' obyasnyat tsennosti 'brachnosti, mnogodetnosti, tselomudriya,'" Verstka.ru, August 22, 2024, https://verstka.media/semyevedenie-vvedut-v-programmu-s-novogo-uchebnogo-goda-news.
19. "Valentina Tereshkova: 'Ukreplenie semyi – vazhneyshee gosudarstvennoe delo," Orenburg.er.ru, June 1, 2015, https://orenburg.er.ru/activity/news/valentina

-tereshkova-ukreplenie-semi-vazhnejshee-gosudarstvennoe-delo.
20. Olga Mamikonyan, "V RGSU razrabotali parametry naloga na bezdetnost'," Forbes.ru, October 4, 2024, https://www.forbes.ru/forbeslife/522575-v-rgsu-razrabotali-parametry-naloga-na-bezdetnost.
21. Anna Ryzhkova and Regina Gimalova, "'Eto li ne patrioticheskoe chuvstvo, kogda chuzhykh detei ne byvaet i vse nashi?' Maria Lvova-Belova," Verstka, March 15, 2023, https://verstka.media/lvova-belova-profile.
22. "Vstrecha s Mariey Lvovoy-Belovoy," Kremlin.ru, October 27, 2021, http://kremlin.ru/events/president/news/67015.
23. Alena Shapovalova, "Lvova-Belova rasskazala o nastroenii detey Donbassa v rossiiskikh semyakh," Lenta.ru, November 2, 2022, https://lenta.ru/news/2022/11/02/family/.
24. Lydia Kelly, "Russia's Birth Rate Slides to Lowest in Quarter Century in 2024," Reuters, September 9, 2024.
25. "Zhena mobilizovannogo Maria Andreeva rasskazala ob uvol'nenii iz-za statusa 'inostranogo agenta,'" MediaZona, August 5, 2024, https://zona.media/news/2024/08/05/mariya_andreeva.

BIBLIOGRAPHY

BOOKS

Alexievich, Svetlana. *U voiny ne zhenskoe litso.* Vremya, 2016.
———. *Vremya sekondhend.* Vremya, 2016.
Alliluyeva, Svetlana. *Dalekaya muzyka docheri Stalina.* Alistorus, 1983.
———. *Dvadtsat' pisem drugu.* 1967. http://lib.ru/MEMUARY/ALLILUEWA/letters.txt.
———. *Only One Year: A Memoir.* Translated by Paul Chavchavadze. HarperCollins, 1969.
Alyokhina, Maria. *Riot Days.* Henry Holt, 2017.
Applebaum, Anne. *Gulag: A History.* Anchor, 2004.
Babel, Isaac. *Sobranie sochinenii v trekh tomakh.* Azbuka-Atticus Press, 2012.
Baker, Peter, and Susan Glasser. *Kremlin Rising: Vladimir Putin's Russia and the End of Revolution.* Potomac, 2007.
Bebel, August. *Woman Under Socialism.* Translated by Daniel de Leon. Schocken, 1971.
Beckerman, Gal. *When They Come for Us, We'll Be Gone: The Epic Struggle to Save Soviet Jewry.* Houghton Mifflin Harcourt, 2010.
Beevor, Antony. *The Second World War.* Little, Brown, 2012.
———. *Stalingrad.* Penguin, 2007.
Beizer, Michael, ed. *From the Revolutions of 1917 to the Fall of the Soviet Union.* Most Kultury, 2017.
Belton, Catherine. *Putin's People: How the KGB Took Back Russia and Then Took on the West.* Farrar, Straus and Giroux, 2020.
Blotsky, Oleg. *Doroga k vlasti: Kniga vtoraya.* Osmos Press, 2002.
Borenstein, Eliot. *Men Without Women: Masculinity and Revolution in Russian Fiction, 1917–1929.* Duke University Press, 2000.
Brezhneva, Luba. *The World I Left Behind: Pieces of a Past.* Translated by Geoffrey Polk. Random House, 1995.
Browning, Christopher. *Ordinary Men: Reserve Battalion 101 and the Final Solution in Poland.* Revised edition. Harper Perennial, 2017.
Buckley, Mary, ed. *Perestroika and Soviet Women.* Cambridge University Press, 1992.
Clements, Barbara Evans. *Bolshevik Feminist: The Life of Alexandra Kollontai.* Indiana University Press, 1979.
———. *Bolshevik Women.* Cambridge University Press, 1997.
———. *Daughters of Revolution: A History of Women in the USSR.* Harlan Davidson, 1994.
Conquest, Robert. *The Great Terror: A Reassessment.* Oxford University Press, 1990.
Dodolev, Yevgeni. *Delo Galiny Brezhnevoy: Brillianty dlya printsessy.* Algoritm, 2013.
Du Plessix Gray, Francine. *Soviet Women: Walking the Tightrope.* Doubleday, 1990.
Elwood, Ralph Carter. *Inessa Armand: Revolutionary and Feminist.* Cambridge University Press, 1992.

Engel, Barbara Alperin. *Women in Russia, 1700–2000*. Cambridge University Press, 2004.
Freeze, Chaeran Y., and Jay M. Harris, eds. *Everyday Jewish Life in Imperial Russia: Select Documents, 1772–1914*. Brandeis University Press, 2013.
Gammer, Moshe. *Muslim Resistance to the Tsar: Shamil and the Conquest of Chechnia and Daghestan*. Frank Kass, 1994.
Gessen, Masha. *Words Will Break Cement: The Passion of Pussy Riot*. Penguin, 2014.
Gevorkyan, Natalia, et al. *Ot pervogo litsa: Razgovory s Vladimirom Putinym*. http://www1.lib.ru/MEMUARY/PUTIN/razgowor.txt_with-big-pictures.html.
Ginzburg, Eugenia. *Krutoi marshrut: Khronika vremyon kul'ta lichnosti*. Agenstvo FTM, 2018.
Goldman, Wendy Z. *Women, the State, and Revolution: Soviet Family Policy & Social Life, 1917–1936*. Cambridge University Press, 1993.
Gorbachev, Mikhail. *Memoirs*. Doubleday, 1996.
———. *Perestroika: New Thinking for Our Country and the World*. Harper & Row, 1988.
Gorbacheva, Raisa. *Shtrikhi k portretu*. Fond Gorbacheva, 2009.
———. *Ya nadeyus'. . .* Kniga, 1991.
Gracheva, Margarita. *Shchastliva bez ruk: Real'naya istoria lyubvi i zverstva*. Komsomol'skaya pravda, 2020.
Grossman, Vasily. *A Writer at War: A Soviet Journalist with the Red Army, 1941–1945*, edited and translated by Antony Beevor and Luba Vinogradova. Vintage Books, 2007.
———. *Zhizn i sudba*. Eksmo, 2013.
Haustov, V. N., ed. *Delo Beria: Prigovor obzhalovaniu ne podlezhit*. Mezhdunarodny fond "Demokratia," 2012.
Hill, Fiona, and Clifford G. Gady. *Mr. Putin: Operative in the Kremlin*. Brookings, 2015.
Hoffman, David. *The Oligarchs: Wealth and Power in the New Russia*. Public Affairs, 2011.
Hosking, Geoffrey. *The First Socialist Society: A History of the Soviet Union from Within*. Second enlarged edition. Harvard University Press, 1996.
Judt, Tony. *Postwar: A History of Europe Since 1945*. Penguin, 2005.
Kollontai, Alexandra Mikhailovna. *Izbrannye stat'i i rechi*. Izdatel'stvo politicheskoi literatury, 1972.
Kane, Eileen. *Russian Hajj: Empire and the Pilgrimage to Mecca*. Cornell University Press, 2015.
Kenez, Peter. *Red Advance, White Defeat: Civil War in South Russia, 1919–1920*. New Academia Publishing, 2004.
Kennan Warnecke, Grace. *Daughter of the Cold War*. University of Pittsburgh Press, 2018.
Khrushchev, Nikita. *Khrushchev Remembers*, translated and edited by Strobe Talbott. Little, Brown, 1970.
———. "O kulte lichnosti i ego posledstviakh: Doklad Pervogo sekretarya TsK KPSS tov. Khrushcheva N. S. XX s'ezdu Kommunisticheskoi partii Sovetskogo Soyuza, 25 fevralya 1956." *Izvstia TsK KPSS*, 1989, no. 3.
Khrushcheva, Nina L. *The Lost Khrushchev: A Journey into the Gulag of the Russian Mind*. Tate Publishing, 2014.
Khrushcheva, Nina P. "Mama's Notebooks," in *Memoirs of Nikita Khrushchev*, vol. 2, *Reformer (1945–1964)*, edited by Sergei Khrushchev; translated by George Shriver and Stephen Shenfield. Pennsylvania State University Press, 2006.
King, Charles. *Odessa: Genius and Death in a City of Dreams*. W. W. Norton, 2011.

Knight, Amy. *Beria: Stalin's First Lieutenant.* Princeton University Press, 1995.
Kon, Igor. *Klubnichka na beryozke: Seksual'naya kul'tura v Rossii.* Vremya, 2010.
———. *Seksualnaya kultura v Rossii: Ocherk istorii russkoy seksualnoy kultury s dokhristianskikh vremen do sovremennosti.* Izdatelstvo AST, 2019.
Kotkin, Stephen. *Stalin: Paradoxes of Power, 1878–1928.* Penguin Press, 2014.
———. *Stalin: Waiting for Hitler, 1929–1941.* Penguin Books, 2018.
———. *Steeltown, USSR: Soviet Society in the Gorbachev Era.* University of California Press, 1992.
Krylova, Anna. *Soviet Women in Combat: A History of Violence on the Eastern Front.* Cambridge University Press, 2010.
Lapidus, Gail Washofsky. *Women in Soviet Society: Equality, Development, and Social Change.* University of California Press, 1978.
Lebina, Natalia. *Muzhchina i zhenshchina: Telo, moda, kul'tura, SSSR - ottepel'.* Novoe literaturnoe obozrenie, 2018.
Livi-Bacci, Massimo. "On the Human Costs of Collectivization in the Soviet Union." *Population and Development Review* 19, no. 4 (1993): 743–66. www.jstor.org/stable/2938412.
Malia, Martin. *The Soviet Tragedy: A History of Socialism in Russia, 1917–1991.* Free Press, 1994.
McNeal, Robert H. *Bride of the Revolution: Krupskaya and Lenin.* University of Michigan Press, 1972.
Mozokhin, Oleg. *Politburo i delo Beria: Sbornik dokumentov.* Kuchkovo Pole, 2012.
Myers, Steven Lee. *The New Tsar: The Rise and Reign of Vladimir Putin.* Alfred A. Knopf, 2015.
Noggle, Anne. *A Dance with Death: Soviet Airwomen in World War II.* Texas A&M University Press, 1994.
Okunevskaya, Tatiana. *Tatianin den'.* Vagrius, 2005.
Orlova, Raisa. Vospominanie o neproshedshem vremeni, 1985. http://avtorsha.com/text_336.html.
Pavlichenko, Lyudmila. *Lady Death: The Memoirs of Stalin's Sniper*, edited by Alla Igorevna Begunova; translated by David Foreman. Greenhill Books, 2018.
Perlstein, Rick. *Before the Storm: Barry Goldwater and the Unmaking of the American Consensus.* Nation Books, 2009.
Pipes, Richard. *The Russian Revolution.* Knopf, 1990.
Pleshakov, Constantine. *Stalin's Folly: The Tragic First Ten Days of World War II on the Eastern Front.* Houghton Mifflin, 2006.
Reagan, Nancy, with William Novak. *My Turn: The Memoirs of Nancy Reagan.* Random House, 1989.
Remnick, David. *Lenin's Tomb: The Last Days of the Soviet Empire.* Vintage Books, 1994.
Rosenberg, Chanie. *Women and Perestroika: Present, Past and Future for Women in Russia.* Bookmarks, 1989.
Rosenberg, William G., ed. *Bolshevik Visions: First Phase of the Cultural Revolution in Soviet Russia*, part 1: *The Culture of a New Society: Ethics Gender, the Family, Law and Problems of Tradition.* University of Michigan Press, 1984, 1990.
Rubinstein, Joshua. *The Last Days of Stalin.* Yale University Press, 2016.
Rubinstein, Joshua, and Vladimir P. Naumov, eds. *Stalin's Secret Pogrom: The Postwar Inquisition of the Jewish Anti-Fascist Committee.* Translated by Laura Esther Wolfson. Yale University Press, 2001.

Ryan, Michael. *Doctors and the State in the Soviet Union.* Palgrave Macmillan, 2016.
Sebag Montefiore, Simon. *Stalin: The Court of the Red Tsar.* Knopf, 2007.
Sebestyen, Victor. *Lenin: The Man, the Dictator, and the Master of Terror.* Pantheon, 2017.
Slezkine, Yuri. *The Jewish Century.* Princeton University Press, 2004.
Smith, Sebastian. *Allah's Mountains: The Battle for Chechnya.* Tauris Parke, 2006.
Smolkin, Victoria. *A Sacred Space Is Never Empty: A History of Soviet Atheism.* Princeton University Press, 2018.
Stites, Richard. *Revolutionary Dreams: Utopian Vision and Experimental Life in the Russian Revolution.* Oxford University Press, 1989.
———. *The Women's Liberation Movement in Russia: Feminism, Nihilism, and Bolshevism, 1860–1930.* Princeton University Press, 1978.
Sullivan, Rosemary, *Stalin's Daughter: The Extraordinary and Tumultuous Life of Svetlana Alliluyeva.* Harper, 2015.
Taubman, William. *Gorbachev: His Life and Times.* W. W. Norton, 2017.
———. *Khrushchev: The Man and His Era.* W. W. Norton, 2003.
Tolokonnikova, Nadya. *Read & Riot: A Pussy Riot Guide to Activism.* HarperOne, 2018.
Trotsky, Leon. *The History of the Russian Revolution.* Translated by Max Eastman. University of Michigan Press, 1967.
Uborevich, Vladimira. *14 pisem Elene Sergeevne Bulgakovoy*, edited by Yuri Kantor. Vremya, 2009.
Uborevich, Vladimira, interviewee. "Film Two." Mira. Doch' Komandarma Uborevicha, by Vladimir Meletin. *Kultura,* January 29, 2012. http://tvkultura.ru/video/show/brand_id/37545/episode_id/229173/video_id/229173/.
Urlanis, Boris. *Wars and Population.* Progress Publishers, 1971.
Utrata, Jennifer. *Women Without Men: Single Mothers and Family Change in the New Russia.* Cornell University Press, 2015.
Vasilieva, Larisa. *Kremlin Wives.* Translated by Cathy Porter. Arcade Publishing, 1994.
Vilensky, S. S., et al., eds. *Deti gulaga: 1918–1956, dokumenty.* Mezhdunarodny Fond "Demokratia," 2002.
Viola, Lynne. *Peasant Rebels Under Stalin: Collectivization and the Culture of Peasant Resistance.* Oxford University Press, 1996.
Volovich, Khava. "Vospominaniya." https://topliba.com/books/589526.
Wood, Elizabeth. *The Baba and the Comrade: Gender and Politics in Revolutionary Russia.* Indiana University Press, 1997.
Zaichik, Irina. "Tatiana Okunevskaya: Chernye rozy moyey zhizni." *Ogonek,* May 4, 1997.
http://www.bafdigital.org/veteran/5255; https://www.yadvashem.org/untoldstories/database/index.asp?cid=646.

ARTICLES

"Belaya magia dlya chernogo mersedesa." *Novy Vzlgyad,* February 15, 1992.
"Glava SK otmetil rost nasiliya v priemnykh semyakh posle dekriminilizatsyi poboev." TASS, February 6, 2018.
"Jailed Russian Rapper Summoned to Recruitment Center." RFE/RL Russian Service, January 8, 2024. https://www.rferl.org/a/russia-rapper-vacio-party-jail-draft/32765966.html.
"Life Has Been a Drama to Russian-Born Actress." *Chicago Tribune,* June 21, 1985.

"Lukin predlagaet otpustit' 'prokaznits', pevshykh nepristoynye pesni v khrame, 8 marta." Interfax, March 7, 2012.
"Madonna Gives Support to Russia's Imprisoned Pussy Riot at Moscow Show Despite Threats of Violence." Associated Press, August 8, 2012.
"Matvienko prizvala menyat' patriarkhal'nyi mentalitet." Lenta.ru, July 25, 2019.
"Obrashchenie Prezidenta Rossiiskoy Federatsii." Kremlin.ru, February 24, 2022. http://kremlin.ru/events/president/news/67843.
"Patriarkh Kirill: Pravoslavnye lyudi ne vykhodyat na demonstratsii." VFM.ru, February 1, 2012. https://www.bfm.ru/news/169330.
"Polet Vladimira Putina so sterkhami." *Kommersant*, September 6, 2012.
"Pomoshchnitsa deputata iz Krasnoyarska poluchila prava admina v chate zhen mobilizovannykh i udalila ego iz–za prizivov k mitingu." Mediazona, November 15, 2023. https://zona.media/news/2023/11/15/wayhome.
"Poslanie prezidenta federal'nomu sobraniyu." Kremlin.ru, December 12, 2012. http://kremlin.ru/events/president/news/17118.
"Predsedatel' pravitel'stva Rossii V. V. Putin, pribyvshyy s rabochei poyezdkoy v Perm', posetil hokkeinyy match komand Rossiyskoy lyubitel'skoy hokkeynoy ligi, a takzhe pobesedoval s rukovodstvom ligi i predstavitelyami komand." Pravitel'stvo Rossiyskoy Federatsii, February 4, 2012. http://archive.government.ru/docs/18004/.
"Prezident rasskazal ob otkaze alkogol'nogo napitka." Lenta.ru, October 7, 2020.
"'Prigovor chudovishchno zhestokii'. Pediatru Nadezhde Buyanovoy dali 5,5 goda po delu o 'feykakh.'" BBC Russian, November 12, 2024. https://www.bbc.com/russian/articles/c75l4kd2224o.
"Protoierey Chaplin: V 20-e gody nravstvennym delom bylo by 'unichtozhit' kak mozhno bol'she bol'shevikov.'" Gazeta.ru, March 21, 2012. https://www.gazeta.ru/news/lenta/2012/03/21/n_2252589.shtml?updated.
"Putin, belukha, peredatchiki." Interfax, July 31, 2009.
"Putin: Dlya Rossiyi nepriyemlemo chtoby detyam navyazyvali izvrashcheniya." TASS, September 30, 2022. https://tass.ru/politika/15921455.
"Putin prizval ukreplyat' traditsionnye tzennosti v Rossii." RIA Novosti, September 12, 2023. https://ria.ru/20230912/tsennosti-1895771716.html.
"Putin pro belye lentochki kak simvol 'tsvetnoy revolyutsii': Pokhozhy na kontratseptivy." Gazeta.ru, December 15, 2011. https://www.gazeta.ru/news/lenta/2011/12/15/n_2135786.shtml.
"Putin prokommentiroval svoe foto slovami 'na medvede poka ne skakal.'" RBK, March 10, 2018. https://www.rbc.ru/rbcfreenews/5aa3a5599a79472bcf418f32.
"Putin rasskazal, chto emigranty iz Rossii vozvrashchayutsya na rodinu iz–za 'obshchikh tualetov dlya mal'chikov i devochek' v drugikh stranakh." Mediazona, January 16, 2024. https://zona.media/news/2024/01/16/toilets.
"Putin schitaet pravil'nym reshenie suda po delu Pussy Riot." RIA Novosti, October 7, 2012.
"Putin soobshchil, chto zanimaetsya sportom kazhdyy den'." TASS, June 13, 2017.
"Putin sovetuyet ne sudit' strogo uchastnits Pussy Riot." BBC Russian Service, August 2, 2012.
"Putin uveren, chto sport vospityvaet pravil'niye ustanovki." TASS, October 16, 2023.
"Putin zayavil, chto pri bor'be s alkogolizmom 'nel'zya nichego zapreshchat'.'" TASS, August 17, 2022.

"Pyanstvu – boy: Pochemu zhenshchiny zhivut dol'she muzhchin." Vysshaya Shkola Ekonomiki, August 12, 2021.

"Shef politsii Moskvy schel 'plevkom v dushu' aktsiyu Pussy Riot." BBC Russian Service, March 28, 2012.

"Shkolnikam na zanyatiakh po 'Semyevedeniyu' obyasnyat tsennosti 'brachnosti, mnogodetnosti, tselomudriya.'" Verstka.ru, August 22, 2024. https://verstka.media/semyevedenie-vvedut-v-programmu-s-novogo-uchebnogo-goda-news.

"Svyateyshyy Patriarkh Kirill: U nas net budushchego, esli my nachinaem glumit'sya pered velikimi svyatynyami." Patriarchia.ru, March 24, 2012. http://www.patriarchia.ru/db/text/2101850.html.

"Telegram-kanal zhen mobilizovannykh poluchil plashku Fake posle ataki propagandista Solovieva i provlastnogo yurista Remeslo." Agentstvo, December 1, 2023. https://www.agents.media/telegram-kanal-zhen-mobilizovannyh-poluchil-plashku-fake-posle-ataki-propagandista-soloveva-i-provlastnogo-yurista-remeslo/.

"Troe podrostkov zakidali snegom Vechnyi ogon' v Kingiseppe. Vozbuzhdeno delo o reabilitatsii natsizma." Fontanka.ru, January 1, 2025. https://www.fontanka.ru/2025/01/01/74951426/.

Ukaz Prezidenta Rossiiskoi Federatsii ot 09.11.2022 g. No. 809. http://www.kremlin.ru/acts/bank/48502.

"Valentina Tereshkova: 'Ukreplenie semyi – vazhneyshee gosudarstvennoe delo." Orenburg.er.ru, June 1, 2015. https://orenburg.er.ru/activity/news/valentina-tereshkova-ukreplenie-semi-vazhnejshee-gosudarstvennoe-delo.

"V Human Rights Watch zayavili o negativnykh posledstviyakh dekriminalizatsyi poboev v RF." Interfax, October 25, 2018.

"Vladimir Putin prinyal uchastie v XIX Yezhegodnom zasedanii Mezhdunarodnogo diskussionnogo kluba 'Valdai'. Stenogramma plenarnoy sessii." Valdai Discussion Club, October 27, 2022. https://ru.valdaiclub.com/events/posts/articles/vladimir-putin-prinyal-uchastie-v-xix-zasedanii-kluba-valdai/.

"Volodin prizval devochek varit' borsch. Video." RBC.ru, December 6, 2023. https://www.rbc.ru/politics/06/12/2023/657059179a794725e38f705d.

"V. Putin izvinilsya pered veruyushchimi za 'pank moleben' gruppy Pussy Riot." RBC.ru, March 7, 2012. https://www.rbc.ru/society/07/03/2012/5703f46f9a7947ac81a65a03.

"V. Putin nashel dve amfory na dne morya." RBC.ru, August 10, 2011. https://www.rbc.ru/society/10/08/2011/5703ea9e9a79477633d36618.

"V Rossii zaveli pervoe ugolovnoe delo ob 'LGBT-ekstremizme'." RBC.ru, March 18, 2024. https://www.rbc.ru/politics/18/03/2024/65f877509a794776142bd004.

"Vladimir Putin postavil tsel' priobshchit' k sportu 40 protsentov rossiyan." *Rossiyskaya gazeta*, April 13, 2012.

"Vstrecha s Mariey Lvovoy-Belovoy." Kremlin.ru, October 27, 2021. http://kremlin.ru/events/president/news/67015

"White Scarves and Flowers: Wives and Mothers of Mobilized Soldiers Take Resentment to the Kremlin." *Moscow Times*, January 16, 2024. https://www.themoscowtimes.com/2024/01/16/white-scarves-and-flowers-wives-and-mothers-of-mobilized-soldiers-take-resentment-to-the-kremlin-a83720.

"Zakrytie Vsemirnogo festivalya molodezhy." Kremlin.ru, March 6, 2024. http://www.kremlin.ru/events/president/news/73515.

Albats, Yevgenia. "Reporter poluchil zadanie: Rodit'!" *Moskovskie novosti*, July 17, 1988.
——. "Reporter zadanie vypolnila." *Moskovskie novosti*, January 1, 1989.
Baklanov, Alexander, translated by Nikita Buchko. 'Radical terrorists from Chechnya'! Billionaire Arkady Rotenberg's divorce is uglier than his ex-wife realized, it turns out." *Meduza*, July 26, 2021.
Barringer, Felicity. "Soviet Tongues Wag over Raisa Gorbachev." *New York Times*, December 2, 1987.
Bessonov, M. "Protiv vymyslov o tserkovnoy date." *Gudok*, April 11, 1987.
Borisenko, Lyubov. "Parad izvineniy." *Novaya Gazeta Europe*, December 26, 2023. https://novayagazeta.eu/articles/2023/12/26/filipp-kirkorov-kseniia-sobchak-i-lolita-izvinilis-za-uchastie-v-pochti-goloi-vecherinke-nasti-ivleevoi
Bucher, Greta. "Free and Worth Every Kopeck: Soviet Medicine and Women in Postwar Russia." In *The Human Tradition and Modern Russia*, edited by William B. Husband. Scholarly Resources, 2000.
——. "Struggling to Survive: Soviet Women in the Postwar Years." *Journal of Women's History* 12, no. 1 (2000): 137–59.
Buckley, Mary. "Glasnost and the Woman Question." In *Women and Society in Russia and the Soviet Union*, edited by Linda Edmondson. Cambridge University Press, 1992.
Butterfield, Fox. "At Wellesley, a Furor over Barbara Bush." *New York Times*, May 4, 1990.
Cavalli, Anna. "Buntarka ot meditsyny: Kak Nadezhda Suslova stala pervoy zhenshchinoy-vrachom v Rossii." *Forbes Woman*, February 9, 2021.
Chernova, Natalia. "Matushka vseya Rusi." *Novaya Gazeta*, July 1, 2020. https://novayagazeta.ru/articles/2020/07/01/86097-matushka-vseya-rusi.
Chernyshova, Elena. "Poyavilos' video s otdykha Putina I Shoigu v tayge." RBK, September 26, 2021. https://www.rbc.ru/politics/26/09/2021/614f995a9a794731cb0c770b.
Clark, Charles E. "Literacy and Labour: The Russian Literacy Campaign Within the Trade Unions, 1923–27." *Europe-Asia Studies* 47, no. 8 (1995): 1327–41.
Davidson, E. S., and L. T. Benjamin. "A History of the Child Study Movement in America," in *Historical Foundations of Educational Psychology: Perspectives on Individual Differences*, edited by J. A. Glover and R. R. Ronning. Springer, 1987, 41–60.
Dixon, Robyn, Francesca Ebel, and Natalia Abbakumova. "Have Babies for Russia: Putin Presses Women to Embrace Patriotism over Feminism." *Washington Post*, June 30, 2024.
Doktorov, Boris. Interview with Tatyana Zaslavskaya. *Sotsiologicheskii zhurnal* 3 (2007). https://cdclv.unlv.edu/archives/Interviews/zaslavskaya_07.html.
Egorova, Daria. "'Na nego zhestochayshim obrazom davili.' V SIZO pogib direktor turfirmy 'Men Trevel.'" Radio Svoboda, January 4, 2025. https://www.svoboda.org/a/na-nego-zhestochayshim-obrazom-davili-v-sizo-pogib-direktor-turfirmy-men-trevel-/33263010.html.
Elder, Miriam. "What Does Pussy Riot Mean Now?" BuzzFeed, February 7, 2014. https://www.buzzfeed.com/miriamelder/what-does-pussy-riot-mean-now.
Fedorenko, Natasha. "Otkuda vzyalsya spisok professii, zapreshchennykh dlya zhenshchin, i chto s nim budet teper'." *Theory & Practice*, July 8, 2019.
Ferris-Rotman, Amie. "Putin the Pro-Choice Champion." Coda, September 20, 2018. https://www.codastory.com/disinformation/traditional-values/putin-prochoice-champion/.
Gallagher, James P. "The Sad Fall of Brezhnev's Widow." *Chicago Tribune*, April 30, 1995.

Gogua, Irina. "Family Stories." *Ogonek*, March 4, 2014.
Gorbacheva, Raisa. "Foros: 73 chasa pod arestom. Iz dnevnika zheny prezidenta." Gorbachev Fund. https://www.gorby.ru/raisa/diary/.
Harden, Jeni. "'Mother Russia' at Work: Gender Divisions in the Medical Profession." *European Journal of Women's Studies* 8, no. 2 (2001): 181–99.
Hiatt, Fred. "Desperately Seeking Their Sons: Russians Go to Chechnya to Learn Children's Fate." *Washington Post*, January 15, 1995.
Ioffe, Julia. "The Cheating Cheaters of Moscow: How Infidelity Has Become Accepted and Even Expected." *Slate*, December 1, 2010.
———. "How Three Young Punks Made Putin Blink." *New Republic*, August 17, 2012.
———. "Net Impact," *New Yorker*, March 28, 2011.
———. "Prokhorov's Smile, Putin's Tears." *New Yorker*, March 4, 2012.
———. "Pussy Riot v. Putin: A Front Row Seat at a Russian Dark Comedy." *New Republic*, August 6, 2012.
———. "The Tragedy of Navalny," *Puck*, February 19, 2024. https://puck.news/the-tragedy-of-navalny/.
———. "Two Russian Women on a Sochi Train." *New Republic*, February 11, 2014.
Kanygin, Pavel. "Khachaturyan. Tantsy s pistoletom." *Novaya Gazeta*, December 21, 2018.
Keating, Joshua. "Alicia Silverstone Writes to Putin, Demands Vegan Meals for Pussy Riot Defendant." *Foreign Policy*, August 15, 2012.
Khabidulina, Ekaterina. "'Rotatsiya ne predusmotrena': Kartapolov nazval sroki vozvrashcheniya mobilizovannykh domoy." Forbes.ru, September 15, 2023.
Kishkovsky, Sophia. "Tatyana I. Zaslavskaya, Adviser to Gorbachev, Dies at 86." *New York Times*, September 3, 2013.
Kolesnikov, Andrey. "Kit sezona." *Kommersant*, August 26, 2010.
Kon, Igor. "Zachem nuzhny otzy?" *Literaturnaya gazeta*, February 28, 1973.
Konstantinova, Anna. "'Rabotaem, sestry'. Kto vedet kanal zhen mobilizovannykh 'Put' domoy,' chego oni khotyat i chem riskuyut." Mediazona, December 6, 2023. https://zona.media/article/2023/12/06/sisters.
Koshechkina, Varvara. "Shoigu dolozhil Putinu o zavershenii mobilizatsii." Lenta.ru, October 28, 2022.
Litvinova, Dasha. "Russian Lawmakers Move to Further Restrict Transgender Rights in New Legislation." Associated Press, July 13, 2023.
Lukas, J. Anthony, "Stalin's Daughter Called Indian Village a Paradise." *New York Times*, March 20, 1967.
McCuaig, Kerry. "Effects of Perestroika and Glasnost on Women." *Canadian Woman Studies* 10, no. 4 (1989): 11–14.
McDermid, Jane, and Anya Hillyard. "In Lenin's Shadow: Nadezhda Krupskaya and the Bolshevik Revolution," in *Reinterpreting Revolutionary Russia: Essays in Honour of James D. White*, edited by Ian D. Thatcher. Palgrave Macmillan, 2006.
Michaels, Sean. "Franz Ferdinand and Red Hot Chili Peppers Voice Support for Pussy Riot." *Guardian*, July 24, 2012.
Motyzlevskaya, Polina. "Deputat Butina poprosila proverit' vecherinku Ivleevoy na LGBT-propagandu." *Kommersant*, December 21, 2023. https://www.kommersant.ru/doc/6413694
Murphy, Matt. "Russian Parliament Bans Gender Reassignment Surgery for Trans People." *BBC News*, July 14, 2023.

Nakachi, Mie. "N. S. Khrushchev and the 1944 Soviet Family Law: Politics, Reproduction, and Language." *East European Politics and Societies* 20, no. 1 (February 2006): 40–68.

Navalny, Alexey. "Pro Pussy Riots." LiveJournal, March 7, 2012. https://navalny .livejournal.com/690551.html.

Novikova, Inna. "Andrei Kormukhin: Zakonoproekt 'O semeino-bytovom nasilii'— dyavol v detalyakh." *Pravda*, December 2, 2019. https://www.pravda.ru /society/1455616-kormuhin/.

Oganov, Grigory. "Perestroika i 1000-e kreshcheniya Rusi." *Sovetskaya kul'tura*, June 18, 1988.

Pertsev, Andrei. "'K prezidentu lyudi s ulitsy priiti ne mogut Pomnite, Putin nedavno vstretilsya s materyami soldat - a okozalos', chto mnogie iz nikh svyazany s vlastyami? 'Meduza' vyyasnila, kak Kreml' gotovil eto sobytie." Meduza, December 3, 2022. https://meduza.io/feature/2022/12/03/k-prezidentu-lyudi-s -ulitsy-priyti-ne-mogut.

Pyatin, Alexander, and Anastasia Lyalikova. "Byvshaya zhena Rotenberga obratilas' v politsiu iz-za 'zakhvata' villy vo Frantsii." *Forbes Russia*, July 24, 2021.

Ramakrishnan, Aditi, et al. "Women's Participation in the Medical Profession: Insights from Experiences in Japan, Scandinavia, Russia, and Eastern Europe." *Journal of Women's Health* 23, no. 11 (2014): 927–34.

Rankin-Williams, Amy. "Post-Soviet Contraceptive Practices and Abortion Rates in St. Petersburg, Russia." *Health Care for Women International* 22, no. 8 (2001): 699–710.

Reid, Susan E. "Cold War in the Kitchen: Gender and the De-Stalinization of Consumer Taste in the Soviet Union under Khrushchev." *Slavic Review* 61, no. 2 (Summer 2002): 211–52.

Remnick, David. "Perestroika Nurtured at Siberian Think Tank." *Washington Post*, February 10, 1990.

Rubin, Mikhail, Dmitri Sukharev, Roman Bodanin, and Svetlana Reiter. "Chem boleet Putin? Rassledovanie k 70-letiyu Vladimira Putina." *Proekt*, April 1, 2022. https:// www.proekt.media/investigation/chem-boleet-putin/.

Ryzhkova, Anna, and Regina Gimalova. "'Eto li ne patrioticheskoe chuvstvo, kogda chuzhykh detei ne byvaet i vse nashi?' Maria Lvova-Belova." *Verstka*, March 15, 2023. https://verstka.media/lvova-belova-profile.

Schafer, Susanne M. "Nancy, Raisa in 'Mexican Standoff.'" Associated Press, June 1, 1988.

Scully, Emer. "Putin's Old Judo Partner, 68, Wins Latest Round of Battle with His Ballet Teacher Ex, 39, over £27m Surrey Mansion Complete with Tennis Courts, Swimming Pool and Its Own Panic Room." *Daily Mail*, November 10, 2021.

Shmaraeva, Elena. "Gulag dlya samykh malen'kikh." Mediazona, September 26, 2014.

Shohat, Yehuda, and Elad Zeret. "Himmler's Letters Revealed: 'I'm Going to Auschwitz. Kisses.'" Ynetnews.com, January 26, 2014. https://www.ynetnews.com/articles /0,7340,L-4481014,00.html.

Smirnov, Sergey. "Eks-supruga Arkadia Rotenberga registriruet brend Rotenberg." *The Bell*, August 14, 2019.

Smith, J. Y. "Raisa Gorbachev, Last Soviet First Lady, Dies." *Washington Post*, September 21, 1999.

Stanley, Alessandra. "Nazran Journal; Mothers Act to Save Their Sons from War." *New York Times*, February 11, 1995.

Sukhova, Svetlana. "Tamara Pletnyova: Predstavlenie ob orderakh." *Ogonek*, October 28, 2019. https://www.kommersant.ru/doc/4117361.

Temkina, Anna. "The Gynaecologist's Gaze: The Inconsistent Medicalisation of Contraception in Contemporary Russia." *Europe-Asia Studies* 67, no. 10 (2015): 1527–46.

Thompson, Nicholas. "My Friend, Stalin's Daughter: The Complicated Life of Svetlana Alliluyeva." *New Yorker*, March 24, 2014.

Urlanis, Boris. "Beregite Muzhchin!" *Literaturnaya gazeta*, July 24, 1968.

———. "Bezotzovshchina." *Literaturnaya gazeta*, January 7, 1970.

Vinokurova, Ekaterina, and Olga Kuzmenkova. "Dolzhen byt' gosudarstvennyy ideal sem'yi." Gazeta.ru, June 5, 2013. https://www.gazeta.ru/politics/2013/06/05_a_5368589.shtml?updated.

Walker, Edward W. "Islam in Chechnya." *Contemporary Caucasus Newsletter*, no. 6 (Fall 1998). Berkeley Program in Soviet and Post-Soviet Studies, University of California, Berkeley.

Womack, Helen. "Beria's Mistress Comes Out of the Closet." *Independent*, July 25, 1993.

Yakovenko, Dmitry. "Igor Rotenberg snova stal milliarderom." *Forbes Russia*, August 2, 2021.

Zhirnov, Yevgeni. "Peredal emu gazetu v kotoroy lezhali obligatsii." *Kommersant Vlast'*, December 10, 2012.

Zinkina, Yulia, and Andrey Korotaev. "Razryv v ozhidaemoy prodolzhitel'nosti zhizni muzhchin i zhenshchin: Obzor geneticheskikh, sotsial'nykh i tsennostnykh faktorov." *Demograficheskoe obozrenie* 8, no. 1 (2021): 106–26.

REPORTS

"Chislo umershikh v trudosposobnom vozraste po osnovnym klassam i otdel'nym prichinam smerti na 100 tys. naselenia sootvetsvuyushchego pola i vozrasta, yanvar'–dekabr' 2019 god, predvaritel'nye dannye po date registratsii v organakh ZAGS, bez ucheta okonchatel'nykh meditsinskikh svidetel'stv o smerti." Federal'naya sluzhba gosudarstvennoy statistiki, March 4, 2020.

"Natsional'nyy reyting trezvosti subyektov Rossiiskoy Federatsii – 2017." Trezvaya Rossiya.

Poznyak, Vladimir, and Dag Rekve. "Global Status Report on Alcohol and Health 2018." World Health Organization, Geneva, Switzerland, 2018.

"Zabolevaemost' naselenia po osnovnym klassam boleznei v 2000–2021 gg. (zaregestrirovano zabolevaniy u patsientov s diagnozom ustanovlennym v pervye v zhizni), Dannye Minzdrava Rossii, raschet Rosstata." Federal'naya sluzhba gosudarstvennoy statistiki, November 20, 2022.

Zaslavskaya, T. I. "Obshchestvennoe mnenie o problemakh rabotayushchikh zhenshchin." Levada Center Archives, Moscow, April 17, 1990.

———. "Zhenshchina v semye." Levada Center Archives, December 20, 1989.

VIDEOS

"'Bylo mnogo ranenykh, oni prosto tam istekali krov'yu!'" Kak zhena rossiiskogo mobilizovannogo pytalas' vernut' muzha s peredovoy." *Nastoyashchee vremya*, November 12, 2022. https://www.currenttime.tv/a/32127060.html.

"'Eto dolzhno delat'sya rukami kontraktnoy armii.' Zhena mobilizovannogo – o voyne, razocharovanii v Putine i popytkakh vernut' muzha domoy." *Nastoyashchee vremya*, November 24, 2023. https://www.currenttime.tv/a/32697107.html.

Matveeva, Garadzha. "Devchonki PUSSY RIOT zakhvatyvayut transport." November 6, 2011. https://www.youtube.com/watch?v=qEiB1RYuYXw.
———. "Gruppa Pussy Riot zhzhet putinskiy glamur." November 30, 2011. https://www.youtube.com/watch?v=CZUhkWiiv7M.
———. "Pussy Riot na Krasnoy Ploshchadi – pesnya 'Putin zassal.'" January 20, 2011. https://www.youtube.com/watch?v=7kVMADLm3js.
———. "PUSSY RIOT poyut politzekam na kryshe tyurmy." December 14, 2011. https://www.youtube.com/watch?v=mmyZbJpYV0I.
"Russia: Chechnya: Russian Mothers Brave Front Line." Associated Press, January 9, 1995. https://www.youtube.com/watch?v=bEOKwoLjmJ8.
"Tatyana Golikova vystupaet na VMF-2024: Pryamaya translyatsiya." *Komsomol'skaya Pravda*, March 6, 2024. https://www.youtube.com/watch?v=r43jKpOHngs.
"Ukrainian Woman Offers Seeds to Russian Soldiers So 'Sunflowers Grow When They Die'—Video." *Guardian*, February 25, 2022. https://www.theguardian.com/world/video/2022/feb/25/ukrainian-woman-sunflower-seeds-russian-soldiers-video.
"Vstrecha s materyami voennosluzhashchikh – uchastnikov SVO." Kremlin.ru, November 25, 2022. http://www.kremlin.ru/events/president/news/69935.

PERIODICALS
Gudok
Izvestia
Krokodil
Kommersant
Kommersant Vlast'
Lenta.ru
Literaturnaya gazeta
Ogonek
Pravda
TVRain.ru

ARCHIVES
Blavatnik Archive (digital)
NKVD Archive, Moscow
USB Archive, Odessa

INDEX

abortion
  in the Gulag, 78
  healthcare provided during, 255–56
  illegal, 9, 93, 149, 154, 166, 168
  legalization of, xii, 42–43, 191, 364
  rates, 254
  restrictions, 358, 424, 431, 433
  in the United States, 254, 282–83, 288
  Zalkind on, 51
adoption, 49, 432–33
adultery, 167, 202–3
Afghanistan invasion, 251, 408
Aganbegyan, Abel, 222–23, 224
agricultural production, 164, 219–20, 251
Akhmatova, Anna, 84–85, 88–91, 143, 346, 430
Akmolinsk Camp for Wives of Traitors to the Motherland, 74
Albats, Yevgenia, 256–59, 390, 392, 394, 395–96, 397, 404
alcohol consumption, 195, 198, 319, 320, 326–27, 330–31
Alexander I, 336
Alexander II, 5
Alexander Nevsky Monastery, 25
Alexievich, Svetlana, 90, 134
alimony, 26, 50
Alliluyev, Joseph, 240, 246–47
Alliluyev, Sergei, 64
Alliluyeva, Anna Sergeyevna, 63, 66, 74
Alliluyeva, Katya, 246–47
Alliluyeva, Kira, 81
Alliluyeva, Nadezhda (Nadya), 172, 242
  career, 64–65
  death, 67–68, 139, 141, 142, 182
  Khrushchev and, 63, 65
  Lenin and, 64
  Stalin and, 63–68, 308
Alliluyeva, Svetlana
  Beria rumors, 153
  Churchill and, 139, 204
  defection, 210–11, 238–46
  father's death, 159–60, 163, 204–5
  on her mother's character, 66
  and Kapler, 142–43
  marriages and family life, 143–44
  mother's death and funeral, 67, 68, 139
  press coverage, 239–41
  relationship with father, 139–45, 153
  return to Moscow, 246–48
  Singh and, 204–8, 210
  in the United States, 239–46, 248
  Wright and, 241–44
Alliluyeva Charitable Trust, 243
All-Union Center for the Study of Public Opinion, 259
alpinism, 185
Altai wapiti, 332–33
Alyokhina, Masha
  arrest and trial, 348–55, 357
  birth and early years, 345–46
  hunger strike, 362–63
  imprisonment, 359–63
  Mediazona, 368
  pardon, 363
  Pussy Riot, 346–47, 367
America. *See* United States
Amnesty International, 348
anarchists, 4, 30, 364
Andreev, Ivan, 406, 409–11, 413–14, 419, 433–34
Andreeva, Maria, 406, 407, 409–11, 413–14, 415–16, 419, 430, 433–34
Andropov, Yuri, 225
Anti-Corruption Foundation, 377, 390, 396, 420
anti-Jewish violence, 34–37, 120–26
anti-Semitism, 123, 143–44, 181–84, 212–13, 265–66
Applebaum, Anne, 77

INDEX

April Theses, 5
Arbatova, Maria, 339
Armand, Alexander, 14, 16, 44
Armand, Inessa, 93, 262, 342, 366, 432
   abortion support, 42
   arrest, 20
   birth and early years, 14, 17
   Central Committee nomination, 28
   death, 43–44
   education, 20
   exile, 13, 16, 20
   as head of Zhenotdel, 27–28, 29
   Krupskaya and, 13, 16–17
   Lenin and, 13–14, 16, 20, 29
   marriage and family life, 14, 16
   Marxism, 20, 23
   philanthropy, 15–16
Armand, Vladimir, 16
Armenia, 265
Ashurkov, Vladimir, 397, 398
assassinations and plots, 5–6, 18, 30–32, 70, 96, 400

babas, 12, 27, 29, 59
Babel, Isaac, 35–36, 120
Babi Yar massacre, 125–26
Baker, James, 269
Baltic republics, 34, 122, 221, 251
Barskaya, Olga, 37
   abortions, 255–56, 283
   birth and early years, 190–91, 192, 193
   career, 267, 285–86
   education, 214–16, 255, 266–67, 282, 283
   Ioffe and, 216–17
   marriage and family life, 217, 266, 267–68
   pregnancy and childbirth, 253–55, 281–82
   relationship with Emma, 275–76, 426–28
   young adult years, 212, 213
Barsky, Pavel, 53
Barsky, Yura, 52–55, 58–60, 125, 185–86, 190–93, 195, 212, 267, 279, 435
Bastrykin, Alexander, 381
Batalina, Olga, 372–73, 375
BBC, 271, 273

Bebel, August, 6–7, 11
Beckerman, Gal, 213
Bedny, Demian, 32
Belarus, 34, 36, 97, 122, 251, 280, 393
Bellingcat, 400
Berdichev, 120–21
Berezniki penal colony, 359
Beria, Lavrentiy
   arrest, 146–47
   Chizhova rape, 147–49, 154
   Drozdova rape, 149–51, 155–57
   execution, 147, 152
   sexual predation, 146, 152–55
   trial, 151–52, 157–58
Berlin, Isaiah, 241
Berlin Wall, 251, 316
Berlusconi, Silvio, 403
Beylin, Alexander, 85
Beylin, Dmitry (Dima), 86, 125, 185, 190
birth certificates, 166–69
birth control, 9, 42–43, 51, 166, 191, 253–54, 433
birth rates, 433
Black Maria (NKVD car), 72, 85–86
black market, 201, 208
Bolshevik Revolution, xi, 23–24, 33–34, 181, 239, 261–62
Bolsheviks and Bolshevism
   Civil War propaganda, 97–98, 162
   Jewish sympathizers, 35
   opposition to Church, 264
   revolutionary plans, 4–5
   social reforms, 24–26
   underground, 16
   views of women, 12, 28, 42–43, 74–75, 93–94, 261–62
Bolshoi Ballet, 209, 264, 265
Borusyak, Lyubov, 294
Bosh, Evgenia, 97
Botkin Hospital, 192, 213–14, 285
Brajesh Singh Hospital, 241
Brekhman, Bella, 187, 188, 281
Brezhnev, Leonid, 233, 290
   coup against Khrushchev, 199, 212
   death, 208
   field wives, 134
   marriage and family life, 200, 202, 208–9

mistresses, 202–3
Viktoria and, 202, 208, 308
Brezhnev, Yakov, 203
Brezhnev, Yuri, 208
Brezhneva, Galina, 202, 209–10
Brezhneva, Luba, 201, 203, 208, 209
Brezhneva, Viktoria, 199, 200, 202–3, 208, 210, 308
Bride of the Revolution (McNeal), 20–21
Brodsky, Joseph, 186
Brokaw, Tom, 226
Browning, Christopher, 123
Bruk, Abram, 86, 87
Bruk, Alexander (Sasha), 87
Bruk, Anatoly (Tolya), 113, 119, 129–31
Bruk, Efim, 86–87, 181
Bruk, Emma, 215, 267, 268, 280, 299, 376
  abortions, 191, 254
  Barsky and, 185–86, 212, 279
  Beria rumors, 146, 153, 158
  career, 191–93, 213–14, 267
  death, 434–35
  education, 179–80, 184–85
  family lost to Holocaust of the East, 126
  health issues, 426–28
  Larichev and, 275, 284
  marriage and family life, 190–93, 275, 287
  relationship with Olga, 275–76, 426–28
  romantic life, 213, 214
  United States trips, 281–84, 427
  during World War II, 113, 118–19, 129–31
Bruk, Isaak, 86, 113, 114, 117–18, 123–24, 129, 183–84, 191, 266, 268, 435
Bruk, Neonila, 87
Bucher, Greta, 189, 194–95
Buddhism, 265
Budnitskii, Oleg, 35
Bugaychenko, Dasha, 323–24
Bugaychenko, Lyuda, 321–24
Bulgakova, Elena Sergeyevna, 81
Burdonsky, Alexander, 247
Buryatse, Boris, 210
Bush, Barbara, 249–50, 252, 274
Bush, George H. W., 249, 252, 274
Butina, Maria, 424

cafeterias, 41–42
Cameron, David, 354
cannibalism, 135
Capital (Marx), 18
capitalism
  free-market economy, 45, 285, 317, 350
  grocery stores and, 340
  marriage in, 7
  perestroika, 222–24
  as source of women's oppression, 10
Cathedral of Christ the Savior, 336–38, 347, 402
Catherine the Great, 25, 34
censorship, 123, 163, 418
Center Against Extremism, 344
Central Committee, 23, 27, 28, 32, 71, 199, 220, 226, 270, 285
Central Executive Committee, 77
Central Scientific Research Institute of Leather Footwear Industry, 52
Chaplin, Charlie, 101
Chechen war, 408–9, 417
Cheka, 30, 32, 96, 417
chelnaki (merchants), 321
Chernenko, Konstantin, 225, 402
child abandonment, 50, 166
child-bearing and -rearing, 10, 11, 41–42, 77–80, 135–36, 256–59. *See also* family laws
childcare, 7, 9, 10, 41–42, 187
child support, xii, 25, 50, 167
Chizhova, Valentina, 147–49, 154, 157
Choral Synagogue, 181
ChSIR ("family members of traitors to the Motherland"), 74–75, 81–82
Churbanov, Yuri, 209
Churchill, Winston, 101, 139, 204
CIA, 238, 239
"civilized patriarchy," 295
Civil War, 33, 35–36, 38, 42, 43, 69, 96, 97, 162
class differences, 8–9, 65. *See also nomenklatura*
Claudia (nun), 336
Clements, Barbara Evans, 10, 27
Cold War, 175, 239
collective farms, 219–20, 221, 231, 251, 318

collectivization, 10, 134, 164
Committee of Soldiers' Mothers, 408–9, 416–17, 418, 429
Commonwealth of Independent States, 281
Communist Party, 27–29, 45, 93, 113, 160–61, 266, 372
Communist Youth League (Komsomol), 92–93, 94, 99, 184, 230
complete families, 194
Constituent Assembly, 30, 31
constitution (1918), 95
Construction Institute, 56
contraception, 9, 42–43, 51, 166, 191, 253–54, 433
cooperatives, 252
corporal punishment, 360–61
corruption, 15, 209, 341, 349, 350, 377
Cossacks, 35, 36–37
Covid, 427–28
Crimea, 52, 59, 97, 125, 177, 269, 270, 280, 407, 422
Crimean War, 215
criminal justice system, 356, 366, 371–72
Cuban missile crisis, 174

Davtyan, Mari, 382–84, 387, 388
death camps, 120–26
deficit goods, 251–52
democracy, 317, 372, 417
Denikin, Anton, 35
Denisenko, Mikhail, 195, 319–20, 324
divorce, xii, 8, 9, 10, 26, 50, 93, 167, 170, 358
Dokukin, Sasha, 106
domestic violence legislation, 371–73, 375, 378, 381–83, 387–89
Domontovich, Alexandra. *See* Kollontai, Alexandra
Donbas, 407, 422, 425
"double burden" of women, 172, 188, 196, 260
Drozdova, Valentina (Lyalya), 149–51, 152, 155–58
Dudayev, Dzhokhar, 408
Duma, 305, 358, 372, 373, 388, 415
Durov, Pavel, 419
Dybenko, Pavel, 29, 45

economy, 219–24, 231, 251–53, 285, 316, 317
education, 7, 26, 38, 41, 93–94, 133, 176, 431
Einigkeit (periodical), 123
Eisenhower, Mamie, 172
Ekho Moskvy, 392
elections
　fraud, 345
　free, 30
　Kremlin control over, 359
　presidential, 289, 347, 430
Eleonora (friend), 300, 301–2
Elwood, R. C., 20
Engels, Friedrich, 7, 10, 11
Erofeev, Venedikt, 339
espionage, 71, 87, 96, 143, 147, 152, 309, 311, 313, 424
executions, 6, 18, 31–32, 72, 75, 97, 147, 215, 227, 272
Extraordinary Commission for the Liquidation of Illiteracy (LikBez), 39, 227

family laws
　1918 Family Code, 49
　1936 Family Law, 93
　Khrushchev's, 165–70, 187
　KZOBS, 168
　Putin's, 431–32
family planning, 42–43, 254
family policy, 25–26
Family Studies curriculum, 431
famine, 38, 67, 135, 284
fatherlessness, 193–98, 422
February Revolution (1917), 4
Federation Council, 372, 387, 388
femininity, states of, 295–97
feminism
　American, 253, 288, 363–64
　among the upper-class, 8, 11–12
　decline of, 320
　as an extreme ideology, 300
　opposition to, 341
　punk, 343–45
　second-wave, 249, 342
　Soviet, 295, 339, 366–67
　Western ideas of, 364–66

field wives, 134
financial crisis (2008), 294
financial fraud, 361
Finland Station, 4
Fitzpatrick, Sheila, 13
Five-Year Plans, 58, 164
Ford, Henry, 101
"former people," 49
Frank Lloyd Wright Foundation, 242–44
fraud, 345, 361, 394, 420
freedom of conscience, 264
freedom of speech, 168, 419
free-market economy, 45, 285, 317, 350
FSB, 289, 340, 394, 397, 400, 417
Fyodorova, Zoya, 154, 155

Gagarin, Yuri, 264
Gaidar, Yegor, 284–85
Gamarnik, Viktoria (Veta), 69–70, 71, 72–73, 75, 82
Gamarnik, Yan, 69–70
Gandhi, Mahatma, 205
Gapchenko, Natasha, 286
gender identity, 424
Georgia, 64, 140, 141, 217, 241–42, 247, 265, 280
Gessen, Masha, 338, 342, 357
Gindin, Mikhail, 136
Gindina, Asma, 103–5, 128, 131–32, 136
Ginzburg, Eugenia, 75–77, 78–79, 90, 200, 360
Glamour (periodical), 363–64
glasnost, 82, 247, 256, 266
"glass-of-water" theory, 49
Glinka, Mikhail, 265
Gogua, Irina, 66, 67
gonorrhea, 15
Gorbachev, Mikhail Sergeyevich, xiii
  collapse of Soviet Union, 280–81, 295
  coup against, 269–75
  glasnost policy, 247, 256, 266
  perestroika policy, 225, 227, 238, 250–53
  political career, 230
  Raisa and, 225–27, 228–30, 233–37, 269–75
  summit with Bush, 249–50
  on women, 408–9

World Congress of Women, 259, 262–63
Gorbacheva, Irina, 230, 233, 270, 272, 274
Gorbacheva, Raisa, 393
  abortion, 229
  Barbara Bush and, 249–50, 252
  birth and early years, 227–28
  career, 232–34
  education, 228, 229, 230–32
  Gorbachev and, 225–27, 228–30, 233–37, 269–75
  health issues, 274
  Nancy Reagan and, 235–37
  reforms, 417
  state Church celebrations, 264
  Wellesley commencement, 249–51, 252
Gorbatenko, Svetlana, 411–12
Gorbunova, Yulia, 382
Gorky Institute of World Literature, 206
Grachev, Dimitry, 369–71, 374–76, 378, 379–80, 384
Gracheva, Margarita (Rita), 369–71, 374–76, 378, 379–81, 384–86, 388, 389
Great Fatherland War. *See* World War II
Great Terror, 70–72, 84–85, 113–14, 180–81
Great War (World War I), 3, 23, 26, 34–35, 52, 97, 161
Gromyko, Andrei, 265
Grossman, Ekaterina, 121–22
Grossman, Vasily, 120–22, 123
Grozev, Christo, 400–401
guerrilla actions
  Pussy Riot's, 344–45, 346–47, 367
  Voina's, 340–41
Gulag, 58, 70, 71, 72, 74, 81, 147, 264
  men's experiences, 75, 77
  pregnancy and motherhood in, 77–80
  women's experiences, 75–80, 81–82
Gulag (Applebaum), 77
Gulag Archipelago, The (Solzhenitsyn), 75, 90
Gumilev, Lev, 84–85
Gumilev, Nikolai, 84

Guriev, Sergei, 397
Guthrie, Woody, 101

Harper's Bazaar (periodical), 393, 395
healthcare
  abortion, 255–56
  dispensary-based system, 191–92
  focus on men, 198
  maternal, 10, 24, 256–59
  heart disease, 329–31
Hell of Treblinka, The (Grossman), 120–22
Hero Mother, 166, 431
Hero of the Soviet Union, 99, 133
higher education, xii, 176, 261, 431
Higher School of Economics, 319, 324, 330
Himmler, Heinrich, 123
Hitler, Adolf, xii, 35, 92, 114, 116, 133, 181
Holocaust of the East, 120–26
Hosking, Geoffrey, 265
household appliances, 171, 188, 241, 252–53
housing, 171, 187
Human Rights Watch, 381–82
Hungary, 173, 251

#IDidntWanttoDie campaign, 378, 381
Ignatov, Nikolay, 203
illiteracy, 38–39
incomplete families, 194
infanticide, 9, 166
infant mortality, 258
infidelity, 294, 322
inflation, 38, 200, 285
Institute of World Economics and International Affairs, 205
intelligentsia, 14, 16, 256, 305
Intermediary project (Tolstoy), 17
International Criminal Court, 432
International Women's Day, 3, 210, 306, 408
Investigative Committee, 373, 381
Ioffe, Bluma, 177
Ioffe, Dina, xi, 266, 267
Ioffe, Mendel, 177
Ioffe, Mikhail (Michael), 128–29, 187, 188, 215, 255, 267–68

Ioffe, Nathan (Nota), 111–12, 115, 120, 125, 128, 178
Ioffe, Samuel (Monya), 111–12, 115, 119–20, 125, 128–29, 178
Ioffe, Sonya, 177, 179, 189
Ioffe, Yasha, 111–12, 114–15, 120, 125, 178–79, 187–89, 279, 281
Iskra (periodical), 21
Islam, 265
Israel, 181, 182, 212, 290, 291
"Ivan Susanin" (Glinka), 265
Ivleeva, Anastasia, 424–25
Izvestia (periodical), 239

Jewish Anti-Fascist Committee, 181, 182–83
Jewish people
  anti-Semitism, 123, 143–44, 181–84, 212–13, 265–66
  arrests of prominent, 180–81, 182–83
  Babi Yar massacre, 126, 127
  emigration, 34, 275–76
  ghettos, 125
  Great Terror, 180–81
  Holocaust of the East, 120–26
  Mensheviks, 88
  Pale of Settlement, 34–35, 120, 181
  pogroms, 34, 35, 265, 268, 275
  quotas, 215–16
  stereotyping of, 213
journalism, 376–79, 417
Journey into the Whirlwind (Ginzburg), 75–77, 200
Judt, Tony, 175–76
A Just Russia, 372

Kabaeva, Alina, 403
Kalinin, Mikhail, 77
Kaplan, Fanny, 30–32
Kapler, Aleksei, 142–43, 240
Kashin, Oleg, 397
Kats, Olga, 414–16
Kats, Sasha, 414–15, 416
Kazakhstan, 74, 116, 202, 322
Kenez, Peter, 35
Kennan, Christopher, 239
Kennan, George, 238–39, 241
Kennan, Joan, 239

Kennedy, Jackie, 173
Kennedy, John F., 173
Keohane, Nannerl, 249, 250
KGB, 96, 199, 200, 209, 220, 223, 240, 256, 264, 268, 270, 272, 273, 290, 309–17, 417
Khachaturyan, Angelina, 378–79
Khachaturyan, Krestina, 378–79
Khachaturyan, Maria, 378–79
Khachaturyan, Mikhail, 378–79
Khodorkovsky, Mikhail, 351
Khrushchev, Leonid, 162
Khrushchev, Nikita Sergeyevich, xiii, 139, 141, 212, 220, 221
    Alliluyeva and, 63, 65
    Beria arrest, 146–47, 149, 151–52
    Brezhnev's coup against, 199
    death, 200
    de-Stalinization plans, 160–61, 163
    family law, 165–70, 187
    legacy of, 174
    monetary reform, 192
    Nina Petrovna and, 161–63
    population growth plans, 164–72
    Secret Speech, 82, 160
    Stalin and, 65
Khrushchev, Rada, 170
Khrushchev, Yulia, 162
Khrushcheva, Nina Petrovna, 68, 160–63, 170–74, 199–200, 203, 208, 226
Kirbasova, Maria, 408
Kirilenko, Andrei, 234
Kirilenko, Elizaveta, 234
Kirill, Patriarch, 347, 388, 389
Kirov, Sergey, 70
Knight, Amy, 155
kolkhozy (collective farms), 219–20, 231, 251
Kollontai, Alexandra, xii, 93, 161, 173, 253, 262, 295, 342, 366
    as ambassador, 45–46
    birth and early years, 5
    disdain for feminism, 8, 11–12
    education, 5
    exile, 6, 49, 51
    as head of Zhenotdel, 44–45, 162
    on labor conscription, 41
    Lenin and, 5, 44–45

    marriage and family life, 5–6, 29, 45
    Marxism, 6
    Palace of Motherhood, 24–25, 28–29, 256
    People's Will, 5–6
    return from exile, 4–5
    social reforms, 24–27, 174, 432
    as "Valkyrie of the Revolution," 5
    views on sex, 10–11, 49–51, 170
    Zhenotdel, 27
Kollontai, Vladimir, 5
Kolokoltsev, Vladimir, 349
Komskaya, Brokha-Pesya (Bronya), 111–12, 114–15, 119–20, 125, 128–29, 178, 187, 215
Komsomol, 92–93, 94, 99, 184, 230
Kon, Igor, 197
Koptyug, Valentin, 219, 223
Kopylova, Olga, 293, 295–97
Kormukhin, Andrei, 388
Korotaev, Andrey, 330–31
Kossior, Stanislav, 74
Kosygin, Alexei, 206, 207, 239
Kotkin, Stephen, 47–48, 68, 71, 72, 152, 254
Krasnaya Zvezda (periodical), 120
Kremlin, 32, 65, 66, 180, 213, 281, 351, 372, 399, 413
Kremlin Palace, 402
Krieger, Lyuba, 126
Krieger, Polina, 126
Krieger, Zhenya, 126
Krivonogikh, Svetlana, 404
Krupskaya, Nadezhda, 93, 161, 170, 172, 173, 250, 253, 342, 366
    abortion support, 42
    Armand and, 13, 16–17
    arrest, 19
    birth and early years, 17
    Central Committee nomination, 28
    exile, 19
    as first lady, 40–41, 64
    health issues, 40–41
    Lenin and, 18–22, 31–32, 40, 41, 44, 46–48, 64, 68, 402
    LikBez program, 39
    marriage and family life, 12, 13
    Marxism, 18–22

Krupskaya, Nadezhda (*continued*)
    political career, 40–41
    portrayals of, 20–22
    Stalin and, 46–47, 70
    teaching career, 17–19
    wartime activities, 23
Krylenko, Nikolai, 32
Krylova, Anna, xii, 103
Kryuchkov, Vladimir, 273
Kudryavtsev, Konstantin, 401
Kuzmina, Alexandra, 183
Kuznetsova, Anna, 358

labor camps, 58, 70, 71
labor conscription, 41–42
labor force
    men in, 194–95
    women in, 4, 194–95, 260–61, 268
labor strikes, 3–4, 12, 20, 24, 251
Larichev, Oleg, 275, 284
Latvia, 122
laundries, 41–42
Laverchenko, Tamara, 202
Lenin, Alexander, 18
Lenin, Maria, 40
Lenin, Vladimir, xiii, 4–5, 11, 47–48, 262, 295
    abortion support, 42
    Alliluyeva and, 64
    April Theses, 5
    arrest and imprisonment, 19, 46
    assassination attempt, 30–32
    on collectivized homes, 10
    coup, 23–24
    death, 48–49
    on divorce, 8, 170
    exile, 19, 402
    in hiding, 23
    Inessa and, 13–14, 16, 20, 29, 43–44
    Kollontai and, 5, 44–45
    mausoleum, 63, 337
    Mikhelson factory speech, 30
    Nadezhda and, 12, 13, 18–22, 31, 40, 41, 44, 46–48, 64, 68, 402
    NEP, 45
    opposition to Church, 264
    Stalin and, 45, 46–49
    strokes, 46–48

War Communism, 38
    withdrawal from Great War, 26
    on women, 12
Leningrad Music Hall, 307
Leningrad State University, 307
Lenin Library, 180
Lenin Prize, 192
Lenin's Testament, 47–48
Lensovet Theatre, 306
Lesha (villager), 318–19, 326–28
Let's Bring the Boys Home (*Vernyom rebyat*), 414, 416
Let's Talk (YouTube channel), 377–78, 381–82
Levada Center, 349
Levinson, Alexey, 321
Levitan, Yury, 130
Leyla (friend), 300–301
LGBT people, 372, 423–26
Liepa, Maris, 209
Life Academy, 293–98, 302
Ligachev, Yegor, 247–48
LikBez program, 39, 227
Limonov, Eduard, 339
literacy, 12, 17–18, 38–39
Literaturnaya gazeta (periodical), 193, 195–97
Lithuania, 122, 265
Litvinov, Maxim, 213
Litvinov, Pavel, 213–14
Litvinova, Flora, 213–14
Litvyak, Lidia, 103, 133
lonely mothers, 189–90, 232
Lvova-Belova, Maria, 432–33

Madonna, 354
Make Your Husband a Millionaire (Renar), 300
Malakhov, Andrey, 379–80
Male State, 379
Malenkov, Georgy, 171
Mann, Horace, 41
March of Maternal Compassion, 408
marriage
    bourgeois, 7–8, 10, 11, 25, 50
    civil, 364
    common-law, 50, 166–69
    desire for, 293–3

to foreigners, 206–7
legal age for, 25, 51
love triangles, 14
open, 60
as a religious institution, 8–9, 25
sham, 6
snokhachestvo tradition, 9
socialist, 10
state recognition of, 25–26, 166–69
women taking husband's names, 286–87
Marx, Karl, 5, 6, 7, 11, 18
Marxism, 6–8, 45, 95. *See also* Social Democratic Party
maternity leave, xii, 10, 25, 165, 194–95, 255, 409
Matvienko, Valentina, 387–89
Mayakovsky, Vladimir, 339
McNeal, Robert, 20–22
Medal of Maternal Glory, 166
Medals of Motherhood, 166
Mediazona, 368
Meduza, 412–13
Medvedev, Dmitry, 332, 337, 340, 345, 347, 417
Medvedevo, 318–20, 324–28
Meir, Golda, 181–82
Memorial, 417
men
  alcohol consumption, 195, 198, 319, 320, 326–27, 330–31
  behavior of in times of economic crisis, 321–22
  competition for, 294–97
  fatherlessness, 193–98, 422
  functions of, 299
  gender imbalance, 134–36
  during Great Terror, 72
  Gulag experiences, 75, 77
  heart disease, 329–31
  housework and, 187, 188, 260
  infidelity, 294, 322
  life expectancy, 197, 319, 329–31
  "male butterflies," 168, 197
  manliness, 330–31
  masculinity crisis, 195–97, 309, 320, 331
  military training, 95–96

  suicide, 319, 320, 331
  toxic masculinity, 364–65
  war casualties, 175–76
  as the "weaker sex," 197–98
  in the workforce, 194–95
  World War II front, 110
Mendelson, Kirill, 214
Mendelson, Misha, 214, 279
Mensheviks, 5, 88
menstrual products, 252
#MeToo movement, 366
Meyerhold, Vsevolod, 74
MGB. *See* Ministry of State Security
Michurin-Raver, Mark, 147
Mikoyan, Anastas, 159–60
Mikoyan, Ashkhen, 159–60
military
  draft, 109, 406–7, 410–16, 422, 423
  Order 0099, 99
  recruitment of women, 92–95, 98
  training, 95–96, 133
  unisex, 95
  volunteer recruitment, 414
  Western attitudes about women in, 101–2
Military Medical-Surgical Academy, 215
Ministry of Defense, 409, 410, 414, 418, 434
Ministry of Foreign Trade, 208
Ministry of Health, 253, 329
Ministry of Justice, 433
Ministry of Social Welfare, 24
Ministry of State Security (MGB), 147, 150
Ministry of the Interior (MVD), 148, 209, 373, 415, 424
miscarriages, 9, 189, 194, 254, 288
Mitterrand, François, 226, 234
Mizulina, Elena, 372–73, 375
Mlynář, Zdeněk, 229–30
Moldova, 86, 202, 217
Molotov, Vyacheslav, 92, 98–99, 114, 182
Mongayt, Anna, 392
monogamy, 11, 51
Mordovia penal colony, 359, 363
Morozov, Grigory, 143–44
Morozov, Joseph, 143–44
Moscow Architectural Institute, 81

Moscow Conservatory, 267
Moscow Metro, 174
Moscow News (periodical), 253, 256
Moscow Society for Improving the Lot of Women, 14
Moscow State Pedagogical Institute, 38, 230
Moscow State University, 180, 191, 219, 227, 339, 403
Munich Security Conference, 420, 428
Muslims, 265, 301

Nadaraia, Sardion, 154
Nakachi, Mie, 165, 166, 168
Narkompros, 41
nationalism, 265–66, 349, 397
Navalnaya, Dasha, 393, 394, 395, 396, 399, 405, 420
Navalnaya, Yulia
  arrests, 405, 429
  birth and early years, 393
  education, 393
  marriage and family life, 393–96, 403–4
  Navalny and, 393–98, 420–21
  Navalny's poisoning, 390–93, 399–401
  opposition leadership role, 428–30
  poisoning, 400
  radicalism, 397–98
Navalny, Alexey
  Anti-Corruption Foundation, 377
  death, 421, 428–30
  hunger strike, 405
  imprisonment, 346, 395, 398, 405, 417, 420–21
  legal career, 394–95
  marriage and family life, 393–96, 403–4
  mayoral campaign, 395, 398
  opposition activism, 346, 377, 395, 397–98, 404, 421–22
  opposition to Pussy Riot action, 347, 350
  poisoning, 390–93, 396, 399–401, 420
  support for Pussy Riot, 355
  Yulia and, 393–98
Navalny, Zakhar, 393, 395, 396, 399, 405, 420

Nazis
  death camps, 120–26
  fall and surrender, 130–31
  Soviet invasion, 81, 92, 112–18, 127, 134, 165, 336
  Stalin's son captured by, 64
  women's roles, 94–95
Nehru, Jawaharlal, 205
Nekrasov, Nikolay, 17, 430
NEP, 45
Nevsky Prospect, 3–4
New Economic Policy (NEP), 45
Nicholas II, 3, 16, 23
nigilistki (nihilists), 6
Nikulshina, Veronika, 367
NKVD, 68, 71–72, 73–75, 85–86, 90, 96, 112–13, 117–19, 140, 147, 256, 272, 417
no-fault divorce, xii
nomenklatura, 65, 200–204, 208, 209, 290
normalcy, 349–50
Novichok, 391, 399, 400
"Novosibirsk Manifesto," 222–24
nuclear policy, 173–74

October Revolution. *See* Bolshevik Revolution
Odessa, 33, 34, 37, 86, 87, 100, 161
Ofitserov, Pyotr, 398, 405
Okunevskaya, Tatiana, 153, 154, 155
oligarchs, 289–90, 305–6
Olympics, 331, 333, 354, 363
"On Labor and Luxury" (Tolstoy), 17
Order 0099, 99
Orlova, Raisa, 94
orphanages, 49–50, 75, 78–79, 165
Osoaviakhim, 98, 100–102

Palace of Motherhood, 24–25, 28–29, 256
Palazhchenko, Pavel, 237
Pale of Settlement, 34–35, 120, 125, 181
Palestine, 181
Pamyat, 266
paramilitary training, 94–95
Parkhomenko, Sergey, 392, 404–5
parliament, formation of, 16
Party Congresses, 40, 48, 71
  Tenth, 44–45

Twentieth, 159–60, 226
Twenty-Seventh, 225, 226–27, 238, 247
patriarchy, 12, 14, 195, 259–60, 295, 422
Pauker, Karl, 66
Pavlichenko, Lyudmila, 100–102, 133, 303
Pchelintsev, Vladimir, 101
peasants
   babas, 12, 27, 29, 59
   kolkhozy, 219–20, 231, 251
   marriage, 9
pedagogy, 38
Pelevin, Victor, 339
penal system, 359–63
pensions, 318, 325, 327
People's Commissariat for Popular Enlightenment (Narkompros), 41
People's Will, 5–6
perestroika, 222–24, 225, 227, 238, 250–53, 264, 266
performance art, 340–41, 344–45, 346–47, 367
Perovskaya, Sofia, 5–6, 31, 32, 215
Peskov, Dmitry, 348
Peters, Lana. *See* Alliluyeva, Svetlana
Peters, Olga, 244–46, 247, 248
Peters, Svetlana, 241–42
Peters, Wesley, 241–45
Petliura, Symon, 35
Petrova, Irina, 286–87
Pevchikh, Maria, 400
philosophy of small deeds, 14–15
Plekhanov University, 393
Pletnyova, Tamara, 388
Podvoisky, Nokolai, 95
pogroms, 34, 35, 265, 268, 275
Poland, 34, 108, 115, 120, 122, 161–62, 173, 251, 280
police forces
   Cheka, 30, 32, 96, 417
   FSB, 289–90, 340, 394, 397, 400, 417
   KGB, 96, 199, 200, 209, 220, 223, 240, 256, 264, 268, 270, 272, 273, 290, 309–17, 417
   MGB, 147, 150
   NKVD, 68, 71–72, 73–75, 85–86, 90, 96, 112–13, 117–19, 140, 147, 256, 272, 417
Politburo, 143–44, 148, 225, 234, 239

political prisoners, 4, 31, 77–80, 81, 143, 350, 359
Polozov, Nikolai, 353
Polytechnic Institute, 176
Popova, Alyona, 380–81, 387, 388
population growth, 42, 164–72
populism, 5, 6, 30
Prague Spring, 213, 230, 346
Pravda (periodical), 27, 65, 95, 96, 109, 142, 180, 183, 200
pregnancy, 9, 77–80
Presidium, 146, 152, 157, 159, 165, 172, 199, 203, 265
private property, elimination of, 7
Proekt (media outlet), 332, 404
Prokhorova, Irina, 383
propaganda, 377, 416
   anti-religious, 264
   assassinations and plots, 70
   Civil War, 97–98
   Narkompros, 41
   Nina Petrovna's work in, 162–63, 173
   on Pavlichenko, 101
   RT, 399
   on single mothers, 168–69
   against The Way Home, 418–19
   women in the army, 96
   on World War II, 108
   Zhenotdel campaign, 27–28, 29
property ownership, 7, 14, 25, 125
prostitution, 7–8, 10–11, 15–16, 49–50, 51
protests, 3–4, 345–46, 357, 373, 387, 394, 395, 405, 418
Provisional Government, 4, 23, 24, 31, 97
Pryakhin, Georgiy, 226, 227, 231–32, 237
punk feminism, 343–45
Pussy Riot
   arrests and trials, 348–55, 356–57
   Cathedral of Christ the Savior action, 336–38, 347
   formation of, 343–44
   Glamour Woman of the Year issue, 363–64
   guerrilla actions, 344–45, 346–47, 367
   public opinion of, 349–50
   Putin and, 338, 348–50, 354–55, 357
Putin, Vladimir, 309

Putin, Vladimir Vladimirovich (Volodya), 392, 409, 427
  alcohol consumption, 329
  appeal to women, 334–35
  birth and early years, 309
  censorship laws, 418
  church attendance, 337
  demographic policy, 341
  divorce, 402–3
  domestic violence legislation, 371–72, 373, 381–83, 389
  elections, 289, 347
  family laws, 431–32
  "healthy lifestyle" policy, 331–33
  KGB career, 290, 309–17, 381, 403
  love of sports, 331, 333
  Lyuda and, 306–12, 402
  marriage and family life, 312–13, 314–15, 402–5
  masculinity, 309, 333–35
  on masculinity crisis, 331
  Medvedev and, 340, 345
  oligarchy and, 289–90
  outdoor hobbies, 308, 332–33
  pardons, 363
  pension reform, 325
  physical health, 329, 332–33
  presidential terms, xii, 345
  Pussy Riot and, 338, 348–50, 354–55, 357
  skrepy speech, 357–59, 423
  "traditional values" diktat, 423–26
  war with Ukraine, 407, 411–18, 422–23, 430–31
  West's fixation on, xiii, 333
  as Yeltsin's successor, 306, 340
Putina, Lyudmila (Lyuda), 305, 337
  car accident, 317
  career, 307, 316
  divorce, 402–3
  education, 307
  in Germany, 313–15
  marriage and family life, 312–17
  Putin and, 306–12, 402
Putina, Maria, 309, 311, 313–14, 317

Rabotnitsa (periodical), 17, 19, 20, 215, 347, 379

radicals, 4
Radio Moscow, 173
Rankin-Williams, Amy, 254
rape, 35, 74, 78, 147–51, 152
Raskova, Marina, 99, 103, 133
Ravich, Olga, 96
Reagan, Nancy, 235–37
Red Army, xii, 26, 36, 56, 71, 72, 92, 95–103, 113–14, 133–34
Red Banner Institute, 312–13
Red Square, 63, 68
Red Star (periodical), 120
Red Terror, 32
Registration of Acts of Civil Status (ZAGS), 25
Reikh, Zinaida, 74
religion, 264–65, 349, 358. *See also* Russian Orthodox Church
Remeslo, Ilya, 419
Renar, Larisa, 297–300, 302–3, 383
"Requiem" (Akhmatova), 84–85, 88–91
Revolution Day, 63, 142
revolutionaries, 4, 5, 13, 19, 21, 23, 31, 76, 215, 366
Revolutionary Tribunal, 32
Ride, Sally, xii, 174
Ring, Khana-Batya, 36, 108–10, 116–17, 124, 127–28, 176, 188, 281, 434
Ring, Sonya, 109, 127–28
Rodchenko Art School, 342, 343
Roldugin, Sergei, 311
Romanov dynasty, 3, 430
Ronin, Andryusha, 195
Ronina, A., 195, 197
Rosgvardiya, 415
Rossiya Bank, 404
Rotenberg, Alina, 289–93, 301
Rotenberg, Arkady, 289, 291, 292
Rotenberg, Igor, 289, 291–92
Rotenberg, Natalia, 292
RT, 399
Rudenko, Roman, 157–58
Russian Empire
  illiteracy, 38–39
  land, 422
  marriage, 8–9
  Pale of Settlement, 34, 265
  prostitution, 15–16

Russian Federation
 alcohol consumption in, 319
 creation of, 281
 criminal justice system, 356, 366, 371–72
 democracy, 317, 372
 economy, 285
 Orthodox Christianity, 337, 348–52
 2008 financial crisis, 294
 war with Ukraine, 406–7, 410–18, 422–23, 430–31
Russian Orthodox Church, xii, 8–9, 14, 25, 35, 239, 264–66, 336, 347, 349, 358, 387–88, 424, 425, 432
Russian Revolution (1905), 16, 30
Russian Revolution (1917), 3
"Russianness," 265–66
russkii narod ("Russian people"), 265–66

Samoilov, David, 205
Samutsevich, Katya
 arrest and trial, 348–55, 356–57
 Cathedral of Christ the Savior action, 337–38
 imprisonment, 360
 Pussy Riot, 346–47
 Voina, 342–43
Sarkisov, Rafael, 147–49, 150–51, 152, 153, 154, 156–57
Sazonov, Misha, 325–27, 328
Sazonov, Nastia, 326
Sazonov, Zhenya, 325
scientific atheism, 264
Second Medical Institute, 215
second-wave feminism, 249, 342
Secret Speech, 82, 160
Segal, Asya, 106–7
Segal, Ida, 92, 98–99, 105–7, 132–33
Segal, Nelya, 106–7
Serge, Victor, 97
sexual violence, 35, 74, 78, 147–51, 152
sexuality, 10–11, 49–50, 288, 423–25
sexually transmitted disease, 15, 76, 135, 157
Shelter for Downtrodden Women, 15
Sheremetyevo Airport, 281, 284, 417
shestidesyatniki generation, 185, 223, 229, 230, 275

Shevkunov, Tikhon, 388
Sheykina, Inna, 371, 375–76, 380
Shikhman, Irina (Ira), 376–79, 384, 386
Shimeliovich, Boris, 183
Shlyapnikov, Alexander, 44–45
Shoigu, Sergei, 332
Shostakovich, Dmitri, 169
Shpinel, Nora, 184
Shutova, Katya, 361–62
Silver Age, 84
Silverstone, Alicia, 354
Singh, Brajesh, 204–8, 210, 239
single mothers, 166–69, 189–90
Six-Day War, 212
skrepy (spiritual bindings), 357–59, 373, 423
slave labor, 360
Smirnov, Vanya, 184
snipers, 96, 100, 133, 303
snokhachestvo tradition, 9
Snow Revolution, 345
Sobchak, Anatoly, 316–17
"Sober Russia" project, 327
Sobol, Lyubov, 396, 398
Social Democratic Party, 16, 19, 20, 21, 23
Socialist Revolutionaries (SRs), 30–32
socialists and socialism, 4–5, 223–24
sociology, 221, 230
Sokol, Nastia ("Baby Goat")
 arrest and trial, 348–55, 357
 imprisonment, 360
 Pussy Riot, 344–47
 Voina, 339
Sokologorskaya, Lyubov, 352–53
Sokolov, Oleg, 388
Soloviev, Vladimir, 418–19
Solzhenitsyn, Aleksandr, 75, 90
Sorokin, Vladimir, 339
Soviet Academy of Sciences, 219, 222, 260–61
Soviet Ukraine, 36
Soviet Union
 abortion in, 42–43, 254
 Bolshevik Revolution, xi, 23–24, 33–34, 181
 Civil War, 33, 35–36, 38, 42, 43, 69, 96, 97
 Cold War, 175, 239
 collapse of, 30, 90, 280–81, 285, 295, 321–22, 417

Soviet Union (*continued*)
   competition with United States, 175–76
   economy, 219–24, 231, 251–53, 316
   as a "fairy-tale country," 26, 34, 253
   Great Terror, 70–72, 84–85, 113–14
   Holocaust of the East, 120–26
   nationalism, 265–66
   perestroika policy, 224
   postwar, 175–76
   social reforms, 41–42, 174
   women in the workforce, 194–95, 260–61
   women's rights in, xi
   World War I, 3, 23, 34–35, 52, 97
   World War II, xii, 81, 92–93, 99–107, 108–26, 127–36
space exploration, xii
spies and spying, 71, 87, 96, 143, 147, 152, 309, 311, 313, 424
Spiridonova, Maria, 30
sports, 331, 333
Sputnik, 174
St. Basil's Cathedral, 346–47
St. Petersburg State University, 388
stagflation, 200–201
Stalin, Joseph, xiii
   annexation of Baltic republics, 221
   anti-Semitism, 123, 143–44, 181–83, 184
   death, 72, 77, 82, 144–45, 146, 184, 220, 229
   exile, 63
   Five-Year Plans, 58, 164
   Great Terror, 70–72, 74, 84–85, 113–14
   indictment, 159–60
   Khrushchev and, 65
   Kirov assassination, 70
   Krupskaya and, 46–47, 70
   Lenin and, 45, 46–49
   in Lenin's Testament, 47–48
   marriage and family life, 63–64, 65, 139, 141
   Nadya and, 63–68, 308
   opposition to Church, 264
   Politburo, 143–44
   retribution methods, 151
   school segregation, 133
   stroke, 139
   Svetlana and, 139–41, 143–45
   view of women, 140–41
   World War II, 99, 101, 108, 114, 116, 129, 131
Stalin, Vasily, 66, 139, 141, 142, 247
Stalin, Yakov, 63–64, 139, 142
Stalina, Svetlana. *See* Alliluyeva, Svetlana
Stasova, Elena, 28
State Committee on the State of Emergency, 271, 281
Stites, Richard, 4, 20, 38–39, 50
Stone, Oliver, 332
suicide, 319, 320, 331
Supreme Soviet, 336
Suslov, Mikhail, 206–7
Suslova, Nadezhda, 214–15
Svanidze, Kato, 63
syphilis, 15, 76, 157
Syrova, Marina, 351, 355, 356

Taliesin, 241, 242, 243–44
Taratuta, Julia, 365–66
Tartakovskaya, Khinya, 103, 217–18, 276
   career, 177–79, 187–88
   dementia, 434
   education, 175–78
   emigration, 281
   family lost to Holocaust of the East, 124, 126
   Ioffe and, 178–79, 187–89
   marriage and family life, 187–90, 279–80, 287
   during World War II, 108–10, 116–17, 127, 131
Tartakovsky, Grisha, 108–9, 116, 127
Tartakovsky, Moisei, 36, 108–10, 116–17, 123–24, 127, 176, 178–79, 187, 434
Tartakovsky, Rakhil, 109, 217
Tartakovsky, Wolf, 36, 108–9, 217–18
TASS, 265, 404
taxes
   on the childless, 165, 189, 257, 431
   on one- and two-child families, 166, 189
Telegram, 414–15, 418–19, 430
Tereshkova, Valentina, 174, 431
Thatcher, Denis, 225

Thatcher, Margaret, 225–26, 234, 301
Third Communist International (Comintern) Congress, 45
Third Reich, 95
Tikhonova, Ekaterina, 403
Tikhonova, Katya, 314, 317
Timofeevna, Evgenia, 314–15
Titaev, Kirill, 356
Titarenko, Alexandra, 227
Titarenko, Lyudmila, 228
Titarenko, Raisa Maksimovna. *See* Gorbacheva, Raisa
Tolokonnikov, Andrei, 338–39
Tolokonnikova, Ekatrina, 339
Tolokonnikova, Nadezhda (Nadya)
    arrest and trial, 338, 348–55
    birth and early years, 338–39
    education, 339
    feminism, 341–42, 364, 366–67
    hunger strike, 362–63
    imprisonment, 359, 362–63
    Mediazona, 368
    pardon, 363
    Pussy Riot, 338, 343–47, 367–68
    Verzilov and, 339, 341–43, 367–68
    Voina, 339–43
Tolstoy, Leo, 15–16, 17, 241
Tonia (villager), 318–19, 326–27
Tonia/Antonina (villager), 320, 326
torture, 74, 87, 152, 256
toxic masculinity, 364–65
trade unions, 44
Trotsky, Leon
    death, 48
    on Krupskaya, 21
    in Lenin's Testament, 47–48
    on Petrograd women's strike, 4
Trump, Donald, 424
Tsikhanouskaya, Sviatlana, 393
Tukhachevskaya, Svetlana, 75, 82
Tukhachevsky, Mikhail, 75

Uborevich, Nina Vladimirovna, 69, 73–75, 82–83
Uborevich, Vladimira (Mira), 69, 71, 72–75, 81–83, 90
Ukraine, 74, 97, 321
    Brezhnev's career in, 202
    children kidnapped from, 432–33
    famine, 67
    Holocaust of the East, 120–26
    independence, 251
    Jewish Civil War deaths, 34–36
    Khrushchev's career in, 171–72
    Nina Petrovna's work in, 162
    pogroms, 35
    war with Russia, 406–7, 410–18, 422–23, 430–31
    World War II, 108–10, 115, 121–26
Ukrainian Academy of Sciences, 53
Umansky, Alexander (Shura), 53–62, 85–86, 88, 125–26, 185, 191, 267
Umansky, Andrey, 60, 125
Umansky, Lida, 59–61, 125
United Russia, 345, 372, 413
United States
    abortion in, 254, 282–83, 288, 358
    agricultural production, 164, 220
    baby boom, 164, 170
    Cold War, 175, 239
    feminism, 253, 288, 364–65
    household appliances, 171, 188, 241
    housing, 171
    Jewish emigration to, 31, 34, 36, 87
    Khrushchev's tour of, 172
    mothers and housewives, 171
    Nina Petrovna's trips to, 172–74
    Raisa Gorbachev's trips to, 235–37, 249–50
    schools, 41
    Soviet sniper tour of, 101–2, 133
    Svetlana's defection to, 210–11, 238–46
    "traditional values" in, 424
    war effort, 110
    women in the military, 101
    women in the workforce, 260, 286
    women's education, xi
Universal Military Training (Vsevobuch), 95–96
Urlanis, Boris, 193–94, 197–98, 319
U.S. Congress, 101
USSR. *See* Soviet Union

Vacio, 425
Venediktov, Alexey, 392

venereal disease, 15, 135, 360
Verstka (periodical), 388
Verzilov, Gera, 362, 367
Verzilov, Petya, 337, 339–40, 344–45, 346, 348, 350, 354–55, 362, 367–68
veterans, 25, 133–34
Vinogradov, Vladimir, 139
Virganskiy, Anatoly, 269, 270, 271, 272–73, 274
Voina, 339–43, 367
Volkova, Violetta, 352
Volovich, Eleanora, 79–80, 81
Volovich, Hava, 79–80, 81, 90
Volunteer Army, 35
Volyanskaya, Lia (Sexy Lia), 334–35
Vorontsova, Irina, 419
Vorotnikov, Oleg, 339, 340, 342
voting rights, xii, 25

wage gap, 9–10
Wagner Group, 415
Walker, Alice, 249–50
War Communism, 38
War of 1877, 215
Washington Post, 223
The Way Home (*Put'domoi*), 416, 418–19
Weisser, Dora, 38
Weisser, Ethel, 33, 36–37
Weisser, Eva, 37
Weisser, Gersh, 36–37, 131
Weisser, Hannah, 37, 130
Weisser, Leah/Lena, 37, 38, 126
Weisser, Rivka (Riva), 191, 212, 266
    abortions, 254
    anti-Semitism against, 183–84
    birth and early years, 33–34
    and Bruk, 86–87
    career, 113, 180, 183, 184
    death, 268, 435
    education, 37–39, 86
    family lost to Holocaust of the East, 126, 218
    family lost to pogroms, 268
    Great Terror and, 86, 87
    Lenin's funeral, 49
    LikBez program, 39
    NKVD and, 112–13, 117–19, 129–31

paramilitary training, 94
parents' murders, 36–37
Wellesley College, 249–51, 252, 253
White Army, 35, 43, 96, 97
White Chocolate (pop group), 335
White House, 273
"woman question," 6–8, 14
Woman Under Socialism (Bebel), 7
women
    alcohol consumption, 319, 330–31
    in the army, xii, 95–9103, 133–34
    babas, 12, 29, 59
    class differences, 8–10
    competition among for men, 294–97
    doctors, 214–16
    "double burden," 172, 188, 196, 260
    education, xi, 176
    emancipation of, 49, 259
    gender imbalance, 134–36
    during Great Terror, 72, 74–75
    Gulag experiences, 75–80, 81–82
    housewives, xii–xiii
    labor conscription, 41–42
    labor strikes, 3–4, 12, 20
    life expectancy, 197, 319, 329–30
    literacy rates, 38–39
    military recruitment, 92–95, 98
    military training, 95–96, 133
    "moral obligation" to have children, 42
    in Nazi Germany, 94–95
    new socialist, 10–11
    nigilistki (nihilists), 6
    paramilitary training, 94–95
    penal colonies, 359–61
    rape, 35, 74, 78, 147–51, 152
    retirement, 221
    rights of Soviet, xi
    Russian Revolution started by, 3–4
    single mothers, 166–69, 189–90
    states of femininity, 295–97
    in tsarist Russia, 8–11
    veterans, 133–34
    voting rights, 25
    war effort, 110
    in the workforce, 4, 194–95, 260–61, 286
    working in the criminal justice system, 356

Women's Army Auxiliary Corp, 101
Women's Battalion of Death, 97
Women's Medical Institute, 215
Women's Section of the Central Committee, 27
Wonderzine, 365, 366
Wood, Elizabeth, 8, 12, 14
Workers' Opposition, 44–45
working class, 8, 11–12, 22, 38, 44, 49, 112, 187
World Congress of Women, 259, 262–63
World Cup, 367
World War I (Great War), 3, 23, 26, 34–35, 52, 97, 161
World War II, xii, 81, 92–93, 99–107, 108–26, 127–36
Wright, Frank Lloyd, 241, 243
Wright, Olgivanna, 241–44

Yabloko, 393
Yakir, Iona, 75
Yakir, Pyotr, 75, 82
Yandex, 280
#YaNeBoyusSkazat (#ImNotAfraidToTell) campaign, 378
Yarmysh, Kira, 390
Yeltsin, Boris, 266, 273, 274, 285, 289, 305–6, 340, 417
Yeshchenko, Anastasia, 388
Yezhov, Nikolai, 70, 71

YouTube, 377, 396
Yulia (manicurist), 371, 384, 386

Zakharova, Maria, 426–28
Zalkind, Aron, 50–51
Zaslavskaya, Tatyana, 219–24, 227, 230, 231, 259–62, 396
zdorovyy obraz zhizni ("ZOZh"), 331–33
Zdravomyslova, Elena, 295, 320, 331
Zemlyachka, Rozalia, 97
Zhdanov, Andrey, 144
Zhdanov, Ivan, 390–91
Zhdanova, Katya, 144
Zhemchuzhina, Polina, 67, 181–82
Zhenotdel, 27, 29, 39, 41, 44–45, 162, 231
Zhukov, Georgy, 134
Zinkina, Yulia, 330–31
Zinoviev, Grigory, 32
Zuckerman, Brokha (Buzya), 125, 185, 190, 192, 279, 427
    career, 52–53, 56–58
    in Crimea, 52, 53–54
    death, 267
    Great Terror and, 85–86
    marriages and family life, 53, 62
    in Moscow, 52–53, 54–57
    and Umansky, 53–62
Zuckerman, Eva (Evochka), 52, 53, 54, 85–86, 185
Zuckerman, Tsinusya, 52, 125
Zyuganov, Gennady, 305